Trade-Related Agricultural Policy Analysis

World Scientific Studies in International Economics

(ISSN: 1793-3641)

Vol. 38 International Trade, Distribution and Development: Empirical Studies of Trade Policies
by Paul Brenton (The World Bank, USA)

Vol. 39 Evolving Patterns in Global Trade and Finance
by Sven W. Arndt (Claremont McKenna College, USA)

Vol. 40 Shadow Banking Within and Across National Borders
edited by Stijn Claessens (International Monetary Fund, USA), Douglas Evanoff (Federal Reserve Bank of Chicago, USA), George Kaufman (Loyola University Chicago, USA) & Luc Laeven (International Monetary Fund, USA)

Vol. 41 Modeling Developing Countries' Policies in General Equilibrium
by Jaime de Melo (FERDI, France & University of Geneva, Switzerland)

Vol. 42 Developing Countries in the World Economy
by Jaime de Melo (FERDI, France & University of Geneva, Switzerland)

Vol. 43 Farm Policies and World Markets: Monitoring and Disciplining the International Trade Impacts of Agricultural Policies
by Tim Josling (Stanford University, USA)

Vol. 44 Non-Tariff Barriers, Regionalism and Poverty: Essays in Applied International Trade Analysis
by L. Alan Winters (University of Sussex, UK)

Vol. 45 Trade Law, Domestic Regulation and Development
by Joel P. Trachtman (Tufts University, USA)

Vol. 46 The Political Economy of International Trade
by Edward D. Mansfield (University of Pennsylvania, USA)

Vol. 47 Trade-Related Agricultural Policy Analysis
by David Orden (Virginia Polytechnic Institute and State University, USA)

The complete list of the published volumes in the series can be found at
http://www.worldscientific.com/series/wssie

47 World Scientific Studies in International Economics

TRADE-RELATED AGRICULTURAL POLICY ANALYSIS

Editor

David Orden

Virginia Polytechnic Institute and State University, USA

World Scientific

NEW JERSEY • LONDON • SINGAPORE • BEIJING • SHANGHAI • HONG KONG • TAIPEI • CHENNAI • TOKYO

Published by

World Scientific Publishing Co. Pte. Ltd.
5 Toh Tuck Link, Singapore 596224
USA office: 27 Warren Street, Suite 401-402, Hackensack, NJ 07601
UK office: 57 Shelton Street, Covent Garden, London WC2H 9HE

Library of Congress Cataloging-in-Publication Data
Orden, David.
Trade-related agricultural policy analysis / by (author): David Orden (International Food Policy Research Institute, USA). -- First edition.
pages cm. -- (World Scientific studies in international economics, ISSN 1793-3641 ; v. 47)
Includes bibliographical references and index.
ISBN 978-9814616218 (hardcover) -- ISBN 9814616214 (hardcover)
1. Agriculture--Economic aspects. 2. Agriculture and state. 3. Commercial policy. 4. International trade. I. Title. II. Series: World Scientific studies in international economics ; v. 47.
HD1415.O65 2015
338.1'873--dc23

2014021354

British Library Cataloguing-in-Publication Data
A catalogue record for this book is available from the British Library.

In-house Editor: Alisha Nguyen

Typeset by Stallion Press
Email: enquiries@stallionpress.com

Contents

About the Editor

David Orden is Professor and Director of the Global Issues Initiative (GII) of the Institute for Society, Culture and Environment (ISCE) at Virginia Polytechnic Institute and State University. He joined the university faculty in 1983 and since 2003 has also held the position of Senior Research Fellow at the International Food Policy Research Institute (IFPRI). He is engaged in active research and public policy education programs on the economics and political economy of agricultural domestic support policies, international trade negotiations, and technical barriers to trade. Professor Orden has been a Visiting Fellow at the University of New South Wales in Australia (1990), Chairman of the International Agricultural Trade Research Consortium (1996–1997), and Visiting Professor at Stanford University (1998–1999). His book Policy *Reform in American Agriculture: Analysis and Prognosis* (co-authored by Robert Paarlberg and Terry Roe) received the American Agricultural Economics Association Quality of Communication Award in 2000. A second book *Food Regulation and Trade: Toward a Safe and Open Global System* (co-authored with Tim Josling and Donna Roberts) was published in 2004 by the Peterson Institute for International Economics. He has recently co-edited a volume on the World Trade Organization (WTO) monitoring and discipline of domestic farm subsidies *WTO Disciplines on Agricultural Support: Seeking a Fair Basis for Trade* (with David Blandford and Tim Josling, Cambridge University Press, 2011) and a special issue of *The World Economy* (with John Beghin) addressing nontariff measures affecting food and agricultural trade and competitiveness. In December 2013, Orden received a two-year USDA-NIFA grant for further work in the regulation and competitiveness area (with Everett Peterson and Jason Grant, Virginia Tech). Since July 2011, he has served as director of capacity strengthening for the IFPRI Pakistan Strategy Support Program, a multi-year USAID-funded program for research and outreach to support agricultural development and economic policies initiatives of Pakistan's federal Ministry of Planning, Development and Reforms.

Contributors

David Blandford, Professor, Department of Agricultural Economics, Sociology, and Education, Pennsylvania State University, USA

Frédéric Bouchet, Professor, Economics Department, American Public University System, USA

Lars Brink, Independent Policy Analyst, Ottawa, Canada

Fuzhi Cheng, Commodity Market Analyst, Noble Group, Connecticut, USA

Caesar B. Cororaton, Research Fellow, Institute for Society, Culture and Environment, Virginia Tech, USA

Paul L. Fackler, Professor, Department of Agricultural and Resource Economics, North Carolina State University, USA

Timothy Josling, Emeritus Professor, Stanford University, USA

George W. Norton, Professor, Department of Agricultural and Applied Economics, Virginia Tech, USA

Robert Paarlberg, Betty Freyhof Johnson Class of 1944 Professor of Political Science, Wellesley College, USA

Everett B. Peterson, Professor, Department of Agricultural and Applied Economics, Virginia Tech, USA

Donna Roberts, Associate Director, Market and Trade Economics Division, Economic Research Service, United States Department of Agriculture, USA

John C. Robertson, Senior Policy Adviser, Federal Reserve Bank of Atlanta, USA

Terry Roe, Professor, Department of Applied Economics, University of Minnesota, USA

Joachim Schleich, Professor, Department of Management and Technology, Grenoble Ecole de Management, France

Richard H. Snape (deceased), Professor, Department of Economics, Monash University, Australia

Carl Zulauf, Professor, Department of Agricultural, Environmental, and Development Economics, Ohio State University, USA

Preface

It is both satisfying and also humbling and a little sobering to have the opportunity to put together in a single volume a collection of papers that span the course of my career in agricultural policy analysis. It seems even a bit odd to collect such a volume in an era of instantaneous Google search, RePEc, and ResearchGate recovery of academic papers, and the availability of seminar presentations and other events through online video postings. Still, none of these mechanisms offer quite the same opportunity to juxtapose and draw out the interrelationships of the accumulated work.

In this context, I want to thank the co-authors (in many cases, first authors) of the papers include in this volume. Without engagement through interactions within a school of thought to which one's efforts contribute, the work doesn't culminate and cross-fertilize into a whole of much meaning. The co-authors, some lifelong friends others distant over time but brought together by this set of papers, are the first tier of that school of thought for me. It has been an opportunity and pleasure to work with each of them. A favorite shelf in my office is filled with additional publications from these friends and other colleagues.

Two institutions, Virginia Polytechnic Institute and State University (Virginia Tech) and the International Food Policy Research Institute (IFPRI), have provided my long-term academic home. I am appreciative in both cases for these supportive environments from which I have learned a great amount.

I also thank my wife Denise and close and extended family for the support they have provided over many years. This is my home in a larger sense that has made this book possible.

David Orden
July 2015

Acknowledgments

We would like to gratefully acknowledge the following journals, publishers and institutions for granting their permissions to reproduce the chapters in this book:

Journals

Agricultural Economics

Chapter 4: Cheng, Fuzhi and David Orden. "Exchange Rate Alignment and Producer Support Estimates (PSEs) of India." *Agricultural Economics* 36 (2007): 231–241.

American Journal of Agricultural Economics

Chapter 2: Robertson, John C. and David Orden. "Monetary Impacts on Prices in the Short Run and Long Run: Some Evidences from New Zealand." *American Journal of Agricultural Economics* 72:1 (February 1990): 160–171.

Chapter 3: Orden, David and Paul L. Fackler. "Identifying Monetary Impacts on Agricultural Prices in VAR Models." *American Journal of Agricultural Economics* 71:2 (May 1989): 495–502.

Chapter 10: Zulauf, Carl and David Orden. "The Political Economy of the 2014 Farm Bill," *American Journal of Agricultural Economics* (doi: 10.1093/ajae/aav028: August 2015, forthcoming; Chapter 10 is an extended version).

Chapter 11: Bouchet, Frédéric, David Orden and George W. Norton. "Sources of Growth in French Agriculture." *American Journal of Agricultural Economics* 71:2 (May 1989): 280–293.

Chapter 17: Peterson, Everett B. and David Orden. "Avocado Pests and Avocado Trade." *American Journal of Agricultural Economics* 91:2 (May 2008): 321–335.

Review of International Economics

Chapter 12: Schleich, Joachim and David Orden. "Environmental Quality and Industry Protection with Noncooperative versus Cooperative Domestic and Trade Policies." *Review of International Economics* 8:4 (November 2000): 681–697.

Publishers

CABI

Chapter 8: Orden, David. "U.S. Agricultural Policy: The 2002 Farm Bill and WTO Doha Round Proposal," in *WTO Negotiations and Agricultural Trade Liberalization: The Effect of Developed Countries' Policies on Developing Economies* (Eugenio Diaz-Bonilla, Soren E. Frandsen and Sherman Robinson, editors). Cambridge, MA: CABI, 2006: 80–102.

Cambridge University Press

Chapter 5: Brink, Lars. "The WTO Disciplines on Domestic Support," in *WTO Disciplines on Agricultural Support: Seeking a Fair Basis for Trade* (David Orden, David Blandford and Tim Josling, editors). Cambridge University Press, 2011: 23–60.

Chapter 9: Blandford, David and David Orden. "United States," in *WTO Disciplines on Agricultural Support: Seeking a Fair Basis for Trade* (David Orden, David Blandford and Tim Josling, editors). Cambridge University Press, 2011: 97–152.

University of Chicago Press

Chapter 6: Orden, David. "Agricultural Interest Group Bargaining over the North American Free Trade Agreement," in *The Political Economy of Trade Protection* (Anne O. Krueger, editor). University of Chicago Press, 1996: 71–84.

Chapter 7: Orden, David, Robert Paarlberg and Terry Roe. *Policy Reform in American Agriculture: Analysis and Prognosis*. University of Chicago Press, 1999: 165–195.

Institutions

Centre for International Economic Studies

Chapter 14: Snape, Richard H. and David Orden. "Integrating Import Risk and Trade Benefit Analysis," in *The Economics of Quarantine and the SPS Agreement* (Kym Anderson, Cheryl McRae and David Wilson, editors). Adelaide: Centre for International Economic Studies, 2001: 174–80.

Peterson Institute for International Economics

Chapter 15: Josling, Timothy, Donna Roberts and David Orden. *Food Regulation and Trade: Toward a Safe and Open Global System*. Washington DC: Peterson Institute for International Economics, 2004: 13–34.

Chapter 16: Josling, Timothy, Donna Roberts and David Orden. *Food Regulation and Trade: Toward a Safe and Open Global System*. Washington DC: Peterson Institute for International Economics, 2004: 35–76.

World Bank

Chapter 13: Cororaton, Caesar B. and David Orden. "Pakistan," in *Agricultural Price Distortions, Inequality and Poverty* (Kym Anderson, John Cockburn and Will Martin, editors). Washington DC: World Bank, 2010: 209–246.

Chapter 1

Introduction

David Orden

This book brings together a set of sixteen papers addressing agricultural domestic support policies and the regulation of agriculture production and food processing and distribution with significant implications not only within the implementing country but also for world markets. It has always been my view that the objective that motivates and inspires good agricultural policy analysis, that is to say the ultimate goal of agricultural policy, is a smoothly-operating, globally-integrated, progressive and liberalized agricultural regime. This outcome is sought in order to provide the world as a whole in an efficient and sustainable manner with a diverse and secure food supply, from basic commodities that reduce hunger and malnutrition to refined products that enrich differentiated consumer choice and well-being. An essential mechanism in achieving this integrated global regime as the ultimate policy goal is open international trade. Yet, it is also the case that the interventions and regulations countries adopt toward their agricultural and food sectors are more often than not rooted in deep domestic concerns not trade relations per se. Hence, the volume title and its focus on *Trade-Related Agricultural Policy Analysis*.

In grappling with agricultural policy, the included papers are organized around four themes. The first section focuses on identifying macroeconomic effects, specifically through monetary policy and exchange rates, on agricultural prices, and thus their impacts on the sector and interactions with agricultural support measures. The second section reviews the evolution of U.S. agricultural policy over the twenty years since the establishment of the World Trade Organization (WTO) in 1995 in the context of its Agreement on Agriculture and subsequent negotiations to discipline agricultural support policies multilaterally. The third section provides three illustrations, two empirical studies and one theoretical, of the need to look at policy interventions from a multi-dimensional perspective. The fourth section addresses the regulation of food safety and quality, issues that are central to contemporary agricultural and food policy debates and play a key role in determining international trade flows.

Most of the included papers have an empirical focus, but the issues they address are generalizable across time and space. Diverse research methods are applied. The focus is largely on the United States, but several chapters related to other economies are also included. A group of the papers have an institutional focus, specifically laying out the disciplines, through rules and specific commitments, that the WTO provides for agricultural domestic support and the regulation of product safety and quality as they affect trade. A recurring theme through the book emphasizes the political economy of policy determination. These sixteen papers were prepared at various times over a thirty-year period (1985–2015). There are fifteen co-authors, four of whom were Ph.D. students and the work presented reflects their dissertation research, and one of the papers was prepared independently by a contributor to an edited volume.[1]

Given the diverse coverage by timing and topics of the chapters, the purpose of this Introduction is to provide a non-technical overview of the book in several dimensions. First, it elaborates the framework of the included analysis. Second, each chapter is placed in context of the policy issues and related research into which it fit at the time it was first published. Third, key findings of the chapters are highlighted and some of the complexities of the issues addressed and methods used are touched upon. Fourth, some *ex post* integration of the chapters is provided adding additional context and drawing out the relevance of the analysis to the current agricultural policy agenda.

For many academics and policy practitioners toiling within the framework of seeking an integrated world food regime, D. Gale Johnson's 1973 book *World Agriculture in Disarray* is one of the classic sources of

[1]Co-authors who were graduate students at Virginia Tech at the time the research in the included chapters was undertaken are Frédéric Bouchet, Fuzhi Cheng, John C. Robertson and Joachim Schleich.

guidance. It laid out a simple but fundamental premise that a global excess cost was being borne because too much food was produced in the wrong place, and too little in others, as a result of misguided policy decisions. A lot of progress has been made on agricultural policy since the publication of this critical assessment, but there remains a great deal still to be accomplished. It is hoped that this book offers both some perspective and utility to readers, helping to place into context their endeavors to advance agricultural policy research and outcomes.

Macroeconomic Impacts on Agriculture

Macroeconomic impacts on agriculture have been a longstanding concern of agricultural policy analysts and within the agricultural sector. One particular focus has been non-neutral effects of monetary policy and exchange rates. A basic idea is that agriculture faces more flexible prices than other sectors, resulting in greater fluctuations, and hence shifts in relative prices, in response to monetary policy shocks. This idea underlay arguments by George Warren (1928) that tight monetary policy had been detrimental to agriculture in years prior to the Great Depression. The monetary arguments never faded from discussion of agricultural policy in developing countries, but lay more dormant during the 1950s and 1960s in the United States as agricultural policy insulated the sector with intervention prices and supply controls after the introduction of New Deal policies in the 1930s and 1940s. By 1973, however, U.S. macroeconomic policy, affected in part by inflation related to the Vietnam War, was unable to sustain a fixed exchange rate and the dollar was devalued then floated against other currencies, ushering in the era of flexible exchange rates of the last four decades.

In a classic 1974 article "The Exchange Rate and U.S. Agriculture," G. Edward Schuh made the argument that through the late 1960s and early 1970s an overvalued U.S. dollar had depressed U.S. agricultural prices, exports and sector performance. This stood on its head the general perception of overvaluation of U.S. agricultural resources due to the farm support policies. Agricultural prices and exports shot up in the early 1970s with floating of the dollar and the macroeconomic impacts Shuh highlighted became the focus of extensive policy analysis. Subsequent macroeconomic instability included stagflation through the 1970s, and subsequent tightening of monetary policy starting in 1979 to squeeze down high inflation rates. This was followed by a collapse of U.S. agricultural prices, exports, income and land values in the early 1980s.

The flex-price argument of Warren was revived in the renewed debate about macroeconomic impacts on U.S. agriculture, prompted in part by an influential model proposed by Rudiger Dornbusch (1976) showing that the exchange rate would overshoot its long-run equilibrium value in response to a monetary contraction or expansion. One vein of the analysis of macroeconomic impacts focused on using parsimonious econometric time-series models to measure the effects of monetary shocks on agricultural prices and other sectoral indicators. This literature drew on several new developments in empirical macroeconomics. First, Chris Sims (1980) had pioneered the use of small vector autoregressive (VAR) models and the dynamic impulse response functions to contemporaneous shocks as an alternative to large, heavily over-identified simultaneous equation system models that had previously been dominant. Second, the issue of stationarity of macroeconomic time series and its implications for model specification received heightened attention. A key argument in the latter development was that non-stationary series could have stationary cointegrating equilibrium relationships, in which case modeling in differences of the series lost valuable information while modeling in levels was inefficient. The alternative specification when there was evidence of cointegration was a vector error-correction (VEC) model that explicitly estimated the long-run stationary relationship along with the dynamic paths of the variables subject to the long-run restriction.

Chapter 2, published in 1990, applies the cointegration approach to evaluate the relationships between the money supply and indices of agricultural versus manufacturing goods prices for the small, trade-dependent New Zealand economy. At the time of its publication, the main cointegation tests available were the Engle-Grange (1987) bilateral tests; these were subsequently followed by more complete systems approaches of Soren Johanesen (1991) and later others. The Engle-Grange tests provided evidence of two cointegrating relationships between money and the price series. The long-run neutrality of money, with each price level proportional to the money supply, was not rejected. Imposing these long-run relationships, the analysis shows evidence of a positive shock to the money supply causing agricultural prices to rise in the short run compared to manufacturing prices, consistent with agricultural prices being relatively flexible and short-run overshooting of the exchange rate. In this analysis, manufacturing price shocks appear to be accommodated in the long run by monetary policy, while agricultural price shocks dampen out with no long-run effects on the money supply or price levels.

One of the critiques that arose of the VAR models is that no econometric model escapes the discipline of structural identification being required to draw relevant inferences. The Choleski decompositions of the contemporaneous error covariance matrix imposed on early VAR models (including the model in Chapter 2) provided such a structural identification, but rested on the restrictive assertion that the structural errors that drove dynamics of the economy affected the included variables recursively (and the model is just identified, thus imposing no testable over-identifying restrictions). Ben Bernanke (1986) had challenged this approach and proposed alternative structural identifications of macroeconomic VAR models that allowed simultaneity among the included variables within the contemporaneous period, be it a year, quarter or month.

Chapter 3, published in 1989, explores the effects of monetary policy and other macroeconomic shocks on U.S. agricultural prices employing the technique Bernanke pioneered. The chapter describes recursive representations of money supply and demand as somewhat implausible (in a three-variable model without an interest rate such as Chapter 2, the identifying restriction is that money supply is perfectly inelastic within the contemporaneous period). In Chapter 3, a partially-complete structural identification is imposed in which the contemporaneous (within a quarter) money supply is responsive to interest rates, while contemporaneous money demand responds to interest rates and other variables in a seven-variable model also including real output, the price level (GNP deflator), oil prices, the exchange rate, and an index of agricultural prices. Within this model (specified in levels), the estimated contemporaneous and dynamic effects of a money supply shock look plausible. A positive money supply shock lowers the interest rate, the U.S. dollar depreciates and output expands for several quarters. Agricultural prices rise relative to the overall price level in the short run, but the estimated results do not suggest that monetary shocks were the dominant source of agricultural price instability over the period for which the model is estimated (1975:1 to 1988:1) which corresponds to the period on macroeconomic instability described above. If structural identification is limited to recursive models, the results suggest the most plausible interpretation is to identify money supply shocks with a shock to the interest rate ordered before the quantity of money in the Cholski decomposition, but this interpretation rests on the somewhat implausible identifying restriction that contemporaneous money demand is perfectly interest-rate inelastic.

Chapter 4, published in 2007, approaches the issue of macroeconomic impacts on agriculture from the somewhat different conceptual perspective of exchange rate misalignment and its effects on agricultural prices and the measurement of levels of agricultural support. The application is to India. This chapter again employs cointegration time-series models, in this case applied to equilibrium real exchange rate determination (the exchange rate of the Indian rupee versus the U.S. dollar adjusted for inflation within each country). The Johansen systems cointegration tests and long-run identifying restrictions on two cointegrating relationships evident among the series are used to relate the real exchange rate to five determinants: domestic industrial productivity, government expenditures as a percentage of GDP, world interest rates, the terms of trade (export prices relative to import prices), and a measure of openness of the economy. Macroeconomic policy as measured by domestic credit enters the model only as having short-term effects on its dynamics, highlighting the emphasis on real versus nominal determinants of the exchange rate in the long run. The empirical results suggest the rupee was overvalued relative to its long-run equilibrium value by 8 percent or more from 1986–1992, then moved closer to equilibrium (deviations of less than 4 percent) during 1993–2002.

To evaluate the effects of exchange rate misalignment on agricultural incentive and measures of agricultural support, Chapter 4 utilizes Producer Support Estimates (PSEs) for India. The PSE is a well-established measurement to quantifying support for agriculture through border protection (domestic prices above or below equivalent border prices based on world markets) and government budgetary expenditures on support programs. A PSE can be computed for various products and is usually aggregated to an overall national sum, often expressed as a percentage of the domestic value of agricultural production at the farm level. The PSE is best known because of its use since 1987 by the OECD to characterize and compare agricultural support among member countries and, more recently, to provide similar analysis for some key non-member emerging economies (OECD 2013). India has not participated in the OECD support estimation exercise, but Chapter 4 uses PSEs for India developed at IFPRI for the 1986–2002 period (Orden *et al.* 2007). The direct effects on PSEs from agricultural policies are compared to the indirect effects that can be attributed to exchange rate misalignment. A similar approach had been used in a groundbreaking World Bank study that made empirical estimates of the disarray (in D. Gale Johnson's phrase) created by agricultural policies across 18 other developing countries (Kruger, Schiff and Valdes 1991). For India, the PSEs reported in Chapter 4 indicate that aggregate protection or disprotection of agriculture follows a countercyclical pattern, with more protection when world prices are relatively low (as in the 1980s) and less when world prices strengthen (as in the mid 1990s).

The PSEs measure agricultural support at existing domestic prices with the observed exchange rates used to convert world prices to domestic currency values for the border price comparison. The counterfactual exercise of assessing effects on agricultural production incentives and support if exchange rates had been at an equilibrium level has two dimensions. A rupee depreciation, for example, raises the border price in domestic currency given a fixed world price. To the extent that the domestic price remains constant (e.g. a fixed administered price prevails), then measured support for agriculture would decline, but there would not be an improved incentives to produce through a changed domestic output price. Conversely, to the extent that the exchange rate realignment also raises the domestic price, measured support would not be affected but production incentives would improve.

To distinguish between these outcomes Chapter 4 provides estimates of exchange rate pass-through to domestic prices for India using panel data for 11 commodities. Overall, pass-through is relatively high, around 0.8 (80 percent). The initial PSE estimates in Chapter 4 show that overvaluation of the rupee during 1985–1992 created disprotection of Indian agriculture as measured in the PSE evaluated at observed domestic prices. In the three years leading to a macroeconomic crisis and sharp devaluation by India in 1991, the exchange rate effects on the PSE dominated the direct effects of agricultural policies. Using the pass-through estimates, had the exchange rate moved during those years to its equilibrium values and the estimated pass-through occurred, most of the effect of the depreciation would have resulted in improved production incentives (through higher domestic prices) not in lower support as measured in the PSE.

By the early 1990s, macroeconomic instability had diminished for the United States and a long period of relative stability (sometimes termed the Great Moderation) ensued. The intensity of academic and policy focus on macroeconomic impacts on agriculture subsided again for developed countries, while remaining more important for some developing countries with greater macroeconomic misalignments. This long period of relative macroeconomic stability was shaken by the U.S. financial market collapse in 2008 and U.S. and world recession (the Great Recession) and slow growth that followed. In this context, expansionary monetary policy was argued to be necessary to shore up financial markets to avoid deflation and an even deeper economic collapse. An extraordinary expansion of the U.S. money supply ensued, without the inflation that accompanied monetary expansion in the 1970s. For a variety of reasons (discussed further below) U.S. agriculture prospered during this period. One factor was that agriculture as a capital intensive sector benefitted from historically low interest rates during the recession and correspondingly a relatively weak U.S. dollar contributed to export demand and strong farm incomes. But by 2014, the boom period of agricultural prosperity appeared to lose steam, while the U.S. economy showed substantial recovery. Higher interest rates that might ensue, and a stronger U.S. dollar already evident in early-2015 and that would accompany such a shift in monetary policy, could rekindle debate about the relative importance of macroeconomic policy effects on agriculture.

U.S. Farm Policy in International Perspective, 1990–2020

The second section turns to the evolution of U.S. agricultural policy since 1990 evaluated in an international context. Chapter 5 by Lars Brink, published in 2011, lays out the history of GATT negotiations about domestic support programs as one component of the global agricultural protection and subsidization that multilateral agreements would seek to constrain. These negotiations resulted in limited disciplines on domestic support forming one of three pillars of agreement, along with market access (reductions in tariffs and elimination of quantitative border measures) and export competition (limits on export subsidies), reached about agriculture in the Uruguay Round GATT negotiations. The results are in the Agreement on Agriculture that came into effect as one part of the legal texts when the WTO was established in 1995.

As Brink describes, the Agreement on Agriculture distinguishes between agricultural domestic support measures that are subject to commitments that WTO members made to constrain their support levels and those measures that are exempt from these constraints. The Current Total Aggregate Measurement of Support (CTAMS) that sums support counting against the commitment includes both measurements of market price support (MPS) and certain categories of budgetary expenditures. As a negotiated legal construct, the MPS utilized in assessing compliance with WTO commitments differs from the border protection measured by the PSE or other economic measurements of nominal protection. The MPS utilized to ascertain WTO compliance is only calculated when there is a fixed administered price announced for a product by a government. This administered price is compared to a fixed external reference price from an agreed period (1986–1988) not to the prevailing border price as it evolves over time. The MPS construct in the WTO was agreed upon largely at the insistence of the European Union (EU). At the time of the Uruguay Round negotiations, the EU relied heavily on fixed nominal administered prices as support measures. In any given year, administered prices can differ from domestic market prices and border prices can differ from the fixed reference prices. Hence, the WTO definition of MPS has led to a bifurcation in the discussion and comparisons of agricultural support, with one focus on its economic effects while another focus is on WTO legal compliance.

Chapter 5 laid this framework out for the book *WTO Disciplines on Agricultural Support* (Orden, Blandford and Josling 2011) about agricultural policies and WTO compliance of four developed countries/regions (the United States, the European Union, Japan and Norway) and four developing countries (Brazil, China, India and the Philippines). Chapter 5 also describes in depth the more complex rules and commitments that have been discussed in the Doha Round WTO negotiations that were launched in 2002. For developed countries, the commitments tabled in the Doha Round would tighten the limits on agricultural domestic support quite substantially, as Brink describes for the set of revised draft modalities that emerged in the negotiations by December 2008. However, the WTO members have not been able to reach agreement about such modifications to the Agreement on Agriculture, which would have to be agree upon within the context of an overall Doha Round outcome.

Chapter 6 turns to the stakes of U.S. agriculture in the North American Free Trade Agreement (NAFTA) that has been in effect since 1994 along with the WTO Agreement on Agriculture. This chapter, the synopsis from a longer proceedings of an NBER conference on the political economy of American trade protection (Kruger 1996), introduces a theme that runs throughout the remainder of the book—not only what are the economic stakes in various policy decisions but what is the political economy that surrounds these decisions and determines the policy outcomes undertaken? In the case of NAFTA, Canada, Mexico and the United States are important agricultural trade partners. The political economy of achieving the agreement for the U.S. rested largely on its provisions with Mexico, as a bilateral trade agreement with Canada had been reached in 1988.

There are natural economic comparative advantages in agricultural production (for example, basic grains versus winter vegetables) between Mexico and the United States but also strong protection for some of the affected sectors. A stated goal of the NAFTA negotiators was that the agricultural agreement would go further than the WTO in reducing bilateral trade barriers. Domestic support programs were agreed to be in the multilateral WTO domain and not to be negotiable on a regional basis.

Chapter 6 describes the interest group involvement and concessions that went into achieving the NAFTA agricultural agreement. The agreement largely met the stated goal of eliminating all agricultural tariff barriers between Mexico and the United States over a fifteen-year period. That adjustment period is now completed and the Mexico-U.S. provisions of NAFTA stand (compared to other agreements around the world) as one of the deepest liberalizations of agricultural trade on a bilateral or regional basis. However, trade disputes between the NAFTA countries continue for sensitive products under claims of anti-dumping and other administered trade regulation. Agricultural interest groups in the U.S. extracted substantial concession within the NAFTA negotiations by positioning themselves as pivotal in securing passage by Congress of its implementing legislation once those concessions were achieved. One can imagine a different coalition having been put together for NAFTA approval with fewer concessions to agriculture had other groups that opposed the trade agreement pursued a similar strategy.

Chapters 7–10 trace the development of U.S. agricultural support policy through farm bills enacted in 1996, 2002, 2008 and 2014. This evaluation of U.S. farm policy in the WTO-era forms a core component of the book. A shown in Chapter 10 (Table 1), each of these four farm bills was enacted with large congressional majorities — veto proof when one party controlled both bodies of Congress (Republicans in 1996, Democrats in 2008) and smaller but still substantial in 2002 and 2014 when Republicans controlled the House Representatives and Democrats the Senate.

With agriculture a small but relatively prosperous and concentrated sector of the economy, it is plausible to maintain that U.S. farm policy is an equilibrium result of interest group lobbying. This is a conceptualization of the farm bill political process along lines of the formal models of Grossman and Helpman (1994, 1995) in which organized industries seek support from a government that values both campaign contributions and general welfare. Each of the four farm bills enacted since 1996 has been driven by specific contestation among various farm and nonfarm political interests. The chronology of proposals, debate, compromises and enactment is often portrayed as unique when it is occurring but is actually quite similar time and again. The substantive outcome of U.S. farm policy has evolved in directions that have lessened its distortionary effects, with each farm bill to varying degrees turning policy in a different direction while continuing to provide substantial support for farmers. Chapters 7–10 describe the outcomes for each of the farm bills and assesses the underlying forces that drove these decisions in the circumstances of its time.

Chapter 7, taken from *Policy Reform in American Agriculture* (Orden, Paarlberg and Roe 1999), evaluates the unexpected developments in the 1996 Federal Agricultural Improvement and Reform (FAIR) Act, also known informally as "freedom to farm." As described in earlier chapters of that book, by the 1990s U.S. farm policy for most of the major crops had evolved quite far from the New Deal agricultural support programs that had centered on price supports above market-clearing levels, government purchases and storage of crop surpluses, and annual supply control programs to limit supply and control fiscal costs. Farmers had gained increased flexibility about what crops they planted while remaining covered by the support programs and the form of support had evolved into two payment tiers, one provided only on a fixed program base acreage and fixed historical program yield when market prices were below target prices stipulated in a farm bill and the second, more-distortionary payments provide on all output when market prices were below lower support prices known for historical reasons as "loan rates." These reforms are characterized as a cash out of past farm support programs. This cash out left market prices flexible, took the government out of the business of storing excess commodities and made economic sense for an agricultural exporting country. Still the 1990 farm bill retained authority for annual supply controls and the planting flexibility of farmers remained limited.

As described in Chapter 7, the FAIR Act eliminated annual supply controls, provided farmers with planting flexibility on their full program acreage and kept loan rates at what seemed at the time to be relatively low levels below prevailing market prices. The FAIR Act also decoupled farm support payments from production decisions and market prices by unexpectedly replacing payments tied to target prices with fixed direct payments of nearly $5 billion annually based on historical output. The first set of changes extended the cash out reforms that had been occurring since the 1960s, while the fixed direct payments introduced a new element into U.S. support policy. Chapter 7 attributes the extension of the cash out to the election of the first Republican-controlled House of Representatives in forty years along with Republican control of the Senate. Freedom to farm was a longstanding conceptual principle of the Republicans and they sought an end to annual supply controls, more planting flexibility and low loan rates consistent with this view. The introduction of fixed direct payments was a more opportunistic reform. As market prices increased during 1995–1996, the anticipated payments under the target price program evaporated. The fixed direct payments were a way to capture those anticipated expenditures under the budget rules used by Congress in determining the cost of enacted legislation.

In a political environment in which budget battles between the Congress and a Democratic president led to shutdowns of the federal government in November and December 1995, the fixed direct payments were claimed as a reform that reduced program costs. In reality, farm support policy would have cost less with the high market prices at the time if the target price system had been retained. Reform advocates voiced the hope that these payments might be a transition, or buyout, bringing an end to commodity programs, while proponents of farm support noted that Congress remained the final guarantor of a safety net. The farm support permanent legislation with the New Deal type of programs from the 1930s and 1940s that each new farm bill temporarily supplants was kept in place by the FAIR Act, strengthening the case for another farm bill to follow. Reforms in 1996 didn't extend to sugar or dairy, where protection from import competition rather than being a competitive exporter dominated the interests of the industry and congressional farm policy decisions. Nor was the elimination of annual supply controls accompanied by ending long-term, Conservation Reserve Program acreage idling that had an environmental constituency as well as serving to limit production.

By 1998, market prices had fallen sharply and calls arose to abandon freedom to farm. Chapter 8, published in 2006, assesses the 2002 Farm Security and Rural Investment Act (FSRIA) that ensued. By 1998, Congress had enacted temporary additional support for farmers, setting the stage for enhanced expenditures in a new farm bill. The FSRIA reinstitutionalized countercyclical support payments based on target prices, adding a third tier of subsidies to the fixed direct payments and loan rate programs. Coming just at the time when efforts were underway to launch the WTO Doha Round of trade negotiations, the FSRIA was met with a barrage of criticism and equally strident defense by its advocates. Chapter 8 argues that both the severe critics and its staunch supporters overstated their cases. The FSRIA took few constructive unilateral steps toward reduction of U.S. farm subsidies (eliminating peanut production quotas was one), but it retained planting flexibility, did not significantly raise loan rates, and kept the renewed countercyclical payments tied to historical base acres and yields rather than tying the payments to current production decisions. That said, enactment of the new temporary farm support starting in 1998 followed by the 2002 FSRIA caused the U.S. to abandon an initial strong proposal for new WTO subsidy constraints that was tuned more to its support stance under the FAIR Act. Chapter 8 describes the slow evolution of the Doha framework for agriculture that followed, leading to little progress on a new agreement through July 2004.

Chapter 9, published in 2011, presents an analysis of U.S. farm policies through its WTO domestic support notifications, along the lines for which Chapter 5 lays out the basic framework of commitments. The U.S. commitment limit is annual support to $19.1 billion. The decoupled fixed direct payments introduced in 1996 are reflected in the notifications as exempt from counting in the CTAMS; instead they are notified in the "green box" of measures for which the Agreement on Agriculture describes specific criteria that qualify a measure for exclusion because it is defined to have "no, or minimal, trade-distorting effects or effects on production." The U.S. also excludes the countercyclical payments under the 2002 FSRIA from the CTAMS support that is counted against its commitment; in this case by arguing that they are non-product-specific because of planting flexibility and the fixed acreage and yields used to calculate the payments. The non-product-specific classification allows the U.S. to exclude the countercyclical payments because a *de minimis* exemption is provided for support less than 5 percent of the total value of agricultural production. The U.S. notifies the countercyclical payments as non-product-specific even though these payments go only to farmers who historically planted a limited set of crops.

The two exclusions from the CTAMS matter for U.S. compliance because in the low-price years 1999 and 2000 the notified CTAMS exceeded $16 billion, non-product-specific countercyclical payments exceeded $5.4 billion, and total non-product-specific support (which has to stay below the *de minimis* threshold to be exempted and also included crop insurance support payments) exceeded $7 billion. The WTO definition of MPS also matters to the CTAMS: Chapter 9 shows that for U.S. dairy and sugar, the notified MPS was significantly lower than the OECD PSE measure of the nominal value of border protection in almost all years.

As shown in Chapter 9, as late as 2005 the U.S. CTAMS support was nearly $13 billion, the fixed direct payment added $5 billion and *de minimis* non-product-specific support another $6 billion. Prices strengthened in 2006 and 2007, and notified CTAMS and countercyclical support declined accordingly. One proximate cause of the strengthening of prices was the U.S. biofuel policy, which mandated increased blending of corn-based ethanol into the fuel supply. The main ethanol policies are defined by separate legislation from farm bills and are not reflected in agricultural domestic support notifications (see Chapter 9). However, ethanol policy creates another measure by which agricultural prices can be affected. The 2008 Food, Conservation and Energy (FCE) Act was written under high world prices driven by various forces affecting world markets, and under anticipation of continued strong ethanol demand and other factors keeping upward pressure on corn and other grain prices in coming years.

The 2008 FCE Act largely continued the farm support polices set in place in 2002. Despite high prices, farmers remained wary of changes to the existing programs. Their strategy, as in other farm bill debates, was to protect their own funding and, in this case, the structure of their support programs, while seeking a broader coalition to achieve congressional majorities. In 2008, under a Democrat-controlled Congress the prospects for increased funding of conservation programs and nutrition assistance to the poor was as important to passage of a new farm bill as the commodity programs. The Food Stamp program, renamed the Supplemental Nutrition Assistance Program (SNAP), expanded eligibility criteria and signaled a shift from food access to improved nutrition. Eventually the FCE Act was enacted over a presidential veto (see Orden, Blandford and Josling (2010) for a more detailed description of the congressional debate and eventual veto override than provided in Chapter 9).

In terms of the farm support programs, while the fixed direct payments were retained in 2008 they came under scrutiny as critics questioned their legitimacy with high crop prices and eyed reductions to fund other priorities. The sharp rise in prices also led to introduction of a new policy measure able to provide support even if prices remained above the legislated target prices, which remained at their levels set in 2002. For farmers who chose to enroll, this new program, Average Crop Revenue Election (ACRE), made payments tied to current planted acres of a crop when per-acre revenue at the state level fell below a moving average of past revenue. Thus, similarly to the 1996 farm bill that introduced fixed direct payments as a new policy measure under relatively high market prices, the 2008 FCE Act created a new policy measure as a result of relatively high prices. The 2008 innovation addressed revenue variability in a range that was above the level associated with prices that would trigger countercyclical payments because of the high prices in 2008. However, enrollment in ACRE proved modest during

2008–2012 because of several penalties the FCE Act imposed for choice of this program.

Chapter 9 also elaborates in depth on the commitments the U.S. would face under the Doha Round 2008 draft modalities described in Chapter 5. These commitments are shown to significantly tighten the constraints on U.S. support. Nonetheless, a key finding is that if prices remained at future levels forecast by USDA in 2009 the U.S. would have been able to meet the tighter commitments under continuation of the FCE Act through 2016 had the Doha modalities been implemented starting in 2011. Product-specific new commitments on support for cotton, sugar and dairy were exceptions that might have required modification of the FCE Act support policies and expenditures on ACRE would potentially exceed U.S. commitments under the Doha draft modalities if enrollment was high. Lower prices than projected could also create compliance issues for the U.S. This outcome is much less likely under continuation of the commitment only on CTAMS support under the Agreement on Agriculture.

Chapter 10 extends an invited paper presented in January 2015 to assess the five-year Agricultural Act of 2014 that replaced the FCE Act. Similar to the policy process in 1995–1996, the 2014 farm bill debate was mired in disagreements about program design among competing interests within the farm lobby and was enmeshed in a broader deficit-related stand-off between a Republican-controlled House of Representative and a Democrat-controlled Senate and administration. This policy environment resulted in October 2013 in the first federal government shut down since 1995 and caused delay in enacting the new farm bill. The battle over the budget and entitlement spending arose from the deep economic recession and slow recovery after the financial crisis in 2008 and a deep divide over health care legislation. SNAP expenditures rose during the post-2007 economic slowdown (Wilde 2012), averaging $49.9 billion in 2008–2010 then $74.2 billion in 2011–2013. In contrast, the U.S. farm sector experienced a remarkable six years of prosperity. Although crop prices had dipped in 2009 and drought in 2012 caused heavy crop losses, net farm income averaged $74 billion during 2008–2010, increasing to $121 billion during 2011–13. Corn and cotton prices averaged over 40 percent higher during the latter three years, while soybean and wheat prices averaged 27 percent and 14 percent higher.

One consequence of this period of high prices is that premium subsidies and indemnity payments from crop insurance programs increased in relative importance among farm support expenditures, as described in an appendix to Chapter 10. Subsidized crop insurance had been growing in importance since the 1980s, with new types of insurance contracts developed, increased subsidies, a shift by most farmers from yield to revenue policies, and a growing number of crops and total acreage insured. Still, net indemnity payments (insurance payments less farmer-paid premiums) averaged only $2.1 billion during 2007–2010, less than half the level of the fixed direct payments. In contrast, net indemnity payments averaged $9.1 billion for 2011–2013, exceeding direct payments each year, and peaking at $13.3 billion after the 2012 drought.

With high incomes, but facing yield, price and revenue variability, and under pressure to show a reduction in anticipated program costs for renewal of the farm bill, most farm groups endorsed wider calls to eliminate the fixed direct payments as unjustified when farm incomes were high. They opted to defend crop insurance instead and argued that most of the savings from eliminating the fixed payments should go into strengthening insurance and other downside risk safety net programs. This proved the eventual outcome.

Chapter 10 describes the complex set of program options adopted in 2014. The countercyclical payment program and ACRE moving-average revenue support program were revised, embedding higher support parameters. Crop insurance was enhanced, including through a new program to partly cover insurance deductibles. The traditional upland cotton fixed and countercyclical payment measures were redesigned into a new cotton insurance program. This was a reform that allowed the U.S. to resolve a longstanding WTO dispute with Brazil over cotton subsidies, while the domestic industry could also support the reform because of high levels of recent indemnity payments and large premium subsidies for the new program. The dairy support programs were also redesigned into a margin protection program, while the sugar program was left intact; both were outcomes sought by producers. Overall, nearly 80 percent of the savings from eliminating fixed direct payments was captured in anticipated increased safety net spending. The fiscal cost of the farm bill with this enhanced safety net is less certain than with the fixed direct payments. But whatever options they choose from the 2014 farm bill farmers are given increased protection against falling prices or declining revenue. Prices fell sharply during the summer of 2014 but partly recovered later in the year. This is emblematic that the cost of the 2014 farm bill may prove more or less than if the 2008 FCE Ac had been extended. In terms of WTO compliance, the new cotton and dairy programs will increase product-specific AMS support, while the revised countercyclical and revenue programs will increase non-product-specific support. In Chapter 10 it is concluded that neither of these increases is likely to cause compliance problems for the U.S. under the Agreement on Agriculture. But they could lead to dispute cases like the Brazil-U.S. cotton case based on the effects of the subsidies (including crop insurance) on world markets. Expenditures under the Agriculture Act of 2014 also are likely to exceed a number of the potential commitments included in the Doha Round 2008 draft modalities.

Looking back across the four farm bills enacted since the WTO Agreement on Agriculture came into effect, several conclusions can be drawn. The 1996 FAIR Act and the Agricultural Act of 2014 bookend an experience with fixed direct payments that have proven unsustainable politically despite the exempt treatment of this type of payments in the WTO. The U.S. experience with the fixed payments began and ended in years of high crop prices. At the outset, adopting the fixed payments provided farmers with assured support they would otherwise have lost. Conversely, at the end farmers traded those assured payments for enhanced downside risk protection with uncertain levels of support. This latter shift demonstrates that through these two decades of farm policy renewal there is a remarkable core continuity of the long, historical countercyclical design of U.S. farm policy. Likewise, the cash out reforms of planting flexibility, countercyclical payments tied to historical not current production, and relatively low loan rates have largely been sustained. The expanded role of crop insurance, which operates against losses within a production year is consistent with this core countercyclical character of farm support.

A second observation is the limited role that the WTO has played in disciplining U.S. farm support programs. The expansion of subsidies in the 2002 FSRIA left the U.S. in a poor position to argue for significant multilateral reforms in the early phase of the Doha negotiations. Likewise, enactment of the Agricultural Act of 2014 makes it difficult for the U.S. to contribute to attaining limits along lines of the 2008 draft modalities on a global level in the future. What discipline the WTO has imposed has come from dispute settlement, as demonstrated in the Brazil-U.S. cotton case. But these cases are few, protracted, and far between.

What this suggests is that U.S. farm policy will remain for the foreseeable future largely a matter of domestic determination. The farm bill debates are always contestations among interest groups with voices on the margins arguing for more reform or for deeper support. Under differing political and economic circumstances, the outcomes have moved U.S. farm policy in various directions around its core countercyclical character and continuous support for farmers. The farm lobby alone is not sufficient to secure enactment of farm bills, but each time it builds a broader coalition and there are many ways majority congressional votes can be secured. Over the past 20 years, the farm bill coalition has proven robust. Achieving enhanced disciplines on agricultural support and border protection through multilateral negotiations seems uncertain after twelve years of the Doha Round. In contrast, it is near certain there will be future U.S. farm bills. This is a sobering assessment of the political reality of farm policy from the perspective of achieving less disarray in world agriculture, despite the reforms that have made U.S. support less distortionary over time and seem to be permanent.

Policy Interactions

In a world of specialization, research papers often elaborate primarily on a single issue. The third section of the book is composed of three diverse papers with the common theme of assessing interrelated impacts of economic policies. Emergence of the EU as a grain exporter in the 1980s under its Common Agricultural Policy of high administered prices was a source of friction between the U.S. and EU. Disciplining the EU export subsidies utilized to move European grain into world markets with those high domestic prices became a key U.S. objective in the Uruguay Round GATT negotiations.

Chapter 11, published in 1989, examines the effects of EU price policies on French agricultural production in the context of also assessing the impacts of technological change that occurred in this advanced economy over the period 1960–1984. French agricultural output is disaggregated into four categories (cereals, noncereal crops, milk and animal products) and inputs are classified as variable (hired labor, fertilizers/energy and animal feed), quasi-fixed (farm capital and family labor) and fixed (land). A short-run variable profit function is estimated for French agriculture with the quasi-fixed factors held at observed values. This short-run profit function can also be solved to provide information about long-run profit maximization in which the quasi-fixed factors adjust to optimal levels. The model is specified to account for technological change through lagged French public agricultural research expenditures and international technology transfers. This sets up a comparison of effects of the CAP price policies that induce increased output along a supply function versus increased competitiveness of French agriculture through outward movements of that function over time. Four measures of French agricultural support policies were included in the model as additional government interventions and deviations for normal rainfall were included to control for weather variations.

Over the twenty-five year study period, French agricultural output rose substantially. Real output prices declined even with the CAP interventions and variable input prices increased, particularly for hired labor. The econometric model is able to disentangle the observed movements of output and prices to estimate upward-sloping output supply functions and downward sloping variable input demand functions that are price-inelastic in the short run. These functions are more price responsive, but responses are still inelastic, in the long run when the quasi-fixed factors are assumed to adjust to their optimal levels. The model also estimates a strong positive effect of domestic agricultural research and international technology transfers on French agricultural output over time. Using the model estimates, growth in French cereals and milk production between 1960–1962 and 1982–1984 is apportioned among the explanatory variables. The results demonstrate the importance of technological change in French agriculture. Estimated output of cereals from the model grew by nearly 200 percent and milk output by 52 percent over the two decades. Most of this growth was explained by technological change. Had French agricultural prices been at world levels instead of support levels of the CAP, the increase in cereals production would have been 6 percent less and milk production 24 percent less.

In the conclusion of Chapter 11 it is argued that the estimate effects of CAP price interventions indicate that the effects of international negotiations to reduce the high EU support levels at the time could be overstated in the context of the other determinants of European agricultural production, either by competitors anticipating large gains from such an agreement or by those who argued it would be a major concession. A second implication is that Europe might change its view toward agricultural trade liberalization as it continued to become more competitive and thus there might be unexpected progress in trade negotiations. Progress in the multilateral negotiations has not lived up to that possibility. But stating in the early 1990s the EU has undertaken a significant reform of its agricultural support policies, moving almost entirely away from administered prices above world levels as the basis of support and substituting whole-farm fixed direct payments decoupled from prices and planting decisions (Josling and Swinbank (2011) and Josling and Tangermann (2015) among others provide discussions of this transformation). Such a reform of EU agricultural policy was not widely foreseen in the late 1980s, but in retrospect is reform movement in just the direction of domestic policy realignment the analysis of determinants of French agricultural production anticipated.

Chapter 12, published in 2000, is a purely theoretical comparative policy analysis. The Grossman-Helpman (1994, 1995) model of political economy equilibrium when some industries are organized to lobby government for support by offering financial contributions and governments care about contributions and public welfare is extended to introduce environmental externalities and include both first-best policies for addressing the externality (production or consumption taxes or subsidies) and trade policies (tariffs, import subsidies and export taxes and subsidies). The interplay that is demonstrated between policy effects and equilibrium outcomes are suggestive of the importance of growing campaign contributions in U.S. political campaigns and the complexity of trade and global climate change negotiations fifteen years later.

In a normative model without the political economy dimension, Pigovian taxes under the first-best policies would lead to socially optimal environmental outcome for domestic externalities, while trade policies would be used by large-country noncooperative governments to improve their terms of trade (by imposing optimal tariffs) and to address global externalities resulting from production abroad. Trade policies alone would result in sub-optimal environmental quality for a production externality because of the distortions they create for consumers as well as affecting production decisions.

In the extension of the Grossman-Helpman model in Chapter 12, governments choose policies efficiently among those available. In the political economy equilibrium the environmental outcomes are not optimal because a policy measure is used both to address the externality and to accommodate organized industries — for example a production tax would be used to address a negative production externality, but accommodating an organized industry implies a production subsidy (outcomes with consumption externalities are also examined in Chapter 12). Moreover, it is not certain that the first-best policy will result in higher environmental quality than trade policy alone. This is because the first-best policy is more efficient both at addressing the externality and providing support to the organized industry. The equilibrium outcome for environmental quality is uncertain versus the outcome with only trade policy that is less efficient in both respects.

A similar ambiguity arises about cooperative versus noncooperative behavior between the two governments. Cooperating governments avoid imposing costs on each other as they address environmental externalities and support organized industries. However, availability of first-best policy measures will not necessarily lead to better environmental quality than trade policies alone, again because of the combination of environmental and industry contribution objectives the governments have. Moreover, while the governments will always use the most efficient policy measures available, in either the noncooperative or cooperative scenario the organized industries may prefer that only inefficient policies are available since their equilibrium contribution costs as they compete for support with other organized industries may be lower under restricted policy availability.

Chapter 13, published in 2010, provides a second empirical study of policy interaction effects. The World Bank had undertaken a major study of distortions to agricultural incentives and relative protection of agriculture worldwide, expanding on and updating the earlier study led by Kruger, Schiff and Valdes (1991). This study covered 75 developed and developing countries over the period 1955–2007 (Anderson 2009). In a nutshell, what this assessment found was a general trend toward less disprotection of agriculture over time, arising partly from less taxation of agricultural exports among countries and partly from reduced protection of nonagricultural sectors. Using a global computable general equilibrium (CGE) model and the new protection measurements, the World Bank study resulted in an estimated annual gain to the world economy of $233 billion from the reductions in agricultural protection that had occurred and costs to the world from the remaining distortions of $168 billion.

Chapter 13 examines the effects of global and domestic trade liberalization on Pakistan, one of nine countries include in one project of the World Bank study. The framework for this project was to link the global CGE model to more detailed country-level CGE models for each country in order to examine the effects of agricultural and nonagricultural trade liberalization on the nine economies in more depth than the global model allowed. A key focus was on the effects of trade liberalization on poverty, with the country models providing various disaggregations of sectors, factor returns and households in order to measure the poverty impacts. A concordance of the more detailed sectoral specification of the country models to the broader sector aggregates in the global model allowed for cohesive simulation of global (rest-of-the-world) liberalization excluding the specific country, unilateral domestic liberalization by that country, or a combination of both.

The Pakistan model disaggregated the economy into 27 sectors and 19 household groups with different consumption patterns and sources of income (from labor, capital, land and other sources). The policy interaction examined was the effect on the poverty reduction achieved from trade liberalization caused by different taxes raised to keep government revenue constant as tariff receipts were eliminated. The first tax scenario was raising direct (income) taxes, which are paid only by the urban non-poor in Pakistan. Alternatively, indirect (sales) taxes were increased across all goods, in which case the tax burden was spread across all households.

For Pakistan, the impacts of own-country liberalization were significantly larger than the impacts of rest-of-world liberalization and the effects of nonagricultural liberalization were considerable larger than the effects of agricultural liberalization. In the first simulation scenarios, poverty in Pakistan declined by 6.4 percent with full liberalization globally and domestically, and declined by 1.8 percent with liberalization only for agriculture. Thus, most of the poverty-reduction effect came from nonagricultural liberalization. The specifications of each of the nine country models differed, but overall the poverty reduction in Pakistan was larger than the reduction from full liberalization in the other eight countries. Chapter 13 also shows that the extent of poverty reduction in Pakistan is strongly affected by the form of taxation applied. The results with direct taxation include the income transfer effect of government revenue collection being concentrated on the urban non-poor. When an indirect tax is applied instead, poverty is indicated to rise by 0.5 percent with combined nonagricultural and agricultural liberalization. Poverty still declines by 1.2 percent for agricultural liberalization only which involved less loss of tariff revenue and less of a shift to taxes. In conclusion, one has to be careful in attributing poverty effects to trade liberalization without taking associated fiscal policy changes into account. Because of the narrow income tax base only on the urban non-poor in Pakistan, the effects of tax policy decisions along with trade liberalization are highlighted.

Sanitary and Phytosanitary Measures

The fourth section of the book turns to the regulation of agriculture and food production, processing and distribution for health, safety and product quality as it affects international trade. With regulatory responsibilities held by sovereign governments, differences in regulatory measures inevitably arise and international borders become a point at which many regulations differentiate among products. These regulatory measures play an important role in determining trade flows and exporters can be concerned that the regulations impose unnecessary restrictions or costs that serve to protect the domestic industry. Yet many of the health, safety and quality regulations serve legitimate, welfare-enhancing objectives. Again, policies with implications for trade are driven more by domestic concerns than by trade considerations per se. The term non-tariff trade "barriers" seems too strong to apply to this body of regulations and the term health, safety and quality non-tariff "measures" is more appropriate. How to discipline these measures so they do not create unnecessary obstacles to trade has been a concern of national governments and the WTO.

Chapter 14, published in 2001, provides a simple diagrammatic exposition of the difference between the legal obligations of countries under the WTO Agreement on the Application of Sanitary and Phytosanitary Measures (the SPS Agreement) and the economic benefits and costs associated with trade. Under the SPS Agreement, in the presence of non-zero risks to plant, animal or human health from imported products, countries have the authority to set what they deemed are appropriate levels of protection from risks and to restrict trade of products that exceed these risk levels. Diagrammatically, if risk-based costs are measured on the horizontal axis of a graph and other net benefits on the vertical axis, countries can set their level of protection (a vertical line in the graph) anywhere to the right of the vertical axis. The discipline imposed by the SPS Agreement binds countries away from the axis itself: if there is zero risk then SPS measures are prohibited, but such measures are allowed if there is non-zero risk, no matter how negligible. Chapter 13 makes the point that this legal framework does not require further consideration of economic benefits and costs. This leads to conundrums from a benefit-cost analysis perspective. Under the SPS Agreement, a product with risk to the left of the country's appropriate level of protection would be imported even if the risk-based costs exceeded the other net benefits. Conversely, any product with risk to the right of the appropriate level of protection would not be imported even if the other net benefits from trade exceeded the risk-based costs. In short, the SPS Agreement requires a risk-basis for regulations addressing plant, animal and human health, but is not a blueprint for policy determination from an economic perspective.

Chapters 15 and 16 are taken from the book *Food Regulation and Trade: Toward a Safe and Open Global System* (Josling, Roberts and Orden 2004). These chapters elaborate further on the types of regulations utilized to address agricultural and food health, safety and product quality issues and review the disciplines the WTO imposes on these measures. Unlike tariffs or domestic support levels, there are no numerical targets that negotiations on regulatory measures can seek to achieve and enforce. What the WTO sets out to accomplish is more difficult for regulatory measures; to impose disciplines on how countries approach writing the regulations without defining what the regulations are.

Chapter 15 lays out the economic rationales for regulation, offers a classification scheme that distinguishes among these measures along lines that can be significant for assessing their effects on international trade, and distinguishes among different types of regulatory instruments. The rationales for regulation lie in providing public goods (such as disease control that often cannot be accomplished optimally by individual producers) and to facilitate production and exchange by reinforcing confidence in markets and lowering information and transaction costs (such as when food products have credence characteristics that consumers cannot detect). Regulatory interventions are justified economically when they improve social welfare net of costs they impose.

The classification scheme distinguishes among regulatory measures based on goals (risk-reducing or quality-related), attribute focus (content or process attributes of the product), breadth (vertical through a product chain or horizontal across products) and scope (uniform applied to products of all origins or specific to products only of certain origins). The instruments used in regulations are divided into quantitative restrictions such as banning imports from certain countries or regions on a temporary or permanent basis, technical specifications regarding product or process standards, and information remedies requiring mandatory disclosure or setting controls on voluntary claims. Finally, mechanisms for regulatory conformity assessment have to be established.

Having developed this roadmap for categorizing regulations and their application, several complexities of regulatory evaluation are explored in Chapter 15. Both risk-reducing and quality-related regulations can affect domestic or foreign supply by affecting the absolute and relative costs of bringing products into a market. These regulations can also shift consumer demand as willingness to pay for products is affected by knowledge and confidence about the product attributes. For risk-reducing regulations, disagreements arise over scientific evidence of risks. Regulations have to be assessed relative to the appropriate counterfactual situation. A regulation might raise costs of market access, but the alternative in the absence of the regulation might be complete exclusion of the product from a market, not access without bearing those costs. Perceptions of best policy will differ with underlying philosophical approach (a precautionary approach against unknown risks is contrasted with prevention of demonstrated risks) and with levels of accountability should adverse outcomes occur. The diagrammatic comparison in Chapter 14 of risk costs and appropriate level of protection under the SPS Agreement versus benefit-cost analysis is extended to illustrate optimal regulatory decisions that maximize economic benefits net of risk costs. Compared to this optimal decision, both overprotection (too much regulation and too little trade) and underprotection (too little regulation and too much trade) are possible. Political economy capture of regulation by either producer or consumer interest groups can lead to suboptimal policies in either direction. These and other considerations underlie the effort to strengthen international regulatory oversight with the goal of ensuring that agricultural and food regulations do not impede welfare-enhancing trade, and, at the same time, give countries wide latitude to set their health, safety and quality standards.

Chapter 16 presents the provisions embodied in the WTO to work towards this goal. GATT Article XX recognizes the right of countries to adopt restrictions on trade if necessary to achieve legitimate policy objectives such as health, safety or conservation of natural resources. An Agreement on Technical Barriers to Trade signed by some GATT members established obligations to ensure that mandatory regulations, voluntary standards and conformity assessment procedures did not create unnecessary obstacles to trade (this was earlier referred to as the Standards Code but since revised under the WTO is referred to as the TBT Agreement). Creation of the WTO is associated with establishing a more comprehensive set of commitments on regulatory measures and standards, just as it is associated with establishing the first comprehensive set of commitments on agricultural domestic support, protection and export competition. In addition, the WTO encompasses strengthened dispute settlement rules, making it more feasible for countries to seek redress for violation of the multilateral rules by a trade partner.

The commitments governing regulations and standards under the WTO include the GATT articles, a revised TBT agreement, a new SPS agreement, and a new agreement on Trade-Related Aspects of Intellectual Property Rights (TRIPS Agreement). Chapter 16 describes these three agreements, including the role of international standard organizations, and provided one of the early summaries of experiences with their implementation during the first six years of the WTO.

For the SPS Agreement, the key requirement is that measures be based on scientific risk assessment and this requirement has proven critical to judgments reached in dispute cases. The SPS Agreement also encourages use of internationally agreed standards for achieving risk protection (these standards are presumed compliant with corresponding commitments under the SPS Agreement), and to consider harmonization, equivalence and subnational regional applications of risk-reducing regulations. Applied measured are required to be no more trade-restrictive than necessary to achieve a country's appropriate level of protection and are to be notified to the WTO when adopted or modified. The TBT Agreement covers technical regulations, standards and conformity assessment related to objectives such as prevention of deceptive practices and protection of health and safety not covered by the SPS Agreement. Again, measures applied are not to be more trade-restrictive than necessary to achieve a legitimate objective and are to be notified to the WTO. The TRIPS agreement obligates countries to provide enforcement of various types of trade-related intellectual property rights, including protection of geographic indicators (GIs) for commercial identification which are particularly important for agricultural and food products.

The early implementation experience assessed in Chapter 16 demonstrates the beneficial effects that increased transparency and ultimate access to WTO dispute settlement has had on unilateral regulatory decision making, on bilateral consultations and negotiations about disputed measures, and the resolution of a few cases through dispute settlement decisions. It also demonstrates the intractability of some disagreements among countries over what constitutes appropriate regulations, the complexity of regulating the production processes of products that do not result in tangible differences in final product attributes (technically known as non-product-related process and production methods) which are of growing importance in consumers' product perceptions and demand, and continued difference in approaches to recognition of GIs. Another decade of experience with WTO disciplines on regulatory measures has accumulated since Chapter 16 was published. Thousands more notifications of regulations have been made and vetted through the relevant WTO committees, hundreds of issues have been negotiated bilaterally or regionally outside of the WTO, and a small number of additional formal disputes have been adjudicated or are in the dispute settlement process. This additional experience confirms the lessons from the first six years. There is no fixed end point in the disciplining of regulatory measures affecting international trade of agricultural and food products, only a continuing effort to see what improvements can be achieved within a heterogeneous and changing environment among countries in terms of scientific knowledge, demand for product attributes and perceptions of what regulation legitimately should accomplish.

Chapter 17, published in 2008, provides an empirical analysis of one particular case of SPS regulation, the full opening of the U.S. market to importation of Hass avocados from Mexico in 2007. This culminated the reversal over fifteen years of regulatory decision making of a complete import ban that had been in place in earlier decades. The empirical analysis of the avocado case brings specificity to several aspects of the general discussion of trade-related regulatory measures. A simulation model is developed incorporating four key dimensions: supply function estimates for California (the U.S. avocado producing area), Mexico and Chile (another foreign supplier); a range of U.S. Department of Agriculture estimates of pest risks associated with trade; costs of compliance with risk-reducing regulatory measures; and consumer demand from experience under partial opening of the market starting in 1997. The results demonstrate that opening the full U.S. market under a set of SPS measures designed to reduce pest risks in Mexican orchards, packing sheds and during transport to the United States created a trade opportunity with little risk or pest-related losses to domestic producers. Export quantities from Mexico increased by more than 200 million pounds compared to partial opening of the U.S. market. Domestic suppliers' producer surplus declines in face of increased competition but U.S. consumer welfare gains more than offset these losses and a U.S. welfare gain of \$75–\$80 million is projected. Domestic producer surplus losses and consumer and net welfare gains are insensitive to the level of pest risk from trade when the SPS measures are imposed, but with unregulated trade damages to domestic production at the high end of the range of pest risks not only affect domestic producers adversely but drive prices up and result in lower welfare gains than with regulation. What is demonstrated is that appropriate regulations can be designed to achieve economic welfare gains while minimizing trade-related risks to a domestic industry. More generally, the avocado trade case illustrates how a trade agreement such as NAFTA can stimulate trade opportunities that cannot be specified in numeric commitments within the agreement itself and that strong lobbying for protection by domestic interest groups can be overcome. Moreover, in retrospect the simulation model in Chapter 17 underestimated the net beneficial effects of better year-around availability of fresh avocados in the U.S. market. Overall demand, and thus domestic production and imports, proved even more robust after 2007 than the model anticipated. While one cannot make too much of a single case study, for all of these reasons in terms of the broad theme of seeking less disarray in world agricultural markets the avocado case is a very satisfying chapter with which to bring the book to closure.

References

Anderson, K. (editor). 2009. *Distortions to Agricultural Incentives: A Global Perspective, 1955–2007*. London: Palgrave Macmillan and Washington DC: World Bank.

Bernanke, B. S. "Alternative Explanations of the Money-Income Correlation." *Carnegie-Rochester Conference Series on Public Policy* 25 (1986): 49–100.

Dornbusch, R. "Expectations and Exchange Rate Dynamics." *Journal of Political Economy* (1976): 1161–1174.

Engel, R. F. and W. J. Granger. "Co-integration and Error Correction: Representation, Estimation and Testing." *Econometrica* 55 (1987): 251–276.

Grossman, G. and E. Helpman. "Protection for Sale." *American Economic Review* 84 (1994): 833–850.

Grossman, G. and E. Helpman. "Trade Wars and Trade Talks," *Journal of Political Economy* 103 (1995): 675–708.

Johansen, S. "Estimation and Hypothesis Testing of Cointegrating Vectors in Gaussian Vector Autoregressive Models." *Econometrica* 59 (1991): 1551–1580.

Johnson, D. G. 1973. *World Agriculture in Disarray*. London: Macmilllan.

Josling, T, D. Roberts and D. Orden. 2004. *Food Regulation and Trade: Toward a Safe and Open Global System*. Washington DC: Peterson Institute for International Economics.

Josling, T. and A. Swinbank. 2011. "European Union," in *WTO Disciplines on Agricultural Support: Seeking a Fair Basis for Trade* (D. Orden, D. Blandford and T. Josling, editors). Cambridge UK: Cambridge University Press.

Josling, T. E. and S. Tangermann. 2015. *Transatlantic Food and Agricultural Trade Policy: Fifty Years of Conflict and Convergence*. Cheltenham: Edward Elgar.

Kruger, A. O. (editor). 1996. *The Political Economy of American Trade Policy.* Chicago IL: University of Chicago Press.

Krueger, A., M. Schiff, and A. Valdes. *The Political Economy of Agricultural Pricing Policy*. Baltimore, MD: The Johns Hopkins University Press, 1991.

OECD. 2013. *Agricultural Policy Monitoring and Evaluation 2013: OECD Countries and Emerging Economies*. Paris: OECD.

Orden, D., D. Blandford and T. Josling (editors). 2011. *WTO Disciplines on Agricultural Support: Seeking a Fair Basis for Trade*. Cambridge UK: Cambridge University Press.

Orden, D., D. Blandford and T. Josling. 2010. "Determinants of Farm Policies in the United States," in *Political Economy of Distortions to Agricultural Incentives* (K. Anderson, editor). Cambridge UK: Cambridge University Press and Washington DC: World Bank.

Orden, D., R. Paarlberg and T. Roe. 1999. *Policy Reform in American Agriculture: Analysis and Prognosis*. Chicago IL: University of Chicago Press.

Orden, D., F. Cheng, H. Nguyen, U. Grote, M. Thomas, K. Mullen and D. Sun. 2007. *Agricultural Producer Support Estimates for Developing Countries: Measurement Issues and Evidence from India, Indonesia, China and Vietnam*. Research Report 152. Washington DC: International Food Policy Research Institute.

Schuh, G. E. "The Exchange Rate and U.S. Agriculture." *American Journal of Agricultural Economics* 56:1 (February 1974): 1–13.

Sims, C. A. "Macroeconomics and Reality." *Econometrica* 48:1 (1980): 1–48.

Warren, G. F. "Which Does Agriculture Need–Readjustment or Legislation?" *Journal of Farm Economics* 10 (1928): 1–15.

Section I:

Macroeconomic Impacts on Agriculture

Chapter 2

Monetary Impacts on Prices in the Short and Long Run: Some Evidence from New Zealand

John C. Robertson and David Orden

This paper presents support for long-run monetary neutrality based on evidence that individual time series for money, manufacturing prices, and agricultural prices are nonstationary but cointegrated, with a stationary proportional long-run relationship among their levels. Dynamic simulations from a vector error-correction model with this restriction imposed show that monetary shocks shift relative prices in favor of agriculture in the short run and permanently raise nominal prices. Manufacturing price shocks have similar long-run effects but initially place agriculture in a cost-price squeeze, while agricultural price shocks are transitory and have little impact on the other series.

Key words: cointegration, long-run monetary neutrality, unit roots, vector error-correction models.

Whether monetary policy has sustained effects on relative prices has been a crucial question in recent discussions of macroeconomic impacts on agriculture. At issue are whether levels of agricultural and nonagricultural prices respond proportionally to changes in the level of the money supply in the long run, and whether there are predictable deviations from such neutrality in the short run. An important hypothesis concerning these issues is that agriculture is a competitive sector in which its prices are more flexible than those in nonagricultural (fix-price) sectors. Under this hypothesis, it has been argued that expansionary monetary policy favors agriculture and may cause short-run agricultural prices to overshoot their long-run equilibrium levels, while contractionary monetary policy shifts relative prices against agriculture (Bordo; Rausser, Chalfant, and Stamoulis). Alternatively, it has been argued that price shocks arising in oligopolistic nonagricultural sectors, and accommodated by expansionary monetary policy, cause inflation and place agriculture in a cost-price squeeze (Tweeten). The short-run effects of monetary accommodation of supply shocks in agriculture and other competitive sectors have also received attention (Gordon, Van Duyne). None of these arguments about relationships among money and prices in the short run are inconsistent with neutrality in the long run if nominal prices in all sectors eventually reach new equilibrium levels proportional to the money supply. This is the long-run outcome of most theoretical models.

Empirically, a number of recent articles have utilized the impulse response functions from vector autoregression (VAR) models to investigate the relationships among monetary policy and agricultural and other prices in the short run. These articles have presented evidence of non-neutrality in Brazil (Bessler), the United States (Chambers, Orden, Devadoss and Meyers), and Canada (Taylor and Spriggs) but have generally neglected the long-run behavior of money and prices implied by their models. A VAR imposes no testable, theoretically consistent, long-run equilibrium conditions, and estimated long-run results have been viewed in some cases as "nonsensical" (Sims, Mount).

In this paper, the long-run and short-run em-

John C. Robertson is a graduate student and research fellow, and David Orden is an assistant professor, Department of Agricultural Economics, Virginia Polytechnic Institute and State University.

This research was supported in part by the Reserve Bank of New Zealand and in part by the Agriculture and Rural Economy Division, Economic Research Service, U.S. Department of Agriculture.

The authors have benefited from suggestions by Ralph Lattimore, Terry Roe, Robert Myers, Anya McGuirk, John Kitchen, Barbara Craig, and Aris Spanos. An earlier version of this paper was presented at a Reserve Bank seminar and at the 1989 Conference of the Australian Agricultural Economics Society. The authors thank Paul Cruse (Reserve Bank), Rod St. Hill and Bert Ward (Lincoln College), Gary Griffith, Ronald Bewley, and other seminar and conference participants for their comments.

pirical behavior of quarterly levels of money, agricultural prices, and manufacturing prices in New Zealand are analyzed jointly for the period 1963:1–1987:1. The long-run results provide evidence about the theoretical monetary neutrality hypothesis. For New Zealand, the individual money and price series appear nonstationary because of unit roots, as is often the case among aggregate macroeconomic variables (Nelson and Plosser). They also appear cointegrated, so that linear combinations of the series are stationary. Cointegration implies stable equilibrium relationships to which money and prices have a tendency to return (Engle and Granger). The cointegrating relationships found are consistent with long-run proportionality between the level of the money supply and the levels of nominal agricultural and manufacturing prices, and, hence, with neutrality of money in the long run.

Cointegration also has implications for the specification of models of the dynamic relationships among money and prices. These dynamics provide a basis for assessing the various arguments that have been made about short-run deviations from neutrality and are important for New Zealand because of the role of agriculture in the economy. To evaluate these dynamics, while imposing the long-run neutrality restriction, a vector error-correction (VEC) model is specified. In a VEC model, lagged deviations from the long-run equilibrium relationships among the cointegrated variables restrict the interactions within a system of autoregressive equations of first differences of the series. When there is cointegration, a VEC model provides more efficient parameter estimates than a VAR model in levels, while a VAR model in differences ignores information about the levels of the series and is misspecified. Thus, the VEC model provides coherent estimates of the behavior of money and prices in the short and long run. Such inferences are not obtained when support for cointegration among nonstationary series is lacking, as has been the case for money and prices in the United States (Stock and Watson, Orden and Fackler) or for commodity prices among countries (Ardeni).[1]

Organization of the paper is as follows. In the next section, some of the factors affecting the interactions among money and prices in New Zealand are described. In the third section, the stationarity properties of the money and price series are reported and the evidence of long-run monetary neutrality is presented. In the fourth section, the VEC model is specified and short-run non-neutrality hypotheses are evaluated. The final section provides a summary and some conclusions.

Structural Characteristics of the New Zealand Economy

New Zealand is a small and agriculturally trade-dependent nation. The farming sector accounts for around 10% of gross domestic product (GDP) and, including processed agricultural products, around 55% of current account receipts. The economy also contains a well-developed manufacturing sector contributing some 25% of GDP. Hence, the sectoral effects of monetary policy and the dynamic relationships between the farming and manufacturing sectors in terms of relative prices, resource allocation, and profitability are important.

Historically, a variety of policies have served to insulate New Zealand from the world economy. Until 1985, domestic monetary policy and a managed exchange rate were closely coordinated and financial markets were tightly regulated. Nominal exchange-rate adjustments were undertaken periodically to maintain a relatively stable, but overvalued, real exchange rate (Rayner and Lattimore).

The manufacturing sector has received relatively high levels of import protection, primarily based on import quotas rather than tariffs. Protection levels for manufacturing have been well above their levels in other OECD countries. The manufacturing sector has also been characterized by a highly centralized wage-setting process with cost-plus-markup pricing policies (Chapple).

In contrast, the agricultural sector has been primarily an export sector and a price taker in international markets. Although a variety of

[1] With the exception of Taylor and Spriggs, who difference their money and price series, the VAR models of short-run monetary impacts cited above were estimated using levels of potentially nonstationary data. A comparative analysis is beyond the scope of this paper, but it would be interesting to examine the robustness of the estimated dynamics from each of these previous studies with an emphasis on tests for nonstationarity and cointegration and model specification based on the results of these tests. Spriggs is currently evaluating whether cointegration affects the specification of his model and has found evidence of cointegration of money and a number of disaggregated price series in Canada. For the United States, we do not find evidence of cointegration among nonstationary series for money and indices of agricultural and manufacturing prices. Evidence of structural change during the 1963:1–1987:1 period complicates making a direct comparison to our results for New Zealand.

support programs have been implemented, agriculture has received relatively low levels of direct producer assistance (Lattimore). With managed exchange rates, volatility in world prices has been reflected in domestic prices. Some exchange-rate adjustments have been undertaken to insulate domestic agriculture from world price fluctuations (for example, the New Zealand dollar was appreciated in 1972–73 and was depreciated in 1975–76). Agriculture has also been subject to various domestic stabilization programs, particularly in the early 1980s, but these policies have never fully offset changes in world prices (Johnson).

With chronic overvaluation of its currency and protection of its manufacturing sector, New Zealand has experienced continual deterioration of its current account balance since the mid-1970s. Widespread wage-price controls were implemented in June 1982 in an attempt to reduce a high domestic inflation rate. These controls became untenable when government deficits reached 9% of GDP and the current account deficit 4.0% of GDP in 1984. As a consequence, the newly elected Labor Government initiated a broad liberalization of the economy aimed at deregulation of financial markets (including floating the New Zealand dollar in March 1985), reduced levels of regulation and direct assistance to specific industries (including elimination of most producer assistance and stabilization programs for agriculture during 1985), and gradual elimination of the import substitution bias of trade policy through reduction of tariffs and other import barriers.

Long-Run Neutrality

The relationships among money and prices in New Zealand were modeled using quarterly data on the money supply, $M1$, manufacturing prices, IP, and agricultural prices, FP. The data are from the Reserve Bank and Department of Statistics data bases and are transformed by taking logarithms. The measure of money is the level of $M1$ (currency plus demand deposits), and the prices are nominal producer output price indices excluding taxes and subsidy payments. The data are plotted in figure 1. Levels of money and the two price indices have risen over time, with agricultural prices exhibiting more variability than manufacturing prices or money.[2]

Long-run monetary neutrality implies a stable equilibrium relationship in which levels of nominal manufacturing and agricultural prices are proportional to the money supply. However, if the individual series are nonstationary because of unit roots, then linear combinations of the series are generally nonstationary and the series have no tendency to move together over time. The long-run neutrality hypothesis requires that some stationary relationships exist among money and prices, which will be the case when the series are cointegrated. For an N-dimensional nonstationary vector Y_t of cointegrated series, one or more vectors $\alpha_i \neq 0$ exists such that $\alpha_i'Y_t = z_{it}$ is stationary (Engle and Granger). The vector α_i is called a cointegrating vector and the z_{it}'s (the error-correction terms) are deviations from the long-run equilibrium. When the series are cointegrated, the long-run relationship $\alpha_i'Y_t = 0$ will tend to be reestablished after disequilibrating shocks. For the neutrality hypothesis to hold requires in addition that the coefficients of the long-run relationship between money and each price series be unity, so that prices are proportional to money in equilibrium.

Stationarity of the Money and Price Series

Tests to determine the stationarity characteristics of the individual money and price series are summarized in table 1. The null hypothesis is that an autoregressive representation of each series contains a unit root. This hypothesis is tested against the alternative that the autoregressive representation is stationary around a linear time trend. The tests are based on OLS-estimated equations in levels reparameterized as

$$(1) \qquad x_t = \beta_0 + \beta_1 t + \beta_2 x_{t-1} + \sum_{i=1}^{P} \beta_{2+i} \Delta x_{t-i} + e_t,$$

where $\Delta x_{t-i} = x_{t-i} - x_{t-i-1}$. A third-order model was selected for money and manufacturing prices and a fifth-order model for agricultural prices based on Sims' modified likelihood ratio tests. Results of the Dickey-Fuller τ_τ test for a unit root ($\beta_2 = 1$) and Φ_3 test of the joint hypothesis of a unit root with drift but no time trend ($\beta_1 = 0$, $\beta_2 = 1$) are reported. The unit-root hypothesis is not rejected at the 0.10 level for any of the series on the basis of either test. Conditional

[2] The initial data was seasonally unadjusted. Possible seasonality in the series was investigated by examining autocorrelation functions and the joint significance of seasonal dummy variables in univariate forecasting equations for each variable. Only the money supply variable exhibited strong seasonality, which was adjusted for via the Holt-Winter smoothing technique as described in Doan and Litterman.

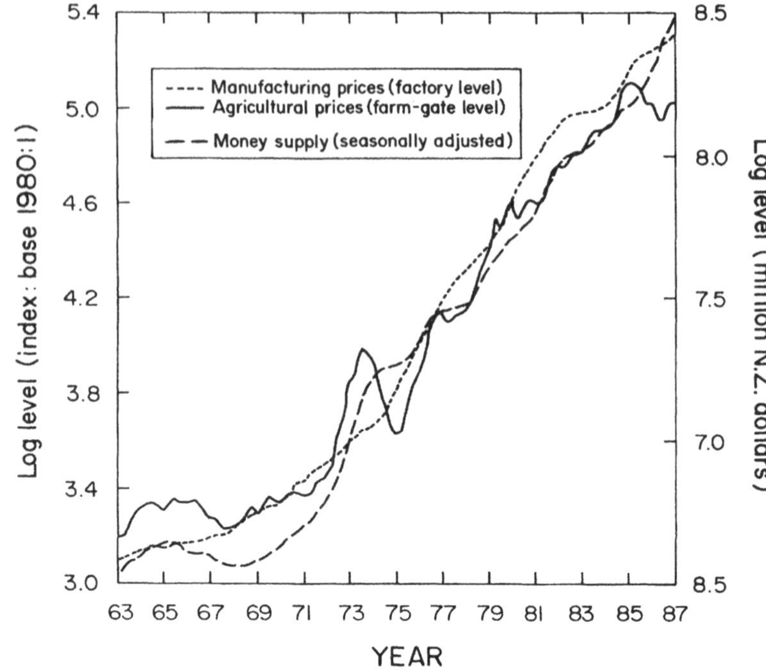

Figure 1. The money supply (*M*1), manufacturing prices, and agricultural prices in New Zealand, 1963:1–1987:1

on this result, a zero drift component is rejected at the 0.05 level for all three series.

Acceptance of the hypothesis that each series contains a unit root is also conditional on the statistical adequacy of the estimated autoregressive models. Therefore, results of several misspecification tests under the null hypothesis (a unit root and drift) are reported in the lower half of table 1. The results generally support the statistical validity of the maintained specifications. The models have reasonable explanatory power, with higher adjusted R^2's and lower estimated regression standard errors for $\Delta M1$ and ΔIP than for ΔFP. Modified Lagrange multiplier tests (denoted *LM*) provide evidence that the errors are not serially correlated (Spanos, p. 542) and skewness-kurtosis tests (denoted *SK*) suggest they are normally distributed (Bera and Jarque). The *ARCH* statistic developed by Engle indicates whether the conditional variances behave autoregressively. The possibility that the variances follow a fourth-order autoregression is not supported, relative to the null that the variances are constant, although there is weak evidence of an *ARCH* effect in the ΔFP equation.

To examine time-dependency of the parameters of the univariate models, tests were undertaken to determine whether the conditional variances are constant over subsamples of relative stability (1964:2–1971:4) and instability (1974:1–1987:1) in the world economy. These tests (denoted *VS*, Spanos p. 484) yielded mixed results; variance stability is rejected for the ΔFP regression residuals at the 0.01 level and the $\Delta M1$ residuals at the 0.05 level. Despite this evidence of instability among the variances, recursive estimation (not shown) indicates quite stable parameter estimates for all three models, except during the 1972–74 period. Moreover, constant variances over the sample and post-sample periods are not rejected when the sample period ends in 1985:4. Chow tests for predictive stability over 1986:1–1987:1 then provide little evidence that changes in the parameters have a

Table 1. Time-Series Properties of Money and Prices in New Zealand

T = 93(1964:1–1987:1)
Stationarity Statistics

Hypothesis	Series		
Unit root	$M1$	IP	FP[f]
Dickey-Fuller (τ_τ)[a] ($\beta_2 = 1$)	−2.545	−2.542	−2.484
Dickey-Fuller (Φ_3)[b] ($\beta_1 = 0,\ \beta_2 = 1$)	4.940	3.489	3.665
Drift[c] ($\beta_0 = 0$, given $\beta_1 = 0,\ \beta_2 = 1$)	2.045***[g]	2.137**	2.833***

Summary and Misspecification Statistics

Statistic	Distribution	Series		
		$\Delta M1$	ΔIP	ΔFP[f]
$\bar{R}^2$		0.64	0.54	0.26
$\sigma\%$		1.13	1.14	4.19
LM	$F(4,83)$	0.90	0.32	1.66
SK	$\chi^2(2)$	0.40	0.77	1.38
$ARCH$	$\chi^2(4)$	3.13	5.08	9.29*
VS[d]	$F(49,28)$	2.02**	1.21	3.62***
$CHOW$[e]	$F(5,84)$	2.08*	0.52	0.89

[a] Significance level of the test statistic based on the distribution reported for T = 100 in Fuller (p. 373); 10% critical value = −3.15.
[b] Significance level of the test statistic based on the distribution reported for T = 100 in Dickey and Fuller; 10% critical value = 5.47.
[c] Test statistic follows standard t-distribution.
[d] Test for conditional variance stability between the subsamples 1964:1–1971:4 and 1974:1–1987:1.
[e] Test for post-sample predictive stability for 1986:1–1987:1 with the model estimated through 1985:4.
[f] For FP, T = 91 (1964:3–1987:1); for ΔFP, distributions of LM, VS, and $CHOW$ are $F(4,81)$, $F(47,24)$ and $F(5,80)$, respectively.
[g] Single asterisk indicates reject null hypothesis at the 0.10 level; double asterisk indicates reject null hypothesis at the 0.05 level; triple asterisk indicates reject null hypothesis at the 0.01 level.

statistically significant impact on the forecasting performance of the models, as shown in table 1. Thus, autoregressive models with time-invariant coefficients provide reasonable representations of the money and price series and the hypothesis that each series contains a unit root is supported.

Cointegration and Neutrality

Tests for cointegration among money, manufacturing prices, and agricultural prices in New Zealand were undertaken conditional on the hypothesis of a unit root and drift in each of the univariate models. Because a cointegrating relationship involves at least two variables, there are at most $r \le N - 1$ linearly independent cointegrating vectors among N variables. In particular, if money is cointegrated with both manufacturing prices and agricultural prices, the cointegrating relationships can be expressed by

$$\alpha' Y_t = Z_t, \tag{2}$$

where

$$\alpha' = \begin{bmatrix} \alpha_1' \\ \alpha_2' \end{bmatrix} = \begin{bmatrix} 1 & \alpha_{12} & 0 \\ 1 & 0 & \alpha_{23} \end{bmatrix}; \tag{3}$$

$$Y_t = \begin{bmatrix} M1 \\ IP \\ FP \end{bmatrix}; Z_t = \begin{bmatrix} z_{1t} \\ z_{2t} \end{bmatrix}.$$

The vectors α_1', α_2' span the space of cointegrating relationships among money and the two prices. Stock has shown that OLS provides consistent estimates of the cointegrating parameters [$-\alpha_{ij}$ in (3)] in static bivariate regressions of current-dated variables in levels (with a constant included to adjust for differences in means). The residuals from these regressions provide estimates of the error-correction terms, and tests for cointegration are based on testing for a unit root in these series of residuals. Long-run monetary neutrality implies $\alpha_{12} = \alpha_{23} = -1$, while any linear combination of the two vectors provides an equivalent expression of cointegration.

Estimates of the cointegrating parameters from bivariate regressions among the money and price series are reported at the top of table 2. For completeness, the results from all possible bi-

Table 2. Cointegrating Vectors and Tests for Cointegration among Money and Prices

T = 93(1964:1–1987:1)

	Dependent Variable					
	*M*1		*IP*		*FP*	
Regressor	*IP*	*FP*	*M*1	*FP*	*M*1	*IP*
Cointegrating regressions						
Estimate of $-\alpha_{ij}$[a]	0.85	0.95	1.14	1.13	1.04	0.86
R^2	0.97	0.97	0.98	0.98	0.97	0.97
Cointegration tests[b]						
Unrestricted model	−2.88	−3.65**[c]	−3.00*	−5.41***	−3.77**	−5.45***
Restricted model ($-\alpha_{ij}$ = 1)	−2.65	−3.69**	−2.65	−3.29**	−3.69**	−3.29**

[a] The coefficient α_{ij} is the only unknown coefficient of a bivariate cointegrating vector [α_i' in (3)] normalized so the coefficient of the dependent variable is one.

[b] Augmented Dickey-Fuller test for a unit root in the residuals from the cointegrating regression. Significance level of the test statistic based on the distribution for T = 100 in Engle and Granger; 10% critical value = −2.91.

[c] Single asterisk indicates reject null hypothesis at the 0.10 level; double asterisk indicates reject null hypothesis at the 0.05 level; triple asterisk indicates reject null hypothesis at the 0.01 level.

variate regressions are reported. The estimated cointegrating parameters are concentrated around a value of one, as implied by the neutrality hypothesis, and reversing the dependent and independent variables produces approximately inverse parameter estimates.[3]

Results of the tests for cointegration are reported in the lower part of table 2. For each test, the null hypothesis is no cointegration and the residuals contain a unit root. The alternative hypothesis is that the variables in the corresponding regression are cointegrated and the residuals are stationary. The tests are based on fourth-order autoregressive models of the residuals with the distribution of the Dickey-Fuller test statistic adjusted for its dependence on the estimated cointegrating parameters.

As shown in table 2, the null hypothesis that the residuals contain a unit root is rejected at the 0.01 level for an *IP*,*FP* regression in either direction. For the *M*1,*FP* regressions, a unit root is rejected at the 0.05 level. The results for *M*1,*IP* are less conclusive, but a unit root in the residuals is rejected at the 0.10 level for one of the regressions. Thus, it appears there are long-run equilibrium relationships among the levels of money and prices. Failure to reject a unit root in the residuals of the *M*1,*IP* regressions at the same level of significance as in the other cases may result from the low power of the tests because, by transitivity, if *IP*,*FP*, and *M*1,*FP* are cointegrated, then, equivalently, *M*1,*IP* are also cointegrated.

[3] The parameter estimates also come close to satisfying the transivity that would arise from determining the coefficient of any third equation algebraically from estimated parameters of the two other equations.

Because the estimated cointegrating parameters are close to unity, the long-run relationships between the level of the money supply and of each of the nominal prices are close to proportional. To test the long-run neutrality hypothesis, the parameters were restricted to unity in the cointegrating regressions and the residuals were tested for unit roots.[4] The results for the restricted models shown in table 2 are generally similar to those shown for the unrestricted model and suggest that the money and price series are cointegrated when the proportionality restrictions are imposed. Cointegration is supported at the 0.05 level for the *M*1,*FP* and *IP*,*FP* regressions; however, cointegration is not supported at the 0.10 level for the restricted *M*1,*IP* relationship.

To further explore the evidence of long-run neutrality from the cointegrating regressions among money and prices, a time series for real GNP, as a measure of output, and the relationship between real GNP and the money supply were also examined. A unit root was not rejected at the 0.10 level in a third-order univariate autoregressive model of the real GNP series (the Dickey-Fuller τ_τ statistic was −2.1). Cointegration tests failed to reject the hypothesis that money and real GNP are not cointegrated at the 0.10 level. With a unit root in each series and no cointegration, a model of first differences of

[4] These tests determine only whether or not the neutrality hypothesis is consistent with stationary equilibrium between money and prices. Formal hypothesis tests on the parameters of the cointegrating vectors are difficult to carry out because the asymptotic distributions of the OLS estimators are nonnormal and depend on nuisance parameters that make a general tabulation of critical values infeasible (Stock).

money and real GNP was specified to evaluate the relationship between their growth rates. Granger causality from growth rates of money to growth rates of real GNP was rejected [$F(3,86) = 2.02$]. This lack of evidence of effects of money on output corroborates the long-run monetary neutrality result apparent in the behavior of money and prices.

Dynamics of Money and Prices

Cointegration among the variables in Y_t has several implications for estimation of dynamic models, inference, and forecasting. It implies rank-reducing restrictions on the coefficients of a moving-average representation of Y_t in first differences and on the coefficients of an autoregressive representation of Y_t in levels. Engle and Granger have shown that a useful way to impose these restrictions is by a vector error-correction model of the form

$$(4) \qquad \sum_{s=0}^{P} A_s \Delta Y_{t-s} = -\gamma Z_{t-1} + U_t,$$

where $A_0 = I$, U_t is a vector of one-step-ahead forecast errors, and γ is an $N \times r$ matrix of parameters ($\gamma \neq 0$). Engle and Granger suggest a two-step procedure for estimating a VEC model using the residuals from preliminary cointegrating regressions as estimates of the error-correction terms.

In a VEC model, one-period-lagged deviations from the long-run equilibrium relationships among the cointegrated variables affect the dynamic interactions in a system of equations of first differences of the series through the γ matrix. In this model, short-run dynamics are flexible, while the long-run constraints among levels of the series implied by cointegration are imposed. The model allows the error-correction process that returns the system to equilibrium to be gradual so it can produce accurate forecasts of responses to disequilibrating shocks over reasonable horizons (Hendry). Because all of the terms in the model are stationary, standard asymptotic results for parameter estimation and hypothesis testing apply and the autoregressive model can be inverted, validating dynamic simulations based on a moving-average representation. Sims, Stock, and Watson have shown that standard asymptotic distribution theory can also be applied to a model in levels involving cointegrated variables. However, a VAR in levels omits the constraints on its parameters implied by cointegration. Hence, a levels model produces long-run forecasts that are consistent but are inefficient (Engle and Yoo). A VAR in first differences is nested within the VEC specification but is misspecified for cointegrated series because it omits the error-correction terms.

Based on the evidence of cointegration among money and prices in New Zealand, the two-step procedure was used to estimate a three-variable VEC model by OLS. First differences of each series were regressed against a constant, the error-correction residuals from the restricted *IP*,*FP* and *FP*,*M*1 cointegrating regressions, and lags of the first differences of each series. A third-order model was chosen based on Sims' modified likelihood ratio tests and Akaike's information criterion, as shown at the top of table 3.

Estimation results and misspecification statistics for each equation in the VEC model are presented at the bottom of table 3. The adjusted R^2s from the estimated forecasting equations are higher, and the equation standard errors are lower, than those reported for the univariate models for $\Delta M1$ and ΔFP. The *LM* tests provide no evidence that the errors are serially correlated, and the *SK* statistics indicate they are normally distributed. There is more evidence of an *ARCH* effect in the $\Delta M1$ equation and less in the ΔFP equation than in the univariate models, and there remains evidence of conditional variance instability in these equations. However, recursive least squares estimates of the parameters (not shown) are again stable (except during 1972–74) and Chow tests for predictive stability over 1986:1–1987:1 provide no evidence of parameter changes having a significant impact on the predictive performance of the model. Overall, these results imply that the VEC model is a reasonably robust statistical model. The evidence from the cointegration tests that a VEC model is an appropriate specification is supported by rejection of the restriction that the coefficients of the error-correction terms are jointly zero. The calculated likelihood ratio statistic (not shown in table 3) is $\chi^2(6) = 14.73$, which is significant at the 0.05 level.

Structural Specification and Simulation Results

To trace the dynamic effects of various shocks, the estimated VEC model was reparameterized to its equivalent formulation in levels. With this reparameterization, the error-correction terms are incorporated into the first-period lagged terms of the autoregression. The model can then be

Table 3. Summary and Misspecification Statistics for the VEC Model

Lag Length Selection

	Number of Lags					
Test	6	5	4	3	2	1
Modified Likelihood ratio test[a]		7.23	9.98	8.36	21.71***[d]	16.93**
Akaike's Information Criterion	−23.74	−23.84	−23.91	−24.00	−23.93	−23.92

Summary and misspecification statistics

Statistic	Distribution	Series		
		$\Delta M1$	ΔIP	ΔFP
$\bar{R}^2$		0.71	0.54	0.40
$\sigma\%$		1.03	1.13	3.73
LM	$F(4,77)$	0.64	0.99	1.07
SK	$\chi^2(2)$	1.70	0.17	1.12
ARCH	$\chi^2(4)$	8.52*	3.07	4.34
VS[b]	$F(41,20)$	2.19**	1.19	3.58***
CHOW[c]	$F(5,76)$	1.99	0.99	1.64

[a] Test statistic follows a χ^2 distribution with 9 degrees of freedom.
[b] Test for conditional variance stability between the subsamples 1964:1–1971:4 and 1974:1–1987:1.
[c] Test for post-sample predictive stability for 1986:1–1987:1 with the model estimated through 1985:4.
[d] Single asterisk indicates reject null hypothesis at the 0.10 level; double asterisk indicates reject null hypothesis at the 0.05 level; triple asterisk indicates reject null hypothesis at the 0.01 level.

inverted to obtain impulse response functions that capture the effects of deviations from long-run equilibrium on the dynamic paths followed by each variable in response to initial shocks.

While tests of the long-run neutrality hypothesis are not dependent on identification of the sources of stochastic deviations from the long-run equilibrium, interpretation of the dynamic relationships from the VEC model requires structural identifying assumptions. Although one must be cautious about structural interpretation because many potential sources of variation are aggregated in the error term of each equation, in the remainder of this analysis the model is interpreted as describing the policy-setting behavior of the monetary authority and reduced-form equations for each sector capturing the likely responses of agricultural and manufacturing prices to shocks of monetary and sectoral origins. Assuming a recursive model then allows a structural interpretation based on a Choleski decomposition of the covariance matrix of the model's one-step-ahead forecast errors.

Impulse response functions showing the responses to one-standard-deviation positive shocks to each variable and their 90% confidence bounds were calculated for the VEC model for several recursive orders using a Monte Carlo integration algorithm with 200 draws from the posterior distribution of each response estimate (Doan and Litterman). The results are essentially invariant to the recursive order and are plotted for the order $M1,IP,FP$ in figure 2 for a twenty-quarter forecast horizon. This model allows money supply shocks the most opportunity to affect the price variables by attributing to the monetary shock any contemporaneous correlations among the forecast errors for money and prices.

The point estimates from the impulse response functions show that the dynamic responses of money and prices depend on the source of the initial shock. The long-run percentage responses to a given shock are approximately equal among the three variables. This reflects the long-run equilibrium imposed by the unitary cointegrating vectors. After any given shock, equality of the point estimates of the impulse responses occurs around thirty quarters.

While further interpretation of the point estimates of the impulse responses shown in figure 2 must be qualified because of their estimated standard errors, the mean responses suggest several observations about the likely time paths of money and prices after specific shocks. In particular, a positive monetary shock raises the levels of the money supply, manufacturing prices, and agricultural prices in the long run. Agricultural prices are immediately responsive to the monetary shock and display some indication of a cylical response pattern, while manufacturing prices start to respond only after a lag of four quarters. With managed exchange rates and agriculture being a price taker in world markets, that positive monetary shocks induce a shift in

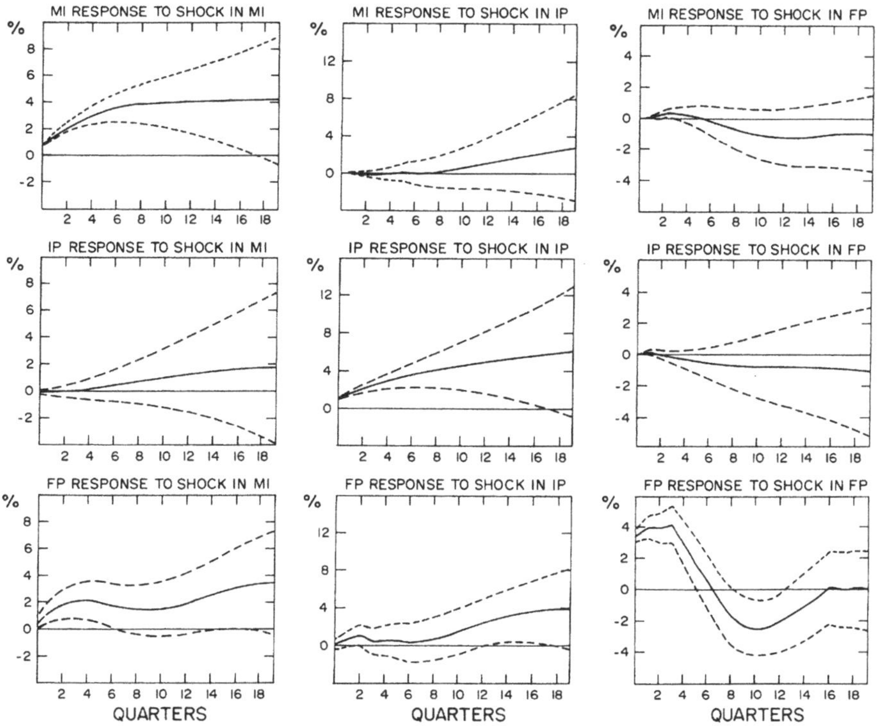

Figure 2. Responses to one-standard-deviation shocks from VEC model of money, manufacturing prices, and agricultural prices

relative prices in favor of agriculture in the short run implies that monetary expansions have been associated with nominal devaluations before domestic manufacturing prices rise. Agricultural prices do not respond more than proportionately or overshoot their long-run equilibrium level in response to a monetary shock, as might be the case if exchange rates were flexible and were to overshoot their long-run equilibrium values in response to monetary policy.

A positive shock to manufacturing prices also raises the levels of all three series in the long run. There is a lag in the response of the money supply and agricultural prices. Because of this delay, the shock to manufacturing prices initially places agriculture in a cost-price squeeze. The response of the money supply suggests a lagged accommodation of the increase in the domestic prices of manufactured goods by the monetary authority, with agricultural prices adjusting simultaneously. This autonomy of manufacturing prices, and subsequent monetary responsiveness, may not persist under the current policies for gradual liberalization of the manufacturing sector, but no evidence of structural change was found through 1987:1.

In contrast to the permanent shift in the level of each series induced by shocks to the money supply or manufacturing prices, following an agricultural price shock a new long-run equilibrium of each series is established around its initial level. The own response of agricultural prices displays a dampening oscillatory pattern. Neither the money supply nor manufacturing prices shows any significant short-run response, so there is a short-run shift in relative prices in favor of agriculture.

The failure to detect an effect of agricultural

prices on the money supply, compared to the long-run responsiveness of the money supply to shocks to manufacturing prices, also has policy implications. The lack of feedback from agricultural prices to the money supply suggests unwillingness of the monetary authority to accommodate world agricultural price shocks. Stabilization programs that retained farm earnings in the Reserve Bank during periods of high world prices and released them during periods of low prices contributed to the ability of the monetary authority to insulate New Zealand from external inflationary and deflationary pressures arising from agriculture. These stabilization programs have been eliminated since 1985. Again, no evidence of structural change was found through 1987:1. However, it remains to be observed whether the dynamic patterns of responses to agricultural price shocks will persist or whether future agricultural shocks will induce greater instability in the money supply or manufacturing prices.

It is interesting to compare the results shown in figure 1 to impulse responses from VAR models specified under alternative assumptions about the stationarity properties of the money and price series. Two VAR models were estimated: a fourth-order model in levels, under the maintained hypothesis of stationarity, and a third-order model in first differences (without the error-correction terms), under the maintained hypothesis of unit roots and no cointegration. The point estimates of the impulse responses from the VAR in levels (not shown but available on request) are generally similar to those from the VEC model. This is not surprising because the parameter estimates from a levels model are consistent for cointegrated nonstationary variables. However, with no long-run restrictions imposed, the point estimates of the impulse responses following any specific shock do not converge to common values in the levels model even after forty quarters.

In contrast, the impulse response functions from a VAR model in first differences are unlike those from the VEC model or the VAR model in levels. Estimates from the differences model (reparameterized to show the impacts of each shock on levels of the variables) suggest both a more-than-proportionate short-run response of agricultural prices to a money supply shock and a short-run tendency for agricultural prices to overshoot their long-run level. The own response to a shock to manufacturing prices is persistent in the differences model and is largely matched by the response of agricultural prices, while the money supply responds more slowly and to a lower level over a long horizon. Own responses to shocks to agricultural prices are also persistent in the differences model but do not induce responses of the money supply or manufacturing prices, suggesting a long-run shift in relative prices in favor of agriculture. Thus, inferences drawn from a VAR model in first differences without the error-correction terms would be different than those drawn from the VEC model.

Summary and Conclusions

In this paper, the stationarity properties of the data have been analyzed in order to test the hypothesis of long-run monetary neutrality and better understand the dynamic relationships among money and prices in New Zealand in the short and long run. Tests for stationarity failed to reject a unit root in autoregressive models of the individual series for money, agricultural prices, and manufacturing prices. The money and price series also appear cointegrated, with parameter estimates from unrestricted cointegrating regressions close to unity. When proportionality among levels of money and prices is imposed on the cointegrating regressions, the evidence is weaker but the restricted error-correction terms (residuals) also appear stationary. These results provide empirical support for the long-run monetary neutrality hypothesis.

Incorporating the restricted error-correction terms in a VEC model provides a description of the dynamic relationships among money and prices consistent with long-run neutrality. Monetary shocks raise the levels of prices in the long run. Agricultural prices respond more quickly than manufacturing prices, but no evidence was found that agricultural prices rise proportionately more than the money supply or overshoot their long-run levels in the short run. Shocks to manufacturing prices induce monetary expansions and place agriculture in a short-run cost-price squeeze, while levels of the money supply and manufacturing prices have not responded to fluctuations in agricultural prices. These results are consistent with the historical insulation of the manufacturing sector in New Zealand and with policies to stabilize the economy in face of external shocks. Monetary responses to shocks to manufacturing prices may moderate under recent liberalization policies, and these policies may leave the economy more exposed to external shocks, but no evidence was found that policy reforms have altered the dynamic patterns among money and prices through 1987:1.

The importance of preliminary evaluation of the stationarity properties of the money and price series is demonstrated in this analysis by a comparison of the impulse response functions from the VEC model to those from VAR models estimated under alternative stationarity assumptions. The VEC model provides more precise long-run estimates than an unrestricted VAR model in levels. The impulse response functions from a VAR model in first differences are less plausible than those of the VEC model.

Some caveats about the results also should be noted. The acceptability of an empirical model is tentative until it has been successfully tested against rival models. The VEC model presented in this paper is a small closed system that omits other theoretically relevant variables and aggregates many potential sources of variation in each of its error terms. Inferences from the model are also limited by the recursive structure imposed and by the relatively wide confidence bounds of the impulse response functions. Assuming that the data are rich enough to reveal the underlying phenomena of interest, postulating larger dynamic models with appealing contemporaneous structures and statistical properties is a priority for future research. These models will further our understanding of monetary effects on agriculture, feedback among sectors, and feedback from the sectors to monetary policy.

[Received April 1988; final revision received May 1989.]

References

Ardeni, P. G. "Does the Law of One Price Really Hold for Commodity Prices?" *Amer. J. Agr. Econ.* 71 (1989): 661–69.

Bera, A. K., and C. M. Jarque. "Model Specification Tests: A Simultaneous Approach." *J. Econometrics* 20(1982):59–82.

Bessler, D. A. "Relative Prices and Money: A Vector Autoregression on Brazilian Data." *Amer. J. Agr. Econ.* 66(1984):25–30.

Bordo, M. D. "The Effects of Monetary Change on Relative Commodity Prices and the Role of Long-Term Contracts." *J. Polit. Econ.* 88(1980):1088–1109.

Chambers, R. G. "Agricultural and Financial Market Interdependence in the Short Run." *Amer. J. Agr. Econ.* 66(1984):12–24.

Chapple, S. "Industrial Pricing and Inflation in New Zealand, 1978–1986." Reserve Bank of New Zealand Disc. Pap. No. G87/5, Dec. 1987.

Devadoss, S., and W. H. Meyers. "Relative Prices and Money: Further Results for the United States." *Amer. J. Agr. Econ.* 69(1987):838–42.

Dickey, D. A., and W. A. Fuller. "Likelihood Ratio Statistics for Autoregressive Time Series with Unit Roots." *Econometrica* 49(1981):1057–72.

Doan, T. A., and R. B. Litterman. *User's Manual, RATS, Version 2.10.* Evanston IL: VAR Econometrics, 1987.

Engle, R. F. "Autoregressive Conditional Heteroscedasticity with Estimates of the Variance of United Kingdom Inflation." *Econometrica* 50(1982):987–1007.

Engle, R. F., and C. W. J. Granger. "Co-Integration and Error Correction: Representation, Estimation, and Testing." *Econometrica* 55(1987):251–76.

Engle, R. F., and B. S. Yoo. "Forecasting and Testing in Co-integrated Systems," *J. Econometrics* 35(1987):143–59.

Fuller, W. A. *Introduction to Statistical Time Series.* New York: John Wiley & Sons, 1976.

Gordon, R. J. "Alternative Responses of Policy to External Supply Shocks." *Brookings Pap. on Econ. Activity* 1(1975):183–204.

Hendry, D. F. "Econometric Modelling with Cointegrated Variables: An Overview." *Oxford Bull. Econ. Statist.* 48(1986):201–12.

Johnson, R. W. M. "The Real Rate of Exchange Revisited: Reflections on Policies Encouraging Competitiveness." Paper presented at the Aust. Agr. Econ. Soc., Lincoln College, New Zealand, Feb. 1989.

Lattimore, R. G. "Economic Liberalisation and Its Impact on Agriculture: The Case of New Zealand." Dep. Agr. Econ., Lincoln College, New Zealand, Aug. 1987.

Mount, T. D. "Policy Analysis with Time-Series Econometric Models, Discussion." *Amer. J. Agr. Econ.* 71(1989):507–8.

Nelson, C. R., and C. L. Plosser. "Trends and Random Walks in Macroeconomic Time Series: Some Evidence and Implications." *J. Monetary Econ.* 10(1982):139–62.

Orden, D. "Agriculture, Trade, and Macroeconomics." *J. Pol. Modeling* 8(1986):27–51.

Orden, D., and P. L. Fackler. "Identifying Monetary Impacts on Agricultural Prices in VAR Models." *Amer. J. Agr. Econ.* 71(1989):495–502.

Rausser, G. C., J. A. Chalfant, and K. G. Stamoulis. "Instability in Agricultural Markets: The U.S. Experience." *Int. Conference of Agr. Econ., Conference Proceedings*, 1985, pp. 595–610.

Rayner, A. C., and R. G. Lattimore. *The Timing and Sequencing of a Trade Liberalisation Policy: The Case of New Zealand.* Washington DC: World Bank, 1987.

Sims, C. A. "Macroeconomics and Reality." *Econometrica* 48(1980):1–48.

Sims, C. A., J. Stock, and M. Watson. "Inference in Linear Time-Series Models with Some Unit Roots." Dep. Econ. Work. Pap., University of Minnesota, Feb. 1988.

Spanos, A. *Statistical Foundations of Econometric Modelling.* Cambridge: Cambridge University Press, 1986.

Stock, J. "Asymptotic Properties of Least Squares Estimators of Cointegrating Vectors." *Econometrica* 55(1987):1035–56.

Stock, J., and M. Watson. "Interpreting the Evidence on Money-Income Causality." *J. Econometrics* 40(1989): 161–81.

Taylor, J. S., and J. Spriggs. "Effects of the Monetary Macroeconomy on Canadian Agricultural Prices." *Can. J. Econ.* 23(1989):278–89.

Tweeten, L. G. "Macroeconomics in Crisis: Agriculture in an Underachieving Economy." *Amer. J. Agr. Econ.* 62(1980):853–65.

Van Duyne, C. "Food Prices, Expectations, and Inflation." *Amer. J. Agr. Econ.* 64(1982):419–30.

Chapter 3

Identifying Monetary Impacts on Agricultural Prices in VAR Models

David Orden and Paul L. Fackler

Since the mid-1970s, a number of studies have used vector autoregressive (VAR) models to evaluate the magnitude and timing of macroeconomic impacts on agriculture. Use of the VAR method has been viewed as a way to obtain empirical evidence about these impacts that might not emerge from more traditional overidentified and less dynamic econometric models. The hope has been that by placing minimal restrictions on VAR models, the true structure of the economic relationships under investigation can be observed.

While the aim is laudable, critics of VAR models have argued that it has had the unfortunate consequence of obscuring some important structural identification issues and seeming to promise that something can be obtained for nothing (Cooley and Leroy, Leamer). They point out that identifying restrictions are required to give economically interpretable meaning to the results of any simultaneous equation model (SEM). In standard practice, identification of VAR models is obtained implicitly by choice of a Choleski decomposition of the covariance matrix of one-step-ahead forecast errors, which is equivalent to imposing a recursive structure for the economy. Of concern is that the recursive structure may not be believable. Further, as Bernanke has observed, examination of ad hoc variants of the recursive order implies a strange set of prior beliefs in which the analyst holds strongly that the system is recursive but is not sure in what order the variables should be arranged.

In response to these concerns, several recent papers have pointed out that identification of VAR models does not have to rely on the assumption that the contemporaneous structure is recursive (Bernanke, Sims). Rather, the distinguishing features of a VAR model are, first, that identification rests on the assumption that distinct, mutually orthogonal behavior shocks drive the economy, and, second, that lagged relationships among the endogenous and exogenous variables (if any) are left entirely unrestricted. Given these features, a VAR model must be identified solely by restrictions placed on the contemporaneous interactions among the variables, but the identifying restrictions do not have to preclude simultaneity.

In this paper, we elaborate on the structural interpretation of VAR models and use this analysis to examine monetary impacts on agricultural prices. We discuss the identification problem and the implications of a recursive structure. We illustrate our points with respect to the three-variable model of money, industrial prices, and agricultural prices that has been used in several articles to evaluate the effects of monetary shocks on price dynamics (Bessler, Devadoss and Meyers). We then introduce a somewhat richer behavioral model of the macroeconomy and its effects. A simultaneous model is shown to offer a more believable identification of monetary policy and other macroeconomic shocks than a recursive model, and monetary impacts on agricultural prices are assessed.

Identification of Dynamic Simultaneous Equation Models

A general specification of a dynamic linear SEM can be given by

$$(1) \qquad Ay_t = \sum_{s=1}^{p} A_s y_{t-s} + Cz_t + Bv_t,$$

where y_t and v_t are both $(k \times 1)$ random vectors, z_t is a $(q \times 1)$ vector of nonstochastic (or strictly exogenous) variables, and A, the A_s, B, and C are matrices of coefficients. The v_t are

---

David Orden and Paul L. Fackler are assistant professors of agricultural economics, Virginia Polytechnic Institute and State University and North Carolina State University, respectively.

The authors wish to thank the Agriculture and Rural Economy Division, Economic Research Service, U.S. Department of Agriculture for partial financial support and Sandra Batie, Jerry Bradshaw, Mark Fisher, Tom Grennes, John Kitchen, Wally Thurman, Douglas Pearce, and participants in a workshop at the Federal Reserve Bank of Minneapolis for helpful comments and suggestions.

assumed to be zero mean, serially uncorrelated, and mutually orthogonal shocks with unit variance. These shocks represent behaviorally distinct sources of variation that drive the economy over time. The rows of A, the A_s, and C model systematic behavioral relationships within the economy. Restrictions imposed on these coefficients describe how the variables in the system interact contemporaneously and with lags, whereas restrictions on B determine the direct impacts of the underlying shocks on the behavioral equations of the system. For example, if one element of v_t is shocks to weather and the model includes agricultural output supply and demand equations, simultaneous effects of weather shocks on supply and demand (the latter through, say, expectations about future prices) would give rise to two nonzero coefficients in the corresponding column of B.[1]

For the structural model (1), a reduced-form representation is obtained by premultiplying by A^{-1}:

$$(2) \qquad y_t = \sum_{s=1}^{p} A_s^* y_{t-s} + C^* z_t + u_t,$$

where $\text{cov}(u_t) = \Omega = A^{-1}BB'A^{-T}$. The u_t are mean zero, serially independent, one-step-ahead forecast errors (conditional on z_t).

In traditional simultaneous equation models, little value is placed on knowledge of B and exclusion restrictions on A, the A_s and C are used to identify the structural parameters. In contrast, the identification of a VAR model utilizes the assumption of the mutually orthogonal behavioral shocks and concentrates all of the identifying restrictions on the A and B matrices. The rationale for focusing attention exclusively on restrictions on contemporaneous interactions is that theory often provides little guidance about lagged behavioral relationships. In particular, past realizations of all variables are often known to economic agents and potentially will be used to form expectations. These expectations provide a link between past and current realizations of all the variables in a given model about which economics has little to say that is not controversial. On the other hand, it may be reasonable to assume that not all agents react immediately to all new economic developments because of information lags or adjustment costs. These minimum delay considerations may provide a useful source of identifying restrictions on the contemporaneous interactions among the variables.

Limiting the identifying restrictions in VAR models to contemporaneous interactions also has an important technical corollary. The reduced-form parameters of the A_s^* and C^* can be estimated efficiently by OLS separately from the contemporaneous parameters. Maximum likelihood estimates of A and B can then be obtained utilizing the OLS estimate of Ω. Because there are $k(k + 1)/2$ free parameters of Ω and $2k^2$ parameters of A and B, an order condition for identification is that $(3k^2 - k)/2$ restrictions be imposed. A recursive model is simply a special case of a just-identified model in which B is diagonal and A is lower triangular when the variables are ordered appropriately.

To illustrate some of the identification issues in VAR models, consider a three-variable model which includes log levels of money, industrial prices, and agricultural prices. The money equation may be interpreted as a money supply function with the shock to that function interpreted as a shift in the money supply, whether by direct Fed policy or due to shocks in financial intermediation. A set of identifying restrictions might then be defined by reasoning that financial variables are highly visible and agents can adjust prices quickly in response to perceived changes in policy. The Fed, on the other hand, can observe industrial price changes only at a lag and is unconcerned about agricultural price shocks. Industrial and agricultural prices are also influenced by other common factors in the short run and agricultural prices by factors unique to agriculture. This implies a recursive model in which the ordering is money, industrial prices, and agricultural prices.

Alternatively, one might identify the effects of a money supply shock by assuming that short-run industrial prices are relatively unresponsive due, for example, to long-term contracts in the labor market. Money supply and demand can be affected by industrial price shocks, as well as by shocks due to unforseen monetary policy and other factors. Finally, agricultural prices are affected by both of these sets of shocks, as well as by shocks that are peculiar to agriculture and do not affect the rest of the economy contemporaneously. This reasoning would lead to a recursive model

[1] There is a redundancy about contemporaneous interactions among the variables in the A and B matrices. Technically, if general nonlinear restrictions were used, there would be no need to describe both matrices explicitly. In practice, however, it may be preferable to place restrictions on both matrices, if such restrictions have a readily interpretable meaning.

ordered industrial prices, money, and agricultural prices.

In terms of the impacts of monetary policy shocks on agricultural prices, the important question concerning either of the above models is whether, in fact, monetary policy shocks are identified. In particular, for both of the identifications the money supply equation excludes the interest rate, and there is no explicit money demand function.

The assumption that is essentially required to justify the omission of the interest rate and identification of the "money" shock with a money supply shift in a three-variable model is that the contemporaneous money supply function is perfectly inelastic. This is illustrated in figure 1, which shows four alternative recursive models of money supply and demand. When money supply is perfectly inelastic (model 2b), only supply shifts are reflected in changes in the quantity of money; while demand shifts, whatever their magnitude, affect just the interest rate. Supply shocks are also fully reflected in changes in the quantity of money when demand for money is perfectly elastic (model 1b). In this case, however, both supply and demand shocks affect the quantity

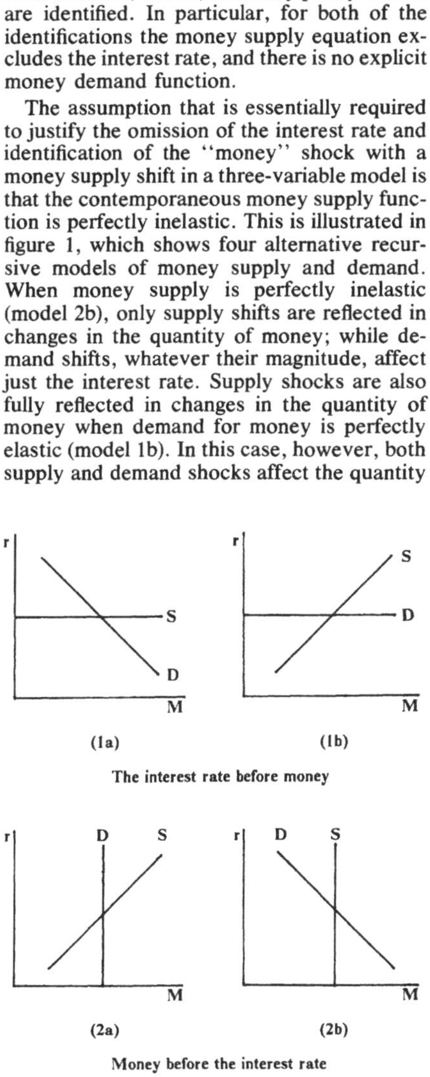

Figure 1. Alternative recursive models of money supply and demand

of money. Hence, when money demand is perfectly elastic, interpreting shocks to the "money" equation as monetary policy requires that demand shocks are negligible relative to supply shocks, an assumption that is not very appealing a priori.

When the three-variable model is expanded to include the interest rate, both money supply and demand shocks can be identified. Imposing a recursive structure again allows each behavioral shock to be associated with the equation for a specific variable. If the interest rate is ordered before money, either money supply or demand is assumed perfectly elastic (models 1a and 1b). The former model implies that the "interest rate" equation is interpreted as a money supply function and the "money" equation, which includes the interest rate as an argument, is interpreted as a money demand function. The latter model implies the opposite interpretation (the "interest rate" equation as demand and the "money" equation as supply). Similar reasoning applies when money is ordered before the interest rate, based on the assumption that money supply or demand is perfectly inelastic. Perfectly inelastic supply implies that the "money" equation is interpreted as the money supply function, as in the three-variable model, while perfectly inelastic demand implies the "interest rate" equation is the money supply function and the "money" equation is the money demand function. Thus, explicit justifications can be provided for particular recursive models. Nevertheless, simultaneous structural specifications are often likely to be more believable.

Two Structural Models of Monetary Impacts on Agriculture

To determine the importance of the identifying restrictions imposed on VAR models of monetary impacts on U.S. agriculture, we specified a seven-variable, quarterly, reduced-form model of macroeconomic variables and agricultural prices, and examined the contemporaneous and dynamic impacts of various behavioral shocks using both recursive and simultaneous structural specifications. The reduced-form model includes quantity and price variables from a domestic goods market (GNP and the GNP deflator) and a domestic money market (M1 and a short-term interest rate). Foreign economies enter the model through the exchange rate ($*/$) and the agricultural sector through agricultural prices. Finally, the model included oil prices as a source of real shocks to the economy.[2] The model was estimated in log levels (except the interest rate, which was in levels) over the period 1975:1–1988:1. For this period, the estimated impacts of a "money" shock in a recursive model with the price level and agricultural prices (not shown) defy interpretation of this shock as a money supply shift because over time the quantity of money rises but the price level falls. The seven-variable model potentially provides a basis for disentangling the various impacts apparently associated with money in the three-variable model.

The within-quarter behavioral parameters from a recursive structural model ordered oil prices (o), the price level (p), output (y), money (m), the interest rate (r), the exchange rate (e), and agricultural prices (a) are shown in table 1.[3] This order reflects the view that among recursive models it is reasonable to assume that output supply is perfectly elastic and money supply is perfectly inelastic within a quarter. Predetermination of the goods market outcome relative to the other variables (except oil prices) reflects an hypothesis of a goods sector with sluggish adjustment.

As shown in table 1, contrary to our prior expectations, a positive sign on the price-level variable in the "output" equation suggests it is an upward-sloping output supply function, with the "price-level" equation being a perfectly elastic output demand function. A structural interpretation contrary to prior expectations also arises from the positive sign of the coefficient on money in the "interest rate" equation. This positive estimated coefficient, although not significant, suggests that the "interest rate" equation is an upward-sloping money supply function traced out by a perfectly inelastic money demand function. Inclusion of the three variables higher in the

[2] The data series are, respectively, GNP in constant dollars (*GNP$*), the total GNP deflator (*PDGNP*), the monthly money supply M1 (*FM1$*) averaged over the quarter, the monthly auction-average interest rate on three-month treasury bills (*FRMTB3MN*) averaged over the quarter, the monthly weighted average of the currencies of 10 countries versus the U.S. dollar (*REXWAFRB*) averaged over the quarter, prices received by farmers for crops, and Saudi crude petroleum prices. Petroleum prices are from International Financial Statistics Commodity Yearbook, except 1986 for which an "unofficial" OPEC price of Saudi crude was taken from *Petroleum Intelligence Weekly*. Prices received by farmers are from USDA, and all other data are from the Wharton data base and were provided to us in the database and automated retrieval system (DARTS) of ARED/ERS/USDA by Ralph Monaco.

[3] The results reported in this paper are derived from a reduced-form model with two lags of each variable, trend, and seasonal constants included in each equation. The Schwartz criteria suggested a reduced-form model with only one lag of each variable in each equation, but Sims' modified likelihood ratio test rejected the one-lag model in favor of the model with two lags (p = .00005). The two-lag model was not rejected by Sims' criterion compared to a model with three (p = .502) or four (p = .121) lags. We estimated the reduced form in levels, rather than differences, despite some evidence of unit roots in univariate models for the individual series and little evidence of cointegration among the variables. The covariance matrix of one-step-ahead forecast errors from a two-lag model in differences is quite similar to the covariance matrix from the levels model. Consequently, estimates of the contemporaneous structural parameters are similar from the two models, although the long-run dynamic responses differ.

Table 1. Contemporaneous Behavioral Equations from a Recursive Model

		Explanatory Variables[a]							
	Dependent Variable	Oil Price (o)	Price Level (p)	Output (y)	Money (m)	Interest Rate (r)	Exchange Rate (e)	Agricultural Price (a)	Standard Error
(1)	o								7.921
(2)	p	.004							0.236
		(.004)							
(3)	y	−.011	.690						0.637
		(.011)	(.376)						
(4)	m	.00005	.525	.296					0.520
		(.009)	(.316)	(.116)					
(5)	r	.010	−.378	.282	.174				0.539
		(.009)	(.334)	(.127)	(.143)				
(6)	e	.021	−.911	−.210	−.530	2.699			2.555
		(.046)	(1.594)	(.614)	(.686)	(.702)			
(7)	a	.046	6.376	.123	1.285	.435	.135		3.314
		(.059)	(2.161)	(.797)	(.901)	(.972)	(.179)		

[a] Standard errors given below the coefficients.

recursive order in the "interest rate" equation also raises a concern. If the "interest rate" equation is interpreted as a money demand function, the estimated coefficients suggest, implausibly, that money demand falls when real output rises.

The inconsistency of the signs of the contemporaneous coefficients of the recursive model with our prior hypotheses for justifying a recursive structure raises the question of whether the estimated effects of specific behavioral shocks will be distorted by failure to allow simultaneity in the model. To examine this question, we estimated a simultaneous structural model using the same reduced form.[4] Estimated contemporaneous structural parameters from this model are shown in table 2, with each equation normalized to reflect its behavioral interpretation.[5] The assumptions that oil prices and the goods market outcome are predetermined for the other variables are retained in the model. Output supply is hypothesized to depend on the price level and oil prices, and output demand only on the price level. The estimated coefficients imply an elastic upward-sloping output supply function and a negative effect of an oil price shock on supply. The coefficient estimates also suggest a less elastic downward-sloping output demand function. The hypothesis of perfectly inelastic demand in the short run cannot be rejected.

In the simultaneous model, money supply is hypothesized to be responsive within a quarter only to oil prices and the interest rate. Money demand is hypothesized to be a function of output, the price level, the interest rate, and the exchange rate. The estimated behavioral coefficients show an upward-sloping money supply function and a downward-sloping money demand function. Money demand also shows inelastic positive responses to changes in real output and, possibly, the price level. The responses of money supply to oil prices and money demand to the exchange rate are insignificant.

The last two equations in the simultaneous model continue to represent foreign economies and agriculture, sectors for which the model is not as fully specified in terms of behavioral equations as it is for the domestic goods and money markets. The "exchange rate" equation may be hypothesized to represent foreign demand for dollars. It includes the price level, the interest rate, the exchange rate, and agricultural prices, but not the level

[4] One can also consider alternative recursive models. As illustrated in figure 1, reversing the ordering of p, y or m, r changes the interpretation of the equation normalized on each of the variables that are switched and shifts the implied elasticity of demand from one extreme to the other. Neither reversal of the recursive order seems more appealing than the order reported in table 1.

[5] We estimated the simultaneous model in GAUSS. The model shown in table 2 has two overidentifying restrictions. A likelihood ratio test does not reject these restrictions (p = .167) and the two-step estimation procedure provides FIML estimators even when the model is overidentified because the identifying restrictions on A and B are implicitly covariance restrictions and have no implications for the autoregressive reduced-form coefficients. See Fackler for details of the estimation strategy and Orden and Fackler for additional discussion of our models and results.

Table 2. Contemporaneous Behavioral Equations from a Simultaneous Model

		Explanatory Variables[a]							
	Dependent Variable	Oil Price (o)	Price Level (p)	Output (y)	Money (m)	Interest Rate (r)	Exchange Rate (e)	Agricultural Price (a)	Standard Error
(Oil sector)	o								7.921
(Output supply)	y	−.022 (.016)	3.531 (1.473)						.926
(Output demand)	y		−1.865 (2.403)						.878
(Money supply)	m	−.009 (.016)				1.442 (.234)			.899
(Money demand)	m		.451 (.395)	.483 (.149)		−.656 (.259)	.046 (.090)		.659
(Exchange rate)	e	−.004 (.061)	−4.260 (3.924)		−1.892 (1.277)	1.896 (1.281)		.580 (.481)	3.068
(Agricultural price)	a	.072 (.075)	5.716 (5.226)	.259 (1.204)		2.806 (2.725)	−.890 (.976)		4.250

[a] Standard errors given below the coefficients.

of domestic output. The exchange rate shows a more elastic response to the price level, a somewhat greater response to money, and a smaller response to the interest rate than in the recursive model; while an increase in agricultural prices now causes the dollar to appreciate (in both models many of the coefficients have relatively large standard errors). In the last equation, agricultural prices continue to show a very elastic response to the price level and a positive response (now elastic rather than inelastic) to the interest rate. Money is not hypothesized to have a direct effect on agricultural prices in the simultaneous model (highlighting the disassociation of monetary policy shocks from the quantity of money variable), while the effect of appreciation of the dollar on agricultural prices is estimated to be negative rather than positive.

Dynamic Impacts of the Behavioral Shocks

Evaluation of the dynamic responses to various behavioral shocks (impulse response functions) under the alternative structural identifications provides a second basis for evaluating the recursive and simultaneous models. For this purpose, the estimated net contemporaneous and dynamic impacts over a two-year period of a money supply shock on all variables are shown in figure 2A, and the effects of all shocks on the price level and agricultural prices are shown in figure 2B. The results for the recursive model are reported under the structural interpretation suggested by the estimated contemporaneous coefficients of the price level in the "output" equation and money in the "interest rate" equation, as discussed above, even though these coefficients were not highly significant. Our discussion of the impulse response functions is limited to three salient points.

First, the results shown in figure 2A demonstrate the importance of interpretation of the shocks based on a structural specification. The effects of a money supply shock on the macroeconomic variables look quite plausible in the simultaneous model. Money expands and, contemporaneously, the interest rate falls and the dollar depreciates. The expansion of

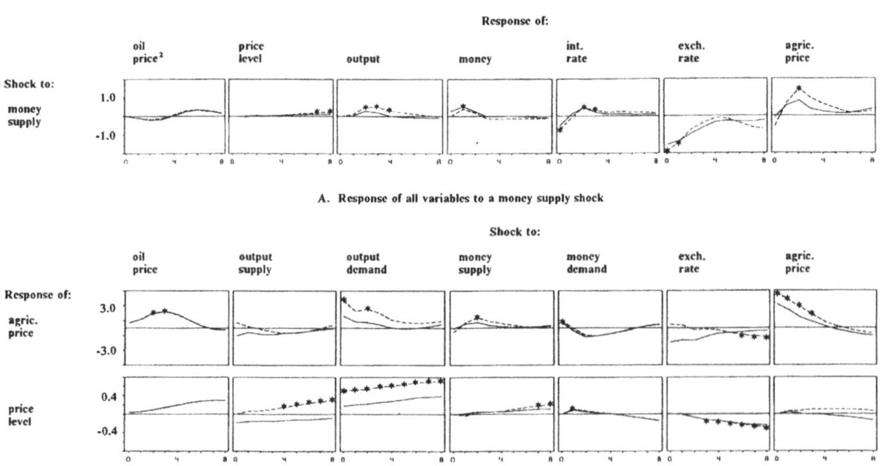

¹ The contemporaneous and lagged responses to positive behavioral shocks of one standad deviation are shown for the simultaneous model (——). Effects of equal shocks are shown for the recursive model (– – –) interpreted as described in the text.
² Response of oil prices are scaled relative to a one-standard-deviation oil price shock in order not to compress the graphs of other responses.
* Coefficient from the recursive model estimated to be significantly different from zero at the 90% confidence level. Confidence bounds were not computed for the coefficients from the simultaneous model.

Figure 2. Impulse response functions from the simultaneous and recursive models[1]

money persists for three quarters, output expands briefly after a lag of two quarters, and the price level rises slowly but persistently. The interest rate rises when output expands, while depreciation of the dollar dampens out slowly. Similar dynamic responses are observed in the recursive model when money supply shocks are identified with the "interest rate" equation. This is not the case if money supply shocks are identified with the "money" equation (the "money" equation is assumed to be a money demand function in the recursive model, and a positive shock, the effects of which are not shown in figure 2, causes money and the interest rate to rise and output to fall over several quarters). In terms of the effects of monetary policy on agriculture, the impulse response functions suggest that positive money supply shocks raise agricultural prices relative to the price level for more than a year; however, the responses shown in figure 2B do not suggest that monetary policy shocks have been the dominant source of agricultural price instability.

A second observation concerns the similarity of many of the impulse response functions between the two models. In particular, the response from the recursive structure seems plausible when the "interest rate" equation is assumed to be a money supply function. However, this interpretation rests on the implausible assumption that within-quarter money demand is perfectly inelastic. Further, as long as the positive coefficient on money in the "interest rate" equation is viewed as evidence of an upward-sloping money supply function, sensible dynamic effects of money supply and demand shocks are not robust to reversing the recursive order of money and the interest rate because this changes the interpretation of each equation (see figure 1) but had little effect on the estimated dynamic impacts of the shocks to the equations.

A third observation about the impulse response functions concerns a persistent difference between the recursive and simultaneous models. Neither the recursive model shown in table 1 nor a recursive model with output ordered before the price level gives very plausible estimates of the effects of an output supply shock. For either model, a positive supply shock causes the price level to rise. This anomalous result in the recursive models makes it appear that positive supply shocks induce inflation and a cost-price squeeze in agriculture. In contrast, in the simultaneous model, a positive supply shock causes the price level to fall. Negative supply shocks raise the price level but agricultural prices rise more than proportionally, so no cost-price squeeze arises.

Conclusions

In this paper we have examined the identifying restrictions needed to make structural interpretations of VAR models and have discussed the use of such models in evaluating monetary impacts on agricultural prices. The distinguishing features of a VAR model are the assumption of mutually orthogonal behavioral shocks and the imposition of identifying restrictions only on contemporaneous behavioral interactions, leaving the lagged relationships unrestricted. Whether VAR models continue to prove useful for policy analysis will depend on whether sensible identifying restrictions can be postulated within this framework. Any recursive order among the variables in a model provides one possible set of identifying restrictions. Recursive orders, however, imply strong assumptions about which variables affect each behavioral relationship and about the elasticities of supply and demand. These assumptions need not be rejected a priori, but their plausibility should be considered explicitly in evaluating the estimated contemporaneous and dynamic impacts from an hypothesized model.

In our analysis, we find reasons to be cautious about recursive models and derive more sensible results from a model with simultaneity in which we do not associate behavioral shocks with the equations for specific variables, as is done when a model is recursive. With respect to the impacts of monetary policy on agricultural prices, identifying policy shocks with the quantity of money variable seems particularly inappropriate during our sample period. If a recursive structure is imposed, it is more reasonable to identify shocks to the interest rate with monetary policy. More generally, there are few good reasons to restrict attention to VAR models with a recursive structure and many good reasons not to do so.

References

Bernanke, B. S. "Alternative Explanations of the Money-Income Correlation." *Carnegie-Rochester*

Conference Ser. on Pub. Pol. 25(1986):49–100.

Bessler, D. A. "Relative Prices and Money: A Vector Autoregression on Brazilian Data." *Amer. J. Agr. Econ.* 66(1984):25–30.

Cooley, T. G., and S. F. LeRoy. "Atheoretical Macroeconomics: A Critique." *J. Monetary Econ.* 16(1985):283–308.

Devadoss, S., and W. H. Meyers. "Relative Prices and Money: Further Results for the United States." *Amer. J. Agr. Econ.* 69(1987):838–42.

Fackler, P. L. "Vector Autoregressive Techniques for Structural Analysis." Dep. Econ. and Bus. Work. Pap. No. 113, North Carolina State University, 1988.

Leamer, E. "Vector Autoregressions for Causal Inference?" *Carnegie-Rochester Conference Ser. on Pub. Pol.* 22(1985):255–304.

Orden, D., and P. L. Fackler. "Identifying Monetary and Other Macroeconomic Impacts on Agricultural Prices in VAR Models." Dep. Agr. Econ. Staff Pap. 88-36, Virginia Polytechnic Institute and State University, 1988.

Sims, C. A. "Are Forecasting Models Usable for Policy Analysis?" *Fed. Res. Bank of Minn. Quart. Rev.* (Winter 1986), pp. 2–16.

Chapter 4

AGRICULTURAL ECONOMICS

Agricultural Economics 36 (2007) 233–243

Exchange rate alignment and producer support estimates (PSEs) for India

Fuzhi Cheng[a,*] and David Orden[b]

[a]*Division of Nutritional Sciences (DNS), 304 Savage Hall, Cornell University Ithaca, NY 14853, USA*
[b]*Markets, Trade and Institutions Division, International Food Policy Research Institute, Washington DC 20006*

Received 13 December 2005; received in revised form 15 September 2006; accepted 26 October 2006

Abstract

This article examines the effects of exchange rate alignment during 1985–2002 on agricultural producer support estimates (PSEs) for India. Based on several time series techniques, the equilibrium exchange rate of the Indian rupee and the corresponding misalignment of the actual rate are estimated and applied to recent PSE calculations. Our results show that the exchange rate was substantially misaligned before a financial crisis and macroeconomic reform in the early 1990s, with subsequent indirect effects on the PSEs. We find a relatively high pass-through of exchange rate movements to domestic agricultural prices, so that removal of the exchange rate misalignment would have improved incentives to Indian farmers during this period. More recently, this indirect exchange rate effect is smaller than the direct effect in the PSEs, indicating the dominance of sectoral-specific policies over economy-wide policies.

JEL classification: F31, Q18

Keywords: Exchange rate; Cointegration; Pass-through; Producer Support Estimate (PSE)

1. Introduction

Agricultural policies in developing countries play a very important role in determining domestic commodity prices and the returns to agriculture. The nature and degree of the policy interventions differ across countries thereby producing different types of impact on producers and consumers. Various agricultural policy indicators (APIs) such as the producer support estimate (PSE) have been constructed to evaluate and monitor these policy changes (Josling and Valdes, 2004). A problem with conventional analyses based on the APIs, however, is that they usually have a sector-specific focus that can miss the important linkages between economy-wide policies and the agricultural sector. By changing the relative prices of importables, exportables, and home goods, some economy-wide policies, such as policies affecting exchange rates, can have impacts on agricultural incentives that might overwhelm those from sectoral policies. The different effects of sectoral and economy-wide policies on agriculture in the developing countries were documented in the study by Krueger et al. (1991).

The relevance of the exchange rate in calculation of PSEs has been pointed out by a number of authors including Harley (1996), Liefert et al. (1996), and Melyukhina (2002). This issue is particularly important for developing countries and economies in transition, since capital surges, macroeconomic instability, and subsequent financial crises, together with delayed or insufficient adjustments in exchange rates, have generated substantial exchange rate misalignments in some cases. Pronounced misalignments of the exchange rate potentially subsidize or tax the agricultural sector and can result in misleading estimates of the level and sometimes the direction of agricultural support as measured by the PSE.

While there is general agreement that use of misaligned exchange rates introduces a bias in PSE calculations, and that this bias can be substantial in some cases, there is much less agreement on the appropriate alternative. Previous studies (e.g., Liefert et al., 1996, for Russia) have used certain "adjusted" exchange rates such as the purchasing power parity (PPP) exchange rate as the "equilibrium" and indicated that exchange rate misalignment had significant impacts on the calculation of the PSEs. Despite plausible results, calculations based on PPP involve a degree of discretion and the results are sensitive to the selection of a base year. Other models of the equilibrium exchange rate are potentially preferred to the PPP approach in PSE estimation (Harley, 1996).

Recently an equilibrium approach that relates the real exchange rate to underlying economic fundamentals has gained

* Corresponding author. Tel.: (607) 255-2684; fax: (607) 255-1033.
E-mail address: fc64@cornell.edu (F. Cheng).

prominence among both practitioners and policy makers to address issues of exchange rate misalignment and to test for over- or under-valued currencies. We apply this approach and analyze misalignment effects on the PSEs of India, a country where agricultural support or disprotection levels are important but exchange rate effects have received little attention. We find a long-run cointegrating relationship between the exchange rate and basic economic fundamentals over the period 1950–2002, as suggested by real exchange rate equilibrium theory. This empirical model suggests the Indian rupee was continuously misaligned in the late 1980s–early 1990s, which contributed to a financial crisis and subsequent macroeconomic reforms during 1991–1993. We also find a relatively high coefficient of pass-through from exchange rate movements to domestic agricultural prices, although less so for basic food grains such as wheat and rice than for other commodities. Applying these results to recently completed PSE estimates by Mullen et al. (2005) for 1985–2002, we find that the misalignment had a substantial effect during the prereform period. Removal of the exchange rate misalignment would have improved incentives to Indian farmers during this era. More recently, the indirect exchange rate effect has been smaller than the direct sectoral effects measured in the PSEs, indicating the dominance of sectoral-specific policies over economy-wide policies.

The article is organized as follows. Section 2 empirically estimates exchange rate equilibrium and misalignment in India. Section 3 discusses the effect of exchange rate misalignment on PSEs, evaluates exchange rate pass-through, and provides estimates of the exchange rate effects on PSEs in India for the period 1985–2002. Summary and conclusions are provided in Section 4.

2. Exchange rate equilibrium and misalignment in India

To address the effects of exchange rate misalignments on agriculture support levels measured by the PSE, the first task is to establish the exchange rate equilibrium. The fundamental difficulty is that the equilibrium value of the exchange rate is not observable. Assessment is further complicated because there exist a variety of models of equilibrium exchange rate determination. Common approaches range from the simple PPP to more sophisticated models such as the Fundamental Equilibrium Exchange Rate (FEER) (Williamson, 1994), the Natural Real Exchange Rate (NATREX) (Stein, 1994), the Behavioral Equilibrium Exchange Rate (BEER) (Clark and MacDonald, 1999) and the Real Equilibrium Exchange Rate (REER) (Edwards, 1989; Hinkle and Montiel, 1999).

The equilibrium exchange rate for the Indian rupee has been modeled using several approaches. Kholi (2003) calculates the equilibrium (nominal) exchange rate of the Indian rupee for postfloating years using PPP with a base rate set at the 1993 level. Results from this study show that the nominal exchange rate moved closely with the PPP rate during the sample period with slight overvaluation. Patnaik and Pauly (2001) use a variant of the BEER approach to derive the equilibrium exchange rate in India. Their results suggest that in the 1990s the equilibrium value of the rupee was essentially determined by the output market. However, due to slow adjustments in this market, the exchange rate was not always in equilibrium. There were periods when the rupee was overvalued or undervalued compared to the long-run rate, but there was a clear tendency to revert to the equilibrium level. Cerra and Saxena (2002) apply the REER approach to study whether the rupee was misaligned before the 1991 crisis through a vector error correction model (VECM). The evidence from this study indicates that the rupee was overvalued in the late 1980s and early 1990s. This overvaluation played a significant role in the macroeconomic crisis which resulted in sharp exchange rate depreciations.

Following Cerra and Saxena (2002) (and Edwards, 1989), this article adopts the REER approach in which the real exchange rate for India is determined by a set of economic fundamentals. The fundamentals identified include four categories: (1) Domestic supply-side factors and particularly the Balassa–Samuelson effect arising from faster productivity growth in the tradable relative to the nontradable good sector; (2) Fiscal policy, such as fiscal deficits as well as changes in the composition of government spending between tradable and nontradable goods; (3) International economic environment, including world interest rate, capital inflows and terms of trade; and (4) Commercial policy such as trade liberalization in terms of a reduction in import tariffs and export subsidies. Time series cointegration is used to test for a stationary long-run relationship between the exchange rate and the economic fundamentals.

2.1. Model description

A system of variables $\mathbf{x}$ consisting of the real exchange rate and the underlying fundamentals is formulated as $\mathbf{x} = [LRER, LPRO, LGEX, WIR, LNCI, LTOT, LOPN]$ with each variable defined as follows. All variables are in logarithms, except for the world interest rate (*WIR*). When index numbers are used, the base year is 2000. Annual data are drawn from the International Financial Statistics of the IMF and supplemented by various issues of the Handbook of Statistics on Indian Economy published by the Reserve Bank of India. The sample period is 1950–2003 for all variables except *LNCI* (1975–2003).

The real exchange rate (*LRER*) is defined as the product of nominal exchange rate and the ratio of consumer price indexes: $LRER = \ln(e \cdot CPI^{US}/CPI)$, where e is the nominal exchange rate and CPI^{US}, CPI are U.S. and India's consumer price indices, respectively. While some other studies have used the multilateral real effective exchange rate, the real exchange rate defined here is a bilateral rate expressed in domestic currencies per U.S. dollar (an increase represents depreciation). This bilateral rate can be readily applied to the later PSE calculations, as world commodity prices are generally denominated in U.S. dollars.

The Balassa–Samuelson effect caused by differential productivity growth in the traded versus nontraded good sectors is approximated by the productivity change variable (*LPRO*). To be consistent with the Balassa–Samuelson theory, an increase in the productivity in the tradable sector relative to the nontradable sector would appreciate the exchange rate, because it creates excess demand for nontradable goods. Following Cerra and Saxena (2002), this variable is proxied by the log of annual growth of the industrial production index (*IPI*):

$$LPRO = \ln(IPI/IPI_{-1}).$$

Government expenditure (*GEX*) as a percentage to GDP is used to capture the effect of fiscal policies: $LGEX = \ln(GEX/GDP)$. Changes in the composition of government consumption affect the exchange rate in different ways, depending on whether the consumption is directed toward traded or nontraded goods. If an increase in government consumption is concentrated in nontraded goods, excess demand in this sector will lead to higher nontraded good price and thus real exchange rate appreciation. Depreciation will occur if expanded government consumption is concentrated in traded goods.

Three variables are defined to capture changes in the international economic environment. First the real world interest rate (*WIR*) is used, which is approximated by the U.S. real interest rate calculated by subtracting the U.S. inflation rate (measured by the CPI^{US}) from the one-year Treasury-Bill rate (*TBR*): $WIR = TBR - (CPI^{US} - CPI^{US}_{-1})/CPI^{US}_{-1}$. Second, the ratio of net capital inflows (*NCI*) to GDP is used: $LNCI = \ln(NCI/GDP)$. It is widely accepted that world interest rate fluctuations and capital flows into and out of the developing countries drive real exchange rate movements. A stylized effect associated with a reduction in the world interest rate or increased capital inflow is real exchange rate appreciation (Fernandez-Arias and Montiel, 1996)

A third international variable is the terms of trade (*LTOT*) defined as the ratio of export price index (export unit value *XUV*) to import price index (import unit value *MUV*): $LTOT = \ln(XUV/MUV)$. Previous studies (e.g., Goldfajn and Valdes, 1999) have shown that the effect of terms of trade on the exchange rate is ambiguous. An improvement in the terms of trade, for instance, through a decrease in the price of importables, increases national income which in turn increases demand for nontraded good leading to real exchange rate appreciation (an income effect). Simultaneously, the movement of production away from importables toward nontradables can depress the price of nontradables causing real exchange rate depreciation (a substitution effect). Therefore the net effect of terms of trade on the real exchange rate depends on the relative magnitude of the income and substitution effects.

Finally, openness of the economy (*LOPN*) is calculated as the ratio of the sum of value of imports (*VM*) plus value of exports (*VX*) to GDP: $LOPN = \ln((VM + VX)/GDP)$. Openness reflects how connected the economy is to the rest of the world and reflects the degree of trade liberalization. Its use as a proxy for trade policy is justified by the difficulty of obtaining good time series data on import tariffs and export subsidies, and also because it may account not only for explicit but also implicit trade policy, for example, quotas and exchange controls. Previous studies have shown that the improvement of a country's openness (decrease in tariff and subsidy) generates a depreciation of real exchange rate due to crowding-in and subsequent reduction in nontradable prices (Goldfajn and Valdes, 1999).

2.2. Long-run exchange rate determination

The Johansen maximum likelihood method (Johansen, 1991) is used to determine the long-run equilibrium exchange rate in India after augmented Dickey–Fuller (ADF) tests on the univariate series indicate that all the variables in the system are I(1) in levels and I(0) in first differences.[1] The Johansen procedure is based on the following *p*th-order VECM:

$$\Delta \mathbf{x}_t = \boldsymbol{\Gamma}_1 \Delta \mathbf{x}_{t-1} + \boldsymbol{\Gamma}_2 \Delta \mathbf{x}_{t-2} + \cdots + \boldsymbol{\Gamma}_{p-1} \Delta \mathbf{x}_{t-p+1} + \boldsymbol{\Psi} x_{t-1} + \boldsymbol{\Pi} D_t + \boldsymbol{\varepsilon}_t \quad (1)$$

where $\mathbf{x}_t$ is a $(n \times 1)$ vector of nonstationary I(1) variables, $\boldsymbol{\Delta}$ is the difference-operator, $\boldsymbol{\Gamma}_i$, $\boldsymbol{\Psi}$ and $\boldsymbol{\Pi}$ are $(n \times n)$, $(n \times n)$ and $(n \times k)$ coefficient matrices, $\mathbf{D}_t$ is a $(k \times 1)$ vector of deterministic terms and $\boldsymbol{\varepsilon}_t$ is a vector of error terms. Suppose that $rank(\Psi) = h$, $0 < h < n$ and there are h cointegrating relationships in $\mathbf{x}_t$. This implies that $\boldsymbol{\Psi}$ can be written in the form

$$\boldsymbol{\Psi} = \mathbf{AB}' \quad (2)$$

for $\mathbf{A}$ an $(n \times h)$ matrix and $\mathbf{B}'$ an $(h \times n)$ matrix. The Johansen procedure provides two tests, the trace and the maximal eigenvalue tests, for the number of linearly independent cointegrating relationships among the series in $\mathbf{x}_t$;

$$\lambda_{\text{trace}}(h) = -T \sum_{i=h+1}^{n} \ln(1 - \hat{\lambda}_i), \quad \text{and}$$

$$\lambda_{\max}(h, h+1) = -T \ln(1 - \hat{\lambda}_{h+1}), \quad (3)$$

where $\hat{\lambda}_i$ are the estimated eigenvalues of matrix $\boldsymbol{\Psi}$.

Before proceeding with the Johansen test, we consider different model formulations. Initially, the vector **x** consists all the variables in the system ($n = 7$). However, difficulty arises because data for variable *LNCI* are only available for the period 1975–2002. The resulting loss of degrees of freedom leads to nonrobust results. *LNCI* is thus dropped from the system and the model is re-estimated using an expanded sample period from 1950 to 2003 ($n = 6$).

The model is further adjusted by taking short-run shocks into account. We follow Edwards (1989) and define an exogenous variable that captures macroeconomic policy, *LDCT*, the log of domestic credit (*DCT*) over GDP: $LDCT = \ln(DCT/GDP)$ (also I(1) in levels and I(0) in first difference by an ADF

[1] The ADF test results are not reported here but are available upon request.

Table 1
Johansen cointegration test results

Null hypothesis	Case I				Case II			
	λ_{trace} test	λ_{trace} (0.95)	$\lambda_{\max}$ test	$\lambda_{\max}$ (0.95)	λ_{trace} test	λ_{trace} (0.95)	$\lambda_{\max}$ test	$\lambda_{\max}$ (0.95)
$h = 0$	151.55*	103.85	68.56*	40.96	147.86*	95.75	68.26*	40.08
$h \leq 1$	82.99*	76.97	38.82*	34.81	79.61*	69.82	38.32*	33.88
$h \leq 2$	44.18	54.08	20.60	28.59	41.29	47.86	20.60	27.58
$h \leq 3$	23.58	35.19	10.65	22.30	20.69	29.80	10.60	21.13
$h \leq 4$	12.92	20.26	9.60	15.89	10.09	15.49	9.23	14.26
$h \leq 5$	3.33	9.16	3.33	9.16	0.87	3.84	0.87	3.84
D	Constant and short-run shocks				Constant and short-run shocks			
Lag length		2				2		
Sample	1950–2003				1950–2003			

Note: * denotes rejection at the 0.05 significance level. Case I: no intercept in the cointegrating equation or the VECM; Case II: intercept in the cointegrating equation and the VECM. h is the cointegrating rank. The lag-length of two is determined by a battery of diagnostic tests on an unrestricted vector autoregression model (VARM) including a χ^2 test for the hypothesis that the i-period lag is zero for each equation separately; a joint LM test for the hypothesis that there is no heteroskedasticity or serial correlation; and a joint χ^2 test for the normality of the errors (not reported but available upon request).

test). Edwards argues that excess supply of domestic credit can proxy inconsistent macroeconomic policies; and when it becomes highly expansive without matching adjustment in the nominal exchange rate, the real rate appreciates in the short run causing overvaluation. The first difference of this variable, $\Delta LDCT$, is included in $\mathbf{D}_t$ to represent such effects. In addition, following Edwards and Savastano (2002), a vector of dummy variables—representing two oil price shocks in the 1970s, and the balance of payment crisis with subsequent exchange rate regime shifts in the early 1990s—is also included in $\mathbf{D}_t$.[2]

Table 1 presents the Johansen cointegration tests for the final model formation under two cases: without and with an intercept (Case I and Case II, respectively). The λ_{trace} and $\lambda_{\max}$ statistics reject the null hypothesis of zero cointegrating rank at the 0.05 significance level for each case. However, the null hypothesis that the cointegrating rank is at most 2 is accepted indicating that there are up to two cointegrating relationships among the variables ($h = 2$).

The existence of multiple cointegrating vectors complicates the interpretation of the equilibrium exchange rates. If the exchange rate variable ($LRER$) appears in two cointegrating vectors then each vector, or any linear combinations of the two, could be treated as a long-run equilibrium exchange rate relationship. However, a likelihood ratio test (Johansen and Juselius, 1990):

$$-2\ln(\hat{L}_R/\hat{L}_U) = -2\ln(Q) = T\sum_{i=1}^{\hat{h}} \ln\left\{\frac{(1-\hat{\lambda}_i^*)}{(1-\hat{\lambda}_i)}\right\}$$

(χ^2 distributed with R and U denoting restricted and unrestricted models) shows that a joint restriction on $\mathbf{B}$ and $\mathbf{A}$ in the form:

$$\mathbf{B}' = \begin{bmatrix} * & * & * & * & * & * \\ 0 & * & * & * & * & * \end{bmatrix} \text{ and } \mathbf{A}' = \begin{bmatrix} * & * & * & 0 & * & * \\ * & * & * & 0 & * & * \end{bmatrix}$$

[2] The dummy variables take the value of 1 in years 1973 (Dummy 1), 1979 (Dummy 2), and 1991, 92, 93 (Dummy 3) respectively, and 0 otherwise.

is not rejected at 0.05 significance level with $\chi^2(2) = 1.93$ (P-value $= 0.38$). In light of this joint test, the first (unrestricted) cointegrating vector, which contains the exchange rate, can be recognized as the equilibrium exchange rate relationship, while the second (restricted) cointegrating vector represents a different long-run relationship for variables excluding the exchange rate. The world interest rate (WIR) can be treated as weakly exogenous to the system. Table 2 presents the restricted cointegration results normalized on $LRER$ and $LPRO$ for the first and second vector, respectively. The two cointegrating vectors can be alternatively presented as

$$\begin{aligned} LRER &= -10.370LPRO + 0.621LGEX + 2.695WIR \\ &\quad + 0.569LTOT + 0.654LOPN + 4.037 \\ LPRO &= 0.042LGEX - 0.548WIR - 0.031LTOT \\ &\quad - 0.030LOPN + 0.250. \end{aligned} \tag{4}$$

For the first cointegrating vector, the negative sign of the variable $LPRO$ for India suggests that an increase in the productivity in the traded good sector relative to the nontraded good sector is associated with real exchange rate appreciation, which is consistent with the Balassa–Samuelson theory. An increase in government expenditure ($LGEX$) causes the rupee to depreciate, suggesting that Indian government expenditures might have a higher content of traded goods, which is consistent with Cerra and Saxena (2002). The positive sign associated with WIR indicates that a reduction in the world interest rate appreciates India's long-run real exchange rate. The positive sign on $LTOT$ suggests the possible dominance of the substitution effect over the income effect and that improvements in the terms of trade depreciate the currency. The volume of trade, or degree of openness, as measured by the variable $LOPN$, confirms previous findings that economic closedness is typically associated with overvaluation, and that external liberalization aimed at reducing tariffs and eliminating trade restrictions causes currency depreciation.

Table 2
Restricted cointegration results

	LRER	LPRO	LGEX	WIR	LTOT	LOPN	Constant
B′							
	1.000	10.370**	−0.621**	−2.695**	−0.569**	−0.654**	−4.037
		(1.345)	(0.078)	(1.104)	(0.184)	(0.076)	
	0.000	1.000	−0.042**	0.548**	0.031*	0.030**	−0.250
			(0.008)	(0.100)	(0.018)	(0.007)	
A′							
	−0.017**	−0.015**	0.016*	0.000	0.049**	0.040**	–
	(0.008)	(0.006)	(0.008)		(0.020)	(0.015)	
	0.011	0.002	0.019**	0.000	−0.011	−0.041*	–
	(0.022)	(0.010)	(0.003)		(0.032)	(0.025)	

Note: Standard errors are in parentheses. ** and * denote significance at the 0.05 and 0.10 levels, respectively.

2.3. Exchange rate equilibrium and misalignment

To calculate the equilibrium exchange rate based on the restricted cointegration results in Eq. (4), we filter the values of the economic fundamentals by the Hodrick–Prescott (H-P) decomposition technique (Hodrick and Prescott, 1997), as the economic fundamentals themselves may be out of long-run equilibrium. The H-P method decomposes these time series into a trend μ_t and stationary component $x_t - \mu_t$ by minimizing:

$$\sum_{t=1}^{T}(x_t-\mu_t)^2+\lambda\sum_{t=2}^{T-1}[(\mu_{t+1}-\mu_t)-(\mu_t-\mu_{t-1})]^2,$$

where λ is an arbitrary constant reflecting the penalty of incorporating fluctuations into the trend.[3]

Fig. 1 compares the actual with the equilibrium exchange rates for 1980–2002. The difference between the two indicates the exchange rate misalignment. The figure shows that the actual real exchange rate of the Indian rupee significantly increased (depreciated) from 1980 to 1993. Large steps of devaluations started in 1988 and continued through 1992. The actual exchange rate shows a persistent overvaluation from 1986 to 1992 compared to the equilibrium rate. Concurrent with the long period of real exchange rate overvaluation was the deterioration of the country's balance of payments, the depletion of foreign exchange reserves, and political turmoil, which triggered the macroeconomic crisis starting in 1991.

The actual real exchange rate came into line with the equilibrium in 1993 after devaluations and as a result of postcrisis adjustments featuring macroeconomic stabilization and structural reforms, especially in the direction of trade and financial liberalization. The combined effects of these measures were evident in the external sector. In the years following the crisis, rising capital inflows and shrinking trade deficits have led to continued accumulation of foreign exchange reserves by India. The actual real exchange rate of the Indian rupee has fluctuated around its equilibrium values with limited degrees of misalignment. As Fig. 1 shows, both the actual and the equilibrium real exchange rates were relatively stable during 1993–2002, with a slight initial appreciation followed by depreciation when the U.S. dollar began to appreciate globally in 1996. In cases of misalignment of the Indian rupee, the actual rate has subsequently moved in the direction of restoring the equilibrium during this period.

[3] Different λs should be used depending on data frequency: larger when the data is monthly and smaller when it is annual. Hodrick and Prescott (1997) suggest a λ of 1,600 for quarterly data. In this analysis of annual data, λ is set equal to 10.

3. Effects of exchange rate alignment on PSEs

3.1. The PSE

According to the OECD, the PSE is "an indicator of the annual monetary value of gross transfer from consumers and taxpayers to agricultural producers" (Portugal, 2002). In nominal terms the PSE can be expressed as the sum of Market Price Support (*MPS*) and Budgetary Payments (*BP*). The calculation of *MPS* is shown in Eq. (5):

$$MPS=\sum MPS_j=\sum\left(P_j^d-P_j^{ar}\right)Q_j \tag{5}$$

where j denotes commodity, P_j^d is the domestic price, P_j^{ar} is the adjusted reference price, and Q_j is the quantity. The adjusted reference price P_j^{ar} is the world market price (either a relevant import c.i.f. price or export f.o.b. price depending on whether the commodity is an importable or an exportable) expressed in domestic currency and adjusted by various transaction costs.[4]

[4] Byerlee and Morris (1993) and Mullen et al. (2005) point out that the selection of a relevant reference price (P^{ar}) depends on the relationship between the adjusted reference prices for imports (P_m) and exports (P_e) and the estimated autarky equilibrium price (P^*) at which the domestic market would clear without trade. It is always the case that $P_m > P_e$ because of international and domestic cost adjustments. P_m is the relevant P^{ar} when $P^* > P_m$, and P_e is the relevant P^{ar} when $P_e > P^*$. But when P^* falls in the spread between the import and export world prices ($P_m > P^* > P_e$) then P^* is the relevant P^{ar}. Mullen et al. is one of a few empirical PSE studies applying this approach to reference price determination, which requires estimation of P^* as well as observation of prevailing domestic and world prices. Other studies assume either P_m or P_e is relevant depending on the trade position of the country for each commodity.

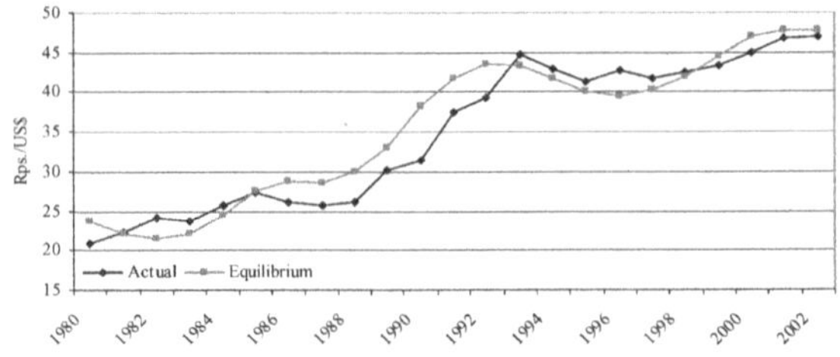

Fig. 1. The actual and equilibrium real exchange rates.

The cost adjustment process differs according to the commodity's trade status (see Mullen et al., 2005, for details), but in either case, the adjusted reference price can be expressed as:

$$P_j^{ar} = P_j^w \times E + ADJ_j \tag{6}$$

where P_j^w is the world market price, E is the nominal exchange rate, and ADJ_j is the domestic cost adjustment factor.

The PSE measure can be expressed on a percentage basis (denoted by $\%PSE$) using $(VOP + BP)$ as the denominator, where VOP is the total value of agricultural production at domestic producer prices:

$$\%PSE = \frac{MPS + BP}{VOP + BP}.$$

Following the terminology of Krueger et al. (1991), we define three types of effects using the percent PSE. The "direct effect" induced by sector-specific policies is defined as the $\%PSE$ calculated using the actual nominal exchange rate E:

$$\text{Direct Effect} = \%PSE(E) = \frac{MPS(E) + BP}{VOP + BP} = \frac{\sum (P_j^d - P_j^{ar}(E))Q_j + BP}{VOP + BP}. \tag{7a}$$

The "total effect" induced by both sectoral and exchange rate policies is defined as the $\%PSE$ calculated using the equilibrium exchange rate E^*, under the *ceteris paribus* assumption holding domestic and budgetary payments constant:

$$\text{Total Effect} = \%PSE(E^*) = \frac{MPS(E^*) + BP}{VOP + BP} = \frac{\sum (P_j^d - P_j^{ar}(E^*))Q_j + BP}{VOP + BP}. \tag{7b}$$

The difference between the total and direct effect captures the "indirect effect" of misalignment of the exchange rate:

$$\text{Indirect Effect} = \%PSE(E^*) - \%PSE(E) = \frac{\sum (P_j^{ar}(E) - P_j^{ar}(E^*))Q_j}{VOP + BP}. \tag{7c}$$

Ignoring domestic cost adjustment (ADJ_j), it can be shown that the indirect effect is $m \cdot \frac{\sum P_j^w E^* Q_j}{VOP+BP}$, where m is the percentage exchange rate misalignment, $m = (E - E^*)/E^*$.[5] The indirect effect is negative if overvaluation occurs ($m < 0$), positive if undervaluation occurs ($m > 0$), and zero if no misalignment exists ($m = 0$).

3.2. Exchange rate pass-through

The effects of realignment of the exchange rate on PSEs depend on the degree of pass-through of appreciation or depreciation movements to domestic agricultural prices and budgetary payments. The empirical literature on exchange rate pass-through to prices is extensive but has mostly focused on the manufacturing industries of developed economies. Among those studies that examine exchange rate pass-through to agricultural commodity prices, some have shown more complete and rapid pass-through to agricultural prices than manufacturing prices (Carter et al., 1990; Xu and Orden, 2002), which is consistent with the view that agricultural commodities operate in competitive flexible-price markets. Other studies have shown incomplete pass-through for some agricultural commodities (Park and Pick, 1996). A number of reasons are offered for such incomplete pass-through from exchange rates. One explanation for this phenomenon is that importing and exporting firms choose to hold prices constant and simply reduce or increase their mark-ups when the exchange rate is changing ("pricing-to-market"). Policy interventions that affect domestic prices, or domestic prices falling between import and export parity would also affect exchange rate pass-through.

To evaluate exchange rate pass-through to domestic agricultural prices in India, we estimate a fixed effects panel regression model in first-difference logarithmic form:

$$\Delta p_{it} = \alpha_i + \theta_t + \sum_{k=0}^{n} \left(\beta_k \Delta e_{t-k} + \gamma_k \Delta p_{it-k}^*\right) + \varepsilon_{it} \tag{8}$$

[5] Ignoring domestic cost adjustment (ADJ_j) simplifies the expressions for the indirect effect. However, in the PSE calculations reported below, ADJ_j is taken into account.

where Δ is difference-operator, p_i and p_i^* are domestic and world prices, respectively, e is the exchange rate, α_i and θ_t represent cross-commodity and time-specific effects, n represents the number of lagged terms, β_k and γ_k are coefficients measuring the contemporaneous or lagged pass-through of exchange rates and foreign prices to domestic prices, and ε_{it} is the idiosyncratic error term distributed with mean zero and variance σ_ε^2. This specification is a variant of the panel regression model proposed by Knetter (1993) to study pricing-to-market behaviour of exporting firms for a particular commodity.[6] If $\sum_{k=0}^{n}\beta$ or $\sum_{k=0}^{n}\gamma$ is not significantly different from one (zero), then there is complete (no) exchange rate or world price pass-through to commodity prices.

The estimation of Eq. (8) is based on a panel dataset that includes 11 commodities covered in a recent PSE study for India by Mullen et al. (2005) for the period of 1985–2002. The commodities include wheat, rice, corn, sorghum, groundnuts, sugar, rapeseed, soybeans, sunflower, chickpeas and cotton, accounting for approximately 50% of total agricultural production in India. Annual data series are used due to the fact that short-run exchange rate changes (monthly or quarterly) may not be fully passed through to prices as they can be treated as temporary. Another reason for using the annual data is that for India higher-frequency data are not available. The exchange rate data are obtained from the previous analysis. Domestic prices and world prices, which are c.i.f. India prices, are taken from Mullen et al. (2005).

Table 3 shows the estimated exchange rate pass-through coefficients (β or $\sum\beta$). Model 1 is a simple pooled regression that does not include either commodity or time effects. Model 2 includes the commodity effect that captures unobserved heterogeneity across commodities (e.g., consumer demands). In addition to the commodity effect, Model 3 also takes into account the time effect that captures common impacts in each time period across all commodities (e.g., national income). Two different lag structures are considered ($n = 0$ or 1).[7] Student-t statistics are provided for the tests that the contemporaneous or aggregated pass-through coefficient is zero, implying no pass-through. Tests are also reported for the contemporaneous or aggregate pass-through coefficient summing to one, which is consistent with complete pass through.

The results in Table 3 show that aggregate exchange rate pass-through to domestic agricultural prices is fairly high for India.[8] Point estimates only differ slightly across the models.

Table 3
Pass-through coefficient by fixed effect panel estimation

	Model 1	Model 2	Model 3
No lag ($n = 0$)			
β	0.82	0.80	0.81
t-stat for $H_0: \beta = 0$	(2.29)*	(2.16)*	(2.45)*
t-stat for $H_0: \beta = 1$	(3.54)*	(3.71)*	(4.42)*
1 lag ($n = 1$)			
$\sum\beta$	0.78	0.77	0.77
t-stat for $H_0: \sum\beta = 0$	(5.62)*	(5.83)*	(5.82)*
t-stat for $H_0: \sum\beta = 1$	(4.21)*	(3.13)*	(3.20)*
Commodity dummies	No	Yes	Yes
Time dummies	No	No	Yes

Note: Calculated t-statistics are in parentheses.
*denotes significance at 0.05 level.

When there is no lag, the contemporaneous exchange rate pass-through coefficient ranges from 0.80 to 0.82. Adding one lag of the exchange rate (and the world price) to the estimation only slightly changes the pass-through. For all model specifications, the pass-through coefficient is significant, indicating that the hypothesis of no exchange rate pass-through is rejected. However, despite high pass-though coefficients, the null hypotheses that they are equal to one, i.e., complete exchange rate pass-through, are also rejected.

3.3. Counterfactual PSEs

A counterfactual measure of the PSE ($\%PSE^{CF}$, where CF denotes "counterfactual") can also be computed under the assumption that the exchange rate (E) moves to its equilibrium (E^*) in a given period. In place of the *ceteris paribus* assumption of Eq. (7b), the exchange rate changes can affect not only the reference prices but also the domestic prices due to exchange rate pass-through. Domestic prices change to $\frac{P_j^d}{1+\beta m}$ when incomplete pass-through (IPT, $0 < \beta < 1$) occurs, where β is the exchange rate pass-through coefficient. Domestic prices remain at P_j^d with no pass-through (NPT, $\beta = 0$), but change to $\frac{P_j^d}{1+m}$ with complete pass-through (CPT, $\beta = 1$).

When there is exchange rate pass-through to domestic prices (complete or incomplete) one may expect that there is also exchange rate pass-through to budgetary payments, even though the magnitude of the these two pass-throughs may differ. In this analysis we consider two cases: Eq. (1) the effect of exchange rate pass-through to budgetary payments is the same as the one to domestic agricultural prices; and Eq. (2) there is no exchange rate pass-through to budgetary payments even though there is pass-through to domestic prices (complete or incomplete). In the first scenario, budgetary payments become $\frac{BP}{1+\beta m}$ with IPT and $\frac{BP}{1+m}$ with CPT, while in the second scenario budgetary payments remain at BP.

A comparison between the direct PSE (based on the actual exchange rate) and the counterfactual PSE (based on equilibrium

---

[6] A panel cointegration method is not used as the hypothesis of a panel unit root is rejected.

[7] Results of aggregate pass-through tests using longer time lags are similar to those with 1 lag.

[8] The panel regression estimation used in this analysis provides a common pass-through coefficient for the 11 covered commodities. Similar estimation methods are used in Mundlak and Larson (1992) who also found a relatively high pass-through coefficient (0.74). In terms of individual commodities, Sharma (2003) reported small exchange rate pass-through coefficients for rice and wheat in India while much higher coefficients were found in Tyers and Anderson (1992) for the same two commodities.

Table 4
A comparison between counterfactual and direct PSE

Pass-through	Counterfactual	Direct effect	Transfer	Nontransfer
NPT	$\frac{\sum\left(P_j^d - P_j^w E^*\right) Q_j + BP}{VOP + BP}$	$\frac{\sum\left(P_j^d - P_j^w E\right) Q_j + BP}{VOP + BP}$	$m\frac{\sum P_j^w E^* Q_j}{VOP + BP}$	0
CPT 1	$\frac{\sum\left(\frac{P_j^d}{1+m} - P_j^w E^*\right) Q_j + \frac{BP}{1+m}}{\frac{VOP}{1+m} + \frac{BP}{1+m}}$	Same as above	0	$m\frac{\sum P_j^w E^* Q_j}{VOP + BP}$
CPT 2	$\frac{\sum\left(\frac{P_j^d}{1+m} - P_j^w E^*\right) Q_j + BP}{\frac{VOP}{1+m} + BP}$	Same as above	$\frac{\sum\left(\frac{P_j^d}{1+m} - P_j^w E^*\right) Q_j + BP}{\frac{VOP}{1+m} + BP} - \frac{\sum\left(P_j^d - P_j^w E\right) Q_j + BP}{VOP + BP}$	$m\frac{\sum P_j^w E^* Q_j}{VOP + BP} - \frac{\sum\left(\frac{P_j^d}{1+m} - P_j^w E^*\right) Q_j + BP}{\frac{VOP}{1+m} + BP} + \frac{\sum\left(P_j^d - P_j^w E\right) Q_j + BP}{VOP + BP}$
IPT 1	$\frac{\sum\left(\frac{P_j^d}{1+\beta m} - P_j^w E^*\right) Q_j + \frac{BP}{1+\beta m}}{\frac{VOP}{1+\beta m} + \frac{BP}{1+\beta m}}$	Same as above	$(1-\beta)m\frac{\sum P_j^w E^* Q_j}{VOP + BP}$	$\beta m\frac{\sum P_j^w E^* Q_j}{VOP + BP}$
IPT 2	$\frac{\sum\left(\frac{P_j^d}{1+\beta m} - P_j^w E^*\right) Q_j + BP}{\frac{VOP}{1+\beta m} + BP}$	Same as above	$\frac{\sum\left(\frac{P_j^d}{1+\beta m} - P_j^w E^*\right) Q_j + BP}{\frac{VOP}{1+\beta m} + BP} - \frac{\sum\left(P_j^d - P_j^w E\right) Q_j + BP}{VOP + BP}$	$m\frac{\sum P_j^w E^* Q_j}{VOP + BP} - \frac{\sum\left(\frac{P_j^d}{1+\beta m} - P_j^w E^*\right) Q_j + BP}{\frac{VOP}{1+\beta m} + BP} + \frac{\sum\left(P_j^d - P_j^w E\right) Q_j + BP}{VOP + BP}$

Note: For simplicity, the formulae shown ignore domestic cost adjustment (ADJ_j) but these adjustments are incorporated in our empirical analysis. NPT: No pass-through; CPT (IPT) 1: Complete (incomplete) pass-through to domestic prices and budgetary payments; CPT (IPT) 2: Complete (incomplete) pass-through to domestic prices, but no pass-through to budgetary payments.

exchange rate) for different exchange rate pass-through scenarios is summarized in Table 4. The difference between the initial direct and new counterfactual measures is denoted as a "transfer" of the indirect effect to the counterfactual measure.

In the case of no exchange rate pass-through (NPT), the difference between $\%PSE^{CF}$ and the initial direct $\%PSE$ is equal to the indirect exchange rate effect shown earlier. This represents a full transfer of the exchange rate effect into the new measure of the PSE, with no change in actual incentives conveyed to producers through the domestic output prices or budgetary payments. The magnitude of the indirect effect, and thus the transfer, is determined by the initial exchange rate misalignment (m).

In contrast, when there is complete exchange rate pass-through to domestic agricultural prices and to budgetary payments (CPT 1), the transfer of the initial indirect effect into the counterfactual PSE measure is zero no matter how much the exchange rate was misaligned. Removing the exchange rate misalignment in this case affects the price incentives producers face but leaves the protection coefficient measured by the initial direct $\%PSE$ unchanged. However, if there is complete pass-through to domestic agricultural prices but no pass-through to budgetary payments (CPT 2), there still exits some degree of transfer even though the pass-through to domestic prices is complete.[9] In the case of incomplete exchange rate pass-through to domestic prices (IPT 1 and IPT 2), no matter whether there is incomplete or no pass-through to budgetary payments, the degree of transfer of the initial indirect effect into the counterfactual direct effect is determined by a combination of the initial exchange rate misalignment (m) and the degree of pass-through (β).

3.4. Direct, indirect, and total PSE effects and counterfactual results

To evaluate the direct, total and indirect effects on PSEs for India we again draw upon the recent analysis of direct PSEs by Mullen et al. (2005) and our analysis of exchange rate equilibrium and misalignment. The actual nominal exchange rates in the analysis are the annual average official rates and the nominal equilibrium exchange rates are derived from the corresponding real equilibrium rates from Section 2.[10] The PSE calculations are based on the 11 covered commodities.[11]

[9] It can be shown that $\%PSE^{CF}$ in Table 4 is a monotonic increasing function of the nominal value of budgetary payments. For the case of complete exchange rate pass-through (CPT), when there is overvaluation ($m < 0$), $\%PSE^{CF}$(CPT 1) is greater than $\%PSE^{CF}$(CPT 2); when there is undervaluation ($m > 0$), $\%PSE^{CF}$(CPT 1) is less than $\%PSE^{CF}$(CPT 2). That is, with either overvaluation or undervaluation, the absolute value of transfer in CPT 2 is greater than that in CPT 1. The same set of arguments can be made for the case of incomplete exchange rate pass-through (IPT).

[10] Specifically, the nominal equilibrium exchange rate is obtained by multiplying the real equilibrium exchange rate by the ratio of India's CPI to U.S. CPI.

[11] Following Mullen et al., the MPS component of PSEs for six commodities (wheat, rice corn, sorghum, groundnuts, and sugar) for which India's trade is small and sometimes switches from imports to exports is calculated using the Byerlee and Morris (1993) procedure to determine the reference prices (see footnote 4). Rapeseed, soybeans, sunflower, chickpeas, and cotton are assumed to be importable in all years. With this approach, the estimated autarky equilibrium price rather than a world price for imports or exports is selected as the relevant reference price in several years for one or more commodities. For example, Mullen et al. estimate that the autarky equilibrium price was

Table 5
Direct, indirect, and total effect by PSE

Period (% misalignment)	I:1985–88 (−8.6%)	II:1989–92 (−11.8%)	III:1993–98 (3.6%)	IV:1999–02 (−2.8%)
Direct	7.7	0.8	−2.9	9.0
Indirect	−3.2	−8.2	1.4	−1.3
Total	4.5	−7.4	−1.5	7.7
Counterfactual (IPT)				
IPT 1	7.0	−1.1	−2.6	8.7
Transfer	−0.7	−1.9	0.3	−0.3
Nontransfer	−2.5	−6.3	1.1	−1.0
IPT 2	6.3	−3.2	−1.9	8.1
Transfer	−1.4	−2.4	1.0	−0.9
Nontransfer	−1.8	−5.8	0.4	−0.4

Note: IPT 1: Incomplete pass-through to domestic prices and budgetary payments; IPT 2: Incomplete pass-through to domestic prices but no pass-through to budgetary payments.

Table 5 shows the direct, indirect and total effects measured by the PSE for the period 1985–2002. The sample period is divided into four distinct subperiods. Period one (I) covers 1985–1988 when the exchange rate started to overvalue with an average overvaluation of −8.6%. Period two (II) represents a sustained overvaluation period from 1989 to 1992 during which the macroeconomic crisis occurred and the exchange rate was under active adjustment. The overvaluation in this period was −11.8%. Period three (III) is postreform from 1993 to 1998, with a slight undervaluation of 3.6%. The last period (IV) is the stable exchange rate period from 1999 to 2002 when the actual exchange rate is close to the equilibrium rate with a slight overvaluation of −2.8%. Fig. 2 illustrates the direct and indirect PSE results on an annual basis.

The direct effects shown in Table 5 and Fig. 2 indicate that the aggregate agricultural protection or disprotection in India follows a counter-cyclical pattern against world prices, which were low in the late 1980s, strengthened in the mid-to-late 1990s, and fell afterwards. Specifically, the direct effect was positive when world commodity prices were low during the first Period (I) but fell and then turned to disprotection when the world prices rose in Periods II and III. In Period IV, the direct effect shows an increase in support as world prices again declined. A similar pattern is observed for the total effect.

The indirect effect caused by exchange rate misalignments has had quite different impacts on India's agriculture than that of the direct effect. On average India's agricultural sector was indirectly penalized by exchange rate overvaluation in Periods I, II, and IV, but subsidized by exchange rate undervaluation in Period III. The indirect effect was greater in the years before and during the macroeconomic crisis when the exchange rate was continuously misaligned, averaging −8.2% in Period II. In the postcrisis years, as a result of decreased exchange rate misalignment following macroeconomic reforms, the indirect effect dampens to less than 2% in absolute value.

Noticeably, the indirect effect of the exchange rate is smaller in absolute value than the direct effect in Periods I, III, and IV, indicating the dominance of sectoral-specific policies over the economy-wide policies reflected in the exchange rate. The opposite happened in Period II, when substantial overvaluation had a large negative effect on incentives facing agricultural producers. This latter result is consistent with the study by Krueger et al. (1991), who found that economy-wide policies such as the exchange rate played a dominant role across a range of developing countries (not including India) in an earlier period to the mid-1980s. More recently India has not experienced sustained periods of significant exchange rate misalignment nor subsequent effects on agriculture as measured by the PSEs.

Estimates of counterfactual PSEs are also shown in Table 5 and Fig. 2 under the assumption of incomplete exchange rate pass-through with a contemporaneous pass-through coefficient of 0.81 obtained from Table 4 (Model 3 with no time lag). The cases of no pass-through (NPT) and complete pass-through (CPT) are not reported explicitly, but they can be inferred from the reported total and direct PSE results under observed exchange rates, as described above.

Since the contemporaneous pass-through of exchange rate movements is relatively high in India, only a small portion of the exchange rate effect remains in the counterfactual PSE under the assumption of incomplete exchange rate pass-through to domestic prices and budgetary payments (IPT 1). For instance, despite a large indirect effect in Period II, only −1.9% out of −8.2% transfers to the counterfactual PSE, with −6.3% disappearing as a result of the exchange rate pass-through. Counterfactually, had this period of misalignment been corrected Indian farmers would have faced better production incentives, with disprotection of only −1.1% instead of −7.4% measured by the total %PSE. The pattern of transfer relative to the nontransfer is somewhat different when there is no exchange rate pass-through to budgetary payments (IPT 2). The magnitude of transfer increases in absolute value in each period but it remains smaller than the nontransfer in Periods I and II while becoming greater in Periods III and IV.

Two additional points help to place the empirical results into context. First, a country's aggregate PSE is widely used in policy discussions and we have presented results for this PSE measure for India. Percentage PSEs can also be computed on a commodity-specific basis, using the MPS computed for that commodity individually and replacing *VOP* and *BP* with the value of production of the single commodity at domestic prices and its share of total budgetary payments. Space limitations preclude a full exposition of these disaggregated results, but the estimates for two basic foodgrains, wheat and rice, are illustrative. For both wheat and rice, similar to the aggregate results, we find a countercyclical policy for India that stabilizes domestic producer prices relative to world price fluctuations. Wheat was

between the import and export adjusted reference prices during the period when world prices fell from 1999–2002, implying no trade would have occurred without policy interventions (see Mullen et al., 2005, for details). Use of these adjustments does not affect the main conclusions we draw about direct and indirect effects on PSEs.

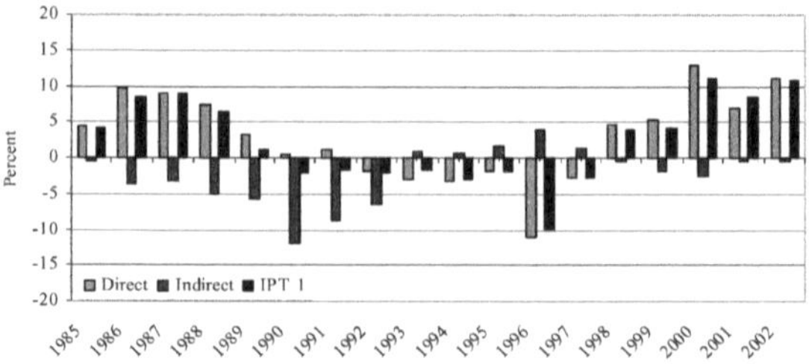

Fig. 2. Direct, indirect, and counterfactual (IPT 1) PSEs

protected in most years during 1985–2002 when the budgetary components of the PSE is taken into account (despite some price disprotection), while rice suffered disprotection throughout the 1990s. Estimates of the exchange rate pass-through for these individual commodities (based on Eq. (8) modified for a single time series) yield smaller coefficients than our aggregate estimate (0.45 and 0.48 for wheat and rice, respectively). Thus, more of the indirect effect on the PSE would be transferred to the counterfactual PSE for these commodities than in the aggregate analysis shown in Table 5. A devaluation, for example, would provide less improvement in price incentive for wheat or rice producers.

The second point of context concerns our approach to aggregation, not dissaggregation. The direct PSEs we report include only the MPS derived for the 11 covered commodities. This approach implicitly assumes that the commodities not covered (in our case, primarily livestock and fruits and vegetables) on average have been neither price-protected nor disprotected. In contrast, the MPS results for the covered commodities are often "scaled up" in PSE studies by dividing the calculated MPS value by the proportion of the value of agricultural output these commodities represent. This latter approach implicitly assumes that commodities not included in the analysis have received, on average, the same level of price protection or disprotection as the covered commodities, which we conclude is not realistic for India. The latter approach magnifies the reported MPS component, and thus our direct PSEs shown in Table 5 and Fig. 2 are smaller than would be reported had the scaling up procedure been invoked.

4. Summary and conclusions

The alignment of exchange rates can have significant impacts on the agricultural sector. In this analysis, a real equilibrium approach to determining exchange rates is applied and effects of exchange rate misalignment on PSEs are evaluated for India for the period 1985–2002. A long-run cointegrating relationship is found between the exchange rate and economic fundamentals. This model suggests that the Indian rupee was continuously overvalued in the mid 1980s to early 1990s. Direct, total and indirect effects on PSEs are compared and three scenarios of exchange rate pass-through are considered: no pass-through, complete pass-through, and incomplete pass-through. Counterfactual PSEs, assuming the exchange rate is in equilibrium in a given year, indicate that the indirect effect is fully transferred to the counterfactual measure when there is no exchange rate pass-through, but that part or all of the indirect effect disappears when exchange rate realignment is partially or fully passed through to domestic agricultural prices and budgetary payments.

The main empirical findings from the PSE calculations indicate that the indirect exchange rate effects counteract the direct effect of sectoral policies for all the sub-sample periods. The indirect effect of exchange rate overvaluation taxed the agricultural sector in India during the periods 1985–1992 and 1999–2002. We estimate a relatively high pass-through coefficient for India based on a fixed effect panel regression model using disaggregate prices of 11 commodities covered in the PSE assessment. Thus, Indian farmers would have faced improved production incentives in the late 1980s and early 1990s had the exchange rate misalignment during this period been corrected. The magnitude of the indirect effects becomes smaller in later periods when the actual exchange rate moves closer to its equilibrium value. Thus, unlike its neighbor China, for which concerns about substantial exchange rate undervaluation remain pervasive, exchange rate misalignment has not recently been a pressing issue for India with respect to either domestic agricultural production incentives or to broader trade and macroeconomic policy. Since the macroeconomic reforms of the early 1990s, Indian farmers have not experienced sharp policy shocks from exchange rate adjustments, nor are they likely to in the near future.

References

Byerlee, D., Morris, M., 1993. Calculating levels of protection: is it always appropriate to use world reference prices based on current trading status? World Dev. 21, 805–815.

Carter, C., Gray, R., Furtan, W., 1990. Exchange rate effects on inputs and outputs in Canadian agriculture. Am. J. Agric. Econ. 72, 738–743.
Cerra, V., Saxena, S., 2002. What caused the 1991 currency crisis in India? IMF Staff Papers 49(3), 395–425.
Clark, P. MacDonald, R., 1999. Exchange rates and economic fundamentals: a methodological comparison of BEERS and FEERS. In: MacDonald, R., Stein, J. (Eds.), Equilibrium Exchange Rates. Kluwer Academic Publishers, Boston.
Edwards, S., 1989. Real Exchange Rates, Devaluation and Adjustment: Exchange Rate Policy in Developing Countries. MIT Press, Cambridge, Massachusetts.
Edwards, S., Savastano, M., 2002. Exchange rates in emerging economies: What do we know? What do we need to know? In: Krueger, A. (Ed.), Economic Policy Reform: The Second Stage. The University of Chicago Press, Chicago.
Fernandez-Arias, E., Montiel, P., 1996. The surge in capital inflows to developing countries. World Bank Econ. Rev. 10, 51–77.
Goldfajn, I., Valdes, R., 1999. The aftermath of appreciations. Q. J. Econ. 114, 229–262.
Harley, M., 1996. Use of the Producer Subsidy Equivalent as a measure of support to agriculture in transition economies. Am. J. Agric. Econ. 78, 799–804.
Hinkle, L., Montiel, P., 1999. Exchange Rate Misalignment: Concepts and Measurement for Developing Countries. Oxford University Press, New York.
Hodrick, R., Prescott, E., 1997. Postwar US business cycles: an empirical investigation. J. Money Credit Bank. 29, 1–16.
International Monetary Fund (IMF), 2005. International Financial Statistics. Washington DC.
Johansen, S., 1991. Estimation and hypothesis testing of cointegrating vectors in Gaussian vector autoregressive models. Econometrica 59, 1551–1580.
Johansen, S., Juselius, K., 1990. Maximum likelihood estimation and inferences on cointegration—with applications to the demand for money. Oxf. Bull. Econ. Stat. 52, 169–210.
Josling, T., Valdes, A., 2004. Agricultural policy indicators. ESA Working Paper 04-04. FAO, Rome.
Knetter, M., 1993. International comparisons of price-to-market behavior. Am. Econ. Rev. 83, 473–486.
Kohli, R., 2003. Real exchange rate stabilization and managed floating: exchange rate policy in India, 1993–2001. J. Asian Econ. 14, 369–387.
Krueger, A., Schiff, M., Valdes, A., 1991. The Political Economy of Agricultural Pricing Policy. The Johns Hopkins University Press, Baltimore.
Liefert, W., Sedik, D., Koopman, R., Serova, E., Melyukhina, O., 1996. Producer subsidy equivalents for Russian agriculture: estimation and interpretation. Am. J. Agric. Econ. 78, 792–798.
Melyukhina, O., 2002. The measurement of the level of support in selected non-OECD countries. In: China and the World Economy: Agricultural Policy Adjustments in China after WTO Accession, OECD.
Mullen, K., Orden, D., Gulati, A., 2005. Agricultural policies in India: producer support estimates, 1985–2002. Discussion Paper, 82, International Food Policy Research Institute, Washington DC.
Mundlak, Y., Larson, D., 1992. On the transmission of world agricultural prices. The World Bank Econ. Rev., 6, 399–422.
Park, T., Pick, D., 1996. Imperfect competition and exchange rate pass-through in US wheat exports. In: Sheldon, I., Abbott, P. (Eds.), Industrial Organization and Trade in the Food Industries, Westview Press, Oxford.
Patnaik, I., Pauly, P., 2001. The Indian foreign exchange market and the equilibrium real exchange rate of the rupee. Global Bus. Rev. 2, 195–216.
Portugal, L., 2002. Methodology for the Measurement of Support and Use in Policy Evaluations. OECD, Paris.
Reserve Bank of India. Handbook of Statistics on Indian Economy (various issues). Mumbai.
Sharma, R., 2003. The transmission of world price signals: the concept, issues, and some evidence from Asian cereal markets. In: Agricultural Trade and Poverty: Making Policy Analysis Count, OECD, 141–159.
Stein, J., 1994. The natural real exchange rate of the US dollar and determinants of capital flows. In: Williamson, J. (Ed.), Estimating Equilibrium Exchange Rates, Institute for International Economics, Washington DC.
Tyers, R., Anderson, K., 1992. Disarray in World Food Markets: A Quantitative Assessment, Cambridge University Press.
Xu, M., Orden, D., 2002. Exchange rate effects on Canadian/US agricultural prices. AAEA Selected Paper.
Williamson, J., 1994. Estimates of FEERs. In: Williamson, J. (Ed.), Estimating Equilibrium Exchange Rates, Institute for International Economics, Washington DC.

Section II:

U.S. Farm Policy in International Perspective, 1990–2020

Chapter 5

The WTO disciplines on domestic support

LARS BRINK

Proposals in international trade negotiations to constrain the domestic support that governments can provide to agriculture attract substantial interest for several reasons. Domestic support makes a country produce and trade differently from how it would if it fully pursued its comparative advantages. Domestic support can also shift a country's comparative advantage over time and thus change its trade profile. The interest in domestic support in the Doha negotiations was fuelled by the potential to strengthen the provisions of the WTO's Agreement on Agriculture, the awareness of interested parties of those provisions and of the size and nature of support they allow governments at home and abroad to provide, and by the consideration many governments give to enacting suitable farm policies that meet their international obligations. This chapter examines the framework of WTO domestic support disciplines in agriculture in several dimensions. Why are disciplines on domestic support part of the Agreement, which is, after all, an international trade agreement? What is the nature of the constraints and how are they being applied? In particular, how do the constraints limit diverse measures of policy support differently in developed and developing countries? What additional constraints may result from the Doha negotiations? And how might new multilateral domestic support constraints accommodate or influence the future development of policy support to agriculture on a global scale?

History of domestic support discipline in the WTO

In the Uruguay Round negotiations in the GATT (General Agreement on Tariffs and Trade) the sense of "domestic" support was in contrast to

Substantial portions of this chapter were part of the author's 2008 presidential address to the Canadian Agricultural Economics Society and are used with permission (Brink 2009). The views expressed are those of the author alone and not those of Agriculture and Agri-Food Canada. The helpful comments of Kym Anderson, May Chow, Dimitris Diakosavvas, Mike Gifford, Tim Josling, Wilfrid Legg, Will Martin, Alex McCalla, Chung Pa, James Rude, and Steve Verheul are gratefully acknowledged. The input by David Orden merits special grateful mention.

the traditional focus on measures applied at the border to impede import access or facilitate exports. Already thirty years earlier the Haberler Report had outlined three elements of what it called agricultural protection (GATT 1958).[1] Measures that directly discourage imports and measures that directly encourage exports were two of those elements. Measures that "directly encourage home production" were the third element. They maintain "the net reward to the farmer above the level which would correspond to the price at which he can sell his product." This distinction between two categories of border measures and a third category of measures not operating at the border was carried into the architecture of the 1994 Agreement in its three pillars of market access, export competition and domestic support.

The Haberler Report also categorized agricultural protection schemes into two groups based on certain of their other characteristics. One group comprises measures that raise the domestic price received by producers and paid by consumers above the world market price. This, the Report clarified, requires also the use of some form of border measure (import protection or export subsidy) in order to insulate the domestic market from the world market. The other group comprises schemes that allow consumers to pay world market prices but raise producers' revenue "by the payment of some form of subsidy." The Agreement would come to distinguish between two groups of domestic support measures along similar lines, viz., market price support (MPS) and non-exempt direct payments.

By the time the Uruguay Round started in 1986, it had become possible after many years of work to account in one indicator for the support provided through a range of measures. This indicator would include support provided through border measures on imports and exports and support provided through domestic measures, whether by payments to producers or by the maintenance of a gap between the domestic price and the border price. Josling's work on such an indicator was pioneering (FAO 1973, 1975), followed by work at the OECD (1987) and the USDA (1987). Although different in some respects, all three indicators bore the name Producer Subsidy Equivalent (PSE) and were conceptually close by accounting for support provided through a wide range of policy measures operating both domestically and at the border.

[1] Professor Haberler was the chairman of a small panel of experts set up by the contracting parties of the GATT to examine, *inter alia*, international trade trends and their implications, including a "widespread resort to agricultural protection."

Based on the PSE and the related development of relevant data, the United States proposed as early as 1987 that aggregate levels of trade-distorting support be brought to zero over ten years (GATT 1987).[2] The measurement of aggregate support would include both domestic and border policies "that directly or indirectly subsidize agriculture." Market price support would be part of the measurement, whether provided through price policies, variable levies, tariffs, export subsidies, export credits, government support of marketing boards, or other mechanisms. Income support and other support would be part of the measurement whether provided as, *inter alia*, deficiency payments, stabilization payments, acreage payments, subsidized crop insurance, fuel subsidies, or other payments to producers. Some policies (certain payments and aid programs) would be excluded on grounds of being production and trade neutral or having only inconsequentially small effects.

Other methods to aggregate support for a product across many policies included the Support Measurement Unit (SMU) and the Trade Distortion Equivalent (TDE). The SMU suggested by the European Communities (EC) would be based on the PSE but adjusted in three significant ways: to include only policies with a significant incidence on trade, mainly market price support and selected direct payments; to recognize the effect of production quotas explicitly, beyond using only the constrained production volume to measure support; and to use a fixed external reference price for the price gap in order to exclude the effects of changes in world market prices and currency values (GATT 1988b). The TDE suggested by Canada would be based on the PSE but modified to exclude non-distorting policies and to adjust the measured support downwards for less distorting policies (selected payments and MPS associated with certain types of production quotas) (GATT 1988a). Canada explained that the TDE derived from the modified PSE of Tangermann, Josling, and Pearson (1987). The EC, the Canadian and the earlier US proposal all accounted for a smaller policy set than did the OECD PSE. The exclusions tended to be based on the extent to which policies were considered not to distort production and trade. These exclusions foreshadowed what was later called the green box exclusions and even *de minimis*.

[2] The United States referred to the work of the GATT's Committee II, culminating in 1962, which "established the links between national farm programmes and the conditions of international agricultural trade" (Josling, Tangermann, and Warley 1996). The United States also referred to FAO (1985) and to OECD (1987), significantly entitled *National Policies and Agricultural Trade*, which had appeared less than two months before the US proposal.

The 1994 Agreement required separate ceiling commitments on market access, export subsidization and domestic support.[3] The commitment in domestic support was based on what was by then called the Aggregate Measurement of Support (AMS), which continued to include both price support and payment support but no longer explicitly accounted for support provided through measures operating at the border, such as tariffs or export subsidies. The scope of the policy aggregation in the measured aggregate support had thus been reduced to aggregating across many kinds of domestic policies but not border policies. The nature of AMS had shifted from what the United States had proposed in 1987, but the fact that commitments would apply to certain kinds of distorting domestic support started to address the need to account for policies not operating at the border, which the Haberler Report had identified in 1958.

Despite their shared ancestry there are many differences between the Agreement's AMS and the OECD PSE (Diakosavvas 2002).[4] The most important one for economic analysis is that the MPS element of an AMS is calculated from the price gap between an administered domestic price and a fixed external reference price based on the years 1986–88. Although the 1987 US proposal did not say so, its kinship with the PSE implied a reference price that would vary from year to year. However, the EC insisted on fixing the external reference price in order for the reduction to be a predetermined amount, which ignores changes in currency values and world market prices. In contrast, the price gap that matters for economic analysis in a given year is the gap between the domestic price and a reference price representing the opportunity cost, i.e., the actual world market price and the currency value of the year to which the analysis pertains.

The AMS and its use present particular challenges for economic analysis, as the country studies demonstrate in the chapters to follow. This stems partly from the terminology used in the Agreement and perhaps also partly from analysts not always being familiar with the nature of the

[3] A commitment is a legally binding undertaking under the agreements of the WTO, such as the Agreement on Agriculture. The Chairman's text of a draft agreement in July 1990 had similarly identified separate commitments in "internal support", "border protection", and "export competition" (GATT 1990). However, for internal support commitments it envisaged an AMS including "any measure which acts to maintain producer prices at levels above those prevailing in international trade." Although this seemed to include also border measures, the eventual Agreement applied the AMS only to domestic measures.

[4] The OECD has been monitoring the agricultural policies of its membership since 1987 and has been reporting annually the Producer Subsidy Equivalent (PSE), re-labeled as the Producer Support Estimate in 1998 (OECD 2009).

Agreement, its rules and associated scheduled commitments. An AMS is literally a measurement of what the Agreement calls support and not a measurement of distortions. Moreover, this support is measured in ways that deviate not only from how support is measured in the PSE but also from its usual representation in economic analysis. A major reason is that a member's AMSs are used as input in determining whether it has satisfied its legal ceiling commitment on certain support in favor of producers. The legal nature of both the agreed-upon domestic support commitment itself and the Agreement's rules about how to calculate various amounts of support effectively override the use of measurement methods that are more directly based on economics and more amenable for use in economic analysis.

The discipline under the Agreement on Agriculture

Key distinctions in constraining domestic support

The rules and implications of the domestic support provisions of the Agreement have proven to be easily misunderstood. Some misunderstandings seem rooted in overlooking the significance of a few key distinctions in these complex provisions. They include distinctions between measures and support, among measures that are classified in different categories, between applied support and a commitment on support, and between applied support that counts towards the commitment and applied support that does not (Brink 2007). Figure 2.1 shows the important distinctions and interactions of the domestic support provisions in the Agreement. These and other provisions of the Agreement related to domestic support are replicated as Appendix A at the end of the book.

Measures and support are two distinct notions in the Agreement. The domestic support commitment of the Agreement applies under Article 6 to all "domestic support measures in favour of agricultural producers" with some exceptions.[5] A ceiling commitment applies to the yearly sum of some of the amounts of support that certain measures provide. Separating exempt from non-exempt measures is behind the popularly known set of green, blue and amber boxes. Although the Agreement does not identify

[5] Unless otherwise indicated, references to articles and annexes refer to the Agreement (see Appendix A).

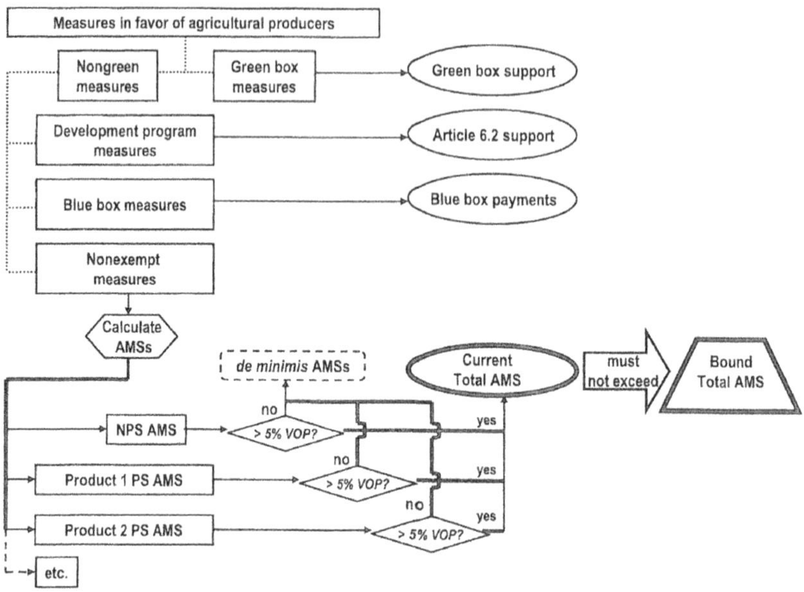

Figure 2.1 Domestic support categories and constraints in the 1994 Agreement on Agriculture

Source: Author's interpretation of the Agreement. The *de minimis* percentages are those of developed countries. AMSs are Aggregate Measurements of Support; NPS is non-product-specific; PS is product-specific; VOP is value of production.

any boxes or colors, it is universally understood that Annex 2 defines the green box and Article 6.5 defines the blue box. The residual subset of measures is less well defined.

Annex 2 requires green box measures to meet "the fundamental requirement that they have no, or at most minimal, trade-distorting effects or effects on production" in order to be exempt from the commitment. Annex 2 also states that the measures shall conform to two basic criteria: the support shall be "provided through a publicly-funded government programme" (which precludes transfers from consumers) and the support "shall not have the effect of providing price support to producers." The text then articulates for twelve types of measures – including nine that involve "direct payments to producers" – the policy-specific criteria and conditions that must be met, together with the basic criteria, for a certain measure to qualify for Annex 2 exemption from the domestic support commitment.

The common shorthand for the measures exempted as green box is that they are not trade distorting. However, Annex 2 does not define "trade-distorting effects or effects on production" nor is there jurisprudence within the WTO on its legal meaning. The policy-specific criteria in Annex 2 leave open the possibility that among the measures meeting these criteria there are some that could have more than a minimal effect on production – in some cases directly and in others by raising agricultural productivity over time. Support through such measures would affect the cost structure of agricultural production, the competitive advantage among countries, and the levels of agricultural output – and thus affect trade. Nonetheless, support through measures that meet the basic and policy-specific criteria of Annex 2 is often said to be non-distorting or only minimally distorting support.

Two kinds of measures are exempt from commitment if they meet certain other criteria or conditions than those of Annex 2. First, trade-distorting measures that meet the criteria in Article 6.5 (blue box payments) are excluded from the commitment. This applies to direct payments under production-limiting programs, and the criteria specified in the Agreement relate to the fixity of area, yields, and livestock heads, and the level of production on which payments are made relative to a base level.

Second, developing countries, but not developed countries, can exempt certain trade-distorting measures if the measures meet the criteria of Article 6.2. No color or box is attached to these measures, but they are often seen as part of a development box relating to special and differential treatment for developing countries.[6] They include investment subsidies that are generally available to agriculture and input subsidies that are generally available to low-income or resource-poor producers, as well as support to encourage diversification from illicit narcotic crops. Developing countries can therefore exempt from commitment certain measures – subsidies on variable inputs – that economic analysis has found to distort production and trade more than market price support, output subsidies, or area payments (OECD 2008).

The Agreement thus identifies three distinct kinds of domestic support measures – green box measures, Article 6.2 measures, and blue box measures – and a non-distinct or residual category of all other measures. The upper left-hand side of Figure 2.1 illustrates this. A measure qualifies for

[6] The Agreement includes a separate Article 15 on the special and differential treatment for developing countries applying to the provisions of the Agreement and to their commitments.

inclusion in a distinct category by meeting that category's criteria. The so-called amber box has no such distinguishing criteria: it consists of the measures that do not qualify for any of the distinct categories.

Another important distinction in the Agreement is between the ceiling commitment on distorting support and the measured applied support that counts towards the ceiling. This distinction has proven particularly difficult to convey in some of the public debate about support levels. A bound tariff and the applied tariff in market access relate to each other in a similar way as the bound ceiling commitment and the measured support in domestic support. However, the measured support that counts towards the commitment is more complicated to express than an applied tariff.

Each member's Schedule of Concessions and Commitments shows the level of the ceiling commitment, called Final Bound Total AMS (FBTAMS).[7] In many cases this level was reached through reductions over several years and each earlier year's bound level also appears in the Schedule without being called final. The FBTAMS commitment consists of a single nominal amount for each year. The year's applied support, measured in certain ways, must not exceed this amount.

The measurement of applied support relies on a number of AMSs. Each AMS is the annual support provided in favor of producers, other than support provided through green box measures (technically the Agreement seems to regard support under Article 6.2 measures and blue box measures as AMS support, although this does not correspond to practice). Separate product-specific AMSs contain the support provided for each product, and a single AMS captures the non-product-specific support provided in favor of agricultural producers in general. The applied support in the AMSs is summed in order to form the year's Current Total AMS (CTAMS). This highlights a crucial distinction: "Aggregate" refers to aggregating support across various policies, such as direct payments, input subsidies, and market price support, and "Total" refers to summing AMSs into a single CTAMS.[8]

[7] The Agreement refers to this as the "Final Bound Commitment Level" (Article 1, see Appendix A). In the section of members' schedules called "Domestic Support: Total AMS Commitments", a column heading refers to "Annual and Final Bound Commitment Levels", where the final entry thus is the Final Bound Total AMS (or FBTAMS) resulting from Uruguay Round implementation or WTO accession. This term is used in the Doha negotiations.

[8] The Agreement defines "Total Aggregate Measurement of Support" and "Total AMS" as a sum of aggregate measurements of support and equivalent measurements of support (Article 1, see Appendix A). It identifies several uses of the term "Total AMS": (a) "Base Total AMS", the support provided in the Uruguay Round base period, (b) "Annual and

CTAMS exempts some AMSs because of the *de minimis* rules: if an AMS is small enough, it need not be included in the calculated sum. To be small enough it can be no more than 5 percent of the product's nominal value of production (VOP) or, for the non-product-specific AMS, the nominal value of total agricultural production. Developing countries use 10 percent (8.5 percent for China). The *de minimis* rules apply to the whole AMS, i.e., an aggregation of support across those measures in effect. The rules do not apply to individual subsidies or support on a measure by measure basis – there is no classification of policies into *de minimis* measures and non-*de minimis* measures.

A *de minimis* allowance can be defined as the amount within which an AMS is excludable from CTAMS. That same amount can also be seen as a *de minimis* threshold, where an AMS switches from *de minimis* status into having to be included in CTAMS. The *de minimis* threshold is different from a commitment. An AMS can increase from zero without any consequence until it reaches the threshold level. When it exceeds that level, the consequence is immediate: the whole AMS (not just the part that exceeds the threshold) is included in CTAMS. There is no obligation to keep an AMS below the threshold if a country has a FBTAMS in its schedule of commitments, in contrast to the legal obligation that CTAMS must not exceed the FBTAMS. Moreover, the *de minimis* threshold is variable because it is a fixed percentage of the nominal VOP, which differs from year to year. If the VOP declines, so does the *de minimis* threshold. If the VOP grows over time, whether through output growth, price increases, inflation or currency depreciation, the *de minimis* threshold also grows. This flexibility is in contrast to the fixity of the nominal value of the FBTAMS commitment.

Many members did not schedule a FBTAMS commitment. Since CTAMS in such cases is constrained to be zero (Article 7), there is no threshold effect: each AMS must simply be kept below the *de minimis* threshold. The absence of a commitment therefore does not preclude

Final Bound Commitment Levels" in the Total AMS section of schedules, i.e., the maximum support permitted to be provided during and after the Uruguay Round implementation period (support limits), and (c) "Current Total AMS", i.e., the level of support actually provided during and after the Uruguay Round implementation period, calculated in a particular way (applied support). To avoid confusion between these uses or with other meanings of "total" we minimize use of the phrase "Total AMS" throughout the book, instead using more explicit expressions to distinguish among FBTAMS (a limit), CTAMS (a measurement of applied support) and other support totals to which we refer at various points.

the provision of support through measures that must be included in an AMS but constrains it to no more than the *de minimis* amount.

An Annex 3 of the Agreement helps to understand what kinds of measures need to be accounted for in an AMS, but Annex 3 is not exhaustive nor is it a definition of the amber box. Annex 3 stipulates that a monetary value of product-specific AMS is to be calculated for each basic agricultural product receiving market price support, non-exempt direct payments, or any other subsidy not exempted from the commitment. Non-product-specific support is to be summed into one AMS in monetary value. Annex 3 gives some basic rules for how to calculate an AMS. "Subsidies" in AMS include budgetary outlays and revenue forgone by governments or their agents. Support at both national and sub-national levels is included in AMS, and specific agricultural levies or fees paid by producers are deducted. Non-exempt direct payments based on factors other than price are measured using budgetary outlays. The measurement of support from other non-exempt measures, including input subsidies, is by government budgetary outlays or by the gap between the price of the subsidized good or service and the market price, multiplied by the quantity of the good or service. The AMS is calculated as close as practicable to the point of first sale of the basic agricultural product. Measures directed at processors are included to the extent that such measures benefit the producers of the basic agricultural product.

Support and subsidies are often interchangeable terms. However, a subsidy has a connotation of a budgetary payment or revenue forgone by government, while support often has a broader meaning. The rules for calculating AMS in Annex 3 require the inclusion of MPS based on a price gap, not on budgetary payments. It is calculated using the gap between a fixed external reference price (based on the years 1986–88) and the applied administered price in a given year, multiplied by the quantity of production eligible to receive the administered price. The term "applied administered price" is not defined in the Agreement. However, including MPS as defined in the AMS is not merely a quibble about words: it demarcates the outer boundaries of the set of support measures that are subject to the Agreement's domestic support discipline. It is also consistent with how some other WTO agreements treat price support: both the GATT and the Agreement on Subsidies and Countervailing Measures (ASCM) make a point of including price support in what they mean by a subsidy (WTO 1995a).

Domestic support notifications and the Committee on Agriculture

The Agreement established a Committee on Agriculture. It is mandated to review the implementation of members' commitments. The review process must be based on the notifications submitted by members and on any requested documentation prepared by the WTO Secretariat to facilitate the process and it provides an opportunity for members to "raise any matter relevant to the implementation" of the commitments. The Agreement is silent on the timing of notification submissions except to say that "any new domestic support measure, or modification of an existing measure, for which exemption from reduction is claimed shall be notified promptly."

The newly-formed Committee on Agriculture adopted notification requirements and formats at its second meeting in 1995 (WTO 1995b). The committee document identifies a need for most members (see below for exceptions) to notify applied domestic support yearly, in addition to the prompt notification of new or modified measures. The yearly notification includes a summary table (called Table DS:1) and tables with supporting material (supporting tables or ST) in a format and numbering system that is common to all members (see Table 2.1). The notification Table DS:1 is a concise statement of the year's CTAMS and the FBTAMS commitment level. The supporting tables (ST DS:1 to 9) give information on the amount of support under each measure, along with calculation methods or data sources. ST DS:1 through ST DS:3 report such information for measures claimed to be exempt from the reduction commitment under Annex 2, Article 6.2 and Article 6.5, respectively. The Committee document lists thirteen categories of green box measures in ST DS:1, adding "other" to the twelve identified in Annex 2.

Calculation of the CTAMS is reported in ST DS:4, which lists and sums the AMSs, including the non-product-specific AMS. The claim for *de minimis* exclusions from the summation into CTAMS is usually made in ST DS:4. Although the substantiation of such a claim requires data on VOP, the notification format does not explicitly require the submission of VOP data. The AMSs listed in ST DS:4 are calculated in ST DS:7 (product-specific AMSs), ST DS:8 (equivalent measurements of support), and ST DS:9 (non-product-specific AMS).[9] ST DS:7 itself draws on ST DS:5 (MPS) and ST DS:6 (certain payments). The required format has column headings for the

[9] The Agreement allows for the use of Equivalent Measurements of Support (EMS) in situations where calculating support with the AMS methodology is impracticable. Annex 4

Table 2.1 *Structure of domestic support notifications*

Table heading	Contents
Table DS:1	Current Total AMS and Final Bound Total AMS Commitment
	Measures exempt from the reduction commitment
Supporting Table DS:1	Green box (Annex 2)
Supporting Table DS:2	Development programs (Article 6.2)
Supporting Table DS:3	Direct payments under production-limiting programs (Article 6.5)
	Current Total AMS
Supporting Table DS:4	Calculation of Current Total AMS
Supporting Table DS:5	Product-specific AMS: Market Price Support
Supporting Table DS:6	Product-specific AMS: Non-exempt direct payments
Supporting Table DS:7	Product-specific AMS: Other product-specific support and total product-specific AMS
Supporting Table DS:8	Product-specific Equivalent Measurement of Support (EMS)
Supporting Table DS:9	Non-product-specific AMS
Table DS:2	New or modified domestic support measures exempt from reduction

Source: WTO (1995b).

reporting period (year), descriptions of the measure, the amount of support, and the levels of price and quantity for measurements based on price gaps.

The Committee on Agriculture document also specifies the intended frequency and timing of notifications, although these guidelines are not legally binding on the member countries. Members with bound commitment levels in domestic support should submit notifications "no later than ninety days following the end of the calendar (or marketing,

specifies the rules for the EMS calculation (see Appendix A). The EU has been the primary member to notify EMS support as part of its CTAMS.

fiscal, etc.) year in question."[10] Members without a FBTAMS commitment should submit "an annual notification", although the Committee can set aside this requirement other than for ST DS:1, 2 and 3. Still more lenient rules apply to least-developed countries (LDCs), which may submit these three supporting tables only once every two years. Further, regarding the new or modified support measures claimed to be exempt under Annex 2, Article 6.2 or Article 6.5 and which the Agreement require to be notified promptly, the Committee specified that they be notified "as far as practicable before such measures are adopted and in any event within thirty days of adoption."

The Committee on Agriculture's notification requirements and formats, including the frequency and timing of notifications, were intended to provide the basis for the Committee's review of members' implementation of commitments, as required by the Agreement. The Committee usually meets four times per year but regular meetings were less frequent for a few years after the launch of the Doha negotiations in 2001.[11] Between 1995 and 2008 the Committee reviewed about 587 original domestic support notifications and more than 100 revisions, corrections, etc. The number would have been larger if more members had adhered to the Committee's notification requirements. This is a cause of concern among members because it makes it impossible for the Committee to carry out its mandate of reviewing members' implementation of commitments. It also complicates or makes impossible the analysis of members' approach to supporting their producers, whether such analysis is desired in the context of the Doha negotiations or in other contexts. Members' concern had by early 2009 reached a level where concrete steps were being discussed in the Committee on how the timeliness of members' submission of notifications might be improved.

The Secretariat's reports on the fifty-three meetings between 1995 and 2008 show that for the domestic support notifications, out of the 2,229 questions members raised, 53 percent concerned green box measures and 47 percent concerned other domestic support issues, such as AMSs. While many questions sought clarification or missing data, others identify issues that could change the CTAMS if the responding member were

[10] An additional thirty days is allowed for submission of a final notification if the initial notification is provisional.

[11] The Agreement specified that negotiations to continue the process of achieving its objectives would be initiated one year before the end of the implementation period (Article 20). These negotiations were integrated into the Doha Round.

to address them as suggested by the questioning member. Often members ask that an exclusion of support from CTAMS be justified by demonstrating conformity with green box criteria or for similar justification of other exclusions. Some notifying members who cannot demonstrate this have then reported the support in question as AMS instead.[12]

The review process in the Committee on Agriculture allows members to raise questions on issues that do not stem from the notifications and exchange information in a more timely setting than if it had to be tied to notifications. The points raised and the underlying arguments in the Committee signal to any member that others are paying attention to whether and how it abides by its commitment and follows the rules of the Agreement. The Committee has no mandate to enforce but only to review the implementation of commitments, which lets some members continue to calculate CTAMS in a particular way in spite of the calculation appearing to others to be inconsistent with the rules of the Agreement.

Dispute settlement involving domestic support

The Committee is not a forum for settling disputes. This is the domain of the Dispute Settlement Body (DSB), which consists of all members of the WTO. It establishes a panel of experts at the request of a complaining member if consultations between the members concerned have failed to resolve the dispute. The panel is essentially an impartial tribunal that hears the arguments of the members involved, which are couched in legal terms with reference to the relevant WTO agreements and which sometimes use economic analysis as supporting evidence. Based on its findings and conclusions and if a rule or commitment has been broken, the panel recommends that the defending member bring its measures into

[12] In its 2005–08 meetings, the Committee on Agriculture reviewed yearly domestic support notifications from six of the eight countries in our analysis, covering altogether twenty-six notified years (submitted by the EU in 2004 and 2006; the US in 2007; Japan in 2005, 2007 and 2008; Norway in 2008; Brazil in 2005 and 2007; and China in 2006). Questions were usually asked at the one or two meetings following the date of the notification. They addressed about 113 different issues and many additional sub-questions were asked in very specific terms. Australia, Canada, the EU, New Zealand and the US raised most of the issues, and the EU and the US were the respondents for most of them, about forty each. More than half of the questions concerned whether certain measures met the relevant criteria of Annex 2. Similar questions were addressed to Brazil whose notification reported use of the development program exemptions. Other questions concerned the measurement of market price support (several countries), EU enlargement, negative AMS (Norway), and the classification of some US support as non-product-specific.

conformity with its obligations. Either side can appeal the panel's recommendations to the Appellate Body based on points of law. The DSB's acceptance of the report of the panel or the Appellate Body makes it a ruling that the defending member must implement as part of its membership obligations.

Considering the high profile of domestic support in the negotiations under both the Uruguay and Doha Rounds and in analysis of the Agreement, surprisingly few disputes about domestic support have been initiated. Prior to 2007 they numbered only two (*Korea – Beef* and *United States – Cotton*) and in neither case was domestic support at the center of the complaint. The fact that most FBTAMS commitments mirrored the high-support 1986–88 base years means that most members' applied support in several years from 1995 onwards has been considerably below their commitment levels, making it more difficult to sustain a claim of FBTAMS violation. The Agreement's "peace clause" (Article 13) precluded through 2003 certain challenges under the ASCM. This may have helped to keep down the number of complaints related to agriculture under the ASCM in the early years of the WTO, but since this clause expired *US – Cotton* has still been the only case of such litigation.

In *Korea – Beef* Australia and the US alleged that Korea's AMS for beef was larger than Korea had calculated, which made its CTAMS exceed the FBTAMS commitment (WTO 2000). The Appellate Body said it was unable to reach a conclusion on this since the panel's work was based on "insufficient factual findings." The panel used a fixed external reference price for 1989–91 instead of 1986–88 as stipulated in Annex 3 to calculate MPS. This may seem to be a technicality but goes to the heart of what the Agreement is: a legally binding instrument and not a blueprint for economic analysis. Nevertheless, *Korea – Beef* did clarify two other domestic support issues. One of these issues relates to the relative strength of the Agreement's different wordings for how to calculate an AMS: "in accordance with" Annex 3 (stronger) and "taking into account" the data and methodology used in establishing the FBTAMS commitment (weaker). The other issue relates to eligible production in calculating a product's market price support under the rules of the Agreement. The quantity that the government has announced is eligible for purchase constitutes the eligible production in this case, even if it then actually purchases only a smaller quantity.

In *US – Cotton* Brazil claimed that the US contravened the ASCM by causing serious prejudice to the interests of Brazil (WTO 2005a). Brazil argued that the Agreement's peace clause did not shelter certain US domestic support programs against such a challenge under the ASCM. The Appellate Body found that this was correct, partly based on the finding that fixed payments under two US programs did not meet the policy-specific green box criteria. Specifically, the criteria under the heading "decoupled income support" do not allow the payment amount to be related to the type of production, a criterion that the US programs could not meet because they prohibited the production of fruits and vegetables on the acreage that determined eligibility for the payments. Support to cotton, when cumulated over several programs and including the fixed payments not qualifying for the green box, was thus found large enough under the rules of the Agreement to disallow the use of the peace clause to shelter against the ASCM challenge in this case. The Appellate Body then found under the ASCM that the effect of numerous price-contingent US subsidies (but not the fixed payments) gave rise to serious prejudice to the interests of Brazil.[13] Subsequent steps in *US – Cotton* have also concerned issues other than the green box compatibility of certain programs. The issues include the implementation of the recommendations of the Appellate Body and the actions that would be permissible under WTO rules. Discussions between the US and Brazil in early 2010 resulted in Brazil agreeing not to impose any of the countermeasures against US trade that had been authorized under dispute settlement rules in exchange for the US agreeing to take several steps. Among these was US funding of technical assistance and capacity building for the benefit of Brazil, perhaps including measures of the kind that many countries report as general services in the green box. The funding would continue until passage of the next US farm support legislation (where cotton programs can be modified) or a mutually agreed solution was reached.

The Appellate Body has reaffirmed in two other disputes that there is a boundary between the domestic support and export subsidy disciplines but that the economic effects of domestic support may spill over to export production. These cases are *Canada – Dairy* (WTO 2001; WTO 2002) and *European Communities – Sugar* (WTO 2004; WTO 2005b; WTO 2005c). A concern was expressed in *Canada – Dairy* that the export subsidy disciplines of the Agreement would be undermined if there was no limit on the exportation of products subsidized under certain domestic schemes. The contrary view was also expressed, namely that it was not for the panel to "collapse" domestic support disciplines into export subsidy disciplines. The Appellate Body believed that if WTO-consistent domestic support

[13] The US fixed and price-contingent payments are described in Chapter 4.

measures were automatically characterized as export subsidies because they produced spill-over economic benefits for export production, the distinction between the domestic support and export subsidy discipline of the Agreement would be eroded. However, the Appellate Body also considered that the distinction between the domestic support and export subsidy disciplines would be eroded if domestic support could be provided without limit for exports. The domestic support provisions of the Agreement along with high levels of tariff protection allow extensive support to producers, compared to the limits imposed through export subsidy disciplines, the Appellate Body explained. It then outlined a technical approach to the export subsidization issue at hand, an approach that it said maintained the export subsidy discipline without erosion while best respecting the integrity of the two disciplines. Giving further attention to the distinction between domestic support and export subsidy disciplines, the Appellate Body later explained that subsidies may be granted in both domestic and export markets, provided that the disciplines imposed by the Agreement on the levels of subsidization are respected. In other words, a particular scheme may provide both domestic support and export subsidies, in which case both the domestic support commitment and the export subsidization commitments need to be complied with.

In *EC – Sugar* the parties expressed concern about any redrawing of the boundary between domestic support and export subsidies or they invoked the Appellate Body's view, stated earlier in *Canada – Dairy*, of the distinction between domestic support and export subsidy disciplines. The Appellate Body considered that its interpretation concerning export subsidization in *EC – Sugar* did not erode the boundary between domestic support and export subsidies recognized under the Agreement. Its interpretation, it said, respects the boundary between the two and operates to ensure that countries provide domestic support and export subsidies in conformity with their obligations. In arbitration this interpretation was expressed as domestic support being the source of the export subsidy that was found to exist in *EC – Sugar*.

In 2007 two cases were initiated where possible FBTAMS violations are central to the dispute (WTO 2007a, 2007b). Following consultations with the US, Canada and Brazil each requested that a panel on US domestic support be established and the DSB established a single panel for the two cases. The background of what has come to be known as the Total AMS (TAMS) case included the complainants' continued frustration over the large amounts of support provided to producers of a fairly small number of crops in the US. Canada argued, for example, that not only was this support large, but the delivery mechanisms were such that production incentives were distorted. The importance placed on domestic support rules and commitments in Doha was also part of the background.

Canada and Brazil contend that the US violated its FBTAMS commitment in almost every year between 1999 and 2005. They argue that the US improperly excludes some support from CTAMS as green box support, such as its fixed payments (earlier found to be non-green in *US – Cotton*) and payments under a large number of programs related to disasters or emergencies, whose conformity with the green box criteria is being tested for the first time in the TAMS case. Canada and Brazil also contend that the US improperly counts some support as part of non-product-specific AMS instead of product-specific AMSs, fails to report some support, and under-reports other support. When the CTAMS is calculated properly, they contend, the US exceeded its FBTAMS commitment by billions of dollars in the years in question (see Chapter 4). The 2008 US farm support legislation replaced some of the measures named in the case with the same measures under new legal authority, eliminated some measures and introduced new ones. While some observers argue that this has reduced the extent of the change in US policy that would flow directly even from an outcome of the case favorable to Canada and Brazil, a clarification of some issues in policy classification and measurement would materialize regardless of the outcome. The intensity of pursuing the case may be linked to developments on domestic support in the Doha negotiations.

The Doha negotiations on domestic support

The Doha negotiations on agriculture follow the three-pillar architecture of the Agreement. By early 2008 the Doha draft modalities provided a blueprint for many of the rules and commitments that members might agree to in the negotiations. Although the draft modalities on domestic support were then modified several times, the modifications were relatively minor and with a few exceptions domestic support was considered a stable element in the version of draft modalities that was reached at the end of 2008 (WTO 2008). These provisions are replicated as Appendix B of this book.

Key distinctions in constraining domestic support under a Doha agreement

The draft modalities propose fundamental changes to the Agreement. They include new ceiling commitments on Overall Trade-Distorting

Domestic Support (OTDS) and on the sum of blue box payments; reductions in FBTAMS commitments and *de minimis* percentages; new limits on product-specific AMSs and on product-specific blue box payments; new rules to govern certain tradeoffs between the limits on product-specific AMS and blue box support; and modification of some green box criteria. In general developing countries would take smaller reductions than developed countries or none at all. Many of the new provisions would not apply to LDCs (thirty-two members in 2008) or to certain other members, according to a large flora of exempting provisions in the draft modalities. Most reductions would be implemented over a number of years, such as five or eight, depending on conditions similar to those determining the size of the reduction. Figure 2.2 shows the structure of the domestic support provisions of the December 2008 draft modalities, also summarized in Table 2.2.

The new ceiling commitment on OTDS would apply for developed and many developing countries to all non-green-box support except support under Article 6.2. This commitment would derive from a Base OTDS established for each member other than least-developed countries and some other developing countries. Base OTDS would take into account both the nominal values of the member's FBTAMS commitment and the size of its agriculture sector as measured by agricultural VOP. The Base OTDS is the sum of the Final Bound Total AMS commitment under the Agreement, 10 percent of the total value of agricultural production (developing countries use 20 percent instead of 10 percent), and either blue box payments during a specified base period or an additional 5 percent of the total value of agricultural production.[14] Twenty-one members would reduce their OTDS commitment from the Base OTDS level, with developing countries making two-thirds of the reductions made by the majority of developed countries.

Under the draft modalities, eighteen of the thirty-one members with FBTAMS commitments would reduce this commitment to a varying extent. The large domestic support commitments of the EU, the US and Japan motivated the idea of harmonizing (tiered) reductions. This concept was initially associated with Canada's delegation (Brink 2001) and is represented in the draft modalities. Harmonization means that the

[14] The 10 percent of historical total VOP in agriculture (developed countries) is sometimes thought, although the draft modalities do not say so, to represent the sum of all product-specific and non-product-specific *de minimis* allowances in a historical period, i.e., 5 plus 5 percent of historical VOP. Once the Base OTDS is established, the origin of the various elements used to establish it no longer matters.

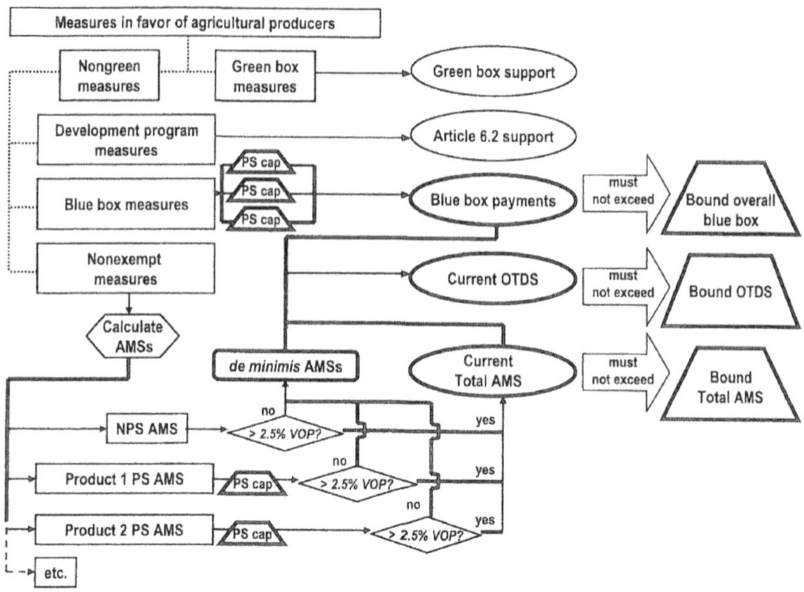

Figure 2.2 Domestic support categories and constraints in the 2008 Doha draft modalities
Source: Author's interpretation of WTO (2008). The *de minimis* percentages are those applying to most developed countries. *De minimis* percentages of 5 percent or 4.2 percent would apply to other developed countries and 10 percent, 8.5 percent or 6.7 percent would apply to developing countries, all based on countries qualifying for inclusion in particular groups. AMSs are Aggregate Measurements of Support; NPS is non-product-specific; PS is product-specific; VOP is value of production.

members with the largest base amounts in the form of Base OTDS and FBTAMS would see the largest percentage reductions. In the Doha draft modalities the size of the reduction would be given by placing a member in one of three tiers according to the size of its base. Some members whose bases are large relative to the size of their agriculture would reduce by more than what would follow strictly from being placed in a particular tier. A fourth tier would provide developing countries with special and differential treatment. The harmonizing nature of the Doha reductions would apply mainly to the developed countries with the largest Base OTDS and FBTAMS. Many developing countries, including those with a very large Base OTDS, would not reduce it at all, even though their Base

Table 2.2 *Summary of the December 2008 Doha domestic support draft modalities*

Establish and reduce OTDS commitment	Base Overall Trade-Distorting Domestic Support (OTDS) is sum of existing FBTAMS commitment and usually 15 percent of value of 1995–2000 agricultural production for developed countries (25 percent and choice of 1995–2004 for developing countries). Many developed countries reduce by 80 percent; 70 percent; 55 percent, if Base OTDS greater than US$60 billion; US$10–60 billion; less than US$10 billion (larger reduction for developed countries in middle tier if Base OTDS exceeds 40 percent of value of production). Some developing countries reduce by 37 percent. Some developed and most developing countries do not reduce, depending on absence of FBTAMS commitment, recent accession or other factors. Differentiation among developing countries regarding need to schedule OTDS commitments.
Reduce FBTAMS commitment	Existing FBTAMS commitment to be reduced. Many developed countries reduce by 70 percent; 60 percent; 45 percent, if existing commitment greater than US$40 billion; US$15–40 billion; less than US$15 billion (developed countries in middle and bottom tier reduce by more if existing commitment exceeds 40 percent of value of production). Some developing countries reduce by 30 percent; most developing countries do not reduce.
Introduce limits on product-specific AMSs	Set limits on AMSs for individual products. Developed countries set limits at product's average 1995–2000 AMS support (1995–2004 product-by-product proportions for US only). Certain provisions for new products. Special formula for cotton. Three more flexible options for developing countries.
Redefine and limit Article 6.5 support (blue box)	Blue box to include also direct payments that do not require production under similar criteria as under production-limiting programs. Total blue box payments limited to 2.5 percent of value of 1995–2000 agricultural production (5 percent and choice of 1995–2004 for developing countries). Special rule for developed country with blue box payments as very large share of 1995–2000 trade-distorting support.
Introduce limits on product-specific blue box payments	Set limits on blue box payments for individual products at product's average 1995–2000 blue box support (special rules for the US only). Flexibility under certain conditions and facility to increase limits on product-specific blue box payment if appropriate reduction in limit on product-specific AMS. Greater flexibility for developing countries.

Table 2.2 (*cont.*)

Reduce *de minimis* percentages	Most developed countries reduce *de minimis* percentage by 50 percent. Some developing countries with FBTAMS commitment reduce by 33 percent. Other developed and developing countries reduce less or do not reduce.	
Modify criteria in Annex 2 (green box)	Base period to be defined, fixed and unchanging for structural adjustment (investment) and regional assistance programs; defined and fixed base period for decoupled income support also to be unchanging. Such base periods to be notified. For developing countries only: General Services to mention certain policies and services related to rural development, such as infrastructure services, drought management and flood control, nutritional security, and issuance of property titles; make criteria less stringent for disaster and insurance programs; accommodate some price policies in the green box with no need to count market price support as AMS support.	
Staging of implementation	Developed countries: OTDS: cut by 33 percent (25 percent for some) on first day, then five annual cuts. FBTAMS: cut by 25 percent on first day (7.5 percent for some), then five annual cuts. *De minimis* percentage: full cut on first day.	Developing countries: OTDS: cut by 20 percent on first day, then eight annual cuts. FBTAMS: cut by 3.3 percent on first day, then eight annual cuts. *De minimis* percentage: full cut by third year.
	All: Limit on blue box total, product-specific AMSs, product-specific blue box payments: mostly in full on first day.	

Source: Author's summary of WTO (2008).

OTDS is large not only because VOP is large but also because the percentage applied to determine it is larger than for the developed countries.

The new ceiling commitment on a member's total of all blue box payments would equal a given percentage of VOP in a historical base period. Developed countries' commitments would generally equal 2.5 percent of the average total value of agricultural production in 1995–2000 (special parameters would be used for members whose support in 1995–2000 included an exceptionally large share of blue box payments). Developing countries would generally use 5 percent and either 1995–2000 or 1995–2004. The Agreement's criteria for excluding blue box payments from the CTAMS (Article 6.5) would be expanded so that certain direct payments that "do not require production" qualify for exemption if they also meet criteria relating to various fixed bases. This broadening of the definition, which was introduced by the US, would accommodate in a redefined blue box its countercyclical payments first legislated in 2002 (USTR 2005).

Under the Doha draft modalities most developed countries would immediately reduce the *de minimis* percentage by 50 percent, from 5 to 2.5 percent. Developing countries with FBTAMS commitments would reduce by two-thirds of the developed country reduction, i.e., from 10 to 6.7 percent. Twenty-one out of 125 members would reduce their *de minimis* percentage to a varying extent under these rules. Developing countries that did not schedule a FBTAMS commitment would not reduce their *de minimis* percentage. A member's *de minimis* allowances would continue to be calculated by applying the *de minimis* percentage to the relevant product-specific or non-product-specific VOP.

The draft modalities would introduce new limits on product-specific AMSs, generally set for developed countries in relation to their applied AMS support in 1995–2000 but with many special rules applying.[15] Developing countries would set their limits on product-specific AMSs in accordance with a variety of rules designed to provide considerable flexibility to those members that did not have large product-specific AMSs in a base period. The draft modalities would also establish new limits on product-specific blue box payments. They would generally be set in relation to past blue box payments but, recognizing that very few members have made such payments in the past, a number of rules allow for the establishment of limits on product-specific blue payments in many other ways. These rules tend to allow more flexibility for developing countries. Certain flexibility is also provided in the special rules applying to the US.

[15] Although not mentioned in the draft modalities, it is understood that product-specific limits would also apply to any future EMSs.

The introduction of product-specific limits mirrors some of the ideas considered in the Uruguay Round negotiations about the measurement and use of AMSs to constrain trade-distorting domestic support on a product-by-product basis. The introduction of an OTDS commitment and a blue box commitment also represent the Uruguay Round ideas of constraining all domestic support other than support under measures that meet certain criteria.

While the draft modalities would generally tighten members' constraints on trade-distorting domestic support, some such support, in particular Article 6.2 support in developing countries (development programs), remains untouched by constraints. Moreover, a plethora of special exemptions or flexibilities would apply to many subsets of members, whether developing or not, such as recently-acceded members, very recently-acceded members, members with or without a FBTAMS commitment, and net food-importing developing countries. Several special rules apply to the US only. Table 2.3 shows the forty conditions affecting members' treatment for OTDS, FBTAMS, blue box and *de minimis*, not counting the many special treatments in product-specific limits. The prevalence of special cases erodes to some extent the ability of the generally strengthened provisions in the draft modalities to effectively constrain future trade-distorting domestic support for a wide range of countries, as subsequent chapters demonstrate in depth.

The Doha draft modalities would make several changes to the Annex 2 criteria for green box measures. For developing countries the non-exhaustive list of general services in the green box would be extended to also mention policies and services related to farmer settlement, land reform programs, rural development and rural livelihood security; among them infrastructure services, drought management and flood control, and nutrition security programs. In addition, developing countries would not need to account for MPS in the AMS when they procure public stocks at subsidized prices in certain situations from low-income or resource-poor producers. This would effectively include some MPS measures in the green box. For all members the draft modalities would introduce more explicit rules to govern any updating of the base period that determines direct payments under decoupled income support, structural adjustment assistance (investment) and regional assistance programs. This tightens the qualifications for including these measures in the green box. The draft modalities would also introduce minor changes to recognize that different programs providing relief from natural disasters operate differently, such as natural disaster payments, crop insurance, and payments for the destruction of animals or crops to prevent certain pests and diseases.

Table 2.3 *Subsets of members identified in the Doha draft modalities on domestic support*

For OTDS commitments	For FBTAMS commitments	For *de minimis* thresholds	For overall blue box commitments
Developed countries (18)			
		General (9)	General (8) Special (1)
Tier 1 (1)	Tier 1 (1)		
Tier 2 with additional effort (1)	Tier 2 with additional effort (1)		
Tier 2 (1)	Tier 2 (1)		
	Tier 3 with additional effort (3)		
Tier 3 (6)	Tier 3 (3)		
			RAM (9)
RAM with FBTAMS commitment (2)	RAM with FBTAMS commitment (2)	RAM with FBTAMS commitment (2)	
SLIRAMET (5)	SLIRAMET (1)	SLIRAMET (5)	
VRAM (2)	VRAM (2)	VRAM (2)	
	Without FBTAMS commitment (4)		
Developing countries (107)			
			General (106) Special (1)
With FBTAMS commitment (10)		With FBTAMS commitment (10)	
	With FBTAMS commitment > $100 million (7)		
	With FBTAMS commitment < $100 million (3)		
NFIDC (4)	NFIDC (4)	NFIDC (4)	
		SLIRAMET (1)	
VRAM (2)	VRAM (2)	VRAM (2)	
Without FBTAMS commitment (91)	Without FBTAMS commitment (91)	Without FBTAMS commitment (90)	

Table 2.3 (*cont.*)

For OTDS commitments	For FBTAMS commitments	For *de minimis* thresholds	For overall blue box commitments
		Support to subsistence and resource-poor farmers (assumed 0)	

Notes: RAM indicates Recently-Acceded Members; SLIRAMET, Small Low Income Recently-Acceded Members with Economies in Transition; VRAM, Very Recently-Acceded Members; NFIDC, Net Food-Importing Developing Countries. Figures in parentheses indicate the number of members in each subset.
Source: Subsets and number of members based on author's interpretation of WTO (2008).

The draft modalities would replace the Agreement's provisions about reviewing the implementation of commitments with a new article designed to enhance the Committee's role in reviewing and monitoring the implementation of the rules and commitments (see Annex M in our Appendix B). This article would also address the notification obligations and formats associated with the new commitments under the draft modalities. Members would need to provide more information in a more timely way on domestic support, under binding rules that would be part of the new agreement itself and not just in the form of hortatory language in a decision of the Committee on Agriculture. The draft modalities pay particular attention to the information to be provided on measures claimed to meet the criteria of the green box. Members would review the effectiveness of the monitoring and surveillance mechanisms, although this would be possible no earlier than three years after the beginning of the new agreement.

Future entitlements to distorting support

Combining the parameters of the Doha draft modalities on domestic support from December 2008 (WTO 2008) with certain data and assumptions makes it possible to estimate each member's future commitments and allowances under a Doha agreement based on these modalities (Brink 2009). For this global overview assessment, Bound OTDS commitments, FBTAMS commitments, overall blue box commitments, and *de minimis* allowances in US dollars were calculated from each member's scheduled Final Bound Total AMS commitment, past blue box payments, past total value of production, and yearly exchange rates. Data were mostly from a series of WTO papers (TN/AG/S/*), notifications to the Committee on Agriculture, and material referred to in acceding members' schedules. A variety of other sources were drawn upon as needed.

Establishing Base OTDS and calculating *de minimis* allowances requires VOP data. VOP from the above sources for a small number of members was complemented with estimates from national sources, the OECD PSE database, or extrapolation. VOP was to the extent possible expressed in the member's currency or in the currency it uses in notifications. A proxy for VOP in the form of value added in agriculture in current US dollars was used for many smaller developing countries (World Bank 2007).[16] This underestimation of VOP by value added leads to an underestimation of Base OTDS and *de minimis* allowances for the developing countries as a group. The *de minimis* allowances were calculated from nominal VOP for 2001–03, which was the most complete data at the time of the analysis, and converted to dollars at average 2001–03 exchange rates. The elements needed to establish a Base OTDS were expressed in the currency of the member's VOP (sometimes different from that of its FBTAMS commitment) and added to form the Base OTDS in dollars, converted as needed at 2006 exchange rates. The reduced OTDS commitments under the draft modalities were calculated in the currency of the member's VOP. The new reduced Final Bound Total AMS commitments were calculated in the currency of the commitment (sometimes different from the local currency or the currency the member uses in notifications). The resulting nominal amounts, when not already in dollars, were converted to dollars using 2006 exchange rates.

The results for most of the individual members are summed and shown as totals or world shares in Table 2.4 for two groups of members: the eighteen developed country and 107 developing country members. The parameters of the draft modalities differ considerably between these groups and dividing into these two groups follows the practice in the negotiations, although it does not reflect the heterogeneity among the developing countries. The analysis does not consider any product-specific limits and does not estimate future applied support – these issues are addressed for selected countries in the chapters that follow.

[16] Throughout the book dollars ($) refers to US dollars (US$) unless otherwise noted.

Table 2.4 *World sums and shares of developed and developing countries for key elements of domestic support disciplines*

	Pre-Doha		Doha	
	Value	World share	Value	World share
	Billion US dollars	%	*Billion US dollars*	%
Final Bound Total AMS			*Limits after reductions*	
All developed countries	155	91	51	82
All developing countries	15	9	11	18
World	170	100	62	100
Blue box			*New limits*	
All developed countries	Not applicable		20	35
All developing countries	Not applicable		36	65
World	Not applicable		56	100
De minimis allowances			*Allowances after reductions*	
All developed countries	66	32	34	21
All developing countries	142	68	131	79
World	208	100	165	100
Overall Trade-Distorting Support (OTDS)	*Base OTDS*		*New limits after reductions*	
All developed countries	274	61	60	27
All developing countries	176	39	165	73
World	450	100	225	100

Notes: There are no blue box limits in the Agreement on Agriculture. World refers to all WTO members.
Source: Author's calculations (Brink 2009).

The world sum of FBTAMS commitments under the Agreement is \$170 billion. Developed countries have the overwhelming share of this sum, amounting to \$155 billion. As discussed by Brink (2009) and further developed in Chapter 3, the twenty-seven-country European Union (EU27) by itself accounts for more than half of the world sum. Because developed countries have most of the FBTAMS commitments and most developing countries have none, developed countries continue to account for a predominant world share of 82 percent even after the seemingly large percentage reductions of the Doha draft modalities. However, after reducing the FBTAMS commitments to their new levels, the developed countries' sum declines to about \$51 billion in a world sum of \$62 billion.

There are no ceilings on blue box payments in the Agreement. The new ceilings established on blue box payments under the draft modalities would sum to \$56 billion for the world, of which developed countries would be entitled to \$20 billion and developing countries \$36 billion.

The *de minimis* allowances under the Agreement sum to \$208 billion for the world, based on the above assumptions. Developed countries' allowances sum to \$66 billion and those of developing countries sum to \$142 billion. Applying the draft modalities reductions in *de minimis* percentages would generate a world sum of \$165 billion, consisting of \$34 billion for developed countries and \$131 billion for developing countries (still based on 2001–03 values of production). Overall, the *de minimis* percentage under Doha would be four times larger for most developing than for developed countries. China's VOP surpasses that of any other member, including the EU27 and the US (see Chapters 3, 4, 9 and 11). In combination with its unchanged 8.5 *de minimis* percentage, China's *de minimis* allowances account for more than one-third of the developing country total under either the Agreement or Doha draft modalities. By comparison, the *de minimis* allowances of the EU27 and US combined fall by nearly one-half (to around \$25 billion, see Brink (2009) and Chapters 3 and 4) under a future 2.5 *de minimis* percentage. The share of China's *de minimis* allowances in the world total, which is about the same as for the EU27 and US together under the Agreement, increases under the Doha modalities to a share that is double that of the EU27 and US together.

Because *de minimis* allowances continue to be calculated from nominal annual VOP, they are larger than shown in Table 2.4 at the higher prices prevailing for most commodities since 2006. VOP and hence the *de minimis* allowances are expected to continue to grow over time for most members. This would increase the contrast between the sums of the *de minimis* allowances of developed and developing countries. Faster growth of agricultural VOP in developing countries would further increase this contrast. To illustrate, suppose the annual growth rate of nominal value of agricultural production is one percentage point among developed countries but two percentage points among developing countries. From 2002 to 2023 the VOP in developed countries would grow by 23 percent and in developing countries by 52 percent, and the *de minimis* allowances in developed and developing countries would increase correspondingly.

The Base OTDSs sum to $450 billion for the world: $274 billion in developed countries and $176 billion in developing countries. The reductions in the draft modalities generate a world sum of OTDS commitments of $225 billion, i.e., a cut by half. Developed countries would be entitled to $60 billion of OTDS support and developing countries to $165 billion. The Doha OTDS limits would make it impossible for most members to increase the sum of blue box payments and AMS support (Current Total AMS and *de minimis* AMSs) to the level it could reach under the Agreement (assuming blue box payments would not exceed historical levels). It would be impossible to reverse the EU policy reforms, and no developed country would be able to raise support as far as in the past in case of a large price decline. The constraint on most developing countries' OTDS support would equal the Base OTDS, without any reduction. Most developing countries have in the past provided little non-green-box support. As subsequent chapters demonstrate for four large middle-income countries, there is scope for relatively large increases from these low past levels in the OTDS and AMS support that developing countries would be able to provide within their limits, as well as through continuation of the Article 6.2 exemption for development programs.

The sum of FBTAMS commitments, blue box limits and *de minimis* allowances for developed countries equals $105 billion under implementation of the Doha draft modalities, compared to OTDS commitments summing to $60 billion. For developing countries the sum of the component constraints is $178 billion, compared to OTDS commitments summing to $165 billion. The draft modalities indicate that for members with Bound OTDS commitments, a lower OTDS commitment overrides the sum of the constraints on the components of applied OTDS support (blue box support, *de minimis* AMS support, and AMS support that counts in CTAMS). When the OTDS commitment is lower than the sum of the constraints on the components, the amount of support provided in one or more of the components has to be less than would be allowed within the component-specific constraint itself.[17] The OTDS commitment would thus constrain many members' future applied OTDS support more tightly than would the sum of the component constraints, particularly so for developed countries but less for developing countries.[18] In many cases the caps on product-specific AMSs and blue box payments would add further effective constraints on the applied support that counts towards the various simultaneous ceilings.

The FBTAMS and OTDS commitments are constant in nominal currency units (such as dollars or national currency) while the *de minimis* allowances increase as nominal VOP increases. Over time the *de minimis* allowances will therefore account for a growing share of most members' entitlements to provide AMS support, although product-specific caps will to some extent limit the generality of this phenomenon. The OTDS commitment is relatively larger for developing countries in general than for developed countries, as a result of the larger percentage of VOP used to establish the Base OTDS and the smaller or absence of reductions from base. Still, the OTDS commitment eventually would bind the effective use of growing nominal *de minimis* allowances by developing countries under a Doha agreement. The developing countries except China remain entitled to support agriculture without any constraint through the not-very-specific criteria of Article 6.2 for development programs, and some may choose to do so if they were constrained by FBTAMS or OTDS commitments.

Summary and conclusions

The difficulties in agricultural trade that the Haberler group was set up to address were to some extent tackled with the introduction of domestic

[17] This rule does not apply to the *de minimis* allowances of recently acceded members. In addition, the OTDS constraint is not as binding as it appears relative to the component constraints for members with a FBTAMS commitment because of the practical impossibility of fully using at the same time all *de minimis* allowances and the FBTAMS commitment (Brink 2006). The sum of all applied *de minimis* AMSs (whether product-specific or non-product-specific) and CTAMS will always in practice be smaller than the sum of all *de minimis* allowances and the FBTAMS commitment. The reason is that there is no *de minimis* AMS for a product for which the AMS is large enough (exceeds the *de minimis* threshold) to be counted in CTAMS. That product's theoretical *de minimis* allowance can thus not be used. The same reasoning applies to the non-product-specific AMS.

[18] Underestimation of the *de minimis* allowances makes little difference for the shares among groups of countries. It does matter, however, when adding the allowances to the draft Doha blue box limits and FBTAMS commitments so this sum of constraints on the components can be compared to the OTDS commitment. It also matters when the allowances are used as the starting point for the above projections to 2023.

support constraints in the WTO's Agreement on Agriculture. Some kinds of distorting support in both developed and developing countries escaped constraints, and the measurement of support through an AMS deviated from other ways of measuring support. The size and nature of the domestic support that WTO member countries provide were made more transparent by the requirement to submit notifications to the Committee on Agriculture. The yearly amounts of support classified by given criteria have to be notified, as does the introduction or modification of measures that are claimed as exempt from the ceiling commitment on CTAMS. Member countries review the notifications in the Committee on Agriculture several times per year. Between 1995 and 2008 the Committee reviewed around 700 domestic support notifications and revisions. They gave rise to more than 2,200 questions in the Committee, divided about equally between questions on annual support and questions on measures claimed as exempt from commitments. However, many member countries' record of adhering to the notification due dates is patchy at best and very poor in some instances.

Doha would introduce more constraints than presently in the Agreement, including a limit on OTDS, a limit on overall blue box payments, and individual limits on product-specific AMSs and on product-specific blue box payments. Many existing commitments and thresholds would be reduced. While Doha would significantly constrain the future distorting support of several members compared to past amounts, special provisions for numerous other members would erode its effectiveness in containing other large amounts of distorting support. Such special provisions would apply to recently-acceded members, very recently-acceded members, certain other recently-acceded members, net food-importing developing countries, and developing countries generally, as well as through special provisions seemingly designed for individual members, whether developed or developing countries.

With few exceptions members have in the past been far below their FBTAMS commitment, including in the eight countries discussed in subsequent chapters. Under a Doha agreement based on the December 2008 draft modalities, several constraints would apply simultaneously to overlapping measurements of distorting support. Most members face only small or no reductions in such constraints, so they would be allowed to provide almost the same amounts and kinds of distorting support as they could have provided in the past. Still, some developed countries in particular who have been close to their FBTAMS commitment or who take significant reductions from the base amounts of the new constraints would not be allowed the same amounts of the same kind of support as they provided or could have provided in the past.

Developing countries as a group and also some developed country members would have considerable room for maneuver between the amounts of distorting support they have provided in the past and what they would be allowed to provide under future constraints. Most developing countries have been unable to provide much or any distorting domestic support in the past, but some developing countries have demonstrated growing ability and willingness to provide such support (Anderson 2009). As the economies of developing countries grow over time, and especially if they grow rapidly, many developing countries will soon approach the same levels of economic wellbeing where the developed countries saw fit in the past to deliver significant support to farmers, often by distorting measures. Some developing countries might choose to use this future capacity to increase domestic support within the rules and commitments governing the use of domestic support and border measures.

The total amounts of distorting domestic support that developing countries could provide within their commitments would remain large with a Doha agreement. Developing countries as a group would be entitled to provide almost three-quarters of the world total of distorting domestic support below the ceilings on OTDS and developed countries as a group slightly more than one-quarter. On some kinds of distorting domestic support developing countries other than China would continue to face no constraint on certain investment and input subsidies. All countries would also be entitled to provide unlimited amounts of support under measures that meet the criteria of the green box, which would encompass a larger set of measures for developing countries than for developed countries.

If some developing countries use their future economic capacity to significantly increase various forms of distorting domestic support to agriculture, some interesting implications could follow. In the past the large amounts of distorting domestic support in some developed countries have generated concerns both in other developed countries and in developing countries. Imagine a world where most developed countries' distorting domestic support was considerably more constrained, and some developing countries had become the large providers of such support. Might low-support developing countries then direct their concerns about policy-driven distortions to the high-support developing countries? Might developed countries, most of which would be constrained to be relatively low-support countries, join the low-support developing countries in voicing their shared concern over the trade distortions caused by large amounts of distorting domestic support in some developing countries? These and related questions – along with more traditional concerns about high levels of support by developed countries – lead to the detailed investigations presented in subsequent chapters for eight selected countries of the size and nature of their past and possible future support under the WTO rules.

References

Anderson, K. (ed.) 2009. *Distortions to Agricultural Incentives: A Global Perspective 1955–2007.* London: Palgrave Macmillan, and Washington, DC: World Bank.

Brink, L. 2001. Establishing domestic support commitments through a harmonization formula. Working Paper 01–2, International Agricultural Trade Research Consortium (IATRC), October. www.iatrcweb.org/publications/working.htm (accessed August 12, 2008).

2006. WTO constraints on US and EU domestic support in agriculture: The October 2005 proposals. *The Estey Centre Journal of International Law and Trade Policy* 7(1): 96–115.

2007. Classifying, measuring and analyzing WTO domestic support in agriculture: Some conceptual distinctions. Working Paper 07–02, International Agricultural Trade Research Consortium (IATRC), April. www.iatrcweb.org/publications/working.htm (accessed August 12, 2008).

2009. WTO Constraints on domestic support in agriculture: Past and future. *Canadian Journal of Agricultural Economics* 57(1): 1–21. DOI: 10.1111/j.1744-7976.2008.01135.x.

Diakosavvas, D. 2002. How to measure the level of agricultural support: Comparison of the methodologies applied by OECD and WTO. In *Agricultural Policies in China after WTO Accession.* Paris: OECD.

FAO (Food and Agriculture Organization of the United Nations). 1973. Agricultural protection: Domestic policy and international trade. Conference, C 73/LIM/9. Rome.

1975. Agricultural protection and stabilization policies: A framework of measurement in the context of agricultural adjustment. Conference, C 75/LIM/2. Rome.

1985. International agricultural adjustment. Fifth progress report. Conference, C 85/21. Rome.

GATT (General Agreement on Tariffs and Trade). 1958. Trends in international trade – A report by a panel of experts. October.

1987. United States proposal for negotiations on agriculture. MTN.GNG/NG5/W/14, 7 July.

1988a. The Trade Distortion Equivalent (TDE): An aggregate indicator of adverse trade effects of measures of support and protection for agriculture. MTN.GNG/NG5/W/46, 23 February.

1988b. Short-term measures (other than immediate measures) in the framework of the measures proposed by the European Communities. MTN.GNG/NG5/W/62, 10 June.

1990. Framework agreement on agriculture reform program – Draft text by the chairman. MTN.GNG/NG5/W/170, 11 July.

Josling, T. E., S. Tangermann, and T. K. Warley. 1996. *Agriculture in the GATT.* New York: St. Martin's Press, Inc.

OECD. 1987. *National Policies and Agricultural Trade.* Paris.

2008. *Agricultural Policy Design and Implementation – A Synthesis.* Paris.

2009. *Agricultural Policies in OECD Countries: Monitoring and Evaluation.* Paris.

Tangermann, S., T. E. Josling, and S. Pearson. 1987. Multilateral negotiations on farm-support levels. *The World Economy* 10(3): 265–281.

USDA (US Department of Agriculture). 1987. Government intervention in agriculture: Measurement, evaluation, and implications for trade negotiations. Foreign Agricultural Economic Report No. 229, Economic Research Service, April.

USTR (US Trade Representative). 2005. Implications of US WTO proposal on trade-distorting domestic support. Doha Development Agenda Policy Brief, October.

World Bank. 2007. World Development Indicators. http://ddp-ext.worldbank.org/ext/DDPQQ/member.do?method=getMembers&userid=1&queryId=6 (accessed May 9, 2008).

WTO. 1995a. *The Results of the Uruguay Round of Multilateral Trade Negotiations – The Legal Texts.* Geneva.

1995b. Notification requirements and formats. G/AG/2, Committee on Agriculture, 30 June.

2000. Korea – Measures affecting imports of fresh, chilled and frozen beef. Report of the Appellate Body, WT/DS161/AB/R and WT/DS169/AB/R, 11 December.

2001. Canada – Measures affecting the importation of milk and the exportation of dairy products. Report of the Appellate Body, WT/DS103/AB/RW, 3 December.

2002. Canada – Measures affecting the importation of milk and the exportation of dairy products. Report of the Appellate Body, WT/DS103/AB/RW2, 20 December.

2004. European Communities – Export subsidies on sugar. Report of the Panel, WT/DS265/R, 15 October.

2005a. United States – Subsidies on upland cotton. Report of the Appellate Body, WT/DS267/AB/R, 3 March.

2005b. European Communities – Export subsidies on sugar. Report of the Appellate Body, WT/DS265/AB/R, 28 April.

2005c. European Communities – Export subsidies on sugar. Award of the Arbitrator, WT/DS265/33, 28 October.

2007a. United States – Subsidies and other domestic support for corn and other agricultural products. Request for Consultations by Canada, WT/DS357/1, 11 January.

2007b. United States – Domestic support and export credit guarantees for agricultural products. Request for Consultations by Brazil, WT/DS365/1, 17 July.

2008. Revised draft modalities for agriculture. TN/AG/W/4/Rev.4, 6 December.

Chapter 6

7 Agricultural Interest Group Bargaining over the North American Free Trade Agreement

David Orden

This paper focuses on the attempts of U.S. agricultural interest groups to influence the outcomes of the North American Free Trade Agreement (NAFTA), which was approved by Congress in November 1993. Agricultural issues have loomed large in world trade discussions since the earlier inception of the Uruguay Round General Agreement on Tariffs and Trade (GATT) negotiations in 1986, and Canada and Mexico are important agricultural trade partners of the United States. For these reasons, the agricultural provisions of NAFTA became an important component of the agreement. Moreover, agricultural interests played a crucial role in the passage of the NAFTA implementing legislation. They were able to win concessions that protect U.S. sugar from Mexican competition and provide transition-period protection to winter fruits and vegetables, and that ensnared the United States in disputes about Canadian exports of wheat and peanut butter. With these concessions, the trade liberalization achieved under NAFTA has resulted in little reform of entrenched domestic agricultural support programs in the United States (or Canada) during the lengthy tariff phaseout periods.

To develop these points, the paper is organized as follows. A brief description of U.S. agricultural trade and support policies is provided, the approaches of the agricultural interest groups toward the negotiations between 1990 and 1992 are examined, and the provisions of the negotiated agreement and estimates of its likely impacts are reviewed. The focus then turns to the side agreements negotiated by the administration of President Bill Clinton after the 1992 elections, the activities of the agricultural interest groups during the con-

David Orden is associate professor of agricultural and applied economics at Virginia Polytechnic Institute and State University.

The author thanks Barbara Craig, Carol Goodloe, and Anne Krueger and other conference participants for helpful comments. He is also indebted to the many participants in the NAFTA debate who shared their insights in interviews and other correspondence.

gressional debate over the implementing legislation, and the final concessions offered to obtain support from agricultural interests. The concluding section addresses some issues raised by the NAFTA outcomes for agriculture.

7.1 Diversity within Agriculture

Agricultural production is only 3 percent of national output but is diffused among many diverse sectors. Grains and oilseeds account for one-fifth of the value of U.S. production, and livestock and poultry products for another one-fifth (International Trade Commission [ITC] 1993). A third group of commodities, important in the NAFTA context, is made up of horticultural products, and a final group are those commodities for which the United States has traditionally imposed import quotas under Section 22 of the Agricultural Adjustment Act of 1935 and its extensions (dairy products, cotton, peanuts, sugar and sugar-containing products).[1]

Grains and oilseeds are generally exported crops, while trade has been less important for livestock and poultry products and most fruits and vegetables (an exception is seasonal winter vegetables, for which imports have a 40 percent market share). Imports of dairy products, cotton, and peanuts have been restricted to less than 2 percent of domestic production, while sugar imports have fallen to 15 percent as domestic output has increased and corn sweeteners have captured a large share of the caloric sweeteners market. Less than 2 percent of dairy products are exported but exports account for more than 40 percent of U.S. cotton and 15 percent of the value of peanut production.[2]

Domestic policy interventions provide high levels of support for some export crops as well as for the Section 22 commodities (see, for example, U.S. Department of Agriculture [USDA] 1994). Support for export crops (including cotton) is provided through supply restrictions, direct payments to producers, floor prices ("loan rates") for government-supported storage, and some export subsidies. Livestock and poultry generally receive few direct support payments and relatively low levels of protection. The support and protection levels have also been relatively low for most fruits and vegetables.

Canada and Mexico are important to U.S. agricultural trade of a number of commodities. Canada produces over one-third of U.S. grain and oilseed imports, including essentially all imported wheat, barley, and soybeans. Canada also produces over 35 percent of U.S. livestock and poultry imports, almost one-third of U.S. imports of peanuts and peanut products, and over one-fourth of imported sugar-containing products. Mexico produces over 90 percent of

1. Section 22 authorizes trade restrictions when imports "render ineffective or materially interfere with" domestic supply-control and price-support programs of the U.S. Department of Agriculture.

2. Dairy products are priced above world levels and are exported with subsidies. Peanut exports arise from a two-tier pricing scheme that allows sales at lower world price levels of U.S. peanuts beyond a quantity produced for the domestic market.

imported winter fruits and vegetables and over 10 percent of livestock imports. Canada and Mexico each account for over 15 percent of the value of U.S. livestock and poultry exports and Mexico receives over one-third of U.S. dairy exports.

7.2 Interest Group Approaches to the Negotiations

When the Mexico-U.S. free trade negotiations were announced in June 1990, President Carlos Salinas and President George Bush articulated a broad mandate for reducing bilateral trade barriers and supporting Mexican reforms in agriculture and other sectors. Nevertheless, there was considerable uncertainty about the extent to which agriculture would be included under the mandate for trade liberalization. This uncertainty was created in part by the high levels of protection provided to many commodities in Mexico and the United States. The subsequent entry of Canada into the negotiations added to the uncertainty, since nontariff trade barriers had not been removed in the 1988 Canada-U.S. trade agreement, as described by Miner (1993). Finally, the Uruguay Round GATT negotiations, which had originally been scheduled to conclude in 1990, remained deadlocked on agriculture.

Faced with all this uncertainty, agricultural interest groups took active roles in seeking to shape the provisions of NAFTA. Among the supporters of relatively comprehensive liberalization were the American Farm Bureau Federation, the National Corn Growers Association, numerous other grain, oilseed, and livestock associations, and many processing industries.[3]

Opponents of liberalization included the National Farmers Union, wheat producers (raising concerns about transportation subsidies and the nontransparency of the pricing policies of the monopolistic Canadian Wheat Board), and protected peanut, sugar, and citrus and other winter fruit and vegetable producers. A strong coalition emerged among the Florida sugar and fruit and vegetable interests. They developed a unified position with the Florida Farm Bureau and the Florida Cattlemen's Association (both eventually broke ranks with their national organizations' support for NAFTA), and the state commissioner of agriculture became an active proponent of their concerns. No similar coalition arose among the Section 22 commodities in general because the dairy and cotton sectors (with current or potential export interests in Mexico) remained less opposed than sugar and peanuts to trade liberalization on a bilateral basis.

3. Descriptions of the positions and activities of the various interest groups are based largely on interviews with representatives of twenty-two of the groups most involved in the negotiations and congressional deliberations, as well as with negotiators and others. These interviews were conducted between August and November 1993. Some initial evaluations of NAFTA by representatives of the agricultural interests are also summarized in the reports of the Agricultural Trade Policy Advisory Committee and the Agricultural Technical Advisory Committees.

7.3 Agricultural Provisions of NAFTA

High-level negotiators for Mexico and the United States agreed in February 1992 that all agricultural products would be included in the long-run provisions for trade liberalization. Canada resisted participation in an agreement of such broad scope for agriculture. It agreed only to negotiate extension to Mexico of the limited provisions similar to those of the 1988 Canada-U.S. agreement.

The negotiating parties announced that they had reached a conclusion to their discussions in August. For Mexico and the United States, the agricultural tariff and market access provisions called for the conversion of all nontariff barriers to tariff-rate quotas (TRQs). Under the TRQs, limited quantities of commodities would receive access under low or zero duties, while imports above these quantities would be subject to over-quota tariffs set to provide initial protection equivalent to the previous nontariff measures. The over-quota tariffs were to be phased out over adjustment periods of ten to fifteen years (see U.S. House of Representatives 1993).

The long-run NAFTA provisions for agriculture accomplished the basic objectives with respect to trade barriers of the broader 1987 U.S. "zero-option" GATT proposal for elimination of trade-distorting border measures and support policies. This result led Hufbauer and Schott (1993), for example, to conclude that there was "laudable progress in the liberalization of farm trade barriers."

One cannot be as sanguine about the short-run NAFTA provisions for agriculture. For the commodities protected by import quotas or licenses, market access levels under the initial TRQs were based on 1989 to 1991 trade quantities and were scheduled to increase at only a 3 percent annual compound rate. Over-quota tariffs provided high levels of protection against additional imports in the short and medium run. Corn, dry edible beans, milk powder, and peanuts were considered particularly sensitive commodities and received fifteen-year adjustment periods.

Intense negotiations also focused on complex protective TRQ transition mechanisms for sugar: Mexico agreed to raise its external sugar tariff to the preexisting U.S. over-quota level by the seventh year of the agreement and subsequently gained potentially unlimited access to the U.S. market if it achieved a net production surplus. Special tariff phaseout and TRQ mechanisms were also developed for citrus and other horticultural products.

The influence of various producer groups on the negotiations is evident from the NAFTA transition mechanisms for agricultural trade. Within the framework of long-run liberalization, likely gainers among U.S. producers confront the lengthy adjustment mechanisms included to protect Mexican farmers. Import-competing U.S. commodities are provided with similar adjustment protection. Given these provisions, the end constraint of complete tariff elimination is crucial to the assertion that the negotiated provisions accomplished long-run bilateral trade liberalization for agriculture.

7.4 Estimated Impacts of the Agreement

Among the quantitative studies of the long-run effects of NAFTA on Mexican-U.S. agricultural trade, Grennes and Krissoff (1993) estimated that U.S. agricultural exports to Mexico (primarily grains, oilseeds, and livestock products) would increase by $485 million annually, and agricultural imports from Mexico by $164 million (primarily horticultural commodities and live cattle). The USDA Office of Economics (1993) asserted a more positive view of NAFTA's potentially beneficial impacts. Incorporating projected demand effects resulting from an increase due to NAFTA of 0.5 percent in Mexico's annual economic growth, the USDA concluded that agricultural exports to Mexico were likely to be more than $2.5 billion higher annually with NAFTA by the end of the fifteen-year adjustment period, while imports of agricultural products from Mexico would increase by $500 to $600 million.

7.5 Side Agreements and Implementing Legislation

After the November 1992 election, the Clinton administration followed through on its campaign pledge to negotiate supplemental (side) agreements with respect to the environment, labor, and import surges. The change in administration gave the agricultural commodity groups that had sought limits on NAFTA's trade-liberalizing provisions the opportunity for a second hearing. In particular, the concerns of the sugar producers were acknowledged by the designated United States trade representative, Mickey Kantor. As early as his January 1993 preconfirmation hearings, he pointed out that the side agreement on import surges would "affect agriculture and particularly be protective, we hope, of the sugar industry" (U.S. Senate 1993). Despite such assurances, the side agreement on import surges that was negotiated by the Clinton administration did not achieve the types of changes in the initial NAFTA provisions sought by some agricultural producer groups.

Faced with growing opposition, President Clinton used a September 1993 signing ceremony for the side agreements to launch an intense campaign for passage by Congress of implementing legislation for NAFTA. Agricultural interest groups played an active role in the ensuing congressional debate.

Among supporters of the agreement, an umbrella support organization called Ag for NAFTA was formed and eventually claimed over 140 member organizations. In addition, the American Farm Bureau Federation and many of the specific commodity associations devoted staff and resources to support passage of the implementing legislation. However, the scale of their activities was relatively modest compared to the widespread efforts among interested parties (see, for example, Grayson 1993). Ag for NAFTA had an initial budget of about $10,000 and its final budget for publicity, advertising, and other expenses was less than $100,000.

The commodities receiving Section 22 protection pursued separate approaches to the implementing legislation based on the particular circumstances of each sector. The National Milk Producers Federation adopted a position of support for the agreement during the summer of 1993 and the National Cotton Council of America endorsed NAFTA in October.

Opponents of NAFTA also continued to mobilize around the implementing legislation. The National Farmers Union made defeat of NAFTA one of its top priorities and was a founding member of the opponents' Citizens Trade Campaign. While not formally aligned with third-party presidential aspirant Ross Perot, who was an active NAFTA opponent, representatives of the farmers union believed he had reduced the prospects for the approval of the agreement.

Among specific commodity groups opposing the agreement, wheat producers continued their break with the other export-oriented grains and held out for resolution of the issues of Canadian transportation subsidies and Wheat Board price transparency.[4] In exchange for their support for NAFTA, the wheat producers sought emergency action under Section 22. This would have allowed the Clinton administration to impose immediate quotas or tariffs on grain imported from Canada rather than await the outcome of an investigation and ruling by the ITC.

Peanut and sugar producer groups also remained opposed to the NAFTA provisions. The sugar producers sought two modifications of the initial agreement: inclusion of corn sweeteners in determining the balance of production and consumption affecting Mexican access to the U.S. sugar market and a ceiling on Mexico's access for the full fifteen-year adjustment period. The sugar producers lobbied the USDA and the Office of the U.S. Trade Representative (USTR) and pressed their case through the Senate sweeteners caucus. They viewed the USTR as sympathetic to their interests but nevertheless committed $500,000 to a campaign to "go hell bent to defeat NAFTA" if the agreement was not revised. Their demands, of course, brought into sharp focus the competing interests of different commodity groups within U.S. agriculture, as well as the relative strength of the Mexican and U.S. negotiating positions.

The Florida coalition, working along commodity lines and through the unified position among agricultural groups within the state, also pressed for further accommodations for sugar, citrus, and other winter fruits and vegetables. The Florida agricultural producers, worked closely with the state's congressional delegation of ten Democrats and thirteen Republicans, which throughout the congressional deliberations almost entirely remained on record as opposed to the agreement.

4. While the wheat growers were clamoring about Canadian policies, the flow of wheat into the United States resulted as much from the U.S. export subsidies discussed by Bruce Gardner in chapter 6 of this volume.

7.6 End Game Concessions

With the fate of NAFTA uncertain as the November 17 vote in the House of Representatives approached, the agricultural commodity groups were positioned to win various concessions. Unlike organized labor and others committed to the defeat of the agreement, most of the agricultural commodity groups had limited their opposition to specific provisions. Moreover, a relatively large number of congressional votes rested at least in part on satisfying the concerns of the agricultural producers.

The end game exploded into public view in early November. Concessions obtained for agriculture in the last two weeks of the debate are summarized in table 7.1.

7.6.1 Initial Concessions

An initial November 3 letter from the U.S. trade representative to Mexico's secretary of commerce indicated that the United States would seek a mutual agreement on accelerated tariff reductions for wine and brandy (USTR 1993). A second and more significant letter confirmed the USTR's understanding that the two parties had recognized that substitution of corn syrup for sugar could "result in effects not intended by either Party" and therefore agreed that consumption of corn syrup would be included in the determination of Mexico's net production surplus. The letter also indicated that notwithstanding previous provisions, Mexican sugar sales in the United States under NAFTA would be capped at 250,000 metric tons through a fifteen-year adjustment period. In short, Mexico had conceded to the demands of the U.S. sugar producers. Subsequently, the sugar industry indicated that it had withdrawn its opposition to NAFTA, a decision expected to influence at least a dozen votes in the House of Representatives.

A third letter between the U.S. and Mexican negotiators addressed the issues raised by the Florida citrus industry. It specified an explicit price-based tariff snapback for citrus. Under the snapback, the United States would apply the prevailing most-favored-nation (MFN) rate of duty on imports from Mexico in excess of specific quantities if the price of fresh concentrated orange juice dropped below an average based on the preceding five years for five consecutive days.

In addition to this modest change from the original NAFTA text, the citrus producers had bargained for several other concessions: that tariffs on all forms of fresh and processed citrus products would receive the minimum 15 percent cut under the still-pending Uruguay Round GATT, that non-NAFTA citrus juices would be reclassified as perishable commodities under U.S. law (expediting future injury claims by the industry), and that foreign citrus products would not receive additional special status under the Generalized System of Preferences (GSP) or the Caribbean Basin Initiative (CBI). The board of direc-

Table 7.1 Final NAFTA Concessions and Assurances to Agricultural Interests

Wine/brandy	United States to seek mutual agreement to accelerated tariff reductions
Sugar	Consumption of corn sweeteners included in the determination of net production surplus Mexican TRQ capped at 250,000 metric tons for the seventh through fourteenth years of the agreement
Citrus	Most-favored-nation rate of duty on imports from Mexico in excess of 70 million gallons annually through 2002 (90 million gallons during 2003–2007) if the price of fresh concentrated orange juice drops below an average based on the preceding five years for five consecutive days GATT tariff cuts on fresh and processed citrus products limited to 15 percent Non-NAFTA citrus juices to be reclassified as perishable commodities to expedite injury claims Citrus products not to receive additional special status under the GSP or the CBI
Fruits and vegetables	Early warning import-surge mechanism GATT tariff cuts limited to 15 percent on tomatoes, peppers, lettuce, cucumbers, celery, and sweet corn Sensitive products not to receive additional special status under the GSP or the CBI Postponement of decertification of methyl bromide for use as a soil fumigant until 2000 Funding for soil and postharvest fumigant research; completion and funding for U.S. Horticultural Research Station, Fort Pierce, Florida Doubled purchases of fresh tomatoes and new purchases of sweet corn for school lunch programs Trade representative assurance of effective price-based and volume-based tariff snapback provisions for fresh tomatoes and peppers
Wheat	End-use certificates to prevent subsidized reexport of Canadian wheat and barley Bilateral consultations to address transportation subsidies and Canadian Wheat Board pricing practices and an ITC investigation of whether imports interfere with the domestic wheat program within sixty days unless the consultations were successful
Peanuts	Bilateral consultations to address the increase in imports of peanut butter/paste from Canada and an ITC investigation of whether imports interfere with the domestic peanut program within sixty days unless the consultations were successful Secretary of agriculture assurance to work vigorously to limit the volume of imports from Canada
Transshipment	Commissioner of customs assurance of at least ten investigations and 350 positions, including 100 new hires, to enforce rules of origin

tors of Florida Citrus Mutual voted to withdraw their opposition to the agreement on November 10 based on these concessions.

As the anti-NAFTA Florida coalition collapsed, other Florida fruit and vegetable producers also sought accommodations. The administration agreed to a range of concessions that included the use of an early warning import-surge mechanism; limits for certain commodities with respect to GATT, the GSP, and the CBI similar to those offered for citrus; an environmentally controversial postponement of decertification and methyl bromide for use as a soil fumigant;

funding for research on soil treatment and postharvest fumigation; and an agreement to increase purchases of fresh tomatoes and sweet corn for school lunch programs. The board of directors of the Florida Fruit and Vegetable Association withdrew its opposition to NAFTA on November 11.

7.6.2 Final Deals

Passage of the implementing legislation remained uncertain less than a week before the scheduled congressional vote, so the administration and its supporters could not relax their efforts. Ag for NAFTA brought fifty to sixty leaders of various member organizations to Washington to lobby, but the real action was with the groups that had been or remained opposed to NAFTA.

The wheat producers engaged in tense late-deal bargaining. Their hope for emergency Section 22 quotas or tariffs was scuttled when, by several accounts, the administration determined that they could not influence many votes. On November 15, however, the president agreed to partially accommodate the producers: he asked that the ITC investigate whether imports from Canada were interfering with U.S. wheat support programs, unless there were successful bilateral negotiations on Canadian policies within sixty days. With this concession, the National Association of Wheat Growers announced, less than thirty-six hours before the House vote, that it would "now work for congressional approval of NAFTA." Five congressmen cited the Wheat Growers' position in support of their final decisions to vote for the implementing legislation.

One of these representatives, Representative Glenn English, was also concerned about illegal transshipment of peanuts and beef through Mexico. To address the continuing opposition to NAFTA by peanut producers and English's concerns, the president committed the administration to bilateral consultations on imports of peanut butter from Canada and to a second ITC investigation within sixty days if necessary. English was assured by the commissioner of customs that there would be "at least ten visits to agricultural processing sites in Mexico," and that "350 positions, including 100 newly hired employees," would be assigned to enforce the NAFTA rules of origin.

Final critical decisions were made by the Florida congressional delegation, which held a closed-door meeting on November 16. Although there may already have been several closet votes for NAFTA, an Associated Press poll had counted only five of the twenty-three members of the delegation as supporting or leaning toward supporting the agreement on the previous day. A pivotal senior member of the Florida delegation was Representative Tom Lewis, who served on the House Committee on Agriculture. To assure Lewis about his concerns required an additional letter from Mickey Kantor specifying that NAFTA contained "effective price and volume-based snapback provisions to deal with increased imports of fresh tomatoes and peppers." The next day, Lewis and twelve other members of the Florida delegation voted with the administration. The NAFTA implementing legislation passed in the House of Representatives by a 234 to 200 majority.[5]

7.7 Conclusions from the NAFTA Outcomes

In drawing inferences about the political economy of trade protection on the basis of the influence of U.S. agricultural groups on the NAFTA negotiations and implementing legislation, a crucial issue is the extent to which a mechanism was provided for overcoming established protection among agricultural sectors and expanding international markets. The decision to seek long-run liberalization of Mexican-U.S. agricultural trade under NAFTA established a strong objective compared to the limited provisions for agriculture in previous bilateral trade agreements and the significant weakening of the U.S. zero-option proposal in the Uruguay-Round GATT negotiations.[6] The subsequent NAFTA provisions for long-run trade liberalization remained largely intact even with the grueling congressional debate. Many of the concessions offered to U.S. agricultural interest groups weaken the NAFTA transition-period provisions only marginally, and other acknowledged concessions to the interest groups are also relatively minor.

This said, the notion that a trade agreement can serve as an avenue for reform of entrenched domestic U.S. agricultural programs fared poorly under NAFTA. Among the protected U.S. commodities, dairy and cotton came to support the Mexican-U.S. agreement only when strong rules of origin were adopted and the absence of any threat to their domestic markets became apparent. Peanut producers fought hard against the agreement and battled in the end for several concessions to sustain their protection.

More egregious than the dairy, cotton, and peanut provisions, NAFTA initially created a trade-diverting common sugar market between Mexico and the United States. The subsequent concessions to U.S. sugar interests exacerbated

5. In addition to the confirmed concessions, there were rumors in the press that the administration would back away from its intention to raise grazing fees on federal lands and that the proposed increase in the cigarette tax to finance health care reform might be scaled back in exchange for support for NAFTA (*Wall Street Journal* 1993a, 1993b). A possible deal that did not seem to be under consideration (despite the importance of the Florida delegation) would have linked the NAFTA vote to stalled negotiations between the government and sugar and fruit and vegetable producers as they sought an out-of-court settlement on a program to restore the Everglades by reducing agricultural runoff. Whatever the NAFTA deals, health care reform failed to come to a vote in the 103rd Congress and Interior Secretary Bruce Babbitt withdrew his proposal to raise grazing fees in December 1994.

6. The Uruguay Round GATT negotiations were finally concluded in December 1993 and Congress approved legislation implementing the agreement in December 1994. The final agreement for agriculture includes provisions for replacing quantitative restrictions, such as Section 22 quotas, with TRQs and for lowering all tariffs by an average of 36 percent over six years. The agreement also reduces but does not eliminate export subsidies, and caps some domestic support payments to farmers. See Sanderson (1994) and International Agricultural Trade Research Consortium (1994) for further discussion.

the initial distortion by essentially stealing from the Mexican producers some of their potential market opportunity while enhancing the potential demand facing U.S. producers. The concessions obtained gutted the agreement for freer bilateral trade, albeit within a protected common market, for at least the next fifteen years. They also raise the question of whether the agreement to allow unrestricted trade in sugar between Mexico and the United States after fifteen years is ultimately credible.

The differences in the NAFTA outcomes with Mexico compared to Canada are also telling. The U.S. export producer groups were successful with respect to Mexico, which has opened itself to substantial reform of its agricultural policies. Mexican agricultural producer groups that might have benefitted from a stronger agreement in terms of their own export opportunities had only limited countervailing power against the pressure for concessions by import-protected U.S. producers. To insure NAFTA's approval, the U.S. government succeeded in pressing these concessions on the Mexican government.

With Canada the story is different. Throughout the NAFTA process, import-competing Canadian agricultural producers were more effective in defending their established protection than the Mexican producers. Canada's participation in NAFTA was largely ignored in the United States except by a few special interests. But to insure passage of the implementing legislation, the Clinton administration made unilateral promises to several U.S. agricultural commodity groups about their perceived grievances over imports from Canada. Thus one outcome of the process was that it prolonged the disputes between the United States and Canada over wheat, peanut butter, and other products.

Given the focus on Mexico in the public NAFTA debate, the unresolved issues with Canada are a surprising outcome. Subsequent to NAFTA's enactment, the United States offered to settle the agricultural trade disputes with Canada by adopting bilateral free trade in agricultural products. When this offer was declined, the United States reached a bilateral agreement with Canada for temporary trade restrictions on wheat and imposed a global TRQ on peanut butter in its final Uruguay Round GATT tariff schedule. Thus, post-NAFTA agricultural trade between Canada and the United States ends up more laded with barriers than before.

On a somewhat different theme, the bargaining power that agricultural groups held toward the end of the NAFTA debate is striking. The agricultural interest groups were well positioned to bargain for concessions because they sought modifications of specific provisions but did not oppose the entire agreement. The concerns of sugar, the Florida coalition, peanuts, or wheat mattered to the outcome of close to thirty congressional votes.

The question that arises is why other groups didn't do more to put themselves in such a position. The concessions made to agriculture toward the end of the debate were not the only concessions offered by the Clinton administration. One wonders, for example, why the AFL-CIO didn't approach the president with concerns about specific industries and seek additional transition-period protection in these areas in exchange for delivering their support for the agreement. One can imagine a very different coalition having been put together to pass the implementing legislation in such circumstances. Agricultural interests could have found themselves irrelevant to the congressional vote, leaving the sugar and wheat producers to make their case elsewhere. Curiously, one doubts these parties to last-minute concessions were the intended beneficiaries of organized labor's political efforts.

References

Agricultural Policy Advisory Committee. 1992. *Report on the North American Free Trade Agreement.* Washington D.C.: Office of the U.S. Trade Representative.

Agricultural Technical Advisory Committees. 1992. *Reports on the North American Free Trade Agreement.* Washington D.C.: Office of the U.S. Trade Representative.

Grayson, George W. 1993. *The North American Free Trade Agreement.* Headliner Series, no. 299, Foreign Policy Association.

Grennes, Thomas, and Barry Krissoff. 1993. Agricultural trade in a North American free trade agreement. *The World Economy* 16, no. 4:483–502.

Hufbauer, Gary Clyde, and Jeffrey J. Schott. 1993. *NAFTA: An assessment.* Washington, D.C.: Institute for International Economics.

International Agricultural Trade Research Consortium. 1994. *The Uruguay Round Agreement on Agriculture: An evaluation.* Commissioned Paper no. 9. St. Paul, Minn.: University of Minnesota, Department of Agricultural and Applied Economics.

International Trade Commission. 1993. *Potential impact on the U.S. economy and selected industries of the North American Free-Trade Agreement.* Publication no. 2596.

Miner, William M. 1993. Agricultural trade under the klieg lights: Domestic pressures and bilateral frictions. Working Paper. Ottawa, Canada: Carleton University, Center for Trade Policy and Law.

Office of the United States Trade Representative (USTR). 1993. Letters from Administration Officials Prepared in Connection with the NAFTA Debate. Transmitted by Ira S. Shapiro (general counsel, USTR) to Senator Daniel P. Moynihan (chairman, Senate Committee on Finance) on 18 November 1993.

Sanderson, Fred H. 1994. The GATT agreement on agriculture. Working Paper. Washington, D.C.: National Center for Food and Agricultural Policy.

United States Department of Agriculture. 1994. *Estimates of producer subsidy equivalents and consumer subsidy equivalents: Government intervention in agriculture, 1982–1992.* Statistical Bulletin no. 913. Washington D.C.: Economic Research Service, December.

———. Office of Economics. 1993. *Effects of the North American Free Trade Agreement on U.S. agricultural commodities.* Washington D.C.: Economic Research Service, March.

U.S. House of Representatives. 1993. *Message from the president of the United States transmitting North American Free Trade Agreement, supplemental agreements and additional documents.* 103rd Cong., 1st sess. H. Doc. 103-160.

U.S. Senate. 1993. Committee on Finance. *Hearings on the anticipated nomination of*

Mickey Kantor, U.S. Trade Representative Designate. 103rd Cong., 1st sess. Senate Hearings 103-12. 19 January.
Wall Street Journal. 1993a. White House hopes to trade changes in grazing-fee plan for NAFTA support. 10 November.
———. 1993b. Anatomy of a victory: "Deals" and sense of Clinton's commitment clinched NAFTA. 19 November.

Chapter 7

The Political Economy of the FAIR Act

David Orden, Robert Paarlberg and Terry Roe

In chapter 4, we described the sequence of policy proposals and political negotiations that led to unexpected domestic farm policy reforms in the 1996 FAIR Act. In this chapter, we step back from the political process to address two fundamental analytical questions about these reforms. First, what were the economic impacts of the FAIR Act on U.S. agriculture? Second, what fundamental economic and political forces drove Congress and the president to adopt the originally rejected Freedom to Farm approach?

At the outset of the farm bill debate, economic analysis suggested that elimination of the existing farm programs in 1995 would result in more efficient resource use and an increase in income derived directly from markets. When the FAIR Act passed, it was thus acclaimed by farm policy proponents and critics alike for freeing agriculture from many of the distorting production incentives spawned by the traditional programs. Yet the higher market prices that helped produce the FAIR Act would have led to fewer production distortions even under those programs, and smaller initial budget outlays as well.

Without a change in party control of Congress, and without an unexpected interlude of rising farm prices in 1995–96, the most important reforms in the FAIR Act would not have been undertaken. Prior to the November 1994 Republican midterm election victory, and prior to the 1995 run-up in commodity prices, few participants in the farm policy process expected radical change, and those that did expect change were not anticipating decoupled support payments. A number of proposals were advanced for eliminating unpaid ARP set asides, and the ascendancy of the Republican Party in Congress heightened the prospects for this reform move. But it was not foreseen that a combination of Republican control of Congress and high commodity prices would eventually trigger an important restructuring of the deficiency payment mechanism for providing support to farmers. We examine the importance of these two coincident events in producing the FAIR Act in 1996 and compare them to a number of other sources of change often considered conducive to reform, which had much smaller impacts at the time. These include the content of the Uruguay Round Agreement on Agriculture and related international negotiations, federal budget pressure, the cumulative structural modernization in agriculture, a diminished potency of the farm lobby, and the emergence of newly dominant ideas favoring a smaller role of the government in the domestic economy (including the farm economy). These other policy-driving forces may prove influential in future years, but they did not prompt the surprising policy changes embraced by Congress in the 1996 FAIR Act.

Economic Impacts of the FAIR Act Reforms

If the FAIR Act is preserved for its scheduled duration from 1996 to 2002, it will deserve to be classified in some important respects as a policy reform victory, certainly as a substantial extension of the limited cash-out reforms previously undertaken. Unlike earlier cash outs, the FAIR Act sought to decouple direct support payments almost entirely from market conditions and farm production decisions. This nearly complete decoupling of payments was the step that had eluded market-oriented reformers on at least two prior occasions—first in 1985, with congressional rejection of the Boschwitz-Boren proposal, then once more in the late 1980s, when international negotiators rejected the zero option proposal in the GATT Uruguay Round. Congress had only partially decoupled support payments from planting decisions and crop yields in the 1985 and 1990 farm bills. The FAIR Act not only fully decoupled support for the former deficiency payment crops, it also eliminated all authority for annual acreage reductions.

Reform Gains from the FAIR Act

From a market-oriented perspective, the main reform features of the FAIR Act provide numerous advantages compared to previous cash outs. In the past, the commodity programs had offered farmers a conflicting mix of incentives, which drove up costs and generated market distortions. Deficiency payments tied to base-acreage production of specific crops created uneconomic incentives for supply expansion and distorted land values, particularly in regions for which the payments constituted a large proportion of net farm income. Simultaneously, supply was constrained by ARPs and, in some cases, by restrictions on planting flexibility on the program acreage bases. Provisions for partial deficiency payments on voluntarily idled land created a further disincentive for efficient production.

The distorting effects of the traditional farm support programs were substantially reduced under the FAIR Act because of the ending of deficiency payments, the decoupling of cash support from production decisions, and the elimination of acreage bases and annual supply controls. Efficiency gains from the decoupling of support and the end to ARPs yield economic benefits for producers and consumers. Earlier limited cash-out reforms had kept some market-distorting program incentives in place, particularly by leaving government policy makers with little means to control expenditure other than by a lapse into damaging production controls. The FAIR Act eliminated this incentive for policy distortion, made the income transfers to farmers explicit and transparent, and allowed low-cost farmers to escape the inefficiency and opportunity cost of idling portions of their land.

Under its production flexibility contracts, the FAIR Act also sought to move closer to the elusive goal of budget certainty, replacing the open-ended deficiency payment entitlements from the 1985 and 1990 farm bills with an explicit cap on most farm support expenditures. Cost overruns had been an embarrassment to past cash-out reforms of farm policy. The FAIR Act not only fixed planned support payments but seemed to offer some increased budget discipline compared to previous years. The total seven-year federal expenditure of $35.4 billion originally authorized for decoupled payments in the FAIR Act implied annual support outlays below the average expenditures under either the 1985 or 1990 farm bill. By this comparison, at least, farm support payments were reduced by the 1996 FAIR Act, and the prospects for more efficient resource allocations within the sector were increased.

Another important reform feature under the FAIR Act was the capping of nominal loan rates at seemingly nonintrusive levels. This would ensure that the period of high farm commodity prices during the mid-1990s did not lead automatically to market-distorting price-support levels and growth in entitlement claims if prices fell. Farm programs had become highly distorting and costly after price supports ratcheted up during the 1970s commodity boom (and general inflation) proved too high in the 1980s. The FAIR Act insulated farm policy from such an automatic growth of intrusive support.

The full decoupling of support payments from prices and production under the FAIR Act also potentially enhanced the bargaining position of the United States for future international trade negotiations. It never made sense from the standpoint of economic efficiency for the United States to engage in supply control, when the European Union (a somewhat higher-cost producer) was going ahead with full production.

By unilaterally abandoning its annual supply-control measures for export crops under the FAIR Act, the United States strengthened its position as a low-cost supplier of grains to world markets. This could indirectly pressure international competitors into parallel reforms.

Having unilaterally adopted fully decoupled support payments in the FAIR Act, the United States also became more persuasive in arguing that its trade partners and competitors abroad—especially the European Union—should do the same, in order to eliminate remaining distortions affecting trade volumes and market prices. Thanks to the FAIR Act, the United States no longer needs the blue box exemption built into the final Uruguay Round Agreement on Agriculture. This might allow U.S. negotiators to argue for repeal of the blue box exemption across the board, and thus perhaps pressure the European Union, which has consistently remained behind the United States in moving toward farm policy reform, into accepting fully decoupled payments as well. Under the MacSharry plan, the European Union finally moved *toward* a cash out in 1992, reducing its intervention price guarantees and compensating farmers with cash payments, while embracing acreage set-aside requirements. When the 1996 FAIR Act ended U.S. set asides, it completed a reversal of the longstanding policy stances of the United States and European Union on annual production controls. With less competitive policies, the Europeans could find themselves more inclined to undertake further reforms.[1]

Limitations of the FAIR Act Reforms

Despite the important accomplishments of eliminating annual supply controls and decoupling support for the former deficiency payment crops from production decisions and market prices, the reform gains made in the 1996 FAIR Act were limited. The FAIR Act is certainly not a cutout of farm programs, because federal government payments to farmers will continue; payments were decoupled, but not terminated.[2]

1. In July 1997, the European Commission made such a reform proposal (called its "Agenda 2000") for decoupled payments. The commission argued that lowering domestic prices to world levels, eliminating export subsidies and acreage set asides, and providing direct compensatory payments to the beneficiaries of the CAP were steps necessary to manage budget costs, avoid surplus accumulations, and pave the way for enlargement of the European Union.

2. One minor exception was that the price-support program for honey was terminated in 1996. This was a clean cutout, but CCC expenditures on the honey program had averaged only $43 million annually since 1985, and government receipts had exceeded outlays in fiscal years 1994 and 1995. Earlier (in 1993) the small wool and mohair support program

Nor is the FAIR Act a guaranteed buyout of farm programs, even though some proponents described it as such.[3] The FAIR Act maintains a baseline of farm program spending for at least seven years and does not repeal the permanent legislation that will automatically trigger a reversion to high price supports and supply controls if Congress fails to take further action in 2002. This almost guarantees new legislation on farm programs. Thus, the institutions and the institutional incentives remain in place to extend decoupled payments, or even to re-implement some of the more intrusive programs and policy instruments that the FAIR Act sought to eliminate.

The FAIR Act also fails to squeeze farmers out of their traditional acceptance of government support. The former deficiency payment programs entailed some restrictions on farmers' production decisions, and participation rates varied among commodities depending on market conditions. The FAIR Act PFC payments, in contrast, are sufficiently generous and free of significant compliance costs—and so easy to claim relative to previous farm program payments—that essentially all of those eligible have opted to take advantage of the offer. As a consequence, rates of participation in the farm support program actually rose under the FAIR Act compared to preceding years.[4] An *enlarged* constituency of beneficiaries thus has become associated with the FAIR Act payments. These beneficiaries may now be more likely to expend political resources to sustain future payments, or to seek some other equivalent support, when the FAIR Act expires.

The FAIR Act that finally emerged from Congress in April 1996 was not as market-oriented a measure as the Freedom to Farm Act originally proposed in August 1995. The floor under market prices set by CCC loan rates was kept at 85 percent of a moving average of past price lev-

---

had also been ended without compensation to farmers, just as support programs for other minor commodities had disappeared in the decades after the Second World War. Wool and mohair support payments had averaged about $100 million from 1985–90, but jumped to nearly twice that level in 1991–93, making them a target for which agriculturalists eventually made a concession in budget negotiations.

3. When the FAIR Act was completed, Terry Francl of the Farm Bureau called it "a $36 billion buyout" (Ingersoll 1996). As we earlier pointed out, a *New York Times* headline on April 5, 1996, read, "Clinton Signs Farm Bill Ending Subsidies." See also Stinson, Coggins, and Ramezani 1998.

4. Under deficiency payments, participation rates for wheat, for example, averaged 87 percent from 1993–95, while for corn the participation rates averaged 81 percent. The USDA ensured that all farmers who were eligible for the new FAIR Act payments were notified of the sign-up criteria, and the participation rate reached nearly 100 percent.

els, although subject to nominal caps, and marketing loans were retained in the final legislation. These price-support interventions constitute supply-enhancing incentives by reducing downward price risk, especially for producers of cotton and rice. The FAIR Act also retained the "three entity" rule, which allows some wealthy farmers to circumvent program payment limitations by establishing eligibility for ostensibly separate operations. Retention of this rule demonstrates how little the FAIR Act did to address equity issues, either through an effective means test or an individual entitlement cap. The PFC payments were calculated for each farm on the basis of past output levels, leaving payments concentrated, as before, among large-scale producers.

As with earlier reform efforts, the FAIR Act did not significantly extend the principle of market deregulation beyond the export-oriented deficiency payment crops. There was no cash out for commodities such as dairy, sugar, and peanuts (and also tobacco, although this crop is handled in separate legislation). The support programs for these commodities escaped convincing reform. Marketing order regulation of regional prices of fluid milk was extended, and TRQs that limit imports of dairy products remain in place. The number of regional milk marketing orders was to be reduced, and price supports for dairy products were scheduled to be phased out by the end of 1999, but the FAIR Act authorized a new Northeast Dairy Compact that increased regional price disparities. Sugar price supports well above world price levels were maintained under the FAIR Act, enforced by TRQs to limit imports. The domestic support price of peanuts was lowered, but also remained well above world price levels—with production quotas still in use and limited options for sale, lease, or transfer of the quotas even among counties within a state.

Changes to U.S. agricultural export policies were also modest under the FAIR Act. The EEP and DEIP were reauthorized with the full funding permitted under the Uruguay Round agreement in 2000–2002.[5] The use of public funds to help agribusiness promote U.S. products in foreign markets was continued, although at a somewhat reduced level.

The FAIR Act also provided authority for some entirely new spending in agriculture, most of it tied nominally to environmental policies.

5. For 1996–99, EEP expenditures were capped below the maximum levels permitted by the Uruguay Round Agreement on Agriculture, but during these years it was expected that high international market prices would make export subsidy spending unnecessary.

The federal role in farm credit markets was reaffirmed, although somewhat tighter rules were written governing the provision of subsidized loans. New "pilot" revenue insurance programs were also authorized—programs that have potentially large production-stimulating consequences and create uncertain budget exposure.

Through renewal of long-term paid land diversions in the CRP, a significant supply-control instrument was extended by the FAIR Act. While supply controls through unpaid annual acreage set asides were eliminated, the total acreage authority for paid CRP contracts was held at its 1995 level of 36.4 million acres—despite strong farm commodity demand and favorable prices for producers at the time. The voluntary nature of the CRP ensures that idling land will continue to be expensive for taxpayers; farmers must forgo the newly decoupled PFC payments on CRP land enrollments, so the commodity programs and the CRP will still be bidding against each other. The secretary of agriculture was given wide discretion in determining the location of future CRP enrollments as existing contracts expired. This did not satisfy the concerns of many environmentalists, who wanted a stronger guarantee that land fragility and off-farm pollution issues would be given priority in the secretary's enrollment decisions. However, because the secretary had made known his intention to maintain the size of the CRP, commodity groups worried about low prices were reassured.[6]

Finally, it was the short-term budget expenditures under the FAIR Act that made it seem least like a bold reform in 1996. When the FAIR Act became law, it increased farm program costs compared to an extension of the 1990 farm bill. As we have described, before market prices increased, the CBO projected that the farm bill title in the 1995 budget reconciliation legislation (essentially the same proposals as the FAIR Act for the defi-

6. While paid acreage idling under the CRP remained intrusive under the FAIR Act, some modest reform gains could be claimed. The 1990 farm bill increased the CRP emphasis on water quality as an environmental consideration, added wildlife habitat, and established a continuous signup program for small areas devoted to practices designated as valuable by the Environmental Protection Agency. CRP enrollments had fallen to 32.8 million acres by spring of 1997, and contracts on 21.4 million acres were due to expire. The USDA enrolled 16.8 million acres in May 1997 (including reenrollments of 11.7 million acres formerly under contract). This was the largest single signup ever. Yet with prices still relatively high, and despite the secretary's assurance, this signup only maintained the CRP at just over 28 million acres—8 million less than the maximum authorized by the FAIR Act. A second signup was conducted in late 1997, increasing the CRP acreage slightly. The distribution of enrolled acres changed only a little among regions as a result of these two post–FAIR Act signups, with the largest change an increase from 27 to 31 percent in the Northern Plains.

ciency payment commodities) would reduce expected budget costs compared to continuation of existing policies by $2.8 billion during fiscal years 1996 and 1997, and by $12.2 billion over seven years. After market prices increased, this calculation had to be redone. In December 1995, the CBO projected that the same farm bill proposals would increase expenditures compared to the 1990 law by $3.9 billion in 1996 and 1997, and would produce a net savings over seven years of just $4.6 billion. These calculations were then redone (by the USDA) once again in mid-1996. Using the high price projections then prevalent, the new calculations showed not only an increase in costs in the short run, but a net increase over the whole seven-year life of the FAIR Act. In mid-1996, USDA calculated that the seven-year cost of the FAIR Act would be a full $25 billion higher than if deficiency payments under the 1990 law had simply been extended (Young and Westcott 1996). Thus, the FAIR Act was perceived at the time as providing a substantial windfall gain to farmers.

Measuring the Efficiency Gains

Along with increased income transfers to farmers, the FAIR Act provided only modest short-run efficiency gains within the U.S. farm sector. Proponents of the FAIR Act emphasized that ending ARPs and decoupling support payments gave farmers greater freedom to respond to market signals, and greater incentives to plant for the market rather than to try to "farm the government programs." For the deficiency payment programs that were reformed most by the FAIR Act, this would have been a measurable benefit at the levels of prices anticipated in February 1995. But the flexibility gains were actually quite small when the FAIR Act came into effect in 1996. With the relatively high farm commodity prices then prevailing, the traditional deficiency payment programs would have provided almost as much freedom to farm.

Prior to the rise in market prices in 1995–96, the CBO projected (in February 1995) that continuation of ARPs under extension of the 1990 farm bill would idle between three and six million acres of corn and cotton base acreage annually during the 1996–2002 period. A larger aggregate acreage was projected to be idled each year under the voluntary set-aside programs, through which farmers could receive deficiency payments even if they didn't produce crops. The voluntarily idled area was expected to exceed twelve million acres annually across all commodities. The CBO made the assumption that CRP land diversions would not extend beyond the termination of the ten-year contracts authorized under the 1985 and 1990 farm bills. Thus, the acreage enrolled in the CRP was projected to decline from nearly thirty-five million acres to less than twenty million.

Various estimates of the economic efficiency gains that could be achieved by eliminating farm program interventions circulated during the 1995–96 farm bill debate. These estimates rested on different assumptions about the amount of ARP and voluntarily idled land that would go into production, the productivity of the previously idled land, and the substitution decisions by producers among commodities—given the expected market prices and the absence of deficiency payments and base-acreage restrictions. A Heritage Foundation study suggested that 95 percent of ARP land and 60 percent of voluntarily idled land would be utilized for program crops if the traditional policies were eliminated (Frydenlund 1995). Analysis by FAPRI noted that ARP acres tended to have below-average productivity and concluded that only 50 to 60 percent would return to production if price expectations remained at the prevailing trend levels. FAPRI also concluded that only 25 percent of voluntarily idled land would return to production at these prices, because producing crops on the voluntarily idled acreage had always been possible (without loss of government payments) if farmers considered it to be profitable.

In an April 1995 analysis, FAPRI provided detailed estimates of the economic effects of an elimination of traditional price-support and supply-control interventions (FAPRI 1995a).[7] In terms of specific commodities, projected acreage of corn increased when ARPs were eliminated, driving prices down slightly. The elimination of acreage controls was projected to allow soybean plantings to rise by several million acres (2 to 4 percent), causing prices to drop by over 5 percent. Wheat acreage, in contrast, was projected to fall by about 3 percent (over two million acres) without the production incentives from deficiency payments, pushing market prices up. Elimination of the traditional programs had more pronounced effects for rice and cotton. Without deficiency payments, rice acreage was projected to fall by 20 percent (about 500,000 acres) despite an increase of more than 10 percent in market prices. Although projected cotton ARPs of 10 percent were eliminated, planted cotton acreage was projected to fall, as farmers switched to alternative crops.

At the aggregate level, FAPRI estimated in April 1995 that total mar-

7. This study was completed before Roberts made his Freedom to Farm proposal, but included analysis of a hypothetical "no program" scenario in which deficiency payments, base acreages, and ARPs were eliminated.

ket receipts for crops and livestock would decline slightly from 1996 to 2002 as a result of eliminating the traditional support programs. The decline in receipts was more than offset, however, by lower production costs. The resulting change in net income (omitting the government payments usually reported in farm income statistics) provides an estimate of the aggregate economic efficiency gains that can be attributed to eliminating the disincentives, restrictions, and incentives associated with the traditional support programs—and to the adoption instead of the input usage, acreages planted, and crop mix that maximized market returns. A gain of $818 million was projected, on average, over the seven years from 1996 to 2002, an increase in net farm income of 4.4 percent.

By the time the FAIR Act was signed into law in April 1996, market prices had risen compared to expectations from the year before. At these higher prices, ARPs would almost certainly have been set to zero for all commodities under the deficiency payment programs. The efficiency gains from eliminating the traditional programs would thus be lower than estimated by FAPRI at least in the short run, because an important part of these estimated gains came from bringing ARP acreage back into production. Higher prices also might have induced more land into production from the voluntary set-aside programs, but this effect cannot be attributed to a change in policy. Under the high prices of 1996–97, few income gains in agriculture could be attributed to the freeing up of production potential because of the shift to FAIR Act decoupled payments.

An important remaining land-use policy issue affecting production efficiency under the FAIR Act is size of the CRP. Here, the limited reach of the FAIR Act in restraining supply-control measures becomes apparent. The 36.4 million acre maximum-enrollment target amounts to continuation of a substantial land diversion under CRP contracts. Maintaining this level of enrollment affects the efficiency of production and, all else equal, puts upward pressure on market prices. FAPRI, for example, raised its assumption about acreage enrolled in the CRP from nineteen million by 2002 in its April 1995 analysis (before Congress extended CRP authority) to thirty million acres by 2002 in a May 1996 assessment of the FAIR Act—even though commodity prices were by then at the highest level in twenty years (FAPRI 1996).[8] Thus, the CRP

8. For wheat alone, CRP acreage that had been projected in the April 1995 FAPRI analysis to fall from 10.8 million acres in 1994 to 4.5 million acres in 2002 instead was projected in May 1996 to remain above 9 million acres, nearly 15 percent of anticipated planted wheat acreage. This FAPRI forecast proved accurate through 1998 when the first two post–FAIR Act CRP signups were completed.

continues to serve as a significant supply-control instrument under the FAIR Act.

Explaining the Politics of the FAIR Act

The policy changes made in the 1996 FAIR Act are relatively straightforward to assess in economic terms, but somewhat more difficult to account for in political terms. Most analyses of U.S. farm politics predating the FAIR Act were geared to an explanation of continuity in U.S. farm policy, not policy change. Some scholars had been willing to consider significant change prior to the FAIR Act, but the legislative politics of 1995–96 did not conform well to their expectations about how that change would occur. With continuous Democratic control of at least one branch of Congress since 1954, Cochrane and Runge argued in 1992, for example, that farm policy change would be extremely difficult without strong presidential leadership determined to "break through the special-interest, legislative bargaining process" (248). But in 1996, the most important policy reforms contained in the FAIR Act came from Congress, and were enacted despite considerable resistance from the president.

Party Control as a Determinant of Farm Policy

Prior to the 1996 FAIR Act, most policy analysts neglected the influence of party control in Congress on the content of U.S. farm policy. B. Delworth Gardner's account of the politics of U.S. agriculture emphasizes changing structures in Congress that had "diminished the role of political parties" and "weakened the influence of party leadership" (1995, 186). Likewise, Browne (1988) acknowledges an early history of party influence in U.S. farm policy debates, but concludes that the influence of party within the Agricultural Committees of Congress had long since been replaced by the influence of bipartisan coalition building, based largely on commodity-by-commodity "issue expertise."

Our review shows Browne was correct to recognize the historical importance for farm policy of party control in Congress. Republicans resisted farm program enactment in the 1920s, before Democratic ascendancy helped pass the Agricultural Adjustment Act of 1933. After the Second World War, the Republican capture of Congress in the midterm elections of 1946 helped facilitate passage of Title II of the 1948 Agricultural Act, a measure that—if it had survived—was designed to put postwar U.S. farm policy on a market-oriented track by lowering support prices. The Democratic recapture of Congress in the November

1948 election then led, by late 1949, to an extension of high price supports fixed at 90 percent of parity. When the Republicans regained control of Congress in the 1952 election, they successfully replaced these high price supports with a lower minimum parity level. In the 1954 midterm elections, the Democratic Party recaptured Congress once again, and farm programs reverted to heavier dependence on supply controls. Thus, during this important early period, the fluctuating fortunes of market-oriented reform efforts corresponded closely to changes of party control in Congress.

After 1954, Democratic control of the House of Representatives was maintained for the next four decades, from January 1955 through December 1994. Because it did not change, the latent importance of party control in Congress was neglected during this period. Most policy analysis *assumed* continuous Democratic control, then focused their attention on other variables within the context of this established majority regime.[9] Party control of Congress only came back into play as a more visible determinant of policy after the November 1994 election.

Party control has a noticeable role in shaping policy because of the powerful legislative assets institutionally provided to leaders of the majority, particularly within the House of Representatives. More than just voting majorities within all committees and on the House or Senate floor, these assets also include committee chair control over the legislative agenda. When the November 1994 midterm election produced Republican Party majorities in both houses of Congress, this powerful agenda-setting authority shifted from Democratic to Republican Party control.[10]

For a shift in party control to produce a significant change in legislative outcomes, two additional conditions are required. Rank-and-file

9. See Shepsle and Weingast 1994 for a discussion of the tendency for political science during these years to underemphasize the party control variable.

10. In the Senate, it is more difficult for the majority party leadership to control the agenda, particularly on the floor, than in the House of Representatives. The still powerful House Rules Committee, which functions in practice as an arm of the majority party leadership, performs a unique gatekeeping role by determining the terms under which bills can be considered for floor debate and final votes. The most important deliberations of the House Rules Committee frequently take place not in the committee room on the third floor of the Capitol, but in the speaker's suite of offices on the second floor, where the speaker, the majority leader, and the majority whip try to bring rank-and-file members into line before the committee meets to adopt a rule for a controversial bill. Minority party members of the Rules Committee can express their objections to a rule, and hope for favorable press attention, but not much more.

party members in Congress must first comply with the preferences expressed by their party leaders. At the outset of the 104th session of Congress in 1995–96, at the moment at which the Republicans savored majority control for the first time in four decades, average rank-and-file Republican members in the House were strongly united behind the party leadership. Republican House members voted in lockstep with one another and with the party leadership over 90 percent of the time. This was the highest level of support within a majority party in the House in more than a dozen years.

Not only must parties vote in a disciplined fashion for a shift in party control to produce a change in legislative outcomes; preferences regarding policy content must also differ between the parties on the key issues in question. In the election campaign of 1994, the Republican House candidates used unified support for their campaign platform, the Contract with America, as a device to drive home where they differed *as a party* from the Democrats. But party differences on agricultural policy were not presented in this 1994 House Republican manifesto, leaving open the question of whether there were such differences, and if so, whether the new Republican majority would make them an issue in 1995–96.

Arguments can be made that party does not matter anymore for farm policy. Inside the Agriculture Committees of Congress, whenever narrow commodity issues are at stake, party differences tend to be trumped by regional loyalties. Members will often be identified as advocates for certain commodities, rather than as Republicans or Democrats. This commodity identity partly reflects personal background, but more often it reflects regional constituent interests.[11]

The durable strength of commodity-based and regional preferences separate from the party label is vividly illustrated by radically changed party control in what used to be called the "solid Democratic South." The Deep South is now a more solid region for Republicans than for Democrats, and a key part of their party power base. Yet, House and Senate Agriculture Committee endorsement for highly protective policies for southern commodities has scarcely been altered by this shift in party alliance. What matters most about the South for agricultural pol-

11. Senator Richard Lugar of Indiana owns a family farm that produces corn, for example, while Representative Charles Stenholm of Texas is himself a cotton farmer. Democratic Senator Kent Conrad of North Dakota speaks for wheat, Republican Senator Jesse Helms of North Carolina for tobacco, Democratic Senator Patrick Leahy of Vermont for the dairy industry in his state, and so on across commodities and regions.

icy is that it still produces cotton, rice, sugar, peanuts, and tobacco—all commodities for which there is a long history of heavy market intervention.

The apparent power of commodity and regional loyalties over party differences also reflects successful recruitment and cultivation of Congress members by narrow commodity-based political action committees (PACs). Across all issues (not just agriculture), members of the House of Representatives tend to rely heavily on PACs for campaign funding; those that win elections receive on average more than 40 percent of their campaign funds from PACs (B. Delworth Gardner 1995). Agricultural PACs gave a total of $15.5 million to members of Congress in 1993–94, making them the nation's third-largest source of PAC money overall. Sugar, dairy, and peanut organizations stood out as especially large contributors, giving $4.1 million. These three commodity PAC groups gave House Agriculture Committee members an average of $18,341 each in 1993–94, and Senate Agriculture Committee members an average of $45,604 (Center for Responsive Politics 1995).

B. Delworth Gardner (1995) describes the differing campaign contribution strategies of various farm-commodity PACs, and finds those that make the largest contributions per million dollars of output sales (in rank order these are sugar, tobacco, cotton, peanuts, and dairy) tend to receive the highest levels of farm program support from Congress. Commodity PACs secure these benefits not by favoring one party over another, but by favoring whichever candidate seems most likely to get elected—which usually means incumbents. As a general rule, contributions to incumbents tend to exceed those to challengers by more than five to one.[12]

And yet, party control still influences farm policy. Party loyalties do not dominate in debates among producer groups, but they emerge as important when the enactment of legislation comes at issue. Farm commodity PACs and lobby groups alone lack the political resources to deliver floor majorities in the House and Senate.[13] Commodity-based

12. Thus, prior to November 1994 more agricultural PAC money went to Democrats than to Republicans, and after the Republican capture of Congress more agricultural PAC money went to the new majority party. During the first six months of 1995, for example, Republicans received 55 percent of sugar industry PAC donations from eighteen different organizations (which gave a total of $660,000), whereas in 1993 Democrats received 62 percent of sugar PAC money.

13. In the Senate, the geographic dispersion of American agriculture still gives farm interests alone surprising political clout. There are few "farm dependent" states, but there remain a large number of states with enough agriculture to be important. B. Delworth

agricultural interests are salient only to a small fraction of the members of Congress, well short of a minimum winning floor coalition. To be enacted, farm bills must be attractive, or at least acceptable, to a mix of constituencies with broader interests. These supporters are drawn from various constituencies, among them farm organizations that are not commodity based, agribusiness, environmentalists, food consumers, and advocates for the rural and urban poor. When this larger set of noncommodity-based farm bill constituencies is surveyed, policy preferences do divide sharply along party lines.

In broad terms across most issues, the Democratic Party still tends to support a significant domestic policy role for the federal government, while the Republican Party tends to favor less government and more of a role for the private sector. These basic differences in party preferences are carried into questions of agricultural policy. On issues of commodity programs, Democrats will often be more comfortable with higher price supports and more intrusive supply controls; this is also the traditional position of the NFU, which claims to represent the smaller-sized, higher-cost farmers who tend to identify themselves as Democrats. Republicans will more often be comfortable with farm income supports that do not constrain full-production agriculture; this is the traditional position of the Farm Bureau, which generally represents larger-sized commercial farmers and export interests. On issues of environmental policy affecting agriculture, Democrats are more likely to welcome land-idling conservation programs and environmental regulation, while Republicans are more likely to favor full production and to object to government environmental regulations, especially those that inconvenience commercial farm operations. On issues of nutrition and consumer protection, Democrats are more likely to argue for well-funded federal nutrition-assistance programs and extensive food safety regulations. Republicans are more likely to argue that business reputations for safety earned in free markets, balanced assessments of regulatory risks and benefits, and allowing crop prices to fall are the best ways to help consumers.

A measure of such divergent party leanings between Republicans and Democrats in Congress can be derived by comparing the "favora-

---

Gardner has listed the "top producing states" for seven different groups of farm program commodities: wheat, feed grains, and soybeans; sugar; cotton; rice; peanuts; tobacco; and dairy products. When these lists are combined, they include thirty-five out of the fifty states.

bility ratings" assigned to key members of Congress by a sample of constituency-linked advocacy groups. Consider the favorability ratings (from 0 to 100) made by six different groups: the AFBF, the NFU, the League of Conservation Voters (LCV), the Libertarian Party (LP), the National Taxpayers Union (NTU), and Bread for the World (BFW). For each of these six lobby groups, the ratings given to Republicans tend to differ sharply from ratings given to Democrats. Republicans tend to be rated high by the AFBF, the LP, and the NTU; and low by the NFU, the LCV, and BFW. Democrats are rated just the opposite: they receive high ratings from the NFU, the LCV, and BFW; and low ratings from the AFBF, the LP, and the NTU.

Table 14 shows the average ratings given to House and Senate committee chairs by these six lobby groups for three different Congresses: the 101st Congress of 1989–90 (the Congress that passed the 1990 farm bill, when all committee chairs were Democrats), the 103rd Congress of 1993–94 (the Congress that passed the Uruguay Round implementing legislation, when all committee chairs were still Democrats), and the 104th Congress of 1995 (the Congress that passed the 1996 FAIR Act, after all committee chairs became Republicans). From these ratings, it is clear that the Republican committee chairs who took over in the 104th Congress were viewed as ideologically distinct from the Democratic

Table 14. Advocacy Group Ratings of House and Senate Committee Chairs

	101st Congress: 1989–90 (Democratic Majority)		103rd Congress: 1993–94 (Democratic Majority)		104th Congress: 1995–96 (Republican Majority)	
	House	Senate	House	Senate	House	Senate
American Farm Bureau Federation	28.7	44.3	21.6	41.6	89.5	92.0
National Farmers Union	79.4	78.3	73.3	85.7	29.2	30.8
League of Conservation Voters	68.5	58.5	73.3	72.1	12.4	16.3
Libertarian Party	11.6	—	9.6	9.4	64.8	74.0
National Taxpayers Union	18.0	28.7	18.5	20.8	82.5	83.6
Bread for the World	74.9	82.7	62.6	79.2	12.9	18.6

Note: Derived from authors' calculations, based on favorability ratings (1–100) periodically published in newsletters by groups listed. Ratings shown are averages for all House and Senate majority party committee chairs. Rankings for 104th Congress are based on 1995 only.

chairs they replaced along every dimension. Key farm bill constituencies thus perceive highly significant differences between Republicans and Democrats.

These significant differences between Republicans and Democrats on farm policy issues do not mean one party is more favorably inclined toward farmers than the other. Both parties have traditionally advocated helping farmers, and in the end both parties tend to support generous farm bills. The capture of Congress by Republicans in November 1994 did not mean farm programs were soon going to disappear. Republicans in Congress had joined Democrats in rejecting the Reagan administration's call to cut out farm programs in 1981 and 1985, and a decade later Pat Roberts used the fact that thirty-three freshman Republicans were dependent on agriculture in their districts to convince the House leadership once again not to cut farm program budgets too severely. Still, the shift in party control did bring a significant movement in congressional preferences away from market-intrusive support programs and toward policies that did not constrain farm production or agribusiness marketing activities.

The Republican Congress Ends Annual Supply Controls

Because the Republican-controlled 104th Congress was more inclined than any Democratic Congress had been toward full production agriculture and agribusiness interests, the new Republican agricultural leadership set as one of its key objectives the elimination of unpaid annual land diversions under ARPs. In the early stage of the farm bill debate, however, another set of preferences brought to Congress by the Republican leadership first had to be addressed. This was the Republican preference (clearly visible in the NTU ratings shown in table 14) for greater federal budget discipline. A few Republican agriculturalists, led by Lugar, wanted this party preference for budget discipline to be applied to farm programs, but a much larger number, led by Roberts, opposed cutting farm program spending sharply. Roberts battled successfully on behalf of agriculturalists (when he broke with the Republican move toward devolution of power back to the states to defend food stamps as a federal entitlement) and emerged as the clear winner in the farm program budget battle.

What forces allowed Roberts and other Republican proponents of farm programs to prevail in this way, over the announced preferences of their own party leadership? The agriculturalists made good rhetorical use of their argument that farm program spending had already been cut disproportionately since 1985. But it was the relatively large number of House Republicans who still cared about farm programs, together with the relatively small savings that agricultural cuts could provide, that finally persuaded the House leadership to yield (including even Majority Leader Dick Armey, earlier the most vocal opponent of farm programs in the entire Congress). House Republican leaders knew the real budget battle of 1995 would take place over the much larger issues of tax cuts, welfare, and health care entitlements. To win this larger partisan battle, every single rank-and-file Republican vote would count. This gave Roberts and the farm district Republicans that he rallied the leverage needed to face down the Budget Committee and save farm programs (plus a variety of agribusiness subsidy programs) from the cuts for which Lugar was calling in the Senate.

Once Roberts and the other Republican agriculturalists had contained the threat of excessive budget cuts, they were faced with the next step in the process: trying to build a unified majority coalition, from their members on the Agriculture Committee, for specific policies affordable within the budget space they had worked so hard to win. Over most of the summer of 1995 this presented itself as a nearly insurmountable political problem. Because of virtually unanimous partisan Democratic opposition to the Republican budget agenda, Roberts knew he needed to craft a farm bill that could win the support of almost every Republican on his committee. A consensus would have to be reached among old-style agriculturalists and new-style budget hawks, and include not only his own midwestern grain constituents—who wanted ARP elimination and greater planting flexibility—but also the southern crop advocates on the committee who were generally opposed to any radical policy change.

In effect, Roberts never solved this coalition-building problem in the summer of 1995. His Freedom to Farm Act was attractive to some of his constituents, solved the budget problem, and made the elimination of ARPs affordable under the CBO rules, but it was blocked by Representatives Emerson, Combest, Baker, and Chambliss. When these Republicans balked, the Freedom to Farm proposal seemed dead. Lugar had likewise failed in the Senate to gain southern Republican support for a much weaker version of reform, one that continued traditional programs for cotton and rice.

Republican control of Congress was therefore not enough, by itself, to go beyond ARP elimination and generate a consensus for decoupled Freedom to Farm payments. Decoupling became politically acceptable only after a second enabling condition emerged in the summer and fall of 1995—the sudden and rapid increase in farm commodity prices. If this commodity price boom had not taken place, the Freedom to Farm Act would not have moved forward. The Republican 104th Congress most likely would have embraced something similar to the bill that actually passed the Senate Agriculture Committee in September 1995, a far more cautious measure that eliminated ARP authority and gave increased planting flexibility to feed grain and wheat producers, but maintained restrictive planting requirements for cotton and rice. This bill retained deficiency payments tied to production and market prices, and met budget requirements by increasing nonpayment acreage to 30 percent.

High Commodity Prices Induce Decoupled Subsidy Payments

Without steadily rising commodity prices in late 1995, Congress would never have been persuaded to embrace Freedom to Farm decoupled payments. Without above-trend prices, in fact, Roberts never would have proposed this approach in the first place.

When the idea of full decoupling had been presented ten years earlier, as the 1985 Boschwitz-Boren plan to replace traditional programs with fixed transition payments, it was firmly rejected by Republicans and Democrats alike. To Republican agriculturalists in Congress, the Boschwitz-Boren decoupling proposal too closely resembled a degrading form of welfare; and to prairie populist Democrats, it had seemed too much like a farm program designed by export-oriented agribusiness firms seeking low inputs costs. Farm commodity prices were also low in 1985, and were falling, making fixed decoupled payments less attractive to farmers as the legislative debate progressed.

Full decoupling of support payments from market prices or production decisions was not considered seriously by Congress as an option when it rewrote farm policy in 1990, and it remained essentially off the table when the 1995 farm bill debate began. In late 1994, Senator Lugar had solicited advice from knowledgeable participants in the farm policy process, and then promulgated a provocative list of fifty-three critical questions to guide hearings on the farm bill. Not one of these questions raised the option of decoupled payments (Lugar 1994).

Numerous experts had been arguing for increased planting flexibility prior to the 1995 farm bill debate, but through the winter and spring almost none advocated decoupling. The privately funded National Center for Food and Agriculture Policy (NCFAP) convened an extensive working group of academicians and leaders of farm organizations early in 1995, hoping to push U.S. farm policy reform. The NCFAP recommendations proposed a budgetary "capping" of farm program entitlements, but did not suggest decoupling (NCFAP 1995). A market-oriented proposal prepared for the Democratic Leadership Council also endorsed a budgetary cap, yet this paper explicitly rejected decoupling as an option, arguing instead for safety net payments that would be made "only when farm revenues fell below levels set by new federal standards" (Runge, Schnittker, and Penny 1995, 39). Fully decoupled payments ("payments to farmers *for being farmers*") were also rejected as a policy "disaster" at a conference of the market-oriented American Enterprise Institute (Wright 1995, 23).

Farm lobby groups were generating new policy ideas of their own just prior to the 1995 debate, but the new concept attracting the greatest attention, an idea pushed by a coalition of Iowa corn growers, was a plan for revenue assurance that would guarantee farmers 70 percent of normal crop income. This "Iowa Plan" represented a sharp break from the traditional method of sending payments to farmers, but it was not decoupling. It was still essentially a deficiency payment scheme, with annual payment guarantees coupled to production levels on individual farms and to market price outcomes. The flexibility contained in the Iowa plan was not especially valued by grain farmers in the more marginal regions of the Midwest where planting options were not so abundant; for this reason, the Iowa plan was resisted by wheat farmers in western Kansas, and hence also by Roberts (Kilman 1994).

Throughout the spring of 1995, as he fought to protect agriculture's portion of the CBO budget baseline, Roberts himself fought almost as hard to defend the reputation of traditional farm policies. He took credit for having earlier helped to devise the deficiency payment programs and was viewed by his colleagues in the House as a "fierce protector of the status quo in agriculture" (Penny 1994). There was no hint before mid-1995 that he was about to advocate a radical decoupling option. Roberts only came to the idea of decoupling in the summer of 1995 because it appeared to solve two problems for him—it neutralized the $6.5 billion in additional program expenditures that the CBO estimated were required for ARP elimination, and it offered aid to his Kansas constituents who had suffered crop damage.

Roberts was not successful at first in his effort to sell the radical idea of fully decoupled payments to his colleagues in Congress. His early advocacy effort revolved too much around a speculative and exaggerated warning of how vulnerable farm spending might be to budget cuts in the future, unless the moneys recently negotiated into the 1995 budget resolution were locked in through fixed payment contracts. This early argument for using decoupling to protect agriculture from future budget cuts was powerful at the time, but it was still not enough to persuade cotton and rice interests in the South, who remained firmly attached to payments tied to existing base acreages and market prices. Thus, when Roberts tried to rally a majority for the Freedom to Farm Act from his committee, internal Republican defections blocked his initiative.

It was not until later, after crop prices continued their sharp rise, that the idea of decoupling became sufficiently attractive, first to southern Republicans in Congress and eventually even to a significant number of Democrats, ensuring its final passage. By November 1995, market prices had risen well above the target price levels set by the 1990 farm bill. At this point it became clear that the Freedom to Farm Act would not just protect farm spending from future budget cuts; it would also bring an immediate *increase* in cash payments to farmers compared to existing law. Once Roberts was able to advocate Freedom to Farm as a way to increase spending on farmers in the short run, he received a more positive response. In just six months' time, a farm bill debate that had begun by making no reference at all to decoupled payments was able to coalesce around the desirability of this radical new plan. An unacceptable option had been transformed into an irresistible choice by rising market prices.

Alternative Explanations for the FAIR Act Outcomes

On the eve of the 1995 farm bill debate, few experienced insiders expected radical policy change. Those that expected change focused not on the variables we have stressed as decisive—party control of Congress and changing market conditions—but instead concentrated on a variety of other circumstances inside and outside the farm sector: the Uruguay Round agreement, federal budget pressure, the cumulative structural modernization in agriculture, the diminished potency of the farm lobby, and the emergence of newly dominant ideas about the appropriate role of the government in the farm sector. These other sources of change may help in future years to strengthen and extend policy reforms, but they had surprisingly little influence upon the 1996 FAIR Act.

The Uruguay Round Agreement on Agriculture

The final 1993 Uruguay Round Agreement on Agriculture does not provide a convincing explanation for U.S. farm policy change in 1995–

96, because the terms of the agreement were carefully written to require no support-level reductions beyond those already undertaken in the 1985 and 1990 farm bills. A reassurance that the Uruguay Round would require no immediate changes in U.S. farm policy was also built into the implementing legislation negotiations in 1994 between the congressional farm lobby and the Clinton administration. The Uruguay Round did have some influence on the pace and direction of policy reform in the European Union, but in the United States the international negotiation functioned more as a source of farm policy continuity than as a force for policy change.

More specifically, the elimination of ARP authority and the switch to decoupled payments achieved in the FAIR Act cannot be represented as a response to the Uruguay Round, because the international agreement was explicitly written to permit payments that were partly coupled to production and prices. The blue box agreement that emerged from the Blair House meeting in 1992 effectively exempted both U.S. deficiency payments and similar EU compensation payments from any Uruguay Round disciplines, on a condition that production-limiting programs such as acreage reductions would accompany those payments. Partly coupled deficiency payments and ARPs thus emerged from the Uruguay Round as privileged policy instruments. When the United States subsequently gave up these instruments in the 1996 FAIR Act, it was not in response to any international obligation or pressure.

In the course of the 1995–96 congressional farm bill debate, the Uruguay Round agreement was almost never mentioned, except in reference to export subsidies, partly because the farm lobby felt it had already secured most of what it could get from the Uruguay Round in the congressional debate of 1994. Reform advocates did occasionally represent the recent Uruguay Round outcome as a reason for U.S. farmers to have new faith in open world markets, but U.S. farm groups demonstrated, in the end, only limited faith in greater market orientation. Under the FAIR Act, the USDA retained its full authority for use of export subsidies up to the Uruguay Round limits, and import-competing commodities remained almost as heavily protected as ever.

Federal Budget Pressure

Federal budget pressures are also unconvincing as an explanation for the key reforms in the FAIR Act. Congressional budget rules certainly helped to drive the outcome, but these rules mostly functioned as a source of opportunity and advantage, not as a constraint, for agriculturalists in Congress.

When the farm bill debate began, Republicans in Congress thought they had a mandate from their 1994 midterm election victory to balance the federal budget by cutting government spending sharply. They learned the limits of that mandate as the year progressed. In agriculture, they first encountered effective resistance from their own internal farm block, led by Roberts. The House leadership eventually accepted less budget discipline in the small area of agricultural programs, in part to ensure the support it needed from farm district members in the much larger budget battle that was looming over tax cuts and federal spending levels. When the House Republican leadership subsequently overreached its mandate on these larger budget issues and lost the budget showdown with the president, fiscal discipline on agriculture was further relaxed. In the Senate, farm program proponents sweetened a bipartisan bill with expanded spending for conservation, nutrition, and other purposes. The allure of spending more through the farm bill eventually became too great, in an election year, for even the House Republican leadership to resist.

Actual budget disciplines thus proved relatively weak in the end, but the budget *rules* used by Congress were highly influential to the final FAIR Act outcome. Without the pay-as-you-go rule (which put a high budget cost on the option of ARP elimination, assuming traditional deficiency payments) and without the constantly obsolescent CBO budget baseline projections (making it possible to capture higher spending with decoupled payments, once market prices started to go up), there would have been no compelling reason for the Republicans to move toward decoupling in 1995. Pay-as-you-go rules alone would probably not have been enough to compel decoupling, even with a Republican Congress.[14] Once prices started rising, however, the baseline capture opportunity made decoupling attractive among Republicans.

The switch to decoupled income support allowed Congress to give farmers larger payments at a time of unexpected high prices, yet it was

14. Again, the compromise proposal forged by Lugar in the Senate offset the cost of ending ARP authority and generated the additional budget savings then being called for (at that point, roughly $13.4 billion over seven years) by placing maximum caps on per-unit deficiency payments and increasing nonpayment (flex) acres from 15 to 30 percent. Had prices been low, or had they been falling during 1995, the final farm bill probably would have adopted these more traditional instruments.

depicted within congressional budget rules as costing the taxpayer less than continuation of the previous programs. The surprising emergence of a lucrative baseline capture opportunity in 1995–96 provided by the rise in world prices meant that real budget discipline was not an influential force behind the 1996 FAIR Act.

The rise of market prices probably would have been enough to alter the final farm bill outcome, but in different ways, had Democrats controlled Congress in 1995–96. By late October 1995, rising prices had given House Democrats an opportunity to put forward their Family Empowerment Act, which raised loan rates to 115 percent of the five-year moving average of past prices, while promising as much budget savings (against the outdated CBO baseline projection) as the Republicans finally settled upon. Other Democrats backed the Fund for Rural America as a means to direct the baseline capture opportunity into expansion of traditional activist and intrusive policies. Democrats in a congressional majority would have found a way to make these expenditures fit into budget constraints, perhaps by pressuring the CBO to count higher loan rates and other generous short-term changes as having no effect on expenditures, because projected market prices were so high. Had these policies been enacted, they would have proven costly later when prices fell, but it was not budget pressure that determined the alternative choice of Freedom to Farm decoupling.

The Cumulative Structural Modernization of Agriculture

The unexpected shift toward decoupled payments under the FAIR Act cannot be attributed to the structural modernization that was continuing in the agricultural sector. The modernization of agricultural production since the Second World War has continuously improved U.S. competitiveness, and led an increasing percentage of farmers to favor cash payments and lessened market intervention over supply controls and high price supports. This systemic change does help explain the progressive movement toward a cash out of farm programs for export crops since the mid-1960s, and the impetus to eliminate remaining annual acreage set asides in 1995–96, a move that enjoyed wide (though not universal) support among farm groups. But the structural transformation that had occurred in agriculture had not led to widespread calls for decoupling when Congress took up the farm bill debate early in 1995. Indeed, outside of the rhetoric of GATT negotiators and a few academic reform advocates, decoupling continued to be held in disrepute.

Diminished Potency of the Farm Lobby

Perhaps the FAIR Act grew out of a long-term systemic change in the demography of the farm sector in a different sense. Honma and Hayami (1986), who use theories of collective action to explain rising levels of farm support despite falling numbers of farmers, posit a limit to this paradoxical result. Their analysis suggests that once farmers represent less than 5 percent of the total population, the political marketplace may start supplying decreasing levels of protection. When the 1995–96 farm bill debate began, farmers numbered under 2 percent of the total U.S. population. For years, it had been commonplace for reform advocates to hope for a policy change based upon "the long, slow erosion of farmers' political clout in Washington" (*New York Times*, 25 July 1994, 1). Reform advocates had in the past consistently overrated the influence of this demographic factor. But were the farm policy changes incorporated in the 1996 FAIR Act a reflection at last of demography-driven farm lobby weakness?

Despite a continued reduction in the number of farmers, the 1996 FAIR Act outcome suggests little in the way of a diminished political clout for farm organizations. For the deficiency payment crops, the most important policy changes in the FAIR Act—the end to unpaid land diversions and decoupling of income payments—provided more, not less, taxpayer money to farmers. For import-competing commodities (sugar and peanuts), farm organizations continued to win head-on battles against well-funded and widely publicized reform initiatives, and dairy policy changes in the FAIR Act added protection for high-cost producers in New England by imposing higher market prices on consumers.

The process through which the FAIR Act was enacted likewise provides evidence of continued farm lobby strength. The original Freedom to Farm proposal did not come from reform-minded crusaders within the new Republican leadership, or from urban-based farm program critics, or even from budget hawks. Freedom to Farm was an idea that came originally from the chair of the House Agriculture Committee, recognized at the time as one of the strongest Republican proponents of traditional farm programs.

The farm bill passage process has traditionally been explained by political scientists as a committee-based logroll. House and Senate agriculturalists use their initial control over the legislation-drafting process to assemble a multifaceted policy package sufficiently generous to a wide enough variety of constituencies to guarantee the minimum winning coalition needed for passage on the floor. This traditional process was somewhat weakened by fiscal pressures in the 1990 farm bill debate, when the reauthorization of farm legislation was ultimately constrained late in the year by a budget reconciliation process that the Agriculture Committees did not completely control, leading to the introduction of nonpayment flex acres as a cost-saving step. Compared to 1990, budget pressures appeared even stronger early in 1995, but a loss of Agriculture Committee control never took place. When Roberts failed in September 1995 to muster a majority within the House Agriculture Committee for a farm title to the Republican budget legislation, he was forced to turn to the House leadership for support, and it seemed the traditional process had been disrupted. Yet, even at this juncture, Roberts and the Republican agriculturalists retained the upper hand. To get the farm-bloc support needed in its larger budget battle, the House leadership backed Roberts in the drafting of a budget reconciliation bill that contained generous provisions for agriculture.

When President Clinton vetoed the budget reconciliation legislation, an even more generous stand-alone farm bill was prepared and quickly passed early in 1996. The bipartisan process used to enact this stand-alone bill conforms closely to the tradition of the committee-based logroll. Thus, the 1996 farm bill process, in its final stages, was closer to the tradition of secure farm lobby control than either the budget reconciliation battle of late 1995, or the budget-driven farm bill process late in 1990. The final legislative outcomes in the 1996 FAIR Act are different from the bipartisan logroll result that would have emerged had Democrats controlled Congress, but a similar logrolling process remains recognizable.

Emergence of Newly Dominant Ideas

A final alternative explanation for the FAIR Act is one based on the power of ideas. Perhaps the move made in the 1996 FAIR Act toward ARP elimination and decoupled payments was a product of more than just clashing interests; perhaps it represented a victory for market-oriented ideas and the notion, expressed even by a Democratic president, that the era of "big government" was over. Hall (1993) has argued that a growing discrepancy between policy outcomes and objectives can trigger either a first-order change (in policy instrument settings), a second-order change (in instruments), or a third-order change (in ideas, goals, and objectives). As the original New Deal idea that the agricultural sector needed help gradually became obsolete, from the Second World War onward the New Deal–era farm programs that were the institutional embodiment of that idea increasingly began to malfunction. Various first-order and second-order policy changes followed accordingly. Was the 1996 FAIR Act at last a third-order change, one that emerged from a larger contestation over fundamental goals and objectives, and one that brought with it a new set of dominant policy ideas?

Some scholars have identified the FAIR Act outcome as part of a larger idea-driven process. Coleman, Skogstad, and Atkinson (1997) argue that the FAIR Act reforms in the United States (and simultaneous farm policy reforms in Canada and Australia) resulted from such a change of ideas. Tweeten and Zulauf (1997) likewise argue that the FAIR Act reflects the emergence of a "new public policy paradigm for agriculture," one that is distinctive because it assumes that a long-term economic equilibrium has very nearly been achieved in the sector, and because it stresses the importance of economic efficiency and off-farm income in place of governmental interventions to boost prices by controlling supply.[15] Yet, it was not the rise to dominance of market-oriented ideas that drove the FAIR Act outcome.

Several features of the 1995–96 farm bill debate indicate that ideas such as small government, market orientation, and an end to supports for agriculture were not yet being embraced within U.S. farm policy. First, if the idea of market orientation had been driving the outcome, reform would have been felt by all crops, not just by the deficiency payment crops, where the budget baseline capture option existed. Second, if (as Hall argues) third-order changes are unlikely to occur without some kind of society-wide contestation and engagement, then there is little to suggest such a fundamental change in 1995–96.[16] There was actually far more social contestation and engagement over agricultural policy at the peak of the inflationary commodity boom of the 1970s (when labor and consumer interests were mobilized against high food prices), or at the depths of the farm crisis of the 1980s (when populist

15. The usage by Tweeten and Zulauf and also by Coleman, Skogstad, and Atkinson of the word *paradigm* is potentially confusing: most natural scientists prefer to use the word more narrowly—to identify new and purely descriptive understandings of unchanging natural realities—rather than broadly to describe a set of ideas, both descriptive and prescriptive, regarding constantly changing social conditions, institutions, and phenomena. See Kuhn 1962 for the etymology of *paradigm* in science.

16. Coleman, Skogstad, and Atkinson argue that their paradigm shift in agriculture was accomplished in 1995–96 through negotiations between state actors and group representatives, rather than through society-wide contestation.

farm groups were mobilized against high debts and low crop prices) than there was during the 1995–96 farm bill debate.

The capture of control of both houses of Congress by the Republican Party, after four decades in the minority, seemed at the time to signal a broad shift toward the idea of smaller government and the culmination of a steady erosion of support for New Deal interventionist approaches. But the Republicans learned the limits to their mandate for change, in their unsuccessful 1995–96 battles with the president over the budget and over entitlement program cutbacks.

If the 1995 Republican mandate had been somewhat stronger, and if a corresponding third-order change had taken place in U.S. farm policy, we can imagine what it might have looked like by recalling the policy ledger briefly touted by Roberts early in 1995. This ledger surfaced at a time when ideas of budget discipline and free market fundamentalism did seem to reign, just after the Republican election victory. The policy ledger, which the Agriculture Committee chair offered as common ground on which both Republican agriculturalists and the new House leadership could stand, promised to lower federal support expenditures and reduce market interventions. Beyond this, farmers were to benefit from elimination of ARPs and greater planting flexibility, from deficit reductions and lower taxes that the Republican Party would champion, from specific tax breaks, from lessening of burdensome regulations, and from strengthening of private property rights. If the market-oriented, small government Republican "revolution" (as the leaders themselves called it) had not been so easily turned back (by Roberts and his supporters for agriculture, among others), this ledger might have emerged as the essential outline of a new American farm policy: a loss of traditional producer supports, compensated by tax breaks and deregulation. This would have been a sharp break from the fundamental assumptions of the New Deal regarding both the role of government and the vulnerability of the farm sector to market forces. Farmers would no longer be protected from the dangers of the market by a benevolent government; they would be protected not from the market but from the regulators and tax collectors of the government itself, and they would be protected not as farmers but as citizens with property rights. The farm bill that passed in 1996 incorporated no such bold reformulation of basic assumptions.[17]

17. When the 105th Congress convened in 1997, short-term budget deficit projections fell mainly due to unexpected tax revenue from a continued robust economy. This allowed the Republican Congress and Democratic president to reach a deal on budget leg-

Outside of the agriculturalists in the Republican Party, the tone of the congressional debate over the 1996 FAIR Act also indicates that old ideas were alive and well. Most Democrats who voted for the FAIR Act did not like decoupling on principle, and many did not vote for the act because it incorporated this objectionable idea. Senator Wendell H. Ford of Kentucky, the minority whip, predicted a "taxpayer revolt" once it became clear that farmers would be paid money whether they planted a crop or not. Senator Tom Daschle, the minority leader, echoed Ford's view, arguing that "it won't take long for journalists to see farmers getting $300,000 for doing nothing" (*Congressional Record* 1996, S868). And Democrat Kent Conrad heaped abuse on the idea of moving toward decoupled payments. On the floor of the Senate, he likened the decoupled payments that the FAIR Act would provide in 1996 and 1997 to the poison-spiked Kool-Aid served by Jim Jones to his deluded followers at their mass suicide in Guyana: "It tastes good on the way down, but when you drink it you're dead" (S728).[18]

Nor was it only the populist wing of the Democratic Party in the Senate that continued to reject decoupled payments. Secretary of Agriculture Glickman remained a champion for traditional policy instruments; he derided the decoupled payments approach both as a dangerous shredding of the traditional safety net, and as a move toward a form of welfare. President Clinton was a steady advocate of the status quo. Throughout the farm bill debate, the president stressed that U.S. agriculture was on an "even footing" and needed no major policy changes. When he finally signed the FAIR Act, he hedged his endorsement with a promise to introduce legislation the following year to recouple some farm programs and payments to the market, to ensure that farmers once

islation that cut some tax rates and raised spending for some social programs—the deal that had eluded congressional leaders in 1995–96. The 1997 budget deal reflected a windfall capture opportunity on a grand scale not unlike the one that rising market prices had made possible in agriculture the previous year: because of increased revenue projections, Congress could claim to be passing legislation to balance the budget while simultaneously changing tax and spending policies in ways that slowed the speed at which that balance would be reached. In the 1997 budget legislation, Republicans were able to deliver some of the reduced estate, capital gains, and health insurance taxes promised in Roberts's 1995 policy ledger. The Republicans remained less successful on their stated objective of providing wide-ranging regulatory relief to farmers.

18. Populist Democrats from the Northern Plains states continued to have good political reasons to resist consolidation of any new ideas that would eventually take farm payments away from their constituents. In the northern plains, farm payments make up a significant share of net farm income, and the idea of unfettered market competition still has limited appeal.

again had a strong safety net. The policy debate in 1995–96 thus reflected a shift in party control and in market conditions much more than an emergence of newly dominant ideas about policy.

The Reform Problem after the 1996 FAIR Act

It required both the Republican recapture of Congress and unexpected high market prices to produce the surprising FAIR Act policy reforms of 1996. The combination of reforms that were passed (ending ARPs and embracing decoupling) and those that failed (retaining export subsidies and market interventions for import-competing crops) reflect the orientation of the new Republican majority and the opportunity created by favorable market conditions, but not a more fundamental shift in dominant policy ideas. Farm lobby groups retained control of the legislative process, offsetting a demographic loss with the usual investments in organization, attention to process, and financial campaign contributions. Federal budget pressure and commitments made by the United States in the Uruguay Round and other international negotiations offered little constraint on domestic policy.

Our earlier review of policy reform efforts in the 1970s and 1980s reinforces the conclusion that the combination of a change in party control of Congress and rising prices was key to determining the farm bill legislative outcome in 1995–96. The early 1970s were also marked by high prices, but market-oriented reforms were frustrated, in part due to continued Democratic control of Congress. Republicans controlled the executive branch of government during these years, and a Republican secretary of agriculture hailed high prices as an opportunity to shed government constraints and plant "fence row to fence row." It would have been relatively painless due to high prices to implement a full cutout of farm program supports in the 1970s, but Democratic control in Congress ensured a different outcome. The Democratic Congress opted to stick with traditional support policies, partly because of the unprecedented rates of inflation at the time. They used the high farm price interlude not to reduce government involvement in agriculture, but to lock in a safety net of target prices and loan rates that ultimately increased budget exposure and required intrusive supply controls when commodity prices subsequently fell.

The farm policy experience of the 1980s is also consistent with the conclusion we have drawn about the importance of party control and market prices. Republicans controlled the executive branch of government in the 1980s, and for a time the Senate as well. The administration pushed for bold policy reforms in 1985, and Senators Boschwitz and Boren introduced their radical scheme to end supply controls and switch to decoupled payments. These reform attempts were blocked in 1985 partly because Democrats still controlled the House, and partly because prices were low (and falling) as the debate proceeded. Falling commodity prices had likewise blocked durable market-oriented reforms much earlier, when a tentative move toward flexible price supports in 1953–54 by the 83rd Congress (Republican by a scant margin), was followed by a reversion to supply controls after Democrats recaptured control of Congress.

Not until forty years later, in 1995–96, was another farm bill written under a Republican House and Senate, this time with the help of the highest prices in two decades. It did not seem to matter, on this occasion, that the executive branch was under Democratic control, and that the president opposed the Freedom to Farm Act. A stand-pat Democratic president could not block a congressional embrace of change in 1995–96, any more than the reform-minded Republican presidents of the 1970s and 1980s could produce policy changes in their day over the objections of a Democratic Congress. Since the original AAA of 1933, in fact, change in U.S. agricultural policy has yet to be determined by the executive rather than the legislative branch of government.

Republican control of Congress without high prices in 1995–96 would have led to a result quite different from the FAIR Act. With Republican control but low prices, the choice, in all likelihood, would have been a cautious budget-cutting version of existing programs (something like the bill that passed the Senate late in 1995). Some Republicans might have championed a wider-ranging agenda for legislative change (along the lines of Roberts's policy ledger), but would have found their mandate limited. Even eliminating ARP supply-control authority would have been much harder for the Republicans had prices been low. Only high prices and a budget baseline capture opportunity enabled the new majority party to deliver more flexibility to their farm sector constituents, simultaneously with more subsidies, through decoupling. This deepened the slow cash out that had long been underway but did not put farm policy on a new strategic path of either a squeeze out, a buyout, or a cutout.

References

Browne, William P. 1988. *Private Interests, Public Policy, and American Agriculture.* Lawrence: University Press of Kansas.

Center for Responsive Politics. 1995. *Down on the Farm: Agricultural Interests and the 1995 Farm Bill* Washington D.C.: Center for Responsive Politics.

Cochrane, Willard W., and C. Ford Runge. 1992. *Reforming Farm Policy: Toward a National Agenda.* Ames: Iowa State University Press.

Coleman, William D., Grace Skogstad, and Michael M. Atkinson. 1997. "Paradigm Shifts and Policy Networks: Cumulative Change in Agriculture." *Journal of Public Policy* 16: 273–301.

Gardner, B. Delworth. 1995. *Plowing Ground in Washington: The Political Economy of U.S. Agriculture.* San Francisco: Pacific Research Institute for Public Policy.

Food and Agricultural Policy Research Institute (FAPRI). 1995a. "Policy Options for the 1995 Farm Bill." Ames: Iowa State University, FAPRI, April 27.

_____. 1996. "FAPRI 1996 Baseline Briefing Paper." CNFAP9-96. Columbia: University of Missouri, Center for National Food and Agricultural Policy, May.

Frydenlund, John. 1995. Freeing America's Farmers. Washington, D.C.: The Heritage Foundation.

Hall, Peter A. 1993. "Policy Paradigms, Social Learning and the State: The Case of Economic Policy Making in Britain." *Comparative Politics* 25: 275–97.

Honma, Masayoshi, and Yujiro Hayami. 1986. "The Determinants of Agricultural Protection Level: An Econometric Analysis." In *The Political Economy of Agricultural Protection,* Kym Anderson and Yujiro Hayami. Sydney: Allen and Unwin.

Ingersoll, Bruce. 1996. "Congress Passes New Farm Bill That Dismantles Subsidy Programs after Much Vote Trading." *Wall Street Journal,* 1 April, A16.

Kilman, Scott. 1994. "The Outlook: Some Farmers Favor Ending Farm Subsidies." *Wall Street Journal* 21 November, 31.

Kuhn, Thomas S. 1962. *The Structure of Scientific Revolutions.* Chicago: University of Chicago Press.

Lugar, R.G. 1994. "Draft Questions for Comprehensive Senate Agriculture Committee Hearings on the 1995 Farm Bill." Senate Committee on Agriculture, Nutrition and Forestry, Washington, D.C.

National Center for Food and Agricultural Policy (NCFAP). 1965. "Report of the Working Group on Price and Income Stability." 1995 Farm Bill Working Group Paper Series. Washington D.C.: National Center for Food and Agricultural Policy.

Runge, C. Ford, John A. Schnittker, and Timothy J. Penny. 1995. "Ending Agricultural Entitlements: How to Fix Farm Policy." Paper prepared for the Progressive Policy Institute, Washington D.C.

Shepsle, K.A., and B.R. Weingast. 1994. "Positive Theories of Congressional Institutions." *Legislative Studies Quarterly* 19, no. 2 (May): 149–79.

Stinson, Thomas F., Jay Coggins, and Cyrus Ramezani 1998. "Was FAIR Fair to U.S. Corn Growers?" Presented at the Annual Meeting of the American Agricultural Economics Association.

Tweeten, Luther, and Carl Zulauf. 1997. "Public Policy for Agriculture After Commodity Programs." *Review of Agricultural Economics* 19, no. 2: 263–80.

Wright, B. D. 1995. "Goals and Realities for Farm Policy." In *Agricultural Policy Reform in the United States*, ed. D. A. Sumner. Washington D.C.: AEI Press.

Young, C Edwin, and Paul C. Westcott. 1996. "The 1996 U.S. Farm Act Increases Market Orientation." Economic Research Service Bulletin 726. Washington D.C.: U.S. Department of Agriculture.

Chapter 8

4 US Agricultural Policy: the 2002 Farm Bill and WTO Doha Round Proposals[1]

DAVID ORDEN

Markets, Trade and Institutions Division, International Food Policy Research Institute, 2033 K Street NW, Washington DC 2006-1002, USA

Introduction

In May 2002 the US Congress enacted and the President signed into law a new 6-year domestic farm bill, the Farm Security and Rural Investment Act (FSRIA). The new law replaced what was known as the 'freedom to farm' legislation of 1996 that received attention when it was enacted for potentially marking the end of US farm subsidies. If Congress had adhered to the 1996 law (formally titled the Federal Agriculture Reform and Improvement (FAIR) Act) in the late 1990s both the level and the year-to-year variability of previous farm support outlays would have been reduced. But when a 3-year run of high crop prices collapsed in 1998, implementing the FAIR Act cost more for price support payments than anticipated and Congress authorized additional support payments on an 'emergency' basis. The 2002 FSRIA continued or expanded the FAIR Act support programmes that provide producer price guarantees and fixed direct payments for wheat, feed grains, soybean and other oilseeds, rice and cotton. It also restored a third tier of counter-cyclical support for a large portion of farm output in place of the emergency payments.

Passage of the new US farm bill was met with derision by domestic policy critics and a barrage of international condemnation. Nobel laureate Joseph Stiglitz disparaged the new farm support law as 'the worst form of political hypocrisy', while Malloch Brown, head of the United Nations Development Program, accused US policy of 'holding down the prosperity of poor people in Africa and elsewhere for very narrow, selfish interests'. In reply, the US House Agriculture Committee offered a strident defence of US farm policy, arguing it was 'important to national security, ensuring a safe, abundant, and affordable domestic food supply'. A document, posted on the Committee's web page, made the claim that 'Critics of US farm policy would cede our food production to unstable places like the Third World', and asked 'but in these times does any American want to depend on the Third World for a safe and abundant supply of food and fibre?'.

These sharply worded and disparate views of the US farm bill are indicative of the festering global conflict over agricultural policies and trade. Yet both severe critics of the FSRIA and its staunch defenders overstate their cases in a situation that is complex in many dimensions. The 2002 US farm bill takes few, if any, constructive unilateral steps toward reduction of subsidies. Nor does it expand the worst subsidy policies as abhorrently as sometimes implied.

Shortly after the FSRIA was signed into law, the USA submitted a proposal on agriculture for the World Trade Organization (WTO) Doha Round negotiations . The initial US proposal was out of step with the extensive support provided to farmers by its new domestic legislation. One provision of the US WTO proposal called for multilateral reductions of all tariffs on agricultural products to 25 per cent or less over a 5-year period. Likewise, the initial US WTO proposal called for consolidation of agricultural support measures into just two categories: exempt support having at most minimal trade-distorting effects on production; and non-exempt support that affects production and would be subject to WTO commitments with a ceiling after 5 years of 5 per cent of the value of aggregate national agricultural output. These were relatively strong proposals for multilateral agricultural policy disciplines.

Unfortunately, the misalignment of domestic farm policy and the early US Doha proposa l soon resulted in subsequent weakening of the US negotiating proposal.[2] In August 2003, the USA joined the European Union in putting forward a proposal deemed by key developing countries as offering too little subsidy restraint. This set the stage for a mid-term collapse of the Doha Round negotiations on agriculture.

To provide some understanding of the origins of this impasse, this chapter provides a brief description of the US farm sector and evolution of US policy in the 1996 FAIR Act. It then focuses on provisions of the 2002 farm bill and the subsequent US position that emerged in the WTO negotiations through the July 2004 framework agreement.

Background on the US Farm Sector and Policies

American agriculture today scarcely resembles the troubled sector of the Depression-era 1930s that led to farm support programmes. The modernization of American agriculture has created a tri-modal farm sector. At one end are the most efficient commercial farms producing the bulk of food and fibre; at the other end are various small farms that account for most of the enumerated units but produce only a small part of output. In the middle is a group of farmers caught in the dynamics of modernization – the mid-sized farms on which there have been substantial investments and on which there remain full-time employment opportunities, but which may lack an adequate resource base to be competitive in face of continuing advances in technology and market integration.

Reforms of farm policy have been undertaken as the production and income of farmers have undergone changes. The basic direction of policy reform has been a shift in policy instruments from acreage supply controls – combined with price supports above market-clearing levels – to less supply intervention and more direct income support, at least for crops that are exported. This policy evolution toward direct payments began in the mid 1960s when price support levels were lowered for maize, wheat and cotton to enhance US competitiveness, and farmers were offered direct payments as compensation. Support payments from the government increased from less that 6 per cent of farm income in the 1950s to over 20 per cent in the 1960s. A second move toward direct payments came in the mid-1980s, when price supports set in anticipation of inflation that did not materialize were reduced, with direct payments once again offered to farmers as compensation. Still further steps in the direction of replacing market interventions with direct payments were taken in the 1996 FAIR Act. Thus, the reform path Congress took in 1996 was the familiar one of a heavily compensated 'cash-out' of farm programmes.[3] Even so, some critical changes in farm programme instruments were made.

Unilateral farm policy reform in the 1996 FAIR Act

The 1996 FAIR Act initiated four unilateral changes in US farm policy compared to previous legislation. First, under the FAIR Act, supported farmers attained flexibility to plant whatever crops they chose (excepting most fruit and vegetables) on 'base acreages'.[4] Second, authority ended for the USDA to require annual acreage idling to limit crop supplies. Third, farmers received fixed income transfers, known as production flexibility contract (PFC) payments, that were based on past production and were independent of current market prices and farmers' planting decisions. These fixed income transfers replaced earlier 'deficiency payments' that had required continued production of the crop for which payments were received. Fourth, the price guarantees made to crop producers for any amount of output through 'loan rates' were capped under the FAIR Act at nominal levels well below market prices prevailing at the time. By 1996, mechanisms had also been put fully in place for most crops that allowed farmers to receive a cash payment (a 'marketing gain' or 'loan deficiency payment' (LDP)) if market prices (determined for each county for wheat, feed grains and oilseeds and by a common 'effective adjusted world price' for rice or upland cotton) were below their loan rate levels. Farmers received these cash payments instead of forfeiting those crops into government-owned storage. Thus the loan rates continued to support prices for producers, but market prices were freed from the loan rate as a floor level and the government was extricated from cumbersome commodity stockpiling.

The changes to farm policy made in 1996 were new partial reforms along the cash-out lines of movemen t toward direct income transfers instead of land idling or government stock-holding to push prices above free market-clearing levels. Farmers responded to the increased flexibility the FAIR Act allowed with substantial movements away from the crops to which deficiency payments previously had been tied, particularly reducing wheat acreage and expanding planting of soybean.

Despite its innovations, the extent to which the FAIR Act put farm policy on a less interventionist or less costly path was uncertain from the outset. The market-oriented policy innovations in the FAIR Act came at a time of high crop prices in 1995 and 1996. It is unlikely that farm policy would have abandoned annual acreage idling had market prices not surged upward . Since prices did rise, agricultural proponents in Congress were able to tout the end to acreage setasides and the introduction of fixed payments as deregulation of a large part of agriculture. Such 'freedom to farm' had been a rallying point for the Republican Party since the 1950s – the last time before 1995 that Republicans had controlled Congress and been in a position to set the farm policy agenda. Yet even Republican proponents of these agricultural policy changes knew full well that while the FAIR Act gave farmers more cropping flexibility it also increased support expenditures in the short term because deficiency payments under the old farm programme were falling as prices rose. Farmers liked the short-term outcomes of the FAIR Act of less regulation of their production and more direct payments. When challenged that the new farm policy neverth eless undermined longer-term support levels, proponent Pat Roberts (Republican, Kansas), then chairman of the House Agriculture Committee, opined that Congress itself was the long-term safety net. This has turned out to be the case.

Re-institutionalizing higher farm support in 2002

After spiking upward in 1995 and 1996, crop prices began to fall in 1997 and remained low through 2001. As prices fell, support expenditures built into the FAIR Act increased automatically because of the price guarantees provided by loan rates. The loan rate-related expenditures jumped up to $1.8 billion in calendar year 1998, then $6.8 billion in 1999, $7.5 billion in 2000 and $6.2 billion in 2001 (Table 4.1).

Once prices fell sharply, the PFC payments and built-in increased expenditures for price guarantees under the FAIR Act provided less support to farmers than would have been available under earlier farm programmes. Critics of freedom to farm decried it as 'freedom to fail', with low prices, reduced support and absence of a strong farm 'safety net'. A Congress closely divided on party lines couldn't resist responding to the criticism, stepping in firstly with 'emergency' legislation and then with supplemental annual appropriations for additional direct payments (called 'market loss assistance' (MLA) payments), as well as with new disaster

Table 4.1. Government payments to farmers 1996-2000 (US$ million). (From USDA.)

	1996	1997	1998	1999	2000	2001	2002 (F)
Pre-FAIR Programmes	-732	-575	-5	na	na	na	na
CAP, Other Env.	2,099	1,950	1,475	1,494	1,615	1,803	1,845
AMTA Payments	5,973	6,120	6,001	5,046	5,049	4,040	9,916
Marketing Loan payments/Gains	0	0	1,792	6,814	7,551	6,172	4,026
Emergency Assistance	0	0	2,841	7,804	8,492	8,405	908
Total*	7,340	7,495	12,380	21,513	22,896	20,727	16,971

*Includes small miscellaneous not shown.
Note: F = forecast, Env. = environmental.

relief and crop insurance subsidies. The effects on support policy were first to speed up delivery of scheduled fixed payments, then to increase their levels by 50 per cent, and finally to double the payments in 1999, 2000 and 2001. Subsequently, the 2002 farm bill locked in new expenditures in the event of low prices.

Support Provisions of the 2002 Farm Security and Rural Investment Act

The final 2002 FSRIA was signed into law by the President on 13 May 2002. Although budget assessments for the legislation were based on its provisions remaining in effect for ten years up until 2011, the new law was only specified for six years (to 2007).5

Three-tiered price and income support for grains, oilseeds, rice and cotton

The final FSRIA incorporates three tiers of support for grains, oilseeds, rice and cotton. Direct payments are continued at rates similar to those provided by PFC payments under the FAIR Act and are added for soybean and other oilseeds, which had not been included in 1996 (Table 4.2). Most loan rates were raised compared to the maximum levels under the FAIR Act for 2002 and 2003, but then the amounts by which the rates went up were reduced for 2004-2007 (Table 4.3). Loan rates were added for several commodities (dry peas, lentils, small chickpeas and groundnuts, as shown in Table 4.3, and for mohair, wool and honey). The FSRIA also fixed the loan rates in nominal terms, removing the discretion of the Secretary of Agriculture to lower the rates based on an average of past market prices that was provided in 1985 – when the government was still taking the supported crops into storage if market prices fell below loan rate levels. Once LDPs and marketing gains came into effect, market prices below loan rates no longer resulted in crops going into government storage, and the pressure to keep loan rates below market price levels was lessened.[6]

Table 4.2. Direct payments.

Crop	1996 Farm Bill rate (in 2002)	2002 Farm Bill rate (2002-2007)
Maize ($/bu}	0.261	0.028
Sorghum ($/bu)	0.314	0.35
Wheat ($/bu)	0.461	0.52
Upland cotton ($/lb}	0.0572	0.0667
Rice ($/cwt)	2.05	2.35
Barley ($/bu)	0.202	0.24
Oats ($/bu)	0.022	0.024
Soybeans ($/bu)	na	0.44
Minor oilseeds ($/lb)	na	0.008
Groundnuts ($/ton)	na	36.00

Table 4.3. Loan rates.

Crop	1996 Farm Bill 2001 rate	2002 Farm Bill 2002-2003 rate	2002 Farm Bill 2004-2007 rate
Maize ($/bu)	1.89	1.98	1.95
Sorghum ($/bu)	1.71	1.98	1.95
Wheat ($/bu)	2.58	2.80	2.75
Upland cotton ($/lb}	0 5192	0.52	0.52
Rice ($/cwt)	6.50	6.50	6.50
Barley ($/bu)	1.65	1.88	1.85
Oats ($/bu)	1.21	1.35	1.33
Soybeans ($/bu)	5.26	5.00	5.00
Minor oilseeds ($/lb)	0.093	0.096	0.093
Groundnuts ($/ton)	na	355.0	355.0
Dry peas ($/cwt)	na	6.33	6.22
Lentils ($/cwt)	na	11.94	11.72
Small chickpeas ($/cwt)	na	7.56	7.43

The target prices in the FSRIA for the new counter-cyclical payments are shown in Table 4.4. In contrast to loan rates, the target prices for most crops were increased after 2003. Counter-cyclical payments are made when the sum of the market price (or loan rate if the market price is lower) and the fixed direct payment is less than the target price. In the final FSRIA, farmers retain flexibility to plant a range of crops – thus they do not necessarily produce the crops for which they receive fixed and counter-cyclical payments. Both the direct fixed payments and counter-cyclical payments are made on 85 per cent of base acreage and 'payment yield' determined under the bill. Each participant has to make a once-only decision about bases and yields that will then determine their payment eligibility for the duration of the FSRIA. The rules in the FSRIA for determining base acreage are the same for both the fixed and counter-cyclical payments, but rules for setting programme yields differ for the two types of payment.

Table 4.4. Target prices.

Crop	2002-2003	2004-2007
Maize ($/bu)	2.60	2.63
Sorghum ($/bu)	2.54	2.57
Wheat ($/bu)	3.86	3.92
Upland cotton ($/lb)	0.724	0.724
Rice ($/cwt)	10.50	10.50
Barley ($/bu)	2.21	2.24
Oats ($/bu)	1.40	1.44
Soybeans ($/bu)	5.80	5.80
Minor oilseeds ($/lb)	0.0980	0.1010
Groundnuts ($/ton)	495.0	495.0

Programme payment yields for direct payments are unchanged for those crops previously covered under PFC payments. However, those farmers who update their base acreage are also given options to update yields for the counter-cyclical payments. This distinction between the two support programme in part reflects WTO considerations. The fixed payments had been reported to the WTO by the USA as Green Box payments that did not affect production. By not allowing yield updating, the USA reduced the likelihood of a challenge to the classification of these payments, even though updating of the base acreage was allowed. The counter-cyclical payments, in contrast, were likely to be reported as an Amber Box policy, similarly to the MLA payments. Even thought they were made on a fixed acreage and yield once a producer enrolls in the support programme, and do not require production of specific crops, the counter-cyclical payments are explicitly linked to market prices. Since the counter-cyclical payments were expected at the time to be reported as WTO Amber Box, no claim of being exempt from commitments was being made, and yield updating did not pose the threat of a challenge to their classification. Of course, because the payments will not necessarily be made on crops actually being produced, the USA was also likely to report these payments as not commodity specific, which made the WTO constraint on their use less binding.7

The final FSRIA includes only modest payment limitations for individual producers. Annual payment limits on direct payments, counter-cyclical payments and marketing loan payments (LDPs and marketing gains) are $40,000, $65,000 and $75,000, respectively. A 'three-entity' rule is retained that allows any individual to receive a full payment directly and up to a half payment from two additional entities. Thus, the maximum payment that an individual can receive is $360,000 per year. Producers with average adjusted gross income over three years of $2.5 million or more are not eligible for payments unless at least three-fourths of their adjusted gross income is from agriculture. For the payments related to loan rates, the limitations on individual eligibility are undermined by special 'commodity certificates' that enable producers who are facing payment limits to continue to benefit from repayment rates below the loan rates.

Divergent programmes for sugar, dairy and groundnuts

The FSRIA continues special programmes for sugar, dairy and groundnuts. These commodities have long been protected by import restrictions and high tariffs. Domestic consumer prices have been sustained above world market prices by also restricting domestic supplies, or by government stockpiling purchases, when necessary. Thus, the support programmes for these three commodities had undergone less of the conversion to direct payments and reduced market intervention by 2002 than had occurred for the main crops. Under the FSRIA, the programmes for sugar, dairy and groundnuts became more divergent.

Sugar

The USA is a large net sugar importer. In 1996, the FAIR Act continued the traditional sugar programme, with domestic sugar price supports fixed nominally at 18 cents per pound for raw cane sugar (about one-half of domestic sugar production) and 22.9 cents per pound for refined beet sugar (the other half of production). Sugar could be forfeited at these rates to USDA's Commodity Credit Corporation (CCC) under 'non-recourse' loans (for which the commodity collateral is accepted in lieu of repayment). Thus, no basic liberalization of the sugar market was achieved, and the loan rates continued to provide a floor under domestic market prices.

As prices for crops fell after 1997, a critical policy point for sugar emerged. By 2000 domestic sugar production, plus minimum imports to which the USA was committed, was about to exceed demand for domestic consumption and private stock-building at the supported domestic prices. To sustain those prices, the CCC accumulated sugar stocks and the USDA offered a sugar 'plough-down', in which it exchanged stockpiled sugar for destruction of some of the planted new sugar beet crop. The alternative of letting the domestic sugar price fall was rejected at this time. To avoid plowing down a growing crop in the subsequent year, a payment-in-kind (PIK) programme was initiated to trade CCC-stockpiled sugar for reduced beet planting. Supply pressure on the sugar market then eased in 2001, lessening political pressure for reform.

In the 2002 FSRIA, domestic producers succeeded in tightening the provisions of the sugar support policies. The loan rates were continued at the same levels as the FAIR Act and other adjustments made the sugar programme more lucrative for producers. The new farm bill reinstated an earlier stipulation that the sugar programme be operated to the extent possible at no net cost to the government.

To make these new sugar provisions operational, authorization for a PIK was continued and authority was restored for USDA to control supply through domestic marketing allotments, but only as long as imports were below 1,360,000 metric tons. The combination of the no-net-cost provision and the constraint on use of domestic marketing allotments – if imports exceeded the level set in the legislation – was designed, in the words of the US producers, to ensure that the USDA and US trade representatives stood 'shoulder to shoulder' with the domestic industry in opposing loosening of import restrictions. Together these provisions tie the hands of policy administrators: imports above 1,320,000 metric tons can not be offset by domestic marketing allotments to sustain the supported price, while allowing imports to exceed this level would induce violation of the no-net-cost provision if CCC stockpiling were to result. Thus, under the FSRIA the sugar programme has to continue to be administered with tight import restraints, which sets the farm bill firmly against sugar trade liberalization.

Dairy

For dairy products, import restrictions under TRQs remain the primary instrument for sustaining domestic prices above world levels. Related dairy provisions of the domestic farm bill are among the most complex among farm programmes. The 2002 FSRIA extends the two main dairy programmes: purchases by the CCC to support the price of milk used for various processed (manufactured) products and federal milk marketing orders that regulate markets for the fluid milk consumed directly. Under the FAIR Act, the dairy price support programme was scheduled to end on 31 December 1999, but it was extended in subsequent legislation. Under the 2002 FSRIA, the milk price support programme is renewed again. Support purchase prices are set to ensure that the market price of milk used in processing averages at least $9.90 per hundredweight. To provide this price support, the CCC is authorized to buy necessary quantities of butter, Cheddar cheese or non-fat dried milk. The Secretary of Agriculture retains the authority to adjust product purchase prices as deemed necessary.

Fluid milk markets are regulated by federal and state milk marketing orders retained under the FSRIA. Milk marketing orders define the relationship between prices of fluid and manufactured dairy products and maintain a regulated geographic price structure.

One modest 'cash-out' innovation under the FSRIA involved a new national dairy payment programme. The Dairy Market Loss Payments (DMLP) programme provided counter-cyclical payments for dairy producers until September 2005. These payments were made to dairy farmers on a monthly basis if the market price of fluid milk (called Class I) in Boston (Federal Marketing Order 1) was less than $16.94 per hundredweight. Payments were limited to 2.4 million pounds of milk per year per operation, which corresponds to the production from a relatively small dairy herd of about 135 cows. With this limit, about 50 per cent of total national milk production was likely to be eligible for the direct payments, but only about 30 per cent of the total production was from the smaller operations that produce less than the 2.4 million pound limit. For these small producers, the counter-cyclical payments created an incentive to expand production at the margin because the per-unit price they received was supported at the target price level. For the larger farms producing about 70 per cent of the milk in the USA, the direct payments programme was essentially decoupled from production -it provided a variable payment on a fixed output that was inversely related to the price of milk. This is similar to the counter-cyclical crop support programme in the FSRIA.

Groundnuts

Groundnuts are a minor crop but evaluation of the changes in policy in 2002 is informative about the economic and political pressures determining farm programmes. Under the 2002 FSRIA a regime of domestic price supports well above world levels for edible groundnuts, combined with long-established quotas on the domestic production eligible for sale in the US market, was scrapped in favour of direct cash payments – a substantial cash-out reform. Under the traditional support programme, domestic quota holders received preferential prices for groundnuts supplied to the domestic market for direct edible use compared to prices received for groundnuts (known as 'additionals') that went into processing (crushing into oil and meal) or were exported. Access to the domestic edible market by foreign competitors was restricted by TRQs. Thus, the traditional groundnut programme created an income stream from higher prices reserved exclusively for those domestic and foreign farmers who had privileged access. Even domestic farmers without quotas were barred from producing groundnuts for the domestic edible market but could produce groundnuts as additionals.

The 1996 FAIR Act had included some policy changes in the groundnut programme. The loan rate for quota groundnuts for the domestic edible market was lowered from $678/ton to $610/ton, a minimum national quota was also eliminated, and geographical production restrictions were partially relaxed.[8] Elimination of the minimum national quota allowed USDA to set an annual quota poundage eligible for the domestic market based on demand estimates. The annual effective quota poundage was reduced from 1.47 million tons for the 1995 crop year to 1.15 million tons in 1996, and averaged 1.24 million tons during 1996-2000. Despite the reduced quota, domestic groundnut production remained nearly constant. The average national production for 1996-2000 was 1.82 million tons, or 99 per cent of the average of 1.85 million tons for the years 1993-1995. As a result, under the FSRIA groundnut producers were selling a relatively smaller proportion of their output at a lower quota support price for domestic consumption, and a relatively higher proportion of their groundnuts at much lower prices in the additionals market.

One reason for the declining effective quota for the domestic edible market was the international trade agreements – to which the USA committed in the 1990s – that increased foreign access to the US groundnut market. Foreign producer access to the US domestic market for groundnuts increased from less than 4 per cent of consumption prior to the 1993/1994 marketing year to over 10 per cent by the 1999/2000 marketing year, due to market access provisions of the WTO and NAFTA. Moreover, under NAFTA the tariff rate for groundnuts is scheduled to decline to zero for Mexico in 2008, so imports are likely to rise. As long as the price in the US domestic market remained above the price in world markets, as it had under the groundnut quota programme, other foreign producers also had incentives to seek additional access in trade negotiations.

The 2002 FSRIA, however, made a fundamental change to the groundnut programme. Under the FSRIA groundnuts receive support through policies similar to other crops. The quota-based dual market structure is replaced with a support programme of direct payments that includes the basic three components: loan rates and related payments, fixed direct payments and counter-cyclical payments. In addition, groundnut quota holders are compensated for their loss of quota rights.

The new groundnut programme is quite lucrative for both former quota holders and for producers of groundnuts that were once sold as additionals. The cash-out has an estimated cost of $4 billion over 10 years. Under the FSRIA, any producer of groundnuts is eligible for a loan rate of $355/ton on all current production. Those who qualify as an 'historic producer' of quota or additional groundnuts are also guaranteed a direct fixed payment of $36/ton and a target price under the counter-cyclical payment programme of $495/ton for the output from 85 per cent of historic groundnut acres and recent yields. Thus, for a traditional producer who continues to grow groundnuts, the minimum average revenue would be $474/ton on a level of production equal to recent output ((0.85) x ($495) + (0.15) x $355 = $474). The traditional groundnut producers also attain planting flexibility. They can receive the fixed payments ($36/ton) and the counter-cyclical payments while growing another crop if that is deemed more profitable. If groundnuts are grown, the new guaranteed revenue is much higher than that received in the past by additional producers, who had only been eligible for a loan rate of less than $200/ton. And for 5 years, the quota holders attain an additional $220/ton. Thus, for 5 years the total guaranteed revenue was $694/ton for a quota owner, compared to $610 under the FAIR Act. After 5 years, guaranteed revenue for a quota holder falls below the previous guarantee, but the quota buy-out of $220/ton for 5 years compares favourably with market prices for many sales of quota rights before the 2002 farm bill was passed. Apparently, these market prices included a discount for the possibility that the groundnut quota programme would not last forever.

There are a number of additional political economy aspects to the cash-out adopted for groundnuts in the USA in 2002. Rising imports and potential trade liberalization that increased foreign access to the domestic edible market were used as arguments to motivate a policy change as being necessary to 'preserve the domestic industry'. The preservation argument was central – the intent of the new groundnut support policy is to sustain the domestic industry, not to cause its demise. The future of the domestic industry can not be guaranteed under the FSRIA because farmers can switch from groundnut production under planting flexibility, whereas under the earlier quota system groundnuts had to be grown to attain the high domestic price. But domestic producers are well compensated for lower market prices under the FSRIA, and incentives for domestic groundnut production are improved for both the traditional growers of additionals and new entrants. In contrast, one group that is disadvantaged by the change in US groundnut policy is foreign producers who had attained TRQ market access. Unlike domestic producers, the foreign producers do not receive any payments as compensation for the lower US domestic groundnut prices. Under the FSRIA, with lower prices access to the US market is of less value to foreign producers, but the USA is better positioned to liberalize groundnut trade. This positioning is quite in contrast to the sugar policies adopted in 2002.

It is noteworthy that US sugar producers did not endorse a cash-out reform similar to groundnuts in 2002, instead opting to tighten restrictions under their traditional price support programme. The sugar producers faced the same farm bill budget as groundnut producers, and could have sought to have some of the money Congress made available for agricultural support used for sugar payments. Sugar potentially faces even more pressure from imports (tariffs on sugar imports from Mexico also are eliminated in 2008 under NAFTA and world sugar prices remain far below the US levels). Sugar producers are widely held to be a more powerful lobby than groundnut producers. The sugar industry didn't seek new cash-out payments under these circumstances; apparently the industry expects to hold on to its current support programme for some time. Yet trade liberalization for agriculture is unlikely to occur without being accompanied by some sort of cash-out for sugar producers in the USA.

Part of the reason the sugar industry did not endorse a cash-out in 2002 lies in the domestic structure of the industry. Cane sugar is characterized by large production units, in Florida in particular, making payment limits per operation a political obstacle to the adoption of direct support. A second reason lies in the prospective short-term cost of a sugar cash-out. For each penny of payments per pound of sugar under a marketing loan programme, the cost is around $180 million, assuming payments on recent levels of output. The PIK programme reduced sugar beet acreage by about 6 per cent in 2001, which, all else being equal, reduced total domestic sugar production by about 3 per cent. If, instead of constraining supply market prices had been allowed to fall below the loan rate with compensating cash payments, the programme cost would have risen from $200 million to as high as $1 billion per year, depending on the price responsiveness (elasticity) of demand. Marketing allotments and PIK programmes were anticipated as being in use for at least several years in 2002, implying that a cash-out would prove costly over this time period. Longer term, the cost would depend on uncertain supply and demand conditions, including future international trade agreements, as well as on the supply and demand responses to lower prices.

Conservation programmes

Conservation and environmental programmes play an important role in agricultural production decisions. Through these programmes, producers receive cost-share, rental and other direct payments in return for using specified farming practices or for setting aside land to aid conservation. The FSRIA continues and, in most cases, expands various conservation/ environmental programmes. The programmes that retire environmentally sensitive land from crop production are extended, but most new expenditures were targeted for conservation measures for livestock operations and land that stays in production.

Idling of farmland under the Conservation Reserve Program (CRP) has been the primary conservation/ environmental programme in effect since 1985. The final FSRIA increased the land-idling authority of the CRP to 39.2 million acres, compared to 36.4 million under the FAIR Act. This increase in CRP acreage will add marginally to its output-reducing effect.

The Environmental Quality Incentives Program (EQIP), which provides technical assistance, cost sharing and incentive payments to assist livestock and crop producers with conservation and environmental improvements, is expanded under the FSRIA. Cost sharing (up to 75 per cent) or incentive payments can be provided for a wide range of practices, including nutrient management, livestock waste handling, conservation tillage, terraces and filter strips. EQIP is unique in its relative focus on livestock producers.

Under the FSRIA, a new Conservation Security Program (CSP) was also initiated. The CSP is focused on land-based practices and specifically excludes livestock waste-handling facilities. Producers will develop and submit a conservation plan to USDA that identifies the resources and designated land to be conserved. The plan can include conservation practices that fall within one of three tiers provided in the programme. Producers entering into first-tier conservation security contracts will receive a base payment for conducting the practices designated in the conservation plan. Producers may also be eligible for bonus payments for implementing additional (tiers two and three) conservation measures.

The new mix of conservation support programmes under the FSRIA calls attention to the policy discretion involved in US programmes regarding acreage idling for environmental purposes. While the USA has maintained the CRP and related long-term land-idling since 1985, it is not under any international obligation to do so. Historically, the USA has enacted conservation land-idling as a supply control measure during times of low prices (the 1930s, the 1960s and again in 1985) and has let these programmes expire when market demand is relatively strong, as in the 1970s. Competitors in world markets don't object to land-idling in the USA, which reduces US production and gives the foreign producers a competitive advantage, but the CRP has been criticized for unnecessarily restricting output and pushing world prices for basic grains higher than otherwise. Were the USA to shift more fully toward support for use of environmental practices on land that continues in production in the future, along the lines of the CSP, output could expand, but competitors in world markets would have little basis for objections under the WTO or other trade agreements.

The conservation programmes of the FSRIA also bring attention to the effects of domestic environmental regulations on agricultural competitiveness.

Should EQIP or CSP payments be considered as production subsidies? Once domestic regulations are enacted, requiring certain environmental performance, producers are obliged to comply. The EQIP expenditures reduce compliance costs of producers. Under an alternative approach, these could be viewed as costs that should be borne by producers (the polluter pays) that might affect agricultural production levels. Thus, the EQIP expenditures can be considered production subsidies, but under WTO rules any subsidies that offset (but do not exceed) environmental costs of measures undertaken by producers are eligible for classification in the Green Box and are exempt from limit comrnihnents. Likewise, subsidies under the CSP are, in principle, offsetting costs related to maintaining environmental quality, and thus qualify as being in the WTO Green Box, even if adoption of the supported practices is not required by domestic regulations.

Trade provisions

The FSRIA continues and modifies programmes designed to develop and expand commercial outlets for US commodities in world markets and to provide international food assistance. Increased emphasis is placed on high-value and value-added products and export programmes oriented toward development of commercial markets. The subsidizing Export Enhancement Program (EEP) is re-authorized in the FSRIA, although this programme has not been used for crops in recent years because of the loan rate payments, which have allowed market prices for crops to fall as low as required in order to make US products competitive in world markets.

For dairy products, US domestic prices can exceed world levels. The Dairy Export Incentive Program (DEIP) is extended and pays cash subsidies that allow dairy product exporters to buy US products and sell them abroad when international prices are below domestic prices. Removing products from the domestic market with the DEIP helps sustain domestic price levels and thus plays a role in the milk price support programme . The DEIP quantities and dollar amounts are subject to WTO limit commitments.

There was also a question of whether total payments for non-exempt crop support under the FSRIA would violate the US Amber Box limit commitment in the WTO Uruguay Round Agreement on Agriculture (URAA). The FSRIA requires the Secretary of Agriculture 'to the maximum extent practicable, to adjust domestic commodity program expenditures to avoid exceeding allowable WTO domestic support ceilings'. Although exceeding the US commitment is possible with very low prices, it is unlikely. The USA may continue to use the de minimis exemption for non-commodity-specific support to reduce the probability that the new FSRIA counter-cyclical payments will count against its WTO constraint. A number of countries are finding other clever tricks that can be used to meet the letter of their WTO commitments without substantially changing the support provided to agriculture.

Finally, the FSRIA introduces several new technical trade barriers. Country of origin labelling was mandated by 2004 for meats and fresh fruit and vegetables. Increased importation for fattening in the USA of feeder cattle from Mexico and feeder pigs from Canada provided much of the impetus for some agricultural producers to lobby for these new rules, but their implementation remained delayed through 2005. In order for livestock to be labelled as a product of the USA, the animals have to be born, raised and processed domestically. The country of origin labelling requirement would impose implementation costs that could reduce access of foreign products to the US market or lead to price discounts for foreign producers. In the case of a few specialty products (catfish and ginseng) the FSRIA includes definitions that preclude foreign products from the domestic market.

The US in the Doha Round: Shifting Away from Reforms After the 2002 Farm Bill

The URAA committed WTO members to further agriculture negotiations starting in 2000. These sectoral negotiations had not progressed very far when they were incorporated into the Doha Round. The Doha negotiations thus offer a test of the hypothesis that the Uruguay Round set the stage for more substantial subsequent agricultural trade liberalization, and possibly the opportunity to strengthen the disciplines on agricultural support and protection .

Agriculture emerged high on the agenda as the Doha Round was launched in November 2001. Adoption shortly thereafter of the costly 2002 US farm bill then drove a wedge between the USA and the Cairns Group of agricultural exporters, and even allowed the EU to fault the USA for increasing subsidies. Despite the setbacks to reform in the 2002 US farm bill and these political considerations, shortly after the farm bill was signed into law the USA submitted a strong initial proposal on agriculture for the Doha Round negotiations.

The initial US proposal called both for changes in the instruments through which reduction commitments are measured and for significant new disciplines on the levels of agricultural tariffs and subsidies. The USA proposed that the linear tariff reduction rules of 1995-2000 be replaced by the use of a 'Swiss formula' for future cuts that would bring high tariffs down more rapidly than low tariffs. A maximum tariff rate of 25 per cent would apply after 5 years. The initial US proposal also called for the Blue Box exemption from WTO limitation commitments to be abolished. Any former Blue Box expenditures were to be subjected, along with other non-exempt support, to an aggregate ceiling of 5 per cent of the total value of agricultural production. The US proposal called for a complete elimination of direct export subsidies and export taxes and phased reductions in controls on agricultural trade by state enterprises. Special safeguard provisions regarding TRQ commodities would be eliminated and clarifications made about the use of export credits (and other forms of implicit trade subsidization) and about how TRQs were administered. The US proposal acknowledged that special and differential treatment would apply to developing countries. These criteria were spelled out in some cases and left vague in others.

Overall, the early US Doha Round proposal, like the US 'zero option' in the Uruguay Round, called for substantial reductions of trade barriers in world agriculture. Yet in several respects, the US proposal was out of step with the extensive support provided to farmers by the 2002 legislation. In other respects, the US proposal was designed not only to bring substantial trade liberalization but to do so in ways that were particularly easy on its own farm programmes. If other countries 'called the US' bluff', the US has relatively few high protective tariffs that would have to reduced sharply with the Swiss formula. It also seemed easy for the US to call for eliminating Blue Box exemption, since the US unilaterally gave up support programmes tied to annual land-idling when it adopted 'freedom to farm' policies eliminating such restrictions (but, as described above, not eliminating paid longer-term land-idling under conservation programmes) in its 1996 farm bill. The burdens of reform called for on export subsidies and state trading enterprises by the US proposal would mostly fall elsewhere. Still, enacting the initial US proposal would have imposed some significant restrictions on it own farm programmes. Bringing down US tariffs on sugar and dairy products would require changes in entrenched domestic support programmes. The proposed limit for non-exempt domestic support of 5 per cent of the aggregate value of total agricultural production would leave the USA with a cap of about $10 billion, just half of its current WTO limitation (not counting *de minimis,* which the US proposal did not address). Meeting that cap would entail reducing support, unless clever new schemes to shield expenditures were concocted. Thus, at face value, the initial US Doha Round proposal could have disciplined the agricultural subsidies and protection of the USA compared to current levels, as well as those of other WTO member countries.

As in the Uruguay Round, most aspects of the US negotiating proposal were looked at favourably by the Cairns Group of developed and developing country agricultural exporters, while the EU and other countries with protected agriculture found it as unacceptable as the earlier zero option had been. The EU put forth its own Doha Round position, calling for a repeat of the linear Uruguay Round tariff cuts (15 per cent minimum and 36 per cent average); reduction of Amber Box expenditures (by 55 per cent), while maintaining the Blue Box exemption; partial elimination of export subsidies (a 45 per cent cut); and provisions related to various concerns such as animal welfare and added protection of geographical indications of product origin under international law. Japan and a few other countries mostly opposed agricultural trade liberalization. Brazil, India and China called for substantial cuts or elimination of domestic support by developed countries, elimination of export subsidies, large cuts in tariffs at least by the developed world (an 'offensive strategy'), and for retaining or expanding various forms of special and differential treatment for developing countries (a 'defensive strategy'). Efforts to forge consensus by striking various compromises among these positions failed to achieve an agreement in spring 2003, as called for in the Doha negotiating schedule.

With the positions of governments far apart, as a September 2003 WTO ministerial meeting in Cancún approached, in August the USA and the EU negotiated a brief framework document; convergences between the USA and the EU, at least in terms of a basic negotiating framework, came earlier in the Doha Round than it had in the Uruguay Round. The US-EU document became the basis for the intended Doha Round mid-term ministerial text, but it met with the strong resistance of the new 'G-20' group of developing countries when presented in Cancún.

The US-EU proposal struck some awkward compromises and was short on details – no levels were specified for the various measures proposed in the negotiating framework, leaving the document at best a template for much contention in the future. For example, the proposal called for reducing Amber Box support policies 'in the range of [] per cent – [] per cent', without providing numbers. One of the biggest changes from the initial US proposal came not only in retention of the Blue Box, but in the weakening of the eligibility criteria for its use by excluding the requirement that these payment s be associated with production limiting programmes. This about-turn in approach represented catching up of the US negotiating stance with changes made in the 2002 farm bill; its renewed counter-cyclical support payments would fit in the redefined Blue Box but not under the original Uruguay Round criteria. More positively, the US-EU proposal called for some reduction in *de minimis* payment limits, a limit of 5 per cent of production value for the Blue Box, and a net limit on Amber Box, Blue Box and *de minimis* of significantly less than their sum in 2004.

On export subsidies, the US-EU proposal called not for full elimination, but only for elimination for unspecified products of interest to developing countries over an indeterminate period, together with unstipulated cuts to expenditures for other commodities. Essentially, this backed off from the stronger initial US proposal at the insistence of the EU. Similar disciplines were to be applied to any trade-distorting elements of government-subsidized export credit programmes. Tariff reductions were to fall into four categories of unspecified relative sizes: those to be reduced to zero, those to be reduced linearly, those to be subject to a Swiss formula and those for a few highly protected commodities that were to be allowed to remain above some maximum level, but only if additional market access were negotiated through TRQs or some other mechanism. The US-EU proposal acknowledged the principle of special and differential treatment for developing countries, allowing lower tariff reductions and longer implementation periods, a new special safeguard for import-sensitive commodities, and promising duty-free access for 'at least [] per cent of imports' from those countries (again unspecified).

Whereas, in the Uruguay Round, the Cairns Group would have voiced objection to a proposal along the US-EU lines, in the Doha Round it was the new block of developing countries, led by Brazil, India, China and South Africa, which orchestrated dissent. The 'G-20' proposal put forward as an alternative in Cancún called for product-specific reductions in AMS Amber Box support, elimination of the Blue Box, a cap on direct income support payments in the Green Box and cuts to *de minimis* support expenditures. It called for reduction of all tariffs of developed countries to some maximum level, expansion of market access under TRQs, an end to special safeguards for developed countries and elimination of all export subsidies. Several of the strongest of these proposals were similar to those put forward by the USA in its initial proposal, but subsequently abandoned. The G-20 also called for continuation of special and differential treatment and a new special safeguard for developing countries.

The collapse of the Cancún conference left it uncertain how far apart the negotiations on agriculture remained. One of the most visible conflicts in Cancún about agricultural trade took place not over the general provisions of the negotiating framework, but over a specific proposal by four low-income African countries (Benin, Burkina Faso, Chad and Mali) to eliminate subsidies and protection for cotton, one of their principal export crops. Building on the concept of products 'of interest to developing countries', these African nations made the argument that cotton was of critical importance to their development and to the livelihood of two million poor farmers, and thus should be subject to liberalization and elimination of subsidies, even in advance of other agricultural trade reform. Until this was accomplished for cotton, the African countries argued that a mechanism should be arranged to provide cash compensation to them for the damage done to their export incomes. A separate case by Brazil against US cotton subsidies was also under review in the WTO dispute settlement process.9

The African cotton case was particularly poignant in 2003 because world prices over the previous few years had been below production-stimulating (Amber Box) US loan rates, so the most egregious form of price-supporting subsidies in a developed country had been in force. But the structure of the US cotton programme, with both guaranteed producer prices and direct and counter-cyclical payments somewhat decoupled from production, differs little from the domestic programmes for other supported crops. Barring US trade negotiators being authorized to take on a contentious internal political battle, they would not be able to accede to such specific liberalization for one crop. The USA is likewise unwilling to open the door to consideration of explicit international compensation payments for damage done by subsidy policies. Not only would international transfers be involved, but compensation for policies that continued in effect differs from the compensation accompanying changes in policy instruments, as has characterized the cash-out of domestic US farm support programmes.

The July 2004 framework agreement on agriculture

The divergent positions that prevented agreement in Cancún continue to demonstrate how difficult it is to achieve multilateral trade liberalization and subsidy reduction for agriculture. In subsequent months negotiations intensified, with the goal of achieving the planned framework agreement by July 2004, before the US presidential elections. In these efforts, both the USA and the EU are constrained by their domestic farm programme commitments and other developed countries (Japan and other members of a group known as the G-10, for example) retain even higher farm support levels. The USA has long been committed to the concept that farm support can be divided between trade-distorting policy instruments and those that provide income transfers without distorting trade. Even the US zero option proposal in the Uruguay Round addressed only elimination of trade-distorting policies, leaving room for unlimited expenditures that were arguably decoupled from production. The WTO panel ruling in the case of Brazil against US cotton subsidies notwithstanding, the USA is not prepared to have its latitude for making domestic support payments constrained very much by a Doha agreement. But in January 2004, the USA returned in part to its earlier position, arguing in particular for a firm date for ending all export subsidies.

The EU has moved more slowly than the USA away from subsidy payments directly tied to farm production and toward income support with less explicit linkages to output. EU partial reforms of the CAP in this direction in July 2003 (see Chapter 2) gave it additional flexibility in its WTO positions, but not enough to accede easily to full elimination of export subsidies. Under pressure to do so, the EU called for export subsidy elimination to be accompanied by strong disciplines on other export assistance, including credit programmes/ guarantees and food aid (both used primarily by the USA), and activities of exporting state trading enterprises.

In the area of tariffs and market access, there remain difficult conflicts between ambitious goals for market opening and continued provision of high levels of protection to various 'special' or 'sensitive' products as designated by importing countries. A multi-tier approach to tariff reductions leaves latitude for substantial tariff differences among commodities and for numerous cases in which any tariff reductions agreed upon do very little to open market access. On top of this, the developing countries, through groups known as the G-33 and G-90, are pressing the case for their own special and differential treatment, including new special safeguards and limited tariff reductions. The net result of these proposals may well turn out looking much more like Swiss cheese – disciplines full of holes for high protection -than like the liberalized regime that would result from application of a tariff-cutting Swiss formula. There is a divergence of views here between advocates of liberalization of agricultural trade and many developing countries and development advocates. Trade liberalization proponents are wary of tariff exceptions, including special and differential treatment, that leave high levels of trade protection in place. Yet many development advocates and governments of developing countries are adamant that they be granted room to retain trade barriers.

By July 2004, after nearly 3 years of Doha negotiations, it proved possible only to reach a very broad WTO framework agreement, leaving many agricultural issues unresolved. The agreement reached on 30 July (Annex A for agriculture) specifies that 'substantial improvements in market access will be achieved for all products', but also that there will be 'flexibilities for sensitive products'. No specifics about the structure of commitments to cut tariffs were agreed upon, except an indication that cuts will be from bound rates, that a tiered approach will be used and that some expansion will be required for TRQs. Developing countries are to receive special and differential treatment on market access commitments in terms of lesser cuts, the ability to designate some commodities as new 'special products', and establishment of a new special safeguard mechanism. LDCs are not required to undertake reduction commitments, but cotton subsidy and market access issues that had been highlighted will be addressed 'ambitiously, expeditiously and specifically' only within the agricultural negotiations, not in a separate initiative as some of the LDCs had sought.

The draft framework agreement calls for elimination 'by a credible end date' of export subsidies and 'parallel' elimination of 'all export measures with equivalent effect'. The agreement calls for elimination of food aid that is not 'in conformity with operationally effective disciplines to be agreed', with the objective to 'prevent commercial displacement'.

The July, 2004 framework agreement calls for an overall reduction in the sum of 'all trade-distorting domestic support', defined to include total AMS, plus allowed *de minimus,* plus the Blue Box, as well as for specific reduction commitments on the three separate components. Total AMS subsidies are to be reduced, with members with the highest levels making 'greater reductions'. Product-specific AMSs are to be capped according to 'a methodology to be agreed' and reductions in total AMS are to 'result in reductions of some product-specific support', whereas in the URAA it is only the total AMS that is bound and reduced. Allowed *de minimis* is to be reduced by a percentage 'to be agreed' in further negotiations. The Blue Box is to be limited not to exceed 5 per cent of the total value of agricultural production of a country during a historical period to be established in the negotiations. The definition of the Blue Box is extended to accommodate new payments in the 2002 US farm bill, by allowing into the Blue Box farm support payments 'that do not require production', as well as the payments originally included when made 'under production-limiting programmes'. No constraints were placed on Green Box expenditures, but the eligibility criteria are to be reviewed for consistency with the included measures having 'at most minimally trade-distorting effect'.

The July 2004 framework agreement provides some limited structure to Doha Round negotiations to follow in 2005, and probably for longer. The framework leaves many key decisions to be made that would determine how ambitious the final Doha Round agriculture agreement will be in opening market access and reducing subsidies. Failure to have agreed to more specificity among such diverse groups as the USA, EU, G-10, G-20, G-33 and G-90 after nearly 3 years of negotiations suggests only limited trade liberalization will emerge from the Doha Round. Inclusion of new protection mechanisms for developing countries reinforces this perception.

Conclusions

The 2002 US farm bill has been widely criticized for increasing subsidies with detrimental effects on competing agricultural producers abroad and for undermining US leadership in achieving liberalized world agricultural trade. A careful assessment shows that the 2002 FSRIA has effects that are nuanced in at least four respects: it raises expenditures compared to 1996 legislation, but not compared to actual 1998-2001 outlays; it maintains planting flexibility,but extends support to new crops and undermines some of the decoupling of subsidy payments from production and market prices that had occurred; it violates the spirit of US trade liberalization rhetoric, but probably not the letter of US WTO commitments; and it continues the policies of wealthy countries that collectively distort agricultural production and world prices, but only marginally worsen the net effects of those policies.

That said, one of the unfortunate consequences of the 2002 farm bill has been a retreat by the USA from a strong reform proposal in the WTO Doha negotiations. The initial July, 2002 US proposal on agriculture called for significant multilateral restraint on subsidies and protection, none of which was undertaken on a unilateral basis in the 2002 US farm bill. This divergence frustrated proponents of further agricultural trade liberalization, who would have preferred sharp unilateral reform action by the USA in 2002 as a clarion call for similar reforms abroad. Movement away from reform in the domestic farm bill was then followed by enunciation by the USA of a common negotiating position with the EU that embodies much less reform than the initial US position.

The cohesion between US domestic policy and its international negotiating position does not preclude progress on agriculture as the multilateral negotiations proceed, but it is an obstacle. The Uruguay Round began under circumstances of another expensive US farm bill of 1985. Despite that expensive bill, the USA started with, and for a long time stuck with, a call for substantial multilateral reform. By the conclusion of those negotiations, with limited progress eventually made, the 1985 farm bill could hardly be considered a key obstacle to the Agreement on Agriculture that was reached. It is to be hoped that substantial additional progress is made on agriculture in the Doha Round. The expensive 2002 US farm bill that precedes the international negotiations, while unfortunate, may not prove the limiting determinant of reforms achieved in a new multilateral agreement for agriculture. But this time it will not be the USA that makes the argument for pursuing those reforms most aggressively.

Notes

[1] A longer version of this analysis of the 2002 US farm bill can be found in Orden (2003).
[2] The Australian Agriculture Minister, Warren Truss, presciently anticipated this outcome when he observed after the 2002 farm bill was enacted that its worst feature might turn out to be 'the way it limits the capacity of the US to take a strong leadership role in trade negotiations'.
[3] Orden, Paarlberg and Roe (1999) describe four alternative approaches that can be pursued to reform farm policy interventions. The four approaches differ in speed of implementation and whether compensation is made to those benefiting from the intervention programmes (a fast, compensated 'buyout' or uncompensated 'cut-out', *versus* a slower compensated 'cash-out' or uncompensated 'squeeze-out'). Of the four, they argue that only a slow reform with substantial compensatory payments (the cash-out) has proved politically viable in the USA.
[4] The term 'base acreage' refers to the acreage on which payment eligibility is determined; 'deficiency payments' refer to subsidies provided on most but not all of farm output when market prices were below a legislated 'target price', and 'loan rates' refer to price guarantees for all output of the covered commodities. The 1990 farm bill had provided limited flexibility under which farmers could shift an optional 10 per cent of their base acreage among crops without that land permanently losing payments eligibility, but eligibility for deficiency payments was suspended on that acreage during years when alternative crops were grown.
[5] For detailed side-by-side comparison of the 1996 FAIR Act and the 2002 FSRIA see ERS/USDA (2002). An additional summary of the main provisions of the FSRIA related to support programmes, conservation and trade is provided by Westcott *et al.* (2002).
[6] Although the Secretary of Agriculture was authorized to do so, loan rates had not been changed under the FAIR Act. Such formula-based rates would have been lower than the maxima specified in the law after market prices dropped sharply from 1998 to 2001.
[7] This is because the payments did not have to count against the Amber Box constraint if they remained under a *de minimis* limit of 5 per cent of the value of agricultural production.
[8] The tight restriction on groundnut production for the domestic edible market had been relaxed only slightly from the original supply control programme of the 1930s to 2001. Until 1996, quota groundnuts had to be grown in the county and state in which the quota had originally been assigned. Under the FAIR Act some quota could be transferred (leased or permanently sold) across county lines within a state. This reform was phased into effect, until a maximum 40 per cent of the state's quota was eligible to move across county lines. This policy change allowed part of quota groundnut production to move from higher-cost production areas to lower-cost areas. The largest shift of production has occurred in Texas, where nearly all of the allowed quota transfer has occurred from Central Texas to West Texas. Fewer transfers of quota across county lines occurred in other states.
[9] In the cotton dispute Brazil challenged numerous aspects of US cotton policies: the fixed, counter-cyclical and loan rate support programmes but also uses of crop insurance, export credits and special payments to processors for use of domestic cotton. A panel ruling made available to the public in September 2004 ruled in favour of Brazil on several counts. The decision was appealed against by the USA, and went to the WTO's Appellate Body, which found that several sections of the cotton programme and related policy provisions violated WTO rules. In March 2005, the Dispute Settlement Body accepted the panel report with the changes suggested by the Appellate Body.

References

ERS, USDA (2002) *The 2002 Farm Bill: Side by Side Comparison with 1996-2001 Farm Legislation.* Available at www.ers.usda.gov

House Agriculture Committee (2002) *The Facts on US Farm Policy.* Accessed September 2002 at www.agriculture.house.gov

Orden, D. (2003) *US Agricultural Policy: The 2002 Farm Bill and WTO Doha Rounds Proposal.* TMD Discussion Paper 109, International Food Policy Research Institute, Washington DC.

Orden, D., Paarlberg, R. and Roe, T. (1999) *Policy Reform in American Agriculture: Analysis and Prognosis.* The University of Chicago Press, Chicago.

Westcott, P.C., Young, C.E. and Price, J.M. (2002) *The 2002 Farm Act: Provisions and Implications for Commodity Markets.* Agriculture Information Bulletin Number 778, Economic Research Service, US Department of Agriculture. Available at www.ers.usda.gov

Chapter 9

United States

DAVID BLANDFORD AND DAVID ORDEN

Domestic support for agriculture by the United States has proven to be contentious in the World Trade Organization and a center of attention in the Doha negotiations. The United States signaled its willingness to accept tighter disciplines on domestic support but insisted on a harmonization of support levels, in effect reducing allowable domestic support in the EU by a greater amount. The US position has also been to require significantly increased market access in other countries, including the emerging markets. In addition to the tension over the level of US domestic support in the Doha Round, several challenges under the WTO dispute settlement process have raised questions about whether the United States is correctly notifying its support to the WTO. Even without a Doha Round outcome, US domestic farm programs will be the subject of international scrutiny.

The first part of this chapter provides a brief review of the political economy of US farm policies, including a synopsis of the Food, Conservation, and Energy (FCE) Act of 2008. The following section discusses US domestic support notifications from 1995–2008. We then assess compliance with the Agreement, including an examination of subsidies that arguably are misclassified, underreported, or omitted from the notifications. The following section provides projections of US support through 2016. These projections are compared to existing support commitments and those proposed in the December 2008 Doha draft modalities. The final section of the chapter provides a summary and conclusions, including a discussion of options for future US policy under tighter WTO constraints.

Helpful comments and suggestions are acknowledged from Anne Effland, David Laborde, Will Martin, Larry Saunders, Randy Schnepf, Bob Young, Ed Young, and Carl Zulauf. Tim Josling was instrumental in the development of the Blandford–Josling WTO simulator used to evaluate projected US subsidies under potential Doha constraints. We thank, in particular, Lars Brink for many constructive comments.

Domestic support in the US

Agriculture in the United States today scarcely resembles the troubled sector of the Depression-era 1930s that led to the introduction of farm support programs. Structural change has created a trimodal farm sector. At one end of the spectrum are highly efficient commercial farms producing the bulk of the nation's food and fiber. At the other end are small farms that account for most of the enumerated units but only a small share of total output. In the middle are a group of farmers caught up in the dynamics of agricultural modernization.[1]

As an exporter of primary agricultural products, the US has maintained a relatively open market. Tariffs on agricultural imports are generally low (with a few exceptions, notably dairy products and sugar) and have been stable, with limited cuts to meet WTO commitments (Blandford, Laborde, and Martin 2008). However, the situation has been more fluid in the domestic support arena due to substantial changes in policy measures since the Agreement on Agriculture came into effect. Annual acreage set-aside to limit supplies, a cornerstone of farm programs since the 1950s, was abandoned in 1996 and was not resurrected during a subsequent period of low commodity prices. Deficiency payments, providing support from the federal government budget and tied to prices and the production of specific crops, were replaced in 1996 by fixed direct payments, decoupled from any direct link to market conditions and current production decisions. Public stockholding and export subsidies to dispose of surpluses have almost disappeared; binding production quotas for peanuts and the entire tobacco price support program have been eliminated with compensatory (buyout) payments being made to producers.

There has also been some reversion in the last decade to subsidies tied to prices or production. Deficiency payments linked to market prices (but less closely than before to planted acreage) were reintroduced in 2002. Biofuel mandates and subsidies have emerged as an influential aspect of US policy in light of the terrorist attacks of September 11, 2001, higher oil prices, and growing environmental concerns about climate change. With agriculture's new battle cry of "food, fiber and fuel" the demand-augmenting and price-stimulating effects of biofuel policies have added a new twist to the debate about the impact of US subsidies on world markets. When grain prices rose rapidly in 2008, concerns not voiced since

[1] The transformation of American agriculture in the twentieth century and the evolution of US farm policy are well described by Gardner (2002 and 2009).

the 1970s were raised against a policy of long-term, subsidized idling of millions of acres of farmland for supply control and environmental purposes under the Conservation Reserve Program (CRP). Biofuel subsidies and mandates subsequently have come under increased scrutiny in terms of their effects on world food prices.

Throughout these various policy changes, the ability of the powerful US farm lobby to command support in the political arena has been evident. Under the FCE Act of 2008, farmers retain a stream of fixed direct payments until 2012 despite back-to-back years of record net farm income in 2007 and 2008. The more trade-distorting price support and countercyclical income support programs were also extended. In addition, the 2008 legislation included an Average Crop Revenue Election (ACRE) revenue-guarantee program under which payments could be substantial in an era of volatile prices. Agriculture also has strengthened its ability to influence agricultural prices through energy policy. The farm sector remains well positioned to receive support in the event of a wide range of contingencies.

US farm policy since the Agreement

Policy measures in the US have evolved over time with direct government payments emerging in the 1980s as a key instrument to compensate farmers for lower support prices. Reforms adopted in the 1996 Federal Agriculture Improvement and Reform (FAIR) Act included a decoupling of payments on eligible base acres from market prices and crop planting decisions, an end to annual acreage reduction (set-aside) programs (ARPs), and the capping of price-support loan rates at low levels.[2] One key factor that drove the FAIR Act reforms was a sharp rise in commodity prices in late 1995 (Orden, Paarlberg, and Roe 1999). As market prices rose above the target prices that triggered payments under the 1990 farm bill, decoupling from prices became a plausible option. In contrast, the Agreement on Agriculture had a minimal impact on the mix of policies

[2] The term "base acreage" refers to the acreage on which payment eligibility is determined; "deficiency payments" refer to subsidies provided on a fixed amount of base-acre output when market prices are below a legislated "target price," and "loan rates" refer to price guarantees for all output of eligible commodities. The 1985 and 1990 farm bills provided limited flexibility for farmers to reallocate part of their base acreage among crops without losing payment eligibility, but deficiency payments were suspended on that acreage if alternative crops were grown. Loan-rate price guarantees can be secured in several ways, resulting in several corresponding loan-rate program benefits, as shown in Table 4.3.

adopted in 1996. Meeting the US commitments under the Agreement required few policy changes and no reductions in the level of support beyond that already undertaken in the 1985 and 1990 farm bills. The main change in the FAIR Act, as Josling, Tangermann, and Warley (1996) observe, was from one non-limited category of farm support to another – from deficiency payments notified in the blue box to fixed direct payments notified in the green box.

In 1995 both short-term and structural factors were viewed as evidence that agricultural prices would remain high throughout the decade. When this scenario proved erroneous and prices fell, calls arose for the virtual rewriting of farm policy to restore the traditional safety net. Supplemental crop market loss assistance (MLA) payments and various disaster relief payments were enacted between 1998 and 2001 and this led the farm lobby to seek a new farm bill a year before the FAIR Act was scheduled to expire.

The Farm Security and Rural Investment (FSRI) Act, signed into law in May 2002, continued fixed direct payments and extended these to soybeans and other oilseeds. The crop market-loss payments that had been appropriated annually were converted into mandatory countercyclical payments (CCPs) tied to market prices. In addition, price-supporting commodity loan rates were raised slightly and several new price supports were added. Thus, the new legislation provided both substantial new support guarantees and familiar policy measures for farm constituents. Nearly $50 billion of new funding was made available for commodity support. However, farmers retained planting flexibility: fixed direct payments and countercyclical payments were based on past production and did not require farmers to grow specific crops.[3]

The conservation and environmental programs included in the FSRI Act highlight another aspect of policy flexibility. The authority for the CRP increased from 36.4 million acres to 39.2 million acres. However, most of the new environmental expenditure went on measures to assist livestock producers and for conservation practices on land that remained in production. Long-term land idling has historically been enacted as a supply control and conservation measure during times of low prices (the 1930s, the 1960s, and again in 1985) and has been allowed to expire when market demand strengthened (during World War II and in the 1970s).

[3] The decoupling of support from production decisions was partly undermined by a one-time option to update the acreage bases determining the direct payments and the base acreage and fixed yield levels determining the countercyclical payments.

Expenditures on the CRP and other environmental payments are notified in the green box, as discussed below. Competitors in world markets typically do not complain about the reduction in US production caused by the CRP. The program has occasionally been criticized by importers for unnecessarily restricting output and keeping world prices higher than otherwise, but this was not an issue with the low prices that prevailed in 2002.

The 2008 FCE Act

As new farm legislation made its way through Congress in 2007, the strategy of farm groups was to protect the structure and funding of the commodity programs, while seeking to build a broader coalition for a congressional voting majority (Orden, Blandford, and Josling 2010). By then, commodity prices had strengthened and were projected to remain sufficiently high to reduce sharply expenditure on price-linked payments during the period covered by the new legislation.

The five-year FCE Act that became law in June 2008 distributes expected mandatory expenditures for the fiscal years 2008–12 in a broadly similar way to that anticipated under an extension of the preceding legislation. An increase in total expected outlays of $5 billion and marginal shifts in spending among categories reflected the effort to attract a broad coalition of political support from proponents of nutrition, conservation, and energy programs and a host of other constituencies.

Projected spending of $41.6 billion on commodity programs for 2008–12 was primarily composed of fixed direct payments that were successfully defended from reductions by traditional recipients of support. Commodity support expenditures were $59.3 billion during the previous five fiscal years and, when the FSRI Act was being written, had been projected to rise to as much as $78 billion (Chite 2007). Hence, although farmers retained their support programs, they did not avoid a squeeze-down of payments under the higher market prices anticipated in the FCE Act. Authority for enrolment of land in the CRP was reduced to 32 million acres, but expenditure authority for other conservation programs increased. Projected total conservation spending reached almost 60 percent of projected commodity support, compared to just one-quarter during the previous five years. In this sense, in the event that high prices were realized, a substantial relative shift would occur towards conservation and the environment in farm program outlays. But farmers remained well-protected if prices proved lower than projected – through retention, and even a marginal strengthening, of the loan-rate and countercyclical tiers of commodity support. The FCE Act also offered new demand-augmenting support for fruits and vegetables, but in the face of opposition from growers did not authorize their production on base acres.[4] It extended dairy support through a Milk Income Loss Contract (MILC) program. New payments to processors of domestic or imported cotton replaced the "Step 2" payments to processors of domestic cotton that had been ruled to be in violation of WTO rules in the *United States – Cotton* case (WTO 2005).

Throughout the debate on the FCE Act most farm groups remained wary of changes to existing programs, despite record prices for farm products in the first half of 2008. Nor was there much budgetary incentive to change policy measures. Relatively high prices and hence low anticipated expenditures on price support were built into the baseline budget projection used by Congress in framing the new legislation (CBO 2007). There was no repeat of the opportunity presented in 1995–96 to reallocate over-estimated projected expenditures for price-dependent payments to fixed payments (Orden, Paarlberg, and Roe 1999). New measures could deliver higher spending in the FCE Act only if their fiscal cost was approved by the Congress, while preserving existing loan rate and countercyclical programs under low projected expenditures came at little political cost to the farm lobby.

With high commodity prices, the fixed direct payments came under scrutiny in the farm policy debate. While the WTO rules encourage decoupling as a way to provide non-distorting support, the US fixed direct payments made up a large share of anticipated support expenditures under the FCE Act. Proponents of other initiatives saw a reduction in these payments as a way to fund their priorities. The payments were retained only after rancorous argument, particularly on the issue of income eligibility limits for recipients, which were tightened modestly in the final Act.

Expenditures on traditional within-year crop and revenue insurance programs, which are subsidized by the government, had expanded in

[4] Domestic producers of fruits and vegetables were concerned about expanded supplies and lower prices and objected to having to compete with farmers that receive payments on base acres. The WTO, without considering any price effects, concluded in the *United States – Cotton* case that the restrictions on planting fruits and vegetables made the US direct fixed payments inconsistent with the green box criterion that decoupled income support payments not be related to production. The FCE Act only includes a small pilot program to allow the production of certain fruits and vegetables (for processing) on base acreage (60,000 acres in seven Midwestern states) with any acreage planted being ineligible for support payments during that year.

the early 2000s. Despite cost-reducing measures in the FCE Act, subsidies were projected to rise because higher commodity prices increase the nominal value of losses from adverse events. Congress had also appropriated disaster relief payments for agriculture in many years. The FCE Act authorized mandatory funding of nearly $4 billion over five years for five disaster relief programs. This was a step towards avoiding a squeeze-down of support by ensuring at least some availability of funds for disaster relief without the need for annual congressional appropriations.

The sharp rise in prices in 2008 also shifted the policy focus towards a new instrument that is capable of providing support even if prices remain relatively high. The FCE Act adopted an optional revenue-guarantee program, the Average Crop Revenue Election (ACRE) program, whose payments are likely to be notified as product-specific trade-distorting support in the WTO. Starting with the 2009 crop, farmers electing ACRE for the duration of the FCE Act incur a 20 percent cut in direct payments and a 30 percent cut in the applicable loan rates for all covered crops. In exchange, if crop revenue for a state (calculated as yield per planted acre times a national price) is below a guaranteed level (based on a moving average of past prices and crop yields) participating producers can benefit. If they incur a loss of revenue for that crop on their farm, producers are provided payments of up to 25 percent of the revenue guarantee. Once the initial per-acre guarantee is established, it cannot vary by more than 10 percent from the previous year's guarantee, moderating any sharp downturn in revenue. Although ACRE payments decline once market-derived revenue stabilizes, compared to traditional programs ACRE raises the price level at which subsidy payments will occur during a transitional period of falling prices. Its proponents acknowledged that ACRE provided an opportunity to avoid a squeeze-down of subsidy payments as a result of high prices. Nevertheless, with the penalty incurred from reduced direct payments and lower loan rates, only 10–20 percent of the acreage of the three largest eligible crops (corn, soybeans and wheat) was enrolled in the program in 2009.

One other change in the 2008 FCE Act proved to affect the US domestic support notifications to the WTO. The United States modified the way that its dairy support program is defined in the FCE Act. This change in definition resulted in a reduced quantity of milk being notified as eligible for market price support (MPS) by the US for 2008 (in September 2010), and hence a reduction in the support subject to its commitment, lessening the constraint on other forms of trade-distorting support.

Table 4.1 *Summary of US domestic support notifications and shadow notification, 1995–2008*

	Notifications						
	1995	1996	1997	1998	1999	2000	2001
Type of support	*Billion dollars*						
Green box	46.0	51.8	51.3	49.8	49.7	50.1	50.7
Blue box	7.0	—	—	—	—	—	—
Current Total AMS	6.2	5.9	6.2	10.4	16.9	16.8	14.5
of which, MPS	6.2	5.9	5.8	5.8	5.9	5.8	5.8
Total *de minimis*	1.6	1.1	0.8	4.7	7.4	7.3	7.1
Product-specific	0.1	—	0.2	0.2	—	0.1	0.2
Non-product-specific	1.5	1.1	0.6	4.6	7.4	7.3	6.8
Total support	60.9	58.8	58.3	65.0	74.0	74.2	72.2
Share of total support	%						
Green box	76	88	88	77	67	67	70
Blue box	12	—	—	—	—	—	—
CTAMS	10	10	11	16	23	23	20
Total *de minimis*	3	2	1	7	10	10	10
Total	100	100	100	100	100	100	100
Value of production (billion dollars)	190.1	205.7	203.9	190.9	184.7	189.5	198.5
Bound Total AMS (billion dollars)	23.1	22.3	21.5	20.7	19.9	19.1	19.1
CTAMS as share of binding (%)	27	26	29	50	85	88	76

Notes: Small differences in totals are due to rounding. — indicates zero.
Sources: US notifications to WTO and authors' calculations.

						Shadow notification
2002	2003	2004	2005	2006	2007	2008
58.3	64.1	67.4	72.3	76.0	76.2	99.6
—	—	—	—	—	—	—
9.6	7.0	11.6	12.9	7.7	6.3	7.1
5.8	5.8	5.8	5.9	6.2	6.2	6.1
6.7	7.8	6.5	6.0	3.6	2.2	4.2
1.6	0.4	0.7	0.1	0.2	0.1	0.1
5.1	7.4	5.8	5.9	3.4	2.0	4.1
74.6	78.8	85.5	91.3	87.4	84.6	110.8
78	81	79	79	87	90	90
—	—	—	—	—	—	—
13	9	14	14	9	7	6
9	10	8	7	4	3	4
100	100	100	100	100	100	100
194.6	216.5	235.7	236.0	246.4	307.0	335.3
19.1	19.1	19.1	19.1	19.1	19.1	19.1
50	36	61	68	41	33	37

Taken together, the measures adopted in the 2008 FCE Act prove the continued strength of the farm lobby. The slight increases in loan rates and the introduction of ACRE in the FCE Act strengthen policy measures coupled to production. The support price increases are likely to be innocuous so long as market prices remain above loan rates, while ACRE opens a new avenue for support.[5] Arguments will be made to extend these trade-distorting safety net programs. With a strong farm lobby continuing to influence US domestic support policies the rules of the WTO could play an important role in influencing future policy decisions.

Notifications of domestic support, 1995–2008

As of the beginning of 2010, the United States had made notifications of domestic support to the WTO for the thirteen years from 1995 to 2007.[6] The notification for green box support is on a federal fiscal year basis (October–September). The product-specific tables for AMS support are on a marketing-year basis. The non-product-specific AMS data relate to both marketing years and fiscal years.[7] As a result, the aggregations used in calculating the notified AMS support include data for a mixture of years.

Table 4.1 provides a summary of US notified support in each year and Figure 4.1 shows the percentage composition of support.[8] Estimates (a shadow notification) are provided for 2008.[9] Total notified support rose

[5] Sugar is an exception because the sugar loan rate is typically above world market prices. The loan rate for raw cane sugar is increased in the FCE Act from $0.18 per pound to $0.1875 in 2012. The Secretary of Agriculture is required to set domestic marketing allotments at no less that 85 percent of estimated quantities for domestic human consumption and to purchase sugar to produce biofuels if necessary to avoid forfeitures of sugar under the loan rate price-support program, thus insulating domestic producers from price pressure due to increased imports.

[6] The notifications are available online in the G/AG/N series of documents (e.g., G/AG/N/USA/66 for the notification for 2006 and 2007).

[7] The periodicity of the estimated data on non-product-specific support is unclear in some cases. It is possible that some of the source data relate to calendar years.

[8] The US notification for 2004 contains an error for the market price support (MPS) calculation for sugar. This was notified as $1,219.8 million, but the correct value is $1,186.0 million, which is used in all the relevant tables and figures in this chapter for numerical consistency.

[9] The principal source of information is the Commodity Estimates Yearbook of the Commodity Credit Corporation for FY2010 – Mid-Session Review July 2009 (USDA 2009a). As discussed below, changes in the way that the dairy support program is defined in the FCE Act affected the eventual US notification of MPS for 2008. Such a change was not incorporated at the time of our estimate of CTAMS, which therefore overstates the notified dairy support.

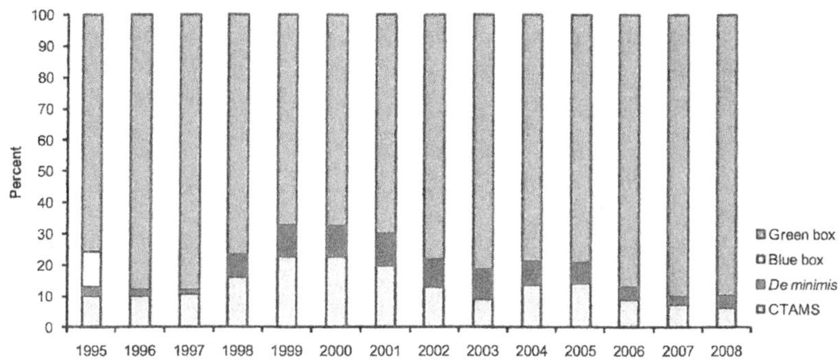

Figure 4.1 US domestic support notifications and shadow notification
Sources: US notifications to WTO and authors' calculations.

from around $60 billion in the mid 1990s to an estimated $111 billion. The largest category is the green box and both CTAMS and non-product-specific AMS support notified as *de minimis* are significant components of total support in some years. Table 4.2–Table 4.5 provide more detail about the components of each category.

Green box support

The green box has expanded from $46 billion in 1995 to an estimated $100 billion in 2008, when it accounted for 90 percent of total notified US support. Table 4.2 shows the components of green box expenditures. Domestic food aid is the most rapidly growing category, accounting for over 75 percent of the green box total in 2008. The main food aid program provides low-income families with benefits that can be used to purchase essentially any grocery item, hence this demand-augmenting program does not favor domestic over foreign producers. Excluding the food aid programs, green box support rose from $8.5 billion in 1995 to $24.7 billion in 2008. In terms of payments to farmers, decoupled income support has been the most important component in the green box. Decoupled income support is composed mostly of fixed direct payments initiated in the 1996 FAIR Act, but also includes peanut and tobacco buyout payments since 2002 and 2004, respectively. Disaster relief and environmental payments have also been important in the green box. Together these three categories totaled almost $13 billion in 2008.

Table 4.2 *Composition of US green box notifications and shadow notification, 1995–2008*

	Notifications					
	1995	1996	1997	1998	1999	2000
	Billion dollars					
General services	6.4	6.6	6.8	7.2	7.7	8.6
Public stockholding	—	—	—	—	—	—
Domestic food aid	37.5	37.8	36.0	33.5	33.1	32.4
Decoupled income support[a]	—	5.2	6.3	5.7	5.5	5.1
Income insurance	—	—	—	—	—	—
Crop insurance/ disaster relief	0.1	0.2	0.2	1.4	1.6	2.1
Producer retirement	—	—	—	—	—	—
Resource retirement	1.7	1.7	1.7	1.7	1.4	1.5
Investment aids	0.1	0.1	0.1	0.1	0.1	0.1
Environmental payments	0.2	0.3	0.3	0.3	0.3	0.3
Regional assistance	—	—	—	—	—	—
Total	46.0	51.8	51.3	49.8	49.7	50.1

Notes: — indicates zero.

[a] Subtracting peanut and tobacco buyout payments, fixed direct payments were $5.3 billion in 2003–04, and $5.2 billion in 2005–08.

Sources: Notifications to WTO and authors' calculations.

							Shadow notification
2001	2002	2003	2004	2005	2006	2007	2008
9.2	10.3	10.9	11.2	11.3	10.8	10.7	10.8
—	—	—	—	—	—	—	—
33.9	38.0	42.4	45.9	50.7	54.2	54.4	75.9
4.1	5.3	6.5	5.3	6.2	6.1	6.1	6.1
—	—	—	—	—	—	—	—
1.4	2.1	1.7	2.0	0.7	1.1	0.9	2.3
—	—	—	—	—	—	—	—
1.6	—	—	—	—	—	—	—
0.1	0.1	0.1	0.1	0.1	0.1	0.1	0.1
0.3	2.5	2.5	3.0	3.4	3.7	3.8	4.4
—	—	—	—	—	—	—	—
50.7	58.3	64.1	67.4	72.3	76.0	76.2	99.6

Table 4.3 *Composition of US Current Total AMS notifications and shadow notification, 1995–2008*

	Notifications					
	1995	1996	1997	1998	1999	2000
	Million dollars					
Market Price Support	6,213	5,919	5,816	5,776	5,921	5,840
Dairy	4,693	4,674	4,455	4,332	4,437	4,377
Sugar	1,108	937	1,045	1,093	1,180	1,133
Peanuts	412	308	315	350	303	330
Other support[a]	—	-22	423	4,616	10,942	11,003
By crop						
Corn	—	—	—	1,534	2,554	2,787
Cotton	—	—	466	935	2,353	1,050
Dairy	-38	17	—	228	223	693
Rice	—	—	—	—	435	624
Soybeans	—	—	—	1,275	2,856	3,614
Tobacco	—	—	—	—	924	519
Wheat	—	—	—	516	974	848
Other[b]	38	-38	-44	129	622	867
By type of measure						
Loan deficiency payments	—	—	3	2,708	6,062	6,192
Marketing loan gains/ payments	—	—	26	1,072	1,830	813
Certificate exchange gains	—	—	—	6	175	619
Commodity loan forfeiture	—	—	—	6	642	20
Cotton user marketing	—	—	416	280	446	237
Milk income loss contracts	—	—	—	—	—	—
Oilseed payments	—	—	—	—	458	921
Emergency payments[c]	—		—	208	683	1,473
Other support[d]	-53	-22	-23	337	567	498
Miscellaneous payments[e]	53	—	—	—	79	231
Current Total AMS	6,213	5,898	6,238	10,392	16,862	16,843

Notes: — indicates zero.

[a] Sum of non-exempt direct payments from notifications supporting table DS:6 and total other support from DS:7.

[b] Other products listed in Table 4.4.

[c] Market loss payments and various disaster assistance from notifications supporting table DS:6.

[d] Total other support from notifications supporting table DS:7 (includes storage payments, commodity loan interest subsidies, bioenergy program payments).

[e] Trade adjustment assistance and other miscellaneous payments.

Sources: US notifications to WTO and authors' calculations.

							Shadow notification
2001	2002	2003	2004	2005	2006	2007	2008
5,826	5,771	5,758	5,832	5,908	6,154	6,238	6,134
4,483	4,509	4,515	4,646	4,794	4,882	5,011	5,007
1,032	1,262	1,242	1,186	1,114	1,272	1,227	1,127
311	—	—	—	—	—	—	—
8,656	3,867	1,193	5,763	7,035	1,588	22	921
1,326	—	—	3,059	4,490	—	—	—
2,810	1,187	435	2,238	1,621	1,365	—	—
—	1,795	222	16	361	162	5	905
763	712	503	131	133	—	—	—
3,623	—	—	—	—	—	—	—
—	—	—	—	—	—	—	—
—	—	—	—	—	—	—	—
135	172	33	318	431	61	16	16
5,400	508	320	3,333	4,750	157	7	4
604	167	87	321	243	8	—	—
1,974	316	306	1,450	1,171	967	—	—
17	658	—	7	4	—	—	—
182	—	—	—	—	—	—	—
—	1,795	221	9	352	157	—	900
—	—	—	—	—	—	—	—
—	110	1	40	90	6	5	5
430	289	257	586	410	293	9	12
49	23	—	17	15	—	—	—
14,482	9,637	6,950	11,595	12,943	7,742	6,260	7,056

Table 4.4 *US CTAMS notifications and shadow notification by product, 1995–2008*

	Notifications					
	1995	1996	1997	1998	1999	2000
	Million dollars					
Apples					99	175
Apricots						2
Avocados						
Barley				84	40	70
Beef, cattle, sheep						
Beef and veal						
Blueberries, wild						
Cattle and calves						
Chickpeas						
Corn				1,534	2,554	2,787
Cotton			466	935	2,353	1,050
Cranberries					20	
Dairy	4,655	4,691	4,456	4,560	4,660	5,070
Dry peas						
Grapes						
Hogs and pigs						
Honey						29
Lentils						
Livestock						
Lychee						
Minor oil seeds						
Canola				8	39	82
Crambe					1	2
Flaxseed				2	11	25
Mustard seed	<0.5	<0.5	<0.5	<0.5	1	<0.5
Rapeseed	<0.5	<0.5	<0.5		<0.5	<0.5
Safflower	<0.5	<0.5	<0.5	<0.5		3
Sesame						<0.5
Sunflower					143	161
Mohair	15				2	2
Oats				20	31	45
Olives						
Onions						
Orchards/vineyards						

2001	2002	2003	2004	2005	2006	2007	Shadow notification 2008
			83	46			
		<0.5	<0.5	<0.5			
1,326			3,059	4,490			
2,810	1,187	435	2,238	1,621	1,365		
4,483	6,305	4,737	4,663	5,155	5,044	5,017	5,913
		14	32	37	30		
	2			11	14		
23				14			
<0.5	<0.5		<0.5				
12							
<0.5							
	2						
55							
	5	4	3	2	1	1	

Table 4.4 (*cont.*)

	Notifications					
	1995	1996	1997	1998	1999	2000
	Million dollars					
Peaches						
Peanuts	415	299	306	340	349	438
Pears						
Pecan trees						
Potatoes						
Rice					435	624
Rye						
Sheep and lamb						
Sorghum				63	154	85
Soybeans				1,275	2,856	3,614
Sugar	1,091	908	1,011	1,055	1,207	1,177
Tobacco					924	519
Tomatoes						
Wheat				516	974	848
Wool	38				9	33
Current Total AMS	6,213	5,898	6,238	10,392	16,862	16,843
Sum of product-specific AMS[a]	6,311	5,937	6,475	10,550	16,891	16,906

Notes: No value either means no notified support or AMS below the *de minimis* threshold for that year. The 2004 MPS for sugar was incorrectly notified as $1,219.8 million; this table uses the correct value of $1,186.0 million; other support in the sugar AMS for 2004 is $62 million.

[a] Includes *de minimis*.

Sources: US notifications to WTO and authors' calculations.

							Shadow notification
2001	2002	2003	2004	2005	2006	2007	2008
305	66			89			
763	712	503	131	133			
22	23						
			130	140			
3,623							
1,061	1,328	1,250	1,248	1,199	1,280	1,236	1,139
	8	7	7	7	7	7	4
14,482	9,637	6,950	11,595	12,943	7,742	6,260	7,056
14,706	11,227	7,386	12,275	13,061	7,913	6,497	7,155

Table 4.5 De minimis *exemptions from CTAMS in US notifications and shadow notification, 1995–2008*

	Notifications					
	1995	1996	1997	1998	1999	2000
	Million dollars					
Sum of AMS support (amber box)	7,696	7,052	7,042	15,134	24,297	24,184
Total *de minimis*	1,483	1,155	804	4,742	7,435	7,341
Product-specific	97	40	236	158	29	63
Non-product-specific	1,386	1,115	567	4,584	7,406	7,278
	%					
De minimis as a share of CTAMS	24	20	13	46	44	44
De minimis as a share of summed AMS support	19	16	11	31	31	30
Major components of non-product-specific *de minimis*				*Million dollars*		
Irrigation projects	380	380	349	349	316	316
Crop and revenue insurance	913	636	119	747	1,514	1,396
Market loss and countercyclical payments	—	—	—	2,811	5,468	5,463
	5% of total value of production (million dollars)					
Non-product-specific threshold	9,506	10,285	10,194	9,544	9,237	9,476

Note: — indicates zero.

Sources: US notifications to WTO and authors' calculations.

							Shadow notification
2001	2002	2003	2004	2005	2006	2007	2008
21,535	16,328	10,187	18,087	18,923	11,343	8,520	11,231
7,052	6,690	3,237	6,491	5,980	3,601	2,260	4,176
224	1,590	436	714	118	171	237	99
6,828	5,101	2,801	5,778	5,862	3,430	2,023	4,077
49	69	47	56	46	47	36	59
33	41	32	36	32	32	27	37
300	300	300	269	269	240	240	240
1,770	2,889	1,862	1,123	756	1,613	801	2,880
4,640	1,804	544	4,288	4,749	1,488	893	864
9,925	9,729	10,824	11,784	11,800	12,321	15,352	16,765

Current Total AMS

Table 4.1 shows that AMS – including the CTAMS plus product-specific and non-product-specific AMSs notified as *de minimis* – can vary substantially from year to year depending on prices and production.[10] In periods when prices are low, such as 1999–2000, support increases markedly in comparison to periods such as 1996–97 when prices of farm products were relatively high.

The notified US CTAMS is composed entirely of product-specific support. Table 4.3 shows the MPS component by major commodity, as well as payments by major commodity and by type of policy measure. The MPS component is based on administered prices (loan rates) that exceed the fixed reference price levels in the US schedule under the Agreement. MPS amounts to roughly $6 billion in most years, with the largest proportion of this (an average of 80 percent over the period) attributed to the dairy program. The MPS for peanuts was eliminated as a result of the buyout of production quotas in the 2002 FSRI Act.

While most of the support for dairy and sugar is provided through MPS, support in CTAMS for most other products is through non-exempt direct payments and other forms of support.[11] The three crops that have benefited most are corn, cotton and soybeans with 28, 26 and 20 percent, respectively, of total payments for 1995–2008. Almost 75 percent of total non-exempt payments and other forms of support were made up of loan deficiency payments (50 percent), certificate exchange gains, and marketing loan gains, which collectively constitute the three principal mechanisms providing price support to US farmers without the government having to take ownership of the products.

The dairy and sugar MPS have consistently accounted for significant shares of the CTAMS. Table 4.3 also demonstrates the influence of market prices on US WTO notifications. When crop prices have been low subsidies included in CTAMS have increased for the major field crops and their share of support has been important. Cotton, which has been particularly

[10] Blue box support is not important for the United States because the deficiency payments for major crops included in this category were eliminated in 1996 by the FAIR Act. The blue box payments shown in Table 4.1 for 1995 were distributed among crops as follows: barley, $151 million; corn, $3,009 million; cotton, $901 million; oats, $12 million; rice, $511 million; sorghum $320 million; and wheat, $2,127 million.

[11] The notable exceptions for dairy are $673 million through a market loss payment in 2000; $1,795 million under MILC payments in 2002; and an estimated $900 million of MILC payments in 2008.

contentious in the WTO negotiations, has accounted for as much as 19 percent of the US CTAMS (in the years 2001 and 2004).

When prices are high, price-linked subsidies decline and this reduces notified support. With high commodity prices, the CTAMS averaged $7 billion in 2006–08. The modest increase from 2007 to 2008 is almost entirely due to higher support for dairy due to lower milk prices and higher payments under the MILC program.[12] Despite some weakening of prices in late 2008, support for crops was not estimated to have increased significantly. The product-specific AMS for almost all products is estimated to be below *de minimis* thresholds in 2007 and 2008. This is in sharp contrast to the situation just a few years earlier, when the notified CTAMS was in the $11–13 billion range (2004–05) and the *de minimis* threshold was exceeded for most of the major crops.

Table 4.4 provides more detailed information on the product composition of the notified CTAMS. If a notification was provided for any product during the period 1995–2007 it is included in the table but any AMS below the *de minimis* threshold is not shown. Product-specific *de minimis* has generally not been a major factor in reducing the US notified CTAMS. One notable exception was an emergency payment to livestock farmers of $1.1 billion in 2002 which was excluded from the CTAMS because of *de minimis* and accounted for most of the increase in product-specific *de minimis* in that year (Table 4.1). The *de minimis* exclusion has also reduced significantly the number of years for which AMS support has been included in CTAMS for a wide range of products. For example, a positive AMS applied to barley in every year with the exception of 2007, but after the application of *de minimis* a barley AMS was included in the CTAMS in only five of the fourteen years.

Table 4.4 reveals that notifications have been made in various years under different headings for related products. For example, notifications have been provided for individual orchard and vineyard crops as well as for an aggregate of those crops; the same applies to livestock. The impact of this on the CTAMS is unclear. For example, it is possible that part of the support notified for livestock in 2002 as *de minimis* would have been counted in the CTAMS if it had been apportioned to individual livestock categories. This is not to imply that the notification was deliberately intended to achieve that effect, but when appropriate data are not

[12] Compared to our shadow estimate the changed definition of the dairy support program in the FCE Act resulted in a reduction of $2.1 billion in the CTAMS due to lower notified MPS. With higher payments than projected for cotton, the final notified CTAMS for 2008 was $6.3 billion.

available the mixing of overlapping product categories in the notifications complicates the issue of identifying accurately the amount of support provided for individual products. This could prove contentious under a Doha agreement with product-specific AMS caps.

Comparison of MPS measurements

Comparisons of the MPS as notified to the WTO to that calculated using the approach adopted by the OECD are shown for dairy (milk) and sugar for 1995–2007 in Figures 4.2 and 4.3. A key difference in the OECD approach is that annual domestic prices (rather than an administered price) are compared to annual international reference prices (rather than a fixed 1986–88 reference price). The pattern of differences between the two measurements is similar for both commodities. The WTO MPS is quite stable in each case and is substantially below the OECD measure in most years. The eligible quantities in the WTO measure are almost identical to total milk and sugar production, so the difference between the two arises from differences in the prices used. The WTO MPS understates the actual protection provided annually to domestic producers by border measures (tariffs, TRQs and for dairy some export subsidies) and domestic supply management (for sugar in some years), reflected in annual domestic prices. In addition to capturing this protection, the OECD MPS reflects changes in the level of protection due to changes in world market prices.

Most of the difference between the WTO and OECD MPS for milk arises from fluctuations in domestic producer prices in comparison to the administered price. The administered price for milk declined from $243 per metric ton in the 1986–88 base period to around $218 per metric ton in 1999. By contrast the producer price was $274 per metric ton in the base period and has increased with annual fluctuations to $403 per metric ton in 2007. Fluctuations in world prices also affect the comparison between the two MPS measurements. The fixed reference price used in calculating the WTO MPS is $160 per metric ton, similar to the corresponding OECD average reference price of $176 per metric ton for 1986–88. By 1995 the OECD annual reference price had risen to $210 per ton and reached $313 per ton in 2007, twice the level of the fixed reference price used in the WTO calculation. Thus, even though the two measures converge during 2005–06, the OECD MPS is based on higher domestic and international prices than those in the WTO MPS. The administered and fixed reference prices used in calculating the WTO MPS in this case only coincidentally reflect the actual price support provided to US dairy farmers.

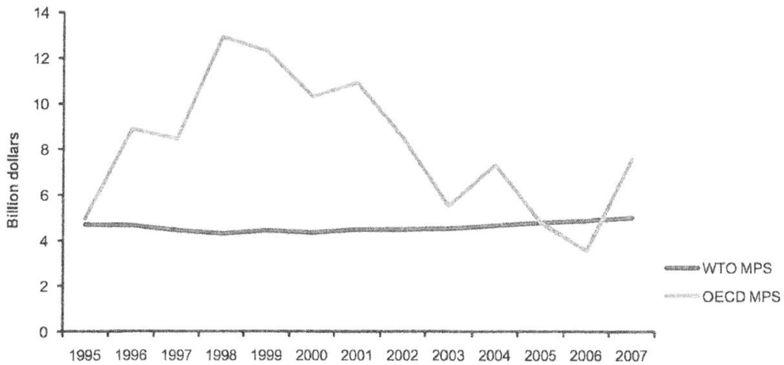

Figure 4.2 US market price support for dairy from notifications and OECD
Source: Authors' calculations based on WTO notifications and OECD statistics.

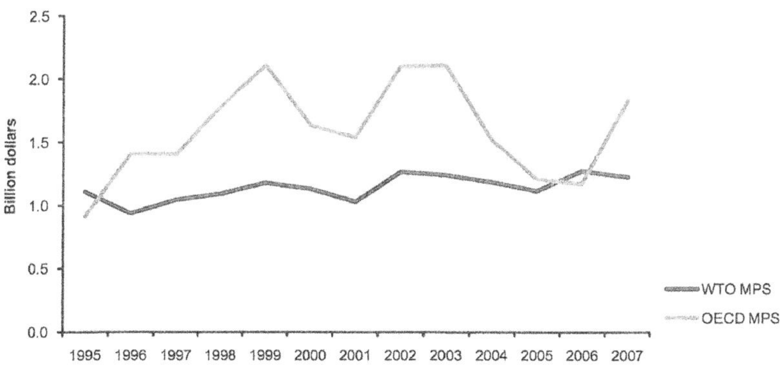

Figure 4.3 US market price support for sugar from notifications and OECD
Source: Authors' calculations based on WTO notifications and OECD statistics.

For sugar, the OECD MPS also exceeds the WTO MPS in most years due primarily to domestic producer prices in excess of the administered price. The latter has been virtually constant (at $396.8 per metric ton, except for $374.8 during 1996–2001 when a penalty under the 1996 FAIR Act was in effect). Producer prices ranged from $47 (2000) to $142 (1996) per metric ton higher.[13] For sugar, the fixed reference price is $231 per metric

[13] Producer prices as reported in the OECD PSE database are below the administered price, ranging from $296 per ton in the 1986–88 base period to $315 per ton in 2007. The WTO

ton for the WTO MPS, while OECD's average international price for the 1986–88 period was $202 per metric ton. By the time the Agreement came into effect in 1995 the international price was $329. It fell as low as $177 in 1999, stayed at or below the fixed reference price through 2004, but was $375 by 2006. For sugar, use of the fixed reference price kept the notified WTO MPS lower than would have been the case with an annual reference price when world prices were low.

On the basis of these results, it might be tempting to dismiss administered prices as playing an insignificant role in US farm policy. Particularly for sugar, this would be a serious error. Sugar imports under a TRQ are carefully managed on a month-by-month basis to keep supply aligned with domestic demand. The management of quantities through the sugar import regime (and sometimes domestic supply control) has been used to keep prices at the processor level above the support level, as reflected in the MPS comparison. Although the government procures very little sugar, the administered price is the policy fulcrum for quantitative management. The industry is keenly aware of the critical policy role played by the administered price. It is defended as the basis for operating the sugar program and border measures in such a way as to avoid sugar being accumulated by the government instead of being sold commercially.

Non-product-specific AMS support

The United States has excluded non-product-specific AMS support from its notified CTAMS under the *de minimis* provision in all years. The *de minimis* exclusion has been extremely important. Table 4.1 shows that *de minimis* support as a whole has accounted for up to 10 percent of total notified support. The total of AMS *de minimis* exemptions was equivalent to roughly 45 percent of the notified CTAMS on average, and almost reached 70 percent in 2002 (Table 4.5). Most of this is non-product-specific support, which has exceeded $4 billion in eight years. However, because of the large total value of US agricultural production (averaging around $220 billion between 1995 and 2008), non-product-specific support would have had to have been at least $1.8 billion greater than the maximum notified amount in order to breach the 5 percent *de minimis* threshold (this calculation relates to the 1999 notification). On average,

administered price and reference price refer to raw cane sugar after mill processing, whereas OECD converts its prices to a farmgate level by multiplying by 0.6 to adjust for processing costs. The producer prices given herein and the OECD MPS in Figure 4.3 are recalibrated to the raw sugar level for comparison to the WTO MPS.

the non-product-specific AMS has been $7 billion below the *de minimis* threshold, and it declined to a relatively low level of $2 billion in 2007.

Several important forms of support are included in the non-product-specific AMS. Crop MLA payments from 1998 to 2001 and countercyclical payments initiated in 2002 alone exceeded $4 billion in five years, most recently in 2005. Crop and revenue insurance subsidies have been another important component, exceeding $1.5 billion in six years. Lesser payments include irrigation subsidies and payments under various emergency assistance and other programs.

The variability in key components of the non-product-specific AMS is also apparent in Table 4.5, and again this relates to price movements. Support increased sharply in the late 1990s as Congress responded to declining prices by authorizing crop MLA payments. These were paid to farmers in proportion to their total eligibility for direct payments and required no specific planting decisions; on this basis they were notified as non-product-specific AMS.[14] The countercyclical payments introduced in the 2002 FSRI Act are directly linked to market prices of specific crops but are based on fixed levels of past output. Again, they have been notified as non-product-specific AMS because the payments are not dependent on annual decisions to plant specific crops. The introduction of these price-responsive forms of support has contributed to an increase in the non-product-specific AMS and has also made it more variable. Since 1998, when MLA payments were first introduced, such support has varied between $0.5 and $5.5 billion. Recently, with prices for major crops relatively high in 2007 and 2008, countercyclical payments have been relatively low, at around $0.9 billion. The non-product-specific AMS is estimated to have increased to $4 billion in 2008, due to larger payments under crop and revenue insurance programs resulting from higher prices and hence higher premium subsidies. The non-product-specific AMS estimated for 2008 was equivalent to 58 percent of the notified CTAMS, thus accounting for over one-third of the non-green box support provided to US farmers in that year.

Consistency of US support with WTO commitments

The sole quantitative commitment on domestic support under the Agreement is the Bound Total AMS. For the United States, this was reduced from $23.1 billion in 1995 to $19.1 billion in 2000 (Table 4.1).

[14] Market loss assistance payments provided for some commodities (e.g., dairy) were notified as product-specific AMS, as noted above.

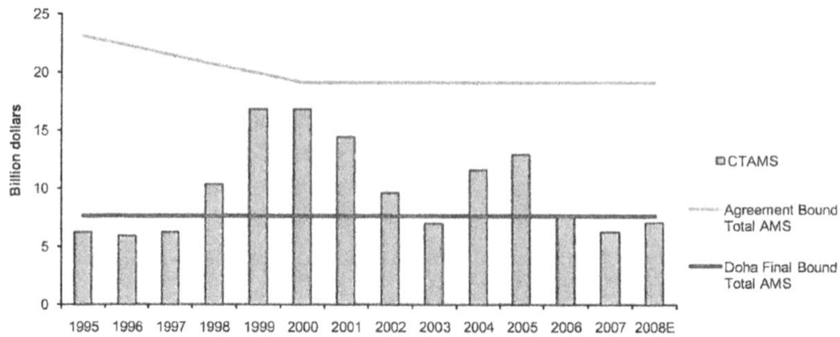

Figure 4.4 US notifications of CTAMS compared with commitments agreed in the Uruguay Round and proposed in the Doha Round

Given the non-product-specific *de minimis* exemption, despite substantial fluctuations in the notified CTAMS the United States has not exceeded its Bound Total AMS under the Agreement (Figure 4.4). However, a significant reduction is being proposed in the Doha negotiations – from $19.1 billion to $7.6 billion. The US notified CTAMS has exceeded the lower figure in eight of the fourteen years from 1995 to 2008. Even with relatively high crop prices in 2007–08, the CTAMS, while comfortably within the binding under the Agreement, is very close to the proposed binding under Doha if there is no change in the method of notifying dairy support. The issues involved in meeting proposed new commitments on support are clearly of major importance for the United States and are examined in more detail below.

Even without a new WTO agreement on agriculture, an important issue for the United States is the notification status of some of its programs in light of the *US – Cotton* case (WTO 2005) and further challenges to its support payments by Brazil and Canada in the Total Aggregate Measurement of Support (TAMS) case (WTO 2007a, 2007b). For the three years with the highest notified CTAMS (1999–2001) US AMS support would have exceeded the Bound Total AMS commitment without the *de minimis* exemption for non-product-specific support, as shown in Table 4.5. The addition of just the MLA payments from the non-product-specific *de minimis* would raise the CTAMS above the ceiling commitment in those years.

The cotton case ruling casts doubt on whether US fixed direct payments, which are currently notified as green box support, qualify for that category because production of some crops (particularly fruits and vegetables) was precluded on the program base acres for which payments are made. Table 4.6 presents two alternative summations of the notified US CTAMS with the inclusion of the fixed direct payments. The United States would have violated its Bound Total AMS in a number of years in each case. If the direct payments were notified as non-product-specific AMS (following the approach used by the United States for counter-cyclical payments) the Bound Total AMS would have been reached or exceeded in five of the fourteen years (1998–2002). In those years, the non-product-specific AMS would have exceeded the *de minimis* threshold and been counted in the CTAMS. Alternatively, if crop MLA and countercyclical payments, as well as fixed direct payments, were counted as product-specific AMS, as some analysts argue, the United States would also have exceeded its commitment in five of the fourteen years (1999–2001 and 2004–05). For these years the sum of the product-specific AMS in the CTAMS is sufficiently high to exceed the Bound Total AMS.

Other alternative subsidy measurement

Beyond the traditional price and income support programs (direct payments, countercyclical payments, and loan-rate program benefits), a number of questions arise on how subsidies are being captured in the US notifications. Here we discuss briefly five categories that may be misclassified, underreported, or omitted from the US notifications. This may become important if support commitments are tightened in a Doha agreement.

Disaster payments

The US notifies various types of disaster payments in the green box, as product-specific support, and as non-product-specific support. The Canadian request for establishment of a panel in the TAMS case listed forty-eight separate disaster programs over the period 1999–2005 (WTO 2007b). Crop insurance and disaster relief payments notified in the green box range from a low of $100 million in 1995 to a high of $2.3 billion in 2008 (Table 4.2). Important questions are whether all disaster programs have been included in the US notifications, whether those notified in the green box satisfied the relevant criteria, and whether annual support through these programs has been measured correctly. Some disaster relief programs could be judged to provide product-specific payments that do not qualify for the green box. Inconsistency with specific green box

Table 4.6 *Alternative summations of US AMS support and fixed direct payments, 1995–2008*

	1995	1996	1997	1998	1999	2000	2001	2002	2003	2004	2005	2006	2007	2008
Fixed direct payments included in non-product-specific AMS														
Hypothetical CTAMS (Billion dollars)[a]	6.2	5.9	6.2	20.6	29.7	29.2	25.4	20.0	7.0	11.6	12.9	7.7	6.3	7.1
As share of ceiling (%)	27	26	29	100	149	153	133	105	36	61	68	41	33	37
Market loss assistance, countercyclical and fixed direct payments included in product-specific AMS														
Hypothetical CTAMS (Billion dollars)[b]	6.2	11.1	12.5	18.9	27.8	27.4	23.2	16.7	12.8	21.1	22.9	14.4	12.3	13.1
As share of ceiling (%)	27	50	58	91	140	143	122	88	67	111	120	75	65	69

[a] Fixed direct payments are only added to the CTAMS and count against the ceiling if their inclusion in the non-product-specific AMS causes it to exceed the *de minimis* threshold. Fixed direct payments exclude buyout payments for peanuts and tobacco that are included in notified green box decoupled income support.

[b] Peanut and tobacco buyout payments not included as product-specific support.

Sources: US notifications to WTO and authors' calculations.

criteria regarding the reference period against which a loss is measured, and the amount of the loss that triggered payments, would be among the reasons for such judgments (see Appendix A for the criteria specified in the Agreement).

Federal tax exemptions for agriculture

US domestic support notifications do not include revenue forgone due to special tax exemptions for agriculture. In its request for a TAMS panel, Brazil identified diesel fuel and gasoline tax exemptions, tax exemptions for agricultural vehicles, and income tax concessions as subsidies that might need to be notified (WTO 2007a). Among the income tax concessions are special capital gains treatment for unharvested crops (notified by the United States as a subsidy under the Agreement on Subsidies and Countervailing Measures (ASCM)), preferential cash accounting rules for farm operations, and preferential availability of income averaging over time. The OECD includes the income tax concession as a payment based on overall farming income and energy subsidies as a payment based on input use in its PSEs. US income tax concessions are reported to have increased from $554 million in 1995 to $1,250 million in 2008, and were as high as $2,456 million in 2003. Energy subsidies, defined as the "value of Federal and State exemptions or reductions in excise and sales taxes on diesel fuel for farmers relative to the standard rate taxes on fuels", are simply reported by the OECD as a constant $2,385 million from 1986 through 2008.

Crop and revenue insurance costs

US notifications for crop and revenue insurance report net indemnities (indemnities minus premiums paid by producers) as non-product-specific support. There are additional expenditures on crop and revenue insurance programs arising from the payment of delivery costs to private insurance agents. The latter are not reported in the notifications, but they have been substantial, averaging about $900 million per year from 1995 through 2008, whereas net indemnities averaged $1,100 million. One can argue that the reimbursements excluded from the notifications are made to companies on behalf of the policyholders (producers of the insured crops), and should therefore be notified as non-product-specific support.

Irrigation and electric power

The US reports interest on the debt for irrigation project construction in its non-product-specific AMS, arguing that "irrigators repay the premium but not the interest." The subsidy has been reported as declining from $380 million in 1995 to $240 million by 2006 (Table 4.5). Arguably, this interest subsidy could be considered part of expenditures "directed to the provision or construction of capital works" and exempt from the AMS calculations under the green box criteria of Annex 2 of the Agreement. Not having claimed that exclusion, the United States might, but does not, include subsidies to agricultural irrigators that arise from lower repayment of capital costs based on assessed "ability to pay" programs. Under these programs a reduced capital cost is charged to farmers and a higher cost is paid by hydroelectric power authorities (again, it might be argued that these subsidies should be in the green box). No notification is made for irrigation subsidies related to maintenance and operating costs (which irrigators apparently pay), nor for the benefits from water charges to farmers that are below those for other users (which is a common practice). No allowance is provided for preferential charges for electricity used by agriculture, either to move water from its source to farmland or for on-farm use of electricity. The extent of subsidies for irrigation and electricity and how these are notified are issues for other countries (see Chapters 8 and 9, India and China). A more systematic and consistent approach to the measurement and notification of these subsidies would be useful in the WTO.

Ethanol

The issue of how ethanol subsidies are notified has become germane. Most important is the forgone revenue from the federal ethanol tax credit to fuel blenders and additional state tax provisions. These tax credits could collectively total $7–8 billion or more on corn-based ethanol alone by 2022. If these amounts were to be counted in the AMS, its nominal level would be substantially higher.

The United States has notified the federal ethanol tax credit to the WTO as an industrial subsidy under the ASCM. However, ethanol is included in the set of products defined as agricultural under the WTO agreements, so the tax revenue forgone could also be appropriately notified under the AMS, with ethanol considered the relevant product. At issue would be the extent to which the tax credit is judged to be a "measure directed at processors" and thus subject to inclusion in the AMS (under Annex 3, paragraph 7 of the Agreement) "to the extent that such measures benefit producers of the basic agricultural product." If ethanol is indeed a "basic" agricultural product, the issue would center on the extent to which the blenders' tax credit is passed through to producers of ethanol.

If ethanol were not to be considered a basic agricultural product, the tax credit to blenders could still be an instrument of domestic support. To the extent that an ethanol tax credit increases corn prices, it might be judged to be a measure directed at processors that affects the price of corn as a basic agricultural product. This would correspond to the way the United States formerly notified Step 2 payments to processors of domestic cotton as part of the cotton product-specific AMS before these payments were eliminated as a result of the *US – Cotton* case.

The use of mandates in conjunction with tax credits raises the issue of whether such a policy is judged a "measure" that could be included among "all . . . domestic support measures in favour of agricultural producers" and thus subject to discipline under the Agreement on Agriculture (Article 6 and Annex 3). As shown by de Gorter and Just (2009), when a mandate is not binding, the tax credit adds substantially to the level of production of ethanol, its price, and the price and output of corn. In contrast, when a mandate is binding, the effects of the tax credit on producers are minimal. In the latter case, it is the binding mandate that influences ethanol and corn production and prices and, one can argue, should be subject to the AMS discipline.

The CTAMS would be composed of a curious mix of policies if ethanol subsidies were included. A common metaphor for US policy has been that it has one foot on the gas pedal and one foot on the brake in terms of production. The "on the gas" part has been the focus of attention regarding the US AMS; that is, what is the value of subsidies that stimulate production? The "on the brake" part has been programs that idle land: these have been notified in the green box for long-term conservation land idling and the blue box for short-term acreage set-asides. With ethanol mandates and subsidies, the new metaphor for agricultural policy would be that it has its feet on two accelerators. But these policy approaches have different effects on world prices, and thus on the interests of various trade partners and constituents within these countries. The traditional accelerator of supply expansion drives world prices down. The new accelerator of demand augmentation, through ethanol policy, drives world prices up. Commodity market events since 2006 have demonstrated the potency of the latter type of policies.

Projected US notifications and WTO constraints

In order to examine the impact of the existing disciplines for agricultural domestic support and of the new disciplines proposed in the Doha negotiations, projections of support under major categories in the US notifications were derived through 2016 using program parameters from the 2008 FCE Act. The projections are based on the domestic support simulator developed by Blandford and Josling (2007). Data for future production and prices are derived primarily from the February 2009 USDA baseline (USDA 2009b). Peanut price projections were derived from the March 2009 CBO budget baseline (Hull, Langley, and Hitz 2009). That is also the source for expenditures under conservation programs and crop and revenue insurance. Overall, the commodity prices used in the projections are relatively high due to a range of factors, including domestic demand for biofuels, and strong overseas demand for US commodities due to income growth, dietary change, and an anticipated weak dollar.

In projecting the CTAMS, two key assumptions are made about future US notifications. The first relates to the notification of the MPS for dairy. As noted earlier, the FCE Act introduced a definitional change in US dairy policy. Prior to the Act the US dairy support program was defined with respect to a support price for milk. That structure was reflected in US notifications because the MPS calculation was applied to total milk production. The FCE Act redefines the program in terms of support for three dairy products: butter, cheddar cheese, and non-fat dry milk. Support prices for these products are set to be consistent with the previous support price for milk ($9.90 per hundredweight). However, as a result of this change the United States eventually notified MPS for dairy for 2008 on the basis of the production of the three products concerned, rather than the total volume of milk. It is clear that the United States will continue to exercise this option in notified dairy support in the future. As noted above the redesign of the dairy support program led to reduction of $ 2.1 billion for 2008 compared to notifying MPS for all milk production that year. In the projections, MPS is assumed to be notified using the new procedure and assuming no subsequent changes to dairy price support policy through 2016 that further reduce the notified MPS.

A second key assumption concerns the ACRE program. This program has the potential to generate large support payments during periods of relatively high prices. Despite an initial modest sign-up rate for the largest-acreage eligible crops in 2009, it is likely that ACRE or similar programs will remain part of US farm policy in the coming years. For this reason, understanding the performance characteristics of this new program versus traditional programs is important. In the projections it is assumed that all acreage is enrolled in the traditional programs. However, the implications of the ACRE program for future notifications are also discussed.

Under the Agreement

Table 4.7 summarizes projected notifications in the various boxes through 2016 under the Agreement. Green box support is projected to increase steadily from $100 billion in 2009 to $118 billion in 2016. This is primarily due to increased expenditures on domestic food assistance programs, with expenditures on conservation programs also projected to increase from $4 billion in 2009 to over $6 billion in 2016. On the basis of these projections, green box support would make up roughly 90 percent of the US total support by 2016, a similar percentage to that in 2008.

The US CTAMS has varied substantially from year-to-year, but the relatively high commodity prices foreseen by USDA and other analysts imply that projected support expenditures for major crops are extremely modest. The notified product-specific AMS for most major products other than dairy and sugar would qualify for *de minimis*. On the basis of these projections, the CTAMS would stay far below the US Bound Total AMS of $19.1 billion. The projected CTAMS would amount to $4.5–$5.0 billion, composed almost entirely of market price support for dairy and sugar.

Over the period 1995–2008 *de minimis* non-product-specific support has been an important component in the US notifications. With the relatively high commodity prices assumed through 2016, there are only modest countercyclical payments for cotton and peanuts. In contrast, crop and revenue insurance subsidies are expected to be high, averaging about $4.7 billion per year due to the higher prices.[15] The projected non-product-specific support in 2016 is $5 billion, including countercyclical payments. This easily falls under *de minimis*. With a projected value of production around $265 billion, there is room for more than $8 billion of additional non-product-specific support without crossing the *de minimis* threshold.

The difference between the notified CTAMS and the Bound Total AMS would be $14.1 billion in 2016, shown in Figure 4.5 as the "Available CTAMS." Domestic commodity programs could provide that much additional notified CTAMS and the United States would still meet its WTO commitment. As long as non-product-specific support was kept under the *de minimis* threshold, additional support in the CTAMS and non-product-specific AMS categories combined could

[15] These estimates of crop and revenue insurance subsidies exclude adjustments estimated by CBO to average $168 million over 2008–11 (due to reduced program costs) and $3,189 million in 2012 (due primarily to delay of some payments to lower the projected five-year cost of the FCE Act).

Table 4.7 *Projected levels of US domestic support under the Agreement, 2009–16*

	2009	2010	2011	2012	2013	2014	2015	2016
	Billion dollars							
Green box	99.7	102.2	104.8	107.6	110.0	112.4	114.8	117.5
Blue box	—	—	—	—	—	—	—	—
CTAMS	4.6	4.6	4.7	4.8	4.9	4.9	5.0	5.0
Total *de minimis*	6.9	6.1	5.6	5.5	5.5	5.6	5.7	5.1
Product-specific	0.2	0.1	0.1	0.1	0.1	0.1	0.1	0.1
Non-product-specific	6.6	6.0	5.5	5.3	5.4	5.5	5.6	5.0
Total support	111.2	113.0	115.2	117.8	120.4	123.0	125.5	127.7

Note: — indicates zero.
Source: Authors' estimates.

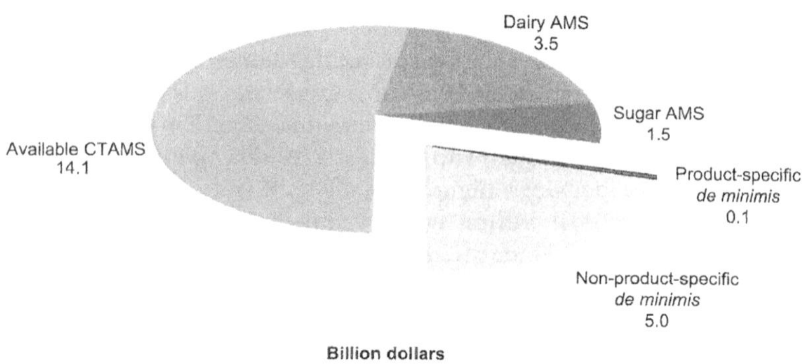

Figure 4.5 Projected composition of US AMS support in 2016 and available CTAMS under the Agreement
Source: Authors' estimates.

be over $22 billion in 2016 without violating US obligations under the Agreement. Additional product-specific support could be provided up to *de minimis* thresholds. The 2008 FCE Act paid little regard to the implications of any future WTO commitments and does not address issues that have been raised by WTO dispute settlement rulings, in particular the consistency of US fixed direct payments with Annex 2 of the Agreement. However, with projected high commodity prices, the fixed direct payments could easily fit within the Bound Total AMS in the future, whether counted as product-specific or non-product-specific support. Likewise, were a judgment made that ethanol blender tax credits (not incorporated into these projections) should be notified in the product-specific AMS category, they could also be included without violating the US limit.

This picture of essentially no constraint on US support under the Agreement could change if prices are not as strong as foreseen by USDA. Nevertheless, prices would have to fall substantially from recent and projected levels to trigger large payments with the loan rates and target prices specified in the 2008 FCE Act.

Under the Doha draft modalities

The United States falls into the second tier of the draft modalities for Base OTDS and Final Bound Total AMS reductions (see Table 2.2). The draft modalities are complicated for the United States, involving several provisions that are either unique or of particular relevance to its situation (WTO 2008). Of note are:

1. the expansion of the blue box criteria to include payments based on 85 percent or less of a fixed and unchanging base level of production – this implies that US countercyclical payments (but not ACRE payments) would be eligible for inclusion in the blue box, rather than being notified as AMS support;
2. a proportionately lower AMS limit for cotton than for other products, with an accelerated reduction schedule;[16]

[16] The United States had not offered a counter-proposal on the special cotton provisions, but it was widely anticipated that they would require further negotiation. When the negotiations broke down in December 2008, the cotton provisions were left unaddressed, so the US position remained undeclared. The special treatment of cotton support also applies to the EU and other cotton producers (see Appendix B).

Table 4.8 *OTDS, CTAMS, blue box and cotton support limits and the* de minimis *allowance for the US under the Doha draft modalities*

	Million dollars
Final Bound Total AMS	19,103.3
Value of production (average 1995–2000)	194,139.3
15 percent value of production	29,120.9
Base OTDS	48,224.2
Final Bound OTDS (after 70 percent reduction)	14,467.3
Final Bound Total AMS (after 60 percent reduction)	7,641.3
FBTAMS as a share of value of production (1995–2000)[a]	5.4%
Blue box limit (2.5 percent value of production 1995–2000)	4,853.5
De minimis	
50 percent immediate reduction	2.5%
Cotton special provisions	
Base AMS for cotton (million dollars)	800.5
Cotton AMS reduction (assuming 60 percent FBTAMS reduction)[b]	82.2%

[a] Tests for less than 40 percent, so additional effort does not apply (Table 2.2 and Appendix B, paragraph 14).

[b] Application of the cotton AMS reduction formula (Appendix B, paragraphs 54 and 55).

Source: Authors' calculations based on WTO (2008).

3. a special provision for the US calculation of other product-specific AMS limits; and
4. a special provision for the calculation of product-specific blue box limits, with a more stringent cap proposed for cotton.

Some of the principal implications of the proposed Doha draft modalities for the United States are summarized in Tables 4.8 and 4.9. The US Base OTDS from which reductions are to be made is $48.2 billion, comprised of the Final Bound Total AMS of $19.1 billion plus 15 percent of the US total agricultural value of production, which averaged $194.1 billion during 1995–2000. With the proposed 70 percent reduction, the final binding for the OTDS is just under $14.5 billion at the end of the proposed five-year implementation period.[17] The 60 percent reduction in the Final Bound Total AMS would

[17] During the December 2008 negotiations a further reduction to $14 billion was discussed.

Table 4.9 *Phased reductions of limits on OTDS, CTAMS and cotton AMS for the US under the Doha draft modalities*

	Immediate	Year 1	Year 2	Year 3	Year 4	Year 5 (Final)
Reduction commitments	*Cumulative proportions of the base to be cut*					
Base OTDS[a]	0.33	0.40	0.48	0.55	0.63	0.70
Final Bound Total AMS[b]	0.25	0.32	0.39	0.46	0.53	0.60
Cotton AMS[c]	0.25	0.25	0.82	0.82	0.82	0.82
Scheduled limits[d]	*Million dollars*					
Bound OTDS	32,310	28,742	25,173	21,604	18,036	14,467
Final Bound Total AMS	14,327	12,990	11,653	10,316	8,978	7,641
Cotton AMS	600	600	142	142	142	142

[a] Initial reduction of one-third, with remainder phased-in in five equal steps (Table 2.2 and Appendix B, paragraph 5).

[b] Initial reduction of 25 percent, with remainder phased-in in five equal steps (Table 2.2 and Appendix B, paragraph 15).

[c] Two-year phase-in period, with higher total reduction percentage than other products (Appendix B, paragraphs 54–56).

[d] Limit applies after reduction at end of year in corresponding column is made.

Source: Authors' interpretation based on WTO (2008).

reduce this cap to $7.64 billion. Total blue blue box payments would be limited to a maximum of $4.85 billion and the product-specific and non-product-specific *de minimis* thresholds lowered immediately to 2.5 percent of production values. The AMS limit for cotton would be reduced by 82.2 percent from a base value calculated as $800 million to $143 million. The cotton limits would have an accelerated phased-in period (20 months) compared to the five-year implementation for the phase-in of reduction commitments for Bound OTDS and Bound Total AMS.

Though the Doha bindings would not come into force for a number of years, it is instructive to examine whether the final proposed commitments would have been binding on past policies as notified. This question was particularly relevant through the early years of the Doha Round WTO negotiations (2001–05) when the broad outlines of possible commitments were being hammered out.[18] In this context, a comparison of the Final Bound OTDS of $14.5 billion to the sum of CTAMS, total *de minimis* and blue box support (Table 4.1) shows that past notified US support would not have been in compliance in the years 1995, 1998–2002 and 2004–05. The CTAMS would have exceeded the Final Bound Total AMS of $7.6 billion in 1998–2002 and 2004–06. The non-product-specific AMS would have exceeded 2.5 percent of the value of production from 1999–2002 and consequently would have been added to the CTAMS in those years. Product-specific cotton support exceeded the proposed limit under the Doha draft modalities every year with the exception of 1995 and 1996 and blue box expenditures in 1995 also exceeded the proposed Doha limit. The implication is that the constraints discussed in the Doha Round would have required policy changes if they had been applied in the past.

Table 4.10 contains calculations for the product-specific AMS limits under the Doha draft modalities for the forty-seven product categories for which an AMS was notified for at least one year since 1995. The sum of product-specific limits is just over $15 billion, almost double the proposed Final Bound Total AMS. Thus, the United States would not be able to provide the full amount of support allowed for each specific commodity while respecting its aggregate commitment.

The implications of the Doha bindings for the US vary by product. Only two of the forty-seven product categories for which an AMS was notified would have a zero AMS binding. These are avocados, for which a small amount of trade-adjustment assistance payments was notified in 2005 and the commodity aggregate beef, cattle and sheep for which a modest amount of assistance under a grant program was notified in 2006. Both of these fall outside the 1995–2004 base period for determining US product-specific caps under the Doha draft modalities, although assistance to beef, cattle and sheep producers could be provided under other categories included in Table 4.10. That is, if the methodology specified in the modalities is applied strictly, some products appear to be eligible for multiple caps (for example, those products notified separately and under aggregates such as livestock and orchards and vineyards).

Two of the products, dairy (with the calculations still based on total milk production) and sugar, would be subject to a special three-year phase-in for the reduction specified in the draft modalities, since their average AMS in the two notifications prior to the December 2008 draft

[18] Sumner (2005) provided an insightful early analysis at that time.

Table 4.10 *Product-specific US AMS bindings under the Doha draft modalities*

	Applicable modalities[a]	Base AMS	Year 1	Year 2	Year 3	Notified AMS 2007
		Million dollars				
Apples	25	76.6	76.6	76.6	76.6	—
Apricots	25	1.8	1.8	1.8	1.8	—
Avocados		—	—	—	—	—
Barley	23	27.4	27.4	27.4	27.4	—
Beef, cattle and sheep		—	—	—	—	—
Beef and veal	25	1,254.8	1,254.8	1,254.8	1,254.8	—
Blueberries, wild	25	1.8	1.8	1.8	1.8	—
Cattle and calves	25	1,255.4	1,255.4	1,255.4	1,255.4	—
Chickpeas	24	0.2	0.2	0.2	0.2	—
Corn	23	1,106.4	1,106.4	1,106.4	1,106.4	—
Cotton[b]	23	1,136.1	600.4	142.5	142.5	—
Cranberries	25	10.7	10.7	10.7	10.7	—
Dairy[c]	23,26	5,030.3	4,947.2	4,864.0	4,780.9	5,016.5
Dry peas	24	34.8	34.8	34.8	34.8	—
Grapes	25	131.2	131.2	131.2	131.2	—
Hogs and pigs	25	512.8	512.8	512.8	512.8	—
Honey	23	2.9	2.9	2.9	2.9	—
Lentils	24	6.1	6.1	6.1	6.1	—
Livestock	25	1,255.4	1,255.4	1,255.4	1,255.4	—
Lychee	25	0.2	0.2	0.2	0.2	—

Table 4.10 (*cont.*)

	Applicable modalities[a]	Base AMS	Year 1	Year 2	Year 3	Notified AMS 2007
		Million dollars				
Minor oil seeds						
Canola	23	15.1	15.1	15.1	15.1	—
Crambe	24	<0.1	<0.1	<0.1	<0.1	—
Flaxseed	24	<0.1	<0.1	<0.1	<0.1	—
Mustard seed	23	0.1	0.1	0.1	0.1	—
Rapeseed	23	<0.1	<0.1	<0.1	<0.1	—
Safflower	23	0.5	0.5	0.5	0.5	—
Sesame	23	<0.1	<0.1	<0.1	<0.1	—
Sunflower	23	35.5	35.5	35.5	35.5	—
Mohair	23	3.1	3.1	3.1	3.1	0.8
Oats	23	9.4	9.4	9.4	9.4	—
Olives	25	2.9	2.9	2.9	2.9	—
Onions	25	35.1	35.1	35.1	35.1	—
Orchards and vineyards	25	798.2	798.2	798.2	798.2	—
Peaches	25	22.0	22.0	22.0	22.0	—
Peanuts	23	249.2	249.2	249.2	249.2	—
Pears	25	14.0	14.0	14.0	14.0	—
Pecan trees	25	11.7	11.7	11.7	11.7	—
Potatoes	25	133.4	133.4	133.4	133.4	—
Rice	23	313.7	313.7	313.7	313.7	—
Rye	25	1.4	1.4	1.4	1.4	—

Sheep and lamb	24	7.0	7.0	7.0	7.0	—
Sorghum	23	42.6	42.6	42.6	42.6	—
Soybeans	23	1,123.7	1,123.7	1,123.7	1,123.7	—
Sugar	23,26	1,257.8	1,213.9	1,169.9	1,126.0	1,235.8
Tobacco	23	142.9	142.9	142.9	142.9	—
Tomatoes	25	86.2	86.2	86.2	86.2	—
Wheat	23	231.4	231.4	231.4	231.4	—
Wool	23	10.1	10.1	10.1	10.1	6.7
Total for all products		16,392.3	15,729.5	15,144.5	15,017.4	6,259.9

Notes: — indicates zero.

[a] See Appendix B for applicable paragraphs.

[b] The effective binding shown for cotton is that implied by the special reduction provisions, but the base value is not adjusted for those provisions.

[c] Dairy binding calculated on the basis of total milk production as notified for 2006 and 2007.

Source: Authors' calculations based on US notifications.

modalities (2006 and 2007) was more than 130 percent of their base levels). The cotton binding would be superseded by additional provisions. In the absence of these provisions the cotton AMS binding would be reduced from a base value of $1.5 billion to a bound value of $1.1 billion over a period of three years. The additional provisions result in a reduction from just over $800 million to a bound value of $143 million over a period of twenty months, as shown in Table 4.9.

Overall, the application of the rules specified in the modalities appears to leave a considerable amount of space for policy flexibility by providing product-specific AMS limits for virtually all important and minor US agricultural commodities, even if the actual notified support for some of these has been small in the past. But it may be difficult to keep within some of the product-specific caps if prices were to fall. The cap on corn at $1.1 billion, compared with a notified AMS well in excess of this value when prices have been low (see Table 4.4), is particularly noteworthy in this respect. A comparison of the data in Table 4.4 on the notifications for 1995–2008 to the product-specific AMS limits in Table 4.10 reveals that no less than 115 of the 153 notified AMS values included in CTAMS (75 percent) would have exceeded the proposed Doha limits (even without any trade-off to the blue box, discussed below). This includes all the notified AMS values for barley, corn, oats, soybeans and wheat. It suggests again that the proposed product-specific AMS limits could be extremely important.

Table 4.11 contains information on product-specific blue box bindings included in the draft modalities. The US limits are based on the maximum potential expenditure on countercyclical payments under the 2002 FSRI Act. The draft modalities include a special provision for the US, allowing base values of product-specific blue box support of either 110 percent or 120 percent of the amounts derived from applying proportionately legislated maximum permissible expenditure under the 2002 FSRI Act to 2.5 percent of average value of production for 1995–2000. Using the lower of the two proposed parameters (110 percent), the product-specific blue box caps would permit support through countercyclical payments equivalent to roughly 61 percent of the legislated maximum. The higher figure (120 percent) yields 66 percent of the maximum. As indicated in Table 4.7, maximum permitted payments within the overall blue box limit would be $4.8 billion. This implies that it would only be possible to exploit the full allowance provided by the individual blue box caps under the lower (110 percent) binding, as shown in Table 4.11.

The draft modalities indicate that countries can elect to increase the blue box binding for individual products by reducing that product's corresponding AMS binding. This is done on a dollar-for-dollar basis, except

Table 4.11 *Product-specific US blue box bindings and the trade-off with product-specific AMS bindings under the Doha draft modalities*

	Base AMS binding[a]	Blue binding 110%	Blue binding 120%	Legislated maximum CCP	AMS binding if blue is increased to maximum[b]
	Million dollars				
Barley	27.4	32.0	34.9	46.7	12.7
Corn	1,106.4	2,359.8	2,574.3	3,224.2	242.0
Cotton[c]	800.5	336.3	366.9	1,376.5	—
Oats	9.4	5.3	5.8	8.7	6.0
Peanuts	249.2	149.5	163.1	200.9	197.8
Rice	313.7	234.9	256.3	323.1	225.5
Sorghum	42.6	106.8	116.5	147.4	2.0
Soybeans	1,123.7	400.4	436.8	550.3	973.8
Wheat	231.4	1,041.1	1,135.7	1,421.5	—
Total	3,904.4	4,666.1	5090.3[d]	7,299.3	1,659.9

Notes: — indicates zero.

[a] It is assumed that the applicable figures for the calculation are the bindings that result after the application of any reduction provisions. This column matches the final product-specific bindings in Table 4.10, with the exception of cotton which is subject to a special provision for its base-period value (see Appendix B, paragraph 55).

[b] For cotton and wheat where insufficient product-specific AMS entitlement exists to reach the legislated maximum CCP, the full AMS entitlement is applied to the blue box.

[c] In the case of cotton, a $1 increase in the blue box entitlement requires a $2 reduction in the AMS; this is applied to the figure in column 1. Cotton blue box bindings are reduced substantially by the paragraph 56 condition.

[d] Total exceeds permitted blue box maximum of $4,853.5 million. Increases in blue box limits only apply if initially scheduled; any subsequent changes would require reductions elsewhere, such that the initial overall blue box limit is not exceeded (Appendix B, paragraph 45).

Source: Authors' calculations based on WTO notifications and WTO (2008).

for cotton where the rate is one dollar of expanded blue box binding for each two dollars given up from the AMS. Table 4.11 analyzes the effect of this provision for the case of the 110 percent initial blue box binding. As shown in the last column, box-shifting from the product-specific AMS to the product-specific blue box could achieve the legislated maxima for all CCP commodities individually except for cotton and wheat (this is without considering any additional constraints imposed by the overall blue box limit). For those commodities the AMS binding is too low to be able to achieve the legislated CCP maximum. In addition, the sum of the individual product bindings would exceed the overall blue box limit. Hence any choice to increase individual bindings to the legislated maximum, which would have to be declared in the initial scheduling of commitments, would imply trade-offs in order to satisfy the overall blue box constraint.

Future compliance with Doha

With buoyant agricultural prices in 2007–08 the prospect of a new era of higher prices has been widely discussed. Price projections are subject to uncertainty, but a shift to higher levels certainly has implications for the tightness of domestic support commitments.

To assess the implications of a Doha agreement in line with the December 2008 draft modalities, the following assumptions were made:

1. The first year for implementation of a new agreement is 2011 with complete implementation by 2015;
2. The Final Bound OTDS, Final Bound Total AMS, blue box and cotton AMS commitments and the *de minimis* threshold and phase-in periods are those shown in Table 4.8 and 4.9;
3. The parameters of US support programs are those of the 2008 FCE Act. Market price support for dairy is assumed to be notified on the basis of the three processed products rather than total milk production. However, possible ACRE revenue-guarantee payments are not included in the basic calculations;
4. The final product-specific AMS bindings included in Table 4.10 are imposed;
5. The 110 percent product-specific blue box bindings (second column in Table 4.11) are applied; and
6. No allowance is made for the transfer of product-specific AMS to product-specific blue box.

Table 4.12 *Projected levels of US domestic support under the Doha draft modalities, 2010–16*

	2010	2011	2012	2013	2014	2015	2016
	Billion dollars						
Green box	102.2	104.8	107.6	110.0	112.4	114.8	117.5
OTDS	10.7	10.3	10.3	10.4	10.6	10.7	10.2
Blue box	—	0.5	0.5	0.4	0.3	0.3	0.2
Current Total AMS	4.6	4.7	4.8	4.9	4.9	5.0	5.0
Total *de minimis*	6.1	5.1	5.0	5.1	5.3	5.4	4.9
Product-specific	0.1	0.1	0.1	0.1	0.1	0.1	0.1
Non-product-specific	6.0	5.0	4.9	5.0	5.2	5.3	4.8
Total support	113.0	115.2	117.8	120.5	123.0	125.5	127.7

Note: — indicates zero.
Source: Authors' estimates.

Table 4.12 summarizes the projected notifications by category. The only change from Table 4.7 is the emergence of a modest amount of blue box payments by switching countercyclical payments from the non-product-specific AMS, and a corresponding reduction in the amount of *de minimis* support under the latter. Figure 4.6 shows how the reductions in the US commitments for the OTDS, the CTAMS, and the overall blue box relate to projected notifications. The reduction in the OTDS ceiling does not become binding even by the end of the implementation period, but the leeway in the commitment, resulting from the limit being higher than projected notifications, is substantially reduced. These projections suggest that in the first year of implementation of a Doha agreement, there would be a roughly $18 billion cushion between the applied OTDS and the bound level. By 2016 this would have declined to around $4.3 billion. The reduction in the Bound Total AMS is also significant, with a decrease in the CTAMS support cushion from over $8 billion in 2011 to less than $3 billion by 2016. Projected blue box payments remain far below the ceiling – the overall blue box limit does not have a constraining effect on the projections since high prices mean that countercyclical payments are low. The analysis also shows that non-product-specific AMS stays below the *de minimis* threshold, but the margin is reduced to roughly $1 billion.

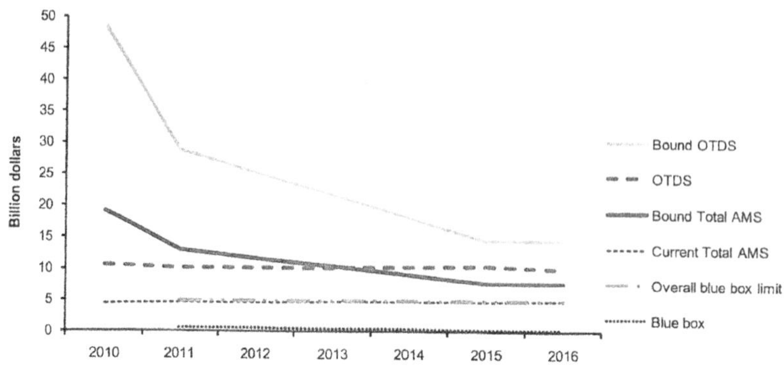

Figure 4.6 Projections and proposed Doha commitments for US OTDS, CTAMS and overall blue box support
Source: Authors' estimates.

AMS support, even within *de minimis* allowances, may also face a limit imposed by the room left within the OTDS binding after accounting for CTAMS and blue box payments.

We also analyzed the implications of the product-specific AMS and product-specific blue box bindings for some of the most important commodities: barley, corn, cotton, dairy (based on total milk production), peanuts, rice, sorghum, soybeans, sugar, and wheat. Our projections suggest that the AMS binding would become operative for dairy and sugar from the first year of the implementation period and throughout. There is a gradual increase in the amount by which the product-specific AMS binding for these commodities is exceeded (Figure 4.7) from around $200 million in 2011 to $400 million for sugar and to $600 million for dairy by 2016. The AMS for sugar is increased by higher sugar administered prices (loan rates) in the FCE Act and by a projected expansion in sugar production. The higher AMS for dairy is attributable to expanding milk production. Our projections also imply that the blue box binding for cotton would be exceeded in the initial years of a new agreement, but higher projected cotton prices eliminate this problem from 2014 onwards.[19]

[19] Earlier projections based on lower cotton prices suggested that both the product-specific blue box and AMS commitments could be binding for cotton (see Blandford, Laborde, and Martin 2008). The potentially binding product-specific dairy limit seems to provide one incentive for the redefinition of dairy support in 2008.

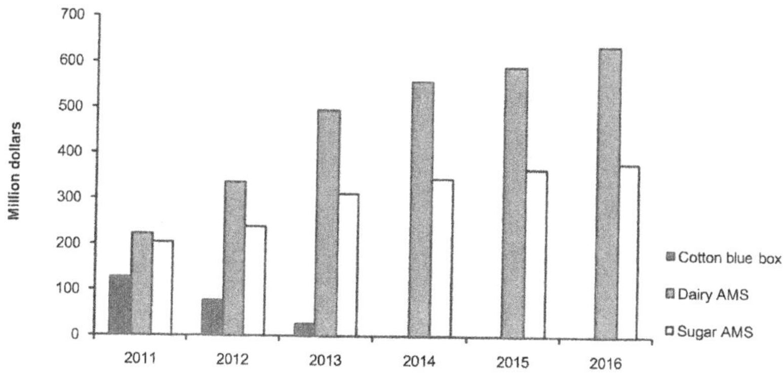

Figure 4.7 Amounts by which proposed US product-specific Doha commitments are projected to be exceeded
Source: Authors' estimates.

In summary, the new Doha commitments would certainly be more stringent than those of the Agreement. They might constrain US farm programs in terms of choice of measures or subsidy levels. Strengthened disciplines would reduce the leeway the US would have for providing trade-distorting support but still provide limited flexibility if prices remain relatively high. The net outcome projected for 2016 is illustrated in Figure 4.8, which shows projected CTAMS, blue box and product-specific and non-product-specific *de minimis* support compared to the potential limit of almost $14.5 billion under a Doha constraint on the OTDS. The difference between the OTDS limit and the sum of projected support is shown as the "Available OTDS." Projected blue box payments (counter-cyclical payments) are only $0.2 billion, well under the modalities cap of $4.8 billion. The CTAMS (dairy and sugar MPS) is projected at $5.0 billion, compared to the proposed cap of $7.6 billion. Product-specific *de minimis* support is negligible and non-product-specific *de minimis* support is projected at $4.8 billion. These projections and caps leave room for various additional OTDS support of $4.3 billion. The latitude for additional support is therefore limited, unless the United States further reduces the notified AMS for dairy and sugar.[20]

[20] The inclusion of a provision in the 2008 FCE Act to divert government purchases of sugar to the production of ethanol opens up the interesting possibility that the sugar program (or some part of it) could be defined as a bioenergy program. This might also be used to

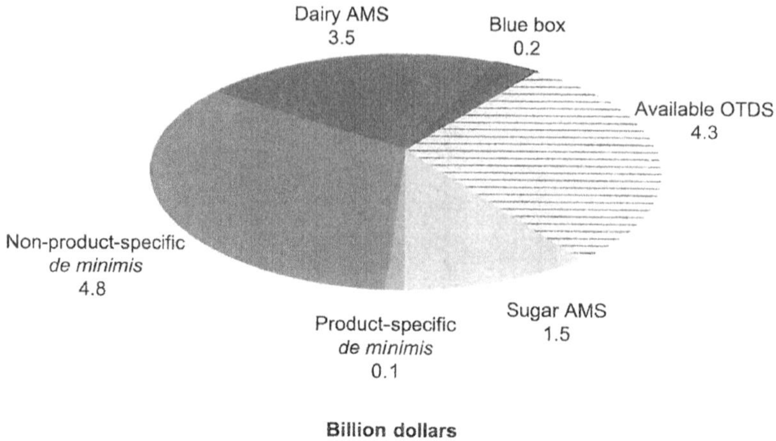

Figure 4.8 Projected composition of US OTDS in 2016 and available OTDS under proposed Doha commitments
Source: Authors' estimates.

Uncertainty due to the ACRE program

Thus far the implications of the new ACRE state revenue-guarantee program have not been considered in the projections of US support. Significant enrollment in the ACRE program and payments triggered by revenue variability could affect compliance with US commitments under the Agreement. The program makes payments when revenue for a crop in a state falls below a moving average of past levels. Payments can be triggered by a decline in the US price, state yields, or a combination of the two. USDA price and yield projections reflect recent trends and exhibit limited variability, so ACRE payments are not triggered using those numbers. However, actual prices and yields inevitably prove more variable than projections. No ceiling exists on guaranteed revenue and ACRE can provide assistance when revenue declines but prices remain above marketing loan and countercyclical support prices. Because ACRE payments are linked to both current prices and production, it is likely that they will be classified as product-specific AMS support.

relieve any pressure on sugar protection that arises from changes in market access (tariffs and tariff-rate quotas) under a new WTO agreement.

The potential magnitude of ACRE payments for corn, soybeans and wheat was examined by Zulauf and Orden (2010). As a counterfactual historical analysis, they assumed for illustration that all the acreage for these crops was enrolled in an ACRE program during 1996–2008 instead of the actual US support programs during that period. They estimated the annual payments that would have been made under ACRE given the changes in annual prices and state yields and acreage that occurred each year.

With ACRE in operation during 1996–2008, there would have been no countercyclical payments. With loan rates reduced by 30 percent in the ACRE program, there also would have been no loan-rate-related payments. Total ACRE revenue guarantee payments would have been only $14.7 billion, in part because in some years higher yields offset lower prices sufficiently such that payments would not have occurred, while the traditional price support programs made payments. The relatively low ACRE payments for 1996–2008 would not have caused the CTAMS to exceed the US commitment under the Agreement in any year. Peak estimated annual ACRE payment for the three crops was $5.2 billion in the 1998 crop year, compared to $3.3 billion in AMS notified for these commodities. Since the 1998 CTAMS was only $10.4 billion the increase due to ACRE would not have violated the US commitment.

In a forward-looking analysis, the potential ACRE payments for the years 2009–12 were estimated given the higher prices for corn, soybeans, and wheat projected by USDA in January 2009 for these crop years. For each year, the analysis considered cases where the percentage changes in prices, yields and acreage compared to USDA's projections matched the percentage changes that took place in one year between 1996 and 2006 (providing eleven such cases of changes). The sum in any crop year of the highest projected ACRE payments to corn, soybeans, and wheat over the sets of applied changes was $14.2 billion, again assuming all acreage is enrolled in the program. Thus, it seems possible that with the higher price levels prevailing since 2007 the United States could exceed its Bound Total AMS of $19.1 billion if market conditions change sufficiently from year-to-year to trigger significant ACRE payments. In contrast, none of the cases of changes in price, yield and acreage triggered countercyclical or loan-rate-related payments for any year when it was assumed that all acreage of corn, soybeans and wheat remained in the traditional support programs during 2009–12.

The possibility of large ACRE payments under some of the cases analyzed poses additional challenges for the United States in meeting potential Doha commitments. The proposed product-specific AMS caps are among the relevant constraints. For corn and soybeans, estimated payments for each crop year exceeded the Doha product-specific caps in three and four of the eleven cases of changes, respectively. For wheat, projected payments exceeded the Doha product-specific cap for seven of the eleven cases for the 2009 and 2010 crop years and for six cases for the 2011 and 2012 crop years. The actual participation rate in ACRE, in addition to future fluctuations in prices and output, will affect the likelihood that ACRE payments would pose a challenge for meeting future Doha commitments. For example, if the share of base acres enrolled in the ACRE program in 2009 (roughly 10–20 percent) remained the same through the mid 2010s, AMS support would likely remain below the Doha product-specific caps. Sign-up rates are high enough that the ACRE program or some variant of it will probably remain part of future US farm support policy. A Doha agreement would make it difficult to design such a program both to stay within the US commitments and attract substantial participation. Thus a Doha agreement could shape future US policy.

Summary and implications for US agricultural policy

This chapter has examined past and proposed US domestic support in the light of existing and potential WTO constraints. In the first section we provided a brief review of US farm policies since the Agreement on Agriculture came into effect, including a synopsis of the Food, Conservation, and Energy Act of 2008. Our review highlights the shifting alignment of US support policies: initially a response to relatively high prices when the 1996 farm bill was enacted with the first US fixed direct payments, then the impact of relatively low prices when policies were reconsidered in the 2002 FSRI Act and price-linked countercyclical payments were re-institutionalized. In 2008, market prices were again strong, but with the exception of the potentially significant ACRE program there was little change in basic support policies. This meant that US price-linked subsidies were projected to fall sharply under the 2008 FCE Act, compared with levels early in the 2000s, with higher subsidies projected for crop and revenue insurance. We also highlighted acreage-idling under the CRP and increased spending on other environmental programs, which are measures in the green box and subject to its rules.

The second section provided an assessment of US domestic support notifications to the WTO from 1995–2007 and a shadow notification estimate for 2008. Green box expenditures for domestic nutrition programs dominate the total dollar value of support notified by the United States. The main notified components for agriculture include fixed direct payments, disaster assistance, and environmental payments in the green box; market price support for dairy and sugar and substantial price-linked expenditures (loan program payments) in the product-specific AMS; and non-product-specific AMS support qualifying for the *de minimis* exemption (crop MLA payments, countercyclical payments, and crop and revenue insurance subsidies). The AMS price-linked payments have varied from a low of near zero (1996, 2007 and 2008) to a high of $9.7 billion in 1999, while crop MLA payments and countercyclical payments varied from $0.5 billion in 2003 to $5.5 billion in 1999.

The US CTAMS has never exceeded the Bound Total AMS of $19.1 billion. It would have done so in some years without the non-product-specific *de minimis* exemption or if US fixed direct payments were included in the AMS as either non-product-specific or product-specific support. We discuss other subsidies that may be underreported, misclassified, or omitted from the notifications, some of which are also at issue in WTO dispute settlement cases. We note that tax credits and mandates related to ethanol production have been largely outside the disciplines of the Agreement and discuss arguments related to their inclusion as trade-distorting support.

We next provided an assessment of projected US support through 2016 and evaluated the extent to which the Agreement or new disciplines in the Doha draft modalities might limit future US policies. With projected high prices the Agreement hardly constrains US policies at all. Reclassified fixed direct payments, large ACRE revenue-guarantee payments, or ethanol tax credits could be accommodated without violating the Bound Total AMS. That is unlikely to be the case if the proposed new Doha disciplines were adopted since the room for maneuver would be more limited. With high prices, the unused support space within the Bound OTDS commitment is projected to be $4.3 billion by 2016 given the way that the US has notified its dairy support after implementing the 2008 FCE Act. If there were no ACRE revenue-guarantee payments, no reclassification of direct payments, and no inclusion of other subsidies, the US would have this limited flexibility to increase support – whether through higher loan rates or by increasing other forms of product-specific support included in the CTAMS, raising target prices for countercyclical payments in the blue box, or through expanding non-product-specific AMS while staying below the *de minimis* threshold. Additional redefinition of the dairy program with a corresponding further reduction in notified MPS could provide more flexibility for increasing loan rates for other commodities by opening additional space within the Bound Total AMS. However, if payments under the ACRE program become significant it seems unlikely that the United States would be able to stay within a reduced Bound Total AMS or meet other Doha commitments.

If the relatively high-price environment foreseen by the USDA continues to materialize, it appears that the United States would have to adapt to the Doha draft modalities by making modest downward adjustments in the support provided by some of its policies. Experience with farm legislation shows that such adjustments would not be easy to make nor politically painless. The proposed product-specific limits, in particular, could further constrain policy flexibility. Sugar poses problems for AMS commitments even if world prices are high because of the way MPS is calculated and notified. The redefinition of the dairy program in the FCE Act might signal that a similar attempt could be made to resolve this issue for sugar without substantive change in the degree of support provided to producers. The stringent modalities for cotton, if adopted, could prove challenging for meeting blue box commitments, even under projected high prices. Other product-specific caps, such as for AMS for corn, would limit support well below levels observed in the 2000s.

The price environment foreseen by USDA and incorporated into our projections may not materialize. Lower prices could prove a challenge. In that case, the Bound Total AMS and some product-specific AMS limits could well be exceeded under a Doha agreement, unless alternatives to current support policies were found. One option would be to use the green box to alter the composition of farm support. Green box support for farmers could be expanded, particularly under the environmental category, or under other categories such as decoupled income support payments or disaster relief payments that satisfy green box criteria. The future status of current US fixed direct payments is in doubt, but payment rules could be modified to ensure green box compliance.

In conclusion, the strengthened disciplines on domestic support in the Doha draft modalities would have the effect of reducing substantially the leeway in the amount of support that can be provided to US farmers while still meeting WTO commitments. A few commodities pose problems even with relatively high prices. The option of redefining support policies to reduce notified MPS further for dairy or for sugar and the possibility of there being some unused support space in other areas (blue box and non-product-specific AMS falling under *de minimis*) provide some amount of flexibility in meeting future WTO commitments. However, if prices were to fall substantially, so that major countercyclical, price support, or ACRE revenue-guarantee payments were triggered, the likelihood of meeting tighter WTO commitments on domestic support under a continuation of existing programs would be substantially reduced. Thus, the tighter Doha commitments could bring significant change in the design of future US domestic support policies for agriculture.

References

Blandford, D., and T. Josling. 2007. US and EU domestic support notifications, 2007–2012. Paper presented at a workshop of the German Marshall Fund of the United States, Washington, DC, September 11.

Blandford, D., D. Laborde, and W. Martin. 2008. Implications for the United States. ICTSD/IPC/IFFPRI Project on Draft Agricultural Modalities. Paper presented at a seminar in Geneva, March 12.

Chite, R. M. 2007. Farm bill budget and costs: 2002 vs. 2007. RS22694, Congressional Research Service. November 7.

Congressional Budget Office. 2008. H.R. 2419: The Food, Conservation, and Energy Act of 2008 – Conference agreement compared to March 2007 CBO baseline, May 12. www.cbo.gov (accessed June 8, 2008).

de Gorter, H., and D. R. Just. 2009. The economics of blend mandates for biofuels. *American Journal of Agricultural Economics* 91(3): 738–750.

Gardner, B. 2002. *American Agriculture in the Twentieth Century: How it Flourished and What it Cost*. Cambridge, MA: Harvard University Press.

2009. Distortions to agricultural incentives in the United States and Canada. In *Distortions to Agricultural Incentives: A Global Perspective 1955–2007*, ed. K. Anderson. London: Palgrave Macmillan, and Washington, DC: World Bank.

Hull, D., J. Langley, and G. Hitz. 2009. CBO March 2009 baseline for CCC & FCIC, February 20. www.cbo.gov (accessed March 10, 2009).

Josling, T. E., S. Tangermann, and T. K. Warley. 1996. *Agriculture in the GATT*. New York: St. Martin's Press Inc.

Orden, D., D. Blandford, and T. Josling. 2010. Determinants of farm policies in the United States, 1996–2008. In *The Political Economy of Distortions to Agricultural Incentives*, ed. K. Anderson. Cambridge University Press.

Orden, D., R. Paarlberg, and T. Roe. 1999. *Policy Reform in American Agriculture: Analysis and Prognosis*. University of Chicago Press.

Sumner, D. 2005. Boxed in: Conflicts between US farm policies and WTO obligations. Trade Policy Analysis No. 32, CATO Institute.

USDA (US Department of Agriculture). 2009a. Commodity Credit Corporation commodity estimates book FY 2010 mid-session review. Presentation 2010–02. Farm Service Agency, July.

2009b. USDA agricultural projections to 2017. Long-term projections report OCE-2008–1. Office of the Chief Economist, World Agricultural Outlook Board.

WTO. 2005. United States – Subsidies on upland cotton. Report of the Appellate Body. WT/DS267/AB/R, 3 March.

2007a. United States – Domestic support and export credit guarantees for agricultural products. Request for the establishment of a panel by Brazil. WT/DS365/13, 9 November.

2007b. United States – Subsidies and other domestic support for corn and other agricultural products. Request for the establishment of a panel by Canada. WT/DS357/12, 9 November.

2008. Revised draft modalities for agriculture. TN/AG/W/4/Rev.4, 6 December.

Zulauf, C., and D. Orden. 2010. The Revenue program option in the 2008 US farm bill: Evaluating performance characteristics of the ACRE program. *Agricultural and Resource Economics Review* 39(3): 517–533.

Chapter 10

Assessing the Political Economy of the U.S. 2014 Farm Bill

Carl Zulauf and David Orden*

Abstract

This chapter assesses the political economy of the 2014 farm bill, which eliminated annual fixed direct payments but offers enhanced downside risk protection against low prices or declining revenue. The farm bill secured substantial bipartisan majorities in a politically contentious Congress. The countercyclical structure of U.S. support is reaffirmed and crop insurance is enhanced as a safety net pillar. Open policy issues include the distribution of benefits among crops, the design of multiple year support around moving-average revenue benchmarks versus fixed references prices, and questions related to crop insurance, including the overall level of premium subsidies. In an international context, we conclude the 2014 farm safety net likely would not have been enacted had multilateral agreement been reached on the 2008 Doha Round negotiating documents; conversely, the 2014 safety net makes achieving those limits more difficult.

Keywords: Agricultural policy, 2014 farm bill, farm subsidies, commodity programs, crop insurance, conservation, WTO

*Carl Zulauf (zulauf.1@osu.edu) is professor in the Department of Agricultural, Environmental and Development Economics at Ohio State University. David Orden (d.orden@cgiar.org) is professor of agricultural and applied economics at Virginia Tech and senior research fellow at the International Food Policy Research Institute. Senior authorship is shared.

This is an extended version of an invited paper "The Political Economy of the 2014 Farm Bill" presented at the AAEA session "The 2014 Farm Bill: An Economic Post Mortem," ASSA Annual Meetings, January 4, 2015, Boston MA and published in the *American Journal of Agricultural Economics* (Orden and Zulauf, 2015). The authors thank participants at presentations at IFPRI, July 16, 2014, the Inter-American Institute for Cooperation on Agriculture (IICA), October 9, 2014, the International Agricultural Trade Research Consortium (IATRC), December 8, 2014, and the ASSA session for helpful comments and

This chapter assesses the domestic and international political economy of the *Agricultural Act of 2014* (P.L. 113-79; 2014 farm bill). Passed in February 2014 after three years of intense debate, it reaffirms through 2018 the longstanding support for U.S. farmers. The debate was framed by large federal budget deficits resulting from a deep economic recession and five years of slow recovery. Given high crop prices and farm incomes during this period of national economic stress, the time may have seemed propitious to lessen the role and fiscal cost of U.S. farm policy. Instead, maintaining public assistance remained a keen objective of farmers and their congressional allies and they mostly succeeded.

The farm safety net that emerged is complex but can be abstracted to a few points. Fixed direct payments of about $4.5 billion annually are eliminated, ending a program of nearly two decades. Countercyclical support, which has a long precedent in U.S. farm policy, is strengthened. Specifically, downside risk protection is increased for both what are termed shallow losses that coincide with the deductible on individual farm insurance and multiple year losses associated with persistent low prices or declining revenue. Also strengthened is the core role for federally subsidized, privately delivered crop insurance for production-period risk. This strengthening of the downside risk safety net highlights the question of what share of U.S. farmers' risk the public should bear. The fiscal cost of the revised safety net is less certain than with fixed direct payments. Costs may prove to be more or less than if the 2014 farm bill had not been enacted.

With agriculture a small but relatively prosperous and concentrated sector of the economy, it is plausible to maintain that U.S. farm policy is an equilibrium result of interest group lobbying.[1] Each farm bill is driven by specific contestation among various farm and nonfarm political

suggestions. A more complete description and discussion of the 2014 farm bill programs is provided in Zulauf and Orden (2014).

[1] Anderson, Rausser and Swinnen (2013) assess alternative theoretical approaches and empirical evidence on the political economy of agricultural policies across political systems. Among concepts they review that are illustrated in our narrative are interest group lobbying, status quo bias, countercyclical bias, aversion to loss, ideology, the role of information, and obfuscation. Comparative governance concepts are not illustrated in this temporal evaluation of U.S. farm bills within a fixed institutional structure.

interests. Yet, farm policy also retains continuity along lines best assessed in retrospect. This is the case for the 2014 farm bill. Significant evolution of risk assistance programs occurred but key past reforms that lessen the distortionary effects of U.S. farm policy were retained, in particular fixed payment bases, planting flexibility, and low loan rates.

Some observers conclude that the extended debate that preceded enactment of the 2014 farm bill signals a loss of political power by the farm lobby. We disagree. The 2014 farm bill reaffirms historical farm support while providing benefits to other traditional constituencies, including conservation and nutrition assistance, as well as new stakeholders. Moreover, permanent legislation is retained, setting the stage for another farm bill starting with stronger protection against downside risks.

In an international context, we conclude the U.S. is unlikely to exceed its World Trade Organization (WTO) domestic support commitment, a topic addressed further by Glauber and Westhoff (2015). Support is more likely to exceed the tighter constraints of the December 2008 WTO Doha Round negotiating documents. Had a Doha agreement been reached, it is unlikely the 2014 farm bill would have been enacted as it is. Conversely, its enactment makes achieving the Doha limits more difficult. In contrast, the WTO rulings in the Brazil-U.S. cotton case led to substantive changes in the safety net for upland cotton.

Change and Continuity in U.S. Farm Policy

As shown in Table 1, the last four farm bills were enacted with large bipartisan congressional majorities; twice veto proof, once needed (2008) and once not (1996). These majorities emerged with differing control of Congress and the presidency. After extensive debates, each bill to varying degrees turned policy in a different direction while continuing support for farmers (Orden Blandford and Josling, 2011). Under the first Republican-controlled Congress in four decades and with rising crop prices, reforms in the 1996 farm bill included an unexpected adoption of fixed direct payments, which decoupled support from prices and planting, and an end to annual supply-control and most public-stock programs. Despite budgetary pressure, the fixed payments allowed farmers to capture support that would have evaporated as market prices rose above target prices. Reform advocates hoped these payments might be a transition, or buyout, bringing an end to

Table 1. Make-up of Congress and 1996 through 2014 Farm Bill Votes

			House		Senate	
Final short title	Public law	President	Party control	Farm bill vote	Party control	Farm bill vote
Federal Agriculture Improvement and Reform Act of 1996	104-127 (4/4/1996)	Clinton	Republican *228R/206D/1I*	318-89 *211R/106D/1I*	Republican *53R/47D*	74-26 *52R/22D*
Farm Security and Rural Investment Act of 2002	107-171 (5/13/2002)	Bush	Republican *222R/211D/2I*	280-141 *141R/137D/2I*	Democrat *49R/50D/1I*	64-35 *43D/20R/1I*
Food, Conservation, and Energy Act of 2008	110-234 (5/22/2008)	Bush	Democrat *202R/233D*	316-108 *216D/100R* (veto override)	Democrat *49R/49D/2I*	82-13 *45D/35R/2I* (veto override)
Agricultural Act of 2014	113-79 (2/7/2014)	Obama	Republican *232R/200D*	251-166 *162R/89D*	Democrat *45R/53D/2I*	68-32 *44D/22R/2I*

Sources: Compiled by the authors based on membership and roll call votes reported at www.congress.gov, www.senate.gov and www.clerk.house.gov.
Notes: Votes are on the farm bill conference report, except 2008 veto override. D is Democrat; R is Republican; I is independent. Party affiliation at the time of the farm bill and yea votes by party in italics. Three House seats were vacant at the time of the 2014 farm bill vote.

commodity programs, while farm program proponents noted that Congress remained the final guarantor of a safety net.

As farm support proponents had argued, Congress stepped in quickly with *ad hoc* payments when prices fell in 1998; the precursor to reviving a price countercyclical program in the 2002 farm bill. Even with low prices and farm incomes, a divided Congress retained planting flexibility and direct payments and did not reintroduce annual supply controls nor raise loan rates significantly.

During the 2008 farm bill debate, a Democrat-controlled Congress prioritized food assistance. The Food Stamp program, renamed the Supplemental Nutrition Assistance Program (SNAP), expanded eligibility criteria and signaled a shift from food access to improved nutrition. Farm groups were generally wary of changes to their safety net. Direct payments were retained, even as critics questioned their legitimacy with high crop incomes and eyed reductions to fund other priorities. The optional Average Crop Revenue Election (ACRE) program embodied several innovations sought by Midwest grain producers including a moving-average revenue benchmark, enacted into law for the first time, and a focus on shallow losses. Enrollment was modest due to a design viewed as complex and a 20% reduction in direct payments if ACRE was elected (Edwards, 2011).

Against this policy background, the 2014 farm bill was framed by divided control of Congress and a largely partisan debate over entitlement programs and fiscal deficits. SNAP expenditures rose during the post-2007 economic slowdown (Wilde, 2012), averaging $49.9 billion in 2008–2010 then $74.2 billion in 2011–2013. In contrast, the U.S. farm sector experienced a remarkable six years of prosperity. Net farm income averaged $74 billion during 2008–2010, increasing to $121 billion during 2011–2013. Corn and cotton prices averaged over 40% higher during the latter three years, while soybean and wheat prices averaged 27% and 14% higher.

With the farm sector prospering, contested direct payments continuing, and crop insurance net indemnity payments rising sharply, support payments reached a politically unstable level. Net indemnity payments averaged $9.1 billion for 2011–2013, exceeding direct payments each year, and peaking at $13.3 billion after the 2012 drought. With high incomes, but facing yield, price and revenue variability, most farm groups endorsed wider calls to eliminate direct payments as unjustified when farm incomes were high. They argued that most of the savings should go into strengthening insurance and other downside risk safety net programs—the eventual outcome.

Similar to the 1996 farm bill, the 2014 farm bill debate became mired in rancor over competing interests within the farm lobby and the broader deficit-related stand-off. In August 2011, as a Republican House squared off with a Democratic Senate and administration, Congress empaneled a super committee to find accord and authorized across the board sequester cuts if it failed. Key farm bill funding deliberations took place in this context but the super committee disbanded without agreement.

The Democratic Senate approved a farm bill in July 2012 but the House leadership never scheduled floor debate on a bill passed that month by its Agriculture Committee. With budget gridlock continuing after the November 2012 elections, the 112th Congress ended with a stop-gap measure to extend most provisions of the 2008 farm bill one year, through September 2013. The sequester cuts took effect in March 2013, including $6 billion over 10 years to projected farm commodity and conservation spending. Ensuing stalemate culminated six months later in the first partial government shutdown since 1995. Only then, in mid-October, did a fiscal truce emerge around continuing appropriations and an extended federal debt ceiling.

The Senate passed a second farm bill in June 2013, moving closer to the 2012 House version of commodity programs. In the House, a conservative caucus vociferously criticized both farm support and nutrition entitlement programs. The House defeated an Agriculture Committee bill then passed separate bills on farm programs and nutrition assistance. SNAP expenditures were reduced 5% ($40 billion), ten times the reduction proposed by the Senate. With this and other disparities, a second one- or two-year extension of the 2008 farm bill was widely expected prior to the fiscal truce. In its wake, under scrutiny to demonstrate the ability to govern, the *Agricultural Act of 2014* became one of the few major bills passed by the 113th Congress.

2014 Farm Bill Programs and Issues

Table 2 summarizes the planted and commodity program (base) acreage for nine major crops that received direct payments under the 2008 farm bill. Table 3 contains key features of the 2014 farm bill commodity and

Table 2. Planted and Base Acres, Crops Receiving Direct Payments, 2012 Crop Year

Crop	Planted acres (million)	Share of principal crop[a] acres	Program (base) acres[b] (million)	Share of program acres
Barley	3.6	1.1%	8.6	3.3%
Corn	97.2	29.8%	84.3	32.6%
Cotton (upland)	12.1	3.7%	17.9	6.9%
Oats	2.8	0.8%	3.0	1.2%
Peanuts	1.6	0.5%	1.5	0.6%
Rice	2.7	0.8%	4.4	1.7%
Sorghum	6.2	1.9%	11.6	4.5%
Soybeans	77.2	23.7%	50.1	19.4%
Wheat	55.7	17.1%	73.7	28.5%
Total	259.1	79.4%	255.1	98.7%

Source: Data from USDA.
Notes: [a]Principal crops include most crops except fruits, nuts and vegetables. Area planted to principal crops totals 326.3 million acres versus 259.1 for the nine crops receiving direct payments. [b]Total base acres for the United States are 258.3 million acres.

crop insurance programs and Table 4 presents some of the key commodity program parameters; for further discussion see, *inter alia*, CRS (2014), U.S. Congress (2014), USDA (2014a), Smith (2014) and Zulauf and Orden (2014).

Crop insurance is enhanced in the 2014 farm bill, including a new county level shallow loss program, the Supplemental Coverage Option (SCO), to partly cover the insurance deductible. The traditional upland cotton and dairy support policies are dramatically redesigned into a new cotton insurance program and dairy margin protection program, while the sugar support program is retained largely unchanged, an outcome also sought by producers. Price and revenue-based commodity programs are revised, embedding higher support parameters. Despite heated debate on recoupling crop program payments to current planting (Zulauf, 2014a), payments largely remain decoupled and farmers retain planting flexibility on fixed program acres (with expanded options for planting fruits and vegetables). The marketing loan program extends price floors coupled to

Table 3. Brief Description of the *Agricultural Act of 2014* Farm Safety Net Programs

Title I: Commodity programs	
Price Loss Coverage (PLC) (revised target price program)	Price commodity program. Payment made if price is below reference price fixed by Congress. No premium is paid but payment made on a fixed historic payment yield and on only 85% of historic program (base) acres.
Agriculture Risk Coverage (ARC) (revised revenue program)	Revenue commodity program with two versions: county and individual. Revenue benchmark changes with yield and market price subject to a minimum price (PLC reference price). Payment occurs if revenue loss is between 14% and 24% of benchmark. No premium is paid but payment is made on only 85% (county) or 65% (individual) of historic program acres.
Marketing Loan (existing program)	Price commodity program. Payment made on current output if price is below loan rate fixed by Congress. Loan rates less than PLC reference prices are retained at 2013 levels except the cotton loan rate reduced from a fixed 52 cents per pound to a range between 45 and 52 cents per pound.
Dairy Margin Protection Program (MPP) (new program)	Replaces dairy price and income support programs. Payment made to participating dairy farmers if margin between milk prices and feed costs is below $4 per cwt with no premium. Option to pay a premium to insure margin up to $8/cwt. Government purchase of dairy products for domestic food programs authorized when margin guarantee payments are triggered.
Sugar (existing program)	Retained largely unchanged; loan rates above world prices protected by import restrictions.
Supplemental Agricultural Disaster Assistance (renewed program)	Authorized retroactively and on a permanent basis four disaster aid programs first authorized in the 2008 farm bill for livestock, farm-raised catfish, honeybees, orchard trees and nursery stock.

(*Continued*)

Table 3. *(Continued)*

Title XI: Insurance programs	
Crop yield and revenue insurance (existing program)	Yield and revenue insurance contracts at the farm enterprise and smaller unit level as well as at county level. Coverage elected by farmer. Farmer pays part of actuarially fair premium, averaging 38%. All planted acres can be insured.
Supplemental Coverage Option (SCO) (new program)	Yield or revenue insurance program that makes indemnity payment if county yield or revenue is between 86% and coverage level elected for underlying individual farm insurance contract. Available if not enrolled in ARC. Farms pay 35% of actuarially fair premium.
Stacked Income Protection Plan (STAX) (new program)	Revenue insurance program for upland cotton only. Insurance indemnity payment received if county revenue is between 90% and coverage level elected for underlying individual insurance contract or can be purchased on stand-alone basis. Farms pay 20% of actuarially fair premium.

Source: Zulauf and Orden (2014).

crop production but at levels well below recent market prices except in the cases of sugar, cotton and peanuts.[2] Options to reallocate program acreage and to update program yields also temper decoupling, but Hendricks and Sumner (2014) find only small production effects from past base updating. In sum, while repeal of direct payments brought a $41 billion reduction in support over 10 years, the fiscal score (Table 5) by the Congressional Budget Office (CBO) at the time the farm bill was enacted projected that nearly 80% of the saving was retained in various farm safety net programs in the commodity and crop insurance titles.

Insights on the impetus to redesign the crop safety net can be gleaned by comparing crop insurance net indemnity payments and direct payments by

[2]The cotton loan rate of 45 to 52 cents per pound is between 55% and 65% of the Olympic average of 2009–2013 market prices, a level higher than for all other crops except sugar (which exceeds the world price) and peanuts (64% of the 2009–2013 market price average).

Table 4. Comparison of Price Parameters for Title I Crop Programs, Major Crops

Crop[a]	Loan rate 2014	Target price 2013	PLC reference price 2014	Estimated ARC price component[b] 2014 crop year
Barley	$1.95	$2.63	$4.95	$5.45
Corn	$1.95	$2.63	$3.70	$5.28
Oats	$1.39	$1.79	$2.40	$3.25
Peanuts	$0.1775	$0.2475	$0.2675	$0.2787
Long-grain rice	$6.50	$10.50	$14.00	$14.17
Medium-/short-grain rice	$6.50	$10.50	$14.00	$17.87
Sorghum	$1.95	$2.63	$3.95	$5.09
Soybeans	$5.00	$6.00	$8.40	$12.27
Wheat	$2.94	$4.17	$5.50	$6.60

Sources: Congressional Research Service (2014), USDA, and authors' calculations.
Notes: [a]Units are $/bushel except for peanuts ($/pound) and rice ($/hundredweight). [b]ARC's price component for the 2014 crop year is the Olympic average for the 2009–2013 crop years of MAX (crop year price, PLC reference price). Crop year prices are from USDA, National Agricultural Statistics Service at its Quick Stats website, August 2014.

state and crop (Glauber, 2012; Zulauf, 2014b). For 42 of 49 states (Alaska not included), their share of net indemnity payments during 2004–2013 was within two percentage points of their share of direct payments. The largely similar distributions by state and high levels of net indemnities in 2011–2013 made it easier for farmers collectively to give up direct payments, while protecting crop insurance. In contrast, the ratio of net indemnity payments to direct payments varies notably by crop: from 12% and 39% for rice and peanuts, respectively, to 92%, 121%, and 135% for corn, cotton, and sorghum. This difference explains in part why rice and peanuts resisted the elimination of direct payments and argued for high target prices, while cotton could opt for an insurance program.

Redesign of Commodity Programs

Reflecting disagreement among farm groups over the design of shallow and multiple year loss programs, the 2014 farm bill authorizes four options.

Table 5. CBO Budget Score Summary, *Agriculture Act of 2014* Estimated FY2014-FY2023 Outlays

	Billions dollars (10-year totals)	
Farm bill title	Estimated outlays	Estimate change from baseline (extension of 2008 farm bill)
Farm support programs	134.3	−8.6
Commodity programs (Title I)	44.5	−14.3
of which		
Repeal Direct Payments		*−40.8*
Repeal Countercyclical Payments		*−1.5*
Repeal ACRE		*−4.7*
PLC		*13.1*
ARC		*14.1*
Dairy Program		*0.9*
Supplemental Disaster Assistance		*3.7*
Crop insurance (Title XI)	89.8	+5.7
of which		
SCO		*1.7*
STAX		*3.3*
Conservation (Title II)	57.6	−4.0
of which		
Conservation Reserve Program		*−3.3*
Conservation Stewardship Program		*−2.3*
Agricultural Conservation Easement		*1.2*
Nutrition (Title IV)	756.4	−8.0
All other titles	8.1	+4.1
Total	956.4	−16.5

Source: Congressional Budget Office (2014).

Shallow loss programs are SCO and Agriculture Risk Coverage (ARC), a revision of ACRE, with county (ARC-CO) and individual (ARC-IC) versions.[3] Multiple year loss programs are Price Loss Coverage (PLC),

[3]ARC differs from ACRE on several key parameters. ARC pays on a share of historical program acres while ACRE generally paid on a share of planted acres. ARC uses county or farm yield; ACRE used state yield. The coverage range is narrower for ARC. The price

a revised price countercyclical program, and the two ARC options. Target prices (renamed reference prices) are mostly increased 30%–50% (ranging from 8% for peanuts to 88% for barley). The resulting reference prices, expressed as a percent of the Olympic average (drop the low and high years) price for the 2009–2013 crop years, range from 68% and 70% for soybeans and corn (reference prices of $8.40 and $3.70 per bushel) to 96% and 99% for peanuts and long grain rice (reference prices of $0.2675 per pound and $14 per hundredweight). The reference prices are fixed values over which Congress exerts control. In contrast, ARC's revenue benchmark is equal to the five-year Olympic moving average of past prices times the five-year Olympic moving average of past yields, but the price entering its price component for any year cannot fall below the fixed PLC reference price. ARC provides assistance of at least limited duration against multiple year losses because a lagged moving average adjusts more slowly than the market in a period of sharply declining revenue and because of the reference price minimum on its price component.

It is unlikely the 2014 farm bill would have been enacted without the four distinct programs favored by various crops and regions. The Midwest, upper Plain states, and South, in general favored the policy design of ARC-CO, ARC-IC, and PLC (complemented by SCO), respectively. Rather than force a common program, the 2014 farm bill allows a one-time irrevocable choice, to be made by the end of March 2015 for the 2014–2018 crop years.

The multi-program outcome implies several farm safety net design issues remain open. For shallow losses, they include whether assistance should be delivered by insurance (SCO) or commodity programs (ARC) and whether farmers should co-pay a share of a premium or receive payment on only a share of acres. For multiple year losses, an important design issue is whether downside risk is capped at a lower value in exchange for assistance for declines in price or revenue from higher levels. PLC provides assistance for low prices that range from the reference price down to the much lower loan rate. ARC provides support at prices above the reference price, but only for a narrower range of losses between 14% and 24% of its revenue

component for ARC eliminates the impact of highest and lowest years on its revenue benchmark but was a simple two-year moving average for ACRE and ACRE had no floor on its price component.

benchmark. Related multiple year loss design issues include whether the focus should be price or revenue and whether policy parameters should be fixed or move with the market. Farm policy has been trending toward targets that move with the market, as illustrated by the increased role of crop insurance and ACRE's moving-average revenue benchmark. Yet a strong proclivity remains among many farm groups and in Congress for fixed parameters to provide downside risk assistance. Its strength is demonstrated by the integration of reference prices into the ARC benchmark.

The inter-temporal support outcomes farmers may face can be illustrated with U.S. yield and price projections in the November 10, 2014 World Agricultural Supply and Demand Estimates (WASDE, USDA 2014b). Using the approach of Zulauf and Schnitkey (2014), these estimates are only indicative because they are based on national average, not county or farm, yields and revenue. For corn, at the projected U.S. average yield (170 bushel per planted acre, 13% above the 2009–2013 yield Olympic average) and the mid-price of the projected range ($3.50 per bushel, 36% below the 2009–2013 price Olympic average), estimated payment for the 2014 crop year from ARC-CO is at its cap, a level of $79 per eligible acre, (85% of program acres), versus payments of $26 per acre from PLC (Figure 1). Assuming (for simplicity of illustration) that yield and price stay constant at projected 2014 levels through 2018, ARC payments remain $79 for 2015, decline to $50 for 2016 and $0 for 2017 and 2018. In contrast, annual PLC payments do not change.[4] This simple comparison illustrates the effects of market oriented versus fixed policy parameters; in particular the temporary nature of support from market oriented (moving average) programs.

Other crops estimated to receive payments for the 2014 crop year at the mid-price projections are sorghum and wheat from ARC-CO and long grain rice and sorghum from PLC. Payments by ARC-CO for corn and PLC for long grain rice are consistent with positions representatives of these crops

[4] Although a simplification from enrollment decisions farmers will make and payments they will receive, SCO does not enter our indicative per acre comparison. SCO was not available for the 2014 crop. Even if it had been, for corn, in particular, SCO payments would not have been triggered at national average prices and yields (with prices falling during the growing season but higher yields, average insured revenue per planted acre at harvest was less than pre-plant expected revenue, but not sufficiently to trigger SCO payments). For subsequent years in our comparison, payments from SCO are precluded by the simplifying assumption for illustrative purposes of constant prices and yields.

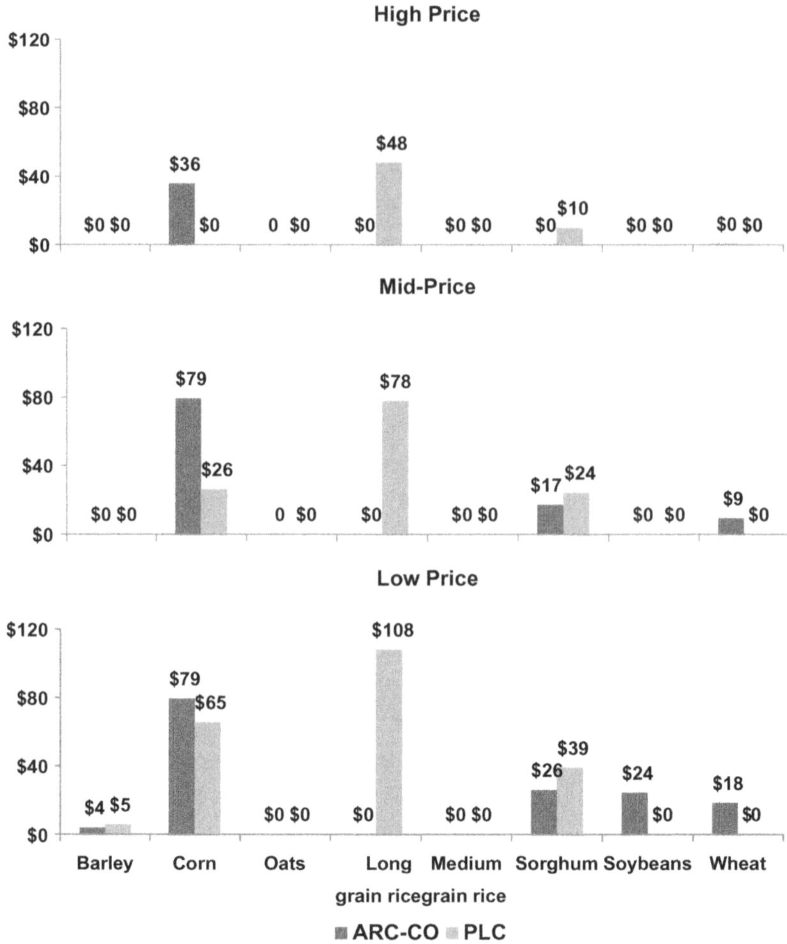

Figure 1. Estimated 2014 crop year ARC-CO and PLC payment per eligible acre (85% of program acres) using November 2014 WASDE U.S. yield and price projections
Source: Authors' calculations.

took during the 2014 farm bill debate. Estimated PLC payments for corn and no payment for medium/short grain rice illustrate both the uncertainty of payments and that outcomes may not align with lobbying positions.

Estimated payments per acre also vary substantially across the WASDE projected price range. At the low-price projection for corn ($3.20), estimated payments for PLC for the 2014 crop year increase to $65 per acre but remains capped at $79 for ARC. At the high-price projection for corn ($3.80), payments drop to $36 per acre for ARC and disappear for PLC.

The notable differences in per acre payments imply a wide range of possible total program costs. At the November 2014 WASDE mid-price projections for the 2014 crop year, ARC-CO costs are $6.3 billion ($5.7 billion for corn) and PLC costs are $0.5 billion if all eligible acres are enrolled in the program that makes the largest per acre payment. Total costs are $2.4 billion for the 2014 crop year if all acres for all crops are enrolled in PLC. If price projections for the 2014 crop remain at the November levels through March 2015, producers may have to decide in their program enrollment decisions whether they prefer support from ARC-CO that, for corn in particular, likely will make large payments in 2015 and 2016; or support that is retained through the 2018 crop year under PLC in the event of market prices below the reference prices that may or may not materialize over the five years of the farm bill.[5] The likelihood of choosing ARC-CO declines with lower prices (from mid to low) for crop year 2014 because there is less short-term advantage and continuation of low prices will seem more likely. Congress has often added support if prices and revenue are sharply lower than anticipated when a farm bill is enacted, as in 1998. But this may prove more difficult to orchestrate politically, at least through 2018, after farmers have made program choices under the stipulation that their decisions cannot be reversed.

Expansion of Insurance

Insurance expenditures, which include premium subsidies, administrative and operating cost reimbursements to private insurance companies and government reinsurance for underwriting gains and losses, are estimated by CBO to increase by $5.7 billion under the 2014 farm bill (Table 5). The

[5] This decision would be acute for corn as follows. Under our simplifying assumptions, corn payments for the 2014 crop with all acres enrolled in ARC-CO would exceed payments if all corn acreage was enrolled in PLC by $3.8 billion at the November WASDE mid-price, but only by $0.9 billion at the WASDE low price. Over the five years 2014–2018, ARC-CO payments would exceed PLC payments for corn by $5.6 billion at the mid-price, but would be less than PLC payments by $5.4 billion at the low price.

evolution since 1980 of crop insurance into a pillar of the farm safety net and several policy issues raised by subsidized insurance are discussed in the appendix.

Other than a loan program, the 2014 farm bill supports cotton only by insurance, including the new shallow loss Stacked Income Protection Plan (STAX). The redesign of cotton support compared to other program crops was driven in large part by the WTO Brazil–U.S. cotton case. In particular, Brazil opposed any fixed reference price for upland cotton, whether through PLC or by incorporation into insurance products. The U.S. cotton industry endorsed replacement of its traditional programs by STAX, both as necessary to seek resolution with Brazil and in anticipation of net indemnities projected by CBO at nearly $3 billion over 10 years. Additional payments will be made if cotton prices fall below the loan rate.

On October 1, 2014, Brazil and the U.S. reached agreement on termination of the long WTO dispute (Schnepf 2014). While this is an institutional success of the 2014 farm bill, the enhanced reliance on insurance raises a number of policy issues. Insurance products do not address multiple year price and revenue risks. If cotton prices were to stay low for several years, any attempt to add assistance (or large loan program payments) could test whether resolution of the WTO cotton case is a meaningful check on U.S. farm policy.

Introduction of the highly-subsidized STAX insurance program specific to upland cotton also may signal the Balkanization of crop insurance as farm bills become a legislative vehicle to negotiate insurance plans differentiated by crop. Its subsidy rate of 80% exceeds the 44% rate for 90% area revenue insurance, 53% for the popular enterprise insurance at its 85% highest coverage level, and the overall average subsidy rate of 62% for existing insurance. Using the argument that the same program was offered to all crops, the U.S. had notified crop insurance expenditures to the WTO as non-product-specific support (net indemnities were notified from 1995 until 2007, then premium subsidies from 2008 onward). STAX is clearly product specific and arguments have long been made that the U.S. crop insurance subsidies are product specific (Zulauf and Orden, 2014). In a decision supposedly not directly related to enactment of the 2014 farm bill, in November 2014 the U.S. indicated it would begin to notify all crop insurance premium subsidies, not just STAX subsidies, as product-specific support. This change to how insurance subsidies will be notified further opens the door to legislating differences among insurance products for different crops.

In eliminating the cotton direct payment and countercyclical programs, Congress converted 17. 9 million cotton base acres to generic base acres. These acres can be planted to any program crop and receive payments by the program elected for that crop. Thus, for generic base acres, program payments may distort planting decisions. Using 2013 USDA cost of production data, returns for nine alternative crops suggest generic base acres may lead to more planted rice and peanuts acres if market prices for program crops are below their reference prices and returns for cotton are low. To put the potential impact in perspective, in 2012 the U.S. planted 2.7 and 1.6 million acres of rice and peanuts, respectively, compared with 11.6 million acres on average to upland cotton over 2010–2014.

Margin insurance also raises issues. The 2014 farm bill authorizes margin insurance for crops, with a program for rice expected in 2015. The new dairy MPP, while a Title I commodity program not a Title XI insurance program, provides milk-to-feed cost margin protection from $4 to $8 per hundredweight and producers can cover 25%–90% of their historic milk production.[6] Farm organizations have tried to reintroduce production costs into safety net programs ever since cost of production adjustment for target prices was removed in the 1980 farm bill. While only initial steps are taken in the 2014 farm bill, it is reasonable to consider that margin insurance might evolve into a dominant insurance product.

A potential issue with margin insurance is the existence of large economies of size in costs of production. For dairy, using USDA cost and return data, the cost per hundredweight of producing milk above feed cost declines from nearly $30 for herds of less than 50 cows to under $7 for herds of more than 1000 cows. The highest insurable $8 MPP margin is effectively less than $6 given a premium of $1.36 and coverage of 90% of historic production. Nevertheless, the variation in cost among farms and likelihood that non-feed cost per hundredweight continue to decline

[6]MPP authorizes government purchases of dairy products to raise prices when margin guarantee payments are triggered (Table 3). An alternative proposal to include supply control measures to manage MPP costs proved controversial and was not adopted.

for larger dairies raise the question of whether MPP guarantees a profit to some farms. A guaranteed profit to large dairy farms would distort the structure of production.

The level of subsidies for crop insurance is a more general issue. As the 2014 farm bill attests, subsidized crop insurance is strongly supported by farmers and in the political arena. Yet, economic analysis is divided over whether any rationale exists for these subsidies (Coble and Barnett, 2012; Goodwin and Smith, 2012).

As discussed in the appendix, the need for public subsidies so crop insurance is available rests upon the cost of providing private insurance exceeding farmers' willingness to pay for it. The two most commonly-cited reasons for the high cost of private crop insurance are significant moral hazard and adverse selection in crop production and high levels of systemic risk. Even if the argument that crop insurance merits subsidies is accepted, significant opportunities exist to reduce crop insurance's current cost.

Moral hazard and adverse selection can be managed using data based on yields of individual farms. Cooper *et al.* (2012) find individual farm yield histories are preferable to current methods USDA's Risk Management Agency (RMA) uses to set premium rates. In contrast, RMA's current method largely reflects county level risk. Using a simulation model incorporating a stylized version of current RMA methods, Cooper *et al.* find an average subsidy rate of approximately 35% is sufficient to have 80% of land insured.

It is well established that idiosyncratic risk can be managed by private insurance markets and thus is not a rationale for public subsidies. Empirical evidence from both the aggregate performance of U.S. crop insurance (see the appendix) and individual farm level (Zulauf *et al.*, 2013) suggest systemic risk is at most 45% of total risk in U.S. crop production. A rule-of-thumb argument might be that the average subsidy rate should not exceed the share of risk that is systemic, which is notably smaller than the current subsidy rate.

Conservation, SNAP and the Broader Farm Bill Coalition

Provisions to bring together a broad political coalition are evident throughout the 2014 farm bill. The environmental focus to farm policy continues.

This is the first farm bill enacted with projected spending higher on the conservation title than the commodity title. Only $208 million of the projected 10-year reductions to conservation program budget authority are slated to occur within the five-year duration of the farm bill. Wetland and highly erodible land conservation are expanded as a condition to receive crop insurance premium subsidies. This latter provision underscores a basic political equilibrium reached in 2014 — that crop insurance cannot be both a farm safety net pillar and excluded from the expectation that farmers protect the environment in exchange for subsidies.

The maximum number of acres in the Conservation Reserve Program (CRP) is reduced but the cap is still 24 million acres in 2018. Thus, both the 2008 and 2014 farm bills continued a program whose elimination could have addressed concerns over high crop prices, in contrast to a fence row-to-fence row planting mentality that dominated during the 1970s period of farm prosperity. The conservation focus is further reinforced by increased CRP acreage in continuous sign-up, continued conservation programs for working lands and livestock facilities, and restored funding that had elapsed under the 2008 farm bill for conservation easements (Ludden and Peace, 2014).

A key rural/urban coalition—between stakeholders in farm support and domestic food assistance programs — survived in 2014 despite intense pressure from political conservatives to reduce expenditures on entitlements and the short-lived separation of nutrition from the farm bill by the House of Representatives. The 2014 farm bill was scored by CBO to reduce projected SNAP outlays by only $8 billion over 10 years, roughly 1%.

An expanding farm/environment/food assistance coalition will be important to the political economy of future farm bills. Opportunities to expand this coalition abound, but so too do challenges, as the U.S. grapples with issues over the role of farm production in nutrition, health, and environmental quality and government programs and regulations in these areas. The consolidated Regional Conservation Partnership Program in the 2014 farm bill provides one avenue for coalition-building opportunities by allowing local, regional or watershed environmental issues to be identified and addressed by leveraging public with private funds.

The 2014 farm bill strengthened other coalition partnerships as well. Combined projected outlays for the forestry, trade, rural development, horticulture, energy, miscellaneous, and research/extension titles increase $4 billion (50%) over 10 years. The farm safety net was extended to more crops and livestock. Notably, disaster aid for livestock, farm-raised catfish, honeybees, orchard trees and nursery stock temporarily authorized in the 2008 farm bill was made permanent at a projected cost of $3.7 billion.

Important to the farm bill coalition is the retention of permanent legislation. Over 250 diverse organizations jointly urged Congress to retain this legislative framework. What they recognize is that permanent legislation creates a powerful incentive to pass a new farm bill, thus providing multiple opportunities to pursue their agendas.

WTO Considerations

While the Doha Round negotiation has faltered, compliance of the U.S. farm safety net programs with the existing WTO disciplines or tighter disciplines that could be negotiated remains an issue. Since ARC-CO and PLC make payments on historic program acres with planting flexibility, they likely will be notified as non-product-specific support. We conclude from simple analysis along lines of our WASDE-based calculations that notified non-product-specific expenditures under the 2014 farm bill are unlikely to exceed the *de minimis* threshold of 5% of total value of agricultural production, and hence to count against the U.S. constraint of $19.1 billion annually on certain domestic support (Zulauf and Orden, 2014).[7] The U.S. decision in 2014 to start notifying crop insurance premium subsidies as product-specific support, removes these support expenditures from the non-product-specific category, making it even less likely than before that ARC and PLC payments will cause the *de minimis* threshold for non-product-specific support to be exceeded. On this basis, we conclude it is unlikely the U.S. will face difficulty meeting its current WTO obligations.

Expenditures under the 2014 farm bill are more likely to exceed several of the proposed limits of the tighter rules and commitments on developed country domestic support under discussion in the December 2008 Doha Round negotiations. The existing support cap would be reduced and

[7]STAX, MPP, payments on generic acres and possibly ARC-IC are likely to be notified as product-specific support.

product-specific caps established, the *de minimis* threshold would fall to 2.5% of total value of production, an aggregate limit and product-specific caps would be placed on the blue box, and blue box and *de minimis* expenditures would count against a new proposed limit on overall trade-distorting support (Brink, 2011). It seems reasonable to conclude that the U.S. would not have enacted the 2014 farm bill as it is, had a Doha agreement been reached in 2008 and phased in over the past six years. Conversely, enactment of this farm bill makes it more difficult for the U.S. to contribute to attaining such limits on a global level in future negotiations.

In contrast, the Brazil–U.S. cotton case may have impacts beyond the U.S. upland cotton safety net. A core complaint by Brazil was that the WTO Agreement on Subsidies and Countervailing Measures specifies that sector-specific government programs cannot cause serious prejudice to the interests of another member by significantly suppressing world prices or otherwise significantly distorting market conditions. By extension, the cotton ruling suggests PLC could be subject to potential WTO challenge if U.S. prices stay below the reference price for an extended period. The ruling also suggests grounds may exist to file a complaint if total U.S. subsidies, including insurance, for a given crop distort trade or suppress world prices. An important policy question that could emerge from such cases is whether the declining level of support associated with moving-average programs such as ARC would be considered in determining trade distortion.

Conclusions

The U.S. farm lobby and broader farm bill coalition demonstrated their continued political power by securing a new farm bill in 2014 under difficult circumstances. A long period of crop prosperity did not bring an end to U.S. support. While not an ironclad assurance on funding, coalition partners now have their basic mandatory programs in place. The farm lobby may receive less support or more support from the enhanced downside risk safety net than from the fixed direct payments it gave up, a one-time card it has played. If expenditures prove lower, eighteen years of fixed direct payments may be the transition out of commodity programs once envisioned by reform advocates. If costs prove higher, it is unclear whether pressure to cut spending will be felt as fiscal deficits fall to a smaller share of GDP in coming years. Moreover, the permanence of permanent farm policy legislation was on display, giving farm and other stakeholders an advantage in securing a next farm bill.

The *Agricultural Act of 2014* both addresses and creates issues in this political economy context. ARC is put on a more even footing with the traditional price countercyclical program than ACRE was in the 2008 farm bill. It is not surprising that a moving-average revenue benchmark program gained stature at a time of high prices and revenue. If expected 2014 crop year prices are not so low through March 2014 as to cause ARC to be stillborn, the 2014 farm bill will provide experience and evidence about whether U.S. farm policy can move further from fixed policy parameters, trading a lower cap on downside risk protection for assistance with declines in price and revenue from higher levels.

A success of the 2014 farm bill is the termination of the WTO Brazil–U.S upland cotton case made possible by shifting from traditional commodity programs to the STAX insurance program. Yet, creation of generic base acres will fuel further debate on decoupling and potentially foreshadows additional lobbying for a return to support tied to current production. STAX may prove costly and upland cotton having a loan rate as its only multiple year loss protection may not hold up. More broadly, the whole structure of available insurance products needs to be monitored. The parameters and size of the public subsidies for insurance could come up and, we argue, should be taken up in the next farm bill debate, if not earlier.

Finally, we have noted two broader contexts that surround the 2014 farm bill. The first is certain optimism that the conservation focus remains central to farm policy and that the 2014 farm bill provides pathways for tackling some of the contentious nutrition, health and environmental policy and regulatory issues surrounding agriculture. Conversely, the 2014 farm bill exacerbates efforts to achieve tighter multilateral disciplines on agricultural support and protection. The U.S. may come to rue this outcome if it leads to impasses on regional trade agreements currently on the table or if newly emerging middle-income countries follow the historical pattern of expanding market-distorting support for their agriculture.

Appendix: Crop Insurance

The high level of spending on crop insurance during 2011–2013, along with policy changes in the *Agricultural Act of 2014*, has stimulated debate over the cost of crop insurance. In particular, economists do not agree if any economic rationale exists to justify public subsidies for crop insurance. From the perspective of economics, provision of these subsidies rest upon the argument that private crop insurance would not be offered without subsidies because the cost of providing private insurance exceeds farmers' willingness to pay for it. The high cost of private crop insurance is commonly attributed to the presence of high reserve load costs resulting from the presence of high administrative costs due to the site specific nature of yield, including the cost of monitoring moral hazard and adverse selection, and to the existence of large systemic losses from widespread weather events (Coble and Barnett, 2012).

In this appendix, we do not attempt to answer the broadest policy question of whether crop insurance subsidies are justifiable economically. Instead, we focus on the narrower question of the implication of the two high cost components of private insurance for public subsidies. Although the 2014 farm bill enhances crop insurance programs, our assessment is that U.S. crop insurance is currently over-subsidized even if subsidies are accepted as economically justified.

Background

The 2014 farm bill enhances public assistance via crop insurance for production-period (pre-planting to harvest) risk, a trend that dates to the early 1980s. Crop insurance operates over the growing season, insuring against losses at harvest compared with expectations before planting. Its yield and price components are reset each year. The growing role of insurance in the U.S. crop safety net reflects in part a shift from yield loss to revenue loss insurance (Figure A.1). Revenue insurance was not offered until the 1996 crop year but now accounts for 85% of insured acres.

Net indemnity payments for insured crop losses (indemnity payments less the premiums paid by farmers) since 2004 are shown in Figure A.2. Although net indemnities spiked in 2008, they were generally a relatively

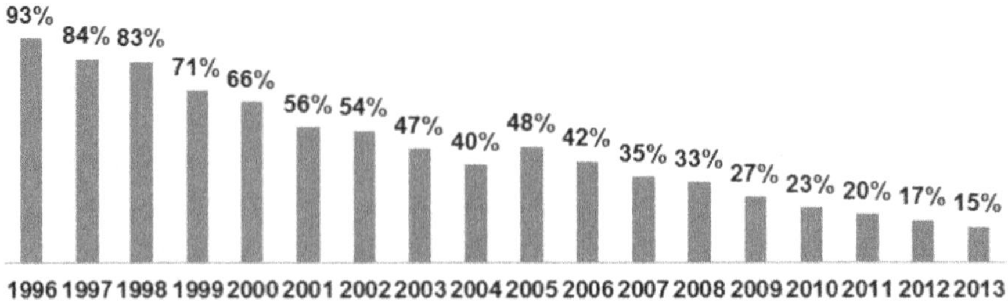

Figure A.1. Share of all insured acres in yield insurance, all crops, U.S., 1996–2013
Source: Authors' calculations using data from USDA, Risk Management Agency.
Note: Yield insurance contracts include Actual Production History (APH), Group Risk Plan (GRP), and Yield Protection (YP).

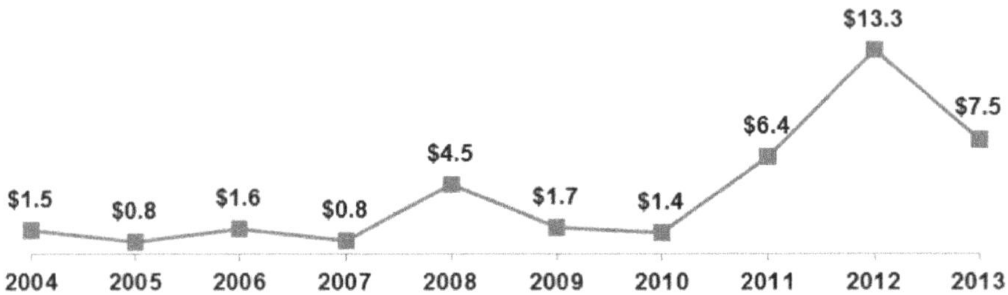

Figure A.2. Net indemnity payments from U.S. crop insurance, 2004–2013 (billion dollars)
Source: Authors' calculations using data from USDA, Risk Management Agency.

small component of total farm support expenditures through 2010. However, in each of the 2011 through 2013 crop years, net indemnity insurance payments to U.S. farms exceeded $6 billion, and thus were larger than direct payments.[8]

Higher net insurance payments reflect in part higher public subsidy rates. The share of premiums paid by farms declined from 74% in the early 1990s to around 38% in recent years (Figure A.3). Major changes in subsidy rates occurred in the *Agricultural Risk Protection Act of 2000* and the 2008 farm bill. The latter made the subsidy rate as high as 80% on

[8]Even though insurance payments exceed farmer-paid insurance premiums summed for all U.S. farms, insurance payments do not exceed premiums paid by each farm that buys crop insurance. An individual farm receives an insurance payment only if it experiences a loss greater than the deductible it elected.

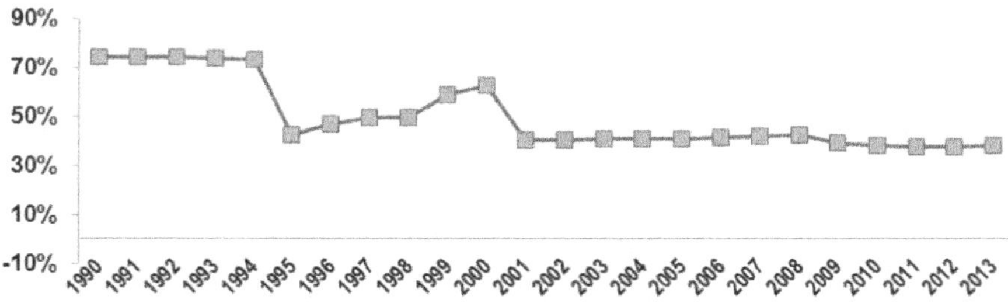

Figure A.3. Share of insurance premiums paid by farmers, U.S., 1990–2013
Source: Authors' calculations using data from USDA, Risk Management Agency.

some coverage levels for enterprise insurance (an enterprise is all acres of a crop of a farm operation in a county). The higher subsidy rate, combined with an expansion in eligible crops and types of insurance, has resulted in more farms buying insurance on more acres. Total insured acres grew from 100 million in the early 1990s to 296 million in the 2013 crop year. A third reason for higher net insurance payments since 2008 is higher crop prices. Higher prices translate into higher expected revenue and thus more insurance payments for a given percentage loss.

Net indemnity payments to farms are only part of the cost to the public of farm insurance programs. The cost of government reinsurance provided to private insurance companies (net underwriting gains and losses) plus government reimbursement to private insurance companies for administration and operation (A&O) costs averaged nearly $1.9 billion annually for the 2009–2013 fiscal years (Shields, 2013).

Policy Issues

The debate over crop insurance subsidies is framed in part by five observations:

1. Other than private hail and fire insurance, U.S. farmers (and farmers around the world) have only purchased crop insurance to any notable extent when public subsidies exist (Wright and Hewitt, 1994; Tweeten and Zulauf, 1997).
2. The higher the subsidy rate the more insurance farmers buy.

3. The U.S. Congress has demonstrated a willingness to increasingly subsidize crop insurance.
4. Economists are divided over the rationale, if any, for crop insurance subsides.
5. No objective-based rationale has been given for the current matrix of subsidies by product and coverage level—it is a political equilibrium matrix negotiated by Congress.

In assessing crop insurance subsidies, it is useful to start with the question, why is farm fire and hail insurance unsubsidized? Fire and hail risk events can substantially reduce yield and revenue, but occur infrequently on a given acre of land. Hail events can affect more than one field in a local area and thus can be spatially correlated. Nevertheless, fire and hail approximate idiosyncratic risks or risks with little correlation of occurrence across potential insurance units. The lack of correlation allows the law of large numbers to be invoked, in turn allowing an actuarially fair premium to be determined and charged. In summary, as reflected by the lack of public subsidies for fire and hail insurance, no economic justification exists for public subsidies for idiosyncratic risk. Private markets can cost effectively deliver such insurance.

Moral Hazard and Adverse Selection as Arguments for Crop Insurance Subsidies

Moral hazard exists when a risk management option alters decisions of the insured so as to increase the probability of collecting a payment. Adverse selection exists when potential users of the risk management option know more about their losses than the provider, allowing them to choose a risk management option when its payout ratio is favorable. Thus, moral hazard and adverse selection increase the cost of private market risk management options. If these costs are high enough, the type of insurance may be affected or insurance may not be offered.

Moral hazard and adverse selection are especially likely in a complex process such as crop production. Farmers make many decisions from planting through harvest that include consideration of risk. Thus, the potential is high that availability of insurance could influence farmers' decisions and that farmers know more about their risks than insurance providers.

Moral hazard and adverse selection are less likely when determinant of payments by risk management programs is outside the control of the insured (Miranda, 1991). Hence, area-wide insurance, such as county insurance, is often championed as a way to reduce moral hazard and adverse selection. However, during the 2013 crop year, county insurance products accounted for only 1.4% of insured U.S. acres.

Moral hazard and adverse selection exist for all private insurance. Techniques for managing them include premiums, co-pays, and deductibles as well as using information to price the riskiness of individual insurance units. Similar tools are available for individual farm crop insurance contracts, including information about the riskiness of production by individual field and individual farmer.

It is not certain how many observations are needed to address the issues of moral hazard and adverse selection, but data for many fields and farmers in the U.S. now exceeds 10 years. This ever-growing data set might allow the use of statistical techniques to combine county and farm specific data to calculate field and farmer specific insurance rates. Cooper *et al.* (2012) examines this approach. They find individual farm yield histories are preferable to current methods used by USDA, RMA to set premium rates. This finding is consistent with observations made by Goodwin (1994) that individual yield histories allow premiums to reflect risk attributes that are idiosyncratic to the operator and land. In contrast, the current method used by RMA largely reflects county level risk. Using a simulation model incorporating a stylized version of current RMA methods, Cooper *et al.* (2012) find an average subsidy rate of approximately 35% is needed so that 80% of land is insured. Their data set is seven county-crop combinations with enough farm level data from the Illinois and Kansas farm management data sets to complete the analysis. At the time of their study, approximately 80% of U.S. cropland was insured.

Systemic Risk as an Argument for Crop Insurance Subsidies

Crop farms are subject to considerable systemic risk or risk that is correlated or held in common by a large number of potential insurance units. Systemic yield risk arises from widespread natural events such as frost, drought, and excess moisture affecting contiguous geographic regions. Systemic price risk arises from both market demand factors and national and international weather conditions. Miranda and Glauber (1997) find that the portfolios of U.S. crop insurers are 20 to 50 times riskier than if yields are stochastically independent across farms. They also find that their portfolio risks are 10 times larger than private insurers offering more conventional insurance lines.

Occurrence of a systemic risk potentially affects enough insured units to cause insurance companies to go bankrupt, which in turn may lead to under-provision, even lack of private insurance. The counter-argument against providing subsidies for crop insurance when systemic risk exists is that the international reinsurance market is large enough to handle the systemic risk associated with crop insurance (Goodwin and Smith, 2012). However, private reinsurance can be expensive and may not be available. Currently, the U.S. government provides a considerable share of reinsurance for companies offering crop insurance to U.S. farms.

The disagreement over the validity of the systemic risk justification for public subsidies for crop insurance should not cloud the prevailing assessment of economics that idiosyncratic risk should not be subsidized. This observation implies an important policy question: How much risk in U.S. crop production is idiosyncratic? Perspective on this question can be gained by examining the share of crop insurance premiums paid as indemnities for losses in various years.

Over the last 10 crop years, a period in which revenue insurance was the dominant insurance product, the ratio of insurance indemnity payments to total premiums (farmer-paid premiums plus premium subsidies) was lowest in 2007 (0.54) and 2010 (0.56), as shown in Figure A.4. Systemic risk was likely low in these two years. Corn, rice, sorghum, soybeans, upland cotton, and wheat accounted for 70% and 79% of insured acres in 2007 and 2010, respectively. In only two of the 12 combinations involving these two years and six crops was U.S. average insured revenue per planted acre at harvest (harvest insurance price times U.S. yield per planted acre) less than the pre-plant expected revenue (pre-plant insurance price times average U.S. yield per planted acre for the 10 preceding crop years). The two exceptions were only -5% for corn in 2007 and -3% for rice in 2010.

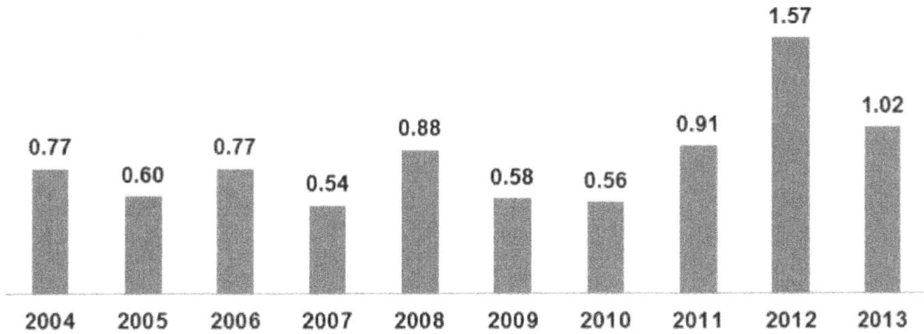

Figure A.4. Ratio of crop insurance indemnity payments to total insurance premiums, U.S., crop years 2004–2013

Source: Authors' calculations using data from USDA, Risk Management Agency.

If all losses in 2007 and 2010 are assumed to result from idiosyncratic risk, then idiosyncratic risk is 55% of all risk in U.S. crop agriculture. Under the argument that idiosyncratic risk should not be subsidized and the assumption that 2007 and 2010 had minimal systemic risk, the 2007 and 2010 observations imply the average U.S. crop insurance subsidy rate should not exceed 45%. In contrast, the average subsidy rate for crop insurance purchased by U.S. farmers in 2013 was 62%.

In a different approach, Zulauf *et al.* (2013) calculated the share of crop revenue loss that is systemic with revenue loss at the county level for Illinois and Kansas management association farms over the 1977 through 2012 crop years. The losses were generated by yield and price risks that occurred between the months in which the pre-plant and harvest insurance prices were determined. Insured revenue loss per acre for the farm and the county in which the farm is located was calculated as follows:

(1) (pre-plant insurance price$_t$ • 5-year average of past yield$_{i,t}$ • coverage level) − (harvest insurance price$_t$ • yield$_{i,t}$)

where t = year, i = farm or county, and the insurance coverage level is 85%, 70%, or 50% (losses greater than 15%, 30%, and 50%, respectively). The highest level of individual insurance a farm can buy is 85% while the lowest is 50%. Crops examined were corn, soybeans, and wheat for both Illinois and Kansas, as well as sorghum for Kansas. Share of farm loss systemic

Table A.1. Share of per acre average Annual Farm Revenue Loss Systemic with County Revenue Loss, Selected Loss Levels, Illinois and Kansas Farm Management Association Farms, 1977–2012

State and Crop	Loss > 15%	Loss > 30%	Loss > 50%
Illinois			
Corn for grain	43%	29%	23%
Soybeans	43%	15%	0%
Wheat	51%	42%	10%
Average	46%	29%	11%
Kansas			
Corn for grain	48%	38%	27%
Sorghum	48%	39%	29%
Soybeans	56%	46%	29%
Wheat	48%	43%	35%
Average	50%	42%	30%

Source: Zulauf, *et al.* (2013).

with the county was calculated as the minimum (farm loss or county loss), expressed as a share of farm loss.

Across the crops, the share of farm loss systemic with county loss averaged 46% for Illinois and 50% for Kansas for farm losses greater than 15% (see Table A.1). Average share declines to 29% and 11% for Illinois and 42% and 30% for Kansas at losses exceeding 30% and 50%, respectively. Thus, the role of systemic risk decreases as the size of the loss increases.

Again, the share of risk that is systemic, even at the smallest loss level, is less than the current average subsidy level for U.S. crop insurance. Moreover, average subsidy level of enterprise insurance, a commonly purchased insurance product, is 80% at the 50% and 70% coverage levels but only 53% at the 85% coverage level. The same pattern of decreasing subsidy levels for higher level of coverage exists for other insurance products. In summary, over-subsidization of existing insurance products increases as the level of loss increases when evaluated from the perspective of the share of risk that is systemic.

In additional analysis, Zulauf *et al.* (2013) find that these results hold for the share of loss that is systemic from the perspective of yield and at other coverage (loss) levels. They also find that the systemic portion of farm risk is lower when evaluated at the state or national level, which might be more relevant to systemic risk causing large losses to private insurers.

Last, an unexpected finding was that the share of risk systemic with the county is generally higher for Kansas than for Illinois, especially at the higher loss levels. Conventional wisdom is that Illinois has more systemic risk, at least for corn and soybeans, since it is a core production area. What this finding likely illustrates is the importance of the variability of weather and the agronomic production environment across space. For example, within a given crop year, rainfall may be more variable within Illinois than Kansas counties, resulting in a lower share of loss being systemic with the county.

Production, Management, and Environmental Impacts of Subsidized Crop Insurance

Even if the systemic risk and moral hazard/adverse selection arguments for publically subsidized insurance are accepted, they are not a full rationale for adopting policy. Adoption depends upon all costs and benefits of a policy.[9] Publically subsidized insurance affects production, management and the environment. The assessment of those impacts that follows is similar in part to the review in Sumner and Zulauf (2012).

Publically subsidized insurance may encourage production and suppress price for three reasons (Nelson and Loehman, 1987). First, because farmers do not pay the full cost of insurance and because financiers may

[9]Tangermann (2011) makes a similar point. He divides risk into three categories. His "catastrophic risks," which "can be considered the market failure level," correspond most closely to what we describe as systemic risk. Tangermann, following OECD analysis, articulates three principles for risk management programs: (1) that public policy should leave as much space as possible for private risk management activities (in particular, government programs should not absorb risks that farmers can manage themselves); (2) that a holistic approach should be taken to evaluating the efficacy of insurance programs within the full complex of farm support policies; and (3) that the distinction should be clear between providing risk management assistance versus providing support more generally. Tangermann concludes that "it is highly questionable whether subsidies to crop insurance are really appropriate" especially in the context of large direct income transfers as occur in the European Union. The shift from direct income support to strengthened risk protection in the 2014 U.S. farm bill will intensify a debate over European versus U.S. forms of support and their effects on domestic producers and world markets.

reduce the cost of operating loans due to a lower chance of default, expected income is higher. Higher net income increases the incentive to plant insured crops, especially crops with higher premium subsidy rates. This impact is similar to that of a price subsidy. Second, risk-averse farmers may plant more acres with insured crops in areas of significant production risk because insurance reduces the financial consequences of large yield losses. Third, because the need to manage large losses is reduced, farmers may focus on increasing average productivity.

Based on a simulation analysis, LaFrance, Shimshack, and Wu (2002) conclude that insurance will not affect land use only when it is actuarially sound and unsubsidized. Lubowski *et al.* (2006) conclude that based on empirical analysis of crop insurance participation and land use, the increase in insurance subsidies during the mid-1990s caused cultivated cropland to increase an estimated 2.5 million acres (0.8%) in the 48 contiguous U.S. states in 1997. Goodwin, Vandeveer, and Deal (2004) found that a 30% decrease in premiums caused less than a 1% increase in Midwest corn acres and about a 1% increase in Northern Plain barley acres. Young, Vandeveer, and Schnepf (2001) also find positive but small production effects. Last, both Babcock and Hennessey (1996) and Smith and Goodwin (1996) report that yield insurance has a small, positive impact on input use.

Risk compensation is another set of distortions resulting from publically subsidized insurance. Risk compensation, which has gained increasing recognition in recent years, is the replacement, in part or whole, of one risk by another risk. For example, publically subsidized insurance may reduce a farmer's incentive to use other risk-mitigating practices, such as crop diversification and risk-reducing production practices. Both Horowitz and Lichtenberg (1993) and Babcock and Hennessy (1996) find that farmers with insurance use less risk-reducing chemicals. A risk compensation impact widely discussed by farmers is that some farmers use subsidized insurance to increase land rents and bids. Risk compensation raises additional questions about the net benefit of subsidized crop insurance to farmers and society.

Last, because risky production areas can overlap with environmentally sensitive areas, the environmental impact of crop insurance is a policy issue. In the most extensive study to date, Lubowski *et al.* (2006) found that subsidized crop insurance increased wind and water erosion by an estimated 1.4% and 0.9% in 1997.

As a group, these studies suggest the distortions resulting from U.S. crop insurance are not large. A possible explanation is that the insurance price is reset each year to reflect existing market conditions. Thus, insurance does not put a floor under market signals, which mitigates its impact on production. A second possible explanation is the existence of production-related constraints. For example, the ability to expand cropland in the U.S. Midwest is limited. Crop rotation considerations and availability of insurance for most alternative crops in many parts of the United States also likely temper the impact of crop insurance on planting decisions. A third possible explanation is that the studies cited above predate the large increase in both insured acres and subsidy level for U.S. crop insurance. A fourth possible explanation is that previous studies have missed certain channels by which publically subsidized insurance may affect crop production (Hennessy, 2014). Those include risk compensation.

In summary, the limited distortions found by existing studies of U.S. crop insurance may or may not be applicable to the current policy and market environment, depending on which of the four proposed explanations are valid and dominant. Additional studies using contemporary data are needed.

Conclusions and Implications

The argument for public subsidies for crop insurance rests upon the observation that, without these subsidies, farmers would not have access to crop insurance. Stated alternatively, farmers' willingness to pay for private crop insurance is less than the cost of providing private insurance, leading to the need for public subsidies to cover the difference. However, economists are divided over whether any rationale exists for crop insurance subsidies.

The two reasons commonly cited for the high cost of private crop insurance are the high level of moral hazard and adverse selection in crop production and the presence of a large degree of systemic risk. This appendix has reviewed both these factors. We conclude that significant opportunities exist to reduce the cost of the current crop insurance program even if the argument that crop insurance would not exist without public subsidies is accepted.

Moral hazard and adverse selection can be managed by making use of the ever-growing data base on the yields of individual farms and land. Using this data to help rate premiums would better align premiums with riskiness at the individual producer and field level.

Idiosyncratic risk is not a rationale for public subsidies since private insurance functions effectively and efficiently in addressing idiosyncratic risk. Empirical evidence is presented from both the aggregate performance of U.S. crop insurance and at the individual farm level that, even if systemic risk is accepted as a rationale for crop insurance subsidies, the current average U.S. subsidy rate is too high.

Combining both actions offers the potential to notably reduce the spending on the premium subsidy for crop insurance. They also offer the potential to better align premium subsidies with the riskiness of individual farmers and individual fields, thus enhancing economic efficiency. The latter action may temper the reduction in the participation in crop insurance from reducing the average premium subsidy by better targeting the premium subsidy so that low risk producers feel crop insurance is a cost effective buy.

References

Anderson, K., G. Rausser and J. Swinnnen. 2013. "Political Economy of Public Policies: Insights from Distortions to Agricultural and Food Markets." *Journal of Economic Literature* 51(2): 423–477.

Babcock, B. A., and D. A. Hennessy. 1996. "Input Demand under Yield and Revenue Insurance." *American Journal of Agricultural Economics* 78(3): 416–427.

Brink, L. 2011. "The WTO Disciplines on Domestic Support" in *WTO Disciplines on Agricultural Support: Seeking a Fair Basis for Trade*, edited by D. Orden., D. Blandford and T. Josling. Cambridge UK: Cambridge University Press.

Coble, K. H. and B. K. Barnett. 2012. "Why Do We Subsidize Crop Insurance?" *American Journal of Agricultural Economics* 95(2): 498–504.

CBO (Congressional Budget Office). 2014. "Letter from D. W. Elmendorf, Director, to the Honorable F. D. Lucas, Chair, House of Representatives Committee on Agriculture (Budget Estimates For 2014 Farm Bill)." January

28. http://www.cbo.gov/publication/45049.

Congressional Research Service (CRS). 2014. "The 2014 Farm Bill (P.L. 113–79): Summary and Side-by-Side Comparison." Report R43076.

Cooper, J., C. Zulauf, M. Langemeier, and G. Schnitkey. 2012. "Implications of Within County Yield Heterogeneity for Modeling Crop Insurance Premiums." *Agricultural Finance Review* 72(1): 134–155.

Edwards, W. M. 2011. "Why Was ACRE a No-Go with Iowa Farmers?" *Choices: The Magazine of Food, Farm, and Resource Issues.*

Glauber, J. 2012. "The Growth of the Federal Crop Insurance Program, 1990–2011." *American Journal of Agricultural Economics* 95(2): 482–488.

Glauber, J. and P. Westhoff. 2015. "The 2014 Farm Bill and the WTO." Paper presented at ASSA annual meetings, January and forthcoming *American Journal of Agricultural Economics*, August.

Goodwin, B. 1994. "Premium rate determination in the federal crop insurance program: what do averages have to say about risk?" *Journal of Agricultural and Resource Economics* 19(2): 382–95.

Goodwin, B. K., M. L. Vandeveer, and J. Deal. 2004. "An Empirical Analysis of Acreage Effects of Participation in the Federal Crop Insurance Program." *American Journal of Agricultural Economics* 86(4): 1058–1077.

Goodwin, B. K. and V. H. Smith. 2012. "What Harm is Done by Subsidizing Crop Insurance?" *American Journal of Agricultural Economics* 95(2): 489–497.

Hendricks, N. and D. A. Sumner. 2014. "The Effects of Policy Expectations on Crop Supply, with an Application to Base Updating." *American Journal of Agricultural Economics* 96(3): 903–923.

Hennessy, D. 2014. "Sodbusting, Crop Insurance, and Sunk Conversion Costs." Seminar presented at the International Food Policy Research Institute, February 28, 2014, Washington, DC.

Horowitz, J. K., and E. Lichtenberg. 1993. "Insurance, Moral Hazard, and Chemical Use in Agriculture." *American Journal of Agricultural Economics* 75(4): 926–935.

LaFrance, J. T., J. P. Shimshack, and S. Y. Wu. 2002. "Crop Insurance and the Extensive Margin." Paper presented at the World Congress of Environmental and Resource Economists, Monterey, CA, June 24–27.

Lubowski, R. N., S. Bucholtz , R. Claassen, M. Roberts, J. Cooper, A. Gueorguieva, and R. Johansson. 2006. "Environmental Effects of Agricultural Land-Use Change: The Role of Economics and Policy." Economic Research Report 25. Washington, DC: USDA Economic Research Service. http://www.ers.usda.gov/publications/err-economic-research-report/err25.aspx.

Ludden, B. and J. Peace. 2014. "Conservation and the Agricultural Act of 2014." Choices: The Magazine of Farm, Food, and Resource Issues (2nd quarter).

Miranda, M. J. and J. W. Glauber. 1997. "Systemic Risk, Reinsurance and the Failure of Crop Insurance Markets." *American Journal of Agricultural Economics* 79(1): 206–215.

Nelson, C. H., and E. T. Loehman. 1987. "Further towards a Theory of Agricultural Insurance." *American Journal of Agricultural Economics* 69(3): 523–531.

Orden, D. and C. Zulauf. 2015. "Political Economy of the 2014 Farm Bill." Paper presented at ASSA annual meetings, January, and forthcoming *American Journal of Agricultural Economics*, August.

Orden, D., D. Blandford and T. Josling. 2010. "Determinants of Farm Policies in the United States," in *Political Economy of Distortions to Agricultural Incentives*, edited by K. Anderson. Washington DC: World Bank.

Schnepf, R. 2014. "Status of the WTO Brazil-U.S. Cotton Case." Congressional Research Service Report R43336, October 1.

Shields, D. A. 2013. "Federal Crop Insurance: Background." Publication 7–5700. Washington, DC: Congressional Research Service.

Smith, V. H. and V. K. Goodwin. 1996. "Crop Insurance, Moral Hazard, and Agricultural Chemical Use." *American Journal of Agricultural Economics* 78(2): 428–438.

Smith, V. C. 2014. "The 2014 Agricultural Act." Issue Paper No. 52. Geneva: International Centre for Trade and Sustainable Development. July.

Sumner, D. A. and C. Zulauf. 2012. "Economic and Environmental Effects of Agricultural Insurance Programs." Council on Food, Agriculture, Resource, and Environmental Economics. http://ageconsearch.umn.edu/bitstream/156622/2/Sumner-Zulauf_Final.pdf.

Tangermann, S. 2011. "Risk Management in Agriculture and the Future of the EU's Common Agricultural Policy." ICTSD Programme on Agricultural Trade and Sustainable Development, Issue Paper 34. Geneva: International Centre for Trade and Sustainable Development.

Tweeten, Luther and Carl Zulauf. 1997. "Public Policy for Agriculture after Commodity Programs." *Review of Agricultural Economics* 19: 263–280.

U.S. Congress. 2014. *Agricultural Act of 2014*. February 7. Washington DC: U.S. Government Printing Office.

U.S. Department of Agriculture (USDA), Economic Research Service. 2014a. "Agricultural Act of 2014: Highlights and Economic Implications."

U.S. Department of Agriculture, Office of the Chief Economist. 2014b. "World Agricultural Supply and Demand Estimates." WASDE-534. November 10.

Wilde, P. E. 2012. "The New Normal: The Supplemental Nutrition Assistance Program (SNAP)." *American Journal of Agricultural Economics* 95(2): 325–331.

Wright, B.D. and J.A. Hewitt. (1994) "All-Risk Crop Insurance: Lessons from Theory and Experience." in *Economics of Agricultural Crop Insurance: Theory and Evidence*, edited by D. L. Hueth and W. H. Furtan. Boston: Kluwer Academic Publishers.

Young, C. E., M. L. Vandeveer, and R. D. Schnepf. 2001. "Production and Price Impacts of U.S. Crop Insurance Programs." *American Journal of Agricultural Economics* 83(5): 1194–1201.

Zulauf, C. 2014a. "The Base vs. Planted Acre Issue: Perspectives, Trade-offs, and Questions." *Choices: The Magazine of Farm, Food, and Resource Issues.*

Zulauf, C. 2014b. State Distribution of Direct vs. Net Crop Insurance Payments, 2004–2013. University of Illinois at Urbana-Champaign, Department of Agricultural and Consumer Economics, April 10. http://www.farmdoc.illinois.edu

Zulauf, C., V. Demircan, G. Schnitkey, A. Barnaby, and K. Herbel. 2013. "Examining Contemporaneous Farm and County Losses Using Farm Level Data." Presented at AAEA Crop Insurance and the Farm Bill Symposium, Louisville, KY, October 8.

Zulauf, C. and D. Orden. 2014. "The U.S. Agricultural Act of 2014: Overview and Analysis." Discussion Paper 01393, International Food Policy Research Institute, December.

Zulauf, C. and G. Schnitkey. 2014. "ARC-CO and PLC Payment Indicator for 2014 Crop Year: October 2014 WASDE U.S. Yield and Price." University of Illinois at Urbana-Champaign, Department of Agricultural and Consumer Economics, October 14. http://www.farmdoc.illinois.edu

Section III:

Policy Interactions

Chapter 11

Sources of Growth in French Agriculture

Frédéric Bouchet, David Orden, and George W. Norton

Growth of French agriculture is addressed with production disaggregated among cereals, noncereal crops, milk, and animal products. Short-run and long-run supply functions are derived from a restricted profit function model in which capital and family labor are assumed quasi-fixed and measures of French public agricultural research expenditures and international technology availability are included. Production is found to be price responsive, but the estimated supply functions are inelastic even when the quasi-fixed factors adjust optimally. Technical change as a source of output growth is also supported. Domestic research is estimated to be the primary cause of increased cereals output over the 1960–84 period, while international technology transfers and domestic research seem to be important for milk production.

Key words: French agriculture, long-run profit function model, price policy, technical change.

Since the slowdown in the growth of world agricultural trade in 1980, the United States and the European Community (EC) have engaged in a series of debates over their respective agricultural policies. High producer prices and the general absence of production controls in Europe have been of particular concern in the United States as world grain stocks have risen and the EC has emerged, with substantial subsidies, as a net cereals exporter. Levels of frustration have increased on both sides of the Atlantic as the United States has responded with its own export-enhancement payments and other costly policies. With current positions difficult to sustain, the United States and some members of the European Community now seek means to limit their conflict and obtain relief from the high costs of their agricultural programs. The reduction of grain stocks resulting from the drought affecting U.S. production in 1988 may lower budget costs temporarily, but it does not lessen the long-run conflict about policy-induced excess supplies.

While permanent budgetary relief is sought in both the United States and Europe, there remain two fundamentally different views of the sources of growth in European agriculture. The U.S. view emphasizes that growth has been created by artificially high prices. European agriculture is seen as cost-noncompetitive, and it is argued that rather dramatic price-support reductions to bring internal prices to world levels would have large effects on agricultural input usage, investment, and output (Schmidt, Frohberg, and Maxwell). The European view emphasizes the political infeasibility of such large price reductions (Bergmann and Petit) and the effects on output growth of factors such as technological change, structural policies, investments in input supply, processing and marketing facilities, and substitution of capital for labor in the modernization process (Petit, Stanton). From this perspective, reduced price supports can have only a limited impact on output, and European agriculture is becoming increasingly competitive over time.

These conflicting views about the sources of growth in European agriculture are addressed

---

Frédéric Bouchet is an economist with the Fédération Nationale Porcine, Paris. David Orden and George W. Norton are an assistant professor and an associate professor, respectively, in the Department of Agricultural Economics, Virginia Polytechnic Institute and State University.

Some of this material was also presented in a contributed paper at the XX International Conference of Agricultural Economists and will appear in the proceedings of that conference.

The authors gratefully acknowledge the International Agricultural Trade Research Consortium for partial financial support and thank Brady Deaton, Michel Petit, Maury Bredahl, and participants in seminars at the OECD and the Economic Research Service, U.S. Department of Agriculture for constructive suggestions during this research. They also would like to thank Jean Marc Boussard and Albert Hayem for assistance in acquiring data on French public agricultural research expenditures, family labor utilization, and farm credit subsidies and Philip Abbott, Maury Bredahl, Michel Petit, G. Edward Schuh, Philip Pardey, Bud Stanton, Barbara Craig, J. Paxton Marshall, and two anonymous reviewers for comments on earlier drafts of this paper.

in this paper by evaluating changes in French agriculture from 1960 to 1984. France accounts for almost 30% of the farm production within the EC and a generally higher share of production of the EC's main export products.

In our analysis, French agricultural output is disaggregated among cereals, noncereal crops, milk, and animal products in a multiproduct variable profit function model. Hired labor, fertilizer and energy, and feeds are the variable inputs. Effects of technological and structural change are compared to the effects of price policies by inclusion in the model of measures of French public agricultural research expenditures, international technology availability, and domestic programs concerning land consolidation, retirement payments for farmers, and farm credit subsidies.

In our model of French agriculture, land is considered a fixed input, while capital investments (buildings and machinery) and family labor are assumed to be fixed at historical levels in the short run but variable and chosen optimally in the long run (quasi-fixed). Using duality results described by Diewert, Lau and, recently, Squires, expressions for the optimal long-run levels of the quasi-fixed factors are derived from the estimated short-run variable profit function and are used to evaluate the long-run elasticities of output supplies and variable input demands with respect to prices and other policies.

The results from our model include estimates of the short-run and long-run impacts of public agricultural research expenditures that are, to our knowledge, the first such estimates available for France and are among few such estimates available for any European country. Our results are suggestive of a very large role for technological change as a source of French agricultural output growth. For cereals, domestic research is found to be the primary cause of increased output. For noncereal crops and milk, growth is attributed to technological change arising from international technology transfers as well as domestic research. Our results also suggest that French agricultural production is price responsive, and more so in the long than short run, but that price responses are inelastic even when capital and family labor adjust optimally. These results have important implications both for agricultural trade negotiations and for agricultural research policies in Europe and the United States.

Background

Growth of French output of selected crop and livestock products between 1960 and 1984 is shown in table 1. Cereals, which accounted for 17.4% of the total value of agricultural output in 1980, showed the largest percentage increase among crop products (269.9%), while production of fruits and vegetables increased the least (4.8%). Among animal products, poultry production (4.9% of the total output value in 1980) increased by 195.8%. Milk production (18.0% of the 1980 total output value) increased by 70.5%. Production of several other animal products showed similar rates of growth.

Real price indices for cereals, noncereal crops, milk, and animal products are shown in figure 1. Due to relatively high inflation rates in France, real output prices have generally fallen, especially since 1975, despite the price intervention policies of the EC. Contrary to common perception, real cereals prices have been variable and exhibit the sharpest downward trend among output prices over the whole period.

Price indices for hired labor, fertilizer-energy, and feeds are shown in figure 2. Real wages of hired labor increased by almost 300% over the 1960–84 period, while real prices of fertilizer-energy and feeds fell slightly even with the 1970s' shocks to energy prices. With the increase of real wages, the French agricultural sector has experienced steady outmigration of labor and a rapid substitution of capital for labor. Utilization of labor decreased by more than 60%, 1960–84. The real value of capital assets (excluding land) increased by more than 90%.

The rapid substitution of capital for labor in French agriculture has been supported by the high priority given to public agricultural research. A public research institute—l'Institut National de la Recherche Agronomique (INRA)—was created in 1946. It encompasses all areas of agricultural research and accounts for more than 95% of public agricultural research expenditures. The budget for INRA (and three smaller public research institutes) has increased in real terms by more than 500% since 1960. The number of research personnel employed by INRA has tripled.

Development of the French agricultural sector has also been affected by European and national price and input policies. Price mea-

Table 1. Value and Growth of French Agricultural Output, 1960–84

Product	Percent of 1980 Total Value	Percent Growth of Output 1960–84
Plant products	46.2	85.6
Cereals	17.4	269.9
Fruits and vegetables	10.6	4.8
Wines	10.1	22.6
Sugar beets	3.1	111.8
Other crop products	5.0	
Animal products	53.8	64.8
Milk	18.0	70.5
Beef and veal	17.1	65.3
Pork	7.0	43.8
Poultry	4.9	195.8
Eggs	2.7	67.8
Other animal products	4.1	

Source: INSEE.

sures included in the European Common Agricultural Policy (CAP) are widely documented (e.g., Harris, Swinbank, and Wilkinson). At the national level, French input policies include a program of voluntary farm consolidation, a group of regional bodies empowered to buy land and resell it with the objective of increasing the size of farms (the Societes d'Amenagement Foncier et d'Etablissement Rural—SAFERs), and the payment of early or supplementary pensions to elderly farmers who retire (the Indemnité Viagere de Depart—IVD). Each of these policies is designed to facilitate modernization of the agricultural sector through consolidation and enlargement of production units. Of 31 million hectares in agricultural use, over 12 million hectares have been consolidated under the voluntary program (Tuppen). Funding levels have limited the effectiveness of the SAFERs and IVD (Chombart de Lauwe).

Public intervention also occurs in the provision of credit to French agriculture. Loans at preferential rates represent between 60% and 70% of the loans administered by the Credit Agricole, which provides about 70% of all farm credit.

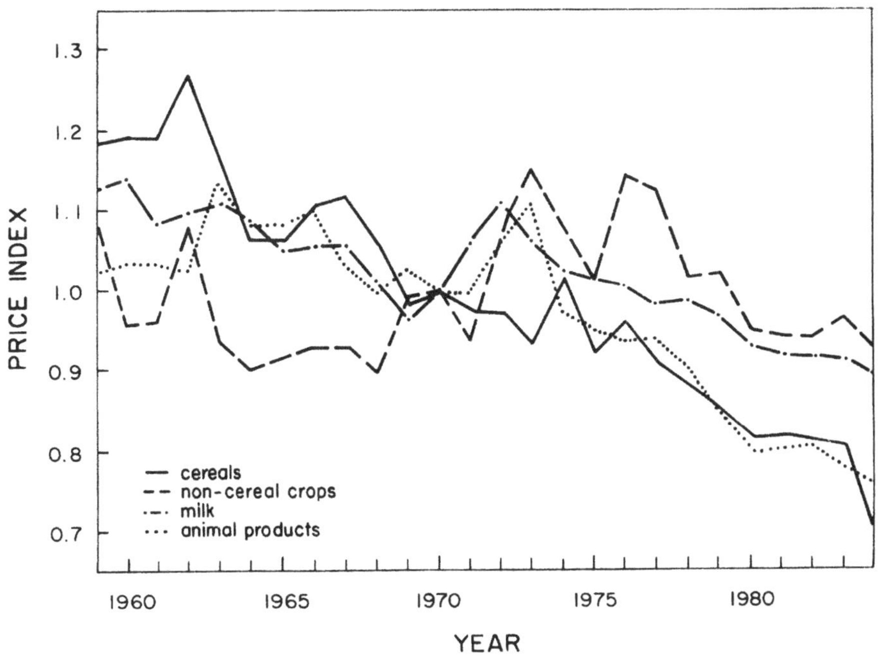

Figure 1. Real French agricultural output price indices, 1959–84

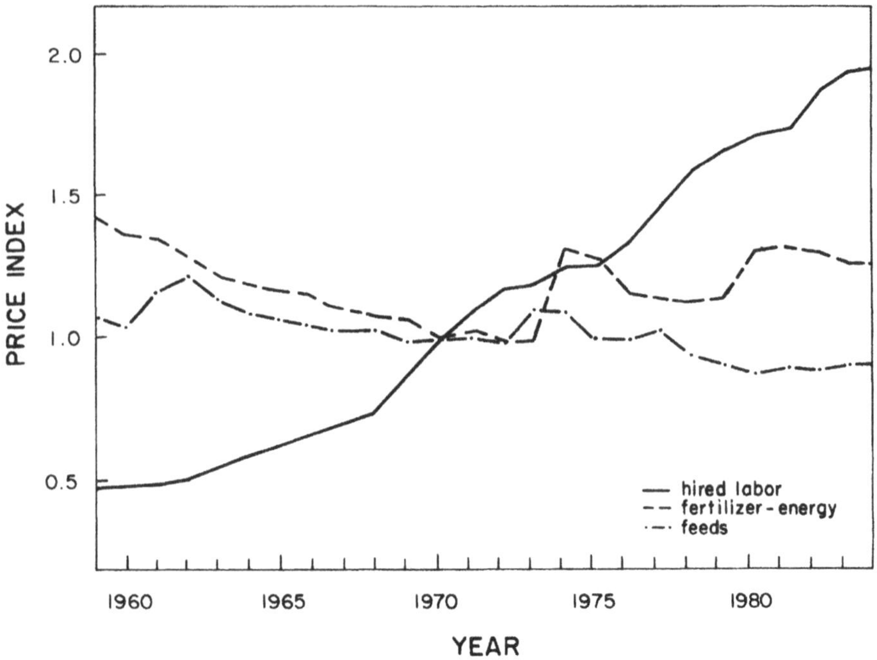

Figure 2. Real French agricultural input price indices, 1959–84

Methodology

The short-run variable (or restricted) multiproduct profit function has been widely used to evaluate input and output price responsiveness in agriculture (e.g., Weaver; Shumway; Antle; Lopez 1984; McKey, Lawrence, and Vlastiun). The effects on output of public agricultural research expenditures and other exogenous factors have been evaluated using production function models by Evenson, Bredahl and Peterson, Cline and Lu, and Mundlak and Hellinghausen, among others, and using profit function models by Huffman, Huffman and Evenson, and Norton. In the studies based on profit functions, demands for variable production inputs have been derived assuming optimization in the short run with levels of other inputs assumed fixed exogenously.

When some of these other production inputs are assumed to be quasi-fixed rather than fixed, the short-run variable profit function model, in which the quasi-fixed inputs are held at given levels, also provides information about long-run profit maximization, in which both variable and quasi-fixed inputs are chosen optimally. Let the short-run profit function be $\Pi = \Pi(P, Z, W)$, where P is a vector of the expected output and variable input prices (P_i:$i = 1, \ldots, m$), Z is a vector of the quasi-fixed inputs (Z_j:$j = 1, \ldots, n$), and W is a vector of the fixed inputs and exogenous factors (W_k:$k = 1, \ldots, s$). Let R be a vector of market prices of the quasi-fixed inputs (R_j:$j = 1, \ldots, n$). At a long-run optimum, the partial derivatives of the variable profit function with respect to the quantities of the quasi-fixed inputs are equal to their long-run equilibrium market prices:

$$(1) \qquad R_j = \frac{\partial \pi}{\partial Z_j} = Z_j(P, Z, W) \qquad j = 1, \ldots, n.$$

By solving equations (1) for the optimal Z_j's, the long-run, profit-maximizing levels of the quasi-fixed inputs, $Z^* = Z^*(P, R, W)$, can be derived. Using relationships among the derivatives and hessian matrices of the restricted and unrestricted profit functions proven by Lau, long-run output supply and variable input demand functions and their respective elasticities can also be obtained. Using these elasticities, the long-run effects of research as well as pricing and other government policies can be assessed.

Empirical derivation of the long-run results from an estimated short-run variable profit function is facilitated by specifying the profit function approximation as a normalized quadratic. The advantage of this functional form is that closed-form expressions can be derived for the optimal levels of the quasi-fixed factors.[1] The quadratic specification of the short-run profit function is

$$(2)\quad \Pi = \beta_0 + \Sigma_i\alpha_i P_i + \Sigma_j\mu_j Z_j + \Sigma_k\delta_k W_k + \tfrac{1}{2}\Sigma_i\Sigma_{i'}\lambda_{ii'}P_iP_{i'} + \tfrac{1}{2}\Sigma_j\Sigma_{j'}\gamma_{jj'}Z_jZ_{j'} + \tfrac{1}{2}\Sigma_k\Sigma_{k'}\chi_{kk'}W_kW_{k'} + \Sigma_i\Sigma_j\eta_{ij}P_iZ_j + \Sigma_i\Sigma_k\phi_{ik}P_iW_k + \Sigma_j\Sigma_k\theta_{jk}Z_jW_k,$$

and the short-run output supply and variable input demand functions are

$$(3)\quad \pm Q_i = \frac{\partial\Pi}{\partial P_i} = \alpha_i + \Sigma_{i'}\lambda_{ii'}P_{i'} + \Sigma_j\eta_{ij}Z_j + \Sigma_k\phi_{ik}W_k \qquad i = 1, \ldots, m,$$

where the sign modifier of Q_i is positive for a supply equation and negative for a variable input demand equation. Equations (1) are linear and can be solved readily for the Z_j^*. When capital ($j = K$) and family labor ($j = L$) are assumed to be quasi-fixed, their optimal levels are

$$(4)\quad \begin{bmatrix} K^* \\ L^* \end{bmatrix} = \frac{1}{\Delta}\begin{bmatrix} \gamma_{LL} & -\gamma_{KL} \\ -\gamma_{LK} & \gamma_{KK} \end{bmatrix} \begin{bmatrix} R_K - \mu_K - \Sigma_i\eta_{iK}P_i - \Sigma_k\theta_{Kk}W_k \\ R_L - \mu_L - \Sigma_i\eta_{iL}P_i - \Sigma_k\theta_{Lk}W_k \end{bmatrix},$$

where $\Delta = \gamma_{KK}\gamma_{LL} - (\gamma_{KL})^2$. By defining the partial derivatives of the optimal capital equation as

$$(5)\quad \delta_{KP_i} \equiv \frac{\partial K^*}{\partial P_i} = -\frac{1}{\Delta}(\gamma_{LL}\eta_{iK} - \gamma_{KL}\eta_{iL}) \qquad i = 1, \ldots, m$$

$$(6)\quad \delta_{KW_k} \equiv \frac{\partial K^*}{\partial W_k} = -\frac{1}{\Delta}(\gamma_{LL}\theta_{Kk} - \gamma_{KL}\theta_{Lk}) \qquad k = 1, \ldots, s$$

and defining partial derivatives of the optimal family labor equation similarly, the long-run output supply and variable input demand functions can be expressed as

$$(7)\quad \pm Q_i^* = \alpha_i + \mu_K\delta_{KP_i} + \mu_L\delta_{LP_i} - R_K\delta_{KP_i} - R_L\delta_{LP_i} + \Sigma_{i'}(\lambda_{ii'} + \eta_{i'K}\delta_{KP_i} + \eta_{i'L}\delta_{LP_i})P_{i'} + \Sigma_k(\phi_{ik} + \theta_{Kk}\delta_{KW_k} + \theta_{Lk}\delta_{LW_k})W_k.$$

Comparing the derivatives of (3) and (7) shows that long-run impacts on output of changes in prices and other exogenous factors consist of the short-run impacts (K and L fixed) plus terms capturing the additional impacts through, respectively, optimal capital and family labor adjustments.

Empirical Specification

The profit function model of French agriculture was estimated using annual data from 1959 to 1984.[2] Prices and other nominal variables were deflated by the price deflator of the French gross national product prior to estimation. Quantities of French agricultural production of cereals (Q_C), noncereal crops (Q_V), milk (Q_M), and animal products (Q_N) were computed from output series published by the Institut National de la Statistique et des Etudes Economiques (INSEE).[3] Output price indices (P_C, P_M, P_V, P_N) were derived from INSEE data provided by the French Ministry of Agriculture. One-year-lagged average mar-

[1] The normalized quadratic is a member of the class of flexible functional forms which provide local second-order approximations to arbitrary functional forms. The output supply and input demand functions derived from a normalized quadratic profit function are linear, and thus the resulting estimates are potentially less stable than those from, say, a translog function. Lopez (1985) also warns that the normalized quadratic imposes restrictive assumptions with respect to quasi-homotheticity and separability between inputs and outputs. Despite these disadvantages, the normalized quadratic is widely used. It has the counterbalancing advantage of being globally convex if it is locally convex. In this analysis, the normalized quadratic also has the advantage over the translog and other flexible forms of allowing for direct solution of equations (1) without having to rely on numerical methods to solve a system of nonlinear equations, as shown above.

[2] Many statistical series are not reported, and data quality is poor for those that are available prior to 1959.

[3] As apparent from table 1, cereals and milk each account for a substantial fraction of French agricultural output, while the noncereal crops and animal products quantities are aggregates among diverse products.

ket prices were used in the model as proxies for expected output prices.

For the fertilizer-energy and feeds inputs, quantity (l_F, l_D) and price (r_F, r_D) data are from INSEE. Employment of hired agricultural labor (l_H) and a series on family labor, adjusted for off-farm work, were obtained from the Ministry of Planning. These series are used in the MAGALI short-run forecasting model of the Ministry of Agriculture (Albecker and Lefebvre) and are more complete than previously published agricultural labor series. The cost of hired labor (r_H) is published by INSEE. It includes wages and social charges paid by farm owners on behalf of farm workers. The wage rate in the industrial sector, which was used as the opportunity cost of family labor (r_L), the total value of farm buildings and machinery (K), and a long-term market interest rate used as the opportunity cost for farm capital (r_K), are also published by INSEE. Series on cultivated acreage (CL) and pasture acreage (PL) are published by the Ministry of Agriculture.

French public expenditures on agricultural research (*RES*) enter the model with a lag structure (several structures were tested and the results are discussed below). Public agricultural research expenditures by INRA and three smaller research institutes were compiled from budgets of the Ministry of Agriculture. These budgets include total expenditures in six categories but not a breakdown of expenditures by commodity. Data on private agricultural research expenditures are not available, nor are consistent data series on expenditures for agricultural extension and the levels of education and training of French farmers. Omission of these variables may bias upward the estimated coefficients of public agricultural research expenditures in our model, since private research may be complementary with public research and extension expenditures and education and training levels of farmers are likely to be positively correlated with research expenditures.[4]

To allow for international technology transfers, the level of total agricultural productivity in the United States was used as a proxy for international availability of technology. In choosing this proxy, our hypothesis is that the United States is a major source of new agricultural technologies applied in France (other sources of international technology transfer, such as among European countries, were not modeled) and we assume that changes in U.S. agricultural productivity reflect to a large extent the availability of these new technologies, whether produced by the public or private sector. A five-year moving average of U.S. productivity was used to account for possible lags in technology transfers and to minimize the effect of random yearly fluctuations. Use of a productivity index, rather than U.S. research expenditures, eliminated the need to measure the lag associated with the effects of U.S. research expenditures on U.S. productivity.

Three French agricultural policy variables related to structural change were also included in the model. These variables were the cumulative area of farmland consolidated under voluntary programs (*REM*) lagged one year, the annual value of farm sales handled by the SAFERs to accommodate farm consolidation (*SAF*), and the annual value of early and supplementary retirement payments made to exiting farmers (*IVD*). A fourth policy variable (*CR*) measures credit subsidies by the ratio of the average loan rate given to farmers to the market rate. This variable was constructed from unpublished data on the amounts of loans given to farmers by the Credit Agricole at market and preferred interest rates.

Finally, the average yearly deviations from normal rainfall (*WEA*) were included in the model to control for weather variations. A dummy variable (*DUM*), with a value of one starting in 1976 and zero otherwise, also was included. This variable proxied for the after-effects of the world oil shock in the early 1970s and an extremely severe drought in France in 1976. These events caused enduring structural changes in the French agricultural production system (Bourgeois).[5]

[4] The research expenditures data series was backcast for the years 1955 to 1958 using a regression of the research series on a constant, a trend, and a dummy variable capturing a faster rate of increase of expenditures before 1970. Lags of research expenditures of up to five years could then be included in the model without losing observations. Five years is a shorter lag length than reported in much of the research evaluation literature (Pardey and Craig). The sum of the coefficients is not likely to be affected too much by truncating the lag length, but individual coefficients are likely to be biased upward because of specification error. Given the purpose of the current study (to assess sources of growth), it is the sum and not the individual coefficients that is important.

[5] Bouchet provides a detailed discussion of each of the variables described in this section and justification for their inclusion in the model.

Short-Run Model

Elasticities at sample means based on the estimated coefficients of the short-run output supply and variable input demand equations and their significance levels (p-values) are reported in table 2a. (Variables are defined in table 2b.) Coefficients of these equations were estimated by normalizing on the feeds price and treating the remaining six equations as seemingly unrelated regressions. The hypothesis that the six equations are derived from profit maximization implies fifteen cross-equation symmetry restrictions. These restrictions were tested jointly, and symmetry was not rejected at a 5% significance level. The cross-price coefficients in the missing (feeds) equation were then obtained by imposing the symmetry conditions, and its own-price coefficient was derived by homogeneity. The remaining coefficients of the feeds equation are not subject to theoretical constraints. After fixing the price terms, these remaining coefficients were estimated by ordinary least squares (OLS).

The own-price elasticities reported in table 2a suggest upward-sloping output supply functions and downward-sloping variable input demand functions for French agriculture that

Table 2a. Estimated Elasticities of the Short-Run Output Supply and Variable Input Demand Functions for French Agriculture and Significance Levels of the Estimated Coefficients

Explanatory Variable	Dependent Variable						
	Q_C	Q_V	Q_M	Q_N	I_F	I_H	I_D
P_C	.34	−.05	.16	.11	.18	.17	.58
	(.22)[a]	(.62)	(.11)	(.15)	(.44)	(.25)	(.30)
P_V	−.16	.66	−.24	−.13	.03	.02	.86
	(.63)	(.02)	(.07)	(.32)	(.93)	(.87)	(.30)
P_M	.18	−.09	.53	−.02	.26	.04	.25
	(.11)	(.06)	(.0008)	(.56)	(.06)	(.65)	(.30)
P_N	.40	−.16	−.007	−.006	−.38	−.19	.19
	(.12)	(.27)	(.54)	(.95)	(.21)	(.19)	(.70)
r_F	−.12	−.007	−.15	.07	−.88	.59	.10
	(.44)	(.92)	(.06)	(.23)	(.03)	(.0003)	(.90)
r_H	−.15	−.006	−.03	.04	.73	−.68	−.05
	(.29)	(.88)	(.68)	(.26)	(.001)	(.005)	(.70)
r_D	−.42	−.23	−.16	−.04	.12	−.06	−1.90
	(.30)	(.30)	(.30)	(.70)	(.90)	(.70)	[b]
L	1.40	.73	.49	.87	1.47	.18	−0.70
	(.12)	(.32)	(.09)	(.04)	(.16)	(.003)	(.60)
K	.72	−.38	.80	.74	2.83	.19	1.50
	(.58)	(.73)	(.09)	(.19)	(.07)	(.61)	(.38)
RES	1.27	.27	.10	.12	−.02	.16	−.04
	(.0001)	(.02)	(.07)	(.09)	(.88)	(.11)	(.92)
USP	.31	1.92	.99	.20			
	(.65)	(.004)	(.02)	(.66)			
CR	−.32		−.14	−.05	.48		.66
	(.05)		(.05)	(.45)	(.02)		(.08)
REM			−.19	.27			
			(.55)	(.49)			
CL	2.27	−.62			−.87	1.28	2.04
	(.04)	(.43)			(.54)	(.03)	(.02)
PL			.75	.37	−.95	−.52	1.19
			(.002)	(.12)	(.13)	(.07)	(.21)
R^2	0.9903[c]	0.9279[c]	0.9908[c]	0.9865[c]	0.9814[c]	0.9988[c]	0.9549[d]

[a] Significance levels (p-values) are reported in parentheses below their respective elasticities. All variables are defined in table 2b and are described in the text.

[b] The p-value of own-price coefficient of the feeds input is not computed. Its p-value is likely to be greater than 0.30 because the variances of the other coefficients in the feeds-input equation are high.

[c] Obtained in first stage of GLS estimation.

[d] Obtained from separate OLS estimation fixing coefficients of output and input prices based on symmetry and homogeneity properties of the system of equations.

Table 2b. Variables of the Model

Variables	Definitions
Q_C	Supply of cereals
Q_V	Supply of noncereal crops
Q_M	Supply of milk
Q_N	Supply of animal products other than milk
I_F	Demand for fertilizer and energy by the agricultural sector
I_H	Demand for hired labor by the agricultural sector
I_D	Demand for feeds by the agricultural sector
P_C	Expected market price of cereals
P_V	Expected market price of noncereal crops
P_M	Expected market price of milk
P_N	Expected market price of animal products other than milk
r_F	Market price of fertilizer and energy
r_H	Wage rate of hired labor in the agricultural sector
r_D	Market price of feeds
L	Family labor in the agricultural sector
K	Capital (buildings and machinery) in the agricultural sector
r_L	Opportunity cost of family labor in the agricultural sector[a]
r_K	Opportunity cost of capital in the agricultural sector[a]
RES	French public agricultural research expenditures
USP	International technology availability
REM	Cumulative amount of land consolidated
IVD	Retirement payments to farmers[a]
SAF	Land sales handled by the SAFERs[a]
CR	Credit subsidies
CL	Area of cultivated land
PL	Area of pasture land
WEA	Average yearly deviations from normal rainfall[a]
DUM	Dummy variable, taking the value 0 through 1975 and 1 afterwards[a]

[a] Not appearing in the report of short-run results above.

are price inelastic in the short run. The estimated own-price elasticities for cereals, noncereal crops, milk, and animal products are .34, .66, .53, and −.006, respectively. The estimated fertilizer-energy, hired labor, and feeds own-price elasticities are −.88, −.68, and −1.90. The own-price elasticities are statistically significant at the 5% significance level with the exception of the cereal-price elasticity (p = .22) and the animal-products elasticity (p = .95).

The estimated cross-price elasticities shown in table 2a suggest complementarities between production of cereals and milk and cereals and animal products that are marginally significant (p = .11 and .15, respectively) and substitutability between noncereal crops and milk (p = .07). Substitutabilities between production of cereals and noncereal crops and milk and animal products that might be expected a priori are not statistically significant. Thus, cross-price elasticities among the outputs seem to be less well estimated than own-price elasticities. Among the variable inputs, hired labor and fertilizer-energy are estimated to be substitutes (p = .0003), while feeds does not show substitutability with the other inputs.

With respect to the quasi-fixed factors, family labor is estimated to have positive effects on production of cereals, milk, and animal products. The estimated elasticities are 1.40, .49, and .87, respectively, with p-values .12, .09, and .04. Capital also has positive effects in the cereals, milk, and animal products equations, with elasticities of .72, .80, and .74, respectively. The statistical significance of the capital elasticity is low in the cereals equation (p = .58) and higher in the equations for milk (p = .09) and animal products (p = .19). Capital has a positive and significant effect (p = .07) on use of fertilizer-energy, while family labor has a positive and significant effect (p = .003) on employment of hired labor.

The elasticities for public agricultural research expenditures reported in table 2a are 1.27, 0.27, 0.10, and 0.12, respectively, in the cereals, noncereal crops, milk, and animal products equations. The associated p-values are 0.0001, 0.02, 0.07, and 0.09. In each case, research expenditures have a positive and significant impact on production, the estimated effect being particularly large for cereals. French public agricultural research expenditures are not significant in the short-run variable input demand equations.

Because of the importance of the research variable, some additional comments on its lag specification are warranted. The estimated effects of public agricultural research expenditures shown in table 2a are based on inclusion of one lag of the research expenditures variable in each equation. Research expenditures were lagged five years in the cereals, milk, and fertilizer-energy equations and four years in the other equations. These lag lengths were selected after a preliminary estimation in which current research expenditures and five years of lagged expenditures were included in each equation without constraints on the lag coefficients. Despite collinearity introduced by inclusion of multiple lags, one or more lagged research expenditure variables were statistically significant in three of the four output equations (the exception was noncereal crops). The final model was estimated with only one lag of research expenditures to reduce collinearity and save degrees of freedom.[6]

International technology transfers, proxied by the five-year moving average of U.S. agricultural productivity, also are estimated to have significant positive effects on French agricultural production. The estimated elasticities of noncereal crops and milk supplies with respect to this measure of international technology availability are 1.92 and .99, respectively, with p-values of .004 and .02. The international technology transfer variable is not significant in the cereals or animal products equation. It is not included in the variable input demand equations because of the limited number of degrees of freedom afforded by the data. When included, it is not statistically significant (the p-values of its coefficient in the fertilizer-energy, hired labor, and feeds equations were, respectively, 0.61, 0.98, and 0.36).

Overall, the French policy variables related to structural change and credit policy are not very robust in our model. Collinearity among the policy variables led to a focus on the cumulative area of farmland consolidated (*REM*) and the measure of credit subsidies (*CR*). These variables were dropped from the final equations when their p-values in initial models were greater than 0.3, unless their exclusion noticeably affected the estimates of other coefficients. With this procedure for model specification, the credit variable has statistically significant effects in four equations ($p \leq .08$), but its negative sign in the input demand equations is difficult to interpret.

Among the remaining fixed and exogenous factors, the allocation of land between crops and pasture has a significant effect on cereals ($p = .04$) and milk ($p = .002$) production. The estimated elasticity of cereals production with respect to crop acreage is 2.27, somewhat larger than expected and suggesting the possibility of measurement error with respect to changes in land quality over time. Yearly deviations from normal rainfall do not enter the final model. Coefficients of the rainfall variable were not statistically significant and their inclusion caused rejection of the cross-price symmetry conditions. These problems are likely because of the inadequacy of total annual rainfall as a proxy for weather conditions affecting agricultural production. The coefficient of the dummy variable for structural changes induced by weather and other shocks in the mid-1970s was statistically significant in three of the output equations and one of the variable input demand equations ($p \leq .05$), and it was retained in these equations.

Long-Run Model

Estimated long-run output supply and variable input demand functions depend on the estimated coefficients of the short-run profit function, as shown in equations (4), (5), (6), and (7). The short-run output supply and variable input demand equations reported in table 2a provide unbiased estimates of some of the required coefficients (the $\alpha_{i'}$'s, η_{iK}'s, η_{iL}'s, $\lambda_{ii'}$'s, and ϕ_{ik}'s). The remaining coefficients of equation (7) must be estimated directly from the equation:

$$(8)\quad \tilde{\Pi} = \beta_0 + \Sigma_j\mu_j Z_j + \Sigma_k\delta_k W_k + \tfrac{1}{2}\Sigma_j\Sigma_{j'}\gamma_{jj'}Z_j Z_{j'} + \tfrac{1}{2}\Sigma_k\Sigma_{k'}\chi_{kk'}W_k W_{k'} + \Sigma_j\Sigma_k\theta_{jk}Z_j W_k,$$

where $\tilde{\Pi}$ is short-run profits minus the terms in the profit function for which the short-run output supply and variable input demand equations provide unbiased coefficient estimates.

Because of the large number of terms in equation (8), it was not feasible to estimate all of the remaining coefficients.[7] To overcome this problem, equation (8) was initially restricted to terms in the variables that were most important in the short-run model: the quasi-fixed factors (capital and family labor), public agricultural research expenditures, and

[6] Imposing specific lag distributions did not prove to be a satisfactory alternative. With an imposed linear distribution, the research expenditures coefficient was statistically significant only in the cereals equation, despite the significance of the coefficient of at least one unconstrained research lag in the cereals, milk, and animal products equations. The cross-price symmetry conditions on the output supply and input demand equations were also strongly rejected when the linear lag distribution was imposed on the research expenditures variables. Imposing a quadratic structure with five lags maintained acceptance of the symmetry conditions, but levels of significance of the coefficients of the research variables were poor (only one coefficient had an associated p-value smaller than 0.15). It is likely that the number of lags (five) is not sufficient to impose a quadratic lag.

[7] There are 2 quasi-fixed inputs (Z_j's) and 10 fixed inputs or other exogenous factors (W_k's). Potentially, the number of coefficients to be estimated is 1 for β, 2 for μ_j, 10 for δ_k, 3 for $\gamma_{j'j'}$, 55 for $\chi_{kk'}$, and 20 for θ_{jk}.

international technology availability. Selected terms were then excluded to reduce collinearity and improve the significance levels of the remaining coefficients (see Bouchet for details). The final estimated coefficients of the profit function and their significance levels are reported in table 3.

The long-run elasticities of the output supply and variable input demand functions are shown in table 4. As noted above, these elasticities are sums of the corresponding short-run elasticities and terms representing the additional effects resulting from optimal adjustments of the quasi-fixed factors [the specific terms are derived easily from equation (7)]. Short-run and long-run elasticities are identical for the fixed inputs and exogenous factors that do not appear in interaction terms with the quasi-fixed factors in the final estimated short-run profit function. This is the case for all of the policy variables, for the variables representing land resources, and for the weather-related variables.

The long-run own-price elasticities shown in table 4 are larger than the short-run own-price elasticities shown in table 2a because of the positive additional effects on outputs of the capital and family labor drawn into the agricultural sector when an output price increases. Nevertheless, the output supply equations remain price inelastic when capital and family labor adjust optimally. The estimated long-run elasticities are .43, .75, .55, and .14, respectively, for cereals, noncereal crops, milk, and animal products.

A comparison of the long-run cross-price elasticities shown in table 4 and the short-run cross-price elasticities shown in table 2a also reveals a consistent pattern. When an output price increases, quasi-fixed inputs are drawn into the agricultural sector. Because these factors are assumed to be homogenously distributed within agriculture, the production of all outputs increases when the use of these factors increases.

Table 3. Estimated Coefficients of the Short-Run Profit Function for French Agriculture

Variable	Coefficient	p-value
Constant	723,246.3	0.13
KK	−0.000105	0.10
LL	−0.037326	0.07
KL	−0.000604	0.67
L RES	−0.000213	0.007
L USP	267.4	0.16
K RES	0.000006	0.006
K USP	16.2	0.16
USP	−1,616,113.3	0.14

Note: As described in the text, the coefficients reported in this table were estimated by subtracting from variable profits those terms of the quadratic profit function for which the output supply and variable input demand equations provided unbiased coefficient estimates. To save space, these latter coefficients are not included in the table.

Table 4. Estimated Elasticities of the Long-Run Output Supply and Variable Input Demand Functions for French Agriculture

Explanatory Variable	Dependent Variable						
	Q_C	Q_V	Q_M	Q_N	I_F	I_H	I_D
P_C	0.43	−0.01	0.20	0.17	0.29	0.25	0.57
P_V	−0.04	0.75	−0.22	−0.07	0.09	0.14	1.09
P_M	0.23	−0.09	0.55	0.08	0.35	0.08	0.26
P_N	0.61	−0.08	0.02	0.14	−0.08	−0.04	0.27
r_F	−0.04	0.06	−0.11	0.13	−0.72	0.65	0.08
r_H	−0.08	0.03	−0.01	0.09	0.80	−0.63	0.01
r_D	−0.51	−0.37	−0.17	−0.07	0.10	0.01	−2.40
r_K	−0.00026	−0.00035	−0.00044	−0.00035	−0.0016	0.00004	−0.0011
r_L	−0.22	0.13	−0.07	−0.13	−0.19	−0.19	0.14
RES	0.96	0.01	0.06	−0.03	−0.09	−0.15	−0.36
USP	2.85	2.46	2.48	2.09	4.86	1.72	0.74
CR	−0.32		−0.14	−0.05	0.48		0.66
REM			−0.19	0.27			
CL	2.27	−0.62			−0.87	1.28	2.04
PL			0.75	0.37	−0.95	−0.52	1.19

Note: The long-run elasticities with respect to prices, public research expenditures, and international technology availability include terms that are nonlinear combinations of estimated coefficients of the short-run variable profit function. Confidence bounds were not computed for these long-run elasticities. Significance levels (p-values) for the remaining elasticities are shown in table 2.

Output supply responses to variable input prices and variable input demand responses to output prices also differ between the short and long run. The elasticities of output supplies with respect to variable input prices are less negative in the long run because of greater input substitution as levels of capital and family labor adjust. Elasticities of variable input demands with respect to output prices are greater in the long run than in the short run because of the increased output response induced by changes in output prices.

The opportunity costs of the quasi-fixed inputs (the interest rate and industrial wages) appear in the long-run output supply and variable input demand equations in place of the levels of capital and family labor. The output supply elasticities with respect to these opportunity costs have the expected negative signs (except for the effect of the wage rate on noncereal crops), but they are quite small for the interest rate. Capital appears to be slightly substitutable for hired labor. Family labor and hired labor appear to be complements.

It was expected that the effects of French public agricultural research expenditures on output would be larger in the long run than in the short run. However, in all cases but one, the long-run output elasticities with respect to research expenditures are estimated to be smaller than the corresponding short-run elasticities. When the long-run effects are decomposed into their three components (the short-run impact and additional impacts coming from adjustments of capital and family labor), French public agricultural research expenditures are estimated to increase the optimal capital stock, yielding positive additional supply effects with respect to research. The opposite is true for family labor: research expenditures are found to be labor saving, which reduces outputs. The estimated long-run negative effects on output levels caused by decreased labor in agriculture outweigh the positive long-run effects from increased capital utilization. This leads to the smaller long-run than short-run elasticities of outputs with respect to public research expenditures.

A similar decomposition of the estimated long-run effects on outputs of international technology availability shows technology transfers to raise optimal levels of capital and family labor. The estimated long-run output elasticities with respect to international technology transfers are therefore larger than the corresponding short-run elasticities.

Cereals and Milk Production

Cereals and milk are the two main products of French agriculture and are two of the principal commodities exported by the European Community. For these two products, output growth from 1960–62 to 1982–84 was apportioned among the explanatory price, quasi-fixed, fixed, and exogenous variables on the basis of the short-run model. This decomposition provides estimates of the output growth that comes from movements in each of the explanatory variables based on the historically observed levels of capital and family labor in French agriculture.[8] Averages over the first and last three observations of each variable were used to prevent yearly fluctuations from having too large an influence on the decomposition among sources of output growth.

The results of the decompositions are shown in table 5. Cereals output is estimated to have increased by 199.8% and milk output by 51.6% over the twenty-year period. These production increases are estimated to be caused primarily by technological change. All else equal, domestic research and international technology transfers would have caused cereals and milk output to increase by 435.4% and 71.0%, respectively. The technology-induced output growth is attributed mostly to French public agricultural research expenditures in the case of cereals. For milk production, the increase in output coming from technological change is attributed to both French public agricultural research expenditures, for growth of 22.3%, and to transfers of technology, for growth of 48.7%. Growth of cereals and milk output attributed to technological change is partially offset by declining real output prices, the rising cost of hired labor, and the decline of family labor in agriculture. In the case of cereals, reduced land utilization and structural change also lower output growth, while land consolidation is estimated to impact negatively on growth of milk output. Credit policies are estimated to play a small role in the growth of output.

The role of price policies requires some fur-

[8] Observed levels of capital and family labor in French agriculture differ from their estimated optimal long-run values in most years. The advantage of a decomposition of output growth on the basis of the short-run model is that estimated output levels are based on actual use of the quasi-fixed factors. The disadvantage is that impacts attributed to changes in prices and other policy variables do not include their long-run effects through their impacts on the optimal levels of capital and family labor.

Table 5. Estimated Sources of Growth for French Production of Cereals and Milk 1960–62 to 1982–84

Explanatory Variable	Cereals		Milk	
	Percent Increase	Percent of Growth	Percent Increase	Percent of Growth
P_C	−18.5	−9.2	−5.8	−11.2
P_V	1.2	0.6	1.2	2.3
P_M	−5.1	−2.5	−9.8	−18.9
P_N	−14.4	−7.2	1.8	3.5
r_F	0.7	0.4	0.6	1.2
r_L	−18.7	−9.3	−2.9	−5.6
r_D	18.5	9.3	4.7	9.2
L	−211.1	−105.6	−50.2	−97.2
K	78.1	39.1	58.0	112.4
RES	412.8	206.6	22.3	43.1
USP	22.6	11.3	48.7	94.4
CR	17.3	8.6	5.4	10.4
REM			−27.8	−54.0
CL	−32.5	−16.3		
PL			5.4	10.4
DUM	−51.1	−25.6		
Total	199.8	100.0	51.6	100.0

ther evaluation. As shown in figure 1, real prices of agricultural outputs have fallen in France despite EC nominal price supports. Everything else constant, the fall in own price is estimated to cause cereals production to decrease by 18.5% and milk production to decrease by 9.8% over the 1960–62 to 1982–84 period. Without EC price supports, cereals and milk production would have been lower in all years because the cereals and milk supply equations have positive own-price elasticities.

As a basis of comparison, French cereals and milk output were simulated under the assumption that domestic prices had been the same as corresponding prices in the United States. The U.S. prices were converted to French equivalents at the average exchange rate over the 1960–84 period. Everything else was assumed unchanged. Under these conditions, it is estimated that the increase in cereals production in France from 1960–62 to 1982–84 would have been almost 6% less and the increase in milk production almost 24% less than occurred under French prices. Based on historical trends in expenditures on public agricultural research and international availability of new technology and our estimates of their impacts on French agricultural production, such a price-induced decline in cereals output growth would be offset very quickly, while the decline in milk output growth would not be offset for more than four years.

Conclusions

There are conflicting U.S. and European views about the sources of growth and competitiveness of European agriculture. These conflicting views shape agricultural trade negotiating positions and will have much to do with accomplishments in discussions such as the current GATT round and with the character of international competition in agriculture that emerges.

This paper has presented short-run and long-run results from a variable profit function model in which French agriculture is aggregated into four outputs, three variable inputs, and two quasi-fixed inputs. Some of the estimated coefficients should be interpreted with caution because of the lack of statistical significance and possible bias, especially in the long run.[9] Nevertheless, various caveats are

[9] Another limitation of this study is the lack of degrees of freedom which impedes more thorough assessment of the research lag. Also, the model abstracts from dynamic considerations. The long-run solution from a static long-run profit function model may differ from that obtained from a dynamic model because long-run functions obtained from dynamic profit maximization are not theoretically constrained to be symmetric in prices (Bouchet). The difference in the solutions from the two approaches may not be very large if the costs of adjustment are independent of the equilibrium stocks of the quasi-fixed factors. This assumption seems reasonable in the current study because labor stickiness in agriculture is caused primarily by forces outside the sector and the costs associated with relocation. These costs are basically independent of the equilibrium amount of labor and capital in agriculture. Nevertheless, the static nature of the model we utilize potentially influences the long-run results.

unlikely to change several of the major results of the analysis or their policy implications. On the issues at stake in the trade negotiations, our analysis of growth in French agriculture cuts in several directions.

Estimates of the short-run output supply functions for French agriculture suggest that agricultural output levels in France are price responsive. This provides support for the view that European price policies have been a source of high European output levels. Lower European prices for agricultural products would reduce European production. However, the responses to price changes are estimated to be inelastic even in the long run when usage of quasi-fixed capital and family labor have fully adjusted to optimal levels. Thus, the view that the persistence of high EC agricultural prices has contributed to increases in output much greater than would have occurred otherwise is not supported by our results.

Moreover, our analysis suggests that French agricultural production has benefited from important technological gains since the early 1960s. Growth of French agricultural output cannot be attributed solely, or even primarily, to high prices. Production has increased despite falling real output prices and rising labor costs.

The importance of technological change in French agriculture has several implications. First, gains from a one-time reduction in farm price levels are likely to prove illusory. If France continues to pursue a strong program of public (and private) agricultural research and continues to adopt new technologies available internationally, then outward shifts of its agricultural supply functions will quickly offset any given downward movement along these functions. The case for negotiating fixed lower prices is weak, from either the point of view of those who might anticipate large gains from such an agreement or from the point of view of those who would like to claim such an outcome would be a major concession.

A second implication of the importance of technological change is that France is achieving a favorable competitive position relative to other producers. If France finds herself in a situation of comparative advantage in agriculture, the French approach to trade negotiations should shift toward a freer market stance in which her comparative advantage would reap the largest benefits. This may pave the way for unexpected progress in trade negotiations. It also implies that competition will remain stiff in its aftermath.

What is suggested is that the United States and the European Community may compete for agricultural export markets in the future largely through the generation and adoption of new technology. On this issue, our results are perhaps the most interesting and the most preliminary, and there is need for additional research. While the technology spillover variable used in the analysis is admittedly imprecise, our results suggest that international transfers of technology play an important role for some commodities but not others. Under these circumstances, competition in world markets will affect domestic perceptions of optimal allocations of research expenditures among commodities. From a global perspective, domestic allocation decisions of individual countries may not be optimal. Additional work on the allocation of public research expenditures in Europe by commodity, on appropriate proxies for international availability of technology, and on the mechanisms, incidence, and magnitude of international technology transfers are warranted. In the interim, our study suggests that development of a sensible international framework for agricultural research among industrial countries will become increasingly important as more explicit trade barriers fade.

[Received March 1988; final revision received August 1988.]

References

Albecker, C., and C. Lefebvre. "Un Modèle Econométrique de l'Agriculture Française (MAGALI)." *Economie Rurale* 165(1985):27–33.

Antle, John M. "The Structure of U.S. Agricultural Technology, 1910–78." *Amer. J. Agr. Econ.* 66 (1984):414–21.

Bergmann, Denis, and Michel Petit. "Modernization of Agriculture in Western Europe after World War II: A Result of Luck, Circumstances or Government Policies?" Paper presented at the International Symposium on Rural Development Strategy, Beijing, China, Oct. 1987.

Bouchet, Frédéric C. "An Analysis of Sources of Growth in French Agriculture, 1960–1984." Ph.D. thesis, Virginia Polytechnic Institute and State University, 1987.

Bourgeois, Lucien. "L'Expansion de la Production Agricole Française Depuis 20 Ans." *Problèmes Economiques*, no. 8 (1983), pp. 14–19.

Bredahl, Maury E., and Willis L. Peterson. "The Productivity and Allocation of Research at U.S. Agricultural Experiment Stations." *Amer. J. Agr. Econ.* 58 (1976):684–92.

Chombart de Lauwe, Jean. *L'Aventure Agricole de la France de 1945 à Nos Jours.* Paris: Presses Universitaires de France, 1979.

Cline, Philip L., and Yao-Chi Lu. "Efficiency Aspects of the Spatial Allocation of Public Sector Agricultural Research and Extension in the United States." *Reg. Sci. Perspectives* 6(1976):1–16.

Diewert, W. E. "Applications of Duality Theory." *Frontiers of Quantitative Economics,* vol. 2, ed. M. D. Intriligator and D. A. Kendrick. Amsterdam: North-Holland Publishing Co., 1974.

Evenson, Robert E. "The Contribution of Agricultural Research to Production." *J. Farm Econ.* 49(1967): 1415–25.

Harris, Simon, Alan Swinbank, and Guy Wilkinson. *The Food and Farm Policies of the European Community.* New York: John Wiley & Sons, 1983.

Huffman, Wallace E. "Research Bias Effects for Input and Output Decisions: An Application to U.S. Cash Grain Farms." *Evaluating Agricultural Research and Productivity,* ed. W. Burt Sundquist, pp. 123–38. University of Minnesota Agr. Exp. Sta. Misc. Pub. No. 52-1987, 1987.

Huffman, Wallace E., and Robert E. Evenson. *Supply and Demand Functions for Multiproduct U.S. Cash Grain Farms: Biases Caused by Research and Other Policies, 1948–1974.* Dep. Econ. Staff Pap. No. 155, Iowa State University, April 1986.

Institut National de la Statistique et des Études Économiques (INSEE). *Annuaire Statistique de la France.* Paris, various issues 1985.

Lau, Lawrence J. "A Characterization of the Normalized Restricted Profit Function." *J. Econ. Theory* 12 (1976):131–63.

Lopez, Ramon E. "Estimating Substitution and Expansion Effects Using a Profit Function Framework." *Amer. J. Agr. Econ.* 66(1984):358–67.

———. "Structural Implications of a Class of Flexible Functional Forms for Profit Functions." *Int. Econ. Rev.* 26(1985):593–601.

McKey, Lloyd, Denis Lawrence, and Chris Vlastiun. "Profit, Output Supply and Input Demand Functions for Multiproduct Firms: The Case of Australian Agriculture." *Int. Econ. Rev.* 24(1983):323–39.

Mundlak, Yair, and René Hellinghausen. "The Inter-country Agricultural Production Function: Another View." *Amer. J. Agr. Econ.* 64(1982):664–72.

Norton, George W. "Evaluating Social Science Research in Agriculture." *Evaluating Agricultural Research and Productivity,* ed. W. Burt Sundquist, pp. 171–92. University of Minnesota Agr. Exp. Sta. Misc. Pub. No. 52-1987, 1987.

Pardey, Philip R. G., and Barbara Craig. "Causal Relationships between Public Sector Agricultural Research Expenditures and Output." *Amer. J. Agr. Econ.,* 9–19.

Petit, Michel. "Economics and Politics in the International Trade of Agricultural Products." Paper presented at International Agricultural Trade Research Consortium, Airlie, VA, Dec. 1987.

Service Central des Enquêtes et Études Statistiques (SCEES). *Annuaire de Statistique Agricole.* Paris: Ministere de l'Agriculture, various issues.

Schmidt, Steven C., Klaus K. Frohberg, and Douglas L. Maxwell. "Implications of Grain Trade Liberalization in the European Community." University of Illinois Agr. Exp. Sta., AERR No. 202, Oct. 1987.

Shumway, C. Richard. "Supply, Demand, and Technology in a Multiproduct Industry: Texas Field Crops." *Amer. J. Agr. Econ.* 65(1983):748–60.

Squires, Dale. "Long-Run Profit Functions for Multiproduct Firms." *Amer. J. Agr. Econ.* 69(1987):558–69.

Stanton, Bernard F. *Production Costs for Cereals in the European Community: Comparisons with the United States, 1977–1984.* Dep. Agr. Econ. AE Res. No. 86-2, Cornell University, March 1986.

Tuppen, John. *The Economic Geography of France.* London: Croom Helm, 1983.

Weaver, Robert D. "Multiple Input, Multiple Output Production Choices and Technology in the U.S. Wheat Region." *Amer. J. Agr. Econ.* 65(1983):45–56.

Chapter 12

Review of International Economics, 8(4), 681–697, 2000

Environmental Quality and Industry Protection with Noncooperative Versus Cooperative Domestic and Trade Policies

*Joachim Schleich and David Orden**

Abstract

This paper characterizes environmental quality and industry protection in a large-country Grossman–Helpman model when production or consumption externalities exist and governments decide noncooperatively or cooperatively on domestic and trade policies. Governments choose policies efficiently from among those available, but competitive lobbies may prefer less efficient regimes. Under restricted policy availability, political-support effects can offset terms-of-trade effects on equilibrium outcomes, and inefficient trade policies can lead to higher environmental quality than efficient domestic policies. If governments cooperate, they can satisfy particular organized industries at lower costs to other lobbies and total welfare. This may result in lower environmental quality than noncooperation.

1. Introduction

Over the last two decades trade and environmental policy issues have gained considerable attention. In this paper, we analyze environmental quality and industry protection in a large-country political economy model when production or consumption externalities exist. The analysis is based on the Grossman–Helpman (G–H) approach, where organized industry lobbies offer financial contribution schedules to affect the policy stances of governments, and the governments decide on their policies given these schedules. We extend previous applications of G–H models under a small-country assumption (e.g., Dixit, 1996; Dixit et al., 1997; Fredriksson, 1997; Aidt, 1998; or Schleich, 1999), to derive equilibrium conditions for single or multiple endogenous domestic and trade policies when the governments of a home and foreign country act either noncooperatively or cooperatively. Our analysis demonstrates several effects of the type of externality and the set of available policies on the equilibrium outcomes. Governments always make efficient policy choices among those available to serve the industry lobbies and, if acting noncooperatively, to address local externalities and exploit international market power.[1] But competitive lobbies may prefer less efficient regimes, and neither use of efficient policies alone nor cooperation by governments necessarily leads to higher environmental quality than use of less efficient policies or noncooperation. These general results are particularly relevant in light of recent trade agreements, which have addressed domestic as well as border policies, and with the emergence of international environmental discussions that parallel more traditional trade negotiations.

When there are production externalities and noncooperative governments have production and trade policies available, production taxes are lower than Pigouvian taxes for organized industries, because production policy is used not only to address the

---

*Schleich: Fraunhofer Institute for Systems and Innovation Research (ISI), Department of Energy Technology and Energy Policy, D-76139 Karlsruhe, Germany. Tel: +49-721-6809-203; Fax: +49-721-6809-272; E-mail: schleich@isi.fhg.de. Orden: Virginia Polytechnic Institute and State University, Blacksburg, VA 24061, USA. Tel: 540-231-7559; Fax: 540-231-3318; E-mail: orden@vt.edu. We are grateful to an anonymous referee for helpful comments and suggestions.

domestic externality but also to satisfy the lobbies with output subsidies. Two related results follow if policy choice is restricted. First, the political equilibrium tax for an exporting country can be *lower* than the Pigouvian tax when governments have only production policies available and there is a local externality (instead of higher, as in Krutilla (1991)) because the political-support effect comes in addition to use of an output tax to address the externality and manipulate the terms of trade. Second, inefficient trade policies, which competitive lobbies may prefer to efficient production policies, can translate into higher environmental quality, as in the small-country model (Schleich, 1999). The reason environmental quality can be higher with trade policies is that, while production policy is more efficient than trade policy for addressing an externality, it is also more efficient for satisfying the political lobby of the polluting industry.

Under cooperation, governments avoid imposing economic costs on each other and are able to satisfy particular industry lobbies at lower costs to the other lobbies and total welfare. An important consequence is that environmental quality may be lower under cooperation than under noncooperation, even though the cooperative equilibrium policies fully reflect the effects of environmental externalities domestically and abroad. Further, an organized industry can be protected in both countries when production policies are available; this is in contrast to the original Grossman–Helpman (1995) result with only trade policy, in which case an industry can be protected in only one country when governments cooperate.

For a consumption externality, when governments act noncooperatively and consumption and trade policies are available, the latter are applied to satisfy the lobbies, while the former address the domestic externality and the distortions arising from the trade interventions. Unlike the outcome for a small country, environmental quality and domestic consumption levels are not socially optimal, whether the governments cooperate or not. When only consumption policies are available, protection for an industry increases with the political power of the industry abroad, since home and foreign governments subsidize consumption to raise the world price. Industry protection is identical across countries when the externality is global and the governments act cooperatively.

2. Equilibrium Policies with a Production Externality

The model is based on Grossman and Helpman (1995) and contains two large countries, home and foreign, with similar political and economic systems. The exposition focuses on the home country, while variables and parameters associated with the foreign country are denoted with an asterisk.

Consumers

The home country population of N residents provide a total labor supply l and have additively separable quasilinear preferences defined over $(n + 1)$ goods. Individual j's utility is $u_j = c_{0j} + \Sigma_{i=1}^{n} u_{ij}(c_{ij}) - u_{Ej}(E)$, where c_{0j} is the consumption of the numéraire good, c_{ij} is the consumption of good i, and $-u_{Ej}(E)$ is the disutility that individual j derives from environmental damage as determined by a negative externality E; that is, $\partial u_{Ej}/\partial E = u'_{Ej} > 0$ with $\partial^2 u_{Ej}/\partial E^2 \geq 0$ for all j. All individuals are assumed to have identical increasing and concave subutility functions. The ordinary demand functions for non-numéraire goods depend only on own prices, $d_i(p_i^d)$, and the marginal utility of income equals one. Indirect utility can be expressed as $v(p^d, y, E) = y + s(p^d) + u_E(E)$, where y represents individual income, $p^d = (p_1^d, p_2^d, \ldots, p_n^d)$ is the vector of non-numéraire consumer prices, and $s(p^d) = \Sigma_{i=1}^n u_i[d_i(p_i^d)] - \Sigma_{i=1}^n p_i^d d_i(p_i^d)$ is consumer surplus from all non-numéraire goods. Individual demands are given by $d_i(p_i^d) = -\partial s/\partial p_i^d$, and total demand for any good i in the home country is $D_i(p_i^d) = Nd_i(p_i^d)$, with $\partial D_i/\partial p_i^d = D_i' \leq 0$.

Production and Industry Lobbies

All sectors produce under perfect competition. The numéraire good is made from labor alone, such that one unit of labor produces one unit of output. Domestic and world prices of the numéraire good are set equal to one, which also fixes the wage rate at one. All other goods are produced from labor and one sector-specific fixed factor, with constant returns to scale in both factors but diminishing returns to the individual factors. This production structure leads to (aggregate) quasi-rents of $\Pi_i(p_i^s)$ to the fixed factor in industry i, where p_i^s is the domestic producer price, and the cross-price effects are zero. Supply for industry i is given by $X_i(p_i^s) = \Pi_i'(p_i^s)$, with $\partial X_i/\partial p_i^s = X_i' > 0$.

The negative environmental externality in the home country E is assumed to be generated by the production activity of one or more non-numéraire goods, with $\partial E(X_i, X_i^*)/\partial X_i = E_X > 0$ for polluting industries in the home country and $E_X = 0$ for nonpolluting industries. The marginal impact of foreign production on the environmental externality in the home country is $\partial E(X_i, X_i^*)/\partial X_i^* = \gamma E_{X^*}$, where $\gamma = 1$ if the externality is global and $\gamma = 0$ otherwise. For simplicity, E_X and E_{X^*} are assumed to be constants.

Owners of the specific factor used in the production of good i have an incentive to lobby for policies that raise p_i^s because a higher price increases their rents. The model does not explain the process of lobby formation; instead it is assumed that only the owners of a subset L of all specific factors is capable of overcoming the free-rider problem and organizing for political action. These lobbies simultaneously and noncooperatively offer financial contributions in order to influence government policies. Initially, we assume that lobbies can influence only the policies in their own country. When each lobby chooses its contributions, it takes into account how all of the government's price interventions affect its members' welfare, including through environmental effects due to impacts on E. Each lobby i chooses its contributions (C_i) to maximize the (aggregate) net welfare of its members

$$W_i(\tau, \theta; \tau^*, \theta^*) - C_i(\tau, \theta; \tau^*, \theta^*) \equiv l_i + \Pi_i + N_i[s - u_E + r] - C_i, \tag{1}$$

where τ is the vector of production policies, and θ is the vector of trade policies in the home country. N_i is the number of people that own specific factor i, l_i is their (aggregate) labor income, and r is the per capita transfer from the revenue generated by the home government's policies.

Government Policies

The government maximizes a weighted sum of contributions from organized industries and total consumer welfare:

$$G(\tau, \theta; \tau^*, \theta^*) = \sum\nolimits_{i \in L} C_i + aW, \tag{2}$$

where the coefficient a captures a tradeoff as perceived by the government.[2] The contributions received by the government are assumed to be used in its re-election campaign or for its own private consumption; these expenditures do not enter subsequent market equilibrium conditions for non-numéraire goods. Total consumer welfare consists of the sum of total labor income, total profits, total consumer surplus, the total disutility derived from the externality, and net government transfers:

$$W(\tau, \theta; \tau^*, \theta^*) \equiv l + \sum_{i=1}^{n} \Pi_i + N[s - u_E + r]. \tag{3}$$

To achieve its objective, the home government can impose *ad valorem* domestic policies τ_i and trade policies θ_i on any of the non-numéraire goods. As in Grossman and Helpman (1994, 1995), Dixit (1996), Fredriksson (1997), Aidt (1998), and Schleich (1999), the set of policies considered is assumed to be predetermined. The policies available include one or more of production, consumption, and trade policies (taxes and subsidies). Given the choice between these three types of policies, any one policy can be substituted by an equal rate combination of the other two. Thus, only two policies can be solved for simultaneously, and any two policies provide a complete set of options. For specificity, when multiple policies are considered we assume that the most efficient environmental policies are available together with trade policies. Alternatively, we assume that only one type of policy is available: either the efficient domestic policy or the trade policy.

In the case of a production externality, production taxes and subsidies are the available domestic policies. Production policies drive a wedge between producer and consumer prices, and trade policies separate domestic producer and consumer prices from world (or offshore) prices p_i^w. The price equilibrium conditions for good i require $p_i^s = (\theta_i/\tau_i)p_i^w$ and $p_i^d = \theta_i p_i^w$, respectively. The net revenue generated by the government's domestic and trade policies (excluding contributions by lobbies) is redistributed evenly on a per capita basis. Thus, the net per capita transfer by the home government is

$$r(\tau, \theta; \tau^*, \theta^*) = \frac{1}{N}\sum_{i=1}^{n} p_i^s(\tau_i - 1)X_i(p_i^s) + \frac{1}{N}\sum_{i=1}^{n} p_i^w(\theta_i - 1)[D_i(p_i^d) - X_i(p_i^s)]. \tag{4}$$

Solution Concept under Noncooperation

Following Goldberg and Maggi (1999), we assume that the lobbies and the governments in each country play a Nash-bargaining game to determine the equilibrium set of feasible contribution functions $\{C_i^0\}_{i\in L}$ and $\{C_i^{0*}\}_{i\in L^*}$ and the equilibrium policy vectors (τ^0, θ^0) and (τ^{*0}, θ^{*0}). Since the lobbies' and the government's preferences are linear in the payments, the political equilibrium policies are independent of the distribution of the equilibrium contributions.[3] The efficiency property of the Nash bargaining solution implies that the equilibrium policies for the home country maximize the joint surplus between the home government and the home lobbies, given by

$$\Omega = aW + \sum\nolimits_{i\in L} W_i, \tag{5}$$

while contributions determine the distribution of this surplus.[4] Substituting equation (4) into (1) and (3), and then (1) and (3) into (5), the first-order conditions for the equilibrium interventions in industry i can be written as

$$\nabla_\beta \Omega = (a + I_{iL})\nabla_\beta \Pi_i + (a + \alpha_L)N\nabla_\beta(s - u_E + r) = 0, \tag{6}$$

where ∇_β denotes the gradient with respect to $\beta = (\tau_i, \theta_i)$, $\alpha_L = \Sigma_{i\in L}(N_i/N) \le 1$ is the degree of organization in the economy (that is, α_L is the exogenous share of the population that owns specific factors in organized industries), and I_{iL} is an indicator variable, with $I_{iL} = 1$ if $i \in L$, and $I_{iL} = 0$ otherwise.

Equilibrium Outcomes for Noncooperative Multiple and Single Policies

When the governments have production and trade policies available, the equilibrium policies for the home country are given implicitly (see the Appendix) by equations (T1a) and (T1b) in Table 1, where $\Phi_i = (I_{iL} - \alpha_L)/(a + \alpha_L)$ depends on exogenous parameters affecting political strength of an industry, $M_i'^* = D_i'^* - X_i'^*/\tau_i^* < 0$, and $\eta_i^* = -p_i^w\theta_i^* M_i'^*/M_i$ is the elasticity of foreign excess supply, which is positive (negative) when the home country imports (exports) good i.[5]

Equations (T1a) and (T1b), together with their foreign counterparts, determine the political equilibrium levels for production and trade policies. The general efficiency property of the G–H model implies that in the political equilibrium the government uses production policies to satisfy the lobbies and to address the externality generated by domestic production, and it uses trade policies to exploit market power and to address the externality generated by production abroad. The equilibrium production policies in equation (T1a) consist of a *political support* term, which will be an output subsidy if the industry is organized ($\Phi_i > 0$) or an output tax if the industry is not organized ($\Phi_i < 0$), and an *environmental effect*, which is a tax that captures the social costs of an additional unit of production.[6] Equation (T1a) implies that the noncooperative political equilibrium production tax is lower than the standard Pigouvian tax for an organized industry; this generalizes similar findings by Fredriksson (1997), Aidt (1998), and Schleich (1999) to the large-country case. The Pigouvian tax emerges only when the political support effect on production policy vanishes, that is when the government weighs total welfare infinitely high ($a \to \infty$), the entire economy is organized ($\alpha_L = 1 = I_{iL}\ \forall i$), nobody is organized ($\alpha_L = 0 = I_{iL}\ \forall i$), or the elasticity of domestic output supply is infinite ($\varepsilon_{X_i p_i^s} = (X_i/p_i^s X_i')^{-1} \to \infty$). Otherwise, the political-support effect implies protection of organized industries in both countries, with protection for an industry only indirectly dependent on the political power of the industry abroad, as the political strength of the foreign industry negatively affects the home industry's profits via a lower world price.

The first term of the equilibrium trade policy in equation (T1b) is the optimal-tariff formula and requires an import tariff or an export tax depending on whether the home country is importing or exporting good i. When foreign production generates a global externality, the second term of equation (T1b) requires an import tariff or an export subsidy. These latter policies lower the world price, which in turn leads to a decrease in the foreign producer price and foreign production. Import tariffs are imposed, and unorganized industries face production taxes, but whether equilibrium production policies (for organized industries) or trade policies (for exporting industries) are taxes or subsidies is ambiguous and depends on the relative magnitudes of the various effects. For example, the subsidizing component of a production policy will be higher, the higher the political weight of the industry lobby (Φ_i); that is, the lower the relative weight of the average consumer (a) and the lower the degree of organization in the economy (α_L), or the more inelastic output supply ($\varepsilon_{X_i p_i^s}$ small, reflecting low deadweight losses). The taxing component of a production policy will be higher, the higher the marginal environmental damage (u_E') and the more pollusive is production (the larger E_X).

Now consider the cases in which only one type of policy (production or trade) is available. In a normative large-country analysis with only domestic policy, Krutilla

Table 1. Noncooperative and Cooperative Equilibrium Production and Trade Policies for Home Country

Policy Availability	Noncooperation: Production Policy		Noncooperation: Trade Policy	
Production and Trade	$\tau_i - 1 = -\frac{\Phi_i X_i}{p_i^s X_i'} + \frac{Nu_E' E_X}{p_i^s}$	(T1a)	$\theta_i - 1 = \frac{1}{\eta_i^*} - \gamma \frac{Nu_E' E_{X^*} X_i'^*}{p_i^w \tau_i^* M_i'^*}$	(T1b)
Production Only (Global Externality)	$\tau_i - 1 = -\frac{\Phi_i X_i}{p_i^s X_i'} + \frac{M_i}{p_i^s (D_i' + M_i'^*)} + \frac{Nu_E' E_X}{p_i^s} + \frac{Nu_E' E_{X^*} X_i'^*}{\tau_i^* p_i^s (D_i' + M_i'^*)}$	(T2)	——	
Trade Only (Global Externality)	——		$\theta_i - 1 = -\frac{\Phi_i X_i}{p_i^w M_i'} + \frac{1}{\eta_i^*} + \frac{Nu_E' E_X X_i'}{p_i^w M_i'} - \frac{Nu_E' E_{X^*} X_i'^*}{p_i^w M_i'^*}$	(T3)

Cooperation

Production and Trade	$\tau_i - 1 = -\frac{\Phi_i X_i}{p_i^s X_i'} + \frac{N u_E' E_X}{p_i^s} + \gamma \frac{N^* u_E'^* E_X}{p_i^s}$ (T4a)	$\theta_i - \theta_i^* = 0$ (T4b)
Production Only (Global Externality)	$\tau_i - 1 = -\frac{\Phi_i X_i}{p_i^s X_i'} + \frac{N u_E' E_X}{p_i^s} + \frac{N^* u_E'^* E_X}{p_i^s}$ (T5)	———
Trade Only (Global Externality)	———	$\theta_i - \theta_i^* = -(\frac{\Phi_i X_i}{p_i^w M_i'} - \frac{\Phi_i^* X_i^*}{p_i^w M_i'^*}) + (N u_E' + N^* u_E'^*)[\frac{E_X X_i'}{p_i^w M_i'} - \frac{E_{X^*} X_i'^*}{p_i^w M_i'^*}]$ (T6)

(1991) derived output taxes for a *local* production externality. He demonstrated that the chosen tax is *higher* than the standard Pigouvian tax when the country is an exporter, because the output tax is also used to affect the terms of trade. In the political economy model herein this result does not necessarily follow.

PROPOSITION 1. *For a local production externality, when noncooperating governments have only production policy available, the political equilibrium tax for an organized exporting industry can be lower than the Pigouvian tax.*

The home country's equilibrium policies are implicitly given by equation (T2) when the governments can only use production policies (setting $\theta_i = \theta_i^* = 1$ in Appendix equation (A1) and $\gamma = 1$ in (A2) yields this result). The first term in equation (T2) has the same structure as the political-support effect in equation (T1a), but the equilibrium level will generally be different. The second term in (T2) is a terms-of-trade effect, which captures the price-responsiveness of composite demand and takes on a positive (negative) value if the home country exports (imports) good *i*. The third term requires a tax to address the externality generated by home production, and the fourth term aims at reducing production of a foreign polluting industry through an output subsidy that lowers the world price. The second and the third terms in equation (T2) are more general representations of the equilibrium tax obtained by Krutilla (1991). Since the first term (political support effect) in equation (T2) is negative for an organized industry and can more than offset the terms-of-trade effect, the equilibrium production policy for an exporting country may be *lower* than the Pigouvian tax. From equation (T2), this is more likely when the political weight of the industry lobby Φ_i is high, the elasticity of output supply ($\varepsilon_{X_i p_i^s}$) is low, or the elasticity of composite demand is large.

When the governments have only trade policies available and the externality is global, the political equilibrium trade policy for the home country is implicitly given by equation (T3) (setting $\tau_i = \tau_i^* = 1$ and $\gamma = 1$ in Appendix equation (A2) yields this result). Without the externality, the equilibrium trade policy is the same as in Grossman and Helpman (1995). The first term in equation (T3) requires an import tariff or an export subsidy to satisfy the lobbies, and the second term (terms-of-trade effect) again takes on the formula of the optimal tariff. With a production externality, the third term requires an import subsidy or an export tax to reduce the externality generated by domestic production, and the fourth term requires an import tariff or an export subsidy to lower foreign production.

Grossman and Helpman (1994) demonstrate for a small-country model that when the distribution of lobbies' contributions is taken into account, political competition may leave the lobbies better off when only less efficient policies are available. This result also applies in a large-country model. The equilibrium contributions of any lobby *i* must match the difference between what the governments and the other lobbies would jointly accomplish if lobby *i* decided not to contribute, and what the governments and the other lobbies receive in equilibrium. With more efficient instruments, this difference will be greater, and each lobby *i* will have to pay more. Thus, competition may result in the lobbies preferring less efficient instruments. Limited policy availability can then be interpreted as the outcome of a prior game that is played between the government and the lobbies.

When policy availability is restricted, the question arises of whether inefficient policies necessarily result in lower environmental quality? As in a small-country G–H model (Schleich, 1999), trade policies alone can lead to higher environmental quality than more efficient production policies alone. Suppose there is no externality, but organized industries lobby for protection. Then, production subsidies will lead to higher equilibrium output prices than trade policies, because the governments can satisfy the lobbies at less deadweight costs (no consumption distortion) to other lobbies and total welfare. Conversely, when there are no lobbies, but there is an externality, the socially optimal production taxes (in the case of a local externality) will result in lower output prices than trade policies, again because of lower costs associated with production policies. Since the two effects work in opposite directions, it is generally ambiguous whether trade policies leads to lower or higher environmental quality than production policies.

Cooperative Policies for a Production Externality

If the governments are able to decide on their policies cooperatively, the joint political support for both governments will be higher, since noncooperative policies impose real costs. Under cooperation, we assume that the equilibrium policies emerge from bilateral negotiations between the home and foreign governments; that domestic and trade policies are determined simultaneously if both are available; and that the lobbies now make their contributions contingent on the outcomes of the negotiations; that is on τ, τ^*, θ, and θ^*. For the negotiations to lead to efficient outcomes for the governments, the equilibrium policy vectors have to maximize the weighted sum[7]

$$A^*G + AG^* = A^*\left(\sum_{i\in L} C_i + aW\right) + A\left(\sum_{i\in L^*} C_i^* + a^*W^*\right), \tag{7}$$

where G is the home government's share of the joint surplus, G^* is the foreign country's share, $A = (\alpha_L + a)$, and $A^* = (\alpha_L^* + a^*)$.[8,9]

When the governments negotiate over production and trade policies, the equilibrium outcomes for the home country are given implicitly by equations (T4a) and (T4b), with corresponding expressions for the foreign production policy (see the Appendix). Production policy is used to address local and global externalities and to satisfy the industry lobbies. The cooperative production policies in equation (T4a) have the same structure, but generally different levels, as the noncooperative outcomes in equation (T1a) if production does not cause a global externality. When there is a global externality, the additional environmental effect on production policies (not on trade policies as in the noncooperative regime) addresses the costs of an extra unit of output on the other country's residents and requires an output tax. For a global externality, when the governments act cooperatively and the industries are equally pollusive (i.e., $E_X = E_{X^*}$), differences in production policies for a given industry arise between countries only from differences in political support effects. Organized industries in both countries obtain protection, and the political strength of the industry in the foreign country affects support in the home country only indirectly through the world price, as under noncooperation. Cooperative trade policies (T4b) are reduced to being equivalent to nonintervention in terms of prices and resource allocations, although domestic trade taxes and subsidies exactly offset by foreign country policies may serve as a mechanism for income transfers between the governments.[10]

Since the governments use production policies to satisfy the demands of the industry lobbies and to address externalities, environmental quality will not be socially optimal at the political equilibrium, even with cooperation. Of particular interest is whether environmental quality will be higher under cooperation compared with noncooperation? The standard result from a normative model is that environmental taxes and environmental quality will increase under cooperation when there is a global externality, because the governments internalize the negative spillovers on other countries' welfare. This result does not follow necessarily when there is lobbying by organized industries.

PROPOSITION 2. *For a global production externality, when cooperating governments have production and trade policies available, environmental quality may be lower than under noncooperation.*

Cooperating governments avoid the costs they impose on each other under noncooperation, but no general conclusions can be drawn as to whether the cooperative equilibrium policies in equations (T4a) and (T4b) result in higher or lower environmental quality than the noncooperative policies in equations (T1a) and (T1b). The overall impact on environmental quality can be divided into four effects. First, cooperating governments no longer apply their policies to affect the terms of trade, either for optimal-tariff reasons or to reduce the externality generated by production abroad. Whether this effect leads to lower or higher environmental quality is indeterminate.[11] Second, for a global externality, cooperating governments take into account the environmental damage imposed by domestic production on consumers abroad. This effect unambiguously results in higher environmental production taxes and higher environmental quality under cooperation. Third, under noncooperation governments support a particular industry lobby without considering negative effects of this support on the lobby in the other country (through a change in the terms of trade). Under cooperation governments take into account the impact of their policies on the other government's ability to satisfy its lobbies: this effect leads to lower output prices under cooperation. Finally, there is a broader political effect. Competing governments can satisfy particular lobbies at lower costs to the other lobbies and total welfare. This political effect translates into higher output prices and lower environmental quality than under noncooperation, and will be stronger, the larger the political weights of the home and foreign organized industries; that is the larger Φ_i and Φ_i^*. Thus, depending on the different magnitudes of the various effects on environmental quality, the overall impact can be production taxes that are lower under cooperation than under noncooperation even for a global externality.

Now suppose that governments acting cooperatively have only one type of policy available. When governments have only production policies available, the equilibrium outcomes with cooperation have the same structure (see equation (T5)) as when there are production and trade policies. With only trade policies, the equilibrium outcomes for the home country are given by equation (T6) when the externality is global (setting $\tau_i = \tau_i^* = 1$ and $\gamma = 1$ in Appendix equation (A11) yields this result). Equation (T6) simplifies to the "trade-talks" result in Grossman and Helpman (1995) when there is no externality. In contrast to the findings shown above when governments negotiate over production and trade policies, when only trade policy is available industry protection depends directly on the difference in the political strength of the home versus the foreign industry, and only the politically more powerful industry can enjoy protection. With an externality, differences in environmental sensitivity (Nu' versus $N^*u'^*$) do not affect the equilibrium trade policies.[12] As under noncooperation, inefficient trade policies alone can result in higher environmental quality than efficient production policies alone. Similarly, whether lobby groups prefer cooperation by governments to noncooperation depends on how much they have to contribute in equilibrium. Thus, lobbies in both countries might prefer noncooperation to cooperation because under the more efficient regime (cooperation) they will have to pay more than under the less efficient regime.

3. Equilibrium Policies with a Consumption Externality

Suppose that consumption rather than production of a non-numéraire good e generates a negative externality such that, for each individual j, $E = \Sigma_{k=1,k\neq j}^{N} c_{ek} + \gamma\Sigma_{k=1}^{N^*} c_{ek}^*$. For $\gamma = 0$ the externality is local, while for $\gamma = 1$ the externality is global. When an individual decides on her level of consumption of good e, she does not take into account the effects of her decision on any other individual's utility.[13] Thus, $E = (N-1)c_e + \gamma N^* c_e^*$, with $\partial E/\partial c_e = (N-1)$ and $\partial E/\partial c_e^* = \gamma N^*$. The government is now assumed to have consumption taxes/subsidies (τ) together with trade policies (θ) available. The price equilibria conditions for good i require $p_i^s = \theta_i p_i^w$ and $p_i^d = \theta_i \tau_i p_i^w$, respectively.

Equilibrium Outcomes with a Consumption Externality

When the governments act noncooperatively and have consumption and trade policies available, the equilibrium outcomes are given implicitly (see the Appendix) by

$$\tau_i - 1 = -\frac{\Phi_i X_i}{p_i^s X_i'} + \delta\frac{(N-1)u_E'}{p_i^s}, \tag{8a}$$

$$\theta_i - 1 = \frac{\Phi_i X_i}{p_i^w X_i'} + \frac{1}{\eta_i^*} - \delta\gamma\frac{N u_E' D_i'^* \tau_i^*}{p_i^w M_i'^*}, \tag{8b}$$

where δ is a dummy variable (with $\delta = 1$ if consumption creates an externality ($i = e$) and $\delta = 0$ otherwise), and $M_i'^* = \tau_i^* D_i'^* - X_i'^* < 0$. Noncooperative governments with consumption and trade policies available use trade policy to satisfy the lobbies, to exploit the terms of trade, and to address a global externality generated by consumption abroad. Consumption policy is applied to counterbalance the distortion arising from use of trade policy to provide industry protection (the first terms of (8a) and (8b) are of equal value and opposite sign) and to address the externality caused by domestic consumption. Whether equilibrium policies are subsidies or taxes depends on the relative magnitudes of the various effects.

For a small country with a local consumption externality, the equilibrium consumption and externality levels are socially optimal, while too much output of organized industries is produced domestically (the last two terms in (8b) drop out for this case; see also Schleich (1999)). By contrast, for a large country, not only is production distorted but also consumption, since the trade and countervailing consumption subsidies affect the world price to the benefit of organized industries.[14]

The equilibrium outcomes when noncooperating governments have only consumption or trade policies available are given in Appendix equations (A5) and (A6), respectively. For a large country with only consumption policy available, the governments again use consumption subsidies to satisfy lobbies indirectly (by pushing up the world price) and to affect the terms of trade. Thus, unlike in the small-country case, environmental quality for a local consumption externality will not be socially optimal in the large-country case. Paralleling the production results above, a political-support effect counterbalances the terms-of-trade effect for an importing country and the political equilibrium consumption tax may be lower than the Pigouvian tax. The political equilibrium trade policy for the home country in equation (A6) differs from equation (T3) only in the environmental effects.

When cooperating governments negotiate simultaneously over consumption and trade policies, the equilibrium policies are given implicitly (see the Appendix) by equations (A14a) and (A14b). With cooperation, trade policies are again used to satisfy organized lobbies, and consumption policies to offset the distortionary impact of the industry protection on consumption. Cooperation leaves no role for terms-of-trade effects in equation (A14b), while political equilibrium trade policies are a function of the relative political-support effects: the politically stronger industry receives higher protection through trade policies. As in the noncooperative regime, when cooperating governments have consumption and trade policies available, the levels of production in both countries are too high, total consumption is too high, and environmental quality is lower than socially optimal. Similar to the case of a production externality, a local or global consumption externality may be greater under the cooperative equilibrium than under noncooperation.

When governments acting cooperatively have only consumption policies available, the externality is global, and N and N^* are large (so $N - 1 \approx N$ and $N^* - 1 \approx N^*$), the equilibrium policies (given by Appendix equation (A15)) are identical for the home and foreign countries. Equation (A15) shows that protection for the home industry increases with the political power of the foreign industry. The sum of the political-support effects requires that both governments subsidize consumption to increase producer prices; these subsidies are counterbalanced by a common level of consumption taxes when there is a global externality, and protection for an industry is the same in both countries.

When the governments have only trade policies available, populations are large, and the externality is global, then home and foreign trade policies are implicitly given by Appendix equation (A16), where $M_i' = \tau_i D_i' - X_i'$ and $M_i'^* = \tau_i^* D_i'^* - X_i'^*$. Equation (A16) shows that for a global consumption externality, just as for a global production externality, only the politically more powerful industry can enjoy protection, differences in the price-responsiveness of demand (D_i' versus $D_i'^*$) and the slopes of the import demand functions affect relative industry protection, while differences in environmental sensitivity across countries do not.

4. Conclusions

This paper characterizes environmental quality and the structure of endogenous industry protection in a large-country Grossman–Helpman model when production or consumption externalities exist, and when governments decide noncooperatively or cooperatively on domestic and trade policies. The political equilibrium policies are expressed as the sum of distinct political-support, terms-of-trade, and local and global environmental effects. Governments choose the most efficient policies from among those available, but lobbies may prefer less efficient policies. When policy availability is restricted, political support effects offset terms-of-trade effects on equilibrium outcomes and inefficient trade policies can lead to higher environmental quality than efficient domestic policies when there is an externality. If governments are able to cooperate, they can satisfy particular industry lobbies at lower costs to other lobbies and total welfare, possibly resulting in higher industry protection and lower environmental quality than under noncooperation. Again, competing lobbies may prefer governments not to cooperate.

The structure of the models developed herein is flexible enough to accommodate a variety of modifications to improve understanding of the political economy of trade and environmental policies. The derived equilibrium policy expressions are only implicit, but whether policy cooperation—through trade negotiations or environmental agreements —leads to higher environmental quality than noncooperation could be assessed for specific functional forms. Further, political equilibrium policies could be analyzed in an extensive form game, where—instead of setting domestic and trade policies simultaneously—one policy is chosen before the other. While the outcome would depend on the order in which policies are chosen, this extension would produce further insight into the strategic aspects between domestic environmental and trade policies.

Appendix

Derivation of the Noncooperative Policy Outcomes for a Production Externality, when the Governments have Production and Trade Policies Available

Substituting equations (1), (2), (3), and (4) into equation (6), and using the world market equilibrium condition, $D_i(p_i^d) - X_i(p_i^s) = -[D_i^*(p_i^{d*}) - X_i(p_i^{s*})]$, together with the price equilibrium conditions and then collecting terms, the first-order conditions for the equilibrium interventions in industry i can be expressed as

$$\tau_i - 1 = -\frac{\Phi_i X_i}{p_i^s X_i'} + \frac{M_i}{p_i^s(\theta_i D_i' + \theta_i^* M_i'^*)} + (\theta_i - 1)\frac{p_i^w}{p_i^s} + \frac{Nu_E' E_X}{p_i^s} + \frac{Nu_E' E_{X^*}\theta_i^* X_i'^*}{\tau_i^* p_i^s(\theta_i D_i' + \theta_i^* M_i'^*)}, \tag{A1}$$

$$\theta_i - 1 = -\frac{\Phi_i X_i}{\tau_i p_i^w M_i'} - \frac{M_i}{p_i^w M_i'^*} - (\tau_i - 1)\frac{p_i^s X_i'}{\tau_i p_i^w M_i'} + \frac{Nu_E' E_X X_i'}{\tau_i p_i^w M_i'} - \gamma\frac{Nu_E' E_{X^*} X_i'^*}{\tau_i^* p_i^w M_i'^*}. \tag{A2}$$

Solving equations (A1) and (A2) simultaneously eventually yields equations (T1a) and (T1b).[15]

Derivation of the Noncooperative Policy Outcomes for a Consumption Externality, when the Governments have Consumption and Trade Policies Available

The first-order conditions for the consumption and trade policies for the home country yield

$$\tau_i - 1 = -\frac{\Phi_i X_i}{p_i^w(\theta_i X_i' - \theta_i^* M_i'^*)} + \frac{M_i}{p_i^w(\theta_i X_i' - \theta_i^* M_i'^*)} + (\theta_i - 1)\frac{\theta_i^* M_i'^*}{\theta_i(\theta_i X_i' - \theta_i^* M_i'^*)} + \delta\left[\frac{u_E'(N-1)}{p_i^s} + \gamma\frac{Nu_E' D_i'^* \tau_i^* \theta_i^*}{p_i^s(\theta_i X_i' - \theta_i^* M_i'^*)}\right], \tag{A3}$$

$$\theta_i - 1 = -\frac{\Phi_i X_i}{p_i^w \tau_i M_i'} - \frac{M_i}{p_i^w \theta_i^* M_i'^*} - (\tau_i - 1)\frac{p_i^s X_i'}{\tau_i p_i^w M_i'} + \delta\left[\frac{u_E'(N-1)\tau_i D_i'}{p_i^w M_i'} - \gamma\frac{Nu_E' D_i'^* \tau_i^*}{p_i^w M_i'^*}\right]. \tag{A4}$$

Solving equations (A3) and (A4) simultaneously yields equations (8a) and (8b). For a global consumption externality, setting $\delta = \gamma = 1$, and $\theta_i = \theta_i^* = 1$ in (A3) or $\tau_i = \tau_i^* = 1$ in (A4), respectively, the equilibrium outcomes when only consumption or trade policies are available are given by

$$\tau_i - 1 = -\frac{\Phi_i X_i}{p_i^w (X_i' - M_i'^*)} + \frac{M_i}{p_i^w (X_i' - M_i'^*)} + \frac{(N-1)u_E'}{p_i^s} + \frac{N u_E' D_i'^* \tau_i^*}{p_i^s (X_i' - M_i'^*)}, \tag{A5}$$

$$\theta_i - 1 = -\frac{\Phi_i X_i}{p_i^w M_i'} + \frac{1}{\eta_i^*} + \left[\frac{(N-1)u_E' D_i'}{p_i^w M_i'} - \frac{N u_E' D_i'^*}{p_i^w M_i'^*}\right]. \tag{A6}$$

Derivation of the Cooperative Policy Outcomes for a Production Externality, when the Governments have Production and Trade Policies Available

Assuming an interior solution, the optimal policies must satisfy the first-order condition

$$A^*\left(\sum\nolimits_{i\in L} \nabla_\beta W_i(\tau, \theta, \tau^*, \theta^*) + a\nabla_\beta W(\tau, \theta, \tau^*, \theta^*)\right) \\ + A\left(\sum\nolimits_{i\in L^*} \nabla_\beta W_i^*(\tau^*, \theta^*, \tau, \theta) + a^*\nabla_\beta W^*(\tau^*, \theta^*, \tau, \theta)\right) = 0, \tag{A7}$$

where now $\beta = \tau_i, \tau_i^*, \theta_i, \theta_i^*$. Thus:

$$\nabla_\beta\{A^*(I_{iL} - \alpha_L)\Pi_i(p_i^s) + A^*A[\Pi_i(p_i^s) + Nr(\tau,\theta,\tau^*,\theta^*) + R + Ns(p^d) \\ + Nu_E(X_e, X_e^*)]\} + \nabla_\beta\{A(I_{iL^*}^* - \alpha_L^*)\Pi_i^*(p_i^{s*}) + AA^*[\Pi_i^*(p_i^{s*}) \\ + N^*r^*(\tau^*,\theta^*,\tau,\theta) - R + N^*s(p^{d*}) + N^*u_E^*(X_e, X_e^*)]\} = 0, \tag{A8}$$

where R is an intergovernmental lump-sum transfer. The first-order condition for the production policy τ_i can be calculated using the market equilibrium condition, partially differentiating the price equilibrium conditions, and substituting equations (1) to (5) together with their foreign counterparts into equation (A8). This yields:

$$A^*(I_{iL} - \alpha_L)X_i\left(\frac{\theta_i}{\tau_i}\frac{\partial p_i^w}{\partial \tau_i} - \frac{p_i^w\theta_i}{\tau_i^2}\right) + A^*A\left[(\tau_i - 1)X_i'\frac{\theta_i}{\tau_i}p_i^w\left(\frac{\theta_i}{\tau_i}\frac{\partial p_i^w}{\partial \tau_i} - \frac{p_i^w\theta_i}{\tau_i^2}\right)\right] \\ + A^*A\left[p_i^w(\theta_i - 1)\left(D_i'\frac{\partial p_i^w}{\partial \tau_i}\theta_i - X_i'\left(\frac{\theta_i}{\tau_i}\frac{\partial p_i^w}{\partial \tau_i} - \frac{p_i^w\theta_i}{\tau_i^2}\right)\right)\right] \\ - A^*A\delta\left[Nu_E'E_X X_i'\left(\frac{\theta_i}{\tau_i}\frac{\partial p_i^w}{\partial \tau_i} - \frac{p_i^w\theta_i}{\tau_i^2}\right) + \gamma Nu_E'E_{X^*}X_i'^*\frac{\theta_i^*}{\tau_i^*}\frac{\partial p_i^w}{\partial \tau_i}\right] \\ + A(I_{iL^*}^* - \alpha_L^*)X_i^*\frac{\theta_i^*}{\tau_i^*}\frac{\partial p_i^w}{\partial \tau_i} + AA^*\left[(\tau_i^* - 1)X_i'^*\frac{\theta_i^*}{\tau_i^*}\frac{\partial p_i^w}{\partial \tau_i}\frac{\theta_i^*}{\tau_i^*}p_i^w\right] \\ + AA^*\left[p_i^w(\theta_i^* - 1)\theta_i^*M_i'^*\frac{\partial p_i^w}{\partial \tau_i}\right] - AA^*\delta\left[N^*u_E'^*E_{X^*}X_i'^*\frac{\theta_i^*}{\tau_i^*}\frac{\partial p_i^w}{\partial \tau_i}\right. \\ \left. + \gamma N^*u_E'^*E_X X_i'\left(\frac{\theta_i}{\tau_i}\frac{\partial p_i^w}{\partial \tau_i} - \frac{p_i^w\theta_i}{\tau_i^2}\right)\right] = 0. \tag{A9}$$

Consolidating terms and solving for $\tau_i - 1$ yields

$$\tau_i - 1 = -\frac{\Phi_i X_i}{p_i^s X_i'} - \frac{\Phi_i^* X_i^*(\theta_i^*/\tau_i^*)}{p_i^s(\theta_i D_i' + \theta_i^* M_i'^*)} - (\tau_i^* - 1)\frac{p_i^w X_i'^*(\theta_i^{*2}/\tau_i^{*2})}{p_i^s(\theta_i D_i' + \theta_i^* M_i'^*)} \\ + [(\theta_i - 1) - (\theta_i^* - 1)]\left[\frac{p_i^w\theta_i^* M_i'^*}{p_i^s(\theta_i D_i' + \theta_i^* M_i'^*)}\right] + \frac{Nu_E' E_X}{p_i^s} \\ + \frac{N^*u_E'^* E_{X^*}X_i'^*(\theta_i^*/\tau_i^*)}{p_i^s(\theta_i D_i' + \theta_i^* M_i'^*)} + \gamma\left[\frac{N^*u_E'^* E_X}{p_i^s} + \frac{Nu_E' E_{X^*}X_i'^*(\theta_i^*/\tau_i^*)}{p_i^s(\theta_i D_i' + \theta_i^* M_i'^*)}\right], \tag{A10}$$

where $M_i' = D_i' - X_i'/\tau_i$ and $M_i'^* = D_i'^* - X_i'^*/\tau_i^*$. A similar expression holds for $\tau_i^* - 1$.

Since the first-order conditions for the home and foreign trade instrument are linearly dependent (Grossman and Helpman, 1995, p. 698), we can derive an expression only for their difference. The first-order condition for the home (or the foreign) trade policy yields

$$(\theta_i - 1) - (\theta_i^* - 1) = -\frac{\Phi_i X_i}{p_i^w \tau_i M_i'} + \frac{\Phi_i^* X_i^*}{p_i^w \tau_i^* M_i'^*} - (\tau_i - 1)\frac{p_i^s X_i'}{p_i^w \tau_i M_i'} + (\tau_i^* - 1)\frac{p_i^{s*} X_i'^*}{p_i^w \tau_i^* M_i'^*}$$
$$+ \frac{(Nu_E' + \gamma N^* u_E'^*)E_X X_i'}{p_i^w \tau_i M_i'} - \frac{(\gamma N u_E' + N^* u_E'^*)E_{X^*} X_i'^*}{p_i^w \tau_i^* M_i'^*}. \quad \text{(A11)}$$

Equation (A10), the equivalent expression for $\tau_i^* - 1$, and equation (A11) determine home and foreign productions policies and the difference between the trade policies. Substituting equation (A11) into the expressions for the production policies and collecting terms yields equation (T4a). Substituting equation (T4a) and a similar expression for the foreign cooperative production policy into equation (A11) yields equation (T4b).

Derivation of the Cooperative Policy Outcomes for a Consumption Externality, when the Governments have Consumption and Trade Policies Available

The first-order condition for the consumption policy τ_i yields

$$\tau_i - 1 = -\frac{\Phi_i X_i}{p_i^w(\theta_i X_i' - \theta_i^* M_i'^*)} - \frac{\Phi_i^* \theta_i^* X_i^*}{p_i^w(\theta_i X_i' - \theta_i^* M_i'^*)} - (\tau_i^* - 1)\frac{\tau_i^* \theta_i^{*2} D_i'^*}{\theta_i(\theta_i X_i' - \theta_i^* M_i'^*)}$$
$$+ [(\theta_i - 1) - (\theta_i^* - 1)]\left[\frac{\theta_i^* M_i'^*}{\theta_i(\theta_i X_i' - \theta_i^* M_i'^*)}\right] + \delta\left\{\frac{u_E'(N-1)}{p_i^w \theta_i}\right.$$
$$\left. + \frac{u_E'^*(N^*-1)D_i'^* \tau_i^* \theta_i^*}{p_i^w \theta_i(\theta_i X_i' - \theta_i^* M_i'^*)} + \gamma\left[\frac{u_E'^* N^*}{p_i^w \theta_i} + \frac{N u_E' D_i'^* \tau_i^* \theta_i^*}{p_i^w \theta_i(\theta_i X_i' - \theta_i^* M_i'^*)}\right]\right\}. \quad \text{(A12)}$$

A similar expression holds for $\tau_i^* - 1$. For the difference in trade policies we get

$$(\theta_i - 1) - (\theta_i^* - 1) = -\frac{\Phi_i X_i}{p_i^w M_i'} + \frac{\Phi_i^* X_i^*}{p_i^w M_i'^*} - (\tau_i - 1)\frac{p_i^d D_i'}{p_i^w M_i'} + (\tau_i^* - 1)\frac{p_i^{d*} D_i'^*}{p_i^w M_i'^*}$$
$$+ \delta\left[\frac{u_E'(N-1)D_i'\tau_i}{p_i^w M_i'} - \frac{u_E'^*(N^*-1)D_i'^*\tau_i^*}{p_i^w M_i'^*} + \gamma\frac{u_E'^* N^* D_i'\tau_i}{p_i^w M_i'}\right.$$
$$\left. - \gamma\frac{u_E' N D_i'^* \tau_i^*}{p_i^w M_i'^*}\right], \quad \text{(A13)}$$

where $M_i' = \tau_i D_i' - X_i'$ and $M_i'^* = \tau_i^* D_i'^* - X_i'^*$. Solving equations (A12), (A13), and the expression for the foreign consumption policy yield

$$\tau_i - 1 = -\frac{\Phi_i X_i}{p_i^s X_i'} + \delta\left[\frac{(N-1)u_E'}{p_i^s} + \gamma\frac{N^* u_E'^*}{p_i^s}\right], \quad \text{(A14a)}$$

$$\theta_i - \theta_i^* = \frac{\Phi_i X_i}{p_i^w X_i'} - \frac{\Phi_i^* X_i^*}{p_i^w X_i'^*}. \quad \text{(A14b)}$$

For a global consumption externality, setting $\delta = \gamma = 1$, $N - 1 = N$, and $N^* - 1 = N^*$ and $\theta_i = \theta_i^* = 1$ in (A12) and the equivalent expression for $\tau_i^* - 1$, the equilibrium outcomes when only consumption policies are available are given by

$$\tau_i - 1 = -\frac{(\Phi_i X_i + \Phi_i^* X_i^*)}{p_i^w (X_i' + X_i'^*)} + \frac{Nu_E' + N^* u_E'^*}{p_i^w}. \tag{A15}$$

Alternatively, setting $\tau_i = \tau_i^* = 1$ in (A13), the equilibrium outcomes when only trade policies are available are given by

$$\theta_i - \theta_i^* = -\left(\frac{\Phi_i X_i}{p_i^w M_i'} - \frac{\Phi_i^* X_i^*}{p_i^w M_i'^*}\right) + (Nu_E' + N^* u_E'^*)\left[\frac{D_i'}{p_i^w M_i'} - \frac{D_i'^*}{p_i^w M_i'^*}\right]. \tag{A16}$$

References

Aidt, Toke, "Political Internalization of Economic Externalities and Environmental Policy," *Journal of Public Economics* 69 (1998):1–16.

Bernheim, Douglas and Michael Whinston, "Menu Auctions, Resource Allocation, and Economic Influence," *Quarterly Journal of Economics* 101 (1986):1–31.

Dixit, Avinash, "Special Interest Lobbying and Endogenous Commodity Taxation," *Eastern Economic Journal* 22 (1996):375–88.

Dixit, Avinash, Gene Grossman, and Elhanan Helpman, "Common Agency and Coordination: General Theory and Application to Government Policy Making," *Journal of Political Economy* 105 (1997):752–69.

Fredriksson, Per, "The Political Economy of Pollution Taxes in a Small Open Economy, *Journal of Environmental Economics and Management* 33 (1997):44–58.

Goldberg, Pinelopi and Giovanni Maggi, "Protection for Sale: An Empirical Investigation," *American Economic Review* 89 (1999):1135–55.

Grossman, Gene and Elhanan Helpman, "Protection for Sale," *American Economic Review* 84 (1994):833–50.

———, "Trade Wars and Trade Talks," *Journal of Political Economy* 103 (1995):675–708.

———, "Electoral Competition and Special Interest Politics," *Review of Economic Studies* 63 (1996):265–86.

Krutilla, Kerry, "Environmental Regulation in an Open Economy," *Journal of Environmental Economics and Management* 20 (1991):127–42.

Schleich, Joachim, "Environmental Quality with Endogenous Domestic and Trade Policies," *European Journal of Political Economy* 15 (1999):53–71.

Notes

1. The general efficiency property of the G–H model was established by Bernheim and Whinston (1986) who showed the existence of an equilibrium that is efficient for the active players, the government and the lobbies. Dixit et al. (1997) demonstrate further that if the government cares about social welfare, and the lobbies play truthful strategies, the political process will result in socially efficient choices from the available set of policies.
2. See Grossman and Helpman (1996) for an endogenous derivation of the government's objective function.
3. Grossman and Helpman (1995) follow Bernheim and Whinston (1986) in modeling the governments' and the lobbies' noncooperative actions as a first-price menu-auction in a common agency game with perfect information. In the first stage of the two-stage noncooperative game, home and foreign lobbies (principals) simultaneously and noncooperatively set their contribution schedules contingent on their own government's (agent) domestic and trade policies. In the second stage, the governments choose their domestic and trade policies simultaneously and noncooperatively given the lobbies' contribution schedules. This procedure results in the same implicit expressions for the equilibrium levels of policy interventions as the Nash-bargaining game.
4. Equation (5) can be obtained from equations (1) and (2).

5. Note that results for the small country case can be obtained for $|\eta_i^*| \to \infty$ ($M_i'^* \to -\infty$).
6. For the remainder of the paper, we mostly limit the interpretation of the equilibrium policies to the cases where the industries are organized.
7. A particular bargaining solution could be imposed to resolve the distribution of the surplus between the two governments from cooperation compared to noncooperation. Outcomes could be derived that would be equivalent to Grossman and Helpman (1995), who apply a modified Rubinstein bargaining solution to characterize intergovernmental transfers.
8. Multiplication by A^* and A, respectively, is necessary to ensure that the home and foreign governments' objectives are measured in the same units.
9. Since we are not concerned about how the joint surplus from cooperation is divided among the governments, we neglect any transfer payments since they do not affect efficiency of the outcomes. To show this, the Appendix allows for intergovernmental transfer.
10. Equation (T4b) only gives the difference (or ratio) in home and foreign trade policies. Since domestic prices are homogenous of degree zero in θ and θ^*, the resource allocations in the two countries and the joint welfare of the governments depend on the ratio of the trade policies only, not on their respective levels. Equation (T4b) shows that in the cooperative political equilibrium the governments apply their trade policies at the same rate, which implies that the resource allocations in both countries are the same as under free trade. However, the levels of the trade policies will affect the division of the surplus from cooperation. An equiproportionate change in trade policies is equivalent to a direct transfer from one country to the other country. The trade policy levels could be determined through a specific bargaining procedure and will depend on the relative bargaining power of the governments.
11. For example, for an industry that is pollusive in both countries, if import tariffs and export taxes are high as each government tries to exploit the terms of trade under noncooperation, then abolishing the trade policies raises production by the exporter and lowers production by the importer, with an effect on the externality that can be in either direction.
12. Differences in pollusiveness, the price-responsiveness of home and foreign supply (X_i' versus $X_i'^*$), and the slope of import demands (M_i' versus $M_i'^*$), which reflect differences in the deadweight costs of the trade policies do affect the equilibrium outcomes in equation (T6).
13. Assuming that N is sufficiently large justifies this assumption.
14. Under noncooperation, additional distortions arise because governments do not take into account the impact of domestic consumption on environmental damage abroad.
15. Further details on this and other derivations are available from the authors upon request.

Chapter 13

Pakistan

Caesar B. Cororaton and David Orden

This chapter analyzes the macroeconomic, sectoral, and poverty implications of the removal of agricultural and nonagricultural price distortions in the domestic markets of Pakistan and in the rest of the world. Our analysis uses the simulated results of rest-of-the-world trade liberalization in the World Bank's global Linkage model (hereafter referred to as the global model; see van der Mensbrugghe 2005) and derives results for rest-of-the-world and own-country liberalization from the Pakistan computable general equilibrium (CGE) model of Cororaton and Orden (2008). The global model incorporates new estimates of assistance to farm industries for various developed and developing countries, including Pakistan, from the World Bank's research project, Distortions to Agricultural Incentives.[1] Using these new estimates, the global model simulates two separate scenarios: one involving full trade liberalization and one involving trade liberalization in agriculture alone. Both scenarios exclude Pakistan. The global model simulations generate changes in the import prices for Pakistan at the border, together with changes in world export prices and shifts in the export demand for Pakistan products. We utilize these results, along with the new estimates of industry assistance in Pakistan generated by Dorosh and Salam (2009), to analyze various liberalization scenarios and measure their impacts on national welfare, income inequality, and poverty using the Pakistan CGE model.

Trade reform entails a fiscal revenue loss to the government because trade taxes are an important source of revenue. We conduct experiments using two alternative tax replacement schemes to retain a fixed fiscal balance: a direct tax on household incomes and an indirect tax on consumption. We are thus able to show how the results differ according to the choice of the tax replacement method.

The simulation analysis is conducted in stages. In the first stage, we run two separate experiments. One experiment involves using the changes in the border prices and the computed shifts in the world export demand for Pakistan products from the global model (see the appendix by van der Mensbrugghe, Valenzuela, and Anderson) as an exogenous shock to the Pakistan model without altering the existing structure of price-distorting policies in Pakistan. The other experiment involves simulating unilateral trade liberalization in Pakistan without incorporating the changes from the global model. In the second stage, we combine these two separate experiments to examine the total effects. We conduct separate experiments in each stage for trade liberalization in all tradable goods sectors and in agriculture only (including lightly processed food). The simulations generate vectors of household income and consumer prices, which we use in conjunction with data from the 2001–02 Pakistan Household Integration Economic Survey (Federal Bureau of Statistics 2003) to calculate the impact on national income inequality and poverty.

The chapter is organized as follows. The next section discusses the structure of agricultural and trade distortions in Pakistan based on the new estimates of industry assistance. The Pakistan CGE model is then outlined. This section covers the model database (which reveals the structure of sectoral production, trade, and consumption), the sources of household income, and the tax structure based on the 2001–02 social accounting matrix (SAM). This is followed by a description of trends in rural and urban poverty in Pakistan. The policy experiments and the results generated by the various modeling scenarios are subsequently discussed in detail. The last section presents a summary of the findings and policy insights. The choice of tax replacement schemes plays an important role in the results we discuss.

Agricultural Policies and Industry Assistance in Pakistan

The period from the 1960s to the mid-1980s involved heavy government intervention in Pakistan (Dorosh and Salam 2009). The government's hand on agricultural markets, trade policies, and the market for foreign exchange depressed the real prices of tradable agricultural commodities. The fixed exchange rate policy during these years, together with high domestic inflation, eroded significantly the competitiveness of the export sectors. However, during these years, the green revolution took place in agriculture. The revolution involved a package of inputs such as seeds, fertilizer, and irrigation that boosted agricultural production through higher farm productivity, Then, from the mid-1980s to the early 1990s, the government started to liberalize the agricultural sector, though it maintained control over the domestic wheat market and imposed high tariffs on vegetable oils and milk products.

Prior to the 1990s, Pakistan had been pursuing an import-substituting industrialization strategy that involved high tariff rates and quantitative import restrictions to promote the manufacturing sector. Then, major reforms were implemented in 1991 and 1997 that involved a series of tariff rate cuts and the phasing out of the quantitative import restrictions. The maximum tariff rates were reduced from 65 to 45 percent, and the number of tariff categories was cut from 13 to 5. This led to a significant drop in government revenue from trade taxes because tariffs had been the major contributor to government funds.

The key policy changes affecting agricultural prices are summarized in the rest of this section, while the policy changes affecting the manufacturing sector are described elsewhere below.

Wheat is the staple food in Pakistan. The wheat market is still heavily controlled by the government through various instruments, including government procurement (to stabilize supply), support pricing (to assist farmers), and ceiling prices (to ensure affordability among consumers). However, Pakistan's trade and pricing policies on wheat effectively tax wheat producers, while providing substantial fiscal subsidies to wheat millers through the government sale of wheat at below market prices (Dorosh 2005).

Government involvement in the market for cotton, which is the largest cash crop in Pakistan, has changed substantially over time. In 1974, the government prevented the private sector from engaging in the international cotton trade, but this changed in 1989, when the private sector was allowed to buy cotton directly from ginners, export, and sell cotton domestically. Also, exports of cotton were subjected to an export tax. After the abolition of the export duty on cotton in 1994, domestic prices were more in line with international prices (Cororaton and Orden 2008). Since the mid-1990s, exports and imports of cotton have been practically duty free, although seed cotton continues to enjoy indirect protection because of import tariffs on vegetable oils that increase the price of cotton seed oil. Otherwise, government intervention has recently been limited to an annual review of the support prices for seed cotton and some public sector procurement to maintain these prices.

Rice is the third largest crop after wheat and cotton. There were heavy controls on rice in the early 1970s when the government instituted a monopoly procurement scheme to limit domestic consumption and expand exports. The two varieties of rice (basmati and the ordinary coarse rice called IRRI rice) are exported. The intervention system still exists but, since 2003–04, government procurement has been minimal. There were no export taxes on rice in the mid-2000s, but imports were subject to a 10 percent customs duty. The average domestic price of rice is below the export price (often about 20 percent) because of quality differences.

The domestic marketing and processing of sugarcane were highly regulated until the mid-1980s. The zoning of sugar mills required farmers to sell sugarcane to mills inside their zone until 1987. There has been no government procurement of sugarcane, but the government annually announces a support price that greatly assists sugarcane and refined sugar production, and it adjusts import tariffs and the related taxes to stabilize domestic prices. There are export bans on sugarcane and refined sugar, but they do little to reduce the high level of assistance to the industry.

There was a minor tax on vegetable oils in the 1970s and 1980s, but, since the 1990s, vegetable oil imports have been taxed heavily. For example, in 2005–06, the tariff was 32 percent on imported soybean oil and 40 percent on palm oil. Likewise, the domestic prices of sunflower oil are considerably higher than the border price. Nonetheless, two-thirds of the edible oil requirements of Pakistan are supplied by imports.

Maize is mainly used as feed in the livestock and poultry sectors. Maize production has expanded rapidly in recent years because of the strong demand for poultry products. The government has not intervened in the production and marketing of maize. However, there are tariffs on imported maize; these range from 10 to 25 percent. Maize was a nontradable crop between 1990 and 2005; thus, import tariffs had only minor effects on domestic prices.

The import tariffs on milk are high. In the 1970s and 1980s, the average protection was estimated at 74 percent, but the extent of protection has diminished, and, in the first half of the present decade, protection averaged about 35 percent (Dorosh and Salem 2009).

The Pakistan CGE Model

This section summarizes the structure of the Pakistan CGE model; more details may be found in Cororaton and Orden (2008). It also discusses the method we use to introduce changes in the model to interface with the results generated by the global model. The model database representing the Pakistan economy is also summarized, along with the key parameters of the model.

Structure of the national model

The Pakistan CGE model of Cororaton and Orden (2008) is calibrated to the 2001–02 SAM constructed by Dorosh, Niazi, and Nazli (2004).[2] The model has 34 production sectors in primary agriculture, lightly processed food, other manufacturing, and services, There are five categories of productive factors: three types of labor (skilled labor, unskilled labor, and farm labor), as well as capital and land. There are also 19 household categories, a government sector, a firm sector, and the rest of the world.

In the model, output (X) is a composite of value added (VA) and intermediate inputs. Output is sold to the domestic market (D) and may also be sold to the export market (E). Goods E and goods D are perfect substitutes. The sources of supply in the domestic market are domestic output and imports (M); substitution between D and M are dependent on the change in the relative prices of D and M and on the substitution parameter in a constant elasticity of substitution function.

The primary factors of production in agriculture are unskilled labor (a composite of the labor of farmers and hired unskilled labor), land, and capital, while, in nonagriculture, they are skilled labor, unskilled labor, and capital. The on-farm labor of farmers is used only in primary agriculture. Other unskilled labor (including by farmers) is mobile across sectors and is employed in agricultural and nonagricultural sectors, while skilled labor is only mobile among nonagricultural sectors. Capital is fixed in each sector; so, the rates of return may differ across sectors.[3] The use of land may shift among agricultural industries.

The sources of household income are factors of production, transfers, foreign remittances, and dividends. Household savings are a fixed proportion of disposable income. According to the SAM, nonpoor urban households pay direct income taxes to the government, while other households do not. Household demand is specified as a linear expenditure system.

The government obtains revenue from direct taxes on household and firm incomes, tariffs, other receipts, and indirect (consumption) taxes on domestic and imported goods. It spends on the consumption of goods and services, transfers, and other payments. We assume a fixed government fiscal balance in nominal terms. Tariff policy reforms result in changes in government income and expenditure, but the government balance is fixed through a tax replacement. We use a direct income tax replacement, but also compare the results under an adjustment via an indirect sales tax replacement on domestic consumption.[4] In either case, the tax replacement is endogenously determined so as to maintain a fixed level of government balance.

Foreign savings are also fixed. The numéraire is a weighted index of the price of value added in which the weights are the shares of the sectoral value added in the base calibration. The nominal exchange rate is flexible. Furthermore, we introduce a weighted price of investment and derive total investment in real prices. We hold total investment in real prices fixed by introducing an adjustment factor in the household savings function. Equilibrium in the model is achieved if the supply and demand of goods and services are equal and if investment is equal to savings.

Linking the global model and the Pakistan model

There are various methods for transmitting the results derived from a global CGE model to a single-country CGE model. Horridge and Zhai (2006) propose, for imports, the use of border price changes from the global model simulation of rest-of-the-world liberalization (that is, without Pakistan). For Pakistan's exports, their proposed scheme is as follows.

The export demand in the Pakistan model is

$$E = E0\left[\frac{PWE0}{PWE}\right]^{\eta}, \tag{13.1}$$

where E is exports; $PWE0$ is international prices; PWE is the free on board (border) prices of Pakistan's exports; η is the export supply elasticity, the value of which is equal to $ESUBM$ (the Armington parameter m the global model); and $E0$ is the scale parameter in the demand function. Because exports and domestic goods are perfect substitutes, the export price in local currency is equal to the local price, which does not include indirect taxes.

The change in the export demand shifter, $E0$, is derived as:

$$E0 = 100 \cdot (a - 1), \tag{13.2}$$

where $a = (1 + 0.01p)([1 + 0.1q]^{[1/ESUBM]})$, in which p is the change in the border export price, and q is the change in the export volume from the global model of rest-of-the-world liberalization, excluding Pakistan (Horridge and Zhai 2006). The purpose of the introduction of the export demand shift calculated in (7.2) is to allow the Pakistan model—not the simpler representation of Pakistan in the global model—to determine export supply behavior and the equilibrium prices and quantities of Pakistan's exports, taking into account the world demand shift in the global model.

Economic structure in the SAM and key parameters in the Pakistan model

Table 13.1 shows the sectoral structure of production and trade in the model based on the 2001-02 SAM. Of the 34 sectors, 12 are primary agricultural sectors (sectors 1 to 12), while sectors 14 to 18, which represent lightly processed food, are part of the broadly defined agricultural sector in this analysis. The nonagricultural sectors include the mining industry (sector 13), other food (sector 19), manufacturing industries (sectors 20 to 27), energy (sector 28), construction (sector 29), and five service sectors (sectors 30 to 34). Among these broad sectoral groupings, agriculture produces 27 percent of the sectoral value added and 28 percent of the

Table 13.1. Elasticity parameters and production structure, Pakistan, 2001–02

	Production											Trade					
	Value added ratio va/x	Value added share	Output share	Capital-labor	Employ-ment	Share (%)			Land output ratio		Indirect tax rate	Elasticities		Exports (%)		Imports (%)	
Sectors	%	%	%	ratio[a]	share, %	Skilled labor	Unskilled labor	Farmers	%	sig_va[b]	%	eta[c]	sig_m[d]	share	intensity[e]	share	intensity[f]
Agriculture		*26.8*	*27.7*		*12.6*									*8.5*		*6.6*	
Primary agriculture		*23.2*	*20.1*		*10.7*									*3.9*		*3.1*	
1. Wheat, irrigated	50.8	1.8	1.8	0.3	1.58		18.86	81.14	27.82	0.75	0.10	5.85	2.93	0.64	3.56	0.30	2.53
2. Wheat, nonirrigated	50.9	0.1	0.1	0.3	0.07		18.85	81.15	27.25	0.75	0.00	5.85	2.93				
3. Paddy, IRRI	60.2	0.2	0.2	0.5	0.10		18.84	81.16	45.35	0.75	0.30	4.45	2.23				
4. Paddy, basmati	60.2	0.5	0.4	0.5	0.12		18.86	81.14	51.27	0.75	0.00	4.45	2.23				
5. Raw cotton	61.2	1.4	1.1	0.3	1.11		18.87	81.13	35.97	0.75	0.04	3.94	1.97				
6. Sugarcane	60.0	1.0	0.8	0.7	0.32		18.87	81.13	46.68	0.75	0.07	5.91	2.96				
7. Other major crops	71.0	2.8	2.0	0.3	2.42		18.87	81.13	38.88	0.75	0.05	3.94	1.97	0.52	2.65	0.60	4.53
8. Fruits and vegetables	64.2	3.6	2.8	0.6	1.75		18.87	81.13	44.37	0.75	0.34	3.94	1.97	1.05	3.78	1.31	6.94
9. Livestock, cattle and dairy	53.2	10.3	9.7	9.0	2.56		100.00			0.75	0.00	3.94	1.97	0.05	0.06	0.70	1.08
10. Poultry	51.6	0.7	0.7	9.0	0.18		100.00			0.75	0.00	3.94	1.97	0.01	0.11		
11. Forestry	82.1	0.3	0.2	0.0	0.12		18.88	81.12	65.68	0.75	0.00	4.31	2.15	0.48	31.36	0.23	25.16
12. Fishing industry	57.1	0.6	0.5	2.3	0.41		100.00			0.75	0.00	4.31	2.15	1.14	23.79	0.00	0.08
Lightly processed food		*3.6*	*7.6*		*1.8*									*4.6*		*3.4*	
14. Vegetable oil	7.9	0.2	1.4	6.7	0.07	60.28	39.72			1.50	0.02	3.94	1.97	0.00	0.02	2.33	19.99
15. Wheat, milled	21.8	1.2	2.8	4.4	0.56	64.94	35.06			1.50	0.02	4.45	2.22	0.51	1.82	0.82	4.31
16. Rice, milled IRRI	30.7	0.2	0.4	3.7	0.12	56.75	43.25			1.50	0.02	4.45	2.22	1.72	46.60		
17. Rice, milled basmati	29.0	0.5	0.8	3.7	0.25	56.77	43.23			1.50	0.00	4.45	2.22	2.34	28.58		
18. Sugar	32.2	1.4	2.2	3.3	0.82	69.96	30.04			1.50	6.75	5.91	2.96	0.03	0.11	0.28	1.89
Nonagriculture		*73.2*	*72.3*		*87.4*									*91.5*		*93.4*	
Mining and manufacturing		*13.2*	*24.2*		*7.9*									*74.1*		*88.2*	
13. Mining	74.6	0.6	0.4	2.3	0.47	85.00	15.00			1.50	14.50	4.31	2.16	0.78	18.61	9.29	80.53
19. Other food	36.9	1.7	2.3	4.7	0.75	61.57	38.43			1.50	44.69	3.94	1.97	12.07	51.47	1.06	12.45
20. Cotton lint and yarn	21.6	1.4	3.3	3.3	0.82	85.52	14.48			1.50	12.05	4.11	2.06	8.97	27.10	0.71	4.27
21. Textiles	22.2	3.6	8.0	2.7	2.43	78.91	21.09			1.50	0.00	4.11	2.06	31.91	39.66	1.61	4.81

(Continued)

Table 13.1. (*Continued*)

	Production											Trade					
	Value added ratio va/x	Value added share	Output share	Capital-labor	Employment	Share (%)			Land output ratio		Indirect tax rate	Elasticities		Exports (%)		Imports (%)	
						Skilled	Unskilled										
Sectors	%	%	%	ratio[a]	share, %	labor	labor	Farmers	%	sig_va[b]	%	eta[c]	sig_m[d]	share	intensity[e]	share	intensity[f]
22. Leather	8.3	0.1	0.5	2.9	0.06	60.36	39.64			1.50	0.00	4.11	2.06	2.27	42.79	0.11	5.21
23. Wood products	36.3	0.7	0.9	1.8	0.57	67.98	32.02			1.50	0.18	4.09	2.04	0.03	0.34	0.56	8.61
24. Chemicals	28.2	0.5	0.9	3.8	0.25	55.16	44.84			1.50	2.58	4.09	2.05	1.38	15.90	11.16	69.89
25. Cement and bricks	55.0	1.4	1.3	7.4	0.42	68.98	31.02			1.50	24.15	4.09	2.05	0.03	0.21		
26. Petroleum refining	19.4	0.6	1.5	2.9	0.36	71.95	28.05			1.50	28.96	4.09	2.05			9.71	50.11
27. Other manufacturing	25.4	2.6	5.0	2.6	1.75	67.99	32.01			1.50	4.39	4.09	2.05	16.61	33.17	54.00	71.03
Other industry		*6.6*	*6.6*		*7.2*									*0.0*		*0.0*	
28. Energy	60.8	3.4	2.8	4.0	1.69	80.00	20.00			1.50	5.02	2.08	1.04				
29. Construction	41.6	3.2	3.8	0.4	5.48	50.00	50.00			1.50	0.16	2.08	1.04				
Services		*53.5*	*41.5*		*72.4*									*17.5*		*5.2*	
30. Commerce	84.0	15.3	9.1	0.4	26.52	20.00	80.00			1.50	0.00	2.08	1.04	0.07	0.07	0.21	0.35
31. Transport	53.9	11.8	10.9	1.5	11.73	20.00	80.00			1.50	0.27	2.08	1.04	17.38	15.88		
32. Housing	81.8	4.9	3.0							1.50	0.03	2.08	1.04				
33. Private services	53.5	12.9	12.0	1.5	12.79	20.00	80.00			1.50	0.00	2.08	1.04	0.01	0.01	5.03	5.98
34. Public services	66.2	8.6	6.5		21.35	100.00					0.00	2.08	1.04				
Total	49.8	100.0	100		100									100.0	10.0	100.0	14.45

Source: Dorosh, Niazi, and Nazli (2004).
Note: va-value added; x-output
a. total labor ÷ total capital
b. *sig_va* = substitution parameter in CES production
c. *eta* = export demand elasticity
d. *sig_m* = substitution parameter in CES composite good
e. export ÷ output
f. imports ÷ composite good

gross value of sectoral output. In the SAM, it accounts for 13 percent of total employment.[5]

There are 19 household groups in the model. The agriculture-based groups are categorized according to household location (Punjab, Sindh, and other Pakistan) and the size of land holdings (large, medium, and small farms; landless small-farm renters, and agricultural workers without land). In addition, there are four nonfarm national aggregates: rural nonfarm poor, rural nonfarm nonpoor, urban poor, and urban nonpoor. Table 13.2 shows the 19 households in the SAM and the corresponding characteristics of the 19 household groups in the Household Integration Economic Survey.

The structure of consumption varies among household groups, A composite sector—livestock, cattle, and dairy—shows the highest share in the consumption basket, varying from 14 percent among large- and medium-farm households in other Pakistan to 25 percent among agricultural

Table 13.2. Model household categories, Pakistan

2001–02 social accounting matrix	2001–02 household integrated economic survey
Large-farm households (Punjab, Sindh, other Pakistan)	Landowners with more than 50 acres
Medium-farm households (Punjab, Sindh, other Pakistan)	Landowners with more than 12.5, but less than 50 acres
Small-farm households (Punjab, Sindh, other Pakistan)	Landowners with less than 12.5 acres
Small-farm renters, landless (Punjab, Sindh, other Pakistan)	No landholdings, but rent land for farm activities
Rural agricultural workers, landless (Punjab, Sindh, other Pakistan)	No landholdings, agricultural workers
Rural nonfram nonpoor	Rural nonpoor, nonfarmers, nonagricultural workers
Rural nonfram poor	Rural poor, nonfarmers, nonagricultural workers
Urban nonpoor	Urban nonpoor
Urban poor	Urban poor

Sources: Dorosh, Niazi, and Nazli (2004); Federal Bureau of Statistics (2003).
Note: The SAM covers three major provinces: Punjab, Sindh, and other Pakistan, which consists of Azad Kashmir, Balochistan, North–West Frontier Province, Northern Areas (Gilgit-Baltistan), Federally Administered, and Federally Administered Tribal Areas.

worker households in Punjab. The other major items in the consumption basket are private services (about 14 percent), transport (about 13 percent), milled wheat (from 4 percent among the urban nonpoor to 12 percent among agricultural workers in other Pakistan), textiles (from 5 percent among large- and medium-farm households in other Pakistan to 7 percent among agricultural worker households in Punjab and the urban poor), other manufacturing (from 1 percent among agricultural worker households in Sindh to 10 percent among large- and medium-farm households in other Pakistan), sugar (from 3 percent among urban nonpoor households to 10 percent among agricultural worker households in other Pakistan), and fruits and vegetables (from 4 percent among large- and medium-farm households in Punjab to 7 percent among agricultural worker households in other Pakistan). Commodities with high foreign trade content are impacted significantly by changes in trade policies and world prices. This has varying effects across household groups because of differences in the household consumption bundles.

The sectoral indirect tax structure is presented in Table 7,1. The highest tax rate, 45 percent, applies to other food, the share of which in the consumption of households is only about 1 percent. Indirect taxes are also relatively high on cement, bricks, and petroleum refining, which generally account for less than 1 percent of direct household consumption, but affect housing and transportation costs. The tax rate on cotton lint and yam is 12 percent, while it is zero on textiles. However, because cotton lint and yarn are major inputs into textile production, an increase in the tax on the former raises the cost of production of textiles. This affects consumers because the share of textiles in the consumption basket is about 5 percent.

Sugar shows the highest tariff rate, 59 percent (Table 13.3). Another commodity showing high tariffs, averaging 55 percent, is livestock, cattle, and diary, which account for a large share in the consumption basket of households. Other agricultural commodities showing high tariffs and substantial consumption shares are milled wheat and vegetable oil. A few primary agricultural and light food processing sectors show low or even negative import tariffs. In contrast, tariffs are uniformly relatively high across the manufacturing sectors.

Overall, the foreign trade sector in Pakistan is not large relative to the domestic sector (Table 13.1). Of the total domestic output, only 10 percent

Table 13.3. Parameters and exogenous demand and price shocks caused by rest-of-the-world liberalization, Pakistan

	Pakistan CGE model	Linkage model	Trade distortions		Full trade liberalization, excluding Pakistan		Agricultural trade liberalization excluding Pakistan	
Sector no.	Sector description	Sector description	Tariff, %	Export tax, %	World import price change, %	Export demand shifter[b]	World import price, % change	Export demand shifter[b]
Agriculture								
Primary agriculture								
1.	Wheat, irrigated	Wheat	–4.9	0.0	2.41	1.0	3.12	1.00
2.	Wheat, nonirrigated	Wheat	–4.9	0.0	2.41	1.0	3.12	1.00
3.	Paddy, IRRI	Paddy rice	0.0	4.0	0.00	1.2	0.00	1.23
4.	Paddy, basmati	Paddy rice	0.0	4.0	0.00	1.2	0.00	1.23
5.	Cotton	Plant-based fibers	4.9	0.0	4.44	1.1	6.68	1.14
6.	Sugarcane	Sugarcane and beets	4.3	0.0	0.00	1.0	0.00	1.00
7.	Other major crops	Other crops	15.3	0.0	–1.91	1.0	0.00	1.01
8.	Fruits and vegetables	Vegetables and fruits	16.5	0.0	–2.93	1.0	–2.62	0.97
9.	Livestock, cattle, and dairy[a]	Cattle, sheep, and so on	55.4	0.0	4.41	1.0	5.17	1.00
10.	Poultry	Other livestock	10.8	0.0	–8.00	1.0	–6.77	0.99
11.	Forestry	Other primary products	14.3	18.1	–0.14	1.1	0.79	1.01

(Continued)

Table 13.3. (*Continued*)

	Pakistan CGE model	Linkage model	Trade distortions		Full trade liberalization, excluding Pakistan		Agricultural trade liberalization excluding Pakistan	
Sector no.	Sector description	Sector description	Tariff, %	Export tax, %	World import price change, %	Export demand shifter[b]	World import price, % change	Export demand shifter[b]
Lightly processed food								
12. Fishing industry		Other primary products	14.3	18.1	–0.14	1.1	0.79	1.01
14. Vegetable oil		Vegetable oils and fats	23.7	0.0	1.78	0.9	0.40	0.93
15. Wheat, milled		Other food, beverages and tobacco	24.9	0.0	0.00	1.0	–1.68	0.97
16. Rice, milled IRRI		Processed rice	0.0	4.0	8.21	1.1	10.18	1.08
17. Rice, milled basmati		Processed rice	0.0	4.0	8.21	1.1	10.18	1.08
18. Sugar		Refined sugar	59.0	0.0	1.62	1.0	3.44	1.00
Nonagriculture								
Mining and manufacturing								
13. Mining		Other primary products	14.3	18.1	–0.14	1.1	0.79	1.01

(*Continued*)

Table 13.3. (*Continued*)

	Pakistan CGE model	Linkage model	Trade distortions		Full trade liberalization, excluding Pakistan		Agricultural trade liberalization excluding Pakistan	
Sector no.	Sector description	Sector description	Tariff, %	Export tax, %	World import price change, %	Export demand shifter[b]	World import price, % change	Export demand shifter[b]
19.	Other food	Other food, beverages and tobacco	24.9	0.0	0.00	1.0	–1.68	0.97
20.	Cotton lint and yarn	Textile and wearing apparel	19.9	1.1	–0.68	1.0	0.48	1.00
21.	Textiles	Textile and wearing apparel	19.9	1.1	–0.68	1.0	0.48	1.00
22.	Leather	Textile and wearing apparel	19.9	1.1	–0.68	1.0	0.48	1.00
23.	Wood products	Other manufacturing	16.6	5.4	–0.38	1.0	0.38	1.00
24.	Chemicals	Other manufacturing	16.6	5.4	–0.38	1.0	0.38	1.00
25.	Cement and bricks	Other manufacturing	16.6	5.4	–0.38	1.0	0.38	1.00
26.	Petroleum refining	Other manufacturing	16.6	5.4	–0.38	1.0	0.38	1.00
27.	Other manufacturing	Other manufacturing	16.6	5.4	–0.38	1.0	0.38	1.00

(*Continued*)

Table 13.3. (*Continued*)

	Pakistan CGE model	Linkage model	Trade distortions		Full trade liberalization, excluding Pakistan		Agricultural trade liberalization excluding Pakistan	
Sector no.	**Sector description**	**Sector description**	**Tariff, %**	**Export tax, %**	**World import price change, %**	**Export demand shifter[b]**	**World import price, % change**	**Export demand shifter[b]**
Other industry								
28. Energy		Services	0.0	0.0	–0.22	1.0	0.19	1.00
29. Construction		Services	0.0	0.0	–0.22	1.0	0.19	1.00
Services								
30. Commerce		Services	0.0	0.0	–0.22	1.0	0.19	1.00
31. Transport		Services	0.0	0.0	–0.22	1.0	0.19	1.00
32. Housing		Services	0.0	0.0	–0.22	1.0	0.19	1.00
33. Private services		Services	0.0	0.0	–0.22	1.0	0.19	1.00
34. Public services		Services	0.0	0.0	–0.22	1.0	0.19	1.00

Source: Linkage model simulations by van der Mensbrugghe, Valenzuela, and Anderson (see the appendix).
a. This is the trade weighted average of cattle, sheep, other livestock, and dairy in the Linkage model.
b. In equation 2, this is $a = (1 + 0.01 * p)(1 + 0.01 * q)^\wedge(1/\mathrm{ESUBM})$; where p is export price change, q export volume change; and ESBUM Arimington elasticity, all from the Linkage model.

goes to the export market. Only 15 percent of the total goods and services available in the domestic market are imported. However, there are large differences across sectors. Within agriculture, the sectors with the highest share of production exported are milled IRRI rice, 47 percent; forestry, 31 percent; and fishing, 24 percent. The shares exported are small in the rest of the agricultural sectors. Within the nonagricultural sectors, other food, at 52 percent, has the highest share of production exported; leather is at 43 percent; textiles, 40 percent; and cotton lint and yarn, 27 percent. The textile sector dominates in exports. In the SAM, textiles account for 32 percent of total exports, cotton lint and yarn for 9 percent, and other food for 12 percent.

Because of the large volume of crude oil imports, the mining sector has the highest share of domestic consumption that is imported, at 81 percent. The share of other manufacturing is 71 percent; of chemicals, 70 percent; and of petroleum, 50 percent. Other manufacturing accounts for 54 percent of overall imports; chemicals, 11 percent; and mining and petroleum refining, each about 9 percent. Except for forestry (25 percent) and vegetable oil (20 percent), the shares of domestic consumption that are imported in the agricultural sectors are well under 10 percent.

Table 13.1 includes the values of key elasticity parameters in the model: the import substitution elasticity (*sig_m*) in the constant elasticity of substitution composite good function and the production substitution elasticity (*sig_va*) in the constant elasticity of substitution value added production function.[6] The values of the export demand elasticity (*eta*) are the Armington parameters of the global model.

The sources of household income in the model are labor income, capital income, income from land, and other income (Table 13.4). Other income is composed of foreign remittances, which is assumed in the SAM to be distributed proportionately among all households, and dividend income, which is earned only by urban nonpoor households. The sources of income vary across household groups. Farm households are dependent on income from land, farm labor, and capital. Other rural households depend on income from unskilled labor and capital. About three-fourths of the income of urban poor households comes from unskilled labor. Urban nonpoor households derive 44 percent of their incomes from other income (composed largely of dividend income) and 33 percent from skilled labor

Table 13.4. Household income sources and income taxes, Pakistan, 2001–02

Households	2001–02 income		2001–02 population		Income sources, %						Direct tax, %
	Total mil Rs	Per capita, PRs, 1,000s	1,000s	% distribution	Labor: Farm	Labor: Unskilled	Labor: Skilled	Capital	Land	Other	
Large-farm households											
–Sindh	19,079	112.9	169	0.12	13.2	0.3	—	31.4	49.8	5.3	—
–Punjab	64,116	173.7	369	0.25	8.6	0.5	—	43.3	42.2	5.4	—
–Other Pakistan[a]	10,755	152.9	70	0.05	9.8	0.2	—	52.4	32.3	5.4	—
Medium-farm households											
–Sindh	44,625	30.4	1,466	1.00	14.5	3.1	—	39.6	37.4	5.3	—
–Punjab	145,995	48.4	3,014	2.07	10.8	4.3	—	52.3	27.2	5.4	—
–Other Pakistan	35,572	34.2	1,040	0.71	14.9	2.9	—	38.2	38.4	5.5	—
Small-farm households											
–Sindh	57,648	14.9	3,873	2.65	6.8	9.0	—	57.9	20.4	5.8	—
–Punjab	318,888	18.1	17,605	12.06	7.9	14.2	—	51.8	20.3	5.8	—
–Other Pakistan	124,985	11.9	10,493	7.19	6.0	11.6	—	63.6	12.5	6.2	—
Small-farm renters, landless											
–Sindh	43,672	7.7	5,682	3.89	11.6	18.7	—	48.5	15.6	5.7	—
–Punjab	45,963	10.7	4,307	2.95	9.0	20.5	—	48.7	16.1	5.8	—
–Other Pakistan	14,970	8.2	1,818	1.25	10.1	14.5	—	55.0	14.7	5.7	—

(*Continued*)

Table 13.4. (*Continued*)

Households	2001–02 income		2001–02 population		Income sources, %						Direct tax, %
					Labor						
	Total mil Rs	Per capita, PRs, 1,000s	1,000s	% distribution	Farm	Unskilled	Skilled	Capital	Land	Other	
Rural agricultural workers, landless											
–Sindh	20,782	6.4	3,241	2.22	—	51.0	—	42.8	—	6.2	—
–Punjab	68,172	12.0	5,693	3.90	—	49.3	—	45.2	—	5.5	—
–Other Pakistan	9,513	14.6	653	0.45	—	18.7	—	76.0	—	5.4	—
Rural nonfarms households											
–nonpoor	400,771	19.8	20,233	13.86	—	43.0	—	49.9	—	7.2	—
–poor	134,398	5.5	24,525	16.80	—	29.7	—	63.4	—	6.9	—
Urban households											
–nonpoor	1,744,119	58.5	29,829	20.44	—	11.9	33.3	10.6	—	44.2	8.4
–poor	181,413	15.3	11,880	8.14	—	76.2	—	18.0	—	5.8	—

Sources: Dorosh, Niazi, and Nazli (2004).

a. Other Pakistan — Azad Kashmir, Balochistan, North–West Frontier Province, Northern Areas (Gilgit–Baltistan), Federally Administered, and Federally Administered Tribal Areas.

income. According to the SAM, it is only the urban nonpoor household group that pays income taxes, amounting to 8.4 percent of their incomes.

Poverty Indicators

The overall poverty rate based on the official national poverty line declined in Pakistan from about 30 percent in the late 1980s to 26 percent in 1990–91. During these years, both urban and rural poverty decreased. However, in 1993–94, the incidence of rural poverty and the incidence of urban poverty started to move in different directions: urban poverty continued to decline, while rural poverty began to rise, thereby widening the poverty gap between urban and rural areas (Figure 13.1). The gap reached a peak in 2001–02, which was largely caused by the crippling drought that severely affected agricultural output that year, together with relatively low international agricultural commodity prices. Almost 70 percent of the people live in rural areas, and, because the majority of these people (40 percent of all households nationally) depend on agriculture for income, the incidence of rural poverty increased to 39 percent that year, while urban poverty was stable at 23 percent.

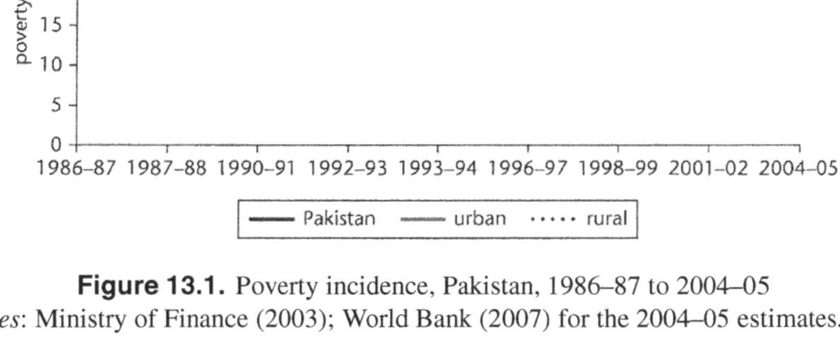

Figure 13.1. Poverty incidence, Pakistan, 1986–87 to 2004–05
Sources: Ministry of Finance (2003); World Bank (2007) for the 2004–05 estimates.
Note: Poverty is defined as the share of the population living below the national poverty line. Official data for 1993–94 indicate that the level of overall poverty was above the incidence of poverty in urban and rural areas; see Ministry of Finance (2003).

There is some disagreement about the accuracy of recent estimates of poverty. For 2004–05, the estimates of the Planning Commission of Pakistan show the overall incidence of poverty declining from the peak of 34 percent in 2001–02 to 24 percent in 2004–05 (Dorosh and Salam 2009). The World Bank (2007) estimates a smaller decline, to 29 percent. Despite the disparity between these estimates (arising primarily because of the inflation factor used in computing the relevant poverty lines), the estimates show the incidence of poverty declining in urban and rural areas in the most recent years, but highlight the large gap between the rural and urban poverty rates. The depth of poverty indicated by the Foster, Greer, and Thorbecke (1984) poverty gap and the squared poverty gap also suggest that the problem of poverty is more severe in rural areas and that this was especially true during the 2001–02 drought (Table 13.5).

Simulations

The first part of this section describes our six policy experiments, while the second part discusses the results. The experiments use direct tax replacement to hold the government fiscal balance fixed. The idea is to

Table 13.5. Poverty estimates, Pakistan, 1998–99, 2001–02, and 2004–05

Poverty index	1998–99	2001–02	2004–05
Poverty incidence			
Pakistan	30.0	31.2	29.2
Urban	21.0	19.9	19.1
Rural	33.8	38.2	34.0
Poverty gap			
Pakistan	6.3	6.5	6.1
Urban	4.3	3.9	3.9
Rural	7.1	8.0	7.2
Square poverty gap, poverty severity			
Pakistan	2.0	2.0	2.0
Urban	1.3	1.2	1.2
Rural	2.2	2.5	2.3

Sources: Ministry of Finance (2003); World Bank (2007) for the 2004–05 estimates.
Note: The table reflects the poverty concepts of Foster, Greer, and Thorbecke (1984).

replace distorting trade taxes with less-distorting income taxes. The fiscal burden falls on urban nonpoor households because, according to the SAM, other household groups do not pay income taxes (Table 13.4). We have also conducted an alternative indirect tax replacement experiment to check the sensitivity of the results to the specification, given that financing a trade reform is a nontrivial issue from the government's point of view (Ahmed, Abbas, and Ahmed 2009). In our analysis, we separate the effects on the economy of reducing distortions in the rest of the world and in domestic markets in Pakistan, and we evaluate the effects of both on income inequality and poverty.

Design of the policy experiments

Table 13.3 shows the sectoral correspondence between the Pakistan model and the global model. It also shows the sectoral tariff rates and export taxes, which, where possible, are based on the set of estimates on nominal rates of assistance for Pakistan by Dorosh and Salam (2009). We use these trade distortions in all our policy experiments. The table presents the changes in border import prices found through the global model under full trade liberalization and agricultural liberalization by the rest of the world, and it lists sectoral export demand shifters calculated on the basis of Equation (7.2). We have used these data as inputs in the six policy experiments we have conducted, as follows:

- *S1A*, full world trade liberalization in all tradable goods sectors by all countries, excluding Pakistan: This experiment uses the results of the global model under full trade liberalization in Table 13.3. It retains all existing trade distortions in Pakistan.
- *S1B*, agricultural price and trade liberalization by all countries, excluding Pakistan: This scenario uses the results of the global model. As with S1A, all existing distortions in Pakistan are retained.
- *S2A*, full goods trade liberalization carried out unilaterally in Pakistan: All Pakistan trade distortions are set to zero. There are no changes in the sectoral border export and import prices or in the export demand shifters because there is no rest-of-the-world trade liberalization.
- *S2B*, agricultural trade liberalization carried out unilaterally in Pakistan: All Pakistan distortions in primary agriculture and in lightly processed

food are set to zero. Similar to S2A, there are no changes in the sectoral border export and import prices and in the export demand shifters because there is no rest-of-the-world trade liberalization.

- *S3A*, full world trade liberalization of all tradable goods, including in Pakistan: This combines S1A and S2A.
- *S3B*, agricultural world trade liberalization, including in Pakistan: This combines S1B and S2B.

In analyzing the results under each of the scenarios, we indicate, first, the effects on poverty for the whole of Pakistan, for rural and urban areas, and for major household groups. The results on poverty include changes in the incidence of poverty and in the depth of poverty measured by the poverty gap and the squared poverty gap. These poverty effects are traced and analyzed through the various determining channels: macro, sectoral, commodity, and factor prices, as well as household incomes. In estimating the poverty effects, we apply the results on household incomes and consumer prices for each of the 19 household groups in the CGE model simulations to the household classifications in the Household Integration Economic Survey. Each of the CGE simulations generates a new vector of household Income and consumer price for each of the groups, which we use to compute new sets of poverty indexes to compare with the baseline indexes.

Simulation results

In this subsection, we present the modeling results of our six policy experiments. We continue the discussion with additional results that show the sensitivity of the core results to changes in the treatment of tax adjustments in the model.

S1A: Trade liberalization by the rest of the world without Pakistan

Full trade liberalization abroad, while retaining all existing trade distortions in Pakistan, causes the overall poverty incidence index to decline by 1.3 percent from its base value, from 31.2 to 30.S (Table 13.6). Households at the bottom of the income ladder benefit the most, as indicated by the greater reduction in the poverty gap (1.6 percent) and the squared poverty gap (1.9 percent). Among rural households, the poorest households—those

Table 13.6. The poverty effects of prospective liberalizations, Pakistan

Indicator	Index in 2001–02	2001–02 population distribution, %	% change from 2001–02 index					
			S1A	S1B	S2A	S2B	S3A	S3B
All Pakistan –P0	31.23		−1.3	−0.1	−5.2	−1.6	−6.4	−1.8
–P1	6.46		−1.6	−0.1	−10.0	−2.3	−11.5	−2.5
–P2	1.97		−1.9	−0.1	−12.1	−2.8	−13.8	−3.0
Gini coefficient	0.34		−0.08	−0.02	−3.3	−0.1	−3.3	−0.2
All Urban –P0	19.86	29.7	−1.5	−0.1	−2.3	−2.4	−0.4	−2.7
–P1	3.91		−1.5	−0.1	−13.3	−3.6	−14.8	−3.7
–P2	1.16		−1.7	−0.1	−16.9	−4.2	−18.3	−4.3
Gini coefficient	0.40		−0.03	−0.01	−2.0	−0.1	−2.0	−0.1
All rural –P0	38.16	70.3	−1.2	−0.1	−7.6	−1.4	−8.6	−1.5
–P1	8.02		−1.6	−0.1	−9.0	−2.0	−10.5	−2.1
–P2	2.47		−2.0	−0.1	−10.8	−2.4	−12.5	−2.6
Gini coefficient	0.26		−0.01	−0.02	−0.2	−0.1	0.2	−0.1
Large- and medium-farm households –P0	22.82	4.0	0.0	0.0	−7.9	3.4	−7.9	3.4
–P1	4.06		−0.7	0.4	−9.9	−4.9	−10.0	5.3
–P2	1.13		−0.7	0.5	−10.5	−5.2	−10.6	5.8
Small-farm households and agricultural workers –P0	37.40	30.6	−1.4	0.1	−8.3	−0.9	−8.7	−0.9
–P1	7.47		−1.3	0.0	−9.3	−1.3	−10.3	−1.3
–P2	2.20		−1.6	0.0	−11.2	−1.7	−12.4	−1.6
Rural nonfarm households –P0	39.89	35.7	−1.1	−0.2	−7.2	−1.9	−8.5	−2.1
–P1	8.71		−1.9	−0.2	−8.9	−2.6	−10.6	−2.8
–P2	2.76		−2.2	−0.2	−10.6	−3.1	−12.6	−3.4

Source: National CGE model simulations by the authors.
Note: P0 = poverty headcount. P1 = poverty gap. P2 = poverty severity.

in the rural nonfarmer group—benefit the most. Thus, rural-urban income inequality is lowered in this scenario also.

What are the forces that drive these reductions in poverty and income inequality? The S1A simulation leads to a real exchange rate appreciation of 1.24 percent (Table 13.7).[7] The terms of trade (the ratio of domestic export to import prices) improve by 1.38 percent in agriculture and by 1.56 percent in nonagriculture. This is because of the lower world import prices of some of the agricultural products, as well as most of the nonfarm goods (Table 13.3).

The import prices of agricultural goods drop by 1.7 percent (Table 13.7), despite the increases in the import prices of livestock, wheat, vegetable oil, and sugar (Table 13.3). This is caused by a number of factors, including the appreciation of the currency; the decline in the border import prices of fruits and vegetables and other major crops (Table 13.3), all of which have relatively large import components (Table 7,1); and the slight reduction in the border import prices of forestry products, which show high import intensity. The domestic prices of farm products decline by 0.3 percent, which is lower than the drop in import prices. This results in more imports of agricultural goods (a rise of 2.4 percent) and a marginal increase in the domestic demand for agriculture (a rise of 0.1 percent). Because the demand for imported and domestic agricultural products increases, the domestic consumption of farm products increases (by 0.2 percent).

Table 13.3 shows that the border import prices of nonagricultural goods decline. This, together with the appreciation of the exchange rate, reduces the import prices of nonagricultural goods by 2.4 percent (Table 13.7). The domestic prices of nonagricultural products also decline, by 0.6 percent, which is lower than the decline in the import prices. Thus, the imports of nonfarm products increase, by 1.0 percent. At the sectoral level, there is a relatively large rise in imports of cotton lint and yarn, textiles, and leather because of the relatively greater decline in the border prices of these products. More imports of nonfarm goods reduce marginally the domestic demand, but, despite this, overall domestic nonagricultural consumption increases by 0.1 percent.

The export prices of farm products decline by 0.3 percent. Because the border prices of these products rise, the decline is caused by appreciation in the exchange rate. There is a slightly greater decrease in the domestic

Table 13.7. Aggregate simulation results of prospective agricultural and nonagricultural liberalization, Pakistan

(% change from the base)

	S1A		S1B		S2A		S2B		S3A		S3B	
Variables	**Ag**	**Nonag**	**Ag**	**Nonag**	**Ag**	**Nonag**	**Ag**	**Nonag**	**Ag**	**Nonag**	**Ag**	**Nonag**
Real GDP	0.15		0.04		0.81		0.26		0.95		0.29	
Real and relative prices												
Real exchange rate	−1.24		−0.13		6.09		1.87		4.79		1.73	
Domestic terms of trade[a]	1.38	1.56	0.98	0.13	12.61	9.37	17.30	−0.84	14.19	11.06	18.52	−0.71
Prices												
Export price in local currency	−0.26	−0.82	0.33	−0.13	−1.92	0.09	−0.63	1.70	−2.16	−0.66	−0.30	1.59
Import price in local currency	−1.70	−2.35	−0.73	−0.24	−12.26	−8.34	−14.49	2.57	−13.74	−10.41	−15.13	2.33
Domestic price	−0.29	−0.55	−0.07	−0.08	−2.47	−1.23	−1.53	1.11	−2.74	−1.69	−1.56	1.06
Output price	−0.29	−0.58	−0.06	−0.08	−2.45	−1.07	−1.50	1.18	−2.73	−1.57	−1.52	1.12
Value added price	0.16	−0.12	0.03	−0.06	−3.14	1.32	−2.88	1.01	−2.98	1.24	−2.79	0.97
Consumer price index	−0.51		−0.11		−2.81		−0.27		−3.24		−0.34	
Volume												
Imports	2.41	0.96	0.89	0.12	22.15	4.45	29.64	−0.48	24.75	5.46	30.42	−0.36
Exports	0.73	−0.16	1.79	0.11	4.78	13.24	6.20	3.07	5.28	13.07	8.00	3.17

(Continued)

Table 13.7. (*Continued*)

Variables	S1A		S1B		S2A		S2B		S3A		S3B	
	Ag	Nonag	Ag	Nonag	Ag	Nonag	Ag	Nonag	Ag	Nonag	Ag	Nonag
Domestic demand	0.09	–0.07	–0.01	–0.02	–0.87	–1.12	–1.05	0.03	–0.76	–1.19	–1.06	0.01
Composite good	0.18	0.12	0.02	0.01	0.09	–0.08	0.20	–0.07	0.30	0.05	0.22	–0.06
Output	0.11	–0.08	0.05	–0.01	–0.69	0.39	–0.82	0.39	–0.57	0.50	–0.77	0.38
Value added	0.07	–0.03	0.03	–0.01	–0.51	0.19	–0.39	0.13	–0.43	0.16	–0.35	0.12
Factor prices												
Farm wages	–0.95		–0.27		–0.58		–2.16		–1.67		–2.44	
Wages of unskilled labor	–0.14		–0.05		1.49		0.47		1.38		0.45	
Wages of skilled labor		–0.04		0.00		2.06		0.73		2.04		0.74
Return to land	–1.00		–0.32		–1.90		–2.52		3.06		–2.85	
Return to capital	1.00	–0.14	0.27	–0.09	–5.02	1.00	–3.80	1.41	–3.92	0.93	–3.41	1.34
Factor prices less inflation												
Farm wages	–0.44		–0.16		2.23		–1.88		–1.56		–2.10	
Wages of unskilled labor	–0.37		–0.05		4.30		0.74		4.61		0.79	
Wages of skilled labor		0.47		0.11		4.87		1.00		5.28		1.09
Return to land	–0.49		–0.21		0.91		–2.25		0.18		–2.51	
Return to capital	1.51	0.37	0.37	0.02	–2.21	3.81	–3.53	1.68	–0.69	4.17	–3.07	1.68

Source: National CGE model simulations by the authors.
Note: Ag = agriculture. Nonag = nonagriculture.
[a]Change in the ratio of domestic export and import prices.

prices of agricultural products. Thus, exports of agriculture improve by 0.73 percent, and the overall output of agriculture increases by 0.11 percent.

The effects on value added, value added prices, and factor prices in agriculture are explained by the changes in sectoral export prices, factor intensities, and import and export intensities. The overall output price of agriculture declines by 0.29, while the value added price increases by 0.16 percent. The difference in the sign is generated by a relatively higher increase in the value added price of milled rice (2 percent) and vegetable oil (1.7 percent).[8] The increase by 1.18 percent in the border export price of milled rice has larger effects on the value added price of milled rice because rice has a high export-intensity ratio (Table 13.1). Although the border import price of milled rice increases more (10,18 percent), this has no effects because there are zero imports. The increase by 1.78 percent in the import border price of vegetable oil increases the value added price of vegetable oil because vegetable oil has a high import-intensity ratio.

Farm wages and the returns to land decline by about 1.0 percent. This is caused by the decline in the output and value added prices in primary agriculture, which employs farmers and uses land. The average rate of return to capital in agriculture improves by 1 percent. This is caused by the increase in the value added price of milled rice and vegetable oil. These sectors are relatively capital intensive, showing capital-labor ratios of 3,7 for rice and 6.7 for vegetable oil (Table 13.1). Because wage rates increase less than value added prices, returns to capital rise. The returns to capital in these sectors increase by more than 2 percent for milled rice and 1.9 percent for vegetable oil. The change in the returns to capital in livestock and poultry is also positive, but smaller. The change in the returns to capital in the other primary agricultural commodities is negative.

The decline in the value added prices in primary agriculture and in nonagriculture lowers the wages of unskilled labor by 0.14 percent. However, because of the increase in the value added prices of milled rice and vegetable oil, the wages of skilled workers decrease by only 0.04 percent. The average returns to the capital used in nonagriculture decline by 0.14 percent.

We have also included the results on factor prices net of the inflation effects. The overall consumer price index, in this experiment decreases by 0.5 percent. Net of the inflation effects, there is a negative result for farm wages and the returns to land, but the other factors show positive net price effects.

All these effects lead to changes in household incomes (Table 13.8). The changes in the nominal incomes of households are negative across groups except rural nonfarmers and rural agricultural workers, the latter because of their heavy reliance on agricultural capital incomes (mostly informal capital), as shown in Table 13.4, and the increase in the average returns to capital in agriculture (1 percent; see Table 13.7). However, the consumer prices for each of the groups decline more rapidly than the drop in nominal incomes because of the greater reduction in import prices. Thus, all household groups realize improvements in real incomes. The largest increases in real incomes occur among rural nonfarmers (0.63 and 0.53 for the nonpoor and poor, respectively; see Table 13.8) and agricultural workers in other Pakistan (0.58 percent). This explains the significant reduction in the depth of poverty in rural areas, particularly among rural nonfarmers.

In the scenario, full trade liberalization by the rest of the world thus reduces both poverty and income inequality. It reduces import prices, especially on commodities that have relatively large shares in the consumption basket of consumers. This translates into declining consumer prices. It also enhances agricultural production relative to nonagricultural production because of improvements in the world price of farm commodities. The poorest nonfarm households in rural areas benefit the most from the improvement in the real wages of unskilled labor and in the returns to capital and from the reduction in consumer prices.

S1B: Agricultural liberalization by the rest of the world

This second experiment incorporates the results of the global model for agricultural liberalization by the rest of the world, while retaining all existing trade distortions in Pakistan. Compared with scenario S1A, the border import prices of some commodities increase more in this scenario. For example, there is a greater increase in the border import prices of wheat, livestock, cotton, milled rice, and sugar (Table 13.3). Furthermore, the border import prices of nonagricultural products increase in this scenario, while they decline in scenario S1A (Table 13.7). Also, for commodities that show declining border import prices, the drop is relatively greater in this scenario compared with scenario S1A. Thus, the increase in the terms of trade for both agriculture and nonagriculture is lower in this experiment compared with scenario S1A. Also, the increase in the terms of trade is significantly lower in nonagriculture than in agriculture in this scenario relative to scenario S1A.

Table 13.6 shows that, while Pakistan's overall poverty incidence index declines marginally, poverty is not reduced across the board. Poverty in urban areas declines, but not all rural households experience a drop in poverty. Rural non-farmers show the highest poverty reduction, but, among farmers and agricultural workers, there is a slight increase in poverty.

What are the factors that drive these poverty results? The import prices of agriculture decline by 0.7 percent (Table 13.7), This is caused by the real exchange rate appreciation of 0.13 percent and the reduction in the border prices of milled wheat, as well as fruits and vegetables, which are import intensive. There are a number of primary agricultural commodities that show relatively greater increases in import prices, but these commodities are not imported. The domestic prices of agricultural goods decrease, but by less than the decline in the import prices of these goods. Thus, the imports of agricultural goods increase by 0.9 percent.

In nonagriculture, the smaller decline in domestic prices relative to import prices leads to a marginal increase in imports by 0.12 percent. This raises slightly the domestic consumption of nonagricultural products.

The increase in the export prices in agriculture by 0.33 percent and the decline in the domestic prices in agriculture by 0.07 percent result in a rise in exports by 1.8 percent. This increases the overall output of agriculture slightly, despite the decline in the domestic demand because of more imports. However, the increase in the exports of nonagricultural goods is not quite sufficient to offset the decline in domestic demand; so, the overall output of nonagriculture declines by 0.01 percent.

The difference in the results between the prices of value added and the output in agriculture is caused by variations in the results across industries within the agricultural sector. The greater increase in the border price of milled rice leads to a higher value added price, which offsets the decline in value added prices in the rest of agriculture. The decline in farm wages by 0.27 percent and the decline in the returns to land by 0.32 percent are caused by the decrease in the value added prices in primary agriculture. There is an increase in the returns to capital in agriculture by 0.27 percent mainly

Table 13.8. Household welfare and price effects of the liberalization in all goods trade by the rest of the world, Pakistan

		S1A			S1B			
Households	2001–02 population distrubution, %	Change in nominal income, %	Change in consumer price, %	EV/ income, %	Change in nominal income, %	Change in consumer price, %	EV/ income, %	Change in nominal income, %
Large-farm households								
–Sindh	0.14	−0.49	−0.51	0.02	−0.24	−0.08	−0.16	−0.53
–Punjab	0.17	−0.35	−0.58	0.23	−0.20	−0.09	−0.11	−0.48
–Other Pakistan	0.01	−0.24	−0.67	0.43	−0.17	−0.13	−0.04	−0.39
Medium-farm households								
–Sindh	0.99	−0.46	−0.51	0.05	−0.20	−0.08	−0.11	−0.61
–Punjab	1.89	−0.30	−0.58	0.28	−0.15	−0.09	−0.06	−0.50
–Other Pakistan	0.75	−0.47	−0.67	0.20	−0.20	−0.13	−0.07	−0.62
Small-farm households								
–Sindh	2.79	−0.19	−0.44	0.25	−0.12	−0.06	−0.06	−0.33
–Punjab	12.87	−0.22	−0.45	0.23	−0.13	−0.09	−0.04	−0.20
–Other Pakistan	5.67	−0.10	−0.46	0.36	−0.09	−0.11	−0.01	−0.19
Small-farm renters, landless								
–Sindh	0.16	−0.22	−0.38	0.16	−0.12	−0.07	−0.06	−0.03
–Punjab	1.50	−0.20	−0.47	0.27	−0.12	−0.10	−0.02	0.00
–Other Pakistan	0.58	−0.18	−0.52	0.35	−0.11	−0.12	0.01	−0.13
Rural agricultural workers, landless								
–Sindh	4.12	−0.01	−0.38	0.37	−0.06	−0.09	0.03	0.87
–Punjab	2.02	0.00	−0.40	0.39	−0.06	−0.09	0.03	0.82
–Other Pakistan	0.86	0.10	−0.48	0.58	−0.04	−0.13	0.09	0.07
Rural nonfarm households								
–nonpoor	17.60	0.11	−0.52	0.63	−0.06	−0.11	0.04	0.94
–poor	18.14	0.06	−0.46	0.53	−0.05	−0.10	0.06	0.35
Urban households								
–nonpoor	22.50	−0.22	−0.53	0.31	−0.11	−0.12	0.01	−7.21
–poor	7.23	−0.09	−0.46	0.37	−0.08	−0.11	0.03	1.49

Source: National CGE model simulations by the authors.
Note: EV = equivalent variation.

S2A		S2B			S3A			S3B		
Change in consumer price, %	EV/ income, %	Change in nominal income, %	Change in consumer price, %	EV/ income, %	Change in nominal income, %	Change in consumer price, %	EV/ income, %	Change in nominal income, %	Change in consumer price, %	EV/ income, %
−2.60	2.08	−1.63	−0.28	−1.34	−1.09	−3.03	1.96	−1.84	−0.32	−1.51
−2.82	2.35	−1.34	−0.16	−1.17	−0.86	−3.31	2.47	−1.51	−0.22	−1.29
−2.94	2.57	−1.11	−0.03	−1.08	−0.64	−3.52	2.90	−1.25	−0.12	−1.12
−2.60	2.00	−1.21	−0.28	−0.93	−1.11	−3.03	1.94	−1.39	−0.32	−1.06
−2.82	2.33	−0.87	−0.16	−0.71	−0.81	−3.31	2.52	−0.99	−0.22	−0.77
−2.94	2.33	−1.25	−0.03	−1.22	−1.14	−3.52	2.40	−1.43	−0.12	−1.30
−2.40	2.08	−0.60	−0.40	−0.19	−0.51	−2.78	2.28	−0.68	−0.43	−0.25
−2.47	2.28	−0.59	−0.53	−0.06	−0.41	−2.84	2.44	−0.68	−0.57	−0.10
−2.37	2.19	−0.37	−0.53	0.16	−0.26	−2.77	2.52	−0.42	−0.60	0.18
−2.16	2.14	−0.53	−0.56	0.03	−0.24	−2.48	2.25	−0.62	−0.59	−0.03
−2.41	2.42	−0.48	−0.52	0.05	−0.19	−2.82	2.64	−0.57	−0.59	0.03
−2.41	2.29	−0.50	−0.44	−0.05	−0.29	−2.87	2.59	−0.58	−0.53	−0.04
−2.08	2.96	0.26	−0.68	0.95	0.91	−2.41	3.33	0.24	−0.73	0.98
−2.19	3.02	0.25	−0.71	0.97	0.87	−2.52	3.40	0.23	−0.76	1.00
−2.20	2.28	0.10	−0.60	0.71	0.24	−2.62	2.87	0.11	−0.70	0.82
−2.68	3.63	0.10	−0.30	0.41	1.12	−3.12	4.25	0.09	−0.37	0.47
−2.23	2.58	0.16	−0.57	0.73	0.47	−2.63	3.11	0.16	−0.64	0.80
−3.13	−4.06	−0.25	−0.11	−0.13	−7.27	−3.57	−3.69	−0.32	−0.19	−0.12
−2.44	3.94	0.38	−0.51	0.90	1.44	−2.83	4.28	0.34	−0.58	0.93

because of the improvement in the value added price of milled rice, a sector which has a high capital-labor ratio. The decline in wages in unskilled labor is smaller than the decline in farm wages because of the increase in the value added price of milled rice, which neutralizes much of the effect of the falling value added prices in the rest of agriculture and in some non-agricultural sectors. Because milled rice requires more skilled labor than unskilled labor (Table 13.1), the increase in the value added price of milled rice also offsets the negative effects arising in the rest of the economy; thus, the wages of skilled labor do not change.

Net of the inflation effects, the changes in factor prices involve declining farm wages and declining returns to land, but otherwise rising factor prices. The nominal income effects are negative among all household groups (Table 13.8), but they are smaller than the effects generated in scenario S1A. Consumer prices decline, but the decline is not sufficient to offset the drop in the nominal incomes of farmers. However, rural nonfarmers and urban households enjoy marginal improvements in real incomes.

In sum, agricultural liberalization by the rest of the world would generate a marginal change in the terms of trade that favors agriculture compared with the results of scenario S1A. Furthermore, although overall import prices decline, the drop is much smaller in the present case than in scenario S1A. This translates into a smaller decline in consumer prices across household groups that is not sufficient to offset the drop in nominal incomes in some groups. These groups—farmers and agricultural workers—experience a slight increase in poverty. Moreover, given the small share of agriculture in the overall trade of Pakistan (less than 10 percent; see Table 13.1), a liberalization only in agriculture has much less impact on the Pakistan economy than a liberalization in all goods trade. Thus, the poverty impact is significantly less in the present case than in scenario S1A.

S2A: The unilateral liberalization of all goods trade by Pakistan

Our third experiment sets all sectoral import tariffs and export taxes in Pakistan to zero and assumes that there are no changes in policies abroad. Table 13.6 shows that this generates a significant drop in poverty, by 5.2 percent overall. There is also a significant reduction in the depth of poverty: the poverty gap drops by 10 percent, and the squared poverty gap drops by 12 percent. However, the incidence of poverty in urban areas increases by 2.3 percent. The detailed results show that the urban nonpoor suffer a decline in incomes because of the additional tax burden. This is the outcome of the tax replacement method, whereby we replace trade-distorting taxes in Pakistan with a less-distorting income tax that falls disproportionately on urban nonpoor households.[9] The rest of the household groups enjoy higher incomes and therefore lower poverty. Overall, income inequality is also reduced.

Most of the effects arise from the elimination of tariffs, although there are also effects because of the dismantling of the export taxes in a number of sectors (Table 13.3). The elimination of tariffs leads to a substantial reduction in import prices. The greatest reduction is in sugar and in livestock, cattle, and dairy because these sectors are exposed to the highest tariff rates. The import prices of vegetable oil, milled wheat, other food, cotton lint and yarn, and textiles also decline notably (Table 13.9). Overall, the import prices in agriculture decline by 12 percent, while, in nonagriculture, the import prices decline by 8.3 percent (Table 13.7).

Domestic prices also decline. However, the decline in domestic prices in most sectors is less than the decline in import prices. Thus, imports in these sectors surge. The imports of sugar increase by 215 percent; livestock, cattle, and dairy, by 99 percent; milled wheat, by 40 percent; other food, by 38 percent; cotton lint and yarn, by 38 percent; textiles, by 33 percent; and leather, by 28 percent (Table 13.9). Other sectors show notable increases as well. Overall, imports in agriculture rise by 22 percent compared with only 4 percent in nonagriculture.

Because world prices are fixed, the decline in prices in Pakistan because of the trade reform increases the country's competitiveness.[10] There is a real depreciation of 6.1 percent in the exchange rate. The results, shown in Table 13.9, indicate that, except for forestry and fishing, the exports of agriculture—primary agriculture and lightly processed food—improve. Overall, agricultural exports expand by 4.8 percent. However, this increase does not offset the displacement effects of the surge in imports by 22 percent. Thus, the overall output of agriculture declines by 0.7 percent. The biggest reductions are in forestry (21 percent), vegetable oil (7 percent), and fishing (5 percent). However, there is an improvement in raw cotton production because of the increase in the output of cotton lint and yarn, as well as textiles (see elsewhere below).

Table 13.9. The sectoral effects of the unilateral liberalization of all goods trade, Pakistan

Sectors	Output		Domestic demand		Composite good		Exports		Imports		Value added		Return to capital
	x	*px*	*d*	*pd*	*q*	*pq*	*e*	*pe*	*m*	*pm*	*va*	*pva*	
Agriculture													
Primary agriculture													
1. Wheat, irrigated	2.2	–2.2	0.6	–2.2	–0.4	–1.9	58.0	–2.2	–30.9	11.2	2.2	–0.9	2.0
2. Wheat, nonirrigated	–0.6	–2.5	–0.6	–2.5	–0.6	–2.5	0.0	0.0	0.0	0.0	–0.6	–1.3	–2.1
3. Paddy, IRRI	0.7	–2.5	0.7	–2.5	0.7	–2.5	0.0	0.0	0.0	0.0	0.7	–1.5	–0.5
4. Paddy, basmati	0.9	–2.6	0.9	–2.6	0.9	–2.6	0.0	0.0	0.0	0.0	0.9	–1.7	0.5
5. Raw cotton	4.3	–2.6	4.3	–2.6	4.3	–2.6	0.0	0.0	0.0	0.0	4.3	–0.8	5.0
6. Sugarcane	–1.3	–2.7	–1.3	–2.7	–1.3	–2.7	0.0	0.0	0.0	0.0	–1.3	–1.8	–3.5
7. Other major crops	–0.2	–1.6	–1.0	–1.6	–0.4	–1.9	32.6	–1.6	13.9	–8.3	–0.2	–1.3	–1.5
8. Fruits and vegetables	–0.8	–1.5	–2.0	–1.5	–0.4	–2.3	32.2	–1.5	15.2	–9.3	–0.8	–1.7	–2.7
9. Livestock, cattle, and dairy	–0.5	–3.3	–0.6	–3.3	0.1	–3.6	41.8	–3.3	99.0	–32.0	–0.5	–5.0	–5.7
10. Poultry	–0.6	–3.6	–0.7	–3.6	–0.7	–3.6	43.9	–3.6	0.0	0.0	–0.6	–5.7	–6.5
11. Forestry	–21.2	–1.9	–3.3	–1.9	–0.3	–3.2	–41.7	–1.9	9.9	–7.5	–21.2	–1.6	0.0
12. Fishing industry	–4.9	–9.2	0.6	–9.2	0.6	–9.2	–18.5	–9.2	–3.4	–7.5	–4.9	–13.7	–19.3

(*Continued*)

Table 13.9. (*Continued*)

Sectors	Output		Domestic demand		Composite good		Exports		Imports		Value added		Return to capital
	x	*px*	*d*	*pd*	*q*	*pq*	*e*	*pe*	*m*	*pm*	*va*	*pva*	
Lightly processed food													
14. Vegetable oil	−6.8	−3.8	−6.8	−3.8	0.1	−7.2	44.8	−3.8	17.7	−14.5	−6.8	−34.9	−37.9
15. Wheat, milled	−0.6	−1.2	−1.1	−1.2	0.2	−1.7	34.8	−1.2	39.6	−15.4	−0.6	0.1	−0.3
16. Rice, milled IRRI	1.5	0.7	−0.1	0.7	−0.1	0.7	3.3	0.7	0.0	0.0	1.5	5.5	6.5
17. Rice, milled basmati	1.3	0.3	−0.3	0.3	−0.3	0.3	5.2	0.3	0.0	0.0	1.3	5.0	5.9
18. Sugar	−1.4	−1.5	−1.4	−1.5	0.0	−2.0	51.5	−1.5	215.2	−33.5	−1.4	−1.2	−2.1
Nonagriculture													
Mining and manufacturing													
13. Mining	−4.0	−8.6	1.1	−8.6	−1.3	−7.5	−21.0	−8.6	−1.9	−7.3	−4.0	−10.4	−15.1
19. Other food	2.6	2.9	6.0	2.9	−1.1	0.2	11.3	2.9	38.1	−15.4	2.6	10.3	12.2
20. Cotton lint and yarn	5.0	1.7	2.5	1.7	3.7	1.1	12.0	1.7	37.5	−11.8	5.0	13.8	17.6
21. Textiles	4.1	1.6	−0.9	1.6	0.8	0.8	12.3	1.6	32.8	−11.8	4.1	9.6	12.6
22. Leather	8.9	−0.5	−0.2	−0.5	1.1	−1.2	22.7	−0.5	27.8	−11.8	8.9	20.0	27.0
23. Wood products	−1.8	−1 7	−1.8	−1.7	−0.5	−2.3	7.2	−1.7	15.9	−9.3	−1.8	−0.3	−1.5
24. Chemicals	−2.5	−4.6	−6.7	−4.6	0.6	−8.0	21.2	−4.6	3.6	−9.3	−2.5	−4.6	−6.2

(*Continued*)

Table 13.9. (*Continued*)

Sectors	Output		Domestic demand		Composite good		Exports		Imports		Value added		Return to capital
	x	*px*	*d*	*pd*	*q*	*pq*	*e*	*pe*	*m*	*pm*	*va*	*pva*	
25. Cement and bricks	–1.4	–4.7	–1.4	–4.7	–1.4	–4.7	21.7	–4.7	0.0	0.0	–1.4	–4.8	–5.7
26. Petroleum refining	–3.8	–4.8	–3.8	–4.8	1.1	–7.1	0.0	0.0	6.3	–9.3	–3.8	–5.5	–7.9
27. Other manufacturing	–0.8	–3.5	–7.9	–3.5	1.0	–7.7	15.5	–3.5	4.7	–9.3	–0.8	0.5	0.0
Other industry													
28. Energy	0.3	–0 5	0.3	–0.5	0.3	–0.5	0.0	0.0	0.0	0.0	0.3	2.7	2.8
29 Construction	–1.7	–2.9	–1.7	–2.9	–1.7	–2.9	0.0	0.0	0.0	0.0	–1.7	1.3	0.1
Services													
30. Commerce	–0.4	0.5	–0.4	0.5	0.4	0.5	11.1	0.5	–5.5	5.7	–0.4	1.5	1.2
31. Transport	1.7	–1.3	–0.6	–1.3	0.6	–1.3	15.2	–1.3	0.0	0.0	1.7	3.4	4.6
32. Housing	0.0	–11.7	0.0	–11.7	0.0	–11.7	0.0	0.0	0.0	0.0	0.0	–13.6	–13.6
33. Private services	–0.4	–0.7	–0.4	–0.7	0.8	–0.3	13.9	–0.7	–6.7	5.7	–0.4	1.2	0.9
34. Public services	–0.7	0.5	–0.7	0.5	–0.7	0.5	0.0	0.0	0.0	0.0	–0.7	2.1	0.0

Source: National CGE model simulations by the authors.

Note: *x* = output, *px* = output price, *d* = domestic demand, *pd* = domestic price, *q* = composite good, *pq* = composite price. *e* = exports, *pe* = export price. *m* = imports, *pm* = import price, *va* = value added. *pva* = value added price.

In nonagriculture, almost all sectors realize positive growth in exports. Overall, exports in nonagriculture increase by 13 percent. The increase in manufacturing exports is also substantial, especially in major export items such as cotton lint and yarn, textiles, other food, and other manufacturing, There is also a notable increase in the exports of services such as commerce, transport, and private services.

For other food, the increase in imports displaces domestic demand by 6 percent. However, this is offset by the increase in exports; thus, the output of other food improves by 2.6 percent, while the output price improves by 2.9 percent. The impact on textiles may be analyzed in relation to the effects on the cotton lint and yarn sector and the raw cotton sector. The increase in textile imports displaces domestic demand by 0.9 percent. However, this is offset by the increase in textile exports; thus, textile output improves by 4.1 percent, while the output price improves by 1.6 percent. Because the cotton lint and yarn sector supplies materials to the textile sector, the improvement in the output of textiles because of the greater exports leads to an improvement in the domestic demand for cotton lint and yarn by 2.5 percent. The increase in both the exports and the domestic demand for cotton lint and yarn leads to 5.0 percent more output and a rise in the output price by 1.7 percent, which, in turn, leads to 4.3 percent more output of raw cotton.

The negative change in the value added prices in agriculture leads to lower prices for factors that are used heavily in agriculture. The wages of farmers decrease by 0.6 percent; the returns to land fall by 1,9 percent; and the average returns to agricultural capital fall by 5 percent.

The average output price in nonagriculture decreases by 1.1 percent, but the value added price improves by 1.3 percent. The increase arises from the notable improvement in the value added prices of leather (20 percent), cotton lint and yarn (14 percent), other food (10 percent), textiles (10 percent), and transport (3 percent) (see Table 13.9). Thus, the prices of the factors used in nonagriculture improve. The wages of unskilled workers increase by 1.5 percent and of skilled labor by 2.1 percent, while the average returns to nonagricultural capital rise by 1 percent. Furthermore, there is a significant decline in the consumer price index. Thus, net of the inflation effects, factor prices improve except for the average returns to the capital used in agriculture.

The nominal incomes of farmers drop (Table 13.8). This occurs largely because of the declines in the wages of farmers, in the returns to land, and in the average returns to capital in agriculture. Because of the higher wages of workers, the nominal incomes of nonfarmers improve except for the nominal incomes of urban nonpoor households. The incomes of the urban nonpoor decline because of the income tax replacement imposed on this group. However, the decline in consumer prices is significant for all groups. This offsets the decline in nominal incomes except in the case of the urban nonpoor.

In sum, all households, except urban nonpoor households, realize an increase in real incomes, which leads to a significant decline in poverty. The urban poor experience the largest increase in incomes and the largest drop in the depth of poverty. Income inequality is reduced.

S2B: Unilateral agricultural liberalization by Pakistan

Our fourth experiment sets only agricultural price distortions in Pakistan at zero, while retaining all nonagricultural trade taxes and assuming no changes in the global model.[11] Overall, the poverty effects are significantly lower in this experiment compared with the S2A scenario. Furthermore, there are differences in the effects across households. Urban households experience a decline in poverty, and, although overall poverty in rural areas declines, large- and medium-farm households face increasing poverty.

The results at the macro, sectoral, factor, and commodity price levels explain these poverty effects. At the sectoral level, the import prices of agriculture drop by 14 percent (Table 13.7). The largest declines are in sugar (36 percent); livestock, cattle, and dairy (34 percent); milled wheat (18 percent); and vegetable oil (18 percent).[12] There is also a reduction in domestic prices, but this is significantly smaller than the drop in import prices. Thus, the imports of agricultural goods surge by 30 percent.

This agricultural liberalization results in a real exchange rate depreciation. Because tariffs and subsidies in nonagriculture are retained, the average import prices in nonagriculture increase by only 2.6 percent, while the domestic prices in nonagriculture increase by 1.11 percent. Thus, the imports of nonagricultural products decline by 0.5 percent. On the other hand, the exports of nonagricultural products improve by 3.1 percent. At the sectoral level, the increase is caused by the strong export effect on leather, wood products, cotton lint and yarn, and commerce. Because world prices are fixed and the domestic and output prices of nonagriculture increase, the increase in nonagricultural exports is caused by the depreciation in the exchange rate. The increase in nonagricultural exports, together with the marginal increase in the domestic demand for nonagricultural products, leads to an improvement in nonagricultural output by 0.4 percent.

The prices of the factors used in agriculture decline. The wages of farmers decrease by 2.2 percent; the returns to land, by 2.5 percent; and the average returns to capital, by 3.8 percent. However, the prices of factors used heavily in nonagriculture improve. We observe a similar pattern in factor prices after we net out the marginal decline of 0.27 percent in the consumer price index.

The nominal incomes of farmers decline, while the nominal incomes of nonfarmers improve. The marginal decline in the consumer price index does not offset the decrease in the nominal incomes of farmers, especially large- and medium-farm households. Thus, the real income of these farm households is lower. However, nonfarmers enjoy higher real incomes, except for the urban nonpoor, among whom real incomes fall slightly as a result of the tax burden they bear. Nonetheless, the additional tax burden is not sufficiently large to push the urban nonpoor below the poverty line (unlike the case of scenario S2A); so, poverty declines in urban areas. Although the overall poverty in rural areas declines, large- and medium-farm households face increasing poverty because of declining real incomes.

S3A: Full trade liberalization by Pakistan and the rest of the world

Our fifth experiment combines the trade liberalization in the rest of the world with that in Pakistan in all sectors. The effects of the unilateral trade liberalization in Pakistan are larger than the effects of the rest-of-the-world trade liberalization. The combined impact on both exports and imports is strongly positive. There is also a large decline in the consumer price index. Factor prices in agriculture decline, but they improve in nonagriculture. However, net of the inflation effects, the only decline in factor returns occurs in the average returns to the capital used in agriculture. The nominal incomes of farmers decline, while the nominal incomes among nonfarmers improve. The large reduction in the consumer price index contributes to an increase in the real incomes of all households except urban nonpoor households.

This scenario generates the largest reduction in poverty. Another point worth highlighting is that, while the incidence of poverty among the urban nonpoor increases, the increase is much smaller in this experiment than in scenario S2A.

S3B: Agricultural liberalization by Pakistan and the rest of the world

Our sixth experiment combines the agricultural liberalization of the rest of the world with that in Pakistan. It turns out that the effects of the reform in Pakistan dominate those of the agricultural liberalization in the rest of the world. There is also an upward response in imports and exports, but in agriculture only. The surge in agricultural imports displaces local production. This results in lower prices for the factors used in agriculture. Factor prices in nonagriculture increase because the sector remains protected. Therefore, farmers have lower incomes, while nonfarmers benefit.

Sensitivity analysis: Indirect versus direct tax replacement

The results discussed above are derived using a replacement income tax. Because the SAM we have used to calibrate the model has an income tax on urban nonpoor households only (Table 13.4), the direct tax replacement puts all the burden of financing the trade reform on this group. As an alternative, we consider, in this subsection, the assessment of indirect taxes to offset the losses in government tariff revenue that are generated by reform. We focus on the poverty effects of these two tax replacement schemes in scenarios S3A (full trade liberalization of all goods in the rest of the world and in Pakistan) and S3B (agricultural liberalization in the rest of the world and in Pakistan).

The effects on real income across households are presented in Table 13.10. In scenario S3A, in which all sectors are liberalized, changing the tax replacement from a direct tax to an indirect tax completely alters the results. Under the direct tax replacement, all households enjoy higher real incomes except urban nonpoor households. This tax replacement scheme therefore redistributes income from the urban nonpoor to the rest of the household groups. These latter household groups benefit from the reduction in consumer prices and from the redistribution of income from the urban nonpoor households. However, if an indirect tax replacement is used,

Table 13.10. Sensitivity analysis of household welfare effects, two tax replacement schemes, Pakistan

Households	2001–02 population distrubution, %	S3A Direct tax	S3A Indirect tax	S3B Direct tax	S3B Indirect tax
Large-farm households					
–Sindh	0.1	1.96	–0.49	–1.51	–1.65
–Punjab	0.2	2.47	–0.08	–1.29	–1.42
–Other Pakistan	0.0	2.90	0.18	–1.12	–1.26
Medium-farm households					
–Sindh	1.0	1.94	–0.75	–1.06	–1.20
–Punjab	1.9	2.52	–0.31	–0.77	–0.92
–Other Pakistan	0.8	2.40	–0.40	–1.30	–1.45
Small-farm households					
–Sindh	2.8	2.28	–0.70	–0.25	–0.40
–Punjab	12.9	2.44	–0.55	–0.10	–0.25
–Other Pakistan	5.7	2.52	–0.56	0.18	0.03
Small-farm renters, landless					
–Sindh	0.2	2.25	–0.92	–0.03	–0.18
–Punjab	1.5	2.64	–0.53	–0.03	–0.13
–Other Pakistan	0.6	2.59	–0.51	–0.04	–0.20
Rural agricultural workers, landless					
–Sindh	4.1	3.33	–0.48	0.98	0.80
–Punjab	2.0	3.40	–0.36	1.00	0.82
–Other Pakistan	0.9	2.87	–0.47	0.82	0.66
Rural nonfarm households					
–nonpoor	17.6	4.25	0.55	0.47	0.29
–poor	18.1	3.11	–0.41	0.80	0.63
Urban households					
–nonpoor	22.5	–3.69	0.63	–0.12	0.10
–poor	7.2	4.28	–0.14	0.93	0.71

Source: National CGE model simulations by the authors.

consumer prices increase because of the taxes, and the burden is shared among all household groups depending upon household consumption structures. There is a reduction in household incomes among most of the groups except the three relatively wealthy groups (the large-farm households in other Pakistan, the rural nonpoor, and the urban nonpoor). Under this tax replacement scheme, there is a significant increase in domestic prices because of the higher indirect taxes.

If the trade liberalization is focused on agriculture only under S3B, the income results are not sensitive to the tax replacement scheme used. This is because the net government budget implications of the elimination of the distortions are not as large in agriculture as in nonagriculture. Thus, the impact on domestic prices through higher indirect taxes is not as significant in the case of agricultural liberalization as in the case of the trade liberalization of all goods. In both tax replacement schemes, farmers, particularly large- and medium-farm households, are negatively affected, while nonfarmers are favorably affected. However, in the direct tax replacement scheme, the urban nonpoor are still negatively affected, while they are favorably affected in the indirect tax replacement scheme.

Table 13.11 presents the poverty results based on this sensitivity analysis. Trade liberalization in all goods globally under the indirect tax replacement scheme is poverty increasing in scenario S3A. This is because of the dec-lining real incomes among most groups. This effect arises largely because of the higher consumer prices resulting from the indirect tax replacement scheme. The higher consumer prices wipe out the gains accruing because of the higher border export prices, the lower border import prices, and the lower tariffs.

Agricultural liberalization alone entails a smaller fiscal burden. Therefore, both the direct income tax replacement scheme and the indirect tax replacement scheme generate favorable effects on poverty. In the case of the indirect income tax replacement scheme, although it increases consumer prices, it does not wipe out the gains achieved through the higher border export prices, the lower border import prices, and the lower trade taxes on agricultural commodities. Because of the negative effects of the agricultural liberalization on domestic agriculture in Pakistan, farmers will be hurt, especially large- and medium-farm households. However, this is a small segment in the total population and exhibits the lowest incidence of poverty (23 percent in 2001–02 compared with 37 percent among

Table 13.11. Sensitivity analysis of poverty effects, two tax replacement schemes, Pakistan

		S3A		S3B	
Households	**2001–02 index**	**Direct tax**	**Indirect tax**	**Direct tax**	**Indirect tax**
All Pakistan					
–PO	31.2	–6.4	0.5	–1.8	–1.2
–P1	6.5	–11.5	1.5	–2.5	–1.8
–P2	2.0	–13.8	1.8	–3.0	–2.2
All Urban					
–PO	19.9	0.4	0.0	–2.7	–2.3
–P1	3.9	–14.8	0.6	–3.7	–2.9
–P2	1.2	–18.3	0.7	–4.3	–3.3
All rural					
–PO	38.2	–8.6	0.6	–1.5	–0.9
–P1	8.0	–10.5	1.7	–2.1	–1.5
–P2	2.5	–12.5	2.1	–2.6	–1.9
Large- and medium-farm households					
–PO	22.8	–7.9	2.2	3.4	3.4
–P1	4.1	–10.0	2.4	5.3	6.0
–P2	1.1	–10.6	2.8	5.8	6.6
Small-farm households and agricultural workers					
–PO	37.4	–8.7	1.5	–0.9	–0.3
–P1	7.5	–10.3	2.2	–1.3	–0.6
–P2	2.2	–12.4	2.6	–1.6	–0.9
Rural nonfarm households					
–PO	39.9	–8.5	0.0	–2.1	–1.5
–P1	8.7	–10.6	1.5	–2.8	–2.2
–P2	2.8	–12.6	1.8	–3.4	–2.7

Source: National CGE model simulations by the authors.
Note: PO = poverty headcount. P1 = poverty gap. P2 = poverty severity.

small-farm households and agricultural workers and 40 percent among rural nonfarmers).

Summary and Policy Implications

In this chapter, we have linked the results of two economic models—the Linkage model of the World Bank and the Pakistan CGE model that we have developed—to analyze and compare the poverty effects of trade liberalization abroad with the corresponding effects of unilateral reform by Pakistan. We have conducted six policy experiments: two rest-of-the-world trade liberalization experiments (full liberalization that covers all goods sectors and agriculture only), two unilateral trade liberalization cases (all goods and agriculture only), and two combined scenarios. The results are evaluated under a direct tax replacement scheme among household incomes; the direct tax is paid only by the urban nonpoor. We also examine an alternative tax replacement scheme, an indirect tax on commodities.

A number of policy insights may be drawn from our simulation results. The impacts on the Pakistan economy and on the extent of poverty in the country from own-country liberalization are significantly larger than the impacts from rest-of-the-world trade liberalization. The effects of agricultural liberalization (both in the rest-of-the-world market and in Pakistan) are considerably smaller than the effects of the liberalization of all goods trade. This is because of the smaller share of agricultural trade in overall exports and imports in Pakistan, in which trade is dominated by nonagricultural products.

The income from trade taxes is a major source of revenue for the government. The trade tax revenue is considerably lower from agricultural commodities than from nonagricultural products. Thus, the elimination of the trade taxes on all tradable commodities creates a large dent in government income and in the fiscal balance. It therefore entails a significant government demand for tax revenue from other sources. The poverty and income effects of full trade liberalization greatly depend upon how the tax replacement is implemented. If an additional tax is imposed on household incomes to generate funds to finance the reduction in trade taxes in all sectors, there is a notable decline of consumer prices and a large income redistribution from urban nonpoor households to the rest of the household groups. There is therefore a considerable decline in the incidence of poverty, in the depth of poverty, and in income inequality. This is because the burden of the additional tax falls entirely on the urban nonpoor, while the rest of the groups benefit from higher real factor prices and larger reductions in consumer prices. However, if the tax replacement is imposed as additional indirect taxes on commodities, consumer prices increase and eliminate the benefits generated from the reduction in trade distortions. In this case, poverty rises.

The trade tax revenue is considerably lower from agricultural commodities than from nonagricultural products. If trade liberalization is focused on agricultural commodities only, the fiscal refinancing requirement is substantially less urgent. The poverty reduction effects, although smaller, are robust to the change in tax policy, that is, poverty is reduced under both tax replacement schemes if only agricultural markets are liberalized.

All these results are derived using a static model. The dynamic impact of trade reform on capital accumulation from the changes in prices has not been accounted for. For example, if the rates of return to capital are high in sectors in which the poor are heavily engaged, this will attract investment, thereby increasing capital accumulation in these sectors and output from these sectors. This would have favorable implications for poverty. (It is also possible that the results would be reversed and would therefore generate negative effects on the poor.) Furthermore, the dynamic effects would have an impact on technological progress, the movement of the labor of farm households into nonfarm employment, factor and total productivity, and the flow of foreign direct investment. These are all empirical issues that are relevant topics for further research.

Notes

1. Estimates of agricultural assistance in Pakistan, based on Dorosh and Salam (2009), are incorporated in the World Bank's Distortions to Agricultural Incentives Project Database (Anderson and Valenzuela 2008). The estimates cover five decades. The representative values for CGE modeling as of 2004 that are used here are available in Valenzuela and Anderson (2008).
2. The specification of the Pakistan CGE model is based on EXTER (see Decaluwé, Dumont, and Robichaud 2000).
3. Cororaton and Orden (2008) include a dynamic analysis in which sectoral capital adjusts over time.
4. The direct tax replacement on household income is specified as:

$$dyh = yh(1 - dtxrh[1 + ndtxrh]),$$

where *dyh* is disposable income; *yh* is income before income taxes; *dtxrh* is the income tax rate at the base; and *ndtxrh* is the income tax replacement. The indirect tax replacement on commodities is specified as:

$$pd = pl(1 + itxr)(1 + nitx),$$

where *pd* is the domestic price; *pi* is the local price before indirect taxes; *itxr* is the indirect tax rate at the base; and *nitx* is the indirect tax replacement.

5. Sectoral informal capital is also in the SAM. The returns to informal capital may be considered primarily as payments to labor outside the formal labor market. However, instead of modeling informal capital separately, we have aggregated it with formal capital. There is no significant underestimation of household incomes because informal capital is still being paid based on the returns to capital. However, this aggregation makes the labor share in agriculture appear relatively low.
6. We have set the sectoral values of the parameter *eta* in the export demand function equal to the Armington elasticities in the global model. The sectoral values of the parameter *sig_e* in the export supply function and the sectoral values of the parameter *sig_m* in the import demand function are half the the values of *eta*.
7. There is no real exchange rate variable in the model. The real exchange rate is defined as the world price, multiplied by the nominal exchange rate, divided by the local price, where the world price is the trade-weighted world import and export prices and the local price is the sectoral output- weighted local prices.
8. Detailed sectoral results are shown only for scenario S2A (see Table 13.9). Detailed comparable sectoral results for the other scenarios are available from the authors on request.
9. In the model, the overall government revenue from tariffs is PRs 154 billion and from export taxes, PRs 15 billion. Total government revenue is PRs 446 billion. The total income of the urban nonpoor is PRs 1.73 trillion.
10. In our model, Pakistan is facing a downward-sloping world demand curve. Because the perfect substitution assumption is imposed between exports and domestic sales in Pakistan, the export supply curve is

horizontal. The decrease in output prices raises export supply, which shifts the horizontal export supply curve downward.

11. The total tariff revenue from agricultural imports is PRs 14.2 billion, while farm export tax revenue is PRs 4,3 billion in the baseline.
12. Detailed sectoral results generated under this scenario are available from the authors upon request.

References

Ahmed, V., A. Abbas, and S. Ahmed. 2009. "Taxation Reforms: A CGE-Microsimulation Analysis for Pakistan." Unpublished working paper, Modeling and Policy Impact Analysis Program, Poverty and Economic Policy Research Network, Université Laval, Quebec.

Anderson, K., and E. Valenzuela. 2008. "Estimates of Global Distortions to Agricultural Incentives, 1955–2007." Data spreadsheet, October, World Bank, Washington, DC. http://go.worldbank.org/YA039F35E0.

Cororaton, B. C., and D. Orden. 2008. *Pakistan's Cotton and Textile Economy: Intersectoral Linkages and Effects on Rural and Urban Poverty*. IFPRI Research Report 158. Washington, DC: International Food Policy Research Institute.

Decaluwé B., J.-C. Dumont, and V. Robichaud. 2000. *Basic CCE Models*. Vol. II of *MIMAP Training Session on CGE Modeling*, Micro Impacts of Macroeconomic and Adjustment Policies Program, International Development Research Centre, Canadian Centre for International Studies and Cooperation, and Université Laval, Quebec, http://www.pep-net.org/fileadmin/medias/pdf/volume2.pdf.

Dorosh, P. 2005. "Wheat Markets and Pricing in Pakistan: Political Economy and Policy Options." Wheat Policy Note, South Asia Rural Development Unit, World Bank, Washington, DC.

Dorosh, P., M. K. Niazi, and H. Nazli. 2004. "A Social Accounting Matrix for Pakistan, 2001–02: Methodology and Results." PIDE Working Paper 2006–9, Pakistan Institute of Development Economics, Islamabad, http://econpapers.repec.org/paper/pidwpaper/2006_3a9.htm.

Dorosh, P., and A. Salam. 2009. "Pakistan." In *Distortions to Agricultural Incentives in Asia*, ed. K. Anderson and W. Martin, 379–407. Washington, DC: World Bank.

Federal Bureau of Statistics. 2003. "Household Integrated Economic Survey: Round 4, 2001–02." Federal Bureau of Statistics, Islamabad. http://www.statpak.gov.pk/depts/fbs/statistics/hies0102/hies0102.html.

Foster, J., J. Greer, and E. Thorbecke. 1984. "A Class of Decomposable Poverty Measures." *Econometrica* 52(3): 761–66.

Horridge, M., and F. Zhai. 2006. "Shocking a Single-Country CGE Model with Export Prices and Quantities from a Global Model." In *Poverty and the WTO: Impacts of the Doha Development Agenda*, ed. T. W. Hertel and L. A. Winters, 94–104. London: Palgrave Macmillan; Washington, DC: World Bank.

Ministry of Finance. 2003, *Economic Survey of Pakistan 2002–03*, Islamabad: Economic Advisers Wing, Finance Division, Government of Pakistan. http://www.accountancy.com.pk/docs/Economic_Survey_2002-03.pdf.

Valenzuela, E., and K. Anderson. 2008. "Alternative Agricultural Price Distortions for CGE Analysis of Developing Countries, 2004 and 1980–84." Research Memorandum 13 (December), Center for Global Trade Analysis, Department of Agricultural Economics, Purdue University, West Lafayette, IN. http://www.gtap.agecon.purdue.edu/resources/res_display.asp?RecordID=2925.

van der Mensbrugghe, D. 2005. "Linkage Technical Reference Document: Version 6.0." December, World Bank, Washington, DC. http://go.worldbank.org/7NP2KKlOH0.

World Bank. 2007. *Pakistan, Promoting Rural Growth and Poverty Reduction.* Report 39303-PK. Washington, DC: Sustainable Development Unit, South Asia Region, World Bank.

Section IV:

Sanitary and Phytosanitary Measures

Chapter 14

10

Integrating import risk and trade benefit analysis

RICHARD H. SNAPE AND DAVID ORDEN*

Economists have long emphasised the gains from international trade, but have acknowledged that there can be external diseconomies, including pest and disease risks, associated with importing plant and animal products. The General Agreement on Tariffs and Trade (GATT), both in the original 1947 version and in the 1994 World Trade Organization (WTO) extension of it, follows this lead, with the general rules constraining trade barriers and facilitating their reduction, but with allowance for exceptions, such as for quarantine purposes.

Quarantine scientists and administrators, environmentalists, and farmers facing threats, competitive and pestiferous, from imports, tend to emphasise the risks to production and the environment from trading, rather than the gains to consumers from imported products. This attitude is reflected in the WTO *Agreement on the Application of Sanitary and Phytosanitary Measures* (SPS Agreement). The emphasis of the SPS Agreement is on the determination of risks from plant and animal imports, the appropriate level of protection against these risks, and securing consistent application of these criteria across similar products and from similar sources. There is little if any scope for distinguishing between products with similar risk according to the level of consumer benefit which would accrue if the products

* Nothing in this paper should be taken as expressing the views of the Productivity Commission or the Australian Government.

were to be imported. Nevertheless the SPS Agreement is written as an "exception" to the general rules of GATT 1994.

Some economists have called for more recognition of the gains from trade - in particular the gains to consumers from imported products - in the application of quarantine laws. A few recent studies have provided estimates of these gains and have shown that the benefits of trade exceed expected costs due to pest risks in certain cases (e.g. James and Anderson 1998, and Chapter 11 in this volume by Orden, Narrod and Glauber). Several chapters in this volume and elsewhere (e.g. Chapter 2 by Roberts and Roberts 2000) also examine conceptual and pragmatic dimensions of the relationship between risk evaluation and cost/benefit analysis in quarantine decisions.

In this chapter we present a simple diagram to illustrate the risk-focused versus cost/benefit approaches to policy decisions about trade of products that may pose SPS risks. In Figure 10.1, the horizontal axis measures the risk (weighted by probabilities) of trading particular products. Several authors have developed 'iso-risk' diagrams, with the economic impact of the imports of pests or diseases (if they were to become established domestically) on one axis and the probability of such establishment and spread on the other (e.g. Chapters 8 and 12 in this volume by Bigsby and Binder respectively). The horizontal axis of our Figure 10.1 is simply the dollar value of their iso-risk curves.

The vertical axis of Figure 10.1 shows the other net benefits from importing products that may carry pests or diseases. These are the traditional gains from trade. For any products which are tested or otherwise treated for quarantine purposes, the costs of treatment or testing should be taken into account in determining this other net benefit. Such testing or treatment would of course also reduce the risk (on the horizontal axis) of that product, as shown for example in movement from D' to D in Figure 10.1.

Figure 10.1: Risks and benefits from trade

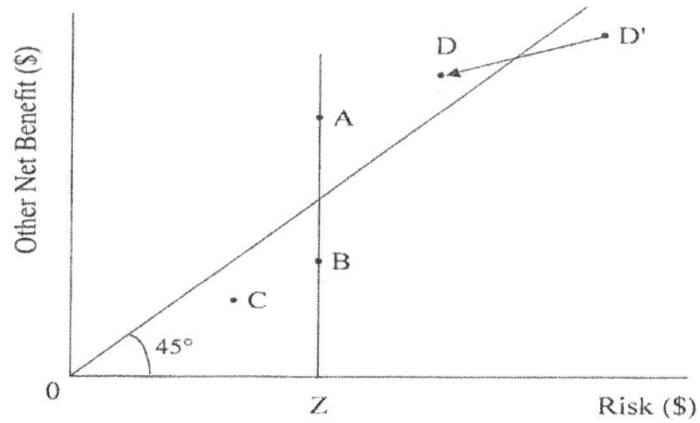

Figure 1

With both the risk and the other net benefits shown in dollar terms (and with consistent time discounting for both) a 45-degree line from the origin indicates the equating of these expected effects of trade. For a neutral policy attitude to risk, this line shows the boundary of positive trade-off of the benefits and risks of imports of particular products. Risk-averse policy would be shown by a steeper curve; risk-loving policy by a flatter one. Based on economic cost/benefit criteria, under a neutral policy attitude toward risk all products with coordinates that are located above the 45-degree line (when the cost-appropriate testing and treatment is accounted for) should be imported. Those products that cannot be raised above the line under any quarantine conditions and treatments should not be imported.

The general rules of the GATT can be viewed as focusing on the vertical axis of Figure 10.1. For products for which there is zero risk, the coordinates lie on this axis and so are above the 45-degree line (at the origin). The general GATT objective for these products is to facilitate the reduction of trade barriers. Reduction of these trade barriers is in the national economic interest of the importing country (leaving aside large-country optimal tariff and similar arguments). But for various political economy reasons, countries often fail to remove trade barriers unilaterally, which is detrimental also to exporters among their trading partners through lost market opportunities. The GATT general rules are an institutional response designed to facilitate mutually beneficial trade barrier reductions. The underlying aim is to achieve the gains from trade by facilitating the international movement among Members of the WTO of products that lie on the vertical axis of Figure 10.1 (involving no risk).

The SPS Agreement as an exception to the GATT general rules can be viewed as predominantly concerned with the horizontal (not the vertical) axis of Figure 10.1. The first aim is to bind countries' policies away from the origin: if there is no credible scientific basis for risk, then quarantine policies are not to be established to limit trade. The second aim of the SPS Agreement is to require countries to select a point on the horizontal axis, such as point Z, that is a standard for their acceptable level of risk or appropriate level of protection (ALOP), and to apply it consistently for all products and for all country sources (including domestic sources). Essentially the aim is to evaluate products relative to a vertical line through point Z – to prevent arbitrary and unjustified quarantine distinctions between products, distinctions that could be used for protection against economic competition. Under the SPS Agreement, products to the left of the vertical line through Z should be permitted; those to the right of Z *may* be prohibited.

Having determined Z, the application of the SPS Agreement would not distinguish between products A and B, even though, on a full cost/benefit analysis, product A should be imported, while product B should not (assuming it is in this location after the best possible quarantine treatment). Even worse from an optimum cost/benefit policy perspective, under the ALOP principle and the specification of point Z, imports of product C would be allowed while those of D would not. By forcing this distinction, the SPS Agreement could preclude a country from implementing a desirable policy from a national cost/benefit perspective.

It may be argued that a product at a point such as D poses no problem as far as the SPS Agreement is concerned because an importing country could decide to relax its quarantine rules to allow the imports of a product with a level of risk above Z, and exporting countries are not likely to complain in such cases. Moreover, if an importing country finds that a large number of products for which it has precluded trade have coordinates like D, it might conclude unilaterally that its ALOP is set too conservatively. A shift of the ALOP to the right would allow more gains from trade to be realised with a consequent increase in risk.[1] Yet there remains concern that many countries have set Z too conservatively, almost indistinguishably from the vertical axis itself. The result may be too many products with coordinates like D that are excluded from trade by quarantine decisions, causing net economic losses.

For the initially chosen Z, a different problem that arises with allowing trade of product D comes through precedent. A WTO Dispute Settlement Panel might later conclude that excluding product C but allowing product D was not consistent with the SPS requirement that an ALOP be applied consistently where similar sources of risk exist.

Quite apart from the precedent set by allowing imports of D products, a problem with respect to trading partners and the potential importing country arises from products with coordinates such as C. Here a decision to exclude is trade restricting, and the decision to exclude cannot be justified under the SPS Agreement in terms of the ALOP set at Z (nor are quarantine procedures justifiable

[1] Digby Gascoine and Ken Forsythe have pointed out that if past quarantine decisions are resulting in products being excluded that lie above the 45-degree line, priority for re-examination should be given to those products whose coordinates are expected to be close to the country's ALOP and furthest above the 45-degree line.

under the Agreement that might reduce risk and move the coordinates of C above the 45-degree line). The problem in this case is that just as countries are not expected to suffer net losses from other trade liberalisation measures under the GATT, no country should be required to bear a burden of risk costs that exceeds the other net benefits from trade (measured for the country as a whole). Yet, that is what application of the principles of the SPS Agreement to product C would require.

Whether excluding products with coordinates such as D or admitting products with coordinates such as C proves more problematic under the SPS Agreement depends on how conservatively the acceptable level of risk is set. The SPS Agreement as interpreted allows for different levels of risk for plant, animal and human health. It may also turn out that the level of risk adopted as acceptable by a country is allowed by WTO Dispute Settlement Panels to be based on scale factors: for example, the dollar value of risk measured relative to the size (e.g. volume of sales) of the industry. These considerations could cause the location of Z to vary among products (or at least among classes of products), but the basic dichotomy would remain between a decision-rule based on setting a level of risk versus a decision rule based on comparing the other net benefits to risks.

Should the SPS Agreement be amended to allow (or even require) Members of the WTO to make quarantine decisions based on cost/benefit assessments instead of ALOP? This would involve not just permitting an adjustment of risk by a scale factor, but also permitting distinctions between products according to the benefits (particularly to consumers) accruing from importing products. This might allow (or even require) countries to adopt best economic policy practices for the benefit of their citizens as a whole, and escape from the emphasis on producer benefits from import restrictions which so often dominate in trade (including quarantine) policy.

But it can also be argued that the purpose of the SPS Agreement is simply to prevent countries from egregious arbitrary and unjustifiable distinctions between products on quarantine grounds, and that if it achieves this it will have achieved a great deal. Taking into account other net benefits of trade could backfire, and open the door to protection against economic competition for particular producers or socio-economic groups in a country.[2] This could undermine what was intended to be achieved under the WTO Agreement on Agriculture. In such event, the alternative decision rule could facilitate what many observers have feared: that as other forms of protection are wound back, economic protection through quarantine provisions could be increased. The best could be the enemy of the good.

References

James, S., and K. Anderson (1998) 'On the need for more economic assessment of quarantine/SPS policies', *Australian Journal of Agricultural and Resource Economics* 42(4): 425-44, December.

Phillips, P.W.B. and W.A. Kerr (2000) 'Alternative paradigms: the WTO versus the biosafety protocol for trade in genetically modified organisms', *Journal of World Trade* 34(4): 63-75, August.

Roberts, D. (2000) 'Sanitary and phytosanitary risk management in the post-Uruguay Round era: an economic perspective', in National Research Council, *Incorporating science, economics and sociology in developing sanitary and phytosanitary standards in international trade,* Washington, DC: National Academy Press.

[2] *Pacé* textiles and clothing protection in developed countries, and Article 26 of the Biosafety Protocol for Trade in Genetically Modified Organisms (Phillips and Kerr 2000, pp. 72-3)

Chapter 15

2

Trade-Related Regulations in the Global Food System

Timothy Josling, Donna Roberts and David Orden

All governments regulate their food sectors extensively. These regulations are set within broader legal frameworks that provide judicial redress in cases of unexpected adverse effects from food production or consumption. Although general legal provisions are an important component of ensuring food safety and quality, the need for specific regulatory measures to buttress this legal framework is widely accepted.

Sound economic reasons exist for food regulations, but the regulatory process is also susceptible to political pressures from narrow interest groups. The result can be ill-advised regulatory measures and levels of protection. Trade frictions arise most frequently when importing countries are prevented by political considerations from implementing the regulatory decisions that emerge from technical rule-making processes. In these cases, exporters feel they are being affected adversely by regulations that restrict their market access for the economic benefit of import-competing domestic producers, or because of unjustified consumer pressures that constrain their ability to offer goods. Thus, although much of the regulation observed in the food sector rests on solid foundations, trade disputes occur when the purpose, severity, or instrumentation of regulations can be questioned.

This chapter sets the stage for analysis of trade-related regulations in the global food system by summarizing the economic rationales for such measures, characterizing regulatory institutions and classifying their outcomes, describing risk assessment and management choices, analyzing the economic effects of regulation on trade, and discussing the political economy of the regulatory overprotection or underprotection that often leads to trade frictions.

Economic Rationales for Food Regulation

A complex system of market, legal, fiscal, and regulatory measures governs the incentives for firms to supply food products that have the safety and quality attributes sought by consumers. Firms that misjudge consumer demand risk losing sales revenue, market share, and their business reputation or brand capital. A country's legal system reinforces the incentives provided by market forces: firms found responsible for contaminated food or consumer fraud may have to compensate plaintiffs seeking legal redress or pay punitive damages.

In many cases, market forces and legal remedies alone provide insufficient incentives for public health and environmental protection. As summarized in John Wilson and Keith Maskus (2002), the economic rationales for some form of government intervention in markets fall broadly into two categories: (1) achieving provision of public goods, and (2) facilitating production and exchange through various means of lowering transactions and information costs. These rationales are especially salient when market failures are associated with the production, processing, distribution, and consumption of food products. The spread of animal and plant diseases, outbreaks of food-borne illnesses, distribution of misleading food labels, or use of production practices that do not reflect contemporary norms may signal the need for corrective measures.

Providing Public Goods

When markets fail, fiscal incentives, such as subsidies or taxes to hasten adoption of new technologies, sometimes offer the best solution. However, mandatory regulatory measures may be needed when the risks associated with products are great, delayed, or imperfectly known, or when no efficient legal system is in place so that citizens find it impossible, costly, or slow to prosecute claims related to domestic or imported goods under product liability or consumer fraud laws. Private firms that violate regulations are subject not only to civil legal liability but also to government penalties, including fines, product recalls, plant closures, new import protocols, or loss of market access.

To the extent that regulations enhance the efficiency of the food sector, they are economically beneficial. Prudent policymakers will weigh the benefits associated with a regulatory action against the costs that it entails. Whatever decision criteria are employed, regulatory choices within countries are primarily national prerogatives, and national institutions occupy the central role in determining, implementing, and enforcing food-sector rules.

Consider, for example, the situation in which the public good provided is a low prevalence of a pest or disease that affects agricultural production. Control of an animal or plant health hazard often cannot be accomplished optimally by individual producers—destroying a diseased animal in one herd, for example, has positive consequences for other herds that will not be realized without government intervention to encourage eradication. Therefore, regulations may be required to achieve the greater production capacity that would result from fewer hazards to crops and livestock. Risk management is a product of activities pursued simultaneously by private agents involved in agricultural production and by related public regulatory agencies. The public agencies will undertake interventions and enforce regulations that determine the overall prevalence of a pest or disease, given private behavior. Private agents will choose their production activities after assessing the prevalence of the hazards they face. The optimal strategies therefore often emerge from joint public- and private-sector efforts to engage in pest and disease control.[1]

Additional complications arise when pests and diseases, by possibly spreading across international borders, threaten international trade opportunities. In such instances, coordination of regulatory policies among countries may be optimal, but often it is not achieved. As a result, quarantines and other restrictions are imposed at national borders, and additional requirements are imposed on production and handling processes within countries, as prerequisites to trade. Tensions persist in the global food system over some of these measures imposed by national governments to protect animal, plant, and human health.

Reducing Transactions Costs

Food regulation also can accomplish desirable objectives under the second rationale—facilitating production and exchange through reduced transactions costs. When information about health or quality attributes is unknown or asymmetrically distributed between producers and consumers, regulations can improve the functioning of markets. Economic theory distinguishes among the search, experience, and credence characteristics of a product—all of which can influence consumers' purchasing behavior (Darby and Karni 1973). Consumers can ascertain search characteristics, such as size of a fruit, through examination before purchase. An experience characteristic, such as how long a product's quality can be maintained or its shelf life, often cannot be determined until after purchase. Consumers accumulate information about the experience characteristics of a food product over time, although with attendant costs of learning. By contrast, consumers cannot determine the existence or extent of a credence characteristic, such as whether the product has pesticide residues or is genetically altered, even after repeated purchases and consumption.

1. Brown, Lynch, and Zilberman (2002) describe the social welfare maximization problem for plant pest control in agricultural production.

When food products have experience and credence characteristics, markets may fail to provide efficient price signals. For example, when provided with imperfect information, consumers may not pay for desired levels of safety or producers may not supply improved safety. In these situations, government regulations can improve market efficiency. Public intervention is justified economically when a food safety measure, such as legally mandated limits on pesticide residues, improves social welfare net of industry costs. Regulated grades, standards, and labeling are other tools available to governments to reduce the transactions costs that impede efficient production and exchange.

Geographical indications (GIs) that identify the producer or region of production are a somewhat unusual tool for remedying information failures in food markets. GIs are a form of intellectual property that has a potential value in the market that is jointly created by private-sector investments in production and marketing and the public laws and regulations that protect these investments. GIs are therefore club goods (excludable but not rival) which organized producers can use to privately appropriate the surplus generated by their application. Some producers have long used GIs, such as "Bordeaux," to command premium prices for their products in domestic and foreign markets. The explosion in global demand for distinctive wines, spirits, and food products over the past decade has heightened interest in their use and attention to their regulation (Maskus 2000).

Food Regulation and Trade

The majority of food regulations are social welfare–enhancing measures that may place legitimate restrictions on trade. Nonetheless, food regulations are increasingly appearing at the center of trade disputes. One difficulty for the global food system is that the incidence of risks or available market information can vary across countries. Thus the benefits of a regulation may exceed its costs in one country but not elsewhere. Another difficulty is that regulations may rest on comparisons of nonmarket benefits with market costs and therefore may be more susceptible than otherwise to challenge by trading partners. But perhaps the most significant problem for the global food system is that both the stringency of regulations and the provision of farm support and protection policies tend to increase among wealthier countries, complicating the political economy of the regulation of food.

Classification of Regulations

Classification of food regulations by their goals, attribute focus, and other dimensions will serve as an initial road map to an otherwise diffuse set of measures at the domestic and international levels. The instruments that make the regulations operative, as well as conformity assessment mechanisms, also can be classified according to their type. Indeed, such classifications provide policymakers and analysts with an organizational framework for discussing trade disputes and for negotiating international regulatory guidelines. They also act as a conceptual foundation for evaluating food regulations and as a guide to specification of economic models to gauge the trade and welfare effects of these measures.

First it is helpful to distinguish between the national and international institutions through which regulations are promulgated and administered and the sets of regulations and directives produced by these decision-making bodies.

Regulatory Institutions

Food regulatory institutions comprise the legislative and executive bodies that formulate laws and directives related to the food sector; the judicial systems by which those laws are adjudicated and enforced; and the administrative agencies that are responsible for implementing the regulatory mandates imposed by laws and executive decisions. National food regulatory institutions have characteristics that reflect the political circumstances and other factors specific to a country. Regulatory institutions therefore differ substantially among countries.

Systematic differences among institutional structures of countries may be reflected in differences in regulatory outcomes. In turn, systematic differences among the outcomes of the regulatory institutions of a given country also may occur as control over institutions shifts among domestic political parties or in response to evolving public expectations. Thus food regulatory institutions can be described in terms of their structure and prevailing philosophy during a particular period of time, though nations can and do make changes in these institutions. Because of national sovereignty, domestic regulatory institutions are themselves rarely the subject of international trade conflicts. International regulatory institutions, including their operating procedures and even philosophical orientation, are more commonly the subject of dispute among nations.

Dimensions of Food Regulations

The substantive output of food regulatory institutions is manifest in the large collections of laws and directives that embody, or lead to, food regulations. A classification of such regulations along four basic dimensions exemplifies the range of options open to countries (see table 2.1). The classification variables are goals, attribute focus, breadth (across

Table 2.1 Classification scheme for food regulations

Dimension	Classification
Goals	*Risk-reducing.* Regulations that ensure an acceptable level of animal, plant, or human health or safety
	Quality. Regulations that provide differentiation of goods based on content and process attributes not directly related to health or safety
Attribute focus	*Content attributes.* Regulations that target material aspects of the product
	Process attributes. Regulations that target the processes by which a product is produced, processed, handled, or distributed
Breadth	*Vertical.* Regulations specific to a single product or closely related products in one or more stages of the marketing chain
	Horizontal. Regulations applied across products that are not necessarily closely related
Scope	*Uniform.* Regulations that apply equally to products of domestic and foreign origin
	Specific. Regulations that apply only to imported products, often only of certain origins

products), and scope (among domestic and foreign goods). Each of these variables distinguishes regulations in some way that can be significant in gauging the impacts of regulatory decisions on international trade.

Goals of Regulations

The classification of regulations by their goals is clearly relevant to the task of evaluating their success. Goals also play a role in identifying the trade rules under which a regulation can be challenged. An important distinction, as noted earlier, is between risk-reducing measures and those aimed at providing the quality or product differentiation that is of interest to consumers but has little to do with risks to health or safety. This distinction is important when considering the significance of risk assessment, risk management, and risk communication in regulatory decision making. As noted, risk-reducing measures are subject to a substantial amount of scientific advice. The public good element provided is a degree of collective security to domestic producers, processors, and consumers. Quality-related regulations, by contrast, are adopted by governments to provide consumers with the information they need to make informed decisions.

Trade difficulties over regulations can become particularly intractable when two goals are addressed by one measure. This is the case in the current dispute over genetically modified foods, where some countries cite food safety and environmental risks in justifying regulations that reflects national food quality preferences related to methods of production. Such linkages of goals are often associated with new technologies: tensions within societies on the desirability of adopting new production and processing techniques can spill over into regulations designated as safety guarantees. Domestic interest groups opposed to the technology would have an incentive to make this link so that they could form coalitions and raise the visibility of the issue on the domestic political agenda. Fusion of goals in the articulation of regulatory measures puts a particular strain on international trade relations and often brings charges of covert protectionism.

Attribute Focus of Regulations

The second way in which to classify food regulations—whether the regulation focuses on a content or process attribute of the product—was also mentioned in chapter 1. Regulations that target content attributes include those that establish requirements for existence or quantity. Examples include requirements for fortification of enriched grain products with folic acid or for a minimum butterfat content for products labeled "ice cream." Measures that target process attributes might indicate the source or origin of the product, such as mandatory country-of-origin labeling, or method of production or processing, such as a requirement for shrimp to be harvested using turtle excluder devices (TEDs).

Regulations that target process attributes are especially prone to controversy. Many consumers value information about the methods used in producing their food, and well-designed regulations can improve the functioning of markets. So, too, can other regulations adopted to help farmers to differentiate their products. These measures target production methods to facilitate the creation of value added at the farm level. Regulations with a process attribute focus, such as organic standards, can establish the means for producers to successfully adopt a higher-profit, higher-cost, consumer-oriented business model that emphasizes product quality and diversity—a potentially attractive alternative to the low-cost, high-volume model required for bulk commodities. Policymakers may intend that such regulations create market-oriented mechanisms to relieve some downward pressures on producer incomes. But such regulations may not improve market performance if they become barriers to trade and their design creates the opportunity for some favored producers to exclude others from the domestic (or foreign) marketplace.

Even those process attribute regulations that arise primarily in response to consumer rather than producer interests can lead to greater trade frictions if the requirements for verifying compliance are viewed as overly prescriptive. Competitive food suppliers usually have private (voluntary) tracking systems and standards in place in response to market and legal incentives. The objectives of these private systems are to improve supply-side management through monitoring production flows and retail activity, to facilitate the development of highly differentiated products for niche markets, and to pinpoint product quality defects (Golan, Krissoff, et al. 2003). Mandatory regulations that increase the required breadth, precision, or depth of a firm's tracking system may increase the reliability of quality claims and therefore benefit attribute-conscious consumers. These regulatory regimes may also benefit some firms if increased consumer confidence leads to increased product purchases (Unnevehr and Nelson 2002). But both domestic firms and a country's trading partners may object to traceability and other regulations when they substantially increase verification costs in instances in which it seems unlikely that consumers would be willing to pay a sufficient premium for the regulated attribute.

Breadth of Regulations

The breadth of coverage among products is a third useful way in which to classify food regulations. The basic choice is between "vertical" regulations, which apply to a single product or closely related products at one or more stages of production and processing, and "horizontal" regulations, which apply across many products that are not necessarily closely related.

Most countries employ a mixture of vertical and horizontal regulations in their food sector, and the distinction is used widely in discussions of the EU body of regulations and directives. Vertical regulations tend to be used when a particular subsector has unique problems or conditions. Horizontal regulations are more feasible if the regulatory issues are general, or if the subsector is widely dispersed.

The choice has implications for the type of measures imposed and the ease of their operation in an open economy. Vertical regulations have certain advantages for the industry concerned, such as creating scale economies or barriers to entry, and tend to be developed with the help of such interests. Horizontal regulations are often more attractive to consumer and environmental groups—for them, the wider breadth is an advantage—and where the industry view is less cohesive.

Both vertical and horizontal regulations can pose challenges in international trade. For vertical regulations, which affect different levels of the production, marketing, and distribution of a product, problems may be associated with the various stages being undertaken in different countries. For horizontal regulations, their application to many products is likely to cause trade tensions unless equivalent regulations are in place among trading partners.

Scope of Regulations

The scope of food regulations refers to whether their application depends on where a product originates. Many food regulations apply to goods from all sources, domestic and foreign—a feature that distinguishes these measures from standard trade policy instruments. Regulations that apply to domestic and foreign goods can be termed "uniform." Still other regulatory measures are applied only to imported goods. Frequently, regulations are directed only at products from certain countries and are therefore termed "specific." These measures are used to mitigate different levels of risk posed by imports from different sources. An importing country may use a variety of regulatory measures to mitigate the risks associated with importing one product from different locations, which inherently raises the prospect of trade disputes arising from claims of discrimination.

The scope of a regulatory measure has implications for who will bear the cost of its imposition. Uniform regulations generally affect the final delivery costs of goods for domestic as well as foreign producers. Domestic interests may nonetheless lobby for socially suboptimal measures that raise their own unit costs if such regulations limit competition (Hoeckman and Leidy 1993). The incentives for such behavior vary with the number and relative size of firms, the production technologies, and the type of good (Thilmany and Barrett 1996). Specific regulations have more potential to segment international markets, fundamentally altering the nature of competition. They may transform a "small" country into a "large" country in international markets or create market power for individual firms (Sumner and Lee 1997).

Instruments Used in Food Regulations

Although some international disputes are best understood in terms of the dimensions of regulations just described, often these disputes revolve around specific policy instruments. An increasing number of instruments are available to governments for implementing food regulations (OECD 1997). This range of instruments can be conveniently divided into quantitative restrictions, technical standards, and informational remedies (see box 2.1).

Quantitative Restrictions

Of the instruments used to implement food regulations, quantitative restrictions, including import bans, are the most explicitly trade-limiting. These restrictions are most appropriate when the risks or uncertainties posed by a hazard are great and alternative measures for effectively reducing the risk to negligible levels are technically infeasible. Such cases

Box 2.1 Trade-based food regulatory instruments

Quantitative restrictions	→	Spatial (national and regional) bans on imports Temporal restrictions (quarantine periods and seasonal access) Export prohibitions
Technical specifications	→	Product standards Process standards
Informational remedies	→	Mandatory disclosure Controls on voluntary claims

arise, for example, when current monitoring and detection technology cannot distinguish between imports of hazardous and nonhazardous products, or when effective treatments or eradication programs do not exist. Import bans are most frequently used to protect livestock, crops, and native species of flora and fauna from foreign pests and diseases.

Total import bans are controversial, but not all import bans entirely prohibit trade of a product from a particular source. Partial bans, such as seasonal or regional bans that do not completely preclude entry of a given product from the exporting country, also are used extensively to protect animal and plant health. Typically, these measures are used when regulatory authorities more fully understand the risk factors, and when a more narrowly targeted ban can effectively reduce the risks to acceptable levels. For example, regulatory authorities can safely implement a seasonal ban that allows imports of certain horticultural products from an exporting country for part of the year if they have detailed knowledge about the effects of climatological factors on the biology of the identified quarantine pests and understand how the host status of the commodity might vary over the growing season. Trade controversies arise when partial bans based ostensibly on technical considerations turn out to preclude all of the otherwise feasible trade opportunities.

Technical Standards

Technical standards stipulate conditions that have to be met to gain access to a particular market. Product standards might specify the nature of the product itself (e.g., size, weight, or chemical composition), or content attributes such as absence of particular diseases and microorganisms. By contrast, process standards stipulate use of certain production, processing, handling, or distribution technologies. As noted earlier, sometimes the goal of a regulation dictates whether a product or process standard is applied, but often this is a choice of regulatory authorities.

Economic theory generally suggests the desirability of product over process standards when feasible, because product standards allow latitude for firms to meet a regulatory goal at the least cost. At times, however, process standards are more efficient because of technical factors or verification cost considerations (Antle 1996). For example, the sequential application of required production methods designed to reduce progressively the likelihood of a certain disease or pest in the final product (known as a "systems approach" to risk management) may be preferable to extensive testing that involves destruction of the final product. Similarly, a process standard designed to reduce microbial contamination in food might be a superior regulatory tool to setting specific product standards, given the expense of microbiological tests and the recurrent nature of the pathogen hazard (MacDonald and Crutchfield 1996, Unnevehr and Jensen 1999).

In principle, any firm in any country willing to expend resources to meet the specified technical standard can export a product to a country setting that standard. But, in practice, technical standards shift comparative costs among producers, and some firms may be prevented from meeting the standard by the absence of satisfactory verification services. Thus, although technical standards appear to be less disruptive of trade than quantitative restrictions, the effect can be very similar. A standard that cannot be reached or can be reached only at a prohibitive cost is equivalent to a ban on imports. It is an empirical question whether technical standards are more trade-restrictive than partial bans. Exporting firms may find that the costs of complying with a foreign standard are prohibitive if it is stringent or varies significantly from a domestic or international standard. Standards can also be written in ways that favor domestic producers—for example, by requiring use of an input more widely available in the home country than in potential exporting countries.[2] It is true, however, that many technical standard regulations affecting trade are uniform and so affect costs for domestic as well as foreign producers.

Informational Remedies

When market failures stem from informational failures, informational remedies may be preferred over other measures. Informational regulations fall into two categories: (1) mandatory disclosure requirements, and (2) controls on voluntary claims. When combined with credible certification institutions, these instruments can transform the experience or credence characteristics of a food product into searchable characteristics, for example when orange juice is labeled "calcium enriched." In theory, the purchasing patterns

---

2. A well-known example is Italy's "pasta purity" regulation, which allowed only products made entirely with durum wheat (grown throughout southern Italy but found in few other areas in Europe) to be marketed under the generic term *pasta*.

of well-informed consumers will then be sufficient incentive for producers to provide the range of quality for which consumers are willing to pay without further government intervention.

Informational remedies have generally been viewed as the least onerous form of government regulation. Alan Sykes (1995) points out, however, that if requirements vary from market to market, manufacturers must incur not only the costs of producing different labels but also the possibly substantial costs of maintaining distinct inventories for each market. Recent initiatives to require additional labeling, particularly for process attributes, can raise verification costs for food manufacturers and simultaneously affect consumer demand. The potentially large market effects that some of these labeling regulations could have, particularly those for genetically modified foods, have made the adoption of mandatory labeling regimes particularly controversial.

Conformity Assessment

Conformity assessment is verification of compliance or equivalence with a food regulation. The requirements for assessing conformity with a measure have two dimensions: (1) specification of the means used to verify compliance or equivalence with a measure,[3] and (2) designation of who is authorized to make the assessment. Authority can be vested in private suppliers' declarations; private, third-party agents; or public (regulatory agency) third parties.

Issues related to conformity assessment are increasingly at the forefront of regulatory debates because of the growing reliance on process standards in the regulation of animal and plant health and food safety. Even among developed countries with high levels of regulatory capacity, different views on the appropriate roles for the private and public sector in conformity assessment have given rise to trade disputes. For developing countries, conformity assessment requirements are often a significant impediment to trade, even when trading partners agree on who will provide various verification services. Inevitably, more administrative discretion is involved in the enforcement of process standards than product standards, so judgments about the capability and integrity of verification services in the exporting country figure importantly in decisions to allow trade. It is not surprising that judgments about such matters often differ between importers and exporters, particularly those from developing countries.

Debate over conformity assessment has also intensified because of the growing number of food quality regulations that target process attributes. The use of private, third-party certification services in the global food

3. This dimension was discussed earlier with respect to the policy instrument chosen to achieve the regulatory goal and the attribute focus of the regulation.

system has grown in recent years because of the large increase in private standards (Caswell, Bredahl, and Hooker 1998). Even so, governments often require public-sector verification of compliance with food quality, as well as food safety, regulations. By contrast, a supplier's declaration of conformity with standards usually suffices for trade in industrial products, particularly in countries with a sound legal infrastructure (WTO 2000c). When use of private services is constrained by regulatory regimes that require public-sector provision of verification services, imports are effectively prohibited from countries that lack adequate public regulatory infrastructure, even if individual foreign firms can meet importers' standards.

Risk Analysis and Appropriate Degrees of Caution

At the heart of many disputes over risk-related food regulations are different interpretations of the role of risk assessment or disagreements on the extent to which scientific evidence provides a sufficient basis for risk management decisions. Not surprising, the countries exporting agricultural products have sought to enshrine scientific evidence as a basis for food regulations. But the science associated with risk analysis often leaves room for substantial uncertainty over the incidence of risk and the effectiveness of proposed management strategies. This uncertainty poses problems for those authorities who ultimately are responsible for the consequences of regulatory decisions. Tension runs high between the governments of exporting countries, which prefer that regulations be based on "objective" criteria to minimize the scope for domestic political manipulation, and the governments of importing countries, which know that they will be held accountable if science "has it wrong" or if low-probability, high-consequence adverse events occur. Further room for dissension among countries emerges because agricultural exporters often have strict import regulations in their own food sectors, aimed at ensuring that pests and diseases do not enter and diminish their production capacity or interfere with their access to foreign markets. These strict regulations by exporters can cause problems in a complex trading world where commercial opportunities for intrasectoral trade exist in many markets. The imposition of strict regulations makes it difficult for exporters to exercise credible leadership toward regulatory actions abroad that they would favor.

Disputes over appropriate levels of risk avoidance recently came to a head in discussions among countries of the "precautionary principle" of risk management.[4] The precautionary principle guides political and

4. Patterson and Josling (2001) have described the evolution of this concept, based on the German sociolegal tradition, as it gained policy recognition in the 1980s with the rapid development of environmental laws.

regulatory action toward strict measures intended as ecological or health safeguards (even in advance of scientific proof or need), and places the onus of proof on those who propose change. This principle can be characterized as a conservative approach to risk management in which regulation anticipates harm that has not already been documented for a given category of products. It does not take into consideration the relative costs and benefits of regulation to industry and the public, including the benefits forgone by delayed approval.

Critics of the precautionary principle as a basis for regulatory decision making for the food system argue that although caution is necessary, it is impossible to eliminate all risks from scientific advances or commerce. The precautionary principle could distort regulatory priorities, stifle important life-enhancing research and industrial competitiveness by creating unnecessary bureaucratic delays or precluding the development of some products, and be used to justify protectionist measures. Critics of the precautionary principle prefer a "preventive" approach that responds to "scientifically proven adverse impacts that have arisen in earlier generations of products" (Tait and Levidow 1992, 221). A "pre-market clearance" approach to regulation, in which new products and processes are screened to ensure they do not give rise to recognized hazards, is considered consistent with adequate risk prevention. Advocates of the preventive approach favor case-by-case and step-by-step procedures, in which different steps in research and production processes are examined according to the specific risks involved in each step and new regulations are based on demonstrated harmfulness. In this way, science and market development can proceed, and in the process accumulated knowledge will help to clarify what risks actually exist. This approach still introduces approval delays as compared with a regime of unregulated science and technology adoption, but it provides more flexibility than a regime based on the precautionary principle.

Trade Effects of Food Regulations

Assessment of the efficiency of regulations in an integrated food system requires estimation of the economic impacts of regulatory measures. It is clear that trade is affected by technical regulations. But less clear is the magnitude of these effects on prices and quantities in markets or on the welfare gains from trade. Complying with regulations entails direct costs that are difficult to ascertain.[5] When a regulation is uniform in scope, the net economic and trade effects can be dominated by the regulation's effects on the costs of domestic firms. Even in these cases, the effects of the regulation on domestic and foreign producers can differ. When the

5. Roberts, Josling, and Orden (1999) discuss more fully the issues raised in this section.

scope of a regulation is specific, it has inherently differential impacts on one or more exporters.

Considerably more information is needed to assess the effects of the various food regulations than is needed to assess the impacts of standard tariffs and nontechnical, quantitative trade restrictions. When the cost differentials between domestic and foreign suppliers are reasonably well known, the "tariff equivalent" of a regulation can be defined as the tariff that would reduce imports by the same amount, but the equivalence should be qualified. Tariffs yield government revenue, whereas regulations impose compliance costs that use up real resources, often at home and abroad.

An additional complexity in evaluating the impacts of food regulations is that, unlike other trade barriers, they have indirect as well as direct effects in markets. Regulations that seek to limit the domestic pervasiveness or prevent the importation of an animal or plant pest or disease-causing organism will typically have an impact on the domestic supply of the products that would be vulnerable to those risks. Such a regulation is conveniently thought to be a means of avoiding an adverse shift in the domestic supply function—a shift stemming from either infection or infestation or the cost of remedial treatment of the affected animals or crops. The regulation translates into decreased imports (or increased exports) in the regulating country. However, even when the regulation applies only to imports it may be misleading to call its effects a trade "distortion," because it could represent the most efficient way of dealing with the state of nature presented by the existence of a hazard.

Many food-sector regulations affect the demand rather than the supply of the product in the importing country. A ban on imports of a food that would pose a health threat can prevent a market collapse caused by eroding confidence in the safety of supply. Likewise, consumer confidence in experience and credence characteristics of foods may be difficult to establish for imported products. If consumers are uncertain whether a food purchase will be of sufficient quality, an alternative product might be purchased instead. In this situation, regulations enhance consumers' voluntary food choices by improving the information on which to base decisions. In either food safety or food quality cases, domestic market demand is affected, and trade without regulation might lead to a net loss in welfare.

The impact of a food regulation on trade thus stems from the direct cost of compliance incurred by domestic suppliers, the indirect impacts of the regulation in question on domestic supply and demand, and its impacts on related foreign excess supplies. The incidence of this cost will depend on market structure and the combination of elasticities of supply and demand. And it will depend on the scope of the regulation.

For an importing country, the imposition of a specific regulation on one source of a traded good may have little net effect if costs from other sources are not affected, but the impact on bilateral trade is likely to be pronounced. The net trade effect on the exporter depends on whether other importers place similar restrictions on the exports in question. If all importing countries restrain the product of a single exporting country through technical regulations, the exporting country would suffer the maximum trade effect. When all supplying countries are similarly restrained, the impact on each supplier is lessened, but it still can be significant.

The propensity for a specific import regulation to cause a trade conflict thus depends to a certain extent on the specificity of the restriction among exporters and the extent to which other importers follow suit. All of this suggests that technical regulations affecting trade are not amenable to simple multilateral reduction negotiations.

Science and Economics in Risk-Reducing Regulations

Quantitative analysis of the effects of food regulation takes into account the circumstances that would prevail in the absence of regulations. Without such information, it is impossible to know to what extent food regulations act as trade barriers, which measures most impede trade, and how best to modify existing regulations to reduce any negative impacts. Such detailed knowledge is sometimes available; at other times, it is not.[6] But a few generalizations can be made on the interface between the science of risk assessment and management and the economic and trade analysis related to risk-reducing regulations.

The regulatory procedures of most countries require that risk-related decision making be based on sequential analysis: first, determine that there is essentially no or minimal risk associated with a proposed regulation, and, second, under that premise, assess its economic impacts. When risk-related decisions are made in this sequential manner, economic considerations become secondary as food regulations are promulgated by agencies depending on the scientific evidence. Under this approach, emphasis is placed on risk reduction rather than on a comprehensive analysis that takes risks and economic costs and benefits into account simultaneously (James and Anderson 1998, Roberts 2000). When the mandate of regulatory authorities to protect the domestic economy from negative sanitary and phytosanitary risks from trade is stated in strong terms, as it often is, then import bans and other severe quarantine measures emerge quite naturally as policy outcomes. A product ban is a high-level intervention to address a risk from imports, but a ban does eliminate the risk to the extent that it stems from legally sanctioned trade.

6. Krissoff, Bohman, and Caswell (2002) and Maskus and Wilson (2001) provide some quantitative studies of the impact of regulations on trade, as do later chapters in this volume.

Figure 2.1 Regulatory underprotection and overprotection

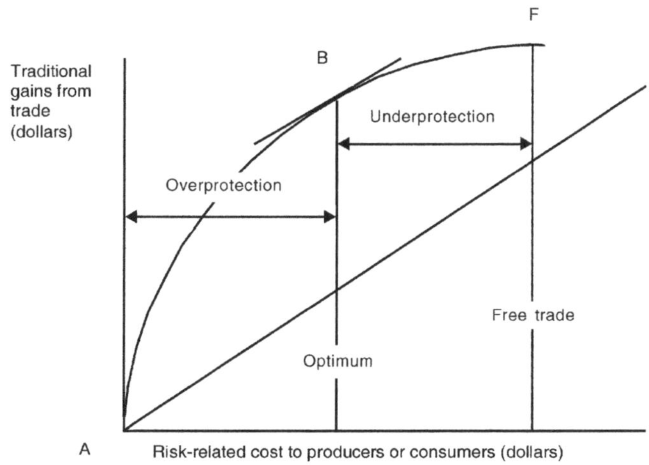

As the global food system becomes more integrated, trade gains ought to enter more fully into the calculus of regulatory agencies. They should incorporate scientific assessments and trade policy analysis in the design of good regulations. Economic analysis of trade should take into account the sensitivity of domestic costs to regulations and the extent to which consumer demand is supported by trust in regulatory decisions. As described earlier in this chapter, trade analysis that views all food regulations simply as "nontariff barriers" is as likely to be as misleading as scientific analysis that considers zero incidence of a risk as necessarily the socially optimal policy.

Richard Snape and David Orden (2001) illustrate these considerations in a simple diagram that forms the basis for figure 2.1. The vertical axis represents the expected traditional gain from trade arising from imports of a product into a particular country. The horizontal axis represents the (monetized) expected cost of the hazard linked with imports. Regulations that achieve trade with coordinates above the 45° line, when the direct and indirect effects on domestic supply and demand are taken into account, are deemed to have passed a benefit-cost test as desirable policy. Snape and Orden contrast this decision criterion with a primarily risk-based rule, which would preclude imports with high benefits relative to costs if they fall to the right of a vertical line representing the cutoff level of acceptable risk. This situation would entail rejecting trade in some cases where the benefit-cost ratio is above one and accepting trade in others (that satisfy the risk-based rule) where the ratio is less than one.

The analysis is extended in figure 2.1 by tracing a risks/benefits tradeoff frontier between domestic risk costs and trade benefits for a range of import protocols. Ignoring benefits in setting regulations can lead to situations in which "too little" trade takes place because the risks are counted but the rewards are ignored. Conversely, if the risks are ignored or discounted relative to the benefits from imports, then "too much" trade occurs. The first situation can arise from mandates within domestic regulatory institutions to base decisions on risk avoidance. Too little protection from risks can occur if authorities either are unaware of the risks associated with trade or are persuaded by commercial interests to downplay their impact.

The risks/benefits trade-off frontier shown in figure 2.1 allows for the specification of an optimal level of protection where the benefits net of risks are the greatest. The curve ABF maps the trade gains and the risk-related costs to producers (or to consumers) from no trade gains and no risk at point A (autarchy) to the maximum trade gain and maximum risk with unregulated free trade (F). Various shapes are possible for the risks/benefits trade-off frontier as import levels rise, but it will generally be concave, as illustrated, because small amounts of trade will tend to produce large economic gains but pose limited risks, whereas the risks may continue to mount with trade even when most of the trade gains have been realized.[7] The optimal point is B, where at the margin the gains to trade (as conventionally measured) just balance the expected loss from the consequences of the importation of the pest or disease. By contrast, the most conservative protocol (point A) would eliminate trade, leading to a lower level of welfare than necessary as trade gains are passed up. The most permissive import protocol (point F) would allow free trade, but again this would not be optimal with a concave trade-off frontier, because the marginal costs of disease prevention or the consequences of pest infestation offset the marginal gains from trade beyond some level of imports.

The simple model of the risks/benefits trade-off in figure 2.1 allows "overprotection" to be defined as a situation in which a relaxation of the regulation would be socially beneficial and "underprotection" as a situation in which more restrictive import protocols would increase expected net social benefits. Measuring the functions involved accurately and calculating the social optimum are a challenge for empirical work, but in principle the concepts of overprotection and underprotection have a precise social meaning.

The integration of risk and economic analysis suggested here can be extended further to account for effects beyond the impacts of import

7. If both benefits and costs depend linearly on the level of trade, then the ABF frontier will be linear as well, and free trade will be optimal if gains from each unit of trade exceed costs. When the ABF curve is convex, net benefits (traditional gains less risk-related costs) fall from A to B and then rise as trade expands toward F. This again gives a corner solution, where no trade has to be directly compared with free trade because no intervening situation is better.

regulations on domestic supply and demand. Consider the case in which an exporting country introduces effective controls over the pest in question. The trade-off curve in figure 2.1 shifts to the left as risks are reduced for each level of trade. The optimum level of imports will also change as benefits from the action of the exporter accrue as an increase in the gains from trade combined with less risk to domestic producers or consumers. If the imposition of an international standard reduces the general risk from imports, the importer could gain considerably from being able to adjust trade to a level where the gains are greater. Thus the optimal policy for a country can only be defined in relation to the policies of other countries and to the existence of effective standards that reduce the riskiness of imports.

Capture of Regulations by Producers or Consumers

One explanation for overprotection by strict import regulations is regulatory "capture" by producer interests who effectively lobby for regulations stronger than are warranted by a full calculation of costs and benefits. The result is protection of domestic producers at the expense of domestic consumers. The regulations that countries have adopted for controlling the spread of animal and plant diseases rely largely on scientific information channeled through national agencies. Pressure on these agencies by those with rent-seeking ambitions has long been recognized as a problem for the trade system.[8] Typically, such situations involve the excessive use of import bans or quarantine restrictions, ostensibly to keep out animal and plant diseases and food-borne pathogens. When domestic producers can influence import regulations and their implementation, then overprotection is likely to be the result, and both consumers and foreign producers lose. The trade system has not been able to provide the full benefits of comparative advantage.

Underprotection can also be a political economy problem. Pressure from overseas interests or importing firms may lead to too much trade in certain products. When exotic pests can come in with trade, the regulatory infrastructure may lag behind the need for vigilance against pathogens. This lag may be of particular importance in some developing countries with limited regulatory capacity, leading at times to underprotection with high costs to domestic agricultural producers in some cases.

8. In a case strangely parallel to the current dispute over the sale of hormone-treated beef from the United States into the European Union, during the tenure of Chancellor Otto Bismarck (1871–90) Germany for many years banned imports of US pork. US pork producers were convinced, apparently with some justification, that the German regulations were unduly restrictive—see Snyder (1945).

Regulations addressing safety of the food supply are subject as well to another type of political pressure. Lack of reliable consumer information can lead to the capture of the regulatory process by consumer-oriented public interest groups. This capture can at times lead to overprotection, if the natural caution of regulators or unfounded public fears are turned into excessive regulation in response to pressure from organized consumer lobbyists. Exporters with safe food to supply can then be shut out of markets. The costs also are borne by those consumers who have to pay a higher price than necessary. Domestic producers may gain from this overprotection, but they can also lose in these situations if the excessively strict import protocol has a counterpart in excessive domestic regulations.

Food regulations that apply process standards are particularly subject to political economy capture. Although such regulations can be distorted to reflect producer interests, their capture by consumer and other groups with various agendas may pose the greater challenge. Much of the onus of sustaining an integrated global food system rests on the independence and credibility of the domestic institutions that implement regulations. If governments allow their food regulatory agencies to be politicized to support narrow interest group agendas, their decisions become susceptible to challenge as unnecessary restraints on trade.

Welfare-Enhancing Regulation of Food Trade

Increased trade is not inconsistent with food safety and quality objectives. Quite the contrary, trade can contribute to the provision of a safe, high-quality food supply. Yet trade tensions arise from different regulatory regimes, and such conflicts appear to be increasing. To avoid a clash between trade, safety, and consumer rights concerns, to the detriment of each, it is important to explore the causes of these tensions.

Trade conflicts over risk-related measures can arise from genuine disagreements about scientific evidence. Sometimes the science is not in place, requiring interim judgments that may be challenged by other countries. More often, the disagreement is over scientific evidence supporting the positions of different governments. Other trade issues arise from an asymmetry of accountability between domestic and foreign suppliers in which foreign suppliers are less directly liable for the unanticipated negative consequences of their products. These issues are found in many areas of international trade, but they are particularly sensitive in the food sector.

A different set of issues arises over quality attributes. Sometimes producers seek recognition of their product identity as a property right, leading to conflict with suppliers of close substitutes. Consumers differ in their levels of demand for information and for standards about food products. Regulatory institutions differ in reliance on mandatory versus voluntary provision of assurances about content and process attributes. From each situation, international trade conflicts easily emerge.

The complexity of the systems of regulations related to the safety and quality of agricultural and food products poses a substantial challenge for trade analysis, negotiations, and dispute resolution. Classification of the differences among national regulatory institutions and their substantive outcomes serves as an initial road map to a dense regulatory maze.

The regulations imposed through various instruments have both direct effects on trade and indirect effects that result from induced shifts in underlying supply and demand. Optimal policies can be described conceptually, but are often difficult to ascertain empirically, and regulatory decision making is subject to political pressure that often results in overprotection for the benefit of influential domestic groups. These considerations underlie the efforts made to strengthen international regulatory oversight and to incorporate comprehensive trade rules into international agreements. The goal is to ensure that agricultural and food regulations do not impede welfare-enhancing trade, and, at the same time, do give countries wide latitude to set their health, safety, and quality standards.

References

Antle, John. 1996. Efficient Food Safety Regulation in the Food Manufacturing Sector. *American Journal of Agricultural Economics* 78, no. 5: 1242–47.

Brown, Cheryl, Lori Lynch, and David Zilberman. 2002. The Economics of Controlling Insect-Transmitted Diseases. *American Journal of Agricultural Economics* 84, no. 2: 279–91.

Caswell, Julie A., Maury Bredahl, and Niel Hooker. 1998. How Quality Management Meta-systems Are Affecting the Food Industry. *Review of Agricultural Economics* 10: 547–57.

Darby, Michael R., and Edi Karni. 1973. Free Competition and the Optimal Amount of Fraud. *Journal of Law and Economics* 16, no. 1: 67–68.

Golan, Elise, Barry Krissoff, Fred Kuchler, Ken Nelson, Greg Price, and Linda Calvin. 2003. Traceability in the U.S. Food Supply: Dead End or Superhighway? *Choices* (2nd quarter). www.choicesmagazine.org/archives/2003/q2/2003-2-04.htm.

Hoeckman, Bernard, and Michael Leidy. 1993. Environmental Policy Formation in a Trading Economy: A Public Choice Perspective. In *The Greening of World Trade Issues,* ed. Kym Anderson and Richard Blackhurst. London: Harvester Wheatsheaf.

James, S., and Kym Anderson. 1998. On the Need for More Economic Assessment of Quarantine Policies. *Australian Journal of Agricultural and Resource Economics* 42, no. 4 (December): 425–44.

Krissoff, Barry, Mary Bohman, and Julie A. Caswell, eds. 2002. *Global Food Trade and Consumer Demand for Quality.* New York: Kluwer Academic/Plenum Publishers.

MacDonald, James, and Stephen Crutchfield. 1996. Modeling the Costs of Food Safety Regulation. *American Journal of Agricultural Economics* 78, no. 5: 1285–90.

Maskus, Keith E. 2000. *Intellectual Property Rights in the Global Economy.* Washington: Institute for International Economics.

Maskus, Keith E., and John S. Wilson, eds. 2001. *Quantifying the Impact of Technical Barriers to Trade: Can It Be Done?* Ann Arbor: University of Michigan Press.

OECD (Organization for Economic Cooperation and Development). 1997. *Regulatory Reform and the Agro-Food Sector.* OECD Report on Regulatory Reform. Vol. 1, *Sectoral Studies.* Paris: OECD.

Patterson, Lee Ann, and Tim Josling. 2001. Biotechnology Regulatory Policy in the United States and the European Union: Source of Transatlantic Trade Conflict or Opportunity for Cooperation? Paper presented at the Western Economic Association International Conference, San Francisco (July).

Roberts, Donna. 2000. Sanitary and Phytosanitary Risk Management in the Post-Uruguay Round Era: An Economic Perspective. In *Incorporating Science, Economic, and Sociology in Developing Sanitary and Phytosanitary Standards in International Trade, Proceedings of a Conference.* Washington: National Academy Press.

Roberts, Donna, Timothy E. Josling, and David Orden. 1999. *A Framework for Analyzing Technical Trade Barriers in Agricultural Markets.* Technical Bulletin 1876. Washington: Economic Research Service, US Department of Agriculture.

Snape, Richard, and David Orden. 2001. Integrating Import Risk and Trade Benefit Analysis. In *The Economics of Quarantine and the SPS Agreement,* ed. Kym Anderson, Cheryl McRae, and David Wilson. Adelaide, Australia: Centre for International Economic Studies.

Snyder, Louis L. 1945. The American-German Pork Dispute, 1879-1891. *Journal of Modern History* 17: 16–28.

Sumner, Daniel, and Hyunok Lee. 1997. Sanitary and Phytosanitary Trade Barriers and Empirical Trade Modeling. In *Understanding Technical Barriers to Agricultural Trade,* ed. David Orden and Donna Roberts. St. Paul: International Agricultural Trade Research Consortium, Department of Applied Economics, University of Minnesota.

Sykes, Alan O. 1995. *Product Standards for Internationally Integrated Goods Markets.* Washington: Brookings Institution.

Tait, Joyce, and Les Levidow. 1992. Proactive and Reactive Approaches to Risk Regulation: The Case of Biotechnology. *Futures* (April): 219–31.

Thilmany, Dawn, and Christopher Barrett, 1996. Regulatory Barriers in an Integrating World Food Market. *Review of Agricultural Economics* 19, no. 1: 91–107.

Unnevehr, Laurian J., and Helen H. Jensen. 1999. The Economic Implications of Using HACCP as a Food Safety Regulatory Standard. *Food Policy* 24: 625–35.

Unnevehr, Laurian J., and Gerald C. Nelson. 2002. Balancing the Costs and Benefits of Labeling and Traceability for GMOs. Paper presented at the Workshop on Labeling Products of Food Biotechnology: Panacea or Hidden Trade Barrier? The European Forum, Institute for International Studies, Stanford University (June 28).

Wilson, John S. 1995. *Standards and APEC: An Action Agenda.* Washington: Institute for International Economics.

Chapter 16

3

Global Food Regulatory Framework

Timothy Josling, Donna Roberts and David Orden

Global governance of food regulation was enhanced with the adoption of new and revised agreements at the conclusion of the Uruguay Round of multilateral negotiations in 1994. These agreements were viewed as critical to prevent governments from resorting to regulatory compensation to appease domestic interests as the Uruguay Round Agreement on Agriculture (URAA) began to put limits on agricultural trade barriers and subsidies. This chapter reviews these agreements, together with other elements of the multilateral governance framework for food regulations. It also evaluates what has been learned and what challenges lie ahead after six years of reporting, consultations, and dispute settlement about such regulations within the WTO.

Multilateral Governance of Food Regulation

The Uruguay Round agreements strengthened the GATT articles, agreements, and case law that had built up to govern the use of technical barriers to trade over the previous 50 years.[1] The negotiators of the original

1. Overall, the Uruguay Round negotiations produced the Final Act, signed in Marrakesh in 1994; the Marrakesh Agreement Establishing the World Trade Organization (or WTO agreement), which serves as an umbrella agreement; the General Agreement on Tariffs and Trade 1994 (known as GATT 1994, which includes the text of the original 1947 GATT articles and subsequent amendments); 16 agreements on goods, services, intellectual property, dispute settlement, and a trade policy review mechanism; and various plurilateral agreements, decisions, and declarations.

GATT treaty recognized the need to subject domestic regulations to international scrutiny so that the strategic application of technical measures by countries would not subvert the commercial opportunities created by lower tariffs and other trade policy reforms. The original GATT treaty set forth various rules designed to limit such abuses. Two GATT articles set out basic prohibitions: Article XI.1 broadly disallows quantitative restrictions, and Article III requires "national treatment" for "like products" to prohibit countries from applying discriminatory internal taxes and regulations to imports. The prohibitions defined by these articles are qualified by GATT Article XX, which recognizes the sovereign right of governments to adopt restrictions on trade if necessary to achieve legitimate policy objectives such as health and safety or conservation of exhaustible natural resources. Subject to the consensus-based approval by all Contracting Parties, a country could request a GATT panel to review a trade complaint. If the panel ruled against the respondent, and the ruling was adopted by consensus, that country could be required to revise its measure, offer compensating trade concessions, or suffer authorized retaliation in the form of higher tariffs on its exports.

The original GATT rules were augmented in the 1973–79 Tokyo Round negotiations, which produced the Agreement on Technical Barriers to Trade (often called the Standards Code). The Standards Code established obligations to ensure that mandatory regulations, voluntary standards, and conformity assessment procedures were not prepared, adopted, or applied to create unnecessary obstacles to trade. These multilateral rules disciplined the use of some protectionist policies.[2] However, neither the original GATT nor the Standards Code was able to stem disruptions of trade in international markets caused by a proliferation of apparently protectionist technical restrictions (Motaal 2002). Moreover, several prominent disagreements over regulations, especially food regulations, remained unresolved in the 1980s.

Three flaws in the pre–Uruguay Round legal infrastructure blunted the effectiveness of the disciplines on technical measures: (1) lack of a single integrated rule system, (2) the GATT's consensus-based dispute settlement process, and (3) ambiguity in the Standard Code's rules for regulations that established requirements for process and production methods (PPMs). Not all Contracting Parties to the GATT had signed the Standards Code, or indeed the other Tokyo Round codes, giving rise to a system sometimes referred to as "GATT à la carte." This system effectively precluded some standards-related disputes from being brought before a GATT panel for resolution. But even if two countries had signed

2. The 1986 Japanese ski standards dispute is one such example. In this case, American and European exporters successfully argued that evidence did not support a Japanese claim that imported skis could not function safely on Japanese snow. The case was settled in formal consultations before reaching a panel (Sykes 1995).

the Standards Code, the consensus-based GATT dispute settlement process allowed either country to block a panel report, or even to deny a request to convene a panel. The third loophole was created by the Standards Code itself, which only disciplined measures that "lay down characteristics of a product such as levels of quality, performance, safety or dimensions." The Standards Code omitted any explicit reference to PPMs in its key provisions, an omission that contributed to the high-profile standoff between the European Union[3] and the United States over the European Union's ban on hormone-treated beef.[4] This unresolved dispute was viewed as one of the more visible failures of the pre–Uruguay Round legal disciplines (Stanton 1997).

To remedy these defects, multilateral disciplines on the use of technical measures were revised, expanded, and strengthened in the Uruguay Round. The Punta del Este Ministerial Declaration launching the negotiations in 1986 stated that the objective was to create disciplines that would minimize the "adverse effects that sanitary and phytosanitary regulations and barriers can have on trade in agriculture." The negotiations therefore produced a new Agreement on the Application of Sanitary and Phytosanitary Measures (SPS agreement), which set out rules for measures that target certain enumerated hazards to animal, plant, and human life and health. The Standards Code was also revised, reappearing as the WTO Technical Barriers to Trade Agreement (TBT agreement). A new Agreement on Trade-Related Aspects of Intellectual Property Rights (TRIPS agreement) imposed obligations to provide minimum protection to a range of intellectual property rights, including geographical indications (GIs) of commercial identity for agricultural products and food. The GATT continued in force as well. Thus the Uruguay Round increased the scope and complexity of the legal infrastructure for food-sector technical regulations and standards, as illustrated in figure 3.1.

3. For a mixture of historical and legal reasons, the European Union is known as the European Communities at the WTO. The responsibility for trade policy rests predominantly with the "first pillar" of the European Union (the second and third pillars deal with foreign and security policy and with justice and home affairs, respectively). The first pillar includes the institutions that govern the economic aspects of the European Union and is based on the same treaty provisions that were established at the time of the founding of the European Communities. Hence, official WTO documents usually reference "the EC," and we therefore use this acronym when citing official WTO documents. However, we follow normal practice by using the term European Union, or EU, to reference the political entity of the 25 member countries. Technically, these member states are also WTO members in their own right, as is the European Union, though they act as one member in WTO matters. (For more information, see "The European Communities and the WTO" at www.wto.org/english/thewto_e/countries_e/european_communities_e.htm.)

4. This omission established the basis for the EU rejection of the US request to establish a technical experts group to evaluate the scientific basis for the hormone ban. See Josling, Roberts, and Hassan (1999) for a complete account of the legal stalemate in the hormones dispute under the GATT agreements.

Figure 3.1 GATT/WTO legal infrastructure for food regulations and standards

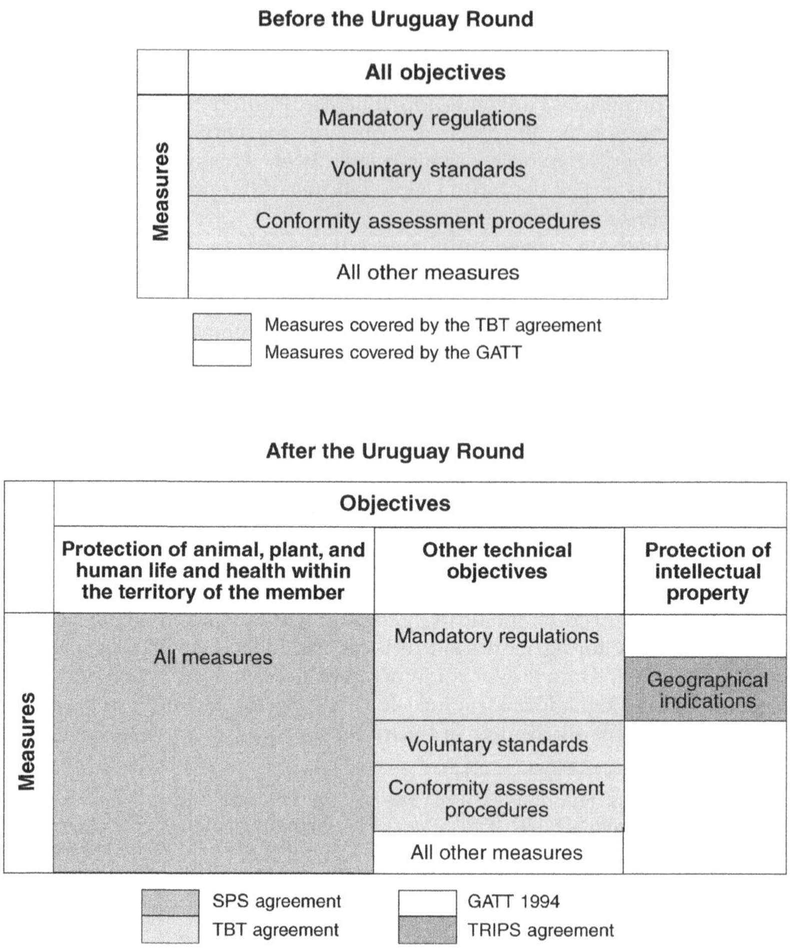

The new dispute settlement rules also adopted in the Uruguay Round are critical to the effectiveness of the various WTO agreements. Under the single integrated rules system of the WTO Understanding on Rules and Procedures Governing the Settlement of Disputes (Dispute Settlement Understanding, or DSU), a single country can no longer block a request for review by a dispute panel or prevent the adoption of a panel's report by the WTO's dispute settlement body.

DSU procedures include formal consultations between the parties to a dispute, followed by examination of the dispute by a WTO panel and review of the panel's decision by the WTO Appellate Body if requested by the parties. If the disputed measure is found to violate WTO provisions, the parties to the dispute may request arbitration to determine a "reasonable period of time" for the respondent to change its policy or, if it does not, to determine the amount of compensation or retaliation due to the complainant (usually in the form of tariff adjustments on other products).

Taken together, the new agreements disciplining technical regulations and standards and the new dispute settlement procedures have spurred more requests for international panels to review food-related measures that restrict trade. This increase has, in turn, heightened the profile of these measures and encouraged closer scrutiny of food regulations by national governments and by WTO committees charged with furthering the implementation of the agreements.

Outside of the GATT/WTO framework, governments have also negotiated multilateral environmental agreements (MEAs), which, in some instances, include mandatory trade provisions, such as the Convention on International Trade in Endangered Species of Wild Fauna and Flora (CITES) and the Convention on Biological Diversity (CBD). To the extent that these MEAs require or authorize trade restrictions among signatories, they can be viewed as a waiver of any GATT obligations that might otherwise prohibit such measures. However, they are potentially in conflict with trade rules to the extent that they authorize otherwise GATT/WTO-illegal trade restrictions against WTO members who are not parties to the MEA (Hudec 1996).

To implement fully its technical agreements, the WTO relies on multilateral standards organizations and also draws on the expertise of other intergovernmental scientific bodies such as the World Health Organization (WHO). Together, the WTO, the multilateral standards and scientific organizations, and, to a lesser extent, the MEAs, along with their principles, rules, standards, and enforcement mechanisms, make up the multilateral governance framework for food regulation. This framework is reinforced by a network of bilateral, regional, and plurilateral trade agreements, which have come to play a role in global food regulation as well. These latter agreements provide the multilateral system with both challenges and opportunities to try out cooperative solutions in a context in which cooperation may come easier.[5]

5. Perhaps the prime example of a bilateral agreement on food regulatory issues is that between Australia and New Zealand. Food safety is regulated jointly through the Australia New Zealand Food Authority (ANZFA), and standards are administered through the Australia New Zealand Food Standards Council (ANZFSC). At the other end of the spectrum of bilateral approaches to food regulations is the attempt to use the transatlantic

The SPS Agreement

The SPS agreement was negotiated on the premise that domestic sanitary and phytosanitary standards based on international norms could reduce trade conflicts and lower transactions costs and that requiring scientific justification for standards that deviated from such norms would make it more difficult for countries to shelter domestic industries behind restrictive health and safety regulations. The SPS agreement maintains a delicate balance between the rights of member countries to determine their health and safety standards and their obligations to other countries as they seek to achieve those national goals.

Basic Provisions

The SPS agreement sets out disciplines for measures that are applied to protect plant, animal, and human health and life within the territory of the importing country from certain enumerated hazards, including pests, disease, and disease-causing or disease-carrying organisms, as well as additives, contaminants, and toxins that might be found in food, beverages, or feedstuffs.[6]

The agreement reiterates the GATT commitments but also sets out additional principles to minimize unnecessary obstacles to trade. They are:

- **Harmonization** (Article 3). Member countries are urged (but not required) to adopt international standards. A country that adopts the standards of designated international standards organizations is presumed to be in compliance with its WTO commitments.
- **Science-based risk management** (Articles 2 and 5). SPS measures must be based on scientific principles and sufficient scientific evidence; more

partnership between the United States and the European Union to resolve differences and increase comity, which has had limited effect—see the discussion of this partnership later in this chapter, and also see Pollack and Shaffer (2001) and Patterson and Josling (2001) for accounts of attempts to solve trade differences arising from regulatory conflicts at a transatlantic level.

Among the more ambitious regional initiatives in the area of food regulations is the Asia Pacific Economic Cooperation (APEC) process (Johnson 1996, Wilson 1995). APEC debated establishing an APEC Food System, which would have included both food safety and trade liberalization instruments. The trade liberalization aspects of the plan have been put on hold, along with other aspects of the APEC program for individual and collective market access improvements, but the food safety part of the program has yielded a framework, the APEC Food Mutual Recognition Agreement, that could facilitate trade in foodstuffs in the Asia Pacific region. Whether this is the start of more substantial cooperation in food regulations remains to be seen.

6. The complete definition is set out in Annex A of the SPS agreement.

particularly, measures must be based on a risk assessment. Measures should be chosen so as to minimize distortions to trade, and be no more trade-restrictive than necessary to achieve a country's "appropriate level of protection." Member countries are to avoid variation in the levels of health protection provided by their measures if the variation creates a disguised restriction on trade. Countries may adopt provisional measures to avoid risks, but they must seek information and carry out a risk assessment to justify permanent use of a trade-restricting measure.

- **Equivalence** (Article 4). A WTO member must accept that the SPS measures of another country are equivalent to its own if it is objectively demonstrated that the other country's measures achieve the member's appropriate level of protection, even if the measures themselves differ.
- **Regionalization** (Article 6). A country is required to allow imports from subnational regions abroad that are free or nearly free of pests or disease.

The obligations of member countries under the SPS agreement are qualified by recognition of national sovereignty. Article 3 of the agreement ensures that any country may choose a measure that differs from the international standard to achieve its appropriate level of protection as long as it complies with the other rules. Thus the SPS agreement takes into account that individual nations may be unwilling to subscribe to uniform standards for all hazards. Implicitly, this principle recognizes that it would not be optimal for them to do so in all cases.

In addition to setting out the rights and obligations of WTO members, the SPS agreement establishes new information exchange and enforcement mechanisms. To maintain transparency about applied measures, members are required to notify their regulations to the WTO and to provide trading partners with an inquiry point. A permanent SPS Committee meets three to four times a year to oversee implementation of the agreement and discuss contentious SPS measures on a continuing basis. The SPS agreement receives additional support through the resolution of conflicts under the rules of the DSU.

Relevant International Standards Organizations

The SPS agreement identifies three intergovernmental standards organizations to help achieve its objectives: L'Office International des Epizooties (OIE) for measures related to animal health and zoonoses affecting both animal and human health, the International Plant Protection Convention (IPPC) for plant health measures, and the Codex Alimentarius Commission (Codex) for food safety measures. These international organizations are given prominence through recognition of the standards they set as a basis for presumed compliance with the agreement. These three scientific bodies also provide channels for technical discussions of inconsistencies and differences among national regulations.

The OIE, IPPC, and Codex differ considerably in their composition and role. The OIE, whose headquarters is in Paris, was established in 1924. It is not affiliated with the United Nations. Its member states finance and run the OIE through an international committee of delegates from those states, a central bureau acts as the executive body, and commissions serve as the deliberative organs. The main commissions are those dealing with epizootic diseases, fish diseases, and standards. OIE issues an International Animal Health Code and an International Aquatic Animal Health Code. The commissions periodically update the codes, discuss protection strategies, and prepare manuals. The OIE also includes working groups and regional offices, as well as a network of laboratories that collaborate with the OIE in testing and certification.

The International Plant Protection Convention was established in 1952 with the objective of ensuring "effective common action to prevent the spread and introduction of pests and parasites affecting plants and plant products and to promote control measures." It is administered by a secretariat attached to the UN Food and Agriculture Organization (FAO) in Rome. Revisions to the convention agreed on in 1979 came into force in 1991. A further revision of the convention was adopted by the FAO Conference in 1997 and aligns the IPPC with the provisions of the SPS agreement (Victor 1998). The latest convention provides for the use of phytosanitary measures to protect the natural environment as well as commercial crops from invasive species. The convention is a treaty that obligates the signatories (currently 110 countries) to take certain steps to guard against the spread of plant pests and diseases. Countries must put in place adequate checks and certification and disinfectant procedures, and they must publish information about such procedures (OECD 1999). The IPPC encourages countries to use the least trade-restrictive policies to protect plant health, avoid unnecessary delays, and be transparent in their use of restrictions.

The Codex Alimentarius Commission was established by the FAO and WHO in 1962 to implement a joint food standards program and to create the Codex Alimentarius, a set of general and commodity-specific standards, guidelines, and recommended codes of practice designed to protect the health of consumers and to ensure fair trade practices (Codex 1999b).[7] The various Codex texts are intended to "guide and promote

7. The Codex Alimentarius Europaeus was established earlier, in 1958, to achieve more consistent methods of food testing among the countries in the European Communities. It was merged with a joint WHO and FAO standards committee on milk standards and reorganized as the Codex Alimentarius Commission (Victor 1998).

the development, implementation and harmonization of definitions and requirements covering food products with a view to facilitating international trade." Proposed norms navigate a complex eight-step process from their introduction to their ultimate approval. Member countries are not required to adopt Codex standards. The existence of international standards, however, has helped those countries that wish to use these standards either as a requirement for imports or as a template for their own regulations.

At present, 165 countries are represented on the Codex, which has an executive committee of 10 members and a small secretariat in Rome. The major work of the Codex is carried out by various subsidiary committees that negotiate the texts and discuss specific problems. Nine of these committees function horizontally, dealing with cross-cutting issues such as labeling or additives, and 16 others are vertical, dealing with specific commodities. Five regional committees focus on issues related to geographic areas.

For much of its existence, the Codex has been regarded as a technical organization that operates at an epistemic level, "largely unaffected by national political interests as well as national and international law" (Veggeland and Borgen 2002, 9). Committees were dominated by scientific experts who worked closely with bodies such as the Joint FAO/WHO Expert Committee on Food Additives (JECFA) and the Joint FAO/WHO Meeting on Pesticide Residues (JMPR). Now, however, because of the heightened legal status of its standards under the SPS agreement and its wide coverage in the area of food standards, the work of the Codex bodies has become especially sensitive. As a result, the prevailing judgment is that of the three standard-setting institutions referenced in the SPS agreement, the SPS agreement has politicized decision making within Codex more than in the other standards organizations. Four specific instances are often cited to support this conclusion: (1) the two-year debate over the 1995 Codex "Statements of Principle," (2) the 1995 vote on Codex beef hormone standards, (3) the 1997 vote on Codex mineral water standards, and (4) the failure of Codex to adopt JECFA's recommended standard for recombinant bovine somatotropin (rbST), a synthetically produced version of a naturally occurring hormone intended to increase milk production.

8. In the debate over the Codex Statement of Principles (formally, the "Statement of Principles Concerning the Role of Science in the Codex Decision-Making Process and the Extent to Which Other Factors Are Taken into Account"), the United States and European Union sought to propagate decision criteria that favored their domestic agricultural policy regimes. The United States and its allies argued that food safety standards should rest solely on scientific evidence, while Europe and its allies sought to introduce a "need" criterion, which held that productivity-enhancing food technologies threatened the livelihoods of economically marginal farmers and were not "needed" in the face of excess global capacity. A compromise resulted in a statement that Codex standards "shall be

In the first matter, compromise language was eventually negotiated.[8] In the second and third matters, the standards for hormone-treated beef (favoring producers in North America, Japan, Australia, New Zealand, and Korea, among others) and mineral water (favoring European producers) were approved by slim majorities rather than by consensus. In the fourth matter, the Codex voted to hold the draft standard for rbST at the last step of the eight-step approval process rather than adopt it as an international standard—an outcome favored by countries that had banned the domestic use of rbST for a variety of reasons unrelated to human health, including consumer concerns, animal welfare concerns, and concerns about the impact of increased milk production on small dairy farmers (Codex 1999a).[9] More recent controversies addressed in the WTO, such as the regulation of genetically modified foods, now routinely spill over into Codex deliberations.

Implementation of the SPS Agreement

The obligations under the SPS agreement address aspects of national regulations that could create trade disputes. Experience has accumulated within the WTO and the standard-setting organizations from which the implementation of the agreement can be evaluated. While hard to quantify, it is apparent that the SPS agreement has generated broad-based regulatory review by many WTO members, both major agricultural exporters and importers, as they determine whether they and their trading partners are complying with obligations. Evidence suggests that regulatory authorities are either unilaterally modifying regulations or voluntarily modifying regulations after technical exchanges (Roberts 1998). To give just two examples of accelerated schedules for making long-standing measures consistent with the obligations in the SPS agreement: in 1997 Japan agreed to rescind its 46-year ban on several varieties of tomatoes grown in the United States after weighing scientific research indicating that they were not afflicted with tobacco blue mold disease, and in 1999 the United States ended a 20-year dispute with four European countries by agreeing

based on the principle of sound scientific analysis and evidence," but, where appropriate, Codex will consider "other legitimate factors" in protecting consumer health and promoting fair trade practices (Codex 2001a). Subsequent efforts by Codex to translate these principles into more specific guidance have achieved some progress, but fundamental differences in approaches to risk management are still evident (Codex 2001b).

9. The United States maintained that JECFA's scientific evaluation should be the only determining factor for the adoption of the rbST standard, and that on the basis of this evaluation the standard should be adopted. Germany (speaking on behalf of the European Union) stated that adoption of the standard "would not be appropriate" (Codex 1999a).

to allow imports of rhododendrons in growing media under a new phytosanitary protocol. More systematic reports, while far from comprehensive, reinforce the anecdotal evidence of a demonstration effect from the SPS agreement. The United States and Australia, respectively, report resolution of 338 and 240 SPS cases in bilateral negotiations over five years (USDA's *SPS Accomplishment Reports* 1996–2000 and *World Food Chemical News* 2001a). Enacting regulatory changes that allow greater market access has become easier now that the SPS agreement assures policymakers that their trading partners must conform to the same science-based principles. The requirements have also prodded authorities to revisit regulations whose longevity could be attributed to simple inertia rather than overt protectionism.

Progress toward realization of the four principles under the SPS agreement—harmonization, science-based risk management, equivalence, and regionalization—also reflects how well the framework of the SPS agreement and supporting institutions has addressed agriculture and food regulatory issues.

Harmonization

The SPS agreement's endorsement of harmonization stems from repeated complaints by exporters that compliance with divergent SPS measures substantially increases the transactions costs of trade. Firms that ship products to several different markets stand to gain if harmonization results in lower production and certification costs on a per unit basis. Harmonization also can benefit consumers—an outcome more likely if the regulatory heterogeneity arises from differences in chance events, informational differences, or interest group capture. Harmonization is less likely to be appropriate if differences in income, taste, and risk are the primary sources of variation in national regulations.

The impact of harmonization on trade appears to be constrained as much by the lack of specific international standards as by normative considerations under the SPS agreement. Of the SPS measures notified to the WTO by members during 1995 to 2002, a majority stated that no international standard existed for the measure. The character of international standards as a public good leads to an expectation of underinvestment in their creation. This underinvestment may lead not only to too few international standards but also to too many outmoded standards, which may account in part for the low adoption rate for those standards that do exist. Over the first four years of the SPS agreement (1995–99), partial or full acceptance of international standards as a percentage of total notified measures was highest for the lower-middle-income countries at 38 percent; followed by high-income countries, 22 percent; lower-income countries, 20 percent; and upper-middle-income countries, 17 percent (Roberts, Orden, and Josling 1999).

The generality of recent international standards also is important in assessing their impact on trade and trade disputes. Over the past decade, international standards organizations have allocated more of their resources to developing meta-standards that identify common approaches to risk identification, assessment, and management than to specific international standards per se. Exporters' anticipated gains from international meta-standards may be smaller than from specific international standards because adherence to the same general guidelines leaves scope for countries to develop different regulatory regimes to manage risks. For example, even countries that adopted the Codex's 1997 "General Principles of Food Hygiene" have had substantive differences in their requirements for reducing microbial risks, as the European Union's decision to ban imports of US poultry meat in 1997 illustrates (Becker 1999). Thus in recent years international standards organizations have contributed more to the trade system by setting out scientific approaches to regulation than by promulgating standards that are identical across countries, implying that the benefits from international standards have accrued more to consumers than exporters.

Science-Based Risk Management

The requirement to base regulations on scientific risk assessment clearly reduces the latitude for disingenuous use of SPS regulatory interventions. In each of the four SPS disputes to reach the WTO Appellate Body since the SPS agreement came into effect, the regulations at issue were judged to violate this requirement.[10] However, the impact of the science-based risk management requirements of the SPS agreement within the WTO extends beyond formal dispute settlement results. The explicit obligation to base measures on science has led to the resolution of many issues in Geneva before they advance to dispute settlement. In particular, food safety measures that discriminate among sources of supply attract close scrutiny, and sometimes appear to lack scientific rationale. For example, an exemption to a ban on sauces containing benzoic acid that Australia had granted to New Zealand during their transition to a common food standards system was replaced with a tolerance level for all imports in response to a Philippine complaint in the SPS Committee. Disagreements over less overtly discriminatory measures have been resolved by means of updated risk assessments. For example, a scientific review led Korea to amend its new food code to exempt poultry meat destined for further processing and cooking from its new zero tolerance standard for *Listeria*, thereby allowing imports of Thai frozen chicken to resume (WTO 2002f).

10. The four cases—EC-Hormones, brought by the United States and Canada; Australia-Salmon, brought by Canada; and Japan–Varietal Testing and Japan-Apples, both brought by the United States—are discussed later in this chapter.

Although the obligation to base measures on risk assessments can often avert trade disputes, it cannot always do so, sometimes because the relevant risk assessments are not available to inform regulatory responses to new hazards. "Emergency" measures have accounted for 17 percent of the total SPS measures notified to the WTO (OECD 2002). Because such measures are generally very trade-restrictive, they often give rise to complaints if importers fail to modify these policies as new evidence emerges.[11] For example, the European Union had to repeatedly petition Argentine regulators before they modified trade restrictions on Belgian chocolate, German milk powder, and Swedish cacao oil butter—long after other countries had lifted bans on these products upon learning that the OIE and the WHO had reaffirmed that existing scientific data did not indicate that dairy products are BSE vectors.

Risk assessments also do not avert disagreements over measures that reflect extremely conservative approaches to mitigating scientifically verified risks. The national sovereignty principle of the SPS agreement entitles countries to adopt measures that achieve their chosen levels of protection, subject to the requirement that measures be no more trade-restrictive than necessary to achieve these levels. In seeking enabling legislation for undertaking WTO obligations, the US Statement of Administrative Action to Congress asserted that this provision, along with other language in the agreement, "explicitly affirms the rights of each government to choose its levels of protection including a 'zero risk' level if it so chooses" (President of the United States 1994). The national sovereignty principle thus provides leeway for countries to adopt measures that achieve incremental reductions in risk regardless of the costs to either their domestic producers and consumers or their trading partners.[12] Conservative measures may be maintained under the agreement even when these measures fail to increase domestic welfare. To cite but one recent example, New Zealand decided to maintain a ban on imports of bone-in poultry cuts from the United States based on an assessment that shipments posed a risk of three introductions of infectious bursal disease in noncommercial (i.e., backyard) chicken flocks per 100 importation years (New Zealand Ministry of Agriculture and Forestry 2000).[13] Such policies may be scientifically

11. Annex B of the SPS agreement requires a country to publish a new regulation in advance of its entry into force "except in urgent circumstances." The procedures for notifying the WTO of these emergency regulations is set out in the SPS Committee's "Recommended Notification Procedures" (WTO 1996).

12. In other words, requiring evidence of some risk precludes application of SPS regulations only in cases that are shown to lie on the vertical axis in figure 2.1, while otherwise allowing countries to choose their level of risk aversion.

13. The OIE regards infectious bursal disease as a hazard "of socio-economic and/or public health importance within countries" (List B) but finds that it lacks "the potential for very serious and rapid spread, irrespective of national borders," and is not a disease "of serious socio-economic or public health consequence" (List A). See chapter 4 for further discussion of the OIE's recommended risk management practices for List A and List B diseases.

justifiable, but nonetheless fail benefit-cost tests by ignoring the benefits of imports to domestic consumers. Such measures are likely to be seen as unreasonable by exporters.

The SPS agreement provides little elaboration of risk management principles to guide resolution of disputes other than the requirement to minimize trade effects for chosen levels of risk reduction. Negotiators of the agreement judged it inappropriate for the WTO to be more prescriptive about risk management, seeing the standards organizations as the better forum for the development of templates for regulatory practices. Guidance has been provided by the OIE, IPPC, and Codex, and internationally recognized standards and procedures may further narrow the scope for trade disagreements.[14] But it is unrealistic to expect that these principles will eliminate disputes over the best course of action to take in regulation, given the scientific evidence. Science is descriptive, not prescriptive. A risk management decision will therefore always require a choice among different policy options, each with different costs and benefits. Options that severely limit market access to achieve extremely incremental health or safety benefits are likely to be contentious, even if based on science.

Equivalence

Article 4 of the SPS agreement requires each WTO member to accept another member's measures as equivalent to its own if the exporting country can demonstrate that its measures achieve the importing country's desired level of SPS protection. This provision recognizes that regulatory flexibility allows countries to allocate scarce resources efficiently rather than identically. The SPS agreement also seeks to promote trade by requiring members, upon request, to enter into consultations for bilateral and multilateral agreements on the equivalence of their measures.

Equivalence determinations mostly involve process standards, because countries are more easily able to compare product standards that stipulate the observable or testable attributes of goods. An enormous number—and arguably a growing proportion—of food safety SPS measures are process standards, as discussed in depth in chapter 5. The SPS equivalence obligation therefore has the potential to yield significant benefits in international markets for products such as cheeses, meats, fresh produce, and seafood—that is, those products for which process standards are the main instruments used to manage microbial risks.

There is no systematic accounting of negotiations of equivalence

14. The Codex's "Working Principles for Risk Analysis" and the Codex "Statement of Principles" noted earlier are two examples of risk management guidance promulgated by an international standards organization for the benefit of its members. The adoption by the Codex reflects a strong desire on the part of member countries to achieve a consensus on some aspects of risk management policy, but these documents have not yet reconciled disagreements over some fundamentals such as the role of precaution and "other legitimate factors" in regulatory decision making.

arrangements to date, but their use is not common in international food trade, despite the conceptual appeal.[15] The administrative burden of equivalence determinations is often significant, involving evaluation of infrastructure, overall program design and implementation, and specific technical requirements. For example, a framework agreement signed by the United States and the European Union in July 1999 to recognize equivalence of some SPS measures for selected animal products[16] required six years of occasionally high-profile negotiations that extended to details such as the color of wall paint in food-processing facilities. Under this agreement, the exporting country must continue to comply with the importing country's measures that are not judged to be equivalent, including several that regulate food and feed additives and animal drug residues. Both the European Union and the United States also recognize the equivalence of some measures for selected meat and dairy products from Australia, Canada, and New Zealand. However, numerous regulatory differences remain in contention, even between countries generally recognized as having rigorous regulatory standards that are rigorously enforced.

Often, differences between countries hinge not only on the equivalence of different process standards themselves but also on how conformance with different standards is ascertained. For example, differences over government and industry roles in certification have held up EU recognition of the equivalence of the US production and inspection systems for food-grade gelatin. Exports from the United States to the European Union have been suspended since June 2000, when the European Commission's new BSE-related regulations came into force. The European Commission has indicated that most US gelatin safety measures are equivalent to corresponding EU measures. However, the European Union has been unwilling to import US gelatin until there is more oversight by the US Food and Drug Administration (FDA) of industry self-certification of compliance with the two "non-equivalent" measures (WTO 2002f).

Given the problems that developed countries have had with equivalence arrangements, developing countries have questioned whether this provision of the SPS agreement will provide many export opportunities for them (WTO 1998c). Some equivalence agreements exist between developing and developed countries, especially for seafood products.[17] However,

15. Although the SPS Committee has urged members to submit information on their bilateral equivalence arrangements, few have done so (WTO 2001b). Gascoine (1999) discusses reasons for limited early use of equivalence in international food trade.

16. The agreement applies to approximately $1 billion in EU exports of dairy products, fish, and meat to the United States, and to a similar value in US exports of fish, hides, and pet food to Western Europe.

17. The European Union, for example, states that 62 countries have been recognized as implementing an equivalent system of inspection and certification for fishery products, and another 41 await equivalence evaluations but can currently export fishery products to individual EU member states on the basis of bilateral agreements (WTO 2002d).

developing countries, echoing the claims of developed countries, have argued that often compliance with domestic measures rather than equivalence of alternative measures is required by importing countries. Even developing countries that have had substantial success as agricultural exporters, such as Brazil, Mexico, and Thailand, have gone on record to note the difficulties in gaining recognition of equivalence (WTO 1999e, 2001d).

Globally, the limited access to developed-country markets for poultry meat illustrates both the potential and challenge of equivalence. Of the 148 WTO member countries (as of September 2003), only 15 are eligible to export fresh, chilled, or frozen poultry meat to the European Union; only 4 can export to the United States; only 1 can ship to Canada; and none are allowed to export to Australia.[18]

Because of a recent decision by the SPS Committee to increase the transparency of equivalence arrangements, a more systematic assessment of the impact of equivalence on global food trade will eventually be possible.[19] Transparency may further the objective of increasing regulatory flexibility, but significant constraints remain nonetheless. First, significant time and resources can be required for equivalence determinations, as the bilateral framework agreement between the United States and the European Union illustrates. According to the United States, the potential for equivalence may be limited because the actual trade benefits often do not justify the administrative burden (WTO 2000a).[20] Second, after recognizing the equivalence of an alternative regulatory regime, national regulators may have to offer the same alternative to domestic producers, requiring in turn new or revised domestic regulations. Finally, if national regulations are specified in legislation, there is little scope for regulators to consider other options without new legislative authority.[21]

18. In addition to the four countries (Canada, Great Britain, France, and Israel) that are permitted to export fresh, frozen, or chilled poultry to the United States, some plants in northern Mexico can reexport US-origin poultry meat to the United States after minimal processing.

19. In 2001 the committee revised its recommended procedures to provide for the notification of equivalence of SPS measures and finalized the notification format in June 2002. In its Decision on the Implementation of Article 4, the committee noted that equivalence could be accepted for a specific measure or measures related to a certain product or categories of products, or on a systemwide basis (WTO 2001a).

20. The United States also has cautioned that equivalence does not imply mutual recognition. Under the equivalence provisions of the SPS agreement, market access is contingent on a scientific determination that an exporter's alternative measure achieves the level of SPS protection required by the importer, not on the reciprocity of such determinations.

21. For example, the US Egg Products Inspection Act of 1970 requires continuous inspection of processed eggs by government inspectors, a standard that is currently met by only one other country (Canada).

Regionalization

The regionalization provision of the SPS agreement is an integral part of a science-based approach to regulating trade, because differences in levels of risks do not always correspond to national political boundaries. Regionalization allows countries to export products from areas where animal or plant health risks are considered negligible, thereby benefiting consumers without jeopardizing the agricultural resource base in the importing country. Chile's decision to allow imports of fresh melons and watermelons from all US production areas except Hawaii is one example of a regional approach to mitigating pest risks (WTO 2000b). By ensuring that geographic eradication or reduced incidence of hazards leads to trade gains, regionalization also provides incentives for additional investments in control measures. Over time, this SPS provision is likely to be of growing importance in international agricultural markets.

As with equivalence, agricultural producers in developing countries face more challenges than developed-country producers in capitalizing on the regionalization provisions, because exports will generally depend on adequate public-sector investments in laboratory, inspection, monitoring, and certification infrastructure. And national regulations will not always be effective: transborder pest or disease controls may be required where there are insufficient natural barriers or where animals, including wildlife, move freely across borders. It is therefore likely that creating or strengthening implementation of regional sanitary and phytosanitary measures across as well as within countries will often be necessary to realize fully the gains from trade. Coordination of this sort requires substantial institutional capabilities (see the discussion of control of FMD in chapter 4).

The TBT Agreement

The TBT agreement sets out rules for mandatory regulations, voluntary standards, and conformity assessment procedures that are not covered by the SPS agreement.[22] Like the SPS agreement, the TBT agreement acknowledges the right of countries to develop product requirements as well as procedures to assess compliance with those requirements. However, it attempts to ensure that the preparation, adoption, and application of these measures do not create unnecessary obstacles to trade. The TBT agreement is becoming increasingly important in global food markets as governments promulgate more regulations and standards in response

22. Article 1.5 of the TBT agreement states that "the provisions of this Agreement do not apply to sanitary and phytosanitary measures as defined in Annex A of the Agreement on the Application of Sanitary and Phytosanitary Measures."

to growing consumer demands for products with specific quality attributes or for information about those attributes.

Basic Provisions

While technical regulations and conformity assessment procedures are covered in the main body of the TBT agreement, standards are covered in the Code of Good Practice for the Preparation, Adoption and Application of Standards (Code of Good Practice) set out in Annex 3 of the agreement. The substantive disciplines of the TBT agreement begin with a list of legitimate objectives for which regulations may be developed. These provisions also delineate the types of evidence that can be used to judge whether the required measures are necessary to fulfilling those objectives:

> Such legitimate objectives are, inter alia: national security requirements; the prevention of deceptive practices; protection of human health or safety, animal or plant life or health, or the environment. In assessing such risks, relevant elements of consideration are, inter alia: available scientific and technical information, related processing technology or intended end-uses of products.

The agreement then sets out key principles for adherence by WTO members. Article 2 of the TBT agreement stipulates that members

- must not discriminate against imported like products from other WTO members;
- must not adopt measures that are more trade-restrictive than necessary to fulfill a legitimate objective;
- must monitor and review measures to address changes in circumstances and objectives;
- must base measures on international standards when available and where appropriate;
- must give positive consideration to recognizing other members' measures as equivalent to their own, even if different, provided that they are satisfied that another country's measures adequately fulfill the objectives of their own regulations; and
- must base measures, where appropriate, on product performance requirements rather than design or descriptive characteristics.

The TBT agreement also requires each country to ensure that its central government standardizing bodies adhere to the Code of Good Practice, which endorses most of the principles found in the TBT agreement itself. WTO members also are to take reasonable measures to ensure that other governmental and nongovernmental standards organizations within their territories accept and comply with the code.[23]

In addition to these disciplines, the TBT agreement sets out information exchange and enforcement mechanisms that are very similar to those established under the SPS agreement. These mechanisms include notification procedures and inquiry points for informing other WTO members of changes in TBT measures, a TBT committee to discuss issues on a continuing basis, and use of WTO dispute resolution mechanisms for resolving conflicts between countries in a timely manner.

Related Standards Organizations

The TBT agreement, unlike the SPS agreement, does not reference specific international standards organizations. Instead, the WTO recognizes the international standards of all of those organizations that adhere to the principles established by the TBT Committee in the Decision of the Committee on Principles for the Development of International Standards, Guides, and Recommendations (WTO 2000c). These principles include transparency, openness, impartiality and consensus, effectiveness and relevance, coherency, and attention to the needs of developing countries.[24]

A diffuse set of public and private organizations promulgate international food standards, either as a principal or as an ancillary undertaking. These organizations include regional institutions such as the United Nations Economic Commission for Europe (UN/ECE); plurilateral institutions such as the Organization for Economic Cooperation and Development (OECD), which operates the Scheme for the Application of International Standards for Fruits and Vegetables and recently has taken responsibility for plurilateral dialogue on the regulation of biotechnology; and multilateral institutions such as the International Dairy Federation (IDF) and the International Organization for Standardization (ISO).

---

23. All nongovernmental as well as governmental standardizing organizations are invited to accept the code and abide by its provisions. Motaal (2002) notes that because most of the organizations that develop standards are nongovernmental, the code was created to bring their work under the purview of the TBT agreement.

24. Not all international organizations that address food regulations meet the criteria laid out by the TBT Committee. The WHO, for example, has not always adopted its standards on the basis of consensus, and other organizations do not provide an opportunity to comment on proposals being considered by WTO countries that are not members of the standards organization. These institutions may nonetheless influence the development of international standards recognized as such by the WTO. For example, the WHO is well positioned to convene expert scientific panels on issues of emerging importance, such as biotechnology and microbial resistance, and to distribute their findings even if the findings are not in accordance with the views of the entire WHO membership.

Public and private institutions often collaborate in the development of international standards. For example, the IDF, a private organization, is the source of draft standards for milk products in the intergovernmental Codex Committee for Dairy Products. Several state and provincial governments have similarly contributed to the development of eco-labeling standards that have been adopted by the ISO, another private organization. In most instances, the international standards themselves are voluntary; when mandatory, only members of the organization are obliged to comply. However, as reference points for the global food system, either by incorporation into national regulations or through voluntary contracts of private firms, such standards have the potential to affect trade significantly.

The Codex, responsible for promulgating standards to promote fair food trade practices as well as to improve food safety, is the foremost multilateral institution in the governance framework for food quality measures. The very first Codex standard (for canned tomatoes) was related to its fair trade mandate rather than food safety. Over the past few years, the Codex has drafted, finalized, or amended international standards or guidelines for quantitative declarations of ingredients, nutrition labeling, health claims, country-of-origin labeling, organic production and labeling, and labeling of genetically modified foods (Codex 2001c). Bodies such as the Codex Committee on Food Labeling have become battlegrounds at the center of some of the most prominent disputes over food regulation within the global trading system.

Implementation of the TBT Agreement

In the implementation of the TBT agreement, the appropriate use of labels for agricultural and food products to signal quality attributes has been one of the most contentious issues among countries. Proposed requirements for country-of-origin labeling for perishable foods, eco-labeling of forestry products, traditional expressions for wine and spirits, labeling for genetically modified products, and other labeling regimes draw objections from members at almost every meeting of the TBT Committee (WTO 2002c). Disagreements over these proposals arise to some extent from uncertainty over the TBT agreement's rules for labeling what have been called "non-product-related process and production methods" (npr-PPMs), regulations that target process attributes not materially evident in the end product. Much of this uncertainty stems from the agreement's definition of a technical regulation. Annex 1 of the TBT agreement defines a technical regulation as a

> [d]ocument which lays down product characteristics or their related processes and production methods, including the applicable administrative provisions, with which compliance is mandatory. It may also include or deal exclusively with terminology, symbols, packaging, marketing, or labeling requirements as they apply to a product, process or production method.

In the view of some WTO members, the ambiguous language used in this definition has called into question the applicability of Article 2 requirements to npr-PPMs. The first sentence refers only to product characteristics or their "related" PPMs. The second sentence, which explicitly mentions labeling, refers to "products" and PPMs without qualification. The lack of a specific reference to npr-PPMs in the definition could be taken to suggest that such measures are not bound by the rules in the TBT agreement per se, although other GATT disciplines might apply. Instead, some countries have taken the lack of explicit mention of npr-PPMs in the definition to imply that such measures are simply not allowed. Other countries have disagreed with this interpretation, arguing that such measures should be, and are, disciplined by the TBT agreement; otherwise, many important regulations—in particular, many of the emerging quality-related process attribute regulations—would be outside its scope (WTO 2001f, 2001g). This unresolved debate poses a serious challenge for the governance of food regulations. The npr-PPMs, or process standards addressing process attributes, are growing in importance in domestic and international food markets (see the more in-depth discussion in chapter 7).

Should a complaint over a labeling regime for an npr-PPM advance to a WTO panel, one factor likely to be relevant is whether the measure discriminated against an imported like product in violation of Article 2 of the TBT agreement. Several GATT/WTO dispute panels have analyzed "likeness" under GATT Article III.4 rules for national treatment, but the meaning of like products under the TBT agreement has not been interpreted by a panel or the Appellate Body. The Appellate Body's first opportunity to examine the meaning of "likeness" under GATT Article III was provided by the European Union's appeal of the panel report in the Canada-EU asbestos dispute in 2001 (WTO 2001c). For this determination of likeness, the judges based their analysis on four criteria that were slightly modified from earlier GATT reports: (1) the physical properties of the products, (2) the extent to which the products are capable of serving the same or similar end uses, (3) the extent to which consumers perceive and treat the products as alternative means of performing particular functions in order to satisfy a particular want or demand, and (4) the tariff classification of the products.[25]

Because of the varying interpretations of the definitions and articles in the agreement, the TBT Committee agreed in 2001 to begin a series of informal meetings to discuss uncertainties about the legitimacy of various

25. The Report of the Working Party on Border Tax Adjustments (BISD 18S/97, adopted December 2, 1970) outlined the initial approach for analyzing "likeness." Based on the first three criteria, this approach has been followed and developed since by several panels and the Appellate Body. The fourth criterion, tariff classification, was not mentioned in this report, but was included by subsequent panels.

labeling policies (WTO 2001g). If countries are unable to agree on a common understanding of the rights and obligations set out in the TBT agreement, the remaining ambiguities may have to be resolved via formal WTO dispute resolution. Although the dispute settlement process may lead to resolution in specific cases, the outcomes would have less generality and less legitimacy than rules produced by deliberate debate among all WTO members.

The TRIPS Agreement

The TRIPS agreement obligates countries to provide "effective and appropriate means for the enforcement of trade-related intellectual property rights" for each type of intellectual property that it covers. The three main kinds of intellectual property instruments are copyright for artistic and literary works; patents and similar devices for inventions, industrial designs, and trade secrets; and trademarks, signs, and geographical indications for commercial identification.

The provisions of the TRIPS agreement of particular importance to global food trade are the international rules for protection of GIs.[26] Although GIs are used for industrial products, such as Silicon Valley microchips, most are used to aid in the marketing of agricultural products. Countries differ considerably in the way their laws handle GIs. Some countries have specific GI laws. Others use trademark law, consumer protection law, marketing law, or common law, or some combination of these. Some countries have formal lists of registered geographical indications. Others do not, preferring to rely on court case histories (based on criteria such as consumer protection) to identify where problems have arisen and been resolved. Although it does not harmonize these national regulations, the TRIPS agreement does establish criteria that domestic regulations must meet. The objective is to avoid trade conflicts that inevitably arise if different countries have different coverage and use incompatible instruments for protection of intellectual property.

Basic Provisions

The TRIPS agreement sets forth the negotiated definition of a GI and provides two different levels of protection for this type of trademark. GIs are defined as "indications which identify a good as originating in the territory of a Member, or a region or locality in that territory, where

26. TRIPS protection for new plant varieties (though not necessarily by patents) and for innovations in microbiology also is important to the world food system, but these forms of intellectual property are beyond the purview of this book. See Watal (2000) for a discussion of these issues.

a given quality, reputation or other characteristic of the good is essentially attributable to its geographic origin."

Article 22 of the TRIPS agreement offers protection for GIs for all goods, requiring countries to provide the legal means for private interests to prevent the use of a designation that is misleading or constitutes unfair competition. GIs for products protected under US law include "Idaho" for potatoes and "Washington State" for apples. Examples of foreign GIs that are protected in the United States are "Roquefort" (for cheeses), "Darjeeling" (for tea), and "Swiss" (for chocolate).

The TRIPS agreement provides additional protection for GIs that identify wines and spirits. Article 23 stipulates that any use by a third party of a wine or spirit GI belonging to another is prohibited—consumer protection or unfair competition does not have to be demonstrated. Moreover, the use of terms including kind, type, style, or imitation in tandem with a wine or spirit GI is prohibited.

Article 24 of the TRIPS agreement sets out two exceptions to the general rules. Countries are not required to extend protection to a GI if the term is the generic name for the product in the importing country. The United States can therefore continue to permit the use of "chablis," "champagne," and "Swiss cheese" as synonyms for white wine, sparkling wine, and Emmenthal-style cheese, because they have been recognized as generic terms under US trademark law.

The second exception is found in Article 24's grandfather provisions for existing product names. An importing country is not required to protect a GI if a trademark was in use in that country before the TRIPS agreement came into effect or before the GI was protected in its country of origin. Protection for existing names for wines and spirits is narrower under the grandfather provisions. Names for these products must have been in continuous use in the importing country for at least 10 years before conclusion of the Uruguay Round to exempt the importing country from its obligation to protect a GI that uses the same product identifier.

Related Governance Institution for GIs

The TRIPS agreement specifically references the World Intellectual Property Organization (WIPO), based in Geneva, as the relevant international body for GIs. The WIPO administers various international agreements that deal partly or entirely with the protection of geographical indications, such as the Lisbon Agreement for the Protection of Appellations of Origin and Their International Registration. The WIPO's Standing Committee on the Law of Trademarks, Industrial Designs and Geographical Indications, composed of representatives of member states and interested organizations, considers new initiatives for the international protection of GIs.

Implementation of the TRIPS Agreement

The TRIPS agreement's wide accommodation of national differences in protection of GIs narrows the scope for successful legal challenges. Thus few complaints about this form of intellectual property have surfaced under the Uruguay Round rules, and only one formal dispute over GIs has emerged over the 1995–2002 period.[27]

This record belies, however, the level of discord over the administration and enforcement of GIs in the world food system. The TRIPS agreement calls for negotiations on two aspects of GI protection, although it does not say when these negotiations should take place, or when they should end. Article 23 calls for negotiations on the establishment of a multilateral centralized registry system for GIs for wines and spirits, and Article 24 requires negotiations aimed at extending the higher level of protection Article 23 accords to wines and spirits to other products. Countries differ widely in their positions in these negotiations.

One set of proposals for the central registry sees the system as essentially a database: Members would report the GIs for wines and spirits that they protect, and other members would take the information into consideration when making a decision about protection under their own systems. Another group of countries have proposed that participating countries be obliged to protect the GIs listed on the central registry, subject to certain conditions. Similarly, WTO members differ widely on extending Article 23 protection to other products. These differences stem from, among other things, diverse interpretations of which product identifiers can be considered GIs and are therefore eligible for protection.

Disagreement even extends to the appropriate WTO venue for negotiations on strengthened GI protection for products other than wine and spirits. The Doha Ministerial Declaration refers to these negotiations as one of many "implementation issues" that "shall be addressed as a matter of priority by the relevant WTO bodies." These bodies are then to report back to the Trade Negotiating Committee, which oversees the multilateral trade talks. Some countries have concluded that this language establishes a mandate for GI extension negotiations as part of the "single undertaking" of the Doha Round, but others see only an obligation to continue discussions in the TRIPS Council, the WTO body that oversees implementation of the agreement. Frustrated proponents of GI extension have thus explicitly linked progress on this issue to the Doha negotiations on agriculture. Proposals for expanding GI protection have been submitted to the agriculture negotiations, casting GI protection as a question of market access for agricultural products (Roberts, Unnevehr, et al. 2001).

27. The formal dispute (DS 174 in table 3.2) involves a US objection to the breadth of GI protection for a Czech Republic beer. It has led to the cancellation of two trademarks of the Anheuser-Busch company in four European countries.

Any assessment of whether strengthening protection for GIs will improve the global food system must consider several issues. Property right holders will benefit if new rules reduce the transactions costs of globally marketing differentiated products. Consumers also may benefit if new rules lead to lower search costs and curbs on misleading claims. However, producers and consumers in some countries may be disadvantaged if repatriation of GIs results in the loss of generic identifiers that consumers have come to associate with a style rather than the origin of a product, such as Dijon mustard. Developing countries that do not produce wine and spirits must weigh whether the benefits of strengthened rules for GI for products of interest to them, such as tea and rice, are greater than increased enforcement costs for protection of domestic and foreign GIs in their home market. These issues are examined at greater length in chapter 6.

Enforcement of the Multilateral Disciplines

The quantitative impact of food regulations on trade and welfare is largely unknown, primarily because systematic information on the regulations themselves is lacking and methods of economic assessment are underdeveloped (Beghin and Bureau 2001, Maskus and Wilson 2001). However, the evidence suggests that disagreements over these measures have become more important over time. This raises the question of whether the mechanisms set up in the WTO have made it easier to solve trade conflicts over technical regulations. Two avenues can be identified within the WTO through which it has had an impact. First, the WTO has provided a forum, primarily through the SPS and TBT Committees, in which members can informally discuss technical barriers to trade and resolve questions or disputes over existing regulations or new measures that have been notified to the WTO. Second, in a small number of cases, formal disputes have been launched under the DSU.

SPS and TBT Notifications and Counter-notifications

The WTO's notification requirements are the cornerstone of the transparency provisions that are intended to facilitate decentralized policing by trading partners to ensure compliance with the substantive provisions of the SPS and TBT agreements. All of the major agricultural exporting and importing countries now routinely notify the WTO of proposed measures.

In fact, between 1995 and 2001 members submitted more than 2,400 SPS notifications to the WTO, far more than submitted under prior GATT obligations.[28] As might be expected given its wider scope, countries have submitted many more notifications under the TBT agreement than the SPS agreement. Between 1995 and 2001, the WTO recorded nearly 4,100 TBT notifications (WTO 2002e). Although agriculture's share of worldwide merchandise trade is about 10 percent (and it accounts for a much smaller share of the economies of developed countries that submitted the majority of TBT notifications), about 800, or 20 percent, of the TBT notifications referenced agricultural products (USDA 2002).

Each notification indicates, among other things, what the proposed measure is, the product or products to which it is applied, whether it is based on an international standard, and when it is expected to come into force. Although the notifications are essentially "regulator to regulator" communications, and more could be done to clarify how these measures might affect trade, the notification process has increased the transparency of national regulatory decisions. This increased transparency contributes to the smooth functioning of the world trading system by facilitating both compliance and complaints by trading partners. Compliance is aided when advance notice of new or modified measures gives firms an opportunity to change production methods to meet new import requirements, thereby minimizing the disruptions to trade flows of such changes. Notifications also give trading partners an opportunity to raise questions or objections to proposed measures in the relevant committee before they are adopted as regulations. In all cases, trading partners can continue to raise objections to measures viewed as violating WTO obligations.[29]

WTO members have taken advantage of this process, registering 187 complaints (or "counter-notifications") in the SPS Committee between 1995 and 2001 (see table 3.1).[30] In the SPS Committee, counter-notifications have been spread among goals related to animal, plant, and human health. A large number of complaints have concerned the regulation of transmissible spongiform encephalopathies (TSEs), which include bovine spongiform encephalopathy (BSE). TSE measures alone accounted

28. Between 1980 and 1990, countries notified the WTO of only 168 measures to prevent risks to public health and safety under the Standards Code, and fewer than half of those notifications concerned SPS regulations (GATT 1990–91).

29. Emergency measures are "notified" after the fact, but they are still subject to the scrutiny of trading partners while they remain in effect.

30. Other WTO committees have formally adopted the term *counter-notifications* to reference complaints or requests for further information. Although the SPS and TBT Committees have not done so, the term is used here to help distinguish the complaints raised in these committees from those that proceed to formal dispute settlement. The complaints are variously recorded under "information from members," "specific trade concerns," and "other business" in the minutes of the SPS Committee meetings (G/SPS/R series) and under "administration and implementation of the agreement" in the minutes of the TBT Committee (G/TBT/M series). These sources are drawn on throughout this analysis.

Table 3.1 Number of complaints about regulations (counter-notifications) brought before the WTO's SPS Committee, 1995–2001

	Regulatory goal of contested measure					
Complaints by	**Plant health**	**Animal health**	**TSEs[a]**	**Human health**	**Other[b]**	**Total**
Developed countries against						
Other developed countries	12	3	23	19	1	58
Developing countries	12	6	15	16	1	50
Multiple countries	0	1	0	0	0	1
Subtotal	24	10	38	35	2	109
Developing countries against						
Developed countries	11	12	10	20	1	54
Other developing countries	7	9	2	3	1	22
Multiple countries	0	2	0	0	0	2
Subtotal	18	23	12	23	2	78
Total	42	33	50	58	4	187

a. Transmissible spongiform encephalopathies, including BSE.
b. Includes complaints about administrative issues and horizontal regulations that reference human, animal, and plant health as objectives.

Source: Authors' tabulation from WTO (2002h).

for more than a fourth of the complaints raised in the SPS Committee since 1995, indicating that BSE has significantly disrupted international trade.[31] The BSE case, which has been an important test for the global health system, is examined in chapter 4.

Developed countries were most often the source as well as the target of counter-notifications that identified SPS regulations as unjustified trade impediments. Measures falling in the TSE and human health categories accounted for more than two-thirds of developed-country complaints. These measures also accounted for nearly three-fourths of the complaints raised against developed countries. The complaints against developed countries by other developed countries (42) outnumbered those by developing countries (30) in these categories, suggesting that access to the

31. The large number of trade disputes is related to the reluctance of countries to relax emergency import restrictions in the light of the human health consequences, the lack of established precedent for many of the health measures put into place, and the fact that cattle, the vector of BSE, provide so many food and industrial products, including meat and milk for human consumption, gelatin for pharmaceutical purposes, semen for breeding, and other by-products used in cosmetics and commercial animal feed, among other things.

same scientific information and technologies still leaves ample scope for disagreement over food safety measures among trading partners with similar per capita incomes.

Whether developing countries have been able to participate effectively in the activities of the various committees has been a concern of the WTO. The incidence of counter-notifications sheds some light on this important institutional question. Developing countries have accounted for just over 40 percent of the counter-notifications, or slightly less than their share of global food trade. A slight majority of the developing country counter-notifications targeted animal and plant health measures.

Contention over labeling in implementation of the TBT agreement has been reflected in labeling requirements being among the principal targets of counter-notifications raised in the TBT Committee. The committee recorded 117 complaints related to 38 labeling regulations in its meetings between 1995 and October 2002 (WTO 2002g). In 2000, during the last formal review of the operation and implementation of the TBT agreement, the committee reiterated that labeling regulations must be consistent with WTO rules in view of the number of disagreements over these measures (WTO 2000c). The large majority of the counter-notifications referenced labeling requirements for agricultural products (102), and the remainder were directed at regulations for industrial products (10) or both agricultural and industrial products (5).

The proposed labeling regimes have drawn objections for various reasons. One reason is that exporters believe compliance costs will be high, even if there are no anticipated impacts on demand. This objection most often applies to labeling that importers require for customs enforcement of other border policies such as tariffs and tariff rate quotas (TRQs).[32] Egypt's proposed regulation requiring the name of the country of origin to be woven into each end of a bolt of cloth falls into this category. Other objections to labeling regimes are related to the regimes' expected market effects. Objections to some proposals, such as the country-of-origin labeling requirements proposed by the United States and Japan for foodstuffs, reflect this concern. Other labeling regimes raise concerns because exporters fear both higher supply costs and significant effects on demand. In this category are the highly controversial notifications of mandatory labeling regimes for genetically modified products by Australia, Brazil, Chile, the European Union, and New Zealand, which collectively were the target of 15 TBT counter-notifications (see chapter 7).

Proposed regimes for labeling process attributes (npr-PPMs), whether mandatory or voluntary, also have been especially controversial. Examples

32. Under the Agreement on Agriculture, TRQs limit the quantity of agricultural imports eligible for a low tariff.

are the voluntary labeling scheme for dolphin-safe tuna proposed by the United States, the mandatory eco-labeling of timber proposed by the Netherlands, and the voluntary labeling of industrial and agricultural products using socially responsible production methods proposed by Belgium. Together, these regimes have accounted for 23 counter-notifications from both developed and developing countries.

WTO Dispute Settlement Cases

Between 1995 and 2002, WTO member countries made 32 formal requests for consultations related to food regulation trade barriers under the DSU. These complaints, which are summarized in table 3.2, account for 11 percent of the total formal DSU complaints for all products under all agreements over this time period.[33] Nineteen of these complaints reference animal or plant health measures, with the balance referencing food safety measures (six), labeling measures (four), environmental measures (two), and geographical indications (one). Formal complaints related to food regulations exhibit the same pattern observed for counter-notifications—developed countries are both the petitioner and respondent in the majority of cases, but not in every case. More recently, over the four years 1999 to 2002, developing countries initiated more complaints (six) than developed countries (five).

Seven complaints related to food system regulation reached a WTO panel ruling and the Appellate Body. Five of these complaints involved SPS measures, and all of them concerned regulations found to have no rationale in terms of risk reduction. In the first complaint (DS 18), Canada challenged Australia's ban on salmon imports imposed ostensibly to prevent the spread of disease in recreational and commercial fish stocks. In separate complaints (DS 26 and DS 48) heard by the same WTO panel, the United States and Canada challenged the scientific basis for the EU ban on growth hormones in beef production. In the fourth complaint (DS 76), the United States challenged Japan's testing requirements regarding treatment effectiveness for all new varieties of selected horticultural products. In the most recent SPS case to go to the Appellate Body (DS 245), the United States challenged Japan's strict phytosanitary regime for imported apples to prevent entry of diseases such as fire blight.

The measures at issue in these cases were imposed by developed countries. In each case, the panel and Appellate Body ruled for the complainants (exporters) on at least some grounds, so these disputed cases have shown

33. It also is notable that 70 percent of the complaints that have cited violations of the TBT agreement over this same period were related to food regulations. Only eight complaints referenced other sectors, including textiles, petrochemicals, and pharmaceuticals.

Table 3.2 WTO disputes over regulation of agricultural product safety and quality, 1995–2002

Dispute number	Petitioner(s)	Respondent	Issue	Agreement(s) referenced in dispute proceedings	Status (through September 2003)
1995					
DS 3	United States	Korea	Measures concerning testing and inspection of agricultural products	GATT, SPS, TBT, URAA	Consultations
DS 5	United States	Korea	Measures concerning shelf life requirements	GATT, SPS, TBT, URAA	Settled
DS 7	Canada	European Communities[a]	Trade description of scallops	GATT, TBT	Settled
DS 12	Peru	European Communities	Trade description of scallops	GATT, TBT	Settled
DS 14	Chile	European Communities	Trade description of scallops	GATT, TBT	Settled
DS 18	Canada	Australia	Measures affecting importation of salmon	GATT, SPS	Panel and Appellate Body ruled against Australia
DS 20	Canada	Korea	Measures concerning bottled water	GATT, SPS, TBT	Settled
DS 21	United States	Australia	Measures affecting importation of salmon	GATT, SPS	Settled
1996					
DS 26	United States	European Communities	Measures affecting meat and meat products (hormones)	GATT, SPS, TBT, URAA	Panel and Appellate Body ruled against EC

(table continues next page)

Table 3.2 *(Continued)*

Dispute number	Petitioner(s)	Respondent	Issue	Agreement(s) referenced in dispute proceedings	Status (through September 2003)
DS 41	United States	Korea	Measures concerning the testing and inspection of agricultural products	GATT, SPS, TBT, URAA	Consultations
DS 48	Canada	European Communities	Measures affecting meat and meat products (hormones)	GATT, SPS, TBT, URAA	Panel and Appellate Body ruled against EC
DS 58	India, Malaysia, Pakistan, Thailand	United States	Import prohibition on certain shrimp and shrimp products	GATT	Panel and Appellate Body ruled against the United States
DS 61	Philippines	United States	Import prohibition on certain shrimp and shrimp products	GATT, TBT	Consultations
DS 72	New Zealand	European Communities	Measures on butter products	GATT, TBT, import licensing	Settled
1997					
DS 76	United States	Japan	Measures affecting agricultural products (varietal testing requirements)	GATT, SPS, URAA	Panel and Appellate Body ruled against Japan
DS 96	European Communities	India	Quantitative restrictions on imports of agricultural, textile, and industrial products	GATT, SPS, URAA	Settled

(table continues next page)

Table 3.2 WTO disputes over regulation of agricultural product safety and quality, 1995–2002 *(Continued)*

Dispute number	Petitioner(s)	Respondent	Issue	Agreement(s) referenced in dispute proceedings	Status (through September 2003)
DS 100	European Communities	United States	Poultry requirements	GATT, SPS, TBT	Consultations
1998					
DS 133	Switzerland	Slovakia	Dairy product imports and transit of cattle (BSE restrictions)	GATT, SPS, import licensing	Consultations
DS 134	India	European Communities	Restrictions on rice	GATT, customs valuation, import licensing, SPS, TBT, URAA	Consultations
DS 137	Canada	European Communities	Measures affecting imports of wood of conifers	GATT, SPS, TBT	Consultations
DS 144	Canada	United States	Certain measures affecting imports of cattle, swine, and grain	GATT, SPS, TBT, URAA	Consultations
1999					
DS 174	United States	European Communities	Protection of trademarks and geographical indications for agricultural products and foodstuffs	TRIPS	United States has requested a panel to hear its complaints
2000					
DS 203	United States	Mexico	Measures affecting trade in live swine	GATT, SPS, TBT, URAA	Consultations

(table continues next page)

Table 3.2 *(Continued)*

Dispute number	Petitioner(s)	Respondent	Issue	Agreement(s) referenced in dispute proceedings	Status (through September 2003)
DS 205	Thailand	Egypt	Import prohibition on canned tuna with genetically modified soy oil	GATT, SPS	Consultations
2001					
DS 210	United States	Belgium	Administration of measures establishing customs duties for rice	GATT, TBT, URAA, Customs Valuation Agreement	Settled
DS 231	Peru	European Communities	Trade description of sardines	GATT, TBT	Panel and Appellate Body ruled against EC
DS 237	Ecuador	Turkey	Certain import procedures for fresh fruit	GATT, GATS, SPS, import licensing procedures, URAA	Settled
2002					
DS 245	United States	Japan	Measures affecting importation of apples	GATT, SPS, URAA	Panel and Appellate Body ruled against Japan
DS 256	Hungary	Turkey	Import ban on pet food	GATT, SPS, URAA	Consultations
DS 263	Argentina	European Communities	Measures affecting imports of wine	GATT, TBT	Consultations

(table continues next page)

Table 3.2 WTO disputes over regulation of agricultural product safety and quality, 1995–2002 *(Continued)*

Dispute number	Petitioner(s)	Respondent	Issue	Agreement(s) referenced in dispute proceedings	Status (through September 2003)
DS 270	Philippines	Australia	Importation of fruits and vegetables	GATT, SPS, import licensing	Under review by panel
DS 271	Philippines	Australia	Certain measures affecting importation of fresh pineapple	GATT, SPS	Consultations

a. See chapter 3, footnote 3.

Source: WTO (2003a).

that the measures of countries with advanced scientific establishments are not immune to challenge.

The two other cases that reached WTO panels and the Appellate Body involved developing-country complainants and pertained to provisions of WTO law dealing with environmental measures (DS 58 filed against the United States by India, Malaysia, Pakistan, and Thailand) and with restrictive identity labeling (DS 231 filed against the European Union by Peru).

In addition to these seven complaints, 25 formal WTO complaints were filed against food-sector regulations during 1995–2002. Two of these complaints have proceeded to WTO panels though not to the Appellate Body as of December 2003: the Philippines complaint against Australian quarantine measures for fresh fruits and vegetables (DS 270) and the US complaint against the EU regime for protection of GIs (DS 174).[34] Ten complaints were settled prior to a panel hearing or the release of a panel report. Thirteen cases related to the regulation of food are technically still pending, although WTO reports indicate that trade has resumed in some instances (WTO 2002h, 2002f). One of these cases involved Egypt's restrictions on Thai tuna packed in soybean oil, which is the first case related to genetically modified food to come before the WTO.

34. The US request for a panel to hear its complaint against the EU GI measures was submitted to the WTO in August 2003. The complaint against Australia's quarantine measures is still under review by a WTO panel.

Rulings about SPS Measures

The formal dispute rulings reveal how different articles of the SPS agreement can be used to evaluate the legitimacy of a measure. The outcome of these cases is summarized in table 3.3.

The bellwether test of the disciplines of the SPS agreement was the challenge by the United States and Canada of the scientific basis for the European Union's ban on growth hormones in beef production, discussed further in chapter 5. The European Union's defense of its measure rested on its claims that the international standards for these hormones did not meet its public health goals and that the ban represented a precautionary approach to managing uncertain risks. The WTO panel concluded, and the Appellate Body upheld the decision, that the European Union's ban violated the provisions of the SPS agreement (McNiel 1998, Roberts 1998). Both the panel and the Appellate Body affirmed the right of WTO members to establish a level of consumer protection higher than the level set by international health standards. The ban was nonetheless judged to be in violation of the SPS agreement, because, in violation of Articles 3.3 and 5.1, it was not backed by an objective risk assessment. The panel and judges also rejected the European Union's use of the precautionary principle in its legal defense, because no explicit reference to this principle appears in the SPS agreement. Article 5.7 of the agreement recognizes a conditional precautionary principle, which allows countries to provisionally adopt measures "on the basis of available pertinent information" while seeking additional information "necessary for a more objective assessment of risk." However, the European Union could not defend its permanent ban by reference to this provision.

The panel also ruled that the EU ban violated Article 5.5, which requires countries to avoid variation in the levels of health protection provided by its SPS measures, if such variation results in discrimination or creates a disguised restriction on trade. The Appellate Body overturned this panel finding. The judges concurred with the panel that EU policies on the use of growth-promoting substances in animals were "arbitrary and unjustifiable" because the European Union allowed their use in pork. However, they disagreed that the ban was "a disguised restriction on trade," perhaps in deference to the fact that the ban arose from public anxieties that emerged in the late 1970s and early 1980s after widely publicized reports of illegal veterinary drug use in Italy and France. Although the Appellate Body was willing to acknowledge that the ban was originally motivated by "consumer concerns" rather than protectionism, the overall outcome of the case suggests that the WTO will rule against measures based on popular misconceptions of risks as well as more overtly discriminatory measures.

In the salmon case, the Appellate Body concurred with Canada that Australia's 1975 ban on imports of fresh, chilled, or frozen (eviscerated)

Table 3.3 Decisions in the four SPS cases heard by WTO panels and the Appellate Body

	European Communities:[a] Hormones— As judged by		Australia: Salmon— As judged by		Japan: Varietal testing— As judged by		Japan: Apples— As judged by	
SPS provision violated	Panel	Appellate body	Panel[b]	Appellate body	Panel	Appellate body	Panel	Appellate body
Article 2.2. Measures must be based on scientific principles and must not be maintained without sufficient scientific evidence.			X	X	X	X	X	X
Article 2.3. Members must ensure that SPS measures do not arbitrarily or unjustifiable discriminate between members where identical or similar conditions prevail.			X	X				
Article 3.1. Members shall base their SPS measures on international standards, where they exist, except as otherwise provided for in Article 3.3.	X							
Article 3.3. Members may adopt SPS measures which result in a higher level of SPS protection than would be achieved by measures based on the relevant international standards, if in accordance with the requirements under Article 5.	X	X						

Article 5.1. Measures must be based on a risk assessment.	X	X	X	X		X	X	X
Article 5.5. Members shall avoid distinctions in levels of SPS protection if such distinctionsresult in discrimination or a disguised restriction on trade.	X			X				
Article 5.6. Measures must be not more trade-restrictive than required.			X		X			
Article 5.7. Members can adopt measures on a provisional basis when scientific evidence is insufficient, but must seek additional information to conduct a risk assessment.					X	X	X	X
Article 7 and Annex B. Measures must be transparent.				X	X			

a. See chapter 3, footnote 3.

b. The original panel, at the request of Canada, reviewed the revised measures adopted by Australia after the Appellate Body's ruling. The panel judged that the revised measures were not in compliance with Australia's obligations under Articles 2.2, 5.1, and 5.6 of the SPS agreement. It also ruled that Tasmania's continuing ban on Canadian salmon imports was in violation of Articles 2.2 and 5.1. Australia has since revised its measures to Canada's satisfaction; the Tasmanian ban is still in place.

salmon from the Northern Hemisphere was inconsistent with the legal obligations set forth in the SPS agreement. The Appellate Body ruled that the report used by Australia to inform its policy decision did not constitute a risk assessment because it did not evaluate the likelihood of entry, establishment, and spread of diseases, nor did it evaluate the potential consequences of these diseases. The Appellate Body agreed with the panel finding that the report contained "general and vague statements of mere possibility of adverse effects occurring; statements which constitute neither a quantitative nor a qualitative assessment of probability." The Appellate Body also concurred with Canada that the ban provided a level of environmental protection that was arbitrarily higher than that provided by other Australian SPS measures, because Australia allows imports of other fish that are potential vectors for the same, or even more virulent, diseases.

The third SPS case to reach the Appellate Body was the varietal testing dispute. At issue were Japanese requirements to test whether methyl bromide treatments effectively exterminate codling moths on each new variety of fruit and walnuts imported into that country. The United States argued that such requirements restricted US exports (the cost of the required trials discouraged exporters from marketing new hybrids in Japan) and were unscientific because Japan could produce no evidence to support the claim that variety is a causal factor of variation in extermination efficacy. The panel and Appellate Body ruled that Japan's phytosanitary measures were not based on a risk assessment or on sufficient scientific evidence, because evidence presented during the proceedings indicated that testing each product, rather than each variety of each product, was sufficient. Japan's argument that the measure was provisional was not accepted since it had been in place for 48 years. Even if the measure had been accepted as provisional, the Japanese requirement for data from an exporter did not fulfill the obligation under Article 5.7 to seek additional information to complete a risk assessment. Finally, the panel and the Appellate Body found that, in violation of Article 7, the measure was not transparent, because it failed to meet the conditions for publication set out in an annex of the SPS agreement.

In the most recent SPS case to reach the Appellate Body, the United States brought its complaint against Japanese requirements for imported apples (including chlorine dip, cold treatment, and orchard inspections by Japanese phytosanitary authorities) to the WTO for resolution. A WTO panel concurred with the United States that these measures violated the SPS agreement, primarily because there was no scientific basis for the requirements. The WTO Appellate Body upheld the panel's findings in November 2003. Most other countries accept the US phytosanitary regime (which includes good commercial production practices, grading and sorting, and visual inspection for pests) as adequate for mitigating the risk of diseases and pests affecting apples, such as fire blight and coddling moth.

The effectiveness of the DSU rulings, as measured by the changes made to importers' policies after a successful challenge, has been mixed. To date, the salmon and varietal testing cases have successfully concluded with changes in the importing country's measures. Japan and the United States are still negotiating a mutually acceptable settlement in the apples case. In the hormones case, the European Union did not fulfill its obligation to bring its measure into compliance with the SPS agreement by a May 1999 deadline, stating that it needed more time to complete risk assessments. The WTO consequently authorized the United States and Canada to increase tariffs on US$128.1 million of EU exports until the European Union complied with the ruling or provided compensation for the ban by lowering other trade barriers. The parties continue to discuss options, such as increased market access for hormone-free beef and labeling, but the case has not yet been settled. Both the ban and the retaliatory tariffs remain in place.

The rulings in these four SPS disputes provide important case law. The four formal WTO rulings on SPS regulations set precedents on the requirement for risk assessment, consistent risk management, the limits on adoption of measures on a provisional basis, and transparency. The outcome of the hormones dispute also raises questions about the capacity of the WTO to resolve disputes about food regulations when intense national political sensitivities are involved.

Rulings about TBT and GATT Articles

The remaining two formal disputes related to food regulations pertain to other provisions of WTO law. The first WTO panel report to examine the compliance of a food regulation (or indeed any regulation) with the TBT agreement involved Peru's complaint against the European Union's regulation of the labeling of sardines (DS 231), which is discussed in detail in chapter 6. The panel found that the EU regulation, which restricted use of the term *sardines* to one species found off the coasts of Europe and Morocco, was in violation of Article 2.4 of the TBT agreement, which requires countries to use international standards except when "ineffective or inappropriate" to "the fulfilment of the legitimate objectives pursued." The panel found that a Codex labeling standard for sardines was both effective and appropriate for meeting the European Union's three stated objectives of market transparency, consumer protection, and fair competition. This case provides some guidance about the status of international standards under the TBT agreement.

The other case, the shrimp/turtle dispute, could have significant implications for food regulations that affect trade, though somewhat less direct. It involved an environmental measure related to food trade. In 1996 India, Malaysia, Pakistan, and Thailand brought a case (DS 58) against US restrictions (Section 609 of Public Law 101-162) on shrimp caught without turtle excluder devices (TEDs) designed to reduce accidental deaths of sea turtles in shrimp trawler nets. The WTO panel and Appellate Body agreed that the objective of the US law was legitimate under Article XX(g) of the GATT, which allows trade restrictions to protect exhaustible natural resources, but faulted the implementation of the policy, which had resulted in arbitrary and unjustifiable discrimination against the complainants in violation of Article XX's preamble. Two years later, on the grounds that the United States had not appropriately implemented the recommendations of the WTO, Malaysia requested that the matter be referred once again to the original panel, as provided for by the DSU. In particular, Malaysia objected to the fact that the United States had chosen to bring its policies into compliance by providing foreign suppliers with TED technology rather than by lifting its import prohibition on shrimp from countries that had not adopted the same conservation policy. The panel and the Appellate Body agreed, however, that US implementation of the rulings and recommendations in the initial case was justified under Article XX(g) of the GATT, noting the ongoing and serious "good faith" efforts of the United States to reach a multilateral agreement with the complainants.

The shrimp/turtle case is one of those in GATT/WTO jurisprudence that calls into question the "product-process doctrine" that was first applied in the 1991 Tuna-Dolphin decision.[35] The effect of this legal doctrine was to make it prima facie GATT illegal for governments to adopt trade-restrictive taxes or regulations based on how the product was produced, unless the production method (such as unsanitary food processing) materially affected the product. Thus regulations prohibiting the sale of imported goods based on how they were produced—even if the same regulations applied to domestic products—would violate GATT Articles III or XI, unless justified under one of the public policy exceptions of GATT Article XX.

The legal reasoning of the shrimp/turtle decision suggests that Article XX exceptions can be available to permit governments to regulate products on the basis of the process by which they were produced. However, it is unclear whether the scope of the Article XX exception validated by the shrimp/turtle decision will extend beyond environmental measures, or even how much precedent this case set. Consequently, some legal scholars have concluded that the product-process doctrine remains a potential "lethal threat" to regulations with a process attribute focus (Hudec 2001).

35. In this dispute, the panel ruled that a US import ban on tuna harvested in ways harmful to dolphins violated either GATT Article III.4 (which requires that the imported product "be accorded treatment no less favorable than that accorded to like products of national origin") or Article XI (which prohibits quantitative restrictions on imports), depending on the characterization of the law. The panel went on to rule that neither of these two GATT violations was excused under GATT Article XX, and thus that the tuna embargo was prohibited by GATT law.

The Doha Development Agenda Negotiations

Despite the intention of the Uruguay Round to provide a durable multilateral framework to discipline the use of food safety and quality regulations, proposals submitted by countries both leading up to and after the Doha Ministerial Conference in November 2001 indicate that a remarkable divergence of views has emerged about this framework. Developing-country proposals signal frustration with the increasingly exigent standards faced by their exports, the new obligations to justify their own regulatory regimes, or both. They worry that without more progress on meeting these challenges, their participation in international trade will be further marginalized. The proposals of some developed countries, however, would likely increase the challenges faced by developing countries. These developed countries argue that the adequacy of current WTO rules has been called into question by new production technologies, new disease outbreaks, and new demands for regulations that are responsive to consumer concerns. They call for modification of WTO rules to give governments more latitude in regulating risks and product differentiation. This approach is advanced as an enlightened strategy for the entry of agriculture into the "century of quality, not quantity."

WTO members agreed at the Doha Ministerial Conference to take concrete steps to improve implementation of the current agreements in order to address some of the issues and concerns of developing countries (WTO 2001e).[36] These steps include initiatives under both the SPS and TBT agreements that came into effect at the Doha Ministerial Conference. Specifically, greater technical and financial assistance is to be provided to developing countries to help them to fulfill their own obligations under these agreements, to increase their participation in the international standards organizations, and to enable them to comply with new SPS and TBT measures in export markets.[37] In addition, countries are committed to developing a program to advance implementation of the equivalence obligation under the SPS agreement. WTO members also will give developing countries more time to comply with their measures—a form of WTO special and differential treatment—as long as staggered implementation allows the importing country to realize its appropriate level of protection.[38]

36. In May 2000 the WTO initiated "implementation negotiations" to address the needs of developing countries after the Seattle Ministerial Conference failed to launch a new round of trade negotiations (WTO 2001e).

37. In September 2002 the World Bank (WB) and the WTO launched an initiative to link aid to trade opportunities to help in the fight against poverty. The joint WB/WTO initiative included a fund called the Standards and Trade Development Facility.

38. Other issues on which no agreement could be reached were referred back to subsidiary WTO bodies (e.g., the SPS and TBT Committees), which will discuss them further and report back to the committee overseeing all trade negotiations in this round.

Beyond these specific initiatives, the Doha Declaration commits WTO members to further negotiations on some issues related to food regulation through several different venues. Most important, the declaration confirms that nontrade concerns will be part of the negotiations on agriculture, in addition to the three Uruguay Round pillars of market access restrictions, export subsidies, and domestic support measures resulting from national farm policies. In the Uruguay Round, countries identified food security and rural development as nontrade concerns that required specific exemptions from the rules set out in the Agreement on Agriculture. In the Doha Round, some developed countries have identified food safety, food labeling, and animal welfare as additional nontrade concerns meriting special treatment. They have proposed modification of rules set out in the agriculture agreement and in other agreements as they apply to agricultural products. Specifically, these countries advocate subsidies for meeting animal welfare standards and increased protection for geographical indications for products other than wines and spirits, explicit recognition of the legitimacy of the precautionary principle, and mandatory labeling of npr-PPMs. Some developing countries have supported these proposals, but most see them as running counter to their interests in the agriculture negotiations by increasing the difficulty of gaining access to developed-country markets and diverting attention from the core agenda of lowering other barriers to trade.

The Doha Declaration also calls for negotiations on trade and the environment that may have implications for the governance of food regulation. The trade and environment negotiation group will address how WTO rules are to apply to WTO members that also are parties to environmental agreements. These negotiations are widely perceived to be a means of clarifying the WTO status of trade measures that might be taken under any of the multilateral environmental agreements, but in particular the Biosafety Protocol of 2000 (also called the Cartagena Protocol), which authorizes use of the precautionary principle in risk management.[39] The Doha Declaration also asks the WTO's Trade and Environment Committee to continue its work on environmental labeling.

In short, although no country has formally proposed reopening the SPS or TBT agreement during the Doha Round of trade negotiations, the WTO is immersed in issues that will further define the global food regulatory governance regime. In view of the many uncertainties about these negotiations, the next chapter turns to more detailed examination of the global regulation of agricultural and food products.

39. The Doha Declaration is careful to note that the negotiations shall not prejudice the WTO rights of any member that is not a party to the MEA in question, and that the outcome shall not add to, diminish, or alter the balance of rights and obligations of members under existing WTO agreements, in particular the SPS agreement. The Biosafety Protocol is discussed in chapter 7.

References

Becker, Geoffrey, 1999. U.S.-European Agricultural Trade: The Veterinary Equivalence Agreement. Report RS20242. Congressional Research Service, July 26.

Beghin, John C., and Jean-Christophe Bureau. 2001. *Quantification of Sanitary, Phytosanitary, and Technical Barriers to Trade for Trade Policy Analysis.* Working Paper 01-WP-291. Ames, IA: Center for Agricultural and Rural Development, Iowa State University.

Codex Alimentarius Commission. 1999a. Report on the 23rd Session Food and Agricultural Organization and World Health Organization, ALINORM 99/37. 1999, Rome. www.codexalimentarius.net/archiVes.asp.

Codex Alimentarius Commission. 1999b. Understanding the Codex Alimentarius. Food and Agricultural Organization and World Health Organization, Rome. www.fao.org/docrep/w9114e/w9114e00.htm.

Codex Alimentarius Commission. 2001a. Procedural Manual. 12th ed. Food and Agricultural Organization and World Health Organization, Rome. www.fao.org/DOCREP/005/U2200E00.HTM

Codex Alimentarius Commission. 2001b. Report of the Sixteenth Session of the Codex Committee on General Principles. ALINORM 01/33A. Geneva: Codex.

Codex Alimentarius Commission. 2000c. *Report on the Twenty-Ninth Session of the Codex Committee on Food Labeling.* ALINORM 01/22A. Geneva: Codex.

Gascoine, Digby. 1999. Harmonization Mutual Recognition and Equivalence: How and What is Attainable. Paper presented at the WHO/FAO Conference on International Food Trade Beyond 2000, Melbourne, Australia, October.

Hudec , Robert. 1996. GATT Legal Restraints on the Use of Trade Measures Against Foreign Environmental Practices. In *"Fair Trade and Harmonization: Prerequisites for Free Trade?* Vol. 2, *Legal Analysis*, ed. Jagdish Bhagwati and Robert Hudec. Cambridge, MA: MIT Press.

Hudec, Robert, 2001. The Product-Process Doctrine in GATT/WTO Jurisprudence. In *New Directions in International Economic Law,* ed. Marco Bronckers and Reinhard Quick. The Hague: Kluwer Law International.

Johnson, Robbin. 1996. APEC and the Global Food System. Paper presented at *Toward a Pacific Rim Food System: Forum on US Agriculture and Food Trade Policy in APEC.* National Center for APEC, Washington State University (April).

Josling, Tim, Donna Roberts, and Ayesha Hassan. 1999. The Beef-Hormone Dispute and Its Implications for Trade Policy. European Forum Working Paper. Stanford University, September.

McNeil, Dale. 1998. The First Case Under the WTO's Sanitary and Phytosanitary Agreement: The European Union's Hormone Ban. *Virginia Journal of International Law* 39: 89–134.

Maskus, Keith E., and John S. Wilson, eds. 2001. *Quantifying the Impact of Technical Barriers to Trade: Can It Be Done?* Ann Arbor: University of Michigan Press.

Motaal, Doaa Abdel, 2002. The Agreement on Technical Barriers to Trade, the Committee on Trade and Environment, and Eco-labelling. In *Trade, Environment and the Millennium,* ed. Gary Sampson and W. Bradnee Chambers. New York: United Nations University Press.

New Zealand Ministry of Agricultural and Forestry. 2000. *Import Risk Analysis: Chicken Meat and Chicken Meat Products.* Wellington, NZ: Biosecurity Authority.

OECD (Organization for Economic Cooperation and Development). 1999. *Food Safety and Quality: Trade Considerations.* Paris: OECD.

OECD (Organization for Economic Cooperation and Development). 2002. *A Survey of Issues and Concerns Raised in the WTO's SPS Committee.* CP/TP/AGR/WP/(2002)21. Paris: OECD.

Patterson, Lee Ann, and Tim Josling. 2001. Biotechnology Regulatory Policy in the United States and the European Union: Source of Transatlantic Trade Conflict or Opportunity for Cooperation? Paper presented at the Western Economic Association International Conference, San Francisco (July).

Pollack, Mark A., and Gregory C. Shaffer. 2001. The Challenge of Reconciling Regulatory Differences: Food Safety and GMOs in the Transatlantic Relationship. In *Transatlantic Governance in the Global Economy,* ed. Mark A. Pollack and Gregory C. Shaffer. Lanham, MD: Rowman and Littlefield.

President of the United States. 1994. Message from the President of the United States Transmitting the Uruguay Round Trade Agreements to the Second Session of the 103rd Congress, Texts of Agreements Implementing Bill, Statement of Administrative Action and Required Supporting Statements, House Document 103–316. Vol 1: 742–63.

Roberts, Donna. 1998. Preliminary Assessment of the Effects of the WTO Agreement on Sanitary and Phytosanitary Trade Regulations. *Journal of International Economic Law* 1, no. 3: 377–405.

Roberts, Donna, David Orden, and Timothy Josling. 1999. WTO Disciplines on Sanitary and Phytosanitary Barriers to Agricultural Trade: Progress, Prospects, and Implications for Developing Countries. Paper presented at the World Bank Conference on Agriculture and the New Trade Agenda from a Developing Country Perspective, Geneva (October).

Roberts, Donna, L. Unnevehr, J. Caswell, I. Sheldon, J. Wilson, T. Otsuki, and D. Orden. 2001. Agriculture in the WTO: The Role of Product Attributes in the Agricultural Negotiations. International Agricultural Trade Research Consortium, Commissioned Paper no. 17. http://iatrcweb.org/Publication/commiss.html (May).

Stanton, Gretchen. 1997. Implications of the WTO Agreement on Sanitary and Phytosanitary Measures. In *Understanding Technical Barriers to Agricultural Trade,* ed. David Orden and Donna Roberts. St. Paul: International Agricultural Trade Research Consortium, Department of Applied Economics, University of Minnesota.

Sykes, Alan O. 1995. *Product Standards for Internationally Integrated Goods Markets.* Washington: Brookings Institution.

USDA (US Department of Agriculture). 2002. Database of Notifications to the Sanitary and Phytosanitary Committee and Technical Barriers to Trade Committee of the World Trade Organization, Foreign Agricultural Service, Division of Food Safety and Technical Services (accessed in October).

Veggeland, Frode, and Svein Ole Borgen. 2002. Changing the Codex: The Role of International Institutions. Norwegian Agricultural Economics Research Institute, Oslo (January).

Victor, David G. 1998. Risk Management and the World Trading System: Regulating International Trade Distortions Caused by National Sanitary and Phytosanitary Policies. In *Incorporating Science, Economic, and Sociology in Developing Sanitary and Phytosanitary Standards in International Trade Proceedings of a Conference* Washington: National Academy Press.

Watal, Jayashree 2000. *Intellectual Property Rights in the World Trade Organization: The Way Forward for Developing Countries.* Oxford: Oxford University Press.

Wilson, John S. 1995. *Standards and APEC: An Action Agenda.* Washington: Institute for International Economics.

World Food Chemical News. 2001a. Quarantine Laws Cited as Way to Gain Market Access. September.

WTO (World Trade Organization). 1996. Recommended Notification Procedures. Committee on Sanitary and Phytosanitary Measures, G/SPS/7, June 11.

WTO (World Trade Organization). 1998c. The WTO SPS Agreement and Developing Countries. Committee on Sanitary and Phytosanitary Measures, G/SPS/W/93, November 5.

WTO (World Trade Organization). 1999e. Summary of the Meeting Held on 7–8 July, 1999, Sanitary and Phytosanitary Committee, G/SPS/R/15, October 29.

WTO (World Trade Organization). 2000a. Equivalence: Submission from the United States. Committee on Sanitary and Phytosanitary Measures, G/SPS/GEN/ 212, November 7.

WTO (World Trade Organization). 2000b. Notification–Chile, Committee on Sanitary and Phytosanitary Measures. Committee on Sanitary and Phytosanitary Measures, G/SPS/N/CHL/56, February 11.

WTO (World Trade Organization). 2000c. Second Triennial Review of the Operation of the Implementation of the Agreement on Technical Barriers to Trade. Committee on Technical Barriers to Trade, G/TBT/9, November 13.

WTO (World Trade Organization). 2001a. Decision on the Implementation of Article 4 of the Agreement on the Application of Sanitary and Phytosanitary Measures, G/SPS/19, October 26.

WTO (World Trade Organization). 2001b. Equivalence: Note by the Secretariat. Committee on Sanitary and Phytosanitary Measures, G/SPS/W/111, July 4.

WTO (World Trade Organization). 2001c. European Communities–Measures Affecting Asbestos and Asbestos-Containing Products. Report of the Appellate Body, WT/DS135/AB/R, March 12.

WTO (World Trade Organization). 2001d. Experience with Recognition of Equivalence: Statement by Thailand. Committee on Sanitary and Phytosanitary Measures, G/SPS/GEN/242, April 6.

WTO (World Trade Organization). 2001e. Implementation-Related Issues and Concerns–Decision of 14 November, WT/MON(01)/17, November 20.

WTO (World Trade Organization). 2001f. Marking and Labeling Requirements: Submission from Switzerland. Committee on Technical Barriers to Trade, G/TBT/W/162, June 19.

WTO (World Trade Organization). 2001g. Minutes of the Meeting Held on 9 October, Committee on Technical Barriers to Trade. Committee on Technical Barriers to Trade, G/TBT/M/25, November 11.

WTO (World Trade Organization). 2002c. Labeling and the Requirements of the Agreement on Technical Barriers to Trade: Framework for Informal, Structured Discussions–Communication from Canada. Committee on Technical Barriers to Trade, G/TBT/W/174, March, 12

WTO (World Trade Organization). 2002d. A Practical Example of Implementation of the Principle of Equivalence: Submission of the European Communities, G/SPS/GEN/304, March 12

WTO (World Trade Organization). 2002e. Seventh Annual Review of the Implementation and Operation of the Agreement, G/TBT/11, February 18.

WTO (World Trade Organization). 2002f. Specific Trade Concerns. Note by the Secretariat. Committee on Sanitary and Phytosanitary Measures, G/SPS/GEN/204/Rev.2, January 16.

WTO (World Trade Organization). 2002g. Specific Trade Concerns Related to Labeling Brought to the Attention of the Committee Since 1995–Note by the Secretariat. Committee on Technical Barriers to Trade , G/TBT/W/184, October 4.

WTO (World Trade Organization). 2002h. Summaries of the Meetings of the Committee on Sanitary and Phytosanitary Measures. Committee on Sanitary and Phytosanitary Measures, G/SPS/R series, 1995–2001.

Chapter 17

Avocado Pests and Avocado Trade

Everett B. Peterson and David Orden

This article evaluates the effects of a November 2004 phytosanitary rule that removed seasonal and geographic restrictions on the importation of fresh Hass avocados from approved orchards in Mexico to the United States. With the remaining systems approach compliance measures in place, pest risks do not substantially increase and U.S. net welfare rises by $77 million. Removal of remaining compliance measures may lead to lower net welfare gains depending on which measures are eliminated and the estimated probabilities of pest infestations.

Key words: avocados, compliance costs, NAFTA, SPS barriers, systems approach.

Technical barriers related to pest risks can block or significantly impede market access for agricultural products. One approach to easing these barriers is to shift from import bans to less restrictive instruments. Such opening of market access may be achieved through a systems approach to risk management, whereby a set of compliance procedures are specified that reduce the pest-risk externality associated with trade of a commodity. Adoption of systems approaches rest on a firm foundation in Article 5.6 of the World Trade Organization (WTO) Agreement on the Application of Sanitary and Phytosanitary Measures (SPS Agreement), which states that Members shall ensure that their measures "are not more trade-restrictive than required to achieve their appropriate level of sanitary or phytosanitary protection" (WTO 1994).

This article develops a multi-season, partial equilibrium model with imperfect product substitution to evaluate the effects of allowing imports of fresh Hass avocados from approved orchards and packing houses in approved municipalities of Michoacán, Mexico, into the United States, under alternative compliance measures to mitigate pest risks. From 1914 until 1997, phytosanitary restrictions precluded entry of Mexican avocados into the conterminous United States due to prevalence of certain avocado-specific pests and fruit flies in Mexico. In November 1997, fresh Hass avocados from Mexico were allowed entry into nineteen northeastern states and the District of Columbia during a four-month period, November through February, under specified pest-management protocols. In 2001, the area approved for imports was expanded by an additional twelve states, and the period of importation was extended to six months, October 15 to April 15. The remaining geographic and seasonal restrictions were eliminated in a November 2004 rule that allowed year-around importation of Mexican avocados initially into forty-seven states (California, Florida, and Hawaii were excluded) and to all states starting in February 2007.

Progressive easing of the avocado import ban demonstrates successful application of a systems approach which has opened the U.S. market to approved Mexican producers and created more than a $100 million annual export industry. However, the compliance costs associated with the regulations remain controversial. Five avocado-specific pests generally not found in the United States (stem weevil, *Copturus aguacatae*; seed weevils *Conotrachelus aguacatae*, *C. perseae*, and *Heilipus lauri*; and seed moth, *Stenoma catenifer*) are prevalent within Mexico's production areas, particularly within noncommercial (backyard) orchards. Additional controversy has focused on four Mexican fruit flies (*Anastrepha fraterculus*, *A. ludens*, *A. serpentine*, and *A. striata*) that adversely affect numerous horticultural crops and are subject to local quarantine and

---

Everett B. Peterson is associate professor, Department of Agricultural and Applied Economics, Virginia Tech. David Orden is professor, Institute for Society, Culture and Environment, Virginia Tech, and senior research fellow, International Food Policy Research Institute (IFPRI).

We gratefully acknowledge funding by the USDA/ERS Program of Research on the Economics of Invasive Species Management (PREISM) and the Agricultural Development Policy Program of the Australian Centre for International Agricultural Research (ACIAR). We thank three anonymous reviewers for their suggestions and have benefited from discussions with many colleagues including Donna Roberts, Frank Filo, Claire Narrod, Suzanne Thornsbury, Eduardo Romano, Barry Krissoff, and Ray Trewin. Carlos Illsley and other growers and U.S. and Mexican phytosanitary officers in Urupan, Mexico graciously facilitated our field research.

Amer. J. Agr. Econ. 90(2) (May 2008): 321–335

DOI: 10.1111/j.1467-8276.2007.01121.x

eradication programs when discovered at U.S. sites. Mexican growers and sanitary authorities acknowledge the presence of the avocado pests but argue they can be effectively controlled in approved commercial orchards with relatively minimal measures, making the U.S. export compliance requirements excessive. They have also argued that Hass avocados are not a host for fruit flies, so the compliance measures required to monitor fruit fly infestations are unnecessary. USDA's Animal and Plant Health Inspection Service (USDA/APHIS) acknowledges that Hass avocados are a "poor" host for fruit flies but not a nonhost, which would justify elimination of the monitoring and control requirements.

The political economy of the controversy over avocado imports from Mexico has been intense. Roberts and Orden (1997) trace the regulatory process back through the 1970s, when Mexico nearly obtained import authorization, to the renewed discussions facilitated by the NAFTA negotiations in 1991, and the heated public hearings surrounding USDA's subsequent 1997 rule. Lamb (2006) further investigates the lobbying costs and political economy of this case in which the domestic industry once used full-page advertisements in major newspapers to assert that the Secretary of Agriculture by exposing it to pest risks was "about to destroy a $1 billion industry." Orden and Peterson (2006) conclude that opening of the U.S. market has required science (evidence of limited risk), opportunity (substantially higher prices in the U.S. market), traceability (to approved orchards), persistence (of the Mexican exporting association), and joint political will (under the NAFTA umbrella).

The economic impacts of avocado imports have been assessed in partial equilibrium simulation models in each of the final rules, but under the assumption that the systems approach adopted eliminated pest risks and without consideration of the exporter's compliance costs or potential trade-related pest damage. Romano (1998), and subsequently Orden, Narrod, and Glauber (2001), incorporate various pest risk and cost estimates into simulation of the 1997 partial opening of the market in a bilateral model with avocados from Mexico and the United States treated as perfect substitutes. Carman, Li, and Sexton (2006) present preliminary econometric evidence incorporating seasonality considerations to evaluate the implications of the initial market opening on likely imports with full Mexican access to the United States.

The analysis in this article extends the previous simulation analysis by explicitly considering compliance costs in Mexico, subsequent pest risks and U.S. producers' control costs and production losses in the event of a trade-related pest infestation. The analysis proceeds along lines suggested by Paarlberg and Lee (1998), Rendleman and Spinelli (1999), Glauber and Narrod (2001), Yue, Beghin, and Jensen (2006), Wilson and Anton (2006), and Calvin, Krissoff, and Foster (forthcoming) for determining optimal policies when there are pest risks associated with domestic or international movement of products. The model builds upon the detailed supply and demand structure utilized by APHIS in the economic analysis for the 2004 rule. The structural specification herein identifies three supply regions (southern California, Chile and Mexico), two seasons (winter and summer), and four domestic (U.S.) demand regions. In contrast to standard *ex ante* policy simulation analysis that uses demand and supply elasticities from the literature, our analysis utilizes post-2004-rule market data from 2005 to 2006 to calibrate and validate the model.

Three alternative compliance scenarios related to the ongoing controversies are examined in the simulation analysis: access to the U.S. market with the systems approach measures in effect as specified in the 2004 rule; additional elimination of the compliance measures directed specifically toward fruit flies; and elimination of all systems approach requirements. Our results show that the current systems approach reduces pest risk to a negligible level even without seasonal or geographic restrictions; fruit fly-related risks are minimal and eliminating the fruit fly compliance measures leads to a slight expected welfare gain; and elimination of all compliance measures for avocado-specific pests and fruit flies raises expected welfare under the average risk probabilities estimated by APHIS, but leads to a reduction of welfare compared to the 2004 rule under higher-risk probabilities. Because our model validation leads to a relatively large elasticity of avocado demand, we also undertake sensitivity analysis using two less-elastic values. The policy conclusions from a comparison among the three scenarios with the two levels of risk probabilities are robust across these alternative demand elasticities.

Framework of the Analysis

The avocado export program is administered jointly by APHIS and Mexico's Sanidad Vegetal (SV). The systems approach for importation of Mexican avocados contained nine different steps or requirements prior to the 2004 rule, as described in table 1. The 2004 rule eliminates the geographic and seasonal restrictions and modifies some of the remaining steps in light of the increased market access provided.

Only the Hass variety of avocados is included in the model because it accounts for nearly 85% of all avocados consumed in the United States. The chosen supply regions account for nearly all U.S. Hass avocado production (California) and over 95% of all Hass avocado imports (Chile and Mexico). The two seasons reflect seasonal production patterns among the suppliers and the restrictions on Hass avocado imports from Mexico prior to the 2004 rule. In season 1 (winter and a period of low domestic supply), Mexican Hass avocado imports were allowed into the specified states while no imports were allowed during season 2 (summer).

U.S. Consumer Demand

The demand for avocados is derived from a weakly separable, nested CES utility function for a representative consumer with purchases partitioned between avocados and everything else. Avocados from each of the three supply regions are assumed to be imperfect substitutes, reflecting observed U.S. wholesale price differentials. The demand specification for avocados in demand region i, from supply region j, in season k is defined as (see Keller 1976):

$$(1) \qquad q_{ij}^{k} = pop_i \left\{ \frac{b_{ki} a_{kij} wp_{kij}^{-\sigma_2} PI_{ki}^{(\sigma_2-\sigma_1)} I_{ki}}{b_{ki} PI_{ki}^{(1-\sigma_1)} + (1-b_{ki})} \right\}$$

where a_{kij} and b_{ki} are shift parameters, wp_{kij} is the wholesale price, σ_1 is the elasticity of substitution between avocados and all other goods, σ_2 is the elasticity of substitution among avocados, I_{ki} is per-capita income, and PI_{ki} is a CES price index defined as:

$$(2) \qquad PI_{ki} = \left\{ \sum_j a_{kij} wp_{kij}^{(1-\sigma_2)} \right\}^{\frac{1}{(1-\sigma_2)}}.$$

Four domestic demand regions are identified in the model to reflect differences in pest-risk susceptibility and per-capita consumption. Demand Region A corresponds to the thirty-one northern states and the District of Columbia, where imports of fresh Hass avocados were allowed by the 2001 rule. This region is not susceptible to outbreaks of any of the pests of concern. Southern California

Table 1. Systems Approach for Avocado Imports from Mexico

System Requirement	Description
Field surveys	Once per year prior to 2004, twice per year under 2004 rule
Trapping activities	1 trap per 10 hectares to monitor for fruit flies
Field sanitation	Remove fallen fruit weekly and prune dead branches
Host resistance	Hass cultivar only
Post-harvest Safeguards	Transport to packinghouse within 3 hours of harvest in screened trucks; transport from packinghouse in refrigerated containers, identity of grower, packinghouse, and exporter must be maintained
Packinghouse inspection	Stems and leaves removed from the fruit. Each fruit labeled with a sticker with registration number of the packinghouse. Inspectors in packinghouses inspect and cut 300 fruit sampled from each shipment. Each truck or container must be secured by Sanidad Vegetal before leaving packinghouse.
Port-of-arrival inspection	Inspectors ensure seals on the trucks are intact and shipment is accompanied by phytosanitary certification. One fruit per box from 30 boxes per shipment are sampled, cut, and inspect.
Geographical shipment restrictions	Shipments limited to 31 states plus District of Columbia (2001 rule); no geographic restrictions by February 2007 (2004 rule).
Seasonal shipment restrictions	Shipping allowed only October 15 to April 15 (2001 rule); no seasonal restrictions under 2004 rule.

Source: USDA/APHIS (2004b).

(Region D) is identified as a separate demand region because nearly all Hass avocado production occurs within this region, and it is susceptible to both avocado pests and fruit flies. The remaining portion of the United States is disaggregated into two regions: Region B, which is defined as the southeastern United States, and Region C, which is defined as the Pacific Northwest, the southwestern United States, northern California, and Hawaii. Region C is defined as a separate region due to its substantially larger per-capita consumption of Hass avocados than Region B.

The geographic area that is susceptible to fruit fly infestation is comprised of all of plant hardiness zones 8–11, which includes all or portions of California, Oregon, Washington, Nevada, Arizona, New Mexico, Texas, Louisiana, Arkansas, Mississippi, Alabama, Georgia, Florida, North Carolina, South Carolina, and Hawaii (USDA/APHIS 2004b). Thus, only a portion of Regions B and C are susceptible to fruit fly infestation. Because no information is available on avocado consumption in the fruit fly susceptible areas in Regions B and C, it is assumed that consumption in susceptible areas is proportional to the region's population in the those areas.

Supply of Californian Avocados

A Constant Elasticity of Transformation (CET) production possibilities frontier (Powell and Gruen 1968) is specified for California because ripe avocados may be left on the tree for many months before harvesting, allowing producers to shift sales between seasons as relative prices change. If a pest outbreak were to occur, the production possibilities frontier would shift inward toward the origin, as the pest outbreak reduces the amount of avocados produced from a given level of avocado specific factors (labor, capital and other inputs). A pest outbreak could also require producers to utilized costly control measures or affect the productivity of the inputs. The revenue function is:

$$(3)\quad R(p,V) = \left\{\delta(p_1 - CP)^{\beta} + (1-\delta)(p_2 - CP)^{\beta}\right\}^{\frac{1}{\beta}} \times [1 - (N_1 + N_2)pcteff * PL]V$$

where δ is a shift parameter, β is a parameter that determines the elasticity of transformation, p_1 and p_2 are producer prices in the first and second season, respectively, V is the level of factors employed, N_i is the frequency of a pest outbreak in season i, CP is expected per-unit cost of control measures, $pcteff$ is the proportion of total acreage affected by an infestation, and PL is the proportion reduction in productivity caused by an infestation.

The expression $(N_1 + N_2)pcteff * PL$ is the expected annual pest-related productivity loss, whose value is restricted to range between 0 and 1 for positive revenue and outputs.[1] The frequency of a pest outbreak depends on the level of imports and will vary across seasons, while the proportion of acreage affected and reduction of productivity on this acreage determines the severity of the loss per outbreak. It is assumed that the productivity loss associated with an outbreak is the same regardless of the season in which it occurs. The expression $(p_i - CP)$ represents the expected net price received by producers after paying for any pest control measures.

The conditional supply functions are the derivatives of equation (3), with respect to the producer prices. As the risk of an outbreak increases, there are two effects on the expected supply in each season. First, the expected reduction in productivity lowers output in each season proportionally. Second, because the supply functions are conditional on the level of the avocado specific factor utilized, a decrease in the expected net producer price will also lead to a reduction in its utilization. A linear supply function is assumed for the level of the aggregate avocado specific factor, and its parameters are chosen to replicate the aggregate supply response for avocados in each supply region.

Frequency of Pest Outbreaks

The frequency (number) of pest outbreaks for each season (1, 2) and demand region is:

$$(4)\quad N = prob1 * prob2 * prob3 * prob4 * prob5 * suscept * Q^{E}_{mex}$$

where $prob1$ is the probability (on a per-pound basis) that a pest infects fruit pre- or post-harvest; $prob2$ that the pest is not detected during harvest or packing; $prob3$ that the pest survives shipment; $prob4$ that the pest is not

[1] As shown below, in our analysis the base values are 20% for PL and 3% for $pcteff$. At these values, it would take more than 166.67 pest outbreaks for the value of $(N_1 + N_2)pcteff * PL$ to exceed one, which is more than estimated in any of our simulations.

detected at port-of-entry inspection; *prob5* that an outbreak occurs if the pest is present; *suscept* is the proportion of the demand region that is susceptible to an infestation; and Q^E_{mex} is the quantity of avocados exported from Mexico to the region. For avocado-specific pests the value of *suscept* equals one for Region D and zero for all other regions. For fruit flies *suscept* equals 0.0, 0.553, 0.806, and 1.0 for Regions A, B, C, and D, respectively. Estimates of the individual probabilities for the cases of no risk mitigation measures implemented and for the systems approach were obtained from the pest-risk assessment undertaken by APHIS in preparation of the 1997 rule (USDA/APHIS 1996).

A range of probability values (minimum, average and maximum) were estimated by APHIS for fruit flies, stem weevils, seed weevils and seed moths.[2] Because of the uncertainty about the true probability values, our simulations are conducted using the estimated average and maximum values. Under the APHIS, average pest risk estimates the net probability of a fruit fly pest outbreak per pound of avocado imports ($prob1 *\cdots *prob5$) is 3.9E−10, with no pest-risk mitigation measures decreasing to 1.2E−13 under the systems approach; while at APHIS's maximum probability values, the corresponding net probabilities are 3.2E−9 and 1.2E−12, respectively. For stem weevils, which have the highest risk probabilities among the avocado-specific pests, under the APHIS average risk estimates the net probabilities are 3.9E−8 with no risk mitigation, decreasing to 2.7E−10 with compliance measures. With the high-risk estimates the net probabilities for stem weevils are 3.2E−7 and 2.3E−9, respectively.

Costs of U.S. Control Measures and Domestic Productivity Losses

Control cost and production losses are considered for avocados due to fruit flies and avocado-specific pests and for other horticultural crops due to fruit flies. For avocados, the expected annual per-unit cost of controlling fruit flies is expressed as:

$$(5)\qquad CP_{ff} = \frac{CP_{inf}(N_1 + N_2)}{y_1 + y_2}$$

where CP_{inf} is the estimated cost of control per outbreak based on an existing regulatory program, the Texas Valley Mexican Fruit Fly Protocol (USDA/APHIS 2000), and y_i is the quantity of avocados produced in season i. We utilize the upper estimate of costs per fruit fly outbreak ($500,000). There is no loss of fruit implying a zero productivity loss. For fruit fly infestations affecting other crops in susceptible areas of regions B, C and D, only the total cost of control per outbreak is utilized.

The potential cost of an infestation of an avocado-specific pest is based on estimates developed by Evangelou, Kemere, and Miller (1993). The general expression for expected annual average per-unit cost of control for avocado-specific pests over the two seasons is:

$$(6)\qquad CP_{ap} = \frac{Z * pcteff}{yield(1 - PL)} \frac{(N_1 y_1 + N_2 y_2)}{(y_1 + y_2)}$$

where Z is the cost per acre; *yield* is output per acre in the absence of pest infestation; and other terms are defined above. Evangelou, Kemere, and Miller estimated that the pesticide and labor costs required to control a weevil (or other avocado) pest infestation were $2,322 per affected acre. Also, an avocado-specific pest infestation was estimated to result in a 20% reduction in fruit production per acre. Based on an average yield of 6,548 pounds of avocados per acre in California during the 1993/1994 to 2003/2004 marketing years, the average cost is $0.443 per pound for the affected acreage.

The total cost of controlling a weevil or other avocado pest infestation also depends on the acreage affected. We follow USDA/APHIS (2000) and consider a mean of 3%. The costs are borne partly by public pest control agencies but in the model are fully reflected in prices received by avocado producers.

Mexican Avocado Supply and Compliance Costs

There are currently nearly 2,200 orchards in nine of the twenty-one municipalities of Michoacán that are approved to export to the United States. These orchards contained over 27,300 hectares in 2005. An average of 2.29 tons per hectare was harvested for export under the U.S. program out of average

[2] The full set of risk probabilities are reported in the Addendum I to Supplemental Risk Assessment (USDA/APHIS 1996). The November 2004 USDA/APHIS pest risk analysis provides only qualitative assessments of the economic impacts of each type of pest infestation.

total production per hectare of 9.7 tons (El Aguacatero).

The export supply of avocados from Mexico to the United States is also represented using a CET revenue function and linear supply function for the aggregate avocado specific factor utilized. Costs incurred by orchards to participate in the U.S. program include increased production costs to obtain export certification, fees paid to their local Junta de Sanidad Vegetal (JSLV) to cover avocado pest surveys and fruit fly trapping, and loss of fruit during field inspections.

The per-pound cost of compliance for Mexican avocado growers is specified as:

(7)

$$GCOST = \frac{[fieldc + pestsurv]ha + gfruit(p_1x_1 + p_2x_2)}{x_1 + x_2}$$

where *fieldc* is the cost per hectare of field sanitation; *pestsurv* is the cost per hectare of JSLV pest surveys; *ha* is the number of hectares in approved orchards; *gfruit* is the proportion of total exports cut and inspected in the field; p_i is the producer price of exported avocados in Mexico in season i; and x_i is the quantity of exports of avocados to the United States in season i. The number of hectares in approved orchards is kept constant at its 2005 level. Estimates of compliance costs under the 2001 and 2004 rules were obtained through field research (Orden and Peterson 2005). Field sanitation and pest surveys performed on the approved hectares regardless of the quantity of avocados exported are a fixed cost to the approved growers (estimated to be \$76.90 for field sanitation; \$76.67 for pest surveys under the 2001 rule and \$130.27 under the 2004 rule). The proportion of fruit inspected and cut in the field is 0.02.

The nearly 300 packing operations in Michoacán range from informal open sheds to modern enclosed facilities using machine sorting and cold storage. Costs for those exporters approved to participate in the U.S. program in 2005 include: investments to establish fruit fly quarantine conditions in their plants; operating costs of providing certification and protection from fruit flies during picking and processing; reimbursements for Mexican inspectors at the packing plants; and fees paid to reimburse APHIS inspection costs.

The per-pound cost of compliance for Mexican avocado exporters is specified as:

(8)

$$PCOST = pinvest + paphisv + \frac{inspect * plants + paphisf + pfruit * (p_1x_1 + p_2x_2)}{x_1 + x_2}$$

where *pinvest* is the estimated cost per pound of packing plant investment (\$0.005); *paphisv* is the variable cost portion of APHIS inspection costs (\$0.009 per pound); *inspect* is the cost of Mexican inspectors per plant (\$12,000); *plants* is the number of packing plants (22); *paphisf* is the fixed cost portion of APHIS inspection costs (\$335,940); and *pfruit* is the proportion of total exports cut and inspected in packing plants (0.004).

Benchmark Data

The initial equilibrium benchmark prices and quantities for the model are averages from the two-year period October 15, 2001 to October 15, 2003. Total consumption of fresh avocados in the United States (581.1 million pounds) is nearly evenly split between the two seasons.[3] California and Chile each provided about 40% of the avocados consumed during season 1, and Mexico provided about 20%. California avocados dominate U.S. consumption during season 2 (accounting for 75%). Wholesale prices of California avocados are substantially higher than prices of Chilean avocados in all demand regions in both seasons, while Chilean and Mexican avocado have similar wholesale prices in Region A during the first season.[4] Weighted average per pound wholesale prices across our four demand regions are \$1.476 during season 1 and \$1.696 during season 2 for Californian avocados, and \$1.176 during season 1 and \$1.413 during season 2 for Chilean avocados. Wholesale price differentials are also evident in Region A during season 1, where direct competition in

[3] Quantity of Californian Hass avocados shipped to each region is based on monthly shipment data from the Avocado Marketing Research and Information Center of the California Avocado Commission. Quantities of avocados imported from Chile and Mexico are taken from U.S. Census Bureau monthly data. Chilean imports are allocated to domestic demand regions proportional to Californian shipments.

[4] Wholesale prices are from Market News Archive, USDA Agricultural Marketing Service, Wholesale Market Fruit Reports (various issues). Producer prices for California avocados are FOB prices reported by the California Avocado Commission. Chilean producer prices are unit import prices reported by USDA's Foreign Agricultural Service (FAS). Mexican producer prices are the average price paid by Mexican packers for fruit shipped to the U.S. from Orden and Peterson (2005).

the market has existed since 1997 (averaging $1.470, $1.10 and $1.080 for Californian, Chilean and Mexican avocados, respectively). Producer prices for Californian avocados were nearly $0.30 per pound higher than for Chilean and Mexican avocados in season 1 and nearly $0.50 per pound higher in season 2.

The marketing margins between producer and wholesale prices for each region in each season are derived by subtracting the producer prices from the wholesale prices. Because only one marketing margin is observed for Mexican avocados, that margin is used for all regions and seasons. The marketing margin for Mexican avocados includes the exporter costs of compliance with the systems approach. For the benchmark export volume the cost of compliance is calculated to be $0.081 per pound for growers (a relatively consequential 15% of producer price) and $0.026 per pound for exporters (5% of wholesale margin). The margins for California and Chile are assumed to remain constant in all model simulations, while marketing margins for Mexican avocados adjust to changes in the exporter per-pound compliance costs.

Model Calibration and Validation

Because one year of market data is available after the 2004 rule, we use this post-reform data to choose the unknown parameters of and validate the model.[5] The elasticities of substitution in the nested CES utility functions and the supply elasticities for California and Chile are chosen such that after calibrating the model (selecting the shift parameters in [1] and [3]) to replicate the benchmark data, the model is able to closely replicate the observed quantities supplied and the average producer price for Californian avocados during November 2005 to October 2006.[6] The Mexican export supply is assumed to be very price-responsive (elasticity of 50) because less than one-quarter of the output from approved orchards is exported to the United States in the benchmark period. Because of limited substitution patterns, the elasticity of transformation in the CET revenue functions is set equal to 0.5 for all suppliers.

The calibration/validation procedure is more complicated than just implementing the elimination of the geographic and seasonal restrictions on Mexican avocado imports because other factors affect the observed market outcomes in the year to which the model is validated. Specifically, there is a substantially higher supply for California and lower supply from Chile in 2005/2006 than in our benchmark period. We interpret the large California supply as a weather-related positive shock, since acreage has been constant over the period from 1994/1995 to 2004/2005, and the 2005/2006 supply is 50% higher than average annual production during that period (California Avocado Commission). Similarly, Chilean avocado production and exports have been increasing since 2000, with nearly 90% of Chilean exports going to the United States (United Nations/FAO 2007). But there is a relatively low supply of avocados from Chile in 2005/2006, which we interpret as a negative supply shock. These shocks are modeled as shifts in the avocado specific factor supply functions during the validation simulation.[7]

The results of the calibration/validation procedure are shown in table 2. A very inelastic California supply, inelastic Chilean export supply and elastic U.S. demand (derived from the elasticities of substitution) were found to result in a close fit to the observed quantities and price. The implied demand elasticity is larger than estimated recently by Carman (2006). Less elastic demand results in too large of a price decline and too small of an increase in consumption in the calibration/validation compared with observed market outcomes. Thus, we believe the larger demand elasticities reasonably reflect recent consumer behavior for fresh avocados. Likewise, the observed market outcomes are only replicated with a quite inelastic California supply.

The main drawback to using this model validation approach is that with only one year of data, it may be possible that multiple combinations of parameter values "fit" the observation. We find that under the proposition that the supply of Californian avocados is very inelastic, as shown by Carman and Craft (1998), and that the export supply of avocados from Mexico is very elastic, given their excess capacity

[5] We thank an anonymous reviewer for directing us to this calibration and validation approach.

[6] Data for 2005/2006 avocado marketing year is obtained from the Avocado Marketing Research and Information Center.

[7] The geographic restrictions that still limited Mexican avocados to forty-seven states in 2005/2006 are modeled by excluding exports to Region D. This provides only an approximation of the geographic restrictions that were in effect since our other demand regions include northern California, Florida, and Hawaii. Without re-specifying the model's demand structure, we could not fully address this discrepancy. The calibration/validation also accounts for population and income growth subsequent to the benchmark period.

Table 2. Model Calibration and Validation

Parameter	Value	Outcomes: Nov 2005 to Oct 2006	Outcomes: Calibration/Validation
Elasticities of substitution			
σ_1	1.75		
σ_2	2.75		
Aggregate demand *(for California avocados)*	−2.06		
Aggregate supply		Million Pounds	
California	0.05	557.2	558.9
Chile	0.50	126.4	132.8
Mexico	50.0	251.3	226.5
Total		934.9	918.2
		Dollars Per Pound	
Producer price *(annual weighted average for California avocados)*		$0.577	$0.601

Data for 2005/2006 avocado marketing year is obtained from the Avocado Marketing Research and Information Center.

to provide avocados to the United States under the system approach, it greatly restricts the possible values of the demand elasticities that would validate the model.

Modeling the Removal of Import Restrictions

Simulating the removal of seasonal and geographic import restrictions for Mexican avocados for the model calibration/validation or the subsequent policy scenarios requires that shift parameters of the CES utility function be adjusted from initial zero values, which were used to match the absence of consumption from Mexico in the benchmark period (Region A in season 2 and for Regions B, C, and D in both seasons). Following Venables's (1987) analysis of trade policy effects on differentiated products, we assume that these demand shift parameter values for avocados from Mexico can be set equal to the shift parameter values for Chilean avocados after the change in import restrictions. In Regions B, C, and D during season 1, the shift parameters for California avocados are set equal to 0.4, and the shift parameters for Chilean and Mexican avocados are both set equal to 0.3. This maintains the initial preference bias for California avocados as indicated in the calibrated value of the initial shift parameters of approximately 0.6 for Californian avocados and 0.4 for Chilean avocados.

In season 2, the shift parameters for Mexican avocados in all regions are set equal to the initial shift parameters for Chilean avocados in the benchmark period, and the preference parameter for California avocados is decreased by the same amount (to preserve summation of the coefficients to one for each demand region in each season). The initial shift parameters for avocados from Chile during season 2 are smaller in value than for season 1 (e.g., in Region A the initial value in season 2 is 0.1756). A larger preference bias for California avocados is justified in the second season due to seasonal production patterns. More fresh avocados are available from California than from Chile and Mexico during the summer months.

In the supply specification the parameter δ equals 1 initially for Mexico because no avocados are allowed to be exported during season 2. In the simulations δ is set equal to 0.6 to match the proportion of Mexico's total worldwide exports during season 1.

Simulation Results

Because the supply shocks accounted for in the calibration/validation are likely to be transitory, we use the benchmark data as a starting point for the policy simulations. The simulation outcomes are not expected to match the observed outcomes for 2005/2006, but to give an assessment of the effect of only the policy change assuming access for Mexican avocados to all fifty states.

In the first scenario the geographic and seasonal restrictions on avocado imports from Mexico are eliminated while maintaining the other compliance measures of the systems approach. This corresponds to implementation of the 2004 rule. In the second scenario the geographic and season restrictions are eliminated

Table 3. Frequency of Pest Outbreaks

	Risk Probability Levels					
	Scenario 1[a]		Scenario 2		Scenario 3	
Frequency of Outbreak	Average	High	Average	High	Average	High
Fruit flies						
Season 1: Region B	1.0E−6	1.0E−5	2.3E−4	2.0E−3	3.6E−3	3.0E−2
Region C	5.0E−6	4.8E−5	1.2E−3	9.8E−3	1.8E−2	1.5E−1
Region D	3.0E−6	2.5E−5	5.9E−4	5.0E−3	9.3E−3	7.8E−2
Season 2: Region B	1.0E−6	7.0E−6	1.8E−4	1.5E−3	2.7E−3	2.3E−2
Region C	4.0E−6	4.1E−5	9.8E−4	8.3E−3	1.5E−2	1.3E−1
Region D	3.0E−6	2.5E−5	6.0E−4	5.1E−3	9.4E−3	7.9E−2
Stem Weevil: Season 1	5.9E−3	4.9E−2	6.0E−3	5.0E−2	9.3E−1	7.8
Season 2	6.0E−3	5.0E−2	6.1E−3	5.1E−2	9.4E−1	7.9
Seed Weevil: Season 1	2.3E−5	2.2E−4	2.4E−5	2.2E−4	7.6E−3	6.9E−2
Season 2	2.3E−5	2.2E−4	2.4E−5	2.2E−4	7.6E−3	7.0E−2
Seed Moth: Season 1	1.0E−6	7.0E−6	1.0E−6	7.0E−6	2.2E−3	2.2E−2
Season 1	1.0E−6	7.0E−6	1.0E−6	7.0E−6	2.2E−3	2.2E−2

[a]Scenario 1 is unlimited seasonal and geographic access with existing compliance measures; Scenario 2 is unlimited access without fruit fly compliance measures; Scenario 3 is unlimited access without all compliance measures.

along with fruit fly monitoring of orchards and quarantine requirements during harvests and packing in Mexico. This is assumed to raise the probability of a fruit fly infestation during pre- or post-harvest (*prob1* in equation 2) from its system approach level (2.5E−06) to its level without the risk mitigation measures (5.5E−04). Other fruit fly and avocado-specific pest-risk probabilities are assumed to remain at their systems approach levels because inspections continue in packing plants and at the U.S. border. In the third scenario all compliance measures that have been applied to avocado imports from Mexico are removed. The risk probabilities are assumed in the third scenario to be at their levels estimated by APHIS with no risk mitigation measures.

Pest Outbreak Frequencies and U.S. Control Costs

The frequencies of expected pest outbreaks are shown in table 3 for the three scenarios. For fruit flies the frequency of an outbreak is very low, less than 5.0E−6 per year, under the average risk probabilities in scenario 1.[8] The frequency increases in scenario 1 by an order of magnitude (to at most 4.8E−5) under the high-risk probabilities. Eliminating the compliance measures specific to fruit flies in Mexico raises the frequency of outbreaks in the U.S. by two orders of magnitude, and eliminating all of the system approach pest control compliance measures raises these risks another order of magnitude. The maximum estimated frequency of a fruit fly outbreak reaches 0.15 in Region C during season 1 in scenario 3. For southern California (Region D) the expected cost of controlling the fruit fly outbreaks never exceeds $0.00024 per pound (in scenario 3, not shown in the tables) when averaged over the quantity of avocados produced. The total cost of fruit fly controls for expected outbreaks in Regions B and C due to importing avocados from Mexico remain low (at most $244,000 for the worst case of high pest-risk probabilities in scenario 3, as shown in table 4).

The expected frequencies are low for outbreaks of avocado-specific pests due to imports from Mexico in scenario 1. Among the avocado pests, stem weevils have the highest frequency of an outbreak by two orders of magnitude. The avocado pest frequencies are not affected directly by removing the fruit fly compliance measures in scenario 2.[9] But in scenario 3, the avocado pest outbreak frequencies rise by two or more orders of magnitude. For stem weevils expected frequency of an outbreak reaches approximately 0.93 per season under the average pest-risk probabilities and 7.8 per season under the high pest-risk probabilities. The

[8] Region C has a higher frequency of fruit fly outbreaks the Region D due to a larger population.

[9] There is a very slight increase in these probabilities due to a small increase in the equilibrium quantity of avocado exports entering Regions D in scenario 2 as compared with scenario 1.

Table 4. Simulated Outcomes for the Three Policy Scenarios

		Simulation Outcomes					
		Scenario 1		Scenario 2		Scenario 3	
	Base Values	Average Risk	High Risk	Average Risk	High Risk	Average Risk	High Risk
Producer prices				Dollars Per Pound			
Season 1: California	0.871	0.666	0.666	0.664	0.664	0.662	0.695
Chile	0.577	0.452	0.452	0.451	0.451	0.447	0.450
Mexico	0.540	0.489	0.489	0.485	0.485	0.462	0.461
Season 2: California	1.101	0.871	0.871	0.870	0.870	0.868	0.901
Chile	0.599	0.537	0.538	0.537	0.537	0.534	0.539
Mexico	0.540	0.570	0.570	0.566	0.566	0.543	0.544
Wholesale price *(weighted annual average)*							
California	1.622	1.400	1.400	1.398	1.398	1.397	1.430
Chile	1.268	1.168	1.168	1.167	1.166	1.163	1.167
Mexico	1.080	1.056	1.056	1.046	1.046	1.010	1.010
Quantities supplied *(annual)*				Million Pounds			
Total	581.071	763.865	763.785	768.710	768.629	787.370	774.863
California	346.011	341.937	341.839	341.905	341.804	339.682	324.142
Chile	176.813	161.505	161.508	161.359	161.363	160.835	161.350
Mexico	58.247	260.423	260.438	265.446	265.462	286.853	289.371
Mexican compliance cost				Million Dollars *(dollars per pound)*			
Growers	4.726 *(0.081)*	8.291 *(0.032)*	8.291 *(0.032)*	7.097 *(0.027)*	7.097 *(0.027)*	0.000	0.000
Shippers	1.541 *(0.026)*	4.791 *(0.018)*	4.791 *(0.018)*	3.540 *(0.013)*	3.540 *(0.013)*	0.000	0.000
California cost of control	0.000	0.027 *(7.9E−5)*	0.228 *(6.7E−4)*	0.028 *(8.2E−5)*	0.237 *(7.0E−4)*	4.274 *(0.013)*	34.276 *(0.106)*
Welfare effects							
Producer surplus							
California		−76.269	−76.401	−76.763	−76.902	−81.586	−102.127
Chile		−16.848	−16.844	−17.002	−16.998	−17.551	−16.998
Mexico		5.093	5.094	5.302	5.302	6.236	6.351
U.S. equivalent variation		153.721	153.646	156.915	156.836	168.441	156.441
Other fruit fly costs		8.0E−06	7.8E−05	0.002	0.016	0.029	0.244
Net U.S. welfare change		77.452	77.245	80.150	79.918	86.826	54.069

expected frequencies of other avocado pest outbreaks remain two orders of magnitude smaller.

When the system approach compliance measures are all removed in scenario 3, the expected costs of control measures born by California orchards become substantial, particularly for the relatively frequent outbreaks of stem weevil. These costs are estimated to be $0.012 per pound of California production at the average risk probabilities. At the high-risk probabilities the seed weevil-related costs and losses reach $0.106 per pound in scenario 3. Thus, terminating all systems approach compliance measures with high pest risks places onto the domestic U.S. industry pest control costs on the same order of magnitude per pound of California avocado sales as the costs borne by Mexican producers and exporters per pound of exports under the 2001 rule.

Market Equilibrium and Welfare Changes

Because Mexican avocados become more available and are relatively less expensive than other avocados in scenario 1, there is a decline in demand for avocados from California and Chile. With the relatively inelastic supply of Californian and Chilean avocados, the drop in demand leads to lower producer and wholesale prices, with only inconsequential differences in the outcomes with average versus high pest-risk probabilities. As shown in table 4, which provides a summary of the results, producer prices for California and Chilean avocados decline in the range of 10–25% in each season (more in season 1 than season 2), and wholesale prices decline by 5–15%. The annual equilibrium quantity demanded and supplied falls by 1.2% for California avocados and by 8.7% for avocados from Chile.[10]

With the increased seasonal and geographic access allowed under scenario 1, annual exports from Mexico increase by 345%, from 58.2 million pounds to 260.4 million pounds. Although increased requirements raise the total compliance costs from $6.3 million to $13.1 million with year-round shipping, the increase in exports lowers the per-pound costs in Mexico to $0.032 for growers and $0.018 for exporters (table 4). These per-pound compliance costs are only 39.5% and 69.2%, respectively, of the benchmark levels. The reduction in compliance costs affects both the net price received by Mexican growers (gross [market] producer price less compliance costs) and the marketing margin on Mexican avocados. The net producer price remains virtually unchanged in season 1, even though the gross price falls by 9.4%. The decline in the gross price in season 1 is due to both supply and demand factors. On the supply side season 1 is the peak of Mexican avocado production and exports, and with a low elasticity of transformation, there is limited ability for Mexican growers to shift exports between seasons. On the demand side, because Mexico had market access in Region A initially, the increase in market access is smaller in season 1 as compared with season 2, where there was no initial market access. In season 2 the larger increase in market access as well as lower seasonal production in Mexico increases the gross and net prices by 5.6% and 7.5%, respectively. The reduction of marketing margins due to the decrease in compliance costs for Mexican exporters translates into a 13.8% larger reduction in the wholesale price of Mexican avocados in season 1 than otherwise and a 25.7% smaller increase in the wholesale price in season 2.

The expected producer surplus for California avocado growers declines by $76.3 million in scenario 1 ($76.4 million for high risks). This decrease reflects the impact of expanded trade and the small effects from expected control costs and losses in output due to pest damage. Expected pest control cost to California avocado growers due to imports from Mexico is only $27,000 with average pest risks and $228,000 with high risks. Pest control costs for fruit flies for other U.S. crops are negligible. Producer surplus also declines by $16.8 million for Chilean avocado growers but increases by $5.1 million for Mexican growers. The relatively small increase in Mexican producer surplus reflects the elastic export supply, which implies that most of the benefits of the policy change are passed on to U.S. consumers. Total U.S. avocado consumption increases from 581.1 million pounds to 763.9 million pounds. The total estimated gain in equivalent variation for U.S. consumers is $153.7 million ($153.6 million for high risks). Net welfare in the U.S. increases by $77.5 million ($77.2 million for high risks).

Eliminating fruit fly monitoring would reduce the field survey costs from $130.27 per hectare in scenario 1 to $85.58 per hectare in scenario 2. This translates into approximately a $0.005 per pound reduction in growers' compliance costs, with shipper compliance costs reduced by an equivalent amount from the elimination of plant quarantine requirements for fruit flies. With the decrease in grower compliance costs, the average annual net price received by Mexican producers increases by $0.001 per pound (0.17% compared to scenario 1), which leads to an increase in Mexican avocado exports by 5.0 million pounds (an 8.6% larger increase in exports compared to the benchmark than in scenario 1).

The average annual wholesale price of Mexican avocados in the United States falls $0.009 per pound (0.8%) as compared with scenario 1. This small reduction, relative to the wholesale prices of Californian and Chilean avocados, leads to only very small changes in equilibrium quantities demanded of Californian and Chilean avocados compared to scenario 1 (32,000 and 146,000 pounds respectively). This small change in quantity demanded is accompanied by a small reduction in producer prices of Californian and Chilean avocado of $0.001 per pound.

Most of the welfare benefits of eliminating fruit fly monitoring accrue to U.S. consumers, who gain an additional $3.2 million in equivalent variation compared to scenario 1. Producer surplus for Californian and Chilean growers declines by about $500,000 and $155,000, respectively, while producer surplus for Mexican growers increases by about $210,000 (for both average or high-risk probabilities). The expected pest control costs in the U.S. remains low at $28,000, with average pest risks and $237,000 with high risks. Net U.S.

---

[10] A complete set of results is available from the authors upon request.

welfare increases by approximately $2.7 million compared to scenario 1 under either average or high risks.

In the third scenario, there are no compliance costs in Mexico, but trade-related pest infestations become frequent enough that expected control cost for California avocado growers increase significantly to $4.3 million with average pest risks.[11] The increase in control costs leads to a reduction in the annual average net price received by California growers of $0.015 per pound compared to scenario 1. In addition the expected infestations of avocado-specific pests lead to a 1.1% productivity loss with average pest risks. With the decrease in the net price and the productivity loss, Californian avocado production falls by 2.3 million pounds as compared with scenario 1. The reduction in Californian producer surplus is about $5 million higher than in scenarios 1 and 2.

Because of the very elastic Mexican export supply, most of the benefits of the elimination of all compliance measures in Mexico are passed on to U.S. consumers. Compared with scenario 1, total compliance costs are reduced by $0.05 per pound. Mexican growers receive a $0.005 per pound increase in their net price, and Mexican exports increase by 26.4 million pounds compared to scenario 1. The gross producer price of Mexican avocados falls by $0.027 per pound. With the reduction in the gross price and exporter compliance costs, the wholesale price of Mexican avocados declines by $0.046 per pound compared to scenario 1.

For average pest risks, the U.S. net gain in welfare is $86.8 million, a gain of $6.7 million and $9.4 million compared to scenarios 2 and 1, respectively. The equivalent variation for U.S. consumers is $168.4 million in scenario 3 with average risks—$11.5 million and $14.7 million higher than for scenarios 2 and 1. Thus, there is an additional domestic welfare gain associated with eliminating all of the system approach compliance measures at the average pest risks estimated by APHIS, in spite of the significant pest-related losses to California avocado growers.

Unlike scenarios 1 and 2, where the use of average or high pest-risk probabilities had little effect on the model results, for scenario 3 there are quite different results under high pest risks. The nearly hundred-fold increase in the expected frequency of stem weevil outbreaks increases the cost of control for California growers to $34.3 million and the trade-related productivity loss from pest infestations to 9.5%. These two effects lead to the equilibrium quantity supplied of California avocados falling by 15.5 million pounds as compared with scenario 3 with average pest risks. This reduction in the equilibrium quantity supplied results in a $0.033 per pound higher wholesale price of Californian avocados as compared with the average pest-risk case. Total avocado consumption falls by 12.5 million pounds as compared with the case with average pest risks, even with the fairly large elasticities of substitution in consumption.

The higher control costs and productivity losses lead to a $20.5 million larger decrease in producer surplus for California growers as compared with scenario 3 with average pest risks. In addition the reduction in avocado consumption results in a $12.0 million lower gain in U.S. consumer equivalent variation, with a slight decline even with higher imports, as compared with scenario 2. The net U.S. welfare gain of $54.1 million in scenario 3 under high pest-risk probabilities is less than the net gains in scenarios 1 or 2 under either average or high-risk probabilities. Thus, it is possible that removing all of the system approach measures for Mexican avocados could lead to a lower net welfare gain than only removing the seasonal and geographic restrictions or these restriction plus the fruit fly monitoring requirements.[12]

Sensitivity Analysis

Sensitivity analyses are conducted to investigate the effects of uncertainty in our estimates of the underlying costs of compliance (for scenarios 1 and 2) and control costs and losses (for all three scenarios) and uncertainty in the supply and demand elasticities. For the costs of compliance, we focus on the two costs with the most uncertainty: costs of field sanitation and packinghouse quarantine. A range of plus and minus 20% above our initial cost estimate is used for field sanitation costs and plus and minus 50% for the cost of packinghouse quarantine. For California control costs

[11] The costs of controlling fruit fly outbreak remain low in scenario 3, regardless of the pest risk probabilities used.

[12] Yue, Beghin, and Jensen (2006) also note the possibility of consumer welfare falling with expanded trade when domestic and imported goods are imperfect substitutes, and trade-related pest outbreaks occur. Orden, Narrod, and Glauber (2001) called attention to this possibility in the case of limited trade but with homogeneous products and perfectly elastic Mexican supply did not find adverse effects on consumers with full market access.

Table 5. Comparison of U.S. Welfare Estimates Across Alternative Demand Elasticity Values

	Simulation Outcomes					
	Scenario 1		Scenario 2		Scenario 3	
Elasticity Estimates[a]	Average Risk	High Risk	Average Risk	High Risk	Average Risk	High Risk
Net U.S. welfare change			Million Dollars			
Carman (−0.4)	71.016	70.859	73.686	73.519	81.395	57.594
APHIS (−0.98)	75.329	75.158	78.036	77.848	85.465	58.669
Validation (−2.06)	77.452	77.245	80.149	79.918	86.826	54.069
California producer surplus						
Carman (−0.4)	−241.951	−241.990	−243.305	−243.347	−249.604	−254.920
APHIS (−0.98)	−144.914	−144.993	−146.003	−146.087	−152.052	−164.027
Validation (−2.06)	−76.269	−76.401	−76.763	−76.902	−81.586	−102.127
U.S. Equivalent variation						
Carman (−0.4)	312.968	312.849	316.992	316.876	331.016	312.660
APHIS (−0.98)	220.244	220.151	224.041	223.947	237.538	222.878
Validation (−2.06)	153.721	153.646	156.914	156.837	168.441	156.441

[a] Alternative demand elasticity estimates obtained from Carman (2006), USDA/APHIS (2004a), and model validation procedure. Values in parentheses are aggregate demand elasticity for California avocados.

and productivity losses, the following are considered: a range of plus and minus 10% for the average avocado yield per acre; a range from 1 to 5% for the acreage affected by each outbreak (plus or minus 2%); and a range of 10–30% for the productivity loss for each outbreak of an avocado-specific pest (plus or minus 10%). Each uncertain parameter is assumed to have an independent uniform distribution, and the sensitivity analysis uses symmetric order three Gaussian quadratures. Arndt and Hertel (1997) have shown that sensitivity analyses conducted using order three quadratures are as accurate as higher order quadratures.

In general, the model results are not sensitive to alternative assumptions about compliance and control costs. For scenarios 1 and 2, with average or high pest risks, the standard deviations for Californian producer surplus, U.S. consumer equivalent variation and net U.S. welfare gains are approximately $0.2 million, $1.1 million and $1.0 million, respectively. As the frequency of pest outbreak increases in scenario 3, the amount of acreage affected per outbreak and the level of productivity loss associated with each outbreak become more important. For average pest risks the standard deviations of the three U.S. welfare measures increase slightly to $1.1 million, $0.8 million and $1.8 million, respectively. Because the frequency of infestation increases by an order of magnitude for high pest risks, the standard deviations increase, respectively, to $9.3 million, $6.7 million and $14.9 million.

Because the aggregate demand elasticity for California avocados obtained from the validation procedure is quite large, we considered two alternative less-elastic specifications of aggregate demand to determine the robustness of the model results.[13] The alternative aggregate demand elasticities are based on recent econometric estimates by Carman (−0.4) and the elasticity utilized in the APHIS economic assessment (−0.98). All scenarios are re-run using these alternative demand elasticities, holding all other parameter values constant.

As shown in table 5, net U.S. welfare gains are smaller with less elastic demand, but the range of estimates does not vary much across the different values. There is substantial variation in producer surplus for California avocado growers and in U.S. equivalent variation. As demand becomes more inelastic, with an inelastic supply of avocados from California, there are larger reductions in prices received by California avocado growers. This leads to larger decreases in producer surplus. However, as long as the producer price decreases are passed onto consumers, as is assumed in the model, then U.S. consumers gain additional benefit from the lower prices of Californian avocados. These two effects nearly offset each other. More inelastic demand also reduces the pest-risk-related losses because the level of

---

[13] We thank one anonymous reviewer for emphasizing sensitivity to the demand elasticity.

exports from Mexico is substantially reduced.[14] Thus, while the alternative demand elasticities affect the distribution of gains and losses, our estimates of pest-risk losses and net U.S. welfare gains across the three policy scenarios are robust to a wide range of demand elasticity values.

Conclusion

A long and contentious dispute between Mexico and the United States over restrictions on importation of Hass avocados has been largely resolved since 1997, by replacing an import ban with trade under a systems approach of mitigation measures designed to reduce fruit fly and avocado-specific pest risks. This article has developed a model to evaluate the effects of fresh Hass avocado imports from Mexico under alternative systems approach measures. We find that eliminating geographic and seasonal restrictions under the November 2004 rule substantially expands trade and lowers Mexican per-unit compliance costs. Pest risks remain low with the other compliance measures still in place. The estimated annual net U.S. welfare gain from eliminating all geographic and seasonal restrictions is approximately $77.4 million. Thus, the benefits from the decision made by USDA in 2004 to allow imports of Mexican avocados without geographic or seasonal restrictions under a systems approach are confirmed when pest risks and related costs are incorporated into the analysis.

Analysis of alternative avocado import pest-risk management policies that eliminate some or all of the remaining compliance measures suggests two additional conclusions. First, the additional U.S. welfare gains from further modification of the systems approach to eliminate fruit fly control measures are modest. Second, entirely abandoning the systems approach would be a questionable decision on pest-risk and economic criteria. This is because our knowledge of the magnitudes of the pest-risk probabilities is not sufficient to rule out a smaller U.S. welfare gain compared to when some or all of the system approach compliance measures are retained. These conclusions hold up over a wide range of alternative demand elasticity assumptions.

*[Received June 27, 2006;
accepted September 20, 2007.]*

[14] Pest-related costs are not shown separately in table 5. The complete set of results is available on request.

References

Arndt, C., and T.W. Hertel. 1997. "Revisiting 'The fallacy of free trade.'" *Review of International Economics* 5(2):221–29.

Avocado Marketing Research and Information Center, California Avocado Commission. "Statistics." Accessed October 2006. Available at http://www.avocado.org/growers/statistics.php.

Calvin, L., B. Krissoff, and W. Foster. Forthcoming. "Measuring the Costs and Trade Effects of a Phytosanitary Protocol: A U.S.-Japanese Apple Example." *Review of Agricultural Economics*, in press.

Carman, H.F. 2006. "Impacts from Imports with Generic Advertising and Promotion Programs: The Hass Avocado Promotion and Research Order." *Review of Agricultural Economics* 28:463–81.

Carman, H.F., and R.K. Craft. 1998. "An Economic Evaluation of California Avocado Industry Marketing Programs, 1961–1995." Giannini Foundation Research Report No. 345, California Agricultural Experiment Station, July.

Carman, H.F., L. Li, and R.J. Sexton. 2006. "Impact of Sequential and Partial Trade Liberalization for Mexican Hass Avocado Imports to the United States during 1998–2004." Paper presented at AAEA annual meeting, Long Beach CA, 23–26 July.

El Aguacatero. 2005. "Avocado Production Summary." Marzo-Abril.

Evangelou, P., P. Kemere, and C.E. Miller. 1993. *Potential Economic Impacts of an Avocado Weevil Infestation in California*. U.S. Department of Agriculture, Animal and Plant Health Inspection Service, Washington DC, August.

Glauber, J.W., and C.A. Narrod. 2001. *A Rational Risk Policy for Regulating Plant Diseases and Pests*. Regulatory Analysis 01-05, AEI-Brookings Joint Center for Regulatory Studies, Washington DC, June.

Keller, W.J. 1976. "A Nested CES-Type Utility Function and Its Demand and Price-Index Functions." *European Economic Review* 9:175–86.

Lamb, R.L. 2006. "Rent Seeking in U.S. Mexican Avocado Trade." *Cato Journal* 26(1):159–77.

Orden, D., and E. Peterson. 2006. "Science, Opportunity, Traceability, Persistence and Political Will: Necessary Elements of Opening the U.S. Market to Avocados from Mexico." In U. Grote, A.K. Basu, and N. Chau, eds. *New Frontiers in Environmental and Social Labeling*. New York: Springer, pp. 133–50.

Orden, D., and E.B. Peterson. 2005. "Assessment of Costs of the 'System Approach' to Export of Mexican Avocados to the United States." Working Paper, Department of Agricultural and Applied Economics, Virginia Tech.

Orden D., C. Narrod, and J.W. Glauber. 2001. "Least Trade-Restrictive SPS Policies: An Analytic Framework is there but Questions Remain." In K. Anderson, C. McRae, and D. Wilson, eds. *The Economics of Quarantine and the SPS Agreement*. Adelaide: Centre for International Economic Studies, pp. 183–215.

Paarlberg, P.L., and J.G. Lee. 1998. "Import Restrictions in the Presence of a Health Risk: An Illustration Using FMD." *American Journal of Agricultural Economics* 80:175–83.

Powell, A.A., and F.H.G. Gruen. 1968. "The Constant Elasticity of Transformation Production Frontier and Linear Supply System." *International Economic Review* 9:315–28.

Rendleman, C.M., and F.J. Spinelli. 1999. "The Costs and Benefits of Animal Disease Prevention: The Case of African Swine Fever in the US." *Environmental Impact and Assessment Review* 19:405–26.

Roberts, D., and D. Orden. 1997. "Determinants of Technical Barriers to Trade: The Case of US Phytosanitary Restrictions on Mexican Avocados, 1972–1995." In D. Orden and D. Roberts, eds. *Understanding Technical Barriers to Agricultural Trade*. St. Paul, MN: University of Minnesota, Department of Applied Economics, International Agricultural Trade Research Consortium, pp. 117–60.

Romano, E. 1998. "Two Essays on Sanitary and Phytosanitary Barriers Affecting Agricultural Trade Between Mexico and the United States." Ph.D. Dissertation, Virginia Polytechnic Institute and State University.

United Nations, Food and Agriculture Organization. "Trade Data." Accessed October 2007. Available at http://faostat.fao.org/.

U.S. Department of Agriculture, Animal and Plant Health Inspection Service (USDA/APHIS). 1996. *Importation of Avocado Fruit (*Persea americana americana*) from Mexico, Supplemental Pest Risk Assessment, Addendum I: Estimates for the Likelihood of Pest Outbreaks Based on the Draft Final Rule*. Washington DC, July.

——. 2000. *Economic Analysis of Options for Eradicating Mexican Fruit Fly (*Anastrepha ludens*) from the Lower Rio Grande Valley of Texas*. Washington DC, March.

——. 2004a. *Economic Analysis Final Rule: Allow Fresh Hass Avocados Grown in Approved Orchards in Approved Municipalities in Michoacan, Mexico, to be Imported Into All States Year-Round* (APHIS Docket No. 03-022-3). Washington DC, November.

——. 2004b. *Importation of Avocado Fruit (*Persea americana *Mill. var. 'Hass') from Mexico: A Risk Assessment*. Washington DC, November.

Venables, A.J. 1987. "Trade and Trade Policy with Differentiated Products: A Chamberlinian-Ricardian Model." *Economic Journal* 97:700–17.

Wilson, N., and J. Anton. 2006. "Combining Risk Assessment and Economics in Managing a Sanitary-Phytosanitary Risk." *American Journal of Agricultural Economics* 88:194–202.

World Trade Organization. 1994. *The Results of the Uruguay Round of Multilateral Trade Negotiations: The Legal Texts.* GATT Secretariat, Geneva, Switzerland.

Yue, C., J. Beghin, and H.H. Jensen. 2006. "Tariff Equivalent of Technical Barriers to Trade with Imperfect Substitution and Trade Costs." *American Journal of Agricultural Economics* 88:947–60.

Index

Lightning Source UK Ltd.
Milton Keynes UK
UKOW06n2108230915

259142UK00005B/79/P

9 789814 616218